THE UNEASY CHAIR

By *Wallace Stegner*

Novels

ALL THE LITTLE LIVE THINGS

A SHOOTING STAR

SECOND GROWTH

THE BIG ROCK CANDY MOUNTAIN

FIRE AND ICE

ON A DARKLING PLAIN

THE POTTER'S HOUSE

REMEMBERING LAUGHTER

JOE HILL

ANGLE OF REPOSE

Short Stories

THE CITY OF THE LIVING

THE WOMEN ON THE WALL

Non-Fiction

BEYOND THE HUNDREDTH MERIDIAN

ONE NATION (with the Editors of *Look*)

THE GATHERING OF ZION

MORMON COUNTRY

WOLF WILLOW

THE SOUND OF MOUNTAIN WATER

THE UNEASY CHAIR: A BIOGRAPHY OF BERNARD DEVOTO

THE UNEASY CHAIR

A Biography of
BERNARD DEVOTO

Wallace Stegner

DOUBLEDAY & COMPANY, INC.
GARDEN CITY, NEW YORK
1974

PHOTO CREDITS:
SOOY Ogden, Utah   photo 2
James Woolverton Mason   photos 30, 31
Pix photo by K. W. Hermann   photo 35
Carl E. Vermilya, staff photographer, *The Oregonian*, Portland, Oregon   photo 43
Other photos courtesy Mrs. Bernard DeVoto

This is a book which in simple justice must be dedicated to the Tribe of Benny—to those who as his friends, companions, colleagues, and antagonists were so constantly bombarded, needled, provoked, challenged, outraged, informed, and enlarged by his conversation and his books.

CONTENTS

Author's Note

First by accident and later through his friendship and example, the curve of my life has touched some of the points that Bernard DeVoto's did. We were both boys in Utah, though at different times and in different towns. We were both Westerners by birth and upbringing, novelists by intention, teachers by necessity, and historians by the sheer compulsion of the region that shaped us. We both made our way eastward to Harvard, with a stop in the Middle West. We were for some years neighbors in Cambridge and colleagues at the Bread Loaf Writers' Conference. The same compulsion that made amateur historians of us made us conservationists as well: we both wrote a good deal on the subject of conservation, and we both served on the Advisory Board for National Parks, Historical Sites, Buildings, and Monuments.

But until I began this biography I had not realized how many of my basic attitudes about the West, about America in general, about literature, and about history parallel his, either because so much of our experience retraced the same curve or because of his direct influence. It would be impossible at this date to say how many of my attitudes have been formed or modified by contact with him; but the debt is considerable, and I freely acknowledge it.

As a consequence of both the parallelism and the confluences of our lives, the making of this biography has meant renewed contact with many mutual friends, and that has been the pleasantest part of the job. I have profited so much, from so many individuals, that a full accounting would bankrupt me. There is even a sense in which this record of Benny's personality and career is a collaborative effort of his friends. Nevertheless, I have done my best to be objective; and though I thank all those who have helped Benny back to life for me, I assume full responsibility for what I have done to their recollections and the ways in which I have arranged or interpreted their memories. I have tried to re-create Benny DeVoto as he was—flawed, brilliant, provocative, outrageous, running scared all his life, often wrong, often spectacularly right, always stimulating, sometimes infuriating, and never, never dull. He was a force in his times, though probably less a force than he would have been if he had represented another region than the Far West, and certainly than he would have been if he had not stood at the passages of Jordan crying, "Say now Shibboleth." He challenged many of the fads and intellectual assumptions of his times, and he never had a gang—he only had friends, and enemies, and those who had to pay attention, however irritated or aggrieved.

For what must have seemed to her an interminable time, ever since 1968, Avis DeVoto has helped me promptly, efficiently, fully; she has corrected my errors and done her best to clarify my obscurities; she has dug into memories that had to be painful, and put herself cheerfully at the disposal of my book, and has trusted me. I not only thank her, I salute her.

For advice, assistance, friendly support, help so generous that sometimes it has humbled me, I say my thanks, collectively but with personal intention, to many people: to Fred Anderson, George Ball, Stewart Ball, Anne Barrett, Fred Bissell, Catherine Drinker Bowen, Sarah Boyden, Carol Brandt, Dr. Mary Brazier, Lila Eccles Brimhall, Fawn Brodie, Paul Brooks, Paul Buck, Constance Bunnell, and Lyman Butterfield; to Ralph Chaney, Henry Steele Commager, and Malcolm Cowley; to Dorothy di Santillana, Scottie Eccles, Paul Ferris, Leon Fetzer, John Fischer, and David Freed; to John Kenneth Galbraith, A. B. Guthrie, Ray B. Hall, W. E. Higman, George Homans, Ida James, Howard and Bessie Jones, and Alfred Knopf; to Eric Larrabee, William Lederer, Richard Lillard, and Dr. Alfred and Julie Ludwig; to Edward Martin, Dave MacDonald, Elizabeth Browning McLeod, Frederick Merk, Kenneth and Eleanor Murdock, Laurette Murdock, and Theodore and Kathleen Morrison; to Talcott Parsons, Mrs. Arthur Perkins, Earl Pomeroy, Ricardo Quintana, Henry Reck, and Dr. Gregory Rochlin; to Mark Saxton, Dr. Herbert Scheinberg, Arthur Schlesinger, Jr., Richard Scowcroft, Robert Shenton, Claude Simpson, William and Julie Sloane, Henry Nash Smith, Carl Spaeth, Howard Stagner, and George Stevens; to Lovell Thompson and Edward Weeks.

Five friends who helped me a very great deal died before the book was finished. I will always owe Robeson Bailey, Helen Everitt, Elizabeth Kennedy, Dale L. Morgan, and Lawrance Thompson the thanks that I should have offered sooner.

To those who willingly read through an early draft in the effort to save me from error, I owe a special debt. They were Avis DeVoto, Anne Barrett, Dr. Lawrence Kubie, Kay and Ted

Morrison, Mark Saxton, Julie and William Sloane, Dr. Herbert Scheinberg, and Arthur Schlesinger, Jr. I will guarantee them some errors in spite of their efforts.

Patricia Palmer, Susan Rosenberg, Julius Barclay, and Ralph Hansen of the Stanford libraries have been cheerful and indispensable in guiding me through the DeVoto papers. Edward Connery Lathem of the Baker Memorial Library of Dartmouth College has exceeded even himself in helpfulness to a peripatetic scholar. In addition, I have benefited from the prompt help of librarians at the University of Montana, Middlebury College, Bread Loaf, the University of Vermont, the University of Utah, and the Weber County Library in Ogden, Utah—librarians whose names I may have miserably and unforgivably forgotten but whose helpfulness I have not.

Much of the work of this book was done under a Senior Fellowship from the National Endowment for the Humanities. The early stages were aided by a grant from the American Philosophical Society. To both of those organizations I give my thanks.

WALLACE STEGNER

Los Altos Hills, California
April 9, 1973

Biography is the wrong field for the mystical, and for the wishful, the tender-minded, the hopeful, and the passionate. It enforces an unremitting skepticism—toward its material, toward the subject, most of all toward the biographer. . . . His job is not dramatic; it is only to discover evidence and to analyze it. And all the evidence he can find is the least satisfactory kind, documentary evidence, which is among the most treacherous phenomena in a malevolent world. With luck he will be certain of the dates of his subject's birth and marriage and death, the names of his wife and children, a limited number of things he did and offices he held and trades he practised and places he visited and manuscript pages he wrote, people he praised or attacked, and some remarks made about him. Beyond that, not even luck can make certainty possible. The rest is merely printed matter, and a harassed man who sweats his life out in libraries, courthouses, record offices, vaults, newspaper morgues, and family attics. A harassed man who knows that he cannot find everything and is willing to believe that, forever concealed from him, exists something which, if found, would prove that what he takes to be facts are only appearances.

Bernard DeVoto
"The Skeptical Biographer"

THE UNEASY CHAIR

Was it fancy, sweet nurse,
Was it a dream,
Or did you really
Take hold of my scalp lock
When I was half asleep this morning
And open up a trapdoor in my skull
And drop a poached egg in among my brains?

Don Marquis, Grotesques

I

THE AMNIOTIC HOME

1 · *"These People Are Not My People"*

Thirty-five miles north of Salt Lake City, spread across the alluvial land between the Wasatch Mountains and the salt marshes of Great Salt Lake, is the city of Ogden, Utah. First settled as the ranch of the mountain man Miles Goodyear, it became a Mormon colony and later a division point on the Union Pacific. After the railroad-building boom of the late 1860s, it replaced another hell-raising town, Corinne, at the north end of Great Salt Lake, as the only Gentile stronghold in Brigham Young's empire. But no determination to be a seat of opposition, intransigence, and heresy could be maintained in the face of Mormon pressure and infiltration. Corinne wound up a ghost town, and Ogden wound up about as mixed as Salt Lake City itself, a city whose politics, economics, and social life were all resultants of the intersection of religious lines of force. By the 1890s, Ogden was substantially under Mormon control. Then the Liberal Party rallied all the varieties of opposition and took some of the control back. So it has gone, a seesaw or a standoff. Just before World War II, when industry and administration were being dispersed, as it were, beyond the Urals, the town acquired some war industry, some additional regional offices of federal bureaus, and the headquarters of the Army's Ninth Corps Area, which had previously been based at the Presidio, in San Francisco. The old Ogden Arsenal, beginning in 1940, was transformed into Hill Air Force Base. For some years, until 1971, Ogden was known in infamy as the address to which the entire West mailed its income-tax returns.

Before it began to be invigorated by these federal transfusions, it was a rather stodgy postfrontier town of 30,000-odd, a transportation-and-mining-created human accretion unworthy of its splendid setting. From its tracks and marshaling yards it straggled uphill through warehouses and a business district based upon an avenue named for President George Washington, and upward through a succession of other presidential avenues as far as Polk. There were some pretentious houses both Mormon and Gentile, many more that were somewhat shabby middle class. After Polk the streets gave out in weeds and sagebrush, and the foothills (or rather the terraces, fossil beaches of ancient Lake Bonneville) lifted toward the Wasatch Mountains, over whose abrupt escarpment an eastern moon, in season, rose to shed imported enchantment.

In the late summer of 1920, in one half of a nondescript duplex house at 2561 Monroe Avenue, one of Ogden's most gifted sons was undergoing a nervous breakdown. What had begun as insomnia and eye trouble had gone on to migraines that split his head like a watermelon and brought on fits of agonized vomiting, and from there to deep depression, helplessness, and panic. If he forced himself to work on the novel whose manuscript was all over his desk, he knew even as he worked that the effort was useless, that the thing was inert, foolish, jejune, dead, worse than bad. During that summer he had written an unkind little article on Senator Reed Smoot and sent it off to Oswald Garrison Villard at *The Nation*, who had once kindly invited him to contribute things from the West. Some time after he mailed the envelope, his depression was instantly cured by a letter from Villard accepting the essay. Next day came an unexplained letter rejecting and returning it. Bottom again. Whenever he ventured outside he walked fearfully, feeling himself watched. Without warning, a cold, sweating dread could rise up out of the hot streets and engulf him. The familiar smells of his town, known from boyhood and sensuously cherished, were a mockery. He could not smell bitter cottonwood or watered lawns or the fruit scents of a passing produce wagon, or even the salt smell of Great Salt Lake that foretold rain, without that irrational panic of the blood. Sometimes he could not force himself to cross a street. Sidewalks humped by tree roots reached for his feet as he fled.

His mother was dead a year. His father was a brilliant, contrary, sometimes lovable, mule-headed eccentric with a paralyzed will. He himself was in process of breaking up with a girl who for a year and a half had enforced his passionate adoration. He had no job, no prospects, no future, no place in this town that imprisoned him. In every face he met he saw ridicule for a man fool enough to imagine himself a writer, and fear of a man overeducated and probably revolutionary. Though he was gregarious, and had friends, the friends who shared his deepest intellectual interests were far off, in another country. To one of them, Melville Smith, he had written in July:

Do not forget that at best I am a spore in Utah, not adapted to the environment, a maverick who may not run with the herd, unbranded, given an ill name. These people are not my people, their God is not mine. We respect, hate, and distrust each other, and though self-defense forces me to take them with much humor, nothing forces them so to take me. You, who have the good fortune to be among that other kind of people, must share your good fortune with me. I am much nearer to you than I shall ever be to Utah.[1]

In his desk drawer, among a handful of personal papers, were a Certificate of Baptism stating that at the age of four, in Omaha, Nebraska, a town with which he had no connection, he had been baptized into the Roman Catholic Church, in which he did not believe; a paper commissioning him as a Second Lieutenant of Infantry, trained and approved to fight in a war that was now over and that he had never got to; a diploma—which he had determined was not real sheepskin—granting him the rights and privileges of a Bachelor of Arts from Harvard College, with honors; and a clipping from the Harvard *Crimson* listing him among the seniors elected to Phi Beta Kappa. One of the things that fretted him during his sleepless nights was that he had never been notified of his election by the Phi Beta Kappa chapter itself, and that the secretary had not replied to his two importunate letters. Was it a fact, then, or an error? Did he or did he not belong, and if he belonged why had they not notified him? Like all the rest of the world, that stuffy scholarly organization that he scorned even while he yearned for its certification seemed to ignore him and deny his existence.

2 · *Fossil Remnants of a Frontier Boyhood*

East of Ogden, several canyons cut into the Wasatch. Of these, Taylor Canyon, Waterfall Canyon, Strong's Canyon, and most especially Ogden Canyon, which led up to the heart of the range and the beautiful circular valley that the mountain men had called Ogden's Hole, were always places of escape and resort. They were wild pathways for hiking boys, and Ogden Canyon offered a fine trout stream, and locations for summer cabins out of the valley heat, and access to a maze of smaller canyons that were almost wilderness.[1] But still another canyon, Weber (pronounced *Wee*ber), opened widely south of the city, and it was no dead-end refuge but a gateway, one of the great gateways of western history. Through it, following down the Weber River, had come one branch of the California Trail as well as part of the Mormon migration. Down it came the transcontinental railroad and the highway that under several names—Lincoln Highway, US 30N, Interstate 80N—has always been a major access route to the Great Basin from the East.

Weber Canyon was the path by which the Outside reached Ogden. Like the moon, it brought word of happenings eastward, and it had seen most of the events and people of the brief, hot past that after a half century or so some Ogdenites began to think romantic. The Mormon lucerne fields and orchards between which railroad and highway passed had been the campsites of a people on the move westward. Before they were ever plowed or planted, they had been fertilized by the casual graves of Indians, mountain men, Morrisite heretics, and apostates rubbed out—rumor said—by Brigham Young's Destroying Angels Bill Hickman, Porter Rockwell, and Hosea Stout. Farther east, beyond where Weber Canyon flattened out into a valley running lengthwise down the range, another pass, called Echo Canyon, came down through the red rock of the Wyoming Plateau, and up there Mormon minutemen had built breastworks, and Mormon cavalry had conducted guerrilla raids that stalled Albert Sidney Johnston's invading army in the Fort Bridger snow in 1857. Through both Echo and Weber canyons the violent, portable camp called Hell on Wheels had passed as the Union Pacific raced westward toward closure with the Central Pacific at Promontory, and during its brief passage had disrupted, dismayed, altered, and made solvent the Mormon hamlets in the Weber bottoms.[2]

In one such settlement, first called Easton and later rechristened Uinta by the railroad, Bernard Augustine DeVoto spent part of his boyhood on his grandfather's farm. Born in Ogden on January 11, 1897, he was incomparably type-cast to represent the social and religious cleavages of the place, for his mother was the daughter of a pioneer Mormon farmer and his father was a vagrant Catholic intellectual, a former "perpetual student" and part-time teacher at Notre Dame.

The boy was born into neither faith, but into the area of conflict between them; and since any conflict between a good Mormon and a faithful Catholic may be expected to end in a draw, it was predictable that he would adhere to neither. Actually, neither of his parents was a good communicant. His mother had backslid into the status that Utah knows as jack-Mormon, and his father, despite all those years at Notre Dame, was not a churchgoer.

Nevertheless Catholicism had the advantage. To one born in the gopher hole of a Utah town, the Roman faith was bound to seem eastern, exotic, aristocratic, especially when it was the ostensible faith of a father whose intellectual capacities and training were superior to those of the people around him. Also, Florian DeVoto was a bitter anti-Mormon, and intellectually he remained a Jesuit. The baptism of young Bernard in Omaha was the doing of Florian's sister Rose, and never took; but when it came time to send his only child to school, Florian concluded that there was no one in Ogden fit to teach that prodigy except the Sisters of the Sacred Heart. He sent Bernard to them, the only boy in a class of girls, until after several years the sisters themselves, finding him a handful and observing that he took a great interest in the opposite sex, suggested that he might now risk the public school.

What Bernard got from his father was not a faith, or even an inclination toward one. By adolescence he was a confirmed agnostic. But he did get a stiff prejudice against the Mormon people, habits, and beliefs, a sense that culture existed only farther east and among people of another kind, and a pronounced, forced-draft hunger for the intellectual life. He really liked his mother's people, found many of them first-rate, loved some of them dearly. But he admitted that the paternal inheritance, for which he had no such affection, was more important to his development. He did not scorn Catholicism as he scorned Mormonism, and not even the humiliating sense of difference he felt as the only boy among all the females of the Sacred Heart Academy could drive him back toward his mother's church, against which he had been early inoculated. His intellectual affiliation remained with his father. He joined him among Mormonism's sworn enemies.

His mother was his protector and his refuge. A family story says that she nursed him at the breast until he was past two years old and running around. But it was his father who took charge of his mind. An embittered failure whose inherited money had been lost in land and mining speculations and whose talents as a linguist and mathematician went to waste in a hole-in-the-wall title-abstract office, Florian DeVoto was "a combination of Heyst, in Conrad's *Victory*, and the Swift who wrote about the Yahoos."[3] A small man and a contentious one, with tiny tiny feet, he gave his son an example of thoroughgoing misanthropy and of an integrity that managed to alienate everyone it touched. He taught the boy to read at age three (according to family tradition, beginning with Pope's *Iliad*).[4] The same perhaps unreliable tradition says that he started to teach Bernard Greek at the same time, but if he did, the teaching took no better than Rose DeVoto Coffman's rites of baptism. There is, however, no doubt that he set the boy at a very early age to a reading of the Greek, Latin, and Italian epics, and so bent the malleable child crookedly across all the conformities of a postfrontier half-Mormon town.

What could Ogden make of a ten-year-old who was reading *Orlando Furioso?* Funny kid.

The gods who really had charge of Bernard DeVoto's boyhood were neither Mormon nor Catholic nor Renaissance humanist. Some goddess of geography had charge of the auspices. Religion, especially the pentecostal sects with which he classed Mormonism, always seemed to him one of the more egregious forms of delusion, but geography was a fact, an important fact with important consequences. It was important that the orchards of his grandfather Samuel Dye ("a perfect peasant, submissive, unimaginative, stolid, industrious, faithful, thorough")[5] lay in irrigated bottom land below a mountain watershed, for that single fact, familiar from infancy, instructed young DeVoto in a basic condition of western life. Even more important was the fact that it lay on one of the main thoroughfares of western history, for history offered the one dependable heritage to a boy born between worlds, in a place which his father's contempt, his own sense of difference, and the literary currents of his time all led him to despise.

Like many who fled the limited and puritanical village, he would not know until he had separated himself from it how much he knew about his home and how much he valued it. Later he said that he had no interest in western history until he left the West, but he had taken in a good deal through the pores.

The curve of his life would be the curve traversed by many of those who made the influential literature of his generation, the curve of spiritual repudiation followed by physical exile followed by a delayed, reluctant, ambiguous return. "The Middle West," said Glenway Wescott, is "a state of mind of people born where they do not like to live."[6] He needn't have limited himself to the

Middle West, or even to America. What Kewaskum was to him, and Sauk Center to Sinclair Lewis, and Cedar Rapids to Carl Van Vechten, and Oak Park to Ernest Hemingway, Indian Creek, Texas, was to Katherine Anne Porter, and Wellington, New Zealand, was to Katherine Mansfield, and Dublin was to James Joyce.

And Ogden, Utah, was to Bernard DeVoto. By the time he graduated from Ogden High School his directions were established, he had been programmed for life. He was precocious, alert, intelligent, brash, challenging, irreverent, literary, self-conscious, insecure, often ostentatiously crude, sometimes insufferable. To Ogden he looked like a cowbird in a robin's nest ("the ugliest, most disagreeable boy you ever saw," says the sister of one of his boon companions).[7] But he was not totally at odds with his place and time. In fact, he embraced frontier toughness as a substitute for—even a challenge to—the piety of the Mormon households in which he was a watched, suspected, and not always welcomed interloper. He played poker, he used tobacco, he *spoke*, at least, of using liquor, and this among people who still observed the Word of Wisdom, the dietary restrictions set forth in Joseph Smith's *Pearl of Great Price*. He acquired, and valued, the casual skills of a western boy who has grown up close to open country but not in the absolute sticks. The opening of Ogden Canyon was no more than three miles from the center of downtown— a few minutes' bicycle ride put a boy at the edge of wildness.

Thus Bernard, a somewhat fat boy in his youth, who tried to play high school football and broke an ankle at it, was a good shot with either rifle or revolver, a good, self-reliant mountain camper and hiker. He slept his share of nights on top of Mount Ogden, and his favorite sport was marksmanship. He spent a lot of time, when he was an officer in the high school ROTC, at the National Guard range, and he never went into the mountains without a cartridge belt and a holstered revolver or automatic. At the same time, he was a pretty good tennis player in what Bill Tilden used to call the "Young Pete Swattem" style.

Through schoolboy and summer jobs he had gained a certain amount of concrete experience. Probably he never worked at as many jobs as he later claimed, or qualified himself as expert in so many skills, but he seems to have sold tickets and muscled baggage on the interurban line between Ogden and Salt Lake, and at several times, including the summer after his graduation from high school, he wrote sports and occasionally other things for the Ogden *Evening Standard*.[8] Thus he could reassure himself in later life that he had been apprenticed in the hard school of professional journalism. It probably delighted him with some glimpses of the non-pious side of Ogden; it probably taught him to get around among different kinds of people, gave him a nose for a story and a certain skill at discovering and ransacking sources of facts. It contributed to confidence, and perhaps to the overconfidence which is one face of insecurity. Later on, warring with the effete and literary in New York, he would belligerently assert his pride in being a "mere" journalist.

The *Standard* may also have contributed to his pose of worldly toughness, as well as to his realism, his contempt for cant, his cynical nose for the taint of hypocrisy, and his expectation of human cussedness. If his father's misanthropy taught him that every man was probably a liar, a cheat, and a thief, and his father's residual Catholicism told him that there existed in the universe and in men an abiding principle of evil that could not be wished or exorcised away, the *Standard* in the summer of 1914 and at odd times later instructed him in some of evil's practical manifestations, exemplars, and victims.

A journalist, he liked to call himself later, and perhaps then. But a very literary one. From his father's bookshelves, which mirrored the tastes of a man "steeped in a culture which had been closed for almost a hundred years," he found his way to fiction, of which his father had little, and to the "advanced" books that gave an overliterary boy a chance to feel superior. He admits that he bought more books than he read, and talked about more than he bought, but he and his two friends Wendell ("Fitz") Fitzgerald and W. E. (Eddie) Higman bought a good many and read some, all tending to persuade them that Ogden was an uncultivated hole and that the fine mind must find its sustenance elsewhere.[9]

The Ramayana, the Koran, Chesterton, Shaw, Wells, Bennett, Galsworthy's plays, the Georgian poets, the Gaelic revivalists, *Sesame and Lilies, Travels with a Donkey*—the list is desperately eclectic, even accidental. Significantly, it does not contain the writers who were already creating the revolutionary attitudes of the twentieth century. Ogden was a long way from the fountain. It was too early for the Rocky Mountains to have heard the rumors of that calculated hatred of the modern which would come to be known as modernism. No echoes of Ezra Pound drifted back this close to his birthplace in Hailey, Idaho. After all, the only guides a young reader had in Ogden in 1914 were a misanthropic intellectual father with a paralyzed will and antiquated tastes, the clerks and attendants at Spargo's Bookstore and the Carnegie Free Public Library (who probably knew less than he), and a tensely literary high school English teacher, herself a victim of the village virus.

Literary affectations in a town that had no use or respect for literature and thought it a sissy occupation not proper for red-blooded males were surely both cause and effect of some of young DeVoto's aggressive non-conformity. What was at first a conscious repudiation became eventually a reflex. If the majority was for something, or the Mormons were for it, or the dominant coterie was for it, or the academic historians or the English teachers or the critics or the political party in power were for it, he was moved to doubt and sometimes denounce it. Intellectually he was no democrat, whatever he might be in political and cultural matters.

Also, being literary in Ogden, he felt his masculinity in question. Hemingway was not the only writer of that generation open to Max Eastman's gibe about the false hair on the chest. With DeVoto, a compensatory aggressiveness began early and lasted. His defense against felt or suspected scorn was to scorn the scorners, preferably in advance, and to scorn them with such confidence, eloquence, and command of relevant facts that they could never get off the floor.

For lack of concrete evidence one must guess about some things, but it does not stretch the probabilities of either DeVoto or Ogden to guess that some people in Odgen thought DeVoto a Wop name, or that Bernard thought they did. Or that the feeling of intellectual superiority generated by his father's teaching, plus his condition of being a sort of Catholic in a Mormon town, brought him at times the desolating sense of being an outsider. The same acquaintance who thought him the ugliest, rudest boy she ever saw says that many Mormon homes were closed to him as a bad influence. After his father's shabby-middle-class living began to decline toward real poverty, a poor Catholic boy might have complex feelings about those who were both Mormon and rich. There is a story that he used to sit on the porch of a girl he was rushing, and spend whole evenings watching the parties that went on in the Eccles house across the street. The Eccles house was big, built in the solidest Mormon fashion of sandstone and brick, with double turrets and a wrap-around veranda, and it occupied a big corner lot on Twenty-sixth and Jefferson. Presumably it was one of the houses that were closed to Bernard DeVoto. He was vocal and bitter about the wild parties that by his reckoning went on there, though in fact the numerous Eccles girls were nice Mormon girls to whom any drink stronger than lemonade would have been sinful and who would probably not have gone out with a boy who smoked.

Cultural outsider, poor boy, intellectual snob, scorned poet, bad influence suspected by the godly, he had many of the standard literary quarrels with his home town. He also had a physical reason for an acute self-consciousness, a reason that like Henry James's accident was not to be discussed.

Though family tradition says he won some sort of beauty contest as a baby, and though early pictures show him with a nose which like his father's was distinctly Roman, a boyhood accident with a baseball or a baseball bat flattened it badly, and the doctor who patched it up bungled the job. A later trip to Omaha for repairs failed to improve his looks. In conjunction with his natural conformation, that squashed nose made people look at him twice. His head was round, his face a full oval. Before he had to start wearing the glasses that were a fixture of his later life, his lively, alert, sardonic, strikingly intelligent brown eyes saved his looks, and it was a remarkable fact that the moment one began to know him his looks were forgotten; but those who did not like him took pleasure in thinking he looked like a goggled ape, his upper lip very long, his nose broad and flat. In his youth, when he was full of himself and aware of exceptional capacities, he must have stared into mirrors with despair for what the realities of his looks did to the gorgeousness of young fantasies.

These last were ardent and various. One kind would have taken him to instant literary fame and confounded the blockheads and snickerers of Ogden. Another would surely have involved the salutary drubbing of bullies, a theme that recurs with regularity in his fiction. A third demonstrably led him through a series of impassioned attachments to one blonde goddess after another. Perhaps he felt the need of some beautiful woman who would look past his face and fall in love with his mind. The fact is, some did; he was by no means a universally scorned Lothario. But one serious difficulty was that they were of Ogden Ogdenish, and he was born both an iconoclast and a show-off. Sooner or later they flounced off their pedestals, or he shoved them off in a disgusted return to realism.

There was one lady who did fall in love with his mind and remained its faithful handmaiden, but she was not one of the nubile ones. In "A Sagebrush Bookshelf" DeVoto wrote:

We must not forget one typical figure who was indigenous to the small town in that stage of culture all over the United States. She was either a high school teacher or a librarian, and she was the pure amateur of books, a woman who lived for literature and waged a bitter warfare against the horny-minded who scorned it. . . . When she found a youth who shared her passion, brought his ideas to her, and at last brought his sonnets too, it would be inevitable for her to serve literature by nurturing this strange blossom in the wasteland. . . . For the youth himself she was a fortress of strength and confirmation; she renewed his identity, armed him against scorn, coddled and mothered him, fiercely led him on to more discriminating taste. . . . Resented, derided, laughed at, she preached the gospel to the Philistines, and if the nation has a wider toleration of literature than it had fifty years ago, if there is a higher percentage of readers, then some thousands of her scattered from the Alleghenies to Puget Sound are one of the primary causes.

DeVoto's literary den mother he identifies only as Mrs. F. He says she had a way, transparent and probably pathetic to a perceptive youth, of sometimes quoting the great as if their golden words had been coined in conversations with herself, but she believed in literature as did no one else in Ogden except perhaps his father. She made it seem "a natural way of life," she loaned books and opened vistas, she sent him to Yeats and Ossian and Fiona Macleod, she introduced him to the emancipated Wells. She nurtured and guided him until he was ready for college, which had to be the University of Utah because it was nearest and cheapest, and in September 1914 she sent him off with her seal upon his brow and all her hopes for vicarious fulfillment in his suitcase. She wrote him regularly, urging and encouraging, commanding him to read Ernest Poole's *The Harbor* or some other indispensable book.

Then, in the spring of 1915, the Mormon-Gentile conflict, which in Utah was a more natural way of life than literature was, surfaced again. A pair of English instructors at the university, one of them Bernard's Freshman English instructor, Wilbert Snow, were fired. Charges flew that the Mormon Church was exerting its customary suppressive influence upon the freedom of the mind and manipulating the university to its own purposes. Fifteen members of the faculty quit in protest, the president of the university stood his ground, the American Association of University Professors investigated and eventually blacklisted the university, the president ultimately resigned. Bernard DeVoto, as a friend of Snow's and one of the young radicals of the campus, had no difficulty choosing his side, though he seems not to have written anything about the incident for any campus publication. Well before the melted lavas had re-formed the crust that permitted business to go on, he had shaken the dust of that "alleged institution" from his feet, had somehow raised the money to go to Harvard, had applied, and had been admitted.

So Mrs. F. lost him to the wider world, where he was more likely to fulfill the hopes she had for him. He escaped from the "culture clubs and chiropractors" of his native city and made his way toward the mysterious and intellectual and literary East from which his father had come. Never mind that his father had come from Indiana. To an Ogden boy, anything east of Cheyenne is back East. In the fall of 1915 the Union Pacific took him up Weber Canyon past his grandfather's farm, and Ogden—so went his resolve—was behind him forever.

3 · Harvard

Naturally he was wrong. Also he was a little scared. If he thought that a year in college in Salt Lake City had made him a man of the world, he could think again. Looked back at from the shadows of ivied Georgian brick, their echoes heard amid the sound of unfamiliar, flattened vowels and obliterated *r*'s, remembered from his bed in Gannet House while the interminable Cambridge rain swished in the street and gurgled in gutters and downspouts, Ogden and Salt Lake City turned out to be merely variants of the same place, the only place he knew, and he turned out to be only another undergraduate away from home for the first time. Cambridge might stimulate him halfway to combustion, but it was shabby under the rain, its people were strangers with cold hearts and indifferent faces, its girls were unpretty, its ways were foreign. His only acquaintance at first was his roommate, Arthur Perkins, neither literary nor a close friend, but an Ogden boy and therefore a support.

A week after he had put Ogden behind him forever, young DeVoto was homesick for it. His homesickness lay much of the time below the level of awareness, probably, but it crops up in the letters he wrote to a girl named Helen Hunter at the University of Utah.[1] Calf letters full of inflated, playful rhetoric, and salted with French and German phrases sometimes misspelled, they were calculated to stimulate envy and reveal how completely Bernard had taken possession of the larger life. They refer casually to plays and concerts, they drop names sure to sound impressive on Thirteenth East Street in Salt Lake City. They report the pieces he has learned on the mandolin, they describe his collection of pipes.

But through the undergraduate brag and the clichés leaks an occasional spasm of self-doubt, and the interest in Utah matters is constant and hungry. He keeps asking about Utah's football team, presumably unreported in the eastern press. He wants news of Ogden people, especially his "ex-wife"—a phrase to describe some lost girl friend. He complains about the Cambridge weather, the Bahston accent, and his room in Gannett, a room like all the other rooms that Washington slept in. "No doubt it has traditions but I should prefer electric light." At midterm exam time he despairs, fearful that he will flunk something. Later he reports that he missed an A in philosophy—the apparent extent of his casualties. He reveals that his eyes have been bothering him (they bothered him off and on all his life, generally when he was in one of his spells of nervous disintegration) and that he has had to get glasses— tortoise-shell. He demonstrates his new philosophic depth by a solipsistic rumination meant to stun the reader with its profundity: In a world so like a dream, who can tell whether dreams and memory are not as real as what we call reality?

Who indeed. For shortly Helen sent some photographs, which, arriving in the depths of the Cambridge winter with its lead skies and gray snow and black ice, detonated a poem. Her pictures, the poet says, call forth the Wasatch, memory, dreams, YOU, into his far-off room, and Lo! Memory and dream of Ogden, Utah, are as real as Gannett House, and a good deal more attractive.

There are other poems, mostly about love in twilight, love in moonlight, and love to music (Helen was a musician, a contralto). The last one is signed "Florien," which was his father's name with an Old French flourish, and which might mean something to a psychoanalyst tracking down a young man who was in turn tracking down his own identity.

But he wasn't always sticky. Helen's confession that she had gone skiing in her father's pants inspired him to burlesque:

> Behold through hovering shadows slowly stealing
> A gliding form endowed with fairy shape.
> Ye Gods! a maid, with all her maiden's feeling,
> And clad, I veil mine eyes, in manhood's drape!
>
> About her limbs paternal garb is clinging,
> And o'er her forehead looms a Stetson felt.
> And I, her bard, must wonder while I'm singing
> Whether she wears suspenders or a belt.

At least once, in these letters to Helen Hunter, he is defiantly confessional. He always valued the outward evidences of accomplishment—medals, prizes, memberships—as if he needed them on his wall to reassure him. Especially in his college days, that need of certification was extreme. When he joined a club called Kappa Gamma Chi, in May 1916, he joined it for reasons that he said had made him an outcast among his Cambridge acquaintances. No prestige attached to that club at Harvard; it was a long long way from Porcellian. But membership would give Bernard status among his intellectual inferiors in Ogden. "At least," he wrote Helen, "I have the grace not to be a hypocrite."

By that time, Helen Hunter had dropped out of the University of Utah to study voice. By October of the following year she was remote enough from his life so that he didn't know whether to address her in Salt Lake City or Chicago. But for a while, when he was least at home in Cambridge and in himself, she was that person he always needed: someone to cling to, not one of the blonde goddesses and not one of the mentally occluded of Utah, but a good companion, a fellow intelligence, somebody trustworthy, unaffected, unconventional, open, western, friendly, a girl from home. And a contralto voice, something that ever after undid him.

Bernard DeVoto came to Harvard a raw western youth impressed with Harvard's intellectual eminence and defensive about Ogden's assumption that literature was sissy. Sometime during his years there, he seems to have observed that not his literary graces but his westernness got him noticed. He may or may not have realized that his westernness was to a considerable extent the crudity that he had scorned as an attribute of his home town. Iconoclasm is easy to undergraduates, and was particularly easy to this boy who had always been an outsider, an unbeliever, a suspicious and sensitive maverick, and a show-off. If at Harvard he sometimes assumed philistine attitudes and emitted coarse guffaws, if he sometimes attacked the ideas of his fellows with a vigor and a gift for invective that some found offensive, let us never forget that Ogden had a hammer lock on him from behind. Ogden forced him to the perception that, for all its advantages, the East was effete, that it lacked the continental view, that its assumptions and prejudices needed a little western fresh air. The literary needed to be told they were sissy.

The more confident he became that his talents and intelligence would stand up against the competition of the best, the more he adopted the western role; and the more western he became, the more he felt it necessary to back up the role with knowledge, to know what it meant to come from the place he came from. It was at Harvard that he began to read about the West, and since the modern West seemed to him simply provincial and unwashed and unworthy of his allegiance, he was diverted to its history, whose violence and boisterousness were as masculine as even Ogden could desire, but whose distance and heroic largeness made it romantic.

Any western American history he wanted to study he had to get outside the curriculum. He did take some history courses, including a course from Harold Laski, the history of religion with George Foot Moore (his interest in pentecostal aberrations coming to the surface), and the history of science with L. J. Henderson[2]; but those represented less a personal interest than the satisfaction of requirements and distributions. In November 1915 he had indicated a disinclination for history courses.[3] For the fact was that the American social history which most interested him, the history of how the country was settled, how people lived, what houses they built and tools they used and skills they practiced and folkways they knew and entertainment they enjoyed, was not yet a common offering of history departments. Political, military, diplomatic, and the newly popular economic history he could have got; social history as a respectable calling would await the work of Arthur Schlesinger the elder (who brought it to Cambridge from Iowa) and some others who would be DeVoto's friends later on. As DeVoto's friend Garrett Mattingly said, you might have to be buried two thousand miles deep in the continent to have a dependable sense of it.[4] Even as an undergraduate, young DeVoto had a sense of it that was denied most of his professors.

If western American social history was outside the canon, something to be learned not from classes but from reading the narratives and autobiographies and reminiscences and letters of those who had experienced it, American literature was hardly more accessible. Despite his later assertions that his first intention was to become a doctor or a psychiatrist, DeVoto's interests seem to have been literary when he came to Harvard, and to have remained so. Thanks to Mrs. F. and Wilbert Snow, his stance was more American, more contemporary, and more creative than Harvard in his time was quite prepared to deal with. As taught at Harvard in 1915, American literature was the preserve of Barrett Wendell, who "studied it as a now-abandoned folkway of the Bostonians."[5] The men who taught writing—Byron Hurlbut, Dean LeBaron Russell Briggs, and Charles Townsend Copeland—were sympathetic teachers through whose classes passed scores and hundreds of the literary young, including Bernard DeVoto, but they were not themselves writers, and they were all older men, considerably removed from the impatient and revolutionary impulses of their students. "In short, the young writer could not get at Harvard either a creator's point of view toward writing or any critical guidance whatsoever through the values, the contradictions, the fads and shams and controversies of the new movement which he hoped to join."[6]

That statement, characteristically unqualified, sounds like the complaint of a student allowed to flounder. DeVoto may have floundered some, adjusting himself to a new place and to standards of excellence well above anything he had ever been held to, but he did not lack for guidance. All three writing teachers were impressed by him and became his good friends, adopting him in almost fatherly fashion; and if they could not steer him confidently among the forming literary tendencies of the time, they could at least encourage in him the skepticism that he already possessed in good measure. If he was looking for something to join, he quickly found out that he did not fit into any gang or coterie—not the Fabians, not the "poor-devil followers of the Russian novelists," and certainly not the aesthetes of whom Malcolm Cowley's account in *Exile's Return* is the standard one. "An oafish kind of cub, lubberly and stammering and Rocky Mountain," upon whom "no kind of form was imposed" until after the War, he admitted that he was "hardly even a hanger-on of this high-church aestheticism . . . with its "perfumed and uncapitalized verse, with some symbol in the stage directions, such as 'Utter darkness,' 'To be accompanied by a hautboy and a lute,' or 'The mist lifts and Christ is seen.' "[7] Through his sophomore and junior years he remained, despite his abiding need for friends, something of an outsider, more oriented to America than to Europe, closer related to the muckrakers and H. L. Mencken than to Pound, Joyce, or the twilight diabolisms of the *Yellow Book*. Like Sinclair Lewis, and for somewhat similar psychological and geographical reasons, he specialized in the Bronx cheer.

His companions were more accidental than chosen. In an effort to ease the isolation of students who transferred from other institutions, Memorial Hall made up tables of such waifs. Some of those with whom DeVoto was thrown by this administrative gesture remained his close associates and in some cases his roommates through his three years in Cambridge. Gordon King from CCNY, Tommy Raysor from the University of Chicago, Dave Snodgrass from the University of California, Kent Hagler from the University of Illinois were four of them. King and Hagler became De-

Voto's closest friends. Snodgrass and Raysor, though less close, were his roommates for a year in Fairfax Hall.[8] King and Raysor were literary, as DeVoto was, but by no stretch of the imagination could any of them have been called a member of an elite.

Outside the groupings created by intellectual and literary currents, he was also apart from some accepted affiliations and loyalties. In so Anglophile a place as Harvard, during the early years of World War I, there was much pro-Ally sentiment, some prowar talk, and an accelerating amount of enlistment in the American Ambulance Service, the Norton-Harjes, or the Red Cross ambulance units that served on the Italian front. The literary were peculiarly susceptible, though their attitude toward the war itself was often what Malcolm Cowley calls "spectatorial." "One might almost say that the ambulance corps and the French military transport were college-extension courses for a generation of writers."[9] A class list would have included Cowley himself, Dos Passos, Robert Hillyer, Edward Weeks, Hemingway, Julian Green, William Seabrook, E. E. Cummings, Slater Brown, Harry Crosby, John Howard Lawson, Sidney Howard, Louis Bromfield, Dashiell Hammett, and a lot more.

But not Bernard DeVoto. Considerably later, reviewing *Exile's Return*, he would scold Cowley for assuming that his ambulance-and-camion crew accurately represented a whole generation.[10] For a while the war was simply not real to DeVoto; it was something in the rotogravure sections and in the headlines. Then there came a time when it moved up a long step and became a personal possibility. At one of Copeland's Monday Nights there was a guest, a journalist from the Manchester *Guardian*, a man whom a year or two later Copey would hate and fear as a Bolshevik, but who in January or February of 1917 was a voice from the threatened Motherland. His name was S. K. Ratliffe. "He sat in the guest's green chair, Copey vis-a-vis, with the yellow light of Copey's oil lamp on him, and a score or so of us young stotes ranged in the brown shadows on the floor. Quite simply and emotionally, but with a fine art—one then much practiced by visiting Englishmen— he told about seeing the troops march off for Folkstone, singing 'Send father and mother, send sister and brother, but for God's sake don't send me,' [and] about following them to France, about simple, isolated, immensely effective *vignettes militaire*. Just as simply and inevitably, he from time to time dropped his narrative, looked round at us through great gleaming spectacles, mildly, reflectively, and remarked, 'I'll see you young men there in a year or two.' It was a perfection of propaganda, of a particular British propaganda that stinks to God, but it did its job. At least, sitting there with a fire burning on the hearth of Emerson and Thoreau and Everett, looking out to bright moonlight on the snowy roofs of Thayer and Holworthy, I heard the tramp and shuffle of those feet and the hoarse singing overseas."[11]

Heard, but did not yet heed. Though shaken for a moment by the contagious idealism of sacrifice, he prided himself that he did not share the hysteria. Gordon King and others, who did share it, argued and pled with him, called him an anarchist, quoted him Plato on the necessities of the state. He held out. And then, about the following November, when Harvard boys began rotten-egging pacifist and anti-war groups, the belligerent and contrary part of DeVoto rose up and told him to join the pacifists. He did, and was called a yellow coward, from the podium, by Copey—Copey who had paid the expenses of at least one Harvard boy to sail off to France and make his sacrifice. Even among friends such as Gordon King and Kent Hagler, he felt the tension of an effort to understand what to them was a monstrous selfishness and indifference.

Writing about it afterward, DeVoto felt that he held out hard-headedly until the actual declaration of war, listened with some skepticism while Copey extolled Woodrow Wilson's war speech as the highest rhetoric ever uttered, and then quite suddenly and coolly, when Harold Laski in History 2 asked how many war-bound students were taking the special examination, realized that he was taking it. Shortly after, he enlisted in the Harvard Regiment, whose barracks were the Freshmen Dormitories, and found himself a patriot while his friend Hagler, held back by a damaged eye and an injured spine, was not.

Whether or not his motives were as clear to him, and as cynically realistic, as this account implies, there is little doubt that he was divided and had to make a choice. The role of American suspicious of entangling European alliances was native to him (and to Ogden); that of pacifist was merely a contrary reflex. For one of DeVoto's temperament, peace is most attractive when one is fighting in its name. And his later commentary tends to play down the youthful idealism by which, in middle life, he was embarrassed. What put him on the road to war was actually a flash flood of generous feeling.

Water, he liked to point out when engaged in the fight against destructive land uses in the West, runs downhill. In an ardently romantic nature, emotions also run downhill, sometimes over all the dams that common sense and cynicism have erected. They took him into the Harvard Regiment on April 6, 1917. The unit trained through the spring in Cambridge and later went to a camp in western Massachusetts. In August it disbanded, freeing its members for further choices. DeVoto went back to Ogden, renewed his love-hate relationship with the town, talked with his parents, and restlessly contemplated the possibility of returning to a war-altered Harvard from which most of his acquaintance would have vanished into uniform singing such songs as were sung on the road to Folkstone. With characteristic anxiety he examined his soul, tested his resolution, analyzed his reasons, doubted and asserted his courage, passionately read the war news, felt the surge of war fever swirling even in that remote mountain town, and finally enlisted. He was posted for training at Camp Devens, Massachusetts.

4 · A Spiritual War

Ricardo Quintana, who served through the summer of 1917 in the Harvard ROTC regiment, recalls DeVoto as the one member of the outfit with whom he could discuss books and ideas.[1] They did not always agree. In fact they rather seldom agreed, and they had a particularly bitter running argument about the reputation and prose style of Henry James, to whom Quintana was addicted and whom DeVoto could not read. Also, there was the characteristic DeVoto aggressiveness and belligerence, and there was that smashed nose "about which one did not inquire." DeVoto seems to have intimidated Quintana somewhat, and probably neither was temperamentally designed for intimate friendship with the other. But they were companions, almost friends, of an accidental kind, and they were brought even closer together after the war. And so one must pay some attention to Quintana's hearsay evidence that in the regular Army, after their paths had diverged, DeVoto was sometimes referred to as "the Chinese bastard."

The "Chinese" is understandable as a not-very-perceptive reference to his face. The "bastard" is enigmatic, and might be read as indicating either an offensive personality or a stiff-backed, drill-sergeant rigor. There is no evidence that either reading is sound. His letters reflect no sense of being hated; and his military service, which is recapturable mainly through his letters to his parents,[2] was remarkable for quite different things from Prussian discipline: for the passion of his dedication, his determination to think well of the democratic, civilian Army, his pride in being a nameless unit among democracy's defenders, the humility with which he accepted basic training and OTC as personal testings and rites of passage that would permit him ultimately to call himself a man. Those who had thought him brash, crude, arrogant, and disagreeable would have been astonished to read his intimate letters.

Whatever he was in the Harvard ROTC, where he was at home among people against whom he knew he could hold his own and to whom he could even feel superior, his attitude as a raw recruit was marked by as much insecurity as cockiness, though now and then the old cockiness comes through his humility like a rocket through a tent roof. His letters to his parents reveal an extraordinary filial tenderness, an affection essentially boyish and dependent, a frequent humble doubt of his own capacities, a reiterated resolve to do well and not disgrace himself or them. He sounds like anything but a Chinese bastard, or any other sort of bastard. If Quintana's hearsay had any basis whatever in fact, and did indeed reflect the response to DeVoto of some of his fellows, then we may take it as a partial explanation of why he went through much of his life with his quills erected. He was never, in the Army or elsewhere, quite safe from the casual, almost anonymous sneer.

But he encountered friendship too, and a comradeship that he valued, and among his old friends an affection that touched him. Once, on a pass, he visited Cambridge and ran into Charles Townsend Copeland in the Yard, and the Copey who had called him yellow put his arms around him, with tears in his eyes, to wish him well as a soldier. He had never quite lost touch with Cambridge, for his cousin Rose now lived there with her husband, the Belgian painter Jean-Marie Guislain. In June 1918 he wrote his parents about one visit:

Last night I walked along the river bank with Jean-Marie, my first night walk along the old familiar path for over a year. You have not known the nights I wrestled with the angels of a thousand faiths, wrestled with them all night long, in the deep shadow of the river, in sight of the steady lights of Anderson Bridge. Those old nights of doubt, of fear, of self-distrust! We needed just this great national peril to bring back the faith and confidence in ourselves we had so surely lost. Last night there was no thought of abnegation, it was sure, certain confidence. The cause has come, and with it the courage which had died.
But oh! the memories came thick. 'Say could that lad be I?'—that gloomy, melancholy, aspiring young chump . . . I must think of myself of those days very tenderly, though, ludicrous as I must have been. Never, I think, has there been greater sincerity, more genuine aspira-

tion. The pity of all things—it used to shake me to the depths till I was one with the night, in tune with the world's sorrow. . . . I now perceive in myself the truth of what my intuition discerned more than a year ago—that finally and most far-reaching the war is a spiritual war, and will in the end have given us a new and lasting gospel.[3]

As a mature man he would have been embarrassed to be called a patriot; he would have scorned being called an idealist. He sounds defenselessly like both, and neither of them much older than the sophomore who used to write love-in-the-moonlight poems to Helen Hunter. Twenty-one he was when he wrote that letter—a very young twenty-one, badly in need of the advice ex-Dean Gay of Harvard later gave him, not to take himself too seriously. But not unattractive. Touching, even.

At Devens, which with its weekend passes to Cambridge was like an overorganized summer camp, Bernard took himself seriously indeed. In the draftees around him he discovered the true heart of America, often disparaged but in the crisis sound. He was not greatly strained by the training, and in rests and off hours he began writing a novel—his second attempt in that direction—in his head. "And what a book it is!" he wrote his parents. "It is the novel of my own country, the wide and ample theatre of the hills, the peaks and valleys, the mountain streams, the railroad, above all the people. *Labor amoris.*"[4]

Labor of love? Above all the people? Something has happened to Ogden since he kissed it good-by, for in this non-book about it, unwritten on the wind of nostalgia, he thinks he touches "depths of feeling which I had not know[n]," and feels that "through it I have somewhat realized myself. . . . Though the book [may] be done away with forever [by] my death in France, still I have made the beginning of my lifelong devotion."

Reading these letters in 1973 one finds it hard to believe that even the young could ever have attitudinized so, with such sad-sweet relinquishment and such willingness to be sacrificed, and with such a blend of elevated patriotism and literary fustian. It is necessary to remember back to such literary warriors as Willa Cather's Pulitzer-prize hero Claude Wheeler, in *One of Ours*. To stand up in a bullet-swept trench and Give All for Civilization with an inspiring word on one's lips—that was the sort of gesture that Bernard DeVoto of 1918 would have found greatly moving, though it would move the college student of 1973 to incredulous snickers. It was the kind of gesture imagined by the literary and the non-combatant. Actual combat had a way of erasing such posing swiftly and for good, along with all those high-sounding phrases that Hemingway's Lieutenant Henry gagged on, words such as "noble" and "in vain."

"What sort of man do these letters show me to be, I wonder?" Bernard asked himself or his parents, with Posterity waiting breathless for a reply.[5] Posterity can now answer. They show him to have been a young literary man of a dewy, prelapsarian time when self-sacrificing devotion was still possible in the United States, and some causes were held worthy of it.

From Devens, at the end of June 1918, he was shipped south to OTC at Camp Lee, Virginia, and there he set world records for taking himself seriously. The winds of Civil War history around him rippled him like a flag; he vibrated to the news of the fighting in France as the American offensive began near Soissons; he grew stern and resolute about the dedication demanded of an officer in the Army of the United States; he yearned to win his commission, presumably so that he might serve his country to the utmost but also because a piece of paper and a bar on each shoulder would be gratification to his ambition and his unsleeping need to be proved worthy.

Finding that he stood up better than many to the grueling routines of Camp Lee, he exerted himself to help others and talk them out of discouragement. When the thermometer, at least according to his report to his parents, rose to 130° one week, and men wilted like miller moths in a gas jet, and one insane captain double-timed his men for ten minutes in the full glare, to make them tough, and brought on a dozen prostrations, eight sunstrokes, and six deaths in his single company,* Bernard DeVoto got through the ordeal on resolution and nerve, and went off to Richmond on a pass, and from the YMCA there wrote home that only his mind, "the glory of my past years," had enabled him to survive. "Thank God for Harvard," he said: it had given him a trained mind, and men with trained minds came through this brutal sort of punishment better than the strongest physical specimens. But almost in the same paragraph he was flexing his muscles with pleasure in their hard fitness, and congratulating himself that he had now proved himself no weakling, "despite the sneers I have experienced in the past."[6]

All these trials, he said, had knocked out of him the cocksureness which had till then been his dominant trait—and shortly was bragging how self-sufficient the army had made him, how he could be sent into the wilderness and create a new civilization with nothing but some iodine and an entrenching tool. And keep

* DeVoto's count, probably exaggerated.

my manuscript novel out of the hands of Fitz's sister, he said. Hereafter show my writing to nobody without a written order from me.

In August he graduated seventh out of his class of one hundred fifty, apologizing to his father for not being first. His commission literally thrilled him; his dress uniform preoccupied him as her first formal gown might preoccupy a girl. He had to wire his family for a loan to put together Sam Browne belt, leather puttees, garrison cap, insignia, and the rest. He instructed them severely to address him henceforth as Bernard A. DeVoto, 2nd Lieut. Inf., and warned them that at any time now he could expect to be ordered overseas.

But in his boyhood he had improved to too good purpose the canyons of the Wasatch and the National Guard firing range in Ogden. He was too good a shot to be wasted on a war. With uncharacteristic wisdom in the utilization of talent, the Army ordered him to Camp Perry, Ohio, as a musketry instructor.

Some would have thought it a reprieve. Most of his companions envied him the prize assignment. To DeVoto, geared up for heroism and self-sacrifice, ready to go forth to battle and death with his puttees shined, his dress uniform immaculate, and his great books unwritten, it was anticlimactic and vaguely sour. He liked the look of the bars on his shoulders, and he tried to feel glad and successful and vindicated, but one conceives him as a little aggrieved, as a man with his head on the block might feel if the headsman suddenly yanked off the blindfold and leaned back smiling upon his axe. *God damn it, what did you stop for? I wanted to see if I could take it without flinching!*

Camp Perry, he hoped, would not hold him long. He did not want to become a Battalion Range Officer. He wanted to train his own outfit (perhaps vaguely visualized as Rough Riders) and lead it to France and do his duty in the final offensive expected next spring. He did not like Camp Perry, or Ohio, or the Middle West, and he was run-down and underweight and trained to a dangerous edge. The Army sent him to Ohio at the beginning of September. On October 5 it ordered him back to the one place in all America where he did not want to go—Camp Lee—and he arrived just in time for the flu epidemic. He said he was the only officer in his unit to stay on his feet through it. On November 11 the Armistice cut short any remaining dreams of military self-sacrifice. On December 8 he was honorably discharged.

Honorably but not quite satisfactorily. Ever after, he obscurely envied those who had made it overseas. He craved that ultimate testing, and envy may have contributed to his distaste for the Lost Generation and the returned aesthetes of the Ambulance Service. In his Harvard dossier he took care to describe his military experience accurately: "Second Lieutenant of Infantry. Domestic service only—not on account of disability."[7]

5·*Harvard'20—as of '18*

Ogden was deep in snow, its raw wind smelling of cinders and coal smoke, its citizens looking and sounding provincial and out of touch and limited to their beyond-the-mountains myopias, their eternal Mormon-Gentile sparrings. Its intellectual tundra was relieved only by the igloo from which bookseller John Spargo dispensed literary handouts to the literate and lost. And his mother, badly hit by the flu, was slowly dying of the pernicious anemia that seemed to be one of its sequelae.

Even if his mother had not been ill, there was no returning to Harvard for nine months, until the following September, but De-Voto was writing the Secretary of the College by January 8. He wanted to know the requirements for returning; he said he needed a scholarship to return at all; he wondered if his last year's grades—four A's and three B's—might earn him one. He requested, almost demanded, that "inasmuch as my course was interrupted only by my desire for national service in the emergency, I should be allowed to finish it as I most desire." What he most desired was to take Dean Briggs's English 5, the most advanced course in writing at Harvard, though he had already taken all the writing courses the letter of the law allowed. Also, wearing a chip on his shoulder against the place he most revered, he complained that he had not received one of the certificates given to Harvard men who left college to join the Army. "I rendered the best national service I was capable of rendering, and I feel that I am fully entitled to such a certificate."[1]

The tone is strained, faintly paranoid, the tone of a sensitive young man touchy about being overlooked or ignored or forgotten. Probably he was still run-down from the Camp Lee experience and smarting from the disappointment of not getting overseas. Or perhaps he only wanted the certificate for his mother.

She was a simple woman, hard-working, ill-educated, intelligent beyond her training, with a lot of her father's stubborn endurance in her. She had escaped the Uinta farm by "working out" in

Ogden, had made a bad marriage that ended in divorce in 1885, and had met and married Florian DeVoto when he was a freight agent on the Union Pacific and she was running a boardinghouse that supported her, her half-grown son Cleveland de Wolfe, and three of her sisters. "Their married life," Bernard wrote some years after her death, "was really noble, which is a word that sits strangely on my lips, and the only happy thing in the life of either one. She lived to be very proud of me, for, of course, a boy in Harvard who was also a lieutenant in the army symbolized dizzy grandeurs to her. She always thought that the poverty in which my dad supported her was the wildest kind of affluence."[2]

She gave her brilliant, captious failure of a husband the kind of steady affection that let him live with his own cynicism and misanthropy, and she gave her brilliant, ambivalent, anxiously cocky son an adoration that could hardly have been greater. Through her lingering illness he helped take care of her, bitterly watching her strength wane and her skin go yellow and her hold on life slip. When she died, on August 3, 1919, she left her husband distraught, gloomy, and burdened with the care of numerous members of her family whom he was too generous not to help and too contentious not to complain about. She left her son exhausted, drained, and bereft of the softest, strongest tie that had bound him to Ogden.

But not the most fervent one. In March, at rehearsals for a play called *Under Cover*, he had met an Ogden High School senior of seventeen—blonde, beautiful, rich, a heartbreaker—who found the returned officer, the interrupted Harvard man, the aspiring writer, more interesting than the Ogden youths she had known. The whole spring and summer while his mother was dying, young DeVoto had been torn between the demands of death and the attractions of life, between grief and adoration. He and this girl, Katharine, had taken a lot of walks and sat out a lot of waning moons, and he had written her more elevated nonsense than even Helen Hunter had inspired,[3] and under the disguise of literary clowning had offered his heart, humbly, on a platter. ("Do I make an egregious ass of myself when I try to tell you how or what I feel? You see, I am not used to letting people see the deeper recesses of my nature. I cannot tell if it be pride or fear that keeps me from sharing myself with more people.") Solemnly he tried to direct her inexperience away from schoolgirl frivolity, he tried to be her guide to great books and high thinking. At times, fairly clearly, he made her impatient; but when they had had a spat he took it so seriously, he wrote her such agonized, exposed midnight letters, he assumed such stances of tragic renunciation and humility, that out of sheer astonishment at such a man, as much as out of affection, she was won back. And they were to be parted soon, he to go back to Harvard, she to attend a finishing school in Yonkers, New York. That parting hung over him in prospect, as fatal as if he had been Aeneas and she Dido. One night before they were to be parted he slept under her window, holding a string whose other end was tied around Katharine's finger. At dawn he pulled the string, awakening her to see the sun rise over the Wasatch.

In September, in a mood somewhere between desolation and exultation, he watched her train pull out of Ogden, and shortly afterward took his own train East.

"A good year, the last year of youth as such," he later called his last Harvard year. He was more mature, had been for sixteen months in abrasive contact with the army of the democracy, had held command and been in responsible charge of men and materials, and had pondered the possibility of death. And he had watched his mother die. "So a lot of the oaf was gone from me. . . . I got more from Harvard in that one year than ever before—or since." Unexpectedly, as one of three hundred returned veterans, he found himself looked up to. The literary climate had changed, the "trance-ecstasy-shrine" mood of prewar Harvard had given way to more hard-boiled attitudes. He and his "advanced" literary contemporaries were onto Huxley, Lawrence, Anatole France, Mencken, O'Neill. "The year I graduated, 1920, was the year of *Main Street, Moon Calf, This Side of Paradise, Smoke and Steel, A Few Figs from Thistles, The Sacred Wood.*"[4]

There are years when a man grows by everything he touches and there seems no lock that the mind cannot pick. Dean Briggs, intensely admiring DeVoto's literary gifts while sometimes dismayed by the forms they took, joined his other writing teachers in predicting a brilliant career. He moved with greater confidence, and so perhaps with greater grace, among Harvard's intellectuals. But his constant companions did not change. He still saw a great deal of Raysor, Snodgrass, King, Quintana, and especially Kent Hagler, and increasingly Melville Smith. He still ate with the same tableful in Memorial Union. Malcolm Cowley, with whose ideas DeVoto later quarreled, says[5] that he did not know DeVoto well at Harvard, because he didn't like the crowd he ran with. It was in fact the same old crowd of transfers and outlanders that he had been seated with when he arrived in 1915. If it was a gang or coterie, it was a gang of knockers and iconoclasts and low-caste intellectuals who, now that patriotism was no longer a moral imperative, had learned to look cynically upon the warped idealisms of war and the callow capacity for belief among undergraduates.

Some had been overseas. In some respects they found college kid stuff, in others they were determined to get the most from its somewhat torn cornucopia. They dared to be critical of professors; they aligned themselves against the paleolithic philological bias of George Lyman Kittredge; they snickered at Babbitt's inner check; they even, some of them, regarded Dean Briggs as a kindly old granny. When Bliss Perry elucidated his theory of literature, according to which experience entered into a man's mind through his senses, circulated around in thought and memory, mixed with other experiences, was sifted and purified and transformed, and emerged finally as art, Bernard DeVoto, in the back row, was heard to remark *sotto voce* that the alimentary canal offered a better analogy.[6]

They were not Flaming Youth, but they had already begun to bubble with the denials, jeers, emancipations, and challenges of the twenties. According to their temper, they were jaundiced, jaded, disillusioned, cynical, hopeful, or merely innocent. Predictably, they turned out as well as any other bunch of bright undergraduates.

The two who dominated the table and gave it its character were the most inclined to idol smashing then, and remained so. They were DeVoto and Kent Hagler, who for all his physical handicaps had finally won or bought his way into the ambulance service and had come out of the war an authentic hero—Croix de Guerre, American Field Service Medal, everything that DeVoto in his secret heart had most craved. Hagler was more serious-minded than he had been before his war experience, a better student, determined to be a chemist. Sometimes he was morose and silent, touched by a hangover of the nihilism that DeVoto thought the only realistic element in the whole Lost Generation stereotype. But he had retained his direct fearlessness, his experimental coolness at committing experience. He drank harder than any of them, he sometimes inhaled ethyl chloride as an intoxicant. For reasons that he did not speak of, but that his close friends assumed had to do with his tubercular spine, he always carried with him a vial of cyanide salts. His wartime adventures, which had been a long way from spectatorial, DeVoto heard mainly from Kent's sister Clarissa, a freshman at Wellesley. They fed a young hunger in him and all the others of that group. In DeVoto especially they evoked a combination of admiration, envy, and respect.

They ran into each other on the corner of Massachusetts Avenue and Dunster Street two hours after DeVoto got off the train from Ogden, and were instantly friends "of the deepest."

"That relationship," DeVoto remarked many years later, "is practically beyond analysis. Below the censor, the relation of man to man is, I doubt not, ambiguous and dark. Above it, it is infinitely more complex than the relation of man to woman, and sometimes fully as intense."[7] Very different, a maverick from the outlands and an aristocrat from the heartland, a literary man and a chemist, a white-stripe veteran and a decorated hero, they satisfied and completed something in each other. They ate together, worked together, toured Boston and the girlie shows and the speakeasies together, spent long evenings of crackers and cheese and bootlegged wine and intimate talk before a birch log in Fairfax, went together out to Wellesley, where Kent's sister lived in a house known as the Bird Cage, and let the hungry Wellesley girls have a look at a man.

It is easy to see some of the things that Kent Hagler gave Benny DeVoto. They were given and received so intensely that more than a dozen years later, DeVoto used them in a modified and ambiguous form as the central theme of his very personal novel *We Accept with Pleasure*. But DeVoto had something of his own to give. Quintana reports him as seeming to have secret, masculine knowledges, as being at ease in a world far rougher than the Yard. His conversation was salty and profane, as if learned from mule skinners. Though only normally obscene, he had the gift of delighting them, when he was aroused, by a most eloquent vernacular. When he chose to spit, he could split a plank. He was full of satirical wit and hearty contempts and humorous gibes: it was as a humorist that some of them thought he had a future.

And the roughhouse West of which he spoke familiarly had its own aura of romance. Remarkable violences had occurred within his sight, or hearing, or reading, or even family. Whether he told them or not—and he probably told Kent Hagler, at least—his mother's first husband had had to take off for Mexico because of his involvement in shady dealings. Later, after she divorced him, he was said to have been killed in a gun fight in Rock Springs. That sort of story, spun off as an aside during an evening's bull session, had an authenticity that caught the attention. Though DeVoto was not himself a person of "unclean" habits, Ricardo Quintana says, Quintana remembers that he seemed to know by name and in some biographical detail a surprising number of pimps and whores and stewbums and broken-down desert rats along Ogden's trackside and down on lower Twenty-fifth Street.

Like Hagler, he seemed to Quintana a man among boys, one who had seen more than he told.

In actual fact, he may have told more than he had seen. Perhaps he had, through the *Evening Standard*, come in contact with some of Ogden's losers and outlaws. More likely, he knew them at second hand, through newspaper-office talk or from the mutterings of his father, a man who thought ill of all mankind but was a soft touch for a bum or a whore down on her luck. One aspect of the literary gift is the capacity to report the experience of others as if it has happened to oneself, and in that direction Mrs. F. had set him an early example. More significantly, he had read a great deal and he knew a lot. He read all the time, hungrily, omnibiblically but with a heavy emphasis on the history of the American frontier and in particular his own region. The novel he had started in his head at Camp Devens was now going onto paper in Dean Briggs's class. It was built on that local history, and it looked as if it was going to stretch to three volumes. So much of a young man's intellectual and emotional life goes into the discovery of who he is and how he got that way. So much of Benny DeVoto's talking and writing in his last year at Harvard was spent in telling the effete about his West, inhabited by men whose heads do grow beneath their shoulders.

Wherever one can re-create it in detail, the academic year 1919–20 seems utterly confident. DeVoto was heading out into something he wanted to do and felt competent to do, and was polishing the tools to do it with, and enjoyed the encouragement of approving teachers and an interested, intimate audience. He said he had written and destroyed two novels, as well as stories, poems, blank-verse plays, and much other apprentice work.[8] The star of the aesthetes, of whom he was contemptuous, had declined. His own tendencies, which were American, continental, and vernacular, seemed to be coming in. He could hardly have graduated from college, it seems, at a more propitious time.

Except that there was that girl in Yonkers.

Like many other Ogden matrons, her mother didn't like him, and never had. The first letters he wrote to Yonkers were in two parts, the first part for her mother's overseeing eye, the second for Katharine's alone. As the school year progressed, Katharine's replies to DeVoto's letters became sparser, lamer, less personal. He rebuked her, questioned her, eventually accosted her with his full hurt feelings and rejected love. They quarreled violently by mail. She retreated into injured silence, which was the sanctuary he had planned for himself but hadn't the character to seek. He came crawling out; she admitted him to a friendship that was a long way short of what he desired. What he said or intimated about her mother offended her; he apologized. While his mind pursued learning and literature, his late-at-night emotions sought Yonkers in an anguish of yearning. What in daylight looked like a confident march toward a literary career looked after dark like a miserable imprisonment. He wrote her poems. He sent her his novelette "The Winged Man," written for Dean Briggs's course, and invited her praise. (It was an Ogden story, thinly disguised, and she would recognize passages of it, some years later, in his first and third novels.)

In the privacy of his rooms, in the occasional outbursts of confidence to his roommates and friends, it was a horrible year, a year of unrest and infatuation. He may have thought of himself in terms of Maugham's *Of Human Bondage;* he may have muttered lines from "*Cynara*" to himself as he pursued sleep.

Upon graduation, he told Garrett Mattingly long afterward, he went down to New York armed with a letter of introduction from Byron Hurlbut, and paid visits to several literary establishments. He said that a New York daily and a national liberal weekly both offered him jobs.[9] There is no knowing what the daily was, but the liberal weekly was clearly *The Nation*,[10] and what it offered him was not a job. What Oswald Garrison Villard apparently said to this young man sent down from Harvard was that he would welcome the submission of articles about the West, with which the young man seemed well acquainted. It was not hard for the young man, desperately inventing reasons for self-confidence, to construe that invitation into a job offer and report it as such and even remember it as such. It is harder for the biographer to imagine what might have been the DeVoto career if it had started with an affiliation to *The Nation*.

If any jobs were offered him, he took none of them. Having graduated in June 1920 "as of the Class of 1918," he took his diploma, which he later compared with his father's Notre Dame degrees and found to be ersatz parchment, made his brief pilgrimage to New York, and then left—not toward any job, not toward Paris and freedom and the five-to-one franc, not toward the Belgian scholarship that he told some people had been offered him but that he had in fact just missed.[11] Not toward any of those things, but straight back to Ogden. He did the precise opposite of what a confident young literary man of provincial origins would have been expected to do in 1920. It was as if Stanley, having located Livingstone at long last, should perfunctorily shake hands with him and start back through the bush.

Why did he do it? Lack of money? It is true he didn't have any, and his occasional applications to his Aunt Rose, who had married wealth, had produced an occasional Eversharp pencil or silk shirt, but no funds.[12] But it was a time when penniless young men in droves were getting to Europe by cattle boat and making a pittance support them on the Left Bank. Or they were flocking to New York armed with just such letters as Hurlbut had given DeVoto, and staying there until they could snag the handrail of the passing Literary Express.

Was it concern for his father, desolate and unkempt in his widowerhood, that drew him back to Utah? Possibly, for all his life DeVoto accepted that sort of family obligation cheerfully and generously. For years he helped support not only his father, but members of his mother's family and finally even members of his wife's. But filial responsibility, especially since he and his father were considerably alike and did not get along, would hardly have taken him back in person, unless he had other reasons for going.

Then he must have gone back to live in the midst of his material, sacrificing the good life and all intellectual companionship for the sake of his projected three decker novel rooted in Ogden's history. Mattingly, who accepts that reason, says that after his return DeVoto spent most of two years "knocking about the West, renewing and extending his acquaintance with the least spoiled parts of the American continent, tracing the old trails of the fur traders and wagon trains, camping among the peaks, adding to the knowledge of the Rocky Mountain frontier which he was soaking up from every book he could lay his hands on."[13] He suggests a Parkmanesque apprenticeship to the firsthand West, but apart from the camping trips it does not seem to have taken place. He read incessantly, that was true—his was a boiler that demanded an enormous woodpile—but there is no evidence that he "knocked about the West" or retraced any trails at all unless the one through Weber Canyon that he already knew like his own street.

He just went back to Ogden and stayed there.

A biographer should guess as little as possible about his subject, and should label his guesses, and probably put them in small type lest they outshine the less colorful truth. So it is in small type, with qualifications, that one makes two guesses: DeVoto went back to Ogden because he was helplessly in love with his blonde high school goddess, and also because he was afraid to go anywhere else.

With his mother dead, there was no one except this brewer's daughter to enforce his physical presence at a time when his Harvard friends were winning graduate fellowships or joyfully dispersing on their cattle boats to pry open the world's oyster. His father, though desolate and seedy, was self-supporting and in reasonable health. If he wanted material about the West, there was more of it in the Widener Library than in all of Utah. Of his own generation, there was only Katharine to draw him ten miles out of his course. It seems likely that he followed her home, dragged helplessly like a toy on a string.

But also one guesses that even if there had been a good job in New York he would not have dared to take it. All through his last year at Harvard, despite the stigmata of success, he was painfully uncertain: he submitted his writings to friends, roommates, that insulated eighteen-year-old girl, professors, classmates, with hope that they would find them good, and near certainty that they would not. He was shakier than anyone knew. The prospect of being ejected out into the world with a career to make—and in a field that Ogden laughed out loud at—with no friendly institution to back him, no family, no potent friends, no army, no college, filled him (one guesses) with panic. One postulates something like his father's paralysis of will. One speculates that DeVoto returned to Ogden partly because with all its limitations it was the only safety he knew or could rely on; and that later he rationalized his flight to sanctuary as a stern dedication to the necessities of his novel. That was a more palatable and pronounceable reason than either panic or an uncontrollable yearning for the brewer's daughter.

In any event, it took him just about two months to crack up. Not impossibly, he had been heading for a crack-up since before his mother's death.

6 · "Between Pauperism and Drugged Dreams"

The early part of the summer he spent renewing his intimacy, and losing it again, and renewing it again, with Katharine. But circumstances and family were against him. By August 4, when Melville Smith wrote saying that he had won a musical fellowship to Paris and urging DeVoto to come along, DeVoto could pretend that the twice-interrupted "engagement" meant nothing any more. But he did not take Smith's suggestion to cut loose and travel. He said he expected to be in Ogden another thirteen months, after which he would be off to New York, Washington, or Boston. His plans, though indefinite as to direction, were precise as to timing, and he wrote with all the appearance of confidence.[1] Confidence was still with him two weeks later, when he was preparing for a four-day camping trip in Skull Creek Canyon, by himself, with only a bedroll and a .32 automatic to weigh him down. But a couple of weeks later he reported that he had contracted malaria on the camping trip and suffered a collapse of the emotional life on his return.[2]

Whether he actually caught malaria is a question. If he didn't he should have, for his girl and tertian malaria belonged together as recurrent fevers. His letter is full of hollow laughter and philosophical disparagement of women. It asserts (DeVoto making the same mileage out of a polite publisher's letter that he had made out of Villard's invitation to contribute) that he could have his novel published "on a royalty basis" but will refuse to let it be printed unless he can revise it into greater sophistication. "It is a disgustingly immature production for one who asserts so much maturity as I." So on one hand he defended his personal standards against the commercialism of the publishing world, but almost simultaneously he was crying out in a letter to Hurlbut that he had spent the summer "making an incoherent ass of myself." The revision was undone, he was suffering from insomnia and nerves as well as his old eye trouble, and he had been losing weight. The tone of that letter is tense and desperate. He said he felt that his mind was slipping. The state of his nerves was somehow described by Poe's line "Red winds are withering in the sky."[3]

By October 22 he had recovered enough to describe his condition to Smith. "I make progress. Slowly and with frequent lapses. My illness, as you now know, was not the venereal disorder you charge me with. It was, is, nervous. A neurosis perhaps. At any rate a compensation for disappointments more stable natures would have ignored. Perhaps, in addition, an excuse, a retreat from work, a subconscious bolstering up of jealousy, inferiority, and then sloth." The "fiction of romantic love," he said, was not likely to impose on him again. Having said that, he launched into an enthusiastic account of his friendship with another seventeen-year-old high school girl, "the daughter of Ogden's only great man." They were accustomed, instead of necking like other young people, to indulge in roughhouse competition. They punched and wrestled, hiked, swam, argued, and fought. He did not hesitate to sock her in the wind. She had loosened two of his front teeth with a left hook. These healthy physical contacts demonstrated the possibility of a wholesome asexual friendship between man and woman.

The mere act of writing about this girl, called "Skinny" by all her friends, revived his spirits. He demanded that Melville send him books from Paris so that he would be able to keep up and not rot on the branch. And then in one leap he went from despondent description of his symptoms and disparagements of romantic love to pure intellectual euphoria. Clearly, even during his emotional upheavals and the discouragement of his exile, his reading had been at work on him. His continental perspective had expanded into a vision. Perhaps without knowing it, perhaps not even believing it, but whistling into the future only to get past the demoralized present, he stated the theme of his productive life, aligned himself against certain fashionable ideas, even anticipated a favorite whipping boy:

I burst [he wrote] with creative criticism of America—I have at last found a kind of national self-consciousness. Not the mighty anvil-on-which-is-hammered-out-the-future-of-the-world. Still less the damned-bastard-parvenu-among-the-nations. But I have begun to see American history with some unity, with some perspective, with some meaning . . . to dare to think from cause to effect, from the past to the present and future, always with this curious new sense of yea-saying youth.

I do not commit the historic folly, from Washington Irving to Van Wyck Brooks, of hearing fiddles tuning up all over America. . . . But I have dared at last to believe that the Nation begins to emerge from adolescence into young manhood, that hereafter the colossal strength may begin to count for the better, as well as for the worse. That indeed we have come to say yea, at last.

And in the facts which alone can show whether we take the turn, or in the study of them, I shall, I think, spend my vigorous years. . . . I believe I have found something into which I may pour that arresting, God-awful emulsion that is I.[4]

Correct on all counts, but premature. And in both its enthusiasm and its prematureness, symptomatic. He never fully got over the tendency to mistake a lightening of his internal cloud cover for the dawn of a new day.

Euphoria and confidence escaped from him and were as if never known. His next letter to Smith, dated November 9, began with the somber news that Kent Hagler had died suddenly in Paris, and then, like a dog to its vomit, he returned to the obsessive subject of his infatuation, the like of which he hoped never to experience again, and came around to his compulsive self-analysis, the needle steadying on true north. "I have a peculiar capacity for suffering in those areas of personality which neither anatomy nor psychology has yet been able to describe, areas inextricably tangled with religion and sex and faith and poetry." He thought, cautiously, that he was safely past "the spiritual lethargy which comes with peculiar oppressiveness to those of our calling—our emotions being our profession, precisely like our more honest sisters, the *filles de joie*."[5]

Having settled on himself, the needle began to fluctuate wildly, even to spin. For what had brought him out of his spiritual lethargy? The perception that all the time while he had been towed at the chariot wheels of the brewer's daughter, the real object of his passion was another girl, named Mattie,[6] a student at the University of Michigan, who had just reappeared in Ogden. The moment she showed up, bam! "Fireworks, lightnings, and millenniums." He would ask her to marry him before long, maybe next summer. Already she had restored his capacity to work, and he was revising the novel with the energy of a fiend. It was now called *Cock Crow*, and nobody had ever done anything like it. For relaxation from it he had joined the American Legion and been elected its chaplain and was playing power games in its local structure of command. He had also been working in the recent presidential campaign, against Harding. And he had recently addressed the University Club on the subject of American liberty and had been asked to resign because of his revolutionary ideas, gleaned mainly from the Declaration of Independence. He believed he was now being shadowed by Department of Justice agents.[7]

A biographer going through this correspondence might conclude that DeVoto was indeed unstable, that he displayed the classic symptoms of a manic-depressive, and that he was even touched with paranoia as well. More likely, drowning in his own lethargy and Ogden's torpor, he was driven to create his own drama and his own eidolons. "It seems that my nature requires some object of adoration—some outlet for the intangible traffic of my commonplace life." But Mattie, who had gone back to Ann Arbor, was no longer available for worship, and anyway, he had already begun to suspect her of being a calculating wench. He thought he had caught her weighing him against other and better possibilities. He felt that she had definitely cooled toward him, and wondered (not implausibly) if his own "half-satirical, half-tender letters" had contributed to the cooling. Though still asserting that he would ask her to marry him, he supposed he would get turned down—she would throw herself away on some fathead. Out of boredom and the need for money, he had taken a job clerking in Spargo's Bookstore on Washington Avenue, but he was uncomfortable there; he felt that people looked at him sardonically as the fellow who had wanted to write.[8] His novel was revised and at the typist's, his restless mind was temporarily without fuel for its combustion. No romantic eidolon being present, his nature demanded drama, more drama than his cynical games at the American Legion or his baiting of the University Club could provide, or even the final and irrevocable end of the Katharine affair, brought on by Katharine's mother. He found it in the mystery of Kent Hagler's death.

For it now appeared, from Clarissa Hagler's distressed letters,[9] that there *was* a mystery. Shortly before his death, Kent had given to a Paris acquaintance a sealed letter, asking that it be mailed to Kent's father if anything happened to Kent. It arrived sometime after the news of Kent's death, and it said, in terms so melodramatic that the Kent Hagler of Harvard would have laughed at it, that he had gone to Paris to track down a man who had mortally wronged him. If he found him he would kill him, or would be killed himself. He wanted his father to understand this purpose, in case news of some accident or fatality reached him.

That note, coming on the heels of the cable saying that Kent was dead of "cerebral congestion," distracted Clarissa Hagler, who had worshiped her brother. She was half convinced that Kent was not dead, that the letter was a cover-up, that he had perhaps killed his enemy and was in hiding, that he was in need of help, in danger. She transferred from her adored brother to her brother's friend all the questions that her anguish suggested.

Nobody, especially a distressed girl, ever asked Bernard DeVoto for help and failed to get it. He always respected trouble, having experienced some of his own. Moreover, Kent Hagler had been his closest friend. The gloom that might have been added to his already crushing depression did not, however, descend. In a way, Kent Hagler's death was a dramatic release.

From Ogden, a third of the world away from Paris and more than two thousand miles from Wellesley, he fired off letters of comfort, assurance, and advice to Clarissa, and to Melville Smith in Paris he wrote asking him to investigate as discreetly as possible all the details and the people involved: Burroughs, the acquaintance in whose room Kent had died, and who had sent the cable; the man who had been given the letter to mail; the tart with whom

Kent had been living (no word to Clarissa of this); the coroner or physician who had made that diagnosis of cerebral hemorrhage; anyone else. He told Melville to check all possibilities of suicide, for he remembered those cyanide salts Kent had used to carry; and of foul play, poison, violence; he wanted him to determine if possible whether this was a case of a frail young man dying of his Bohemian excesses, or whether the note and its melodramatic suggestions really meant something. If Kent had killed himself with drink, cerebral hemorrhage did not seem quite the right fatal outcome, and he was too young a man for cerebral hemorrhage to seem proper in any case.

For several months he kept up a feverish three-way correspondence, feeding to Clarissa only such details as he thought she should know, castigating Melville Smith for his slowness (he said Smith was the sort of man who would start out to get a newspaper and come back months later by way of California), testing Smith's reported facts, framing theories. He found himself becoming more and more an adviser, brotherly or fatherly or something else, to Clarissa. He agreed to edit, as a memorial, Kent's war letters.[10] Partly his motivation was sympathy for Clarissa's trouble and the family's grief, partly it was his own uneasiness about the mystery of Kent's death, partly it was (one guesses) the reassurance that comes with being a protector. Neurotics who become psychiatrists and lost souls who become social workers know the feeling. And lack of generosity to people in distress was a fault of neither Benny DeVoto nor his father. In his brotherly-and-more effort to spare Clarissa any sordid details, in his will to raise up her spirits and give her of his strength, he sounds as noble as the Virginian, and why not? That was the way of his nature and his youth.

But Smith's investigation turned up little.[11] The doctor who had examined Kent said he had seen no signs that the death was not from the cause he assigned it to. Melville had not requested an autopsy while the body was being held in Paris, because that would have brought into the case speculation, newspaper stories, and other things he thought the family should be spared. If there was poison, there was no way now of finding out; and likewise no way of knowing whether it had been put in Kent's cognac by another or by himself. The girl he had been living with knew nothing; Burroughs seemed to be what he said he was, a jewelry salesman having a holiday in Paris; and when he brought Kent's body home at the family's request they, too, found themselves believing his story that he had gone to bed one night leaving Kent reading with a bottle of cognac at his elbow, and had been wakened by the maid crying, "Votr' ami, c'est mort!" Kent had been planning a walking trip next day. Was that in preparation for his hunting down of his enemy? No way of telling. Had the enemy found him first, and killed him? No evidence, and no knowledge among any of Kent's friends that he was on bad terms with anyone. Was the whole thing a delusion, some figment of neurosis or DT's? If so, the possibility of finding out had died with Kent.

So, gradually, what had begun as a mystery tense with possibilities faded and raveled out. The mystery would tease and bother DeVoto for years, and he would eventually write elements of it into his fourth novel and then later amplify the novel with an extended, fictionized recapitulation of the Kent Hagler story, as part of his autobiographical letters to Kate Sterne.[12] But he would never get an answer, never come any closer to solving the mystery than when he wrestled with it through the winter of 1920–21.

As the excitement faded out, Ogden's narcosis and the lethargy and self-doubt of exile seeped in to fill its place. "I am confronted by the terrible truth that I am doing nothing, but am wasting time while life slips away—and the more terrible truth that my ability and even my desire are diminishing," he wrote Melville Smith on February 10, 1921. But the very act of expressing his apathy made him rouse up to deny it. Somehow he would pull out; the things that were in him were not easily killed. Only young hope and optimism had been killed; what could not be done with enthusiasm might be done by sheer doggedness. He had begun his new novel (no word about the first, which still exists as an unpublished manuscript among his papers and which E. H. Balch of Putnam's rejected on April 21), but "one is not credulous. However confident I am of it and however rosy it may sometimes appear, I know to a minim how little it will assay. The difficulties of the environment and the obstacles to work are not the reason for my incredulity. I have obeyed Socrates perhaps too thoroughly, and know myself, a knowledge in which one has no pride."[13]

Thus the winter of his discontent passed, and the spring following, while he fought the sickness of his spirit with the only weapon that seemed even temporarily to heal it: work. Work was all that made Ogden tolerable; work was what the shrinking spirit would stiffen up to when it would stiffen to nothing else. He got on with his new book; he dared to dream of getting back to Cambridge, "the one place where I feel I belong." He got a good deal of pleasure out of his platonic, tomboy relationship with Skinny, that symbol of the peppy, asexual, irreverent, good-scout flapper of the emerging twenties.

But by the beginning of June his incubus had fastened on him again, a new disintegration of nerve and collapse of will that made the summer of 1921 as dreadful to him as the previous fall had been. Kent Hagler's letters were piled on his desk half edited, his novel had stopped on June 2 and could not be made to go again, his hope of returning to Cambridge had had to be given up for lack of three hundred dollars. His life, dependent for its bare necessities on the father with whom he could not get along, had become "an existence between pauperism and drugged dreams." He drank too much Green River redeye.

The physical symptoms of his illness, which had again begun as aggravated insomnia and had progressed through high blood pressure to a functional heart disturbance, were over by August, but he was left in a state of deepest depression. "All the decency and aspiration in me, if indeed I had any, have died," he wrote Melville Smith, his link with the Left Bank Bohemia where young Americans by scores and hundreds were making music and history and love. "Now what is the trouble? It cannot be the environment, for if it were that merely, I should be able to get out. No, it is something less tangible, a subtle motion or influence of the blood . . . not the commonplace wearing down to contented pedestrianism . . . not mediocrity but an inheritance of a different sort, a type of failure without romance or glamor, the cards stacked not from without but from within, a deep internal humiliation and abasement that is still not extraneous or cosmic but personal in origin."[14]

Some of that was perhaps self-dramatizing, some of it may have been merely the fashionable literary Weltschmerz of the period that led Sam Hoffenstein, one of the parodic mouthpieces of the twenties, to exclaim in a momentarily serious poem,

> But now I know how rare a thing, how truly rare
> Is true despair!

One aspect of literary despair in the twenties was its association with an extraordinary ebullience of productive work. One aspect of DeVoto's was that it balked his work, time and again. And we should note the personal acceptance of responsibility. Not the environment, as bad as he thought it, and not his inheritance of his father's paralyzed will or "the characteristic Dye crack-up"[15] from his mother's family, but himself was to blame for his trouble. That honesty was the best thing in him, and it does not matter that he may have got it from literary sources, from William Ernest Henley, who would be the master of his fate and the captain of his soul, or from Othello, who in the crux took by the throat the circumcised dog who had wronged him, and smote him, thus. Wherever he got it, it eventually saved him from the fate of his father and perhaps of Kent Hagler. He chose not to blame fate, nature, or nurture. If he fell apart he blamed himself.

Yet he could not say how the enemy within had come into being, what it was in himself that cut the hamstrings of his ambition and opened the veins of his self-confidence. And self-knowledge, however stubborn, could not gain him control over his life, could neither rouse him out of his numbness nor prevent the closing in of the periodic dread. There was no doctor in Ogden who could help him. He thought—he was fully confident—that he was going mad.

In periods when his illness eased somewhat he did a little work, clerked at Spargo's, took an assignment from the *Standard*, wrote a little on the novel. He saw Skinny off to school in Washington by squiring her through the booths of a carnival sponsored by the Herman Baker Post of the American Legion, winning her Kewpie dolls at the shooting gallery, and walking afterward for several hours, "almost breath-takingly chaste and uninvolved," up one of the canyons.[16] Then, in November, presumably as a substitute or fill-in, he took a job teaching United States history at the North Junior High School.

He discovered that he had a gift for teaching, a gift enhanced by certain personal habits such as his profanity and his talent for the sulphurous phrase. He tickled the boys half to death with his daring, he shocked some girls and fascinated others, he offended parents and fellow teachers and took some pleasure in doing so. Ogden, he said, had "sharpened his social tongue, which was already sharp enough," and had hardened him in his habit of iconoclasm. He stated his opinions of holy matters at 200 per cent of par, he introduced destructive bacteria under the skin of the godly, and the double gratification of having a despised target and a captive audience got him through the winter. He was not the sort of junior high school teacher who was likely to be retained, but by June, when his job ended, he had Skinny to occupy his mind.

She had contracted encephalitis while away at school, had come close to dying, and had come home early to recuperate. Remembering this relationship later, writing about it to another sick girl, Kate Sterne, DeVoto either deliberately embroidered it to make a good story, or reported not so much the truth as his fantasy, or in some act of creation very like the creation of fiction, remade the relationship with Skinny according to the template of his own wishfulness. As he reported, "A queer thing happened at once. We became absolutely essential to each other and yet the exterior of it was just an amused friendship. Neither of us ever told the other, except in rare and momentary oblique allusions, what was wrong with us, but both of us knew damned well—so far as we could know without the vocabulary that I'm now letter-perfect in. We didn't make love to each other, we didn't even, in the language of the period, neck. Only, if I showed up at the hideous sandstone mansion at the corner of Twenty-seventh and Adams at seven-thirty in the morning, noon, or half past nine at night, Skinny quite unhesitatingly grabbed a hat and we were off to walk five or twenty miles or drive twenty or a hundred and fifty. Or I might say goodnight to her at midnight and go home and go to bed. After I'd been asleep an indefinite time I'd sit straight up in bed, recognizing the toot of a certain Willys-Knight horn. At whatever time it was I knew that Skinny had had an attack of the horrors, I'd finish dressing in the car, and we'd be off—not saying much, just deriving some odd and intimate and profound stability from each other."[17]

That fantasy of mutual dependence Skinny herself does not remember—she remembers only the amused friendship. But, like a lot of fictions and fantasies, it *ought* to have been true. DeVoto's platonic friendship with that Ogden girl ("an absolute darling," say all the people who remember her), and its combination with a certain fatherly watchfulness, an understanding of fear and distress, a comprehension of what it means to have the horrors and an absolute dependability as a refuge from them, was the sort of relationship that he established with several women during his life, and brought to a kind of perfection with the tubercular girl Kate Sterne. He liked and admired women, and wanted to be liked by them; and he respected trouble and sympathized with panic. His fictions, both serious and slick, are full of situations involving older, wiser, fatherly-but-not-too-fatherly men and irreverent, tomboy girls who in a crisis are absolute bricks and in the end are absolute darlings. When he wrote about Skinny to Kate Sterne he was outlining a sort of friendship he deeply desired and needed—reporting it as experience and perhaps establishing it as a pattern for his friendship with Kate Sterne herself.[18]

It does not much matter that the story of Skinny as he told it to Kate Sterne was mostly fiction. It was true as wish fulfillment, as romantic daydream. He reports a night when they were driving home from a dance in the canyon, presumably from the Hermitage, a mountain resort that catered to several generations of Ogden young. They were in a topless touring car, the night was mild, Skinny in some filmy sort of dress was sitting quietly, smiling, looking up at the canyon walls. Asked what she was smiling about, she said she had had a silly sort of thought—how nice it was that they could be such good friends, and mean so much to one another, without having to fall in love. A dependable part of the fantasy of admiring young girl and protective older man, but a demoralizing thing to say to the young man who (he told Kate Sterne) had just looked at her and been knocked groggy with the realization that for months he had been fathomlessly in love with her and did not want to be merely her friend and her defense against the horrors.

It is just as well to carry on this story of Skinny as fantasy remade it. His defenses were weak and his options few. He was "a young ass of intense ambition and an even intenser inferiority complex, jobless and hopeless. I regarded my disease, whatever it was, as incurable. I thought I was certain to die of it, or kill myself, or go crazy. It seemed inconceivable that I should ever get out of Utah, and still more inconceivable that I should ever be a sound man or ever do anything to justify my existence. And now in love with Skinny who, besides being all the unutterable things that girls are when you are in love with them, was the daughter of the richest man in Utah."[19]

Well, he said, he determined upon rehabilitation and took a job as a ranch hand on Tom Keogh's desert ranch in the Raft River Valley, in Idaho. Several months before that, in February 1922, he had written Dean Briggs to ask help in finding a teaching job somewhere—anywhere but Utah, somewhere back in the United States. If there were even the most menial job at Harvard, he would take it before anything else, for the Yard and the Square were the most congenial places in the world, and the best places for him to get through his year or two of trial, error, and investigation of his own possibilities.[20]

That letter, like his romantic fantasy of Skinny, stated a major theme, one on which he played variations all his life. He needed no Paris or Left Bank; Cambridge satisfied all his cultural, intellectual, and emotional needs. But he had to escape his village: he could not sit like a snake-charmed rat through another year of it. And he had to prove himself to Skinny as well as to himself. Eastward, therefore, to more privileged earth; but first, a purging through hard outdoor labor.

The night before he was to leave for Idaho, he told Kate Sterne, he and Skinny were again driving, this time with a companion couple. They kept saying, "Aw, Benny, don't go." Skinny said it too, several times. At last he leaned over and said, "All right, I'll stay if you'll marry me."

"Where can we?" said Skinny, with the misleading promptness of dreams.

"Try Brigham City."

She spun the car around and started north up the state road, while the two in the back seat chortled at the idea that Benny was being kidnapped so that he would miss his train.

"Shut up," said the dream Skinny over her shoulder. "I'm not kidnapping Benny, I'm marrying him."

But the county clerk in Brigham City, waked from his first sleep, refused to get dressed and go downtown and issue a license. The elopement was a bust. In the sober morning Benny went off to the Raft River, up among the lava beds, leaving his love behind.

That was the way he remembered it in the late 1930s, when he was being autobioloquacious at the request of Kate Sterne. The original of Skinny writes me that not much of it is true.[21] There were other things in his memory, some of them pretty firmly fixed, that were likewise not true. Many times throughout his life DeVoto, speaking as if from within the guild, cited his experiences as a cowpuncher. He specifically mentioned the Raft River Valley, and at least once he said he had worked cattle somewhere on the Platte.[22] The assiduous biographer finds no evidence that he ever worked on the Platte in any capacity, though it is possible that some high school summer might have been spent there. The biographer also has to conclude that if his cowpunching experience was limited to Tom Keogh's ranch on the Raft River, he was no such hardhanded waddy as he claimed to be. For one thing, Keogh seems to have run sheep, not cattle. For another, DeVoto stayed there hardly long enough to unpack his Levis. His lifelong distaste for horses could have come more plausibly from his never having learned to ride than from wearing out the end of his spine in lonely communion with any little dogies. The fact is, though he had many skills, they were not the skills of a working man, cowboy or other.[23] He was an intellectual driven to pretend that he had all the frontier competences he admired in the mountain men. He had only one: he was a good shot. And though he knew a great deal about cowboys from books, and understood them better than they understood themselves, he knew them from life very little.

He said he barely arrived on the Raft River before the thought of Skinny yanked him back to Ogden. Much more probably, what yanked him back to Ogden was a letter from Northwestern University offering him an instructorship in English. Reprieve. But also exposure and a renewal of panic.

Skinny saw him off on the Overland Limited. His depression had never been deeper, and it was not all due to leaving Skinny. A conviction grew in him that he would never get off the train alive. Watching in still fear out the window as Weber Canyon and then Echo Canyon went by and the train leveled out onto the barren Wyoming Plateau, he felt that he was leaving everything safe. After a long time he took a card out of his pocket and wrote on it his name and address and the name and address of his father, and put it back in the side pocket, where it would be easily found.

And yet there had been a decision made—by him or for him did not much matter. Later, he would conclude that he left his adolescence behind, and began to grow up, somewhere around Thousand Mile Tree.[24]

One thing remained to be done before he committed himself to the chaos of a new life. Perhaps he conceived it, in the slyness of his unconscious, as an alternative or an evasion. What faced him as he forced himself out of Ogden's sluggish safety was a test that melted the joints of his knees and chilled his skin with the sweat of a hopeless inadequacy. Yet to fail it would be to go down for good. So when he arranged to visit the Haglers in Springfield before going on to Northwestern, he might have been preparing an escape. He was fully aware that Clarissa Hagler had transferred to him some of the dependence she had had on her brother Kent. He knew, or persuaded himself, that Kent's mother, literary, charming, imprisoned in downstate Illinois, thought of him as a gifted young man, inheritor and continuer of her son's promise. His imagination told him that she would not discourage a romance between her daughter and her son's friend.

This is guesswork, mainly DeVoto's own, and guesswork, moreover, that is complicated by his fictionizing fantasy—for this, too, is part of the autobiography he wrote for Kate Sterne. In Springfield, he said, he found all as he had half anticipated. Clarissa watched him with suffused eyes, blushed easily, was all but abject in her desire to please. Mrs. Hagler, the most gracefully intelligent and charming woman he had ever met, made her hopes, it seemed to him, perfectly clear. But he had just parted from

Skinny, whose friendship was far from abject, and whose loss was part of his desolation. He had the desperate sense that anything except the abrasive life of ambition and achievement would be fatal, that he must not succumb to what he thought a plain invitation. Perhaps he kept in mind the image of his father, his talents rotted away in that undemanding title-abstract office and his nature gone sour and murky with self-contempt that emerged as a compulsion to insult everyone he talked to.

From the Haglers' affectionate household and from their perhaps fictional invitation he escaped, with promises and half promises, and faced the door that opened on both hope and dread.[25] Everything he told Kate Sterne about Skinny and about the Haglers might have been sugared with self-protective fantasy, but his neurosis was real. He didn't leave it in Springfield any more than he had left it in Ogden. It got off the train with him in Chicago, and it was compounded during the first weeks of his teaching by a loneliness and isolation against which he had no defenses. In December he wrote to Byron Hurlbut back at Harvard, humbly recalling himself to his former teacher, who he was afraid might not remember him. He talked about his eighteen-month breakdown and depression, his inability to write his friends. The Northwestern job that Dean Briggs had found him was, he said, pleasant enough but only a way-station on the road East. "Cambridge and the winter Yard, evenings at your house, the Symphony, talk about a half dozen fireplaces, twilights over the Charles—those things have lined the darkest hours I ever spent with a half-intolerable beauty of reminiscence." Rather vaguely, he proposed sometime to come back and work for an M.A. under Hurlbut's direction. And "Please," he said in closing, writing from his half-furnished little apartment through whose walls leaked the vicious Lake Michigan wind, "please think well of me!"[26]

II

NORTHWESTERN

1 · Students and Epworth Leaguers

Helen Avis MacVicar is a person both fictional and real. In the collegiate novel *I Lived This Story*,[1] written by her Northwestern classmate Betty White, she appears as a young faculty wife sympathetic to student emotional storms—"a minor benevolent character," as she herself says. Within the complexities of a plot that is only remotely referable to her own life, she is unmistakable as Libby Grayson in Bernard DeVoto's 1934 novel *We Accept with Pleasure*. A caricature of her, a not entirely friendly one, figures largely in Helen Howe's Cantabridgian *roman à clef*, *We Happy Few*.[2] Even in real life she struck many people as a "character." Some thought she deliberately tried for shock effects, some thought her so uninhibitedly honest that she produced them without trying. One of her husband's Harvard students, describing her as she appeared to him at the beginning of the thirties, remembers her as "very good looking" and "very sexy-seeming, like Tallulah Bankhead whom she resembled," and as "the only faculty wife who might have said 'horseshit' even to President Lowell."[3]

But that was after her transplantation from the Middle West, and after six or seven years of being married to Benny DeVoto.

In September 1922 she was a Northwestern freshman of eighteen, a girl from Houghton, Michigan, up in the Copper Range. Her good looks were softer then than later, still overlaid with a little baby fat, which was in turn overlaid with a bright layer of sophistication. Making the assertions of her times, she bobbed her hair, smoked cigarettes, wore cloche hats, rolled her stockings below her knees, and spoke her full mind. She had a disconcerting habit of sitting on desks, tables, bookcases, any high perch, with her legs crossed and her nose in a book. In class she favored the front row, making up part of what DeVoto, writing of his educational experiences, referred to as the chorus line.[4]

It may have been her legs he noticed first, without too much distinguishing them from the legs to right and left. But when he gave all his freshmen a test designed to humble them by revealing how little they knew of literature, history, philosophy, and related mysteries, Helen Avis MacVicar came up with the highest score among them.[5] A mind, then. She wasn't reading those books for nothing. He noticed her.

She had already been noticing him.

What she saw, when she first showed up for Freshman English, was an ugly, interesting-looking young man about five feet nine or ten, neither thin nor fat, but rounded-looking and solid. He had a round head, short dark hair parted a little to the right of center, round glasses, round brown eyes that when he smiled were squeezed up into half moons. He smiled much of the time. "Oddly oriental, somehow amphibian,"[6] he sat hunched at his desk and watched them indifferently from between his collarbones until they were assembled. Then he slouched to his feet and addressed them. Betty White, in her novel, describes what she heard and saw from the front row that also contained Helen Avis Mac-Vicar:

"This is Section 27 of English 1," he said in a deliberate voice, "where presumably you will increase in wisdom by cultivating an aversion to the comma fault. Any wandering souls who have erred are invited to leave." He sat on the desk with a magnificent nonchalance of manner, and put one foot in a chair.

"If you were the matured and eager minds your high school certificates make you out to be, we would concern ourselves with writing. Since you are neither adult nor prepared, and since you are here in reluctant obedience to a requirement, we will confine our efforts to learning the rudiments of primary-school grammar. It will be a very tiresome class for you. You will perhaps better understand the world's capacity for dullness." He paused delicately. "On my part, your presence here will fill my life with joy."[7]

And so on. Miss White's freshman heroine, and presumably Miss White herself, thought him a sarcastic and insufferable smart alec, and was sure she was going to hate that class. Perhaps Helen Avis MacVicar thought the same thing. Both changed their minds. For though DeVoto inhabited the classroom with what George Ball, who sat under him four years later, calls "obtrusive informality,"[8] though he roamed around the room, kidded the girls, wisecracked, sat on the desk and swung his leg, they discovered that he took teaching seriously. They had no way of knowing that his sarcasm was not contempt for them, but some aspect of his show-off compulsion, some variant of his cry to Byron Hurlbut: Please think well of me! But they did find him fair in his grades and genuinely enthusiastic when he could give his infrequent A's. His air of supreme, swashbuckling confidence was backed by an apparent familiarity with every book ever written. He had been around, he was in the swim of things, he was rumored to be a writer himself. His opinions were prompt, vehement, and profane, full of great scorns and unexpected admirations. If he baited them and called them halfwits, he also made himself available, in and out of hours. At twenty-five he was not much older than they, but he seemed to them, as he had seemed to Dick Quintana at Harvard, possessed of great worldly knowledge and sophistication, and he was one with the campus rebels in their aversion to the prevailing Methodism of the university, the snoopings of the Dean of Women, and the inhibiting conventions of the campus. He was fond of referring to Evanston as the home base of the W.C.T.U., which it was.

Even before the end of his first year, he had got himself noticed, and by more than his students, for his outspoken contempt for the "big business bigger stadiums" state of mind. He was caustic about the fund-raising campaigns and the willingness, as he saw it, to sell out intellectual standards.[9] He openly doubted that certain highly regarded scholars and administrators could read without their forefingers. Before too long—and it is difficult to date such things, because the memories of those who participated tend to telescope the years, and what they remember may have occurred at any time between 1922 and 1927—there was developing a "DeVoto way of thinking," which alarmed some administrators and exhilarated some students, especially some of the good students and most especially the students interested in writing. These last were capable of relishing a colorful phrase; they were also capable of quoting, stealing, or imitating it. Those who found him most exciting aped even his mannerisms, his way of lighting a cigarette, his wicked and ribald way of exposing hypocrisy. They hung around his apartment, they boxed or played tennis with him, they walked with him by the lake, and they talked, talked, talked. Toward the end of his Northwestern stay the rumor got around that DeVoto was serving liquor to undergraduates, and President Walter Dill Scott, whom DeVoto did not admire, called him in to discuss it. DeVoto in turn demanded that he be allowed to confront and question his accusers, and the charges were quietly dropped.[10] (But *liquor?* says Helen Avis MacVicar, who by that time was Mrs. Bernard DeVoto, and should know. Liquor to *students,* on a salary of seventeen hundred dollars?)

Lewis Ford, in Betty White's novel, is a somewhat idealized version of the Bernard DeVoto who was an English instructor at Northwestern. She makes him close to omniscient in a sardonic way, and endows him with more influence in faculty circles than he actually possessed; but she also makes him the truest intellectual guide her heroine finds at the university, as well as the truest friend. For those whose minds he respected, he was undoubtedly both. Never mind that many, both students and faculty, found him offensive, abrasive, arrogant, profane, and boorish. Those were the conventional and the timid; those were not of the elect.

For it was frankly an elite that he sponsored and encouraged, an elite of knockers and grumblers and iconoclasts and rebels against fraternities and football. "I shall always be grateful to Benny for teaching me to look down at the bastards surrounding me with a sense of great disdain," says George Ball. "I was preoccupied with my own problems of adolescence. I felt quite detached from the life of the campus and could have been morbidly unhappy if Benny had not provided me with the sturdy defense of intellectual snobbery. No doubt it made me insufferable, but it was helpful at the time."[11]

Other students testify that he gave them more than a defense against herd pressures and a contempt for the collegiate inanities that were perhaps the silliest aspect of the revolution of the twenties. For instance, Sarah Margaret Brown.[12]

She was a redheaded, freckled, bright, gaminish journalism student with a disrespectful sense of humor and an ambition to be a writer. She had taken writing courses before, and was used to top grades and terse comments such as "Not bad, but I think your motivation of Charlie's 'organization' is a little inadequate." In the fall of 1923, DeVoto's second year at Northwestern, she signed up for his English D-6 and at once, to establish status, handed him a chunk of the novel she had been writing during the summer.

It came back next day, well marked up and with its whole last page covered by the teacher's large, legible scrawl:

Excellent and distinguished in detail, this work makes me wonder whether your quality may not betray you when the long story of which this is a part is finally assembled. In effect, you are in for some severe self-criticism, and if you value the total effect more than the individual instance, will have to go over this ruthlessly, compressing, always compressing, which means that most of your individual jewels will have to go into the wastebasket. A style so deliberately jeweled would be unendurable at ninety thousand words. All this, however, I will take up with you in conference when I have read the rest of your earlier work.

Sarah Margaret was not used to professors who requested or demanded conferences, nor to professors who wanted to read all her earlier work, nor to professors who read papers so promptly and with such obvious care and wrote comments of such length and specificity. Also, she was a little piqued at the way he shot down the beauties of her prose. She handed him another section. Back it came, plentifully scribbled upon:

Between your first paragraph and the passage beginning at the middle of p. 5 and running to the next page is a distinct cleavage and a fundamental difference. The difference is one between literature and nonsense. The spanking passage is literature—of a high sort. The clamorous dishes and the quaking words are nonsense. A difference, of course, of origin. The first paragraph is a pose—however ornate, however elaborated and dressed up—a pose compounded of K. Mansfield, Amy Lowell, and Walter de la Mare, a bastard-poetic prose which can be brought fully into neither category and is out of place in both, a pseudo-form which has never been genuine from Baudelaire to F. Scott Fitzgerald, or in Wilde or Fiona Macleod or anywhere else in between. Infinitely careful your words are, I have no doubt, infinitely emotive and suggestive—and infinitely artificial. The spanking, however, is *true*. I mean more than that lamentable word usually says nowadays. I mean that this section is veracious, veritistic—that the emotion of Deborah is given life in words—whereas the other was as dead as it was precious. By all means suppress your tendency toward the first, and nourish your tendency toward the second.

Sarah Margaret had no way of knowing that she had caught the tail end of an Ogden outlander's distaste for a generation of Harvard aesthetes. And she was not quite sure whether she was flattered or annoyed. She took one more chance, and handed him another section. It came back promptly, with her spelling of *bacchante* and *Leander* aggressively corrected on its face. On the back page her teacher came at her still-standing literary pretensions like a bowling ball:

If it is quite clear in your mind that this is Deborah's illusion, and if you treat it as such, all right. If, however, it is *your* illusion, if you see anything of classic mythology in the ordinary young man of this generation—any pagan rapture or Grecian grace—anything at all of a parallel or an analogy—then you are deceiving yourself, and rather conventionally. See things in terms of themselves. The so-called pagan joy never existed on earth apart from the pages of Walter Pater and his disciples. Read Frazer.

Overmatched, Sarah Margaret succumbed. She tried to tame her *fin de siècle* style, she found out who Frazer was, and read him (and De la Mare, Fitzgerald, Mansfield, Pater, and all the others he mentioned, even the ones he knocked). His caustic teaching did for her what Mrs. F.'s hushed devotion had done for him: it guided her reading and her mind. She became one of the Devotees. As campus correspondent for Hearst's Chicago *American*, she was always in hot water with the authorities, who were more interested in a good public image than in good news coverage, and that endeared her to DeVoto. So did her unconventional and imaginative ways of following a story. To cover a circus, she once rode in a cart hitched behind a hippopotamus down Michigan Avenue. To do a feature on the Chicago visit of Queen Marie of Romania she got a job as a chambermaid in the queen's hotel and reported gleefully that the queen, like other mortals, left a ring in the tub.

In that sort of japery DeVoto encouraged her and others. Self-consciously against all herd pressures, he also encouraged campus editors in sly or open violations of the campus code. As he began to publish things, his consciousness of being before an audience led him to indulge his gift for a Menckenesque indiscriminateness of satire and a Menckenesque pungency of phrase. As a writer, he began by showing off. As a teacher, he seems to have been trying to do what he felt Harvard had not quite done for him—to give his students guidance among the contradictions, virtues, pretensions, and shams of the new literary freedom. Those who revered him and hung around him looked upon him as invulnerable, a culture hero.

But a lot of that confidence was false. He lived within his defenses and made sorties. When he lounged around the classroom looking wise and uttering sardonic and picturesque wisdoms, neither those who liked him nor those who found him offensive knew that much of the time he was in a clammy, soul-clutching panic, that he taught not from confidence but from demoralizing and nearly constant fear.

Only Helen Avis MacVicar knew that, and she didn't find it out for a long time after she began to go out with DeVoto, in October 1922. Once she knew what he was going through, her somewhat ribald and concealed admiration became a sort of awe. Nearly a half century later, fifteen years after his death, she could still speak of him feelingly as "the bravest damn man I ever knew."

"It seems that my nature requires some object of adoration," he had written Melville Smith from Ogden's Slough of Despond.[13] It also required friends, respect, admiration, the stimulation of good minds, the drama of intellectual attack and defense. Helen Mac-Vicar (who was called Scotty by her friends but whom he preferred to call Avis), being extremely attractive, would do to worship; being intelligent, she was stimulating; being aggressively unconventional, she delighted him; being young, she enlisted his protectiveness; and being his student and disciple, respectful of his authority, she gave him, not deference ("I never deferred very well," she says) but corroboration and support. Especially after she learned about his migraines, sleeplessness, dreads, panics, and fits of suicidal depression, she helped hold him up. And she had enough shakes and uncertainties of her own so that he could feel the support was not all one-sided.

It was part of his curse that when he was not down he was likely to be sky-high. Toward the end of the spring of 1923 he wrote to Byron Hurlbut again—this time not haunted and begging, but manic and full of brag:[14] "Both faculty and students are lyric about me," he told his old teacher, and added, as if he had noticed his own swagger, "Modesty has never been a vice of mine. . . . My mind is as good as there is." He was full of plans. He was going to write all summer, finish his novel, and then write a half dozen short stories to try to supplement his Northwestern salary and the five hundred dollars he could make by teaching an evening class in the School of Commerce. "If I can sell just one to the S.E.P. most of my uncertainties will disappear."

To the unpublished writer it always seems that the first acceptance will prove the rightness of his gamble. Since almost all unpublished writers have to earn their living at some backlog job, the first acceptance looks in anticipation like the brakeman who will uncouple them from drudgery. In the early twenties most American novelists broke in as journalists, and wrote their way out of the city room. As a teacher, DeVoto had one advantage over them: he got a three-month vacation, from which in his manic moods he expected the impossible. By sheer logomancy, now, he converted into certainty what should have been stated as a hesitant possibility. "I have not yet put myself to a test that I did not pass," he told Hurlbut. "I remember how I was assured beforehand that I would never make good at Harvard, in the Army, as a teacher, and that I made good in all three. So, unfamiliar and dubious as the idea is, I begin writing for publication with confidence if not assurance." His aim, he said, was to write his way free of both teaching and the Midwest, and settle down to full-time writing in some New England town.

He confessed (Confessed? He held Hurlbut with his skinny hand) that the reason for these plans was a girl, one he was engaged to marry. She was everything his heart had ever sought or his imagination given shape, everything his mind in its moments of highest aspiration had learned to admire. He admitted that he had come to Evanston with suicide very close to the surface of his thoughts; but from the time he had first begun to know her, back in October, he had moved steadily toward greater stability and self-possession. Beautiful, intelligent, a splendid pianist, she was possessed of the subtlest mind he had ever known, and she wrote better prose than he did. They had been shaped by many of the same experiences: family failure, literary ambition, isolation in soulless backward towns. They wanted the same things. They would gladly subsist on high thinking, literature, music, and a crust.

So skinless a letter, one that so helplessly and trustingly exposed its author's insides, could have embarrassed Hurlbut, a New Englander. It would probably embarrass Avis DeVoto if she read it now—embarrass her or bring her to tears, or both.

They could not be married at once, DeVoto said, because he had set aside the summer as a proving time. He couldn't ask that superb girl to share a life without accomplishments or assured future. He must first demonstrate that he was capable of being and doing what she believed him capable of. In three months he could do it. They would be married sometime between September and February.

But Avis MacVicar demanded no such proof. However he might feel, she could not see herself setting her Rocky Mountain knight such a batch of tests—so many sword-edge bridges crossed, so many castles taken, so many damsels rescued, so many giants and ogres and dragons slain. She was in love with him and had total faith in him. If he was going up into Wisconsin or Michigan and live in a log cabin and write, why should she not go along? Sum-

mer, and shirt-sleeve nights, and the sound of Lake Michigan lip-
ping its shore, and the shadows of the elms that then lined many of
Evanston's streets, were on her side. They were married as soon
as classes ended, and bought a secondhand Ford and a back seat
full of secondhand tires, and took off for a place some colleague
had told them about: Washington Island, off the tip of Wisconsin's
Door County, in Lake Michigan. The summer of testing got combined with honeymoon.[15]

In Detroit Harbor they boarded in a clean, bare hotel run by
clean, bare Icelanders, paying twelve dollars a week apiece. They
walked, swam, fished, played tennis, lived a healthy outdoor life.
DeVoto taught his bride to shoot a .22. There is a photograph
that shows him in his pegged officers' breeches and leather puttees,
carrying on his shoulders an exuberant girl who wears a men's
white shirt and checkered knickers. They look extremely contented
and unhaunted. While Avis walked the beach or talked with fishermen or sat under a tree with a book, Bernard wrote with the
dedication of an acolyte saying his offices. For the first time since
Dean Briggs's class, he felt that he was writing well.

"A neurosis," he told Kate Sterne years later, "is a psycho-
biological adaptation. Ogden, though agonizing, was an amniotic
home. When I finally, God knows how, probably by way of
Skinny, found resolution to act, to get out, to go about my business, I took the indispensable step." By shedding his adolescence,
he said, he had made it possible to begin shedding his infancy.[16]

A Chicago neurologist, though "eighty percent faith healer," had
helped him to understand what was the matter with him. Success at
teaching had given him the beginning of control over the enemy
or coward within. His marriage had steadied him. Now, as if performing a self-prescribed rite of exorcism or therapeutic magic,
he was working out of his emotional labyrinth under an assumed
identity. He was writing about Ogden—not the historical frontier
Ogden of the failed novel *Cock Crow*, but the Ogden of his own
experience.

At Harvard, DeVoto had thrown in his lot with the tribe of
the moderns; he had opted for the American and the vernacular
and the new. So it is not surprising that *The Crooked Mile*,[17]
which at this preliminary stage was called *Mirage*, incorporates
themes and subject matters that his contemporaries found compelling.

It belongs with the whole literature of the revolt from the village, the repudiation of the puritanical, commercialized, sleazy
mean-spiritedness that two generations ago seemed to the literary to

mark the small town in America. "Dullness made God," Sinclair
Lewis called it. Years before Lewis, paraphrasing a famous theory
of the anthropologist Morgan, Clarence King had characterized
the course of American civilization as a progress from savagery
through barbarism to vulgarity. The phrase accurately describes
Bernard DeVoto's intention in his projected trilogy. He was one
who like Willa Cather saw the pioneer period as a more heroic
time, though he was less inclined than she to glorify the pioneers.
But in *The Crooked Mile* all the frontier vigor has been worn out.
We are left with the vulgarity.

Other dust from the winds of the twenties blows through the
novel too. If its protagonist, Gordon Abbey, is a sibling of Claude
Wheeler and Carol Kennicott and George Willard and Krebs and
Alwyn Tower, he is also a somewhat remoter kinsman of Jake
Barnes, a sensitive young man made impotent by the nihilism of
war and its aftermath and driven to pointless hedonism. And when
Abbey joins the revelries of the country-club set in the town of
Windsor, he is not unrelated to Fitzgerald's anguished butterflies.
Windsor/Ogden is both Gopher Prairie and a sort of parochial
Rocky Mountain Babylon.

But Gordon Abbey, however much he may resemble some of
the fictional types of the twenties, resembles Bernard DeVoto
rather more. He is a Harvard-educated man buried in a provincial
town he hates. He in unlike DeVoto in that the town had been
made by his driving father and grandfather, but he has the same
problem of reconciling the cheap, weak, pleasure-loving present
with the more-than-life-sized past, the crude but heroic pioneers
with their degenerated grandchildren. Like DeVoto, Abbey is afflicted with a vague *anomie*, an enervating paralysis of will. He
tries to rescue himself by working with his hands, on the railroad.
He sinks himself in the vicious pleasures of the "gang." He is tied
for a while to a sexy, mindless woman suspiciously like his injured
memory of the brewer's daughter. He is brought back to sanity
by another young woman, one for whom he had thought he had
no amorous feeling. There is a coltish girl who, though she is not
given a major part, is reminiscent of Skinny. There are many
secondary characters whom Ogdenites recognized, or thought they
recognized.

By the end of the novel, Gordon Abbey, saved both by his
education and by the rediscovery of his "Abbey blood," has pulled
his feet out of the quicksand and is slapping down some Windsor
weaklings in a dreams-of-glory fantasy. The elaborate, epigram-
matic, overwitty tone of many of the conversations is the tone

that Betty White heard from the front row of a Northwestern
Freshman English class. And the hatred that Gordon Abbey feels
for Windsor is also a reflection of DeVoto, justified more by his
emotional state than by anything the commonplace, dull town has
been guilty of. One can feel the author's compulsion to despise
the womb from which at great pain he has finally expelled himself, transferring to it, as hatred, the fear and self-doubt that are
still his abiding emotions.

Yet *The Crooked Mile* was an attempt at understanding, too,
as well as a compulsive exorcism and self-justification. It not only
contains a version of the Ogden-hating Bernard DeVoto, warped
and disguised; it contains also a *raisonneur*, a somewhat cynical
historian of the frontier named John Gale, whose quoted comments
link western past and western present and suggest the degeneration
from pirate pioneers to weakling Windsor. Windsor is no part
of the mythic West, absolved from time and change. It is, despite
its exaggerations, a real town, the product of a real historical
development. Its pioneer miners, farmers, and railroad men are not
glorified, except in terms of their energy. In Gale's view, most of
them were only one jump ahead of the sheriff. Yet their vitality
lifts them above their descendants, as the clean spaciousness of the
country they raped makes them and their motives seem mean and
shoddy. The great shadows of Gordon Abbey's arrogant grandfather and piratical father lie over the present. They have a masculine capacity for violence that Bernard DeVoto, aspiring to be a
writer and afraid that writers were sissy, had always more than
half admired and been tempted to imitate.

A mixed book, more personal than it appeared to be, one
that without being confessional was still revealing. It marked the
beginning of a career that would be built upon experience in and
knowledge of the West, and it contained the contradictory elements of impartial historical observation and personal emotional
involvement that would first divide and finally enlarge his work.
In *The Crooked Mile*, and indeed in all the fiction he ever wrote,
DeVoto totally obliterated the Mormon issue. He saw the West
largely, as the final act of a great continental drama, and he saw it
through time, and he had a clear eye for distinguishing fact from
myth. Knowing and understanding it was the task he had set himself at the beginning of his Ogden exile, in the summer of 1920.
But the "God-awful emulsion" that was himself was still cloudy,
it still stained what he poured it into, and would go on doing so
whenever he essayed fiction. It would take him many years and a
shift to another medium before he would bring himself fully to

bear upon his chosen subject. That is to say, his work would remain murky so long as he himself was any part of his subject matter, even in disguise. But he did not know that yet; perhaps he never knew it.

2 · In Print

With an impatience not unknown among young novelists, he was trying to sell his book before he had written it. As yet he had no literary contacts in Chicago—in fact he never did become closely associated with any of the literary community there except Llewellyn Jones of the Chicago *Post* book page.[1] The only publisher he knew even by mail was E. H. Balch, the man who had rejected *Cock Crow*. So in July he wrote Balch that he had another novel nearly done. Balch replied that he would be delighted to read it either for Putnam's or for the new firm he was then organizing, to be called Minton, Balch & Co. But he waited a good while for the manuscript. It was the beginning of January before DeVoto put it in the mail.

A writer who has submitted his book to a publisher is like a Victorian maiden exposing herself to the marriage market. The slightest hint of interest becomes a matter of speculation. Does he? Doesn't he? Will he? Won't he? And what did he mean by that lifted hat, that slight bow, that enigmatic smile? For a man of DeVoto's temperament the suspense of waiting can be excruciating, especially when all the clues must come by mail. The sound of the postman's steps, the tinny clink of the mailbox, bring him alertly out of his chair; the moment of searching through the envelopes for the one that never seems to come is suspense followed by letdown. The very first letter about *Mirage* demoralized them. Balch found the book overlong (How could I have said it any shorter?) and puzzling (Can't the fool read?). He was going to try it on other readers.[2]

For a solid month they waited, disgusted with the days when the mailman left nothing or dropped into their box no more than a letter from Michigan or Utah, and touched with stubborn gloom when he brought back unwanted one of the stories that Bernard kept sending around to the magazines. On February 23 they got the crusher: Putnam's was rejecting the novel. But one glint of hope was in the final paragraph. Balch himself was not ready to give up on *Mirage* and was now having it read for his new firm. Almost abjectly, DeVoto wrote saying that he was very willing to revise. If they found something specifically wrong, he was confident he could fix it.

But each new communication from Balch contained only another version of uncertainty. Some readers liked it, some did not. Some liked parts but not the whole. Some liked the dialogue, some found it strained and overelaborate. Some found the sexy passages too outspoken, some thought them a superb capturing of the modern mood. Most liked the historical and sociological solidity, some disliked the intrusions of John Gale. Balch had never known a novel to stir such contradictory responses. Have patience; he would try yet another reader.

They had patience, or did their best to have, but they had less and less hope. DeVoto taught his classes and went two evenings a week into Chicago for his School of Commerce class, and wrote late and read later, and suffered from insomnia and sinusitis and migraines, and feared them as the precursors of something worse. It was two months, and then three, since Balch's first, puzzled acknowledgment of the manuscript. Hope had died and mummified. And then a telegram. Minton, Balch was taking *Mirage*, with revisions. Letter followed.

A decade or so later, instructing Catherine Drinker Bowen in the art of biography, in how to deal with events that the biographer is pretty sure of but can't document, and in how to move from verifiable fact to imagination, DeVoto had a characteristically positive piece of advice: Put it in the subjunctive. Instead of writing, "He discussed the whole matter with his wife and came to his decision," write, "He *would have* discussed the whole matter with his wife and come to his decision." Easy.[3] One may borrow the suggestion here. There would have been a party at the DeVoto apartment. Word would have got around by grapevine; young faculty friends such as Arthur Nethercot, Garrett Mattingly, Robert S. Forsythe, Ney McMinn, Bob Almy, would have dropped in with cheers and maybe with bottles of bathtub gin and hoarded pseudo bourbon. Favorite students would have got the news and come around. If there was ever liquor served to undergraduates at the DeVotos' it would have been served that night. And if Bernard DeVoto ever felt the sweetness of justification and success and the support of true friends he would have felt it then.

Two things in his immediate letters to Balch are interesting to his biographer. One is his query whether or not Balch would be embarrassed if DeVoto wrote some stories for *The Saturday Eve-*

ning Post.[4] He still needed money, and he still hadn't passed that test he had so confidently announced to Hurlbut. Later he would tell a lot of young writers that if they wanted to be writers of stories for the big slicks they had better make up their minds to devote about two years to learning the trade.[5] In the spring of 1924 he was, by his own timetable, only halfway there, but the euphoria brought on by Balch's telegram told him that sooner or later he would make it.

The second interesting item in his letters is the confession that he was growing a mustache, an endeavor that Balch gravely encouraged. From here we may view the little Frenchified mustache that resulted as an effort by DeVoto, who had always thought himself unattractive but hoped he wasn't, to meet his first public with his best face forward. There would have to be publicity photographs, and these would have made him uneasy, to put it subjunctively. Through the summer, which they again spent on Washington Island, he made the revisions Balch wanted, read the proofs, wrote some stories, and nourished the growth under his nose. He had some photographs taken, and sent them with self-depreciating words to Balch, who wrote back saying that DeVoto was too hard on his own appearance. None of us was a model of beauty; the photographs were fine.[6] They were there on the jacket flap when *Mirage*, rechristened *The Crooked Mile*, came out in October. ("My God!" somebody reported Avis DeVoto as saying, studying years later those photographs in which Benny's lip is jauntily screened. "He looks like an Armenian Jew!" She denies she ever said such a thing. "Matter of fact, I rather liked that mustache.")

What mattered more than youthful self-consciousness about his appearance was the fact that, for the first time, this young man intensely in search of an audience had found one and could consult its responses. He could take pleasure in the Boston *Transcript*,[7] which thought his account of "the senseless round of pleasure that has ceased to be pleasure" excelled Fitzgerald's, which praised his unswerving representation of reality both past and present, which commended his rejection of the sentimental myth of the pioneer, which valued the "new understanding of the West" that he provided. He could argue in his mind with the New York *Times*,[8] which found his novel too long and its focus blurred, and agreed with some of Balch's readers that the dialogue was too witty and tried too often for a "crushing finality." It thought the novel "somewhat adolescent in its overwhelming cynicism," but it gave him billing ahead of Aldous Huxley, Harry Leon Wilson, and

Gouverneur Morris, and credited him with "acute penetration and virile creative ability," certain to make before long a valuable contribution to American literature.

When he looked closer to home, he found the Chicago papers praising him less cautiously, and he would not have cared if their judgment was impaired by a mild regional chauvinism. The *Tribune*[9] said *The Crooked Mile* stood at the top of the fall novels, a book beside which "the novels of those bright young men, the Messrs. Fitzgerald, Benét, Hume et al., seem but the work of schoolboys." And Llewellyn Jones of the Chicago *Post* Literary Review,[10] making a bad guess, thought that DeVoto's novel, if it was as successful as it deserved to be, might mark the end of the fashion that said all first novels must be autobiographical.

All in all, he could not have thought the reception anything but encouraging. He got fan mail, he was denounced by Ogden readers who recognized their town, he achieved the grudging or respectful attention of some Northwestern people who had noticed him previously only because he was rumored to be radical. He was asked to autograph copies of his book at Lord's, and he and Avis were invited to Janet Fairbank's annual New Year's party among writers, opera singers, artists, musicians, wealthy patrons, and influential press. DeVoto had to buy a dinner jacket for some function, that or another, for his old Harvard tails (in his day Harvard men did have tails) were both too shabby and too formal.

3 · *The* Mercury *Mood*

The taste of a modest success doubled DeVoto's addiction to work. What had been his defense against dread and depression was also the natural road for his ambition. His stories had had no luck with the *Post* or with any of the other national magazines he had sent them to, but he had placed one in a new Philadelphia little magazine called *The Guardian*, which brought it out in December 1924.[1] At almost the same time, he became book editor for the Evanston *News-Index*, and in it published the first of the scores of book reviews he would write for that paper during the next three years. Other book-review editors had done their usual type-casting, and on the strength of *The Crooked Mile* he found himself an instant authority on the West. Llewellyn Jones had him review for the Chicago *Post* Frederic L. Paxson's *History of the American Frontier*, and Henry Seidel Canby's new magazine, *The Saturday*

Review of Literature, sent him Stewart Edward White's *The Glory Hole*. Both reviews appeared in December.[2] Envious junior colleagues, stuck in the publish-or-perish treadmill of the university, must have commented on how one break could create others. Four bibliography items in a month! And a novel only two months ago! If they were thinking that way, and they probably were, why, so was Benny DeVoto.

He had already begun a new novel. His ribald, askance view of Mormonism had not prevented him from indulging an interest in the pentecostal faiths. He had read a good deal about the Millerites, the Cumberland Baptists, the Shakers and the Methodist revivalists, the "burnt-over ground" of upper New York State where prophets and St. Johns and Messiahs had passed. He had pondered Joseph Smith, and he had met the descendants of revealed religion in person. He had also read William Dean Howells' last novel, *The Leatherwood God*, which appeared in 1916, when DeVoto was a junior at Harvard, and he had felt that it did not do justice to a rich and most American theme. So this new novel reached back into the midwestern past to follow the career of a religious zealot with echoes of Joseph Dylkes and reminiscent of Peter Cartwright and not unlike Joseph Smith[3] and with a family resemblance to a half dozen others whose lips had been touched with the hot coal of God's message and who had galvanized frontier America's apparently inexhaustible capacity for belief. Consciously or unconsciously, there had been a lot of Bernard DeVoto in *The Crooked Mile*. There was going to be less of him in this, and more of John Gale, the objective historian of the frontier.

But a published book is a stone that its author throws ahead of him as he wades; his next step is often compelled by it, if only because editors in their restless search for talent do type-cast new writers and make snap judgments. In January 1925 DeVoto had a letter from Duncan Aikman, an editorial writer and book-review editor for the El Paso *Times*, inviting him to do, for a book that Aikman was editing, a chapter on the transformation of some frontier town from its original exuberance to its present Rotary dullness.[4]

Theme and slant were predetermined. They had been in the making ever since Ed Howe had begun looking glumly about him in Atchison, Kansas, at the beginning of the 1880s, and they were reaching some sort of expression as gospel in *The American Mercury*, in 1925 less than a year old. DeVoto was in a mood to accept any commission offered him, but this was specially fitted to his hand. He accepted with pleasure. His home town, in which his father reported that John Spargo had sold a hundred copies of *The Crooked Mile*, not always to satisfied customers, was going to get it again.

His essay, entitled "Ogden: The Underwriters of Salvation,"[5] made specific what had been half disguised in *The Crooked Mile*, and brought into the open the Mormon-Gentile tensions that had had no place in the novel. DeVoto played no favorites: he knocked Mormon and Gentile indiscriminately. Ogden, which had once "shouted its maleness to the peaks," had become a place of culture clubs and chiropractors and Keep Kool Kamps. Polygamy, which he thought had been overdiscussed, was breaking down before it was suppressed, but other things broke down just as fast. The color and power and authority of Brigham Young had declined to petty commercialism. Hostility toward the Gentiles had been dropped— it didn't pay. The Homeric conflicts between the railroaders and the Mormons were over. No more of the rowdy and illicit elections by which the Irish had wrested a degree of power from the Church. In their place, conformity, dullness, and a concern for good business. Meanwhile the Mormon people, recruited from the dregs, remained artless, without refinements, afraid of ideas, without appreciation of the glorious mountains they lived among and polluted with their presence. Their smugness as a self-appointed Chosen People was insufferable. Their religion, which, however ridiculous, had once been a burning faith, had become a commercial system, and their President and his Apostles directors in a vast conglomerate corporation.

Bald scorn and name-calling, with enough fact in it to make it uncomfortable. Aikman loved it; so did Balch, who was going to publish Aikman's book. They sent DeVoto's essay to Mencken, thinking he might want it for the *Mercury*. Mencken admired it but found it too long. Nevertheless, that contact would shortly open a door.

Acceleration fed on itself; the harder he worked the harder he was driven to work. Outlining his standard week to Melville Smith early in 1925—four classes, each meeting three days a week, with lectures, papers, conferences, and examinations; two evenings a week at the School of Commerce; five evenings a week on his novel; two book reviews so far this week and another to be written as soon as he signed this letter—he reported with pride what some would have thought Grub Street drudgery. The reviews, most of them for the Evanston *News-Index* and meagerly paid, were surely no part of his obligation to publish. They were by-products of his insomnia and his unexpended energy. During

1925 alone he wrote thirty-three for the *News-Index*, besides ten for the Chicago *Post* and three for *The Saturday Review of Literature*.[6] In all, between the end of 1924 and June 1927, he wrote seventy-nine identifiable reviews for the *News-Index*, many of them involving two or more titles. If the print shop was college for Howells, Mark Twain, and other frontier Americans whom he admired, the book-review page was graduate school for Bernard DeVoto. At odd moments, sliding in to his desk between the novel and some review, he worked on stories and essays.

Yet, for all the frenzy of his effort, he worked against disappointment. His stories did not sell. No editor would take his Ogden essay for magazine publication. Despite its encouraging notices, *The Crooked Mile* was not a commercial success. Balch had optimistically run three small printings. Of these, twelve hundred copies had to be remaindered. Total sales were about three thousand, total earnings only a little more than five hundred dollars.[7] And on May 5 Balch rejected unequivocally DeVoto's second novel, *The Burning Bush*.

Those humiliating failures made ambiguous and unsatisfying his return to Ogden in the summer of 1925, when he went back to claim the small inheritance that his grandfather Dye had left each of the grandchildren.[8] He would have liked to go back—he who had left as a ridiculed nobody and a nervous wreck—on a note of triumph, able to let it be known that in three years he had become a successful college teacher and a published writer, a man spoken of respectfully in cities that made Ogden look like a prairie-dog town. He would have liked to show himself around town in his white feathers, with a beautiful young wife on his wing. Instead, though he did indeed have trophies to show off, he went with the rejected novel like a buried rebuke in his suitcase, and in his mind a compulsion, more burning than ever, to demonstrate himself, prove the indifferent wrong, produce something that could not be overlooked or ignored.

His young wife had an uncomfortable few weeks of living in the house on Monroe Avenue among the eccentricities and half-exasperating, half-lovable contrarieties of Florian DeVoto. She met the Dye tribe, including Bernard's favorite aunts, Mattie and Grace. She was shown off up and down the little city where they could not walk a block without encountering someone who remembered Benny with friendliness, curiosity, dislike, or derision. He would have (subjunctively) nursed in his heart the thought of what the town would say when Aikman's book came out in the fall, and regretted things that he had forgotten to mention, and thought of new ways to lay powder to the foundation of Ogden's imperviousness. For the latter weeks of their stay they took a cottage up Ogden Canyon, and there, while Avis went walking with a pistol for fear of rattlesnakes, Bernard tinkered with *The Burning Bush,* now called *The Great God Boggs,* and brooded about another, the middle volume of the trilogy in which the unpublished *Cock Crow* was the first and *The Crooked Mile* the third. And he made notes for articles about the western past, which exhilarated him as much as the western present depressed him.

One article he wrote as soon as they got back to Evanston. It arose out of Mencken's interest in "Ogden: The Underwriters of Salvation," and it said many of the same things in shorter and blunter terms. This time he took not Ogden but the whole state of Utah for his target. This time he was not going to blow up a sentry post, he was going to bring the whole fortification down. He finished it and sent it to Mencken, and Mencken took it with yells of delight. The booboisie had never been so vigorously thumped. Utah was fresh stuff, a far-flung and more comic version of the Bible Belt. His acceptance made it certain that DeVoto's first substantial contribution to a national magazine, like his first novel and his first essay, would be an uninhibited attack on his amniotic home.

Utah, it should be remembered, was founded by a people fleeing persecution. It repudiated the United States wholesale, denied its jurisdiction, denounced its political system, scorned its representatives, sneered at its opinion, and upset its institutions even unto the institution of monogamous marriage. But following the Church's renunciation of polygamy, which was in turn followed by amnesty and statehood, Utahns developed a desire to be just like everybody else. Mormons didn't wear horns; they were people like you and me. They were, moreover, diligent, faithful, law-abiding, hospitable, and much else. All true. But because Mormonism's commentary upon itself had for so long been an instrument of solidarity because Mormon history was faith promotion and Mormon biography was hero worship and mythology, there existed in many Mormon minds a suspicion that in this chorus of self-praise there was a certain implausibility. Mormons wanted the praise of non-Mormons, if only as corroboration. That is a simplified explanation of why Utah has been until very recently, and certainly was in 1926, extremely sensitive to unfriendly criticism in national magazines. Besides, as DeVoto would have been the first to say, unfriendly criticism was bad for business. Utah wanted boosters, not knockers.

Those were the corned and bunioned toes that Bernard DeVoto, a renegade if there ever was one, deliberately trod on in his essay in *The Taming of the Frontier* and returned to jump up and down on in the essay called "Utah" in the *American Mercury* for March 1926.[9]

It was written as if in answer to a Cambridge lady who had once asked him, "in derision and incredulity," how people lived in Utah. Well, madam, he had said in effect, if you're a run-of-the-mill Mormon you live like a pious cowherd. If you're a Gentile you "spew out a farrago of lies about polygamy." If you're a business-man of either side you break your neck walking soft to avoid hurting business. Peace with profit has been possible between Mormons and Gentiles ever since 1906, when Reed Smoot, an ex-polygamist, was assured his seat in the United States Senate. If you're a cattle-man or other rancher in Utah, you belong to a better race of men, and live a good life.[10] If you're one of the newly rich, you "lead the most swinish life now possible in the United States." Do not take seriously Edgar Lee Masters' theory that Utah fosters the arts, and that an artist would do better to head for Salt Lake than to go to Paris. Utah artists such as Cyrus Dallin and Maude Adams are to be accounted for by the "mere accident of birth." Beauregard, the only Utah painter worth looking at, is unknown in his home town of Ogden. There has never been a Utah writer above the Mutual Improvement[11] level; for most Utahns it is a trial to sign their names. Artistically the state is a desert. "Civilized life does not exist in Utah. It has never existed there. It will never exist there."

As an essay, "Utah" did not amount to much—a few minutes of adolescent yawp, the sort of thing that a bright Northwestern sophomore might publish in the *Purple Parrot* and get put on probation for. But it came on the heels of the unflattering portrait of Ogden in *The Taming of the Frontier*, which had closely followed the thinly disguised portrait in *The Crooked Mile*. And it came in a national magazine, the national magazine that the godless most read and quoted. The three together marked DeVoto as Utah Enemy Number One, the contemporary avatar of all the Missouri Pukes and Illinois mobbers who had attained immortality in the Mormon memory for their persecution of the Saints.

From Ogden, Florian DeVoto wrote happily that many people were furious and some were tickled, most of all Father Cushnahan, whom Bernard had used to assist in the mass. People kept calling up to tell him Bernard had better not come back to Utah. The news-stands were sold out and had hastily ordered several hundred more copies of the *Mercury*. They could have sold a thousand. And in

Evanston Bernard heard that President George Thomas of the University of Utah had written President Scott of Northwestern demanding that DeVoto be fired. I have found no documentary evidence for that rumor, but in the heat of indignation, which was general all over the state of Utah, Thomas may easily have made the suggestion.[12]

Why did DeVoto scourge his home place so immoderately? He knew better. He had once confessed to Melville Smith that it was himself, not his environment, that was to blame for his miseries. His true enemy, an enemy who was a compound of ambition, self-consciousness, envy, and a grinding sense of inferiority, was within. What was more, his vision of America made allowance for nearly everything that he excoriated in Ogden and Utah—made allowance for it and defended it as the inevitable condition of a developing democracy. From the very bottom of his depression, during his first week at Northwestern, in the fall of 1922, he had scolded Smith for taking a Mencken view of America. He had said, in fact, some astonishing things: That Smith and the whole intellectual hierarchy were making a serious mistake in denouncing America for its repressions, its legislated morality, and its prohibition of paganism, and in assuming that the country was necessarily and objectionably anti-art. Art, said DeVoto, had always been under the ban of respectability. In Shakespeare's London the theaters were forbidden, and had to move out onto the riverbank between the brothels and the bear pits. "And if the worst of what you say is true, as it is not, what is the difference? Take this country of ours, of mine at least, with its hundred million people, every one a member of the human race, albeit of a lower species. Repressions, censorship, cramped, fear-ridden lives. Even so. There is your marble. . . . Here is ugliness, apparent everywhere—build with it. Here are beauties, no less genuine for being strange—build with them. Here is a whole continent stuffed with living things. Put your tongue in your pocket and get to work with them."[13]

It was an affirmation that might have come out of the Whitman of *Democratic Vistas* or out of the Lewis Mumford of *The Golden Day*. If DeVoto had been as impartial about his home state as he was about the nation at large, Utah would never have had cause to spit out his name as an abomination. But the heart has its reasons that reason knows nothing of. In spite of what his mind told him, in spite of his reading and his thinking and his hard hold on history and fact, his material twisted in his hands when he himself was part of it, and his reporting acquired the tones of grievance and denunciation. Even Florian DeVoto, not notable for his impartiality, advised him to give up Utah for a while—he had already estranged all his boyhood friends.[14]

Nearly twenty years later DeVoto admitted, in print and in a Utah publication, that his two early articles on Utah were "ignorant, brash, prejudiced, malicious, and what is worst of all, irresponsible." He deplored his youthful tendency to yank out shirttails and set fire to them, and regretted his gift for burlesque and extravaganza, and wished that he had not yielded, for the only times in his life as he saw it, to the "*Mercury* mood." He thought that a lot of what he had said in the twenties would have been legitimate if he had said it differently.[15]

But that recantation came after time had callused over both his youthful intemperance and his sense of grievance. At the time, he relished the howls of the wounded, he relished the notoriety, he relished the sensation of being in the public eye even as a cinder. The outcry from Utah and the extraordinarily warm and encouraging letters from Mencken could persuade him that whether or not anyone took his pentecostal novel, he was beginning to reveal himself as a mind, as a writer, and as a force.

4 · *Stirring Up the Animals*

A writer's mind is to a great extent made, or confirmed, by what he reads. DeVoto, who once described himself as a literary department store, was shaped by the extraordinary range and variety of the books he read, whether with some specific end in view or randomly. During 1926 and 1927 he was reading Civil War history, because his third novel, *The House of Sun-Goes-Down*, began in the defeated South and went West from there as so many ruined Southerners did, and also because he was fascinated by the Civil War as the great crisis in the forming of the American nation, a theme that was increasingly on his mind. Growing by what he fed on, and feeding largely on American history, he hoped sometime to write a history of the war as what he had not yet learned to call a geopolitical event.[1] He had acquired early, and retained, an admiration for Lincoln both as the architect of Union and as the highest political development of the native American mind, the homely and vernacular raised to the level of greatness in politics as Mark Twain raised it to greatness in literature. He was also reading everything he could lay his hands on about the westward movement, a climax of the continentalizing trend, and he was keeping his father busy in the libraries of historically minded friends in Ogden.² This research, too, had an immediate purpose, since *The House of Sun-Goes-Down* went West by the Platte Valley route and settled down in the place called Windsor Springs City, which was Windsor, which was Ogden. Abandoning the trilogy organization, he was utilizing and condensing and correcting some of the material he had used before, in the failed novel *Cock Crow*.

Other kinds of books came at him by way of the random sampling of the reviewer's trade. At the end of 1925, Avis, restless for something to do, had taken over the job of book-review editor of the Evanston *News-Index*, and for a year and a half they wrote the book page together. He did all the books about the West and the frontier—history, fiction, poetry, ethnology, reminiscence, travel, folklore, whatever—plus all the books on American history, plus such fiction as he was interested in, mainly American.

He had a faculty of making use of whatever came to hand, and now he was given opportunity. His pentecostal novel *The Great God Boggs* had finally been taken by Macmillan; the contract came through in April 1926, when he was still ducking the hornets his "Utah" article had stirred up. What was in some ways even more encouraging, Mencken's interest turned out to be real, enthusiastic, and persistent. He was incredibly friendly. Obviously he recognized in DeVoto a kindred spirit, irreverent, ribald, and blessed with the vernacular gift of tongues. In February he had accepted an article called "Sex and the Co-Ed," a topic so red hot that the author thought it best to protect himself and his job with a nom de plume, John August.³ Mencken guaranteed to announce Mr. August in his author's note as "a practicing Christian with high academic dignity."⁴ He was going to lead with "Sex and the Co-Ed" in the May 1926 issue, and he guessed it would "stir up the animals and set them to roaring."⁵

Meanwhile Mencken demanded ideas for other essays. His appetite was insatiable, and his exuberant demand generated an exuberant supply. By March 4, when the Utah animals were at their most stirred up and roaring their loudest, he had informally commissioned four more essays—one on the YMCA in the colleges, one on the mountain men, one on the Mormons, and one on the Icelanders of Washington Island, with their frugal virtues and what seemed to Mencken their delightful water access to an unwatchable Canadian border. Keep this last one discreet, Mencken said; it wouldn't do to get the prohis after them.⁶

Only a few days later, he approved an article on the teaching of English, which he expected would take off some skin, for, "saving only the faculty of education, the English faculty in the average American university contains the worst idiots in the place."[7] Receiving that hint, DeVoto immediately proposed, and had approved, yet another article, predictably destructive, on the Faculty of Pedagogy.[8]

Mencken was a recurrent jackpot. He poured out dimes and quarters every time DeVoto pulled the handle. His openness to suggestion was exhilarating, his co-operativeness prompt, friendly, and humorous. When in March DeVoto got worried that his authorship of "Sex and the Co-Ed" might leak, Mencken wrote him saying, in effect, Be not dismayed. "If you are publicly accused and want to deny the fact, let me know and I'll have my staff perjurer make all the necessary affidavits. He is a clergyman and hence talented."[9]

But baiting the booboisie had its dangers. On April 15 Mencken wrote that the Watch and Ward Society, angered at a *Mercury* article by A. L. S. Wood called "Keeping the Puritans Pure," had been lying in wait for a chance and had now found it in "Hatrack," an article about a small-town Missouri prostitute. It was out to shut off the *Mercury*'s mailing privileges. If it succeeded, if the Post Office Department closed the door, the *Mercury* would be dead. In the circumstances, and while Mencken fought the Watch and Ward on that front, it seemed best not to irritate them with a new offense. So "Sex and the Co-Ed" was being pulled from the May issue at the last minute. In its place would go a piece on learning to play the cello.[10]

Well, DeVoto may or may not have said to himself, you win some and you lose some. "Sex and the Co-Ed," which was only a piece of opportunist satire anyway, could wait. He had other things to do, plenty of other things. One of them, for which he signed a contract on April 23, was a book on Mark Twain that six years later would make his reputation.

On Washington Island, in the summer of 1926, he was a one-man literary factory. Except when put down by his nervous illness, he had always been a prodigious worker. Now everything he worked on was all but guaranteed publication. He finished his part of the revision he and Arthur Nethercot were making of a freshman English text, W. F. Bryan's *The Writer's Handbook*.[11] So much for the academic proprieties and expectations, which he disposed of in about a week. Then he finished a draft of *The House of Sun-Goes-Down* and read proofs on *The Great God Boggs*, now called *The Chariot of Fire*. Probably he read for the book on Mark Twain, a subject that he protested he knew nothing about but that was a logical outgrowth of his study of the frontier and his irritation with some of the things Easterners had said about it. And he worked steadily on his commitments to Mencken, with a cheering section to applaud every step of his advance upon literary notice. For from time to time some of his Northwestern students followed the DeVotos up to Washington Island and turned their room, the beaches, the woods, into a peripatetic Academy.

It was an extension of their Evanston apartment, which was never entirely removed from the spirit of the classroom, but which made of the classroom a place of challenge, discussion, and debate. The DeVotos had established that relationship with chosen students at the very beginning of their marriage—in fact, their marriage had come out of it. It was not a policy or a duty; it simply happened that way. And they took the Academy principle with them wherever they lived. It was a condition of their life in Evanston, in Cambridge, in Lincoln, on Bread Loaf Mountain, in half a dozen little summer villages in Vermont and New Hampshire, and on the shore at Annisquam. The only place where it never developed, White Plains, was the place they most hated. A circle of friends was indispensable to DeVoto's internal well-being. If they were equals and adversaries, fine; he never fled a fight. If they were young and admiring, fine; he never turned down admiration. If they were female and pretty, better yet. If they were young, admiring, female, pretty, and in some sort of nervous or emotional trouble, that was best of all, for then DeVoto could forget himself and become father, priest, and healer.

At summer's end, when the DeVotos returned to Evanston, he drove his accomplishments ahead of him like fat geese bound for market. *The Chariot of Fire* was due in October.[12] In November the *Mercury* would run not only the essay on Washington Island,[13] but the destructive piece on the YMCA, which he had discreetly signed with another pseudonym, Richard Dye.[14] The December *Mercury* would run his prose hymn to the romantic and savage life of the mountain men,[15] and the January *Harper's* would return him to his role as the bad boy of the colleges, with an article called "College and the Exceptional Man," which bluntly advised the exceptional man to drop out and get his education in a more likely place.[16] Other essays were in the works. The contract for the Mark Twain book assured a corner of the future.

To his friends, and some who were not his friends, he looked like the most explosive literary article in the Chicago area. Perhaps to himself as well, for, constantly examining himself as he did, he was capable of being periodically dazzled by the evidence in his favor. To Briggs and Hurlbut, toward the end of 1926, he wrote asking aid in finding a cottage on Cape Cod for the following summer, confiding incidentally that he could now sell everything he wrote and was close to that moment of decision when he would cut his bonds and head for the privileged earth of New England.[17]

He could sell everything he wrote. But in the next sentence he corrected himself. Everything but stories. The only stories the magazines wanted, he said, were the cheap and artificial kind, and he would not write below his own level in order to sell. That rationalization of his single consistent failure was self-protective— all the more so because fiction was what he most wanted to write. In his heart he perhaps agreed with Dean Briggs, who applauded his success with essays but regretted that they depended so much on Mencken and the Mencken tone.[18] Briggs hadn't liked the tone of *The Crooked Mile* either, saying that the cynicism which had begun as dramatic propriety had ended by tainting its author.[19] Actually he had it upside down: the cynicism that had been generated in the author by his quarrel with Ogden, Utah, had ended by tainting his novel. But Briggs unwittingly laid a cold hand on DeVoto's self-confidence when he said that *The Crooked Mile* had made him "question, in spite of fine passages and an underlying idea, whether the novel was your right medium."[20]

That was the judgment of a friendly and fatherly teacher, and could not be ignored or discounted. It had to be proved wrong. DeVoto sent Briggs an early copy of *The Chariot of Fire*, which Briggs found a marked improvement on the first one, more economical, better controlled, and without the cynical taint.[21] But he didn't fall all over himself to praise it, which is what its author would have liked; and as the weeks went by and the reviews came in DeVoto beat his head trying to understand where and how he had failed. He had gone out, as he wrote a Chicago newspaperman named Paul Ferris, "deliberately to wipe the eye of W. D. Howells, whose *Leatherwood God* has always seemed to me a ludicrous failure in one of the finest themes an American has ever had."[22] He knew the frontier, he knew the history and the spirit of revivalism, he thought he understood the psychology of an illiterate riverman who began in evangelical religious fervor and ended up believing himself God and by his martyrdom confirmed his church in the same belief. He thought he understood, from his study of Mormon history, how a community in backwoods Illinois would respond to such a New Jerusalem deity. And he had written, written, written since he was eighteen years old, and if he didn't know how to write now, how could he ever? One part of him told him that the book was more profound and more American than any of the critics saw. Another part told him that it was the failure in fact that it was in the bookstores and among the reviewers. He had to adjust to that failure as he would have had to adjust to a personal humiliation.

"Though I'm not proud of the book, I'm not ashamed of it," he wrote Briggs in April, after he knew the worst. "I feel that it measures up . . . when compared with the other novels of the day, of my contemporaries. Wasn't there pity as well as irony and condemnation in my handling of Boggs? Wasn't there a sense of tragedy, of determined things, of events overwhelming individual wills and characters? Wasn't there, if not forgiveness, at least understanding of the complex passions and terrors of the religions and the men who embraced them? I hope there was."[23]

A note in the margin of the letter, in Briggs's hand, says, "I believe that this is true." But DeVoto would have been little comforted by his old teacher's qualified approval. For about the time he wrote that letter, Macmillan, discouraged by the reception of *The Chariot of Fire* and dissatisfied with the manuscript of *The House of Sun-Goes-Down*, on which they had an option, began to make it clear that they were unwilling to publish the new book as it stood, and wanted extensive revisions, including the rewriting of the whole last section.[24]

To his colleagues and students, DeVoto might look like a literary skyrocket. To himself, in the times when he gave himself a few minutes to think about his discouragements, he looked like a failure exactly where he had invested his spiritual resources and his pride.

And yet he was making money by writing. Thinking of teaching as only a bread-and-butter job to support him and his wife while he wrote his way out of it, he could foresee a time, not impossibly far off, when he could abandon it and be what he wanted to be. He finished for the *Mercury* another piece on the West, "The Great Medicine Road," which was scheduled for publication in May.[25] Whether he knew it or not, he found in the writing of it a subject that would eventually bring out the very highest capacities he possessed, and a method that he would later use with great effect in much longer works. The subject was a segment of the westward movement—what was happening along the Oregon Trail in the time between the rendezvous of 1835 and the great migrations. The method was what he would later call "history by synecdoche," the concentration of large events and movements of population and clashes of attitude and interest within the single, sharp focus of a symbolic action or restricted period of time. When he keyed his

Mercury essay to the deadly duel between Kit Carson and the trapper Shunar at the 1835 rendezvous, he was anticipating what he would do in more intricate ways in *The Year of Decision: 1846,* in *Across the Wide Missouri,* and in *The Course of Empire,* where, respectively, a single year, a single western expedition, and a single exploration are made to illuminate much wider histories.

He probably didn't know yet what he was doing, but he must have known he had done something good. Briggs was enthusiastic, applauding the absence in this essay of the "Mencken tone."[26] And almost immediately, the door that had been opened up by "College and the Exceptional Man" opened wider. He sold to *Harper's* a piece that for years was famous among freshman-English instructors and a sure-fire stimulator of the controversy that is supposed to beget interest and hence interesting themes. The article was called "The Co-Ed: The Hope of Liberal Education," (later rechristened "The Co-Eds: God Bless Them"),[27] and it was an acknowledgment of the part girls like Sarah Margaret Brown, Betty White, and for that matter Helen Avis MacVicar had played in his first five years of teaching. It was not simply a tribute to the chorus line of the front row or an acknowledgment of women's emancipation. It was an assertion, characteristically overstated, that the co-eds were the best part of any student body—eager, interested, alert, skeptical, teachable. "The women think, the men throb."

DeVoto lived to disparage that essay, as he disparaged and refused to reprint other essays on education. But it reinforced his association with *Harper's,* an association that was to be close and warm from that time onward. What was perhaps most pleasing to him, *Harper's* shortly thereafter bought the first short story he sold to a national magazine.

It was called "In Search of Bergamot,"[28] and it dealt with the nostalgic return of a middle-aged man to the little western city where he had been born and where one missed romantic opportunity had left a dissatisfaction at the core of his life. The city was called Custis, but no one who had read about Windsor or who knew Ogden could have mistaken it. Sticking with materials that he knew best, and with feelings and fantasies not too unlike his own, DeVoto with that sale to *Harper's* moved close to the emancipation he was working for. Now! he said (would have said). Finally!

He and Avis rode their exhilaration eastward in June, toward a boardinghouse in Chatham, on Cape Cod, that Dean Briggs had found for them. Behind them they left rumors: That DeVoto was about to be promoted to an assistant professorship. That he had been proposed for promotion but blocked by some of the moss-backs and Epworth Leaguers, who objected to his opinions or his language or his reputed overfamiliarity with students. That he was quitting. That he was going to be fired. That if he *wasn't* promoted there was going to be a big explosion and protest among students and young faculty. Presumably the rumor of promotion was pleas-ant to the DeVotos. Has there ever been a junior faculty man to whom it wasn't the pleasantest of all rumors? But it was not the thing on which his mind gripped with determination. When *Harper's* bought that story, it brought instantly close the possi-bility they had been dreaming about. What was on DeVoto's mind was the summer of renewed testing that lay ahead.

5 · *"One Story to the* S.E.P.*"*

Like a prisoner ransomed, he went straight to Cambridge. He wanted to show Avis the glories of Harvard, walk her through the Yard and along the Charles, display her to people on the faculty who had helped him and wished him well. They did run into Mrs. Hurlbut in the Square, and so had a personal welcoming back to the Cambridge DeVoto had not seen in seven years, but the people he wanted to see most were scattered to summer homes at Marblehead or the Cape or in the country, and the DeVotos' lack of an automobile prohibited visits. Down to Chatham, therefore, where they knew their life would be circumscribed and circum-spect. Their landlady had taken in writers before, and been burned, and had only consented to house them because of Dean Briggs's recommendation. There was no little Academy there, no member of the Tribe of Benny, and none likely. The people they settled among were less open than the Washington Islanders, less friendly. Here they lived among strangers, and felt their difference.

But work, yes. That was a cloth that could be cut to cover any circumstances.

First he finished the revision of *The House of Sun-Goes-Down* and sent it off to Harold Latham at Macmillan. Then he wrote another western essay, entitled "Footnote on the West," in which he said about the entire region, but in somewhat less outrageous terms, approximately what he had previously said about Ogden and Utah. He admitted, humorously, a lot of western limitations, while asserting western largeness, sun, scenery, and space. His West was the Rocky Mountain West, forever distinguishable from the Southwest and the Pacific Coast. It was not the scene of rugged individualism, as was often claimed. It was the precise opposite, the home of people who co-operated or failed. He quoted his earlier invention John Gale to the effect that western individualists had usually found themselves on one end of a rope whose other end was in the hands of a bunch of vigilantes. He found the whole West deficient in art, cultivation, ideas, *mind*, and also unduly under the influence of the booster, a middle-western type that slopped over the borders of its own proper territory. The West, he said, could not respond to boosterism as the Middle West did— it had too many limitations, most of them keyed to the basic fact of aridity. But if it ever learned its limitations, and threw out the boosters, and kept itself out of the hands of eastern capital, and developed itself as its real qualities and not its myths dictated, it would be the greatest home for man on God's footstool.

It is worth pausing a moment on that essay, because, like "The Great Medicine Road" and to a lesser extent "The Mountain Men," it forecast a lifelong subject matter and a persistent attitude compounded of love for the country and contempt for the people who abused or gutted or colonialized it. The West, past and present, would never be far from the center of his preoccupation; his attitude toward it would be the same in the 1940s and 1950s—for example in the 1947 essay "The West Against Itself"—as it was in the summer of 1927. Perhaps influenced by Dean Briggs's objections to the Mencken tone and Mencken's magazine, he sent the article not to the *Mercury* but to *Harper's*, and *Harper's* bought it.[1]

So far, so good. He sat down to write some stories, frankly trying to take the measure of the slick-magazine market. These, like his essays on the West, were a forecast of things to come.

The first one, "Front Page Ellen," is a romantic Washington Island story involving an athletic, beautiful, and reportedly "fast" ex-tomboy and the older man who in her youth taught her to swim, sail, and shoot. One can see Skinny in this Ellen, and one can see some DeVoto fantasies in the natural nobility and gentlemanly scruples and manifold skills of the leading man. And as in all good fantasies and magazine stories, the asexual companionship of girls and men turns out to have been wistfully sexual all the time.

The second story took him back to the town of Windsor and the contrasts between the old and the new West, the old being represented by a leathery old heroine named Mrs. Yancey, whom he would use again several times. Posterity will not preserve those stories, and no critic or biographer could learn much from either, or from both together. But when they are read along with fifty-two others and along with the novels and the *Collier's* serials of later years, there is a recurrence of character, theme, and attitude that cannot be ignored. The stories represent formulas that DeVoto found would work, and hence used many times; but the special formulas he found and repeated suggest a compulsive circuitry in his fantasy, as well as a compulsive geography in which fantasy best throve.

Affecting to despise them, he sent them to Briggs, up at Halfway Pond. Briggs told him they were by no means as bad as he said they were. Certainly if they were to be judged by their success in the marketplace, they passed. *Redbook* promptly took one, and *The Saturday Evening Post* the other.[2]

A year before, he had written to Hurlbut that sale of one story to the *Post* would solve most of his difficulties. Now he had it, along with a sale to *Redbook* and another to *Harper's*. He was more than an essayist; he was a *writer*. Three magazines besides the *Mercury* were open to him. Editors and perhaps audiences acknowledged his authority on the West, which seemed to be in fashion, and on the colleges, which made a convenient and perennial whipping boy. He knew, by now, his capacity for work. A moment of decision came closer with every day.

Just then, Northwestern chose to write informing him that he had been promoted to an assistant professorship. Considering the skin he had taken off some of the people who voted his promotion, it was an act of considerable impartiality, a concession that in the opinion of his colleagues his abilities outweighed his violations of decorum. Promotion meant that he could probably look forward to further promotions, to tenure, to a safe position on a faculty which, if it contained people he despised, also contained his closest friends.

Brought to the choice, DeVoto hardly hesitated. Not even the fact that Latham was maintaining an alarming silence about *The House of Sun-Goes-Down* deterred him. Inevitably there would be times when he half regretted the road not taken. Inevitably he would make efforts to escape the total independence and total insecurity he had elected, would attach himself to several sorts of institution for longer or shorter periods. But the choice he made on Cape Cod in the summer of 1927 was the one that directed his life.

He wrote Northwestern thanking them for their confidence and resigning from the faculty. On September 1 he wrote Hurlbut at Marblehead, telling him that the die was cast. He was coming to Cambridge to live and write.[3]

III

MORE PRIVILEGED
EARTH

---

1 · *Breaking In—and Down*

At the beginning of September 1927, Robeson Bailey was a
Harvard junior working as a counselor in a New Hampshire boys'
camp. He was a member of the Harvard tennis team and a hunter,
an outdoorsman. Also, he was literary and a member of the *Advocate*. In the August *Harper's* he had read and liked a story called
"In Search of Bergamot," by Bernard DeVoto, a writer who was
new to him. In the September issue he found an article by the
same author entitled "The Co-Ed: The Hope of Liberal Education," which he thought so asinine he wrote the editor suggesting
that its author stick to fiction. Shortly he received a reply from
DeVoto himself, to whom *Harper's* had sent his letter. Bailey's
objections, DeVoto said with disarming candor, were absolutely
justified; the article couldn't be defended. He also said that he
was moving to Cambridge within a week or two and would be
glad to have Bailey drop around.[1]

Was that invitation simply the act of a writer who felt friendly
when a reader took the trouble to read him and respond to him,
either with praise or blame? Was it an expression of the generosity
and—one hesitates a moment and goes on—the courtesy that he
displayed all his life to correspondents, answering them promptly,
frankly, and at great length? Or did he ask that unknown Harvard
undergraduate to call because, having brought himself by his own

efforts to the condition and place he had always coveted, he was afraid he would inhabit them unwelcomed and as a stranger? After seven years, he knew hardly anyone in Cambridge except his three old writing teachers. Always urgently in need of friends, companions, and the comforts of acceptance, and remembering long nights of talk before grate fires in the company of his peers and betters, he perhaps imagined himself moving into the role that Copey and Hurlbut had used to play, presiding Socratically and indulgently over the eager discoveries of the young.

Robeson Bailey did call on the DeVotos at 64 Oxford Street, and responded with enthusiasm to the vitality, the profane and friendly openness, the electric stimulation, the curious mixture of intellectual impetuousness and personal vulnerability that he found there. He returned, and brought others; they became a Sunday-afternoon group. Practicing writers were not then so common in Cambridge, or so available to Harvard undergraduates, that DeVoto's friendliness was likely to be refused. And he was very different from any writer these young men had ever seen. He was an outlander, but also he was a Harvard man. He knew Cambridge but belonged to none of its coteries. On many issues and personalities and books his opinions were outspoken to the point of blasphemy, and across Harvard's untroubled intellectual skies he left the vapor trail of a belligerent professionalism. He had hard words for aesthetes and Capital-A Artists, thinkers of beautiful thoughts, abstract theorizers, and writers of cherished prose. He asserted the astringent values of the marketplace. He was bitter and witty at the expense of the teaching profession, at least as practiced in the hinterlands and even sometimes—oh, heresy—in Sever Hall. When he told them that as between pedagogy and prostitution they could have his virtue every time, he made commercialism sound like a declaration of intellectual integrity imperfectly disguised as cynicism.

Neither he nor they questioned why, if teaching so appalled him, he had instantly, upon achieving his freedom, fled to the place that had taught him, and there gathered around him a cluster of extracurricular disciples. None of them asked what it was he was doing when, one Sunday afternoon, he read aloud to them, entire, Shaw's *Caesar and Cleopatra*, and at the end laid the book down into their respectful silence, declaring it the greatest achievement of English drama since Shakespeare. From a distance, a performance like that looks so much like one of Copey's readings as to be indistinguishable from it, and if Copey was not a teacher, what was he?

Cambridge, at least that part of Cambridge tributary to Harvard Square, is a small town, and in 1927 was even smaller. Gossip and rumor go through it as inevitably and thoroughly as earth through an earthworm, and despite the intellectual snobbery which it sometimes denies and on which it ultimately prides itself, it has always looked with interest, often benign interest, on eccentrics, geniuses, and wild men from the Out Beyond who are drawn into its gravitational field and converted into functioning satellites, or who crash on its bleak moonscape. More people than three aging writing teachers and a group of *Advocate* boys were aware of DeVoto's entry into the Cambridge atmosphere. He was as visible as a comet, though for Cambridge tastes a little garish. The story and the article in the August and September *Harper's* that had attracted the attention of Robeson Bailey were followed in the November *Harper's* by "Footnote on the West." The November *Redbook* was rumored to have contained a story. One heard that the November 19 *Saturday Evening Post* had a story. One noticed, thumbing through *The Saturday Review of Literature*, that DeVoto seemed to be a regular contributor of reviews.

And he did not burn out. In the January *Harper's* an essay, "Farewell to Pedagogy,"[2] kissed Northwestern and the teaching profession a simultaneous and untearful good-by. Rumor spoke of another story in the January *Redbook*,[3] though Cambridge did not read *Redbook* and so could not say for sure. The February *Mercury* disturbed a few teaching assistants with "English A,"[4] the essay on the teaching of English that DeVoto had promised Mencken two years before. Through the spring, the *Saturday Review* ran a half dozen more DeVoto reviews.

Little of this, in the Cambridge view, was quite intellectually respectable, however vigorous.[5] The stories were of course potboilers. The reviews, if one examined them carefully, demonstrated a lively mind and a willingness to have opinions on anything from Philip Guedalla to Judge Ben Lindsey, from P. T. Barnum to Ford Madox Ford. The frontier essays had a rather attractive lustiness, and seemed to indicate a considerable knowledge of those vague states to the westward. The essays on education were clearly the work of a mere journalist kicking up a dust. Personally, the man was a sort of professional Western Wild Man, though without the red-flannel shirt and the bearskin coat—something more like the illegitimate offspring of H. L. Mencken and Annie Oakley. And a very pretty wife who seemed determined to outdo him in flaunting her unconventionality. It was perhaps understandable that he must always be snapping his suspenders and asserting his west-

Florian B. DeVoto, father of Bernard DeVoto.

Bernard DeVoto.

Kent Hagler.

Bernard DeVoto, second from left, top row.

Bernard DeVoto.

Gordon King, 1929 or 1930.

Hans Zinsser at Harvard Medical School animal lab in the early 1930s.

L. J. Henderson cottage in Morgan Center, Vermont, where the DeVotos spent the summer of 1931.

Avis DeVoto, George Homans, Al DeLacey at a picnic on Lake Memphremagog, Quebec, 1931.

DeVotos' home on Weston Road in Lincoln, Massachusetts, where they liv
from 1932 to 1936.

Bernard DeVoto and Gordon, Lincoln, Massachusetts, 1932.

One Sunday evening in Lincoln, Massachusetts, 1935 or 1936; Avis DeVoto, Gordon DeVoto, and Florian DeVoto in background.

Sinclair Lewis and Bernard DeVoto.

ern masculinity, but must every other word out of her mouth be "bitch" or "bastard"?

One is partly guessing, but only partly. Aggressive crudity was one of the characteristics Helen Howe gave her pair of midwestern Freudian barbarians in *We Happy Few*. She got it, presumably, either from observation (some years later)[6] or from Cambridge gossip. But she erred in making it unconscious and hence obtuse. It was neither. In so far as it existed—and it did not exist to the extent Miss Howe suggests—it was compulsive and sometimes re- gretted, and the more regretted the more compulsively repeated. One of the things Benny DeVoto never did learn, all his life, was the social sense of how much was enough—how far to go in collo- quialism among those who spoke only the stiffest king's English, how far to go in profanity among those whose mouths had early been sterilized with soap, how far to go in familiarity with re- served strangers or friendly women, when to stop tomahawking the body his intelligence and eloquence had slain, how much to re- sent an apparent slight, how not to turn simple disagreement into insult, how to state his opinions, which were quick, powerful, and sure, without stating them at someone's expense.

One Cambridge friend, one of the white Anglo-Saxon Protes- tant wellborn well-educated women of the kind DeVoto always liked to impress (and shock), the kind he conceived collectively as The Lady, guesses that some people in Cambridge liked and admired the DeVotos immediately, and that many more, put off at first, came to understand and discount the crudity; and that as this happened, the crudity diminished, though it never entirely dis- appeared. That seems to have been true. By 1939, when I first knew them and Cambridge, they had made themselves a secure place, with many warm friends, a few bitter enemies, and nearly universal respect. But that was more than a decade later. In the beginning, he and Avis gave many people the impression of a pro- vocative "modernity" and an unseemly coarseness in language, combined with great intelligence, ambition, and what to Cambridge was a mongrel vigor. Plus what to Cambridge was an obsession with Freud. Hunting the roots of his own panic, DeVoto had read a lot of psychology books and consulted a few healers, and he talked of what was on his mind. As the months went by, that "ob- session" would increase.

At first his contacts seem to have been limited to those whom he already knew, notably Briggs, Hurlbut, and Copeland, and those with whom he established a bond on the basis of his writing or his intellectual interests. These included men interested in the new field of American Literature,[7] especially Kenneth Murdock; those such as Fred Merk and Arthur Schlesinger, who worked in American frontier and social history; and L. J. Henderson, the distinguished, pink-bearded, and woman-hating chemist from whom DeVoto had once taken a course in the history of science and with whom he shared an enthusiasm for the Italian sociologist Vilfredo Pareto. Those plus the group of students who came around on Sunday afternoons.

When Robeson Bailey was elected president of the *Advocate* in April 1928, one of his first acts was to beg a contribution from his friend and mentor. What he got was a stout defense of the Yard and the Square against one of their detractors, Heywood Broun, who had publicly questioned that he should send his boy to Harvard.[8]

Where, asked DeVoto for all Harvard to read, had Broun got his figure of only twelve first-rate intelligences in the whole Boston area? That was simply nonsense, New York envy, Algonquin spleen. And where had he got his obscene notion that the object of education was to "enthuse your students"? Education had a few other purposes than entertaining the sluggish-minded. Speaking for himself, he had found better and richer intellectual fare in Cambridge than he had found anywhere else—and he had lived in New York. (The hell he had, says the skeptical biographer, wishing his subject didn't sometimes weaken a sound position by having to pose as omniscient, omnipresent, and omnibiblical, an expert in everything.) "Some significance . . . may be found in my almost feverish determination to come back to Cambridge," he went on, and here one can make no demur. "Deciding to follow Mr. Broun's way of living, by the pen, I could have gone anywhere on earth, to New York, to Paris, or to Spuyten Duyvil. I didn't. The grain of life here suits me. It is what has been, too pompously, called the intellectual life. . . . I have found it more attractive here than anywhere else I have been. Why? Because of Harvard." He suggested that Mr. Broun quit worrying whether or not to send his boy to Harvard. Send him for advice to Bernard DeVoto, who clearly knew a lot more about Harvard than Mr. Broun did.

It was a characteristic performance, contentious and aimed at a prominent adversary. It also demonstrated that DeVoto could boost as well as knock, and if Cambridge intellectuals who would not have stooped to answer a journalistic slur in the New York *World* may have smiled at being defended by a writer of slick stories for *Redbook* and the *Post*, that did not make the defense less heartfelt. Or less a tactical maneuver in a campaign for acceptance. Again one is guessing, this time from internal evidence. The tone is a little too assured, the assumption of a secure position as a known writer a little too casual, the untruth about having lived in New York a little too transparent. Archie the cockroach was in some such mood when he said he was six feet and went everywhere.

The fact seems to be that DeVoto was apprehensive when he came to Cambridge, and that as the months went by his apprehension became anxiety and his anxiety deepened into the old panic, with all the accompanying symptoms of migraines, insomnia, and demoralization. Cambridge was what he had desired, but Cambridge was not to be won by mere thundering on its gate. He had coveted independence, and had it, but independence was linked to a scary insecurity. He spun his living and support out of his guts like a spider, and whenever he quit spinning long enough to look around, he saw himself hanging over vertiginous space. Even Northwestern, even the drudgery of Freshman English, even the Evanston of the W.C.T.U. and the endowment drives could have seemed a tempting security by comparison. His Mark Twain book, which might win him serious notice and acceptance as more than a writer of slick fiction and popular essays, was constantly put off by more of the potboilers upon which he depended and by which he was trapped. And what if he should wake up some week and find that well pumped dry?

Those were legitimate worries, but they took a good while to come to a head, and meantime there were encouragements. His agent, Cora Wilkenning,[9] continued to sell everything he sent her: stories to his three sure markets,[10] an article on Northwestern—by name this time—to *College Humor*.[11] He made *Who's Who*, and that was the sort of imprimatur he valued. And Macmillan's long procrastination about *The House of Sun-Goes-Down* had been ended by his peremptory demand, the previous December, that they publish the book or release it.[12] As if to make up for their past reluctance, they not only agreed to publish it as it was, but commissioned a little biographical and critical booklet on DeVoto by his former Northwestern friend Robert S. Forsythe, now unhappily exiled at the University of North Dakota.[13] He maintained his ability to scratch up articles out of the soil around him. Thus when an earnest young man wrote him, on the strength of one of his articles, and asked where and how he could get a decent education, DeVoto wrote him a four-page, single-spaced reply, responding with notable generosity to a request that another might have dismissed, and then in a postscript asked for the return of the letter when its recipient had read it: it might make the basis of his next essay.[14]

A hypochondriac about security as he was about his health, he counted his earnings and projected his earning capacity; he bought a little AT&T stock and was nourished by a sense of bank account. And he hoped. Most of all, he hoped about *The House of Sun-Goes-Down*, for until the slow Mark Twain book could be finished (he had not yet even begun writing, but had only read and read and read), the novel was his best chance not only for making money but for establishing legitimacy in Cambridge.

It appeared in May, 1928. The Boston *Transcript* liked it. The New York *Times* thought tepidly that it had carefully drawn characters. Nobody else paid it much attention. The Chicago *Tribune* didn't review it until a month after publication day and then damned it with faint praise. Two months after the book appeared, the New York *Herald Tribune* panned it for its "self-conscious manner" and its addiction to the violent and melodramatic. "What probably was intended to be vividness or color," it said, "frequently becomes mere verbal virtuosity."[15]

Plenty of cause for a gloomy summer. Through May, while he sat through the ordeal of unenthusiastic reviews and even more excruciating neglect, he could feel Cambridge beginning to disintegrate around him. People were preparing for the shore or the country. He could anticipate the Cambridge summer heat, and he hated heat and suffered from it. So when Robeson Bailey, who was staying near Cambridge in order to take a couple of courses and work on the *Advocate*, proposed that they share the farmhouse of a relative of his or his wife, Hetty's, near Harvard, Massachusetts, the DeVotos accepted gratefully and locked their apartment and got out.

But it was a gloomy summer even in the country. The manifest failure of his novel, made abundantly clear by the *Herald Tribune*'s destructive review on July 29, was never off his mind. In several letters he damned book reviewers—doubting that they could read —and Macmillan—asserting that they had never had confidence in the book and had published it under wraps.[16] He was depressed and irresolute; when he tried to exorcise his demons by work, the work disgusted him. For hours he would sit in a window seat staring out into the hot yard.

The best thing about the farm was that it lay in territory rich with memories of sects that had been on terms of familiarity with the Holy Ghost and groups that had tried to plant in America's virgin countryside the perfect human society. Alcott's Fruitlands was only a short distance away, Alcott's school was only as far as Concord. The Millerites had ascended these hills, the gentle and joyous Shakers had lived nearby and come as close as any to perfection, their one error being that in abandoning sex they had abandoned the instrument that might have perpetuated them. The relics of America's heavenward aspirations interested DeVoto, but not enough to rouse him out of his anxieties. An hour after Bailey's car returned him from an expedition, he would be back in the window seat. Avis began to be afraid to leave him alone. She conspired with Bailey to get him playing something.

There was no tennis court on the place, but Bailey, understanding that DeVoto had used to box at Northwestern, brought out some gloves from Cambridge and offered himself as a sparring partner.

"I had done very little boxing," he says. "Gym classes in prep school, and some friendly bouts in the dormitory. My idea was that boxing a friend meant dancing around, feinting a lot, and maybe landing some modest jabs. I went into my dance, but Benny didn't even shuffle. He just stood there, without even putting a guard up. I feinted a left jab to the midriff, and followed with a right cross to the head. It never landed. What did land was my arse on the greensward. It was the hardest punch I ever took—and that includes three or four very serious bare-fisted fights in school and college. I got groggily up and resumed my dance. But Benny began unlacing his gloves. 'Hell,' he said, 'you don't know how to box.' He threw the gloves on the grass and went into the house."[17]

Bailey told that anecdote as an example of how sick DeVoto really was. For though he decided the punch was legitimate, the contemptuous refusal to go on was completely out of character. In health, Benny DeVoto was too kind to humiliate a friend in that fashion. He was a fierce competitor and a bad loser, but he respected an opponent who stood up to him, and he was immensely tender of his friends. He was sick enough, nearly as sick as he had been in Ogden and in his first year at Northwestern. If one were utilizing his own method of history by synecdoche, one could take the blow that set Bob Bailey on his arse as one that also floored Macmillan, a gaggle of book reviewers, and all the hindrances, difficulties, and uncertainties of being a man of letters in Cambridge, Massachusetts.

Somehow he survived the summer, the latter part of which they spent at Hix Bridge, South Westport, Massachusetts, with their Northwestern friend Bob Almy, who had come back to Harvard to complete a Ph.D. With them, for a while, was Betty White, that fetching girl, fond of both DeVotos, and busy with the manuscript that would become *I Lived This Story* and win her a prize of ten thousand dollars from *College Humor*. Pontificating to the attractive young female of the species probably helped restore DeVoto; seeing Northwestern getting another black eye in her novel didn't harm his peace of mind; having to take care of Avis, who had her tonsils out, took his mind off himself; the death of Byron Hurlbut's son turned him outward in friendliness and sympathy. He ended the summer healthier than he had begun it, but not so healthy that he was confident or in good spirits. His application to A. B. Paine for additional information, from the Mark Twain papers, about the relations between Mark Twain and Bret Harte had been turned down, cavalierly, as he thought, and he was smarting with the sense of having to make his own way without the customary literary courtesies. And though during the fall and winter he published three stories in *Redbook*, two in the *Post*, and a story and an article in *Harper's*, he remained anxious about money. To Paul Ferris, the Chicago newspaperman who was one of his first and most faithful fans, he wrote on September 25 that he got only two hundred fifty dollars an article from *Harper's*. They would pay fifty dollars more for stories, but he couldn't afford to sell his stories there. He had to write for Edwin Balmer at *Redbook*, who would take formula stories, or Lorimer at the *Post*, who said he would not but who in fact did. And he had had a bellyful of book reviewing and had broken with Canby, this time for good. (He hadn't.) He had heard that in Chicago Llewellyn Jones and Fanny Butcher both disliked him for things he had said in print. As for his novel, Macmillan had sold only forty-five hundred copies.

The letter was grouchy and discontented, an ominous beginning to the new Cambridge year. As the year progressed his depression deepened and his production fell off. As his production fell off, his money worries were magnified, and as his money worries increased, he sank lower and lower toward the suicidal depression and sweating dread that both he and Avis feared.

Some index of his condition is provided by his bibliography. For 1928 it contains twenty-two items, nine of them reviews.[18] For 1929, which reflects the production of late 1928 and the first half or two thirds of the next year, it contains only eight, three of them reviews.[19] His paying production, the essays and stories he and Avis lived on, dropped from eleven to five.

Probably no more than a bare handful of friends knew about his depression, which sometime during this period put him again under the care of a psychiatrist.[20] To Cambridge at large he probably looked like the same confident dynamo who had blown in from the Middle West in the autumn of 1927. For whether he sold enough to live on or whether he didn't, he looked to be, and was, as busy as a nailer, and at least some of what he was busy on struck Cambridge as far more respectable intellectually than the stuff he lived by.

In January 1929 he proposed to Alfred Knopf a series of reprints of significant books in the American tradition, himself to be general editor and perhaps to do one or two titles. There is no need to look upon that proposal as an effort to achieve respectability in Cambridge, for in this case what might impress Cambridge would satisfy his own deepest intellectual urging. He had been devouring the western shelves of Widener for fifteen months, building upon a body of reading that was already substantial. His Mark Twain book was taking him straight to the frontier, and the frontier was taking him straight into what he felt to be the quintessential America. The books that reflected or expressed America deserved to be in print, and available.

Knopf was receptive. Letters about the projected series went back and forth throughout the winter and spring, until on April 25 DeVoto signed a letter of informal contract for what was tentatively called The Cambridge Bookshelf, to contain, among other things, *The Life and Adventures of James P. Beckwourth*, edited by DeVoto; Melville's *Pierre*, to be edited by Robert Forsythe; a collection of tall tales, to be edited by Franklin Meine, a Chicago rare-book dealer; and a collection from the ladies' books and annuals of the nineteenth century, to be edited by C. J. Furness. Perhaps also an anthology from the joke books; perhaps Nathaniel Tucker's *The Partisan Leader;* perhaps other titles, up to a minimum of ten, perhaps extending to a whole shelf. There had been nothing like it in American publishing. The colleges were stirring with a restlessness to know and teach the American tradition. With luck, the series could ride into the future on the very first wave.[21]

By the end of May the series had been renamed Americana Deserta, on the suggestion of the *Mercury*'s associate editor Charles Angoff,[22] and DeVoto and Meine and Forsythe were already at work. What was at least as important to DeVoto— and just as hard on the production of the potboilers that paid his bills—he had begun at the end of March to write the book he then called *Mark Twain: a Preface.*[23] He was approaching the enviable scholarly condition in which one hand washes the other, every job contributes to every other, one expertness reinforces another. The joke books that he was examining while he hunted for an editor had a clear relation to the backgrounds of Mark Twain. The tall tales that Meine was assembling were the very soil out of which Mark Twain had grown. Every book of social history, every magazine, every reminiscence from the frontier, every old newspaper contributed to his knowledge of the world that had produced the most American of writers. DeVoto and Mark Twain and the entire series of Americana Deserta celebrated a history, a nation, a people, and a set of values which from very early in his life he had instinctively supported against those who ignored, denigrated, or misrepresented them.

He and Avis planned to spend the summer in Conway, New Hampshire, in the New England mountains that he could simultaneously enjoy for their beauty and disparage for their dinkiness. As usual, he expected the summer to result in a year's work. He took with him the Mark Twain manuscript, a chunk of which was published in the *Mercury* at the beginning of June,[24] the *Beckwourth*, and all the busywork of the general editorship, plus plans for enough stories to support them. Even before they left, he knew it was too much. And he was resisting the necessity of the slick stories, for his mind was set on what involved his training and inclination far more. Casting about, he tried to extract from Little, Brown a twenty-five-hundred-dollar advance against the Mark Twain. For a sample, he could point to the "Brave Days in Washoe" chapter in the current *Mercury*. But Little, Brown hung back. In the end DeVoto had to borrow five hundred dollars to get them to Conway.

The Conway house was unattractive, and right on the road. He did not work well there. Before the end of June he was in a state of panic. He had let what interested him take up too much of his attention and had neglected what supported him, and now that he had to write something profitable he got the shakes, wrote badly, couldn't produce. What he most wanted to do would pay him nothing for a long time, and then only a pittance. He tried and failed, tried again and failed, to write something he dared send out. In a week he wrote thirty thousand words, all of them futile and bad. On July 2 he sent an abject, humiliated letter to Byron Hurlbut saying that he was desperate, that he had sold nothing since February, that he was having to dispose of his AT&T stock to pay the Cambridge rent, that he could see no way of getting through the summer. Would Hurbut lend him five hundred dollars at the highest interest rate charged in Massachusetts?[25]

Promptly, without question and at no interest, Hurlbut sent him the money, and that act of friendship, as much as the money itself, steadied him. He was able to grind out a story that *Redbook* bought.[26] Then, with the reassurance of what the banks sometimes call a "peace of mind savings account," he could settle down and work effectively through the rest of the summer.

In the end, it was a good summer and a healthy one. Meine, who was a sort of advance man or John the Baptist in the frontier research, discovered, and DeVoto authenticated, the earliest known publication by Mark Twain, a sketch called "The Dandy Frightening the Squatter."[27] That promised well not only for Meine's collection, but for DeVoto's critical book. He got ahead with the writing, he kept up a drumfire of letters to his editors and to Knopf, he made progress with the editing of *Beckwourth*, the loud and lying mountaineer whose adventures encapsulated the life of a frontier a little earlier and a little farther west than the one that produced Mark Twain.

To a compulsive worker, the details of routine editing can be restful. The questions an editor is faced with are questions that have answers, and finding the answers gives a man a sense of accomplishment without putting him through the strain that creative work entails. He can turn to them when brainfag and exhaustion have blurred his capacity to make something out of nothing, and he does not have to feel that the change has markedly cheapened his effort or wasted his time. To turn from the hardest kind of work to an easier kind is not an added burden, but a refreshment, and your compulsive worker has his soul more gladdened by it than by recreation, which comes to seem frivolous. The summer of 1929, once he put to rest his fear of starvation, was that kind of summer for DeVoto. He had been a "burst" worker. By now he was well on the way to being a burst worker with no letdown between bursts.

In the fall, they returned only for a few weeks to 64 Oxford Street. Beginning on October 1, they had taken a lease on 10 Mason Street, one of four row houses just off Brattle, within minutes of the Yard.[28] The Mark Twain manuscript had gone ahead, Americana Deserta would be launched in the spring with Forsythe's *Pierre* and Meine's *Tall Tales*, both of which were in press. He was about to begin an important article, "The Centennial of Mormonism," for the *Mercury*.[29] His financial condition was still precarious, but the worst time was past; his confidence was up. He could be assured that his last year, however harrowing to his spirit and unprofitable in money, had enhanced him among men he respected. And he could congratulate himself that he was past the necessity of scratching frantically for every dollar in the marketplace that he had to defend because he had chosen it, but that he deplored because it ate too much of his time. He had also escaped from the demoralizing insecurity of total independence. For, beginning with the fall term of the academic year 1929–30, he was a part-time instructor and tutor at Harvard College. His emancipation from pedagogy had lasted exactly two years.[30]

"I know of no more delightful spot on the footstool," he had written to Melville Smith when Smith was spending his postgraduation summer in Concord. "The charm of New England country, a deeply peaceful calm with the assurance of fertility and virtue; contact with a settled civilization; the inertia of a community which has discovered what few American communities have discovered or, I fear, will ever discover—that there is a richness of life in leisure and quiet passing all the fictitiousness and factitiousness of vim and vigor; intelligent people, and even a ripened sunlight. . . ."[31] And in February 1922, when Dean Briggs was trying to find him some menial position at Harvard, he had expressed his determination to get back to New England somehow, if he had to join the Knights of Columbus and work for Mayor Curley.[32]

That particular sacrifice had not been demanded of him, but he had had to get back by his own efforts, and he had found little enough of the richness of life in leisure and quiet that his youthful fantasy had conceived. He had had to struggle with all the fictitiousness and factitiousness of vim and vigor. But he had made it, and now he had finally made it in the terms he had always wanted: an official affiliation with Harvard, a ratified position as one of the elect.

Not inappropriately, his first tutee was as blue-blooded and bluestockinged as all of Boston could produce: George Homans, the son of Henry Adams' favorite niece. I imagine DeVoto feeling as I felt when, a frontier boy born without history, I accepted a Fulbright appointment to Greece and carried culture back to Athens.

2 · *"Functional Justification as Part of an Institution"*

In any career there are periods of consolidation, when, as literally as a mountain climber, a man digs in and makes secure what he has won, before starting up again. In the three years after the autumn of 1929 DeVoto was not less busy than he had been during his first two years in Cambridge; he was simply less dispersed and less harassed, though his bibliography still reflects the necessities of his life. During 1930 he published five stories in the *Post* and *Redbook;* during 1931, when there were heavy drains on him because of the illness of his father back in Ogden, seven; during 1932, three. By now he was a thorough professional. When he needed money he could grind out a story, knowing in advance what it would cost him but knowing he could pay the price. In some stories he returned to Custis/Windsor and his leathery frontier heroine, Mrs. Yancey. More often, he set his stories on Vineyard Sound, at "Olympus University" in the Midwest, in Greater Boston, or at Harvard. He developed a new set of fashionables among whom to continue the romantic formulas of "Front Page Ellen." He created a new set of student characters led by a parody of Bob Bailey called Robeson Ballou, and put them through a lot of Fitzgerald-like high jinks at Boston debutante parties. Material existed all around him; he could convert it when the need arose, and he was visited by no such deep depression as had afflicted him in 1928 and the summer of 1929.

Part of his emotional stability can be laid to the fact of a small, steady paycheck, part to the psychological reassurance of being a functioning member of an institution he respected, part to his satisfaction in his serious writing. The Mark Twain book moved, however slowly, and he was able now and then to cannibalize a chapter for a magazine. In 1931 and 1932 four chapters were published, in *Harper's, The Bookman, The Saturday Review of Literature,* and the *Harvard Graduates' Magazine,*[1] and each of those enhanced him as a scholar with a field, an accepted authority as legitimate as any Ph.D.

Re-established as a teacher, he brought forth a couple more essays on education.[2] He busied himself with the editorial duties of the Americana Deserta series and with the job of finding new titles and new editors. His visibility helped consolidate his position not only in Cambridge and among the professors of American literature scattered across the country, but in the peculiarly intimate world of Boston publishers, who surrounded the Common on three sides and saw each other every weekday noon at the Tavern or St. Botolph's. (When New York publishers came to town, they took you to the Ritz.)

The stock market crash of October 1929 went by him, if one may judge by his writings and correspondence, without making any impression at all—indeed, it was an event that most Americans comprehended only in retrospect, by its trickle-down consequences. That was the way DeVoto comprehended it over a period of two years and more. His first intimation that it might affect his life came when Alfred Knopf, on January 20, 1930, wrote rather brusquely telling him to go slow on signing up any more new editors in Americana Deserta as he had just signed Hartley Grattan to do Timothy Flint's *Recollections of the Last Ten Years*. DeVoto, offended, cited what he thought was Knopf's authorization to go ahead up to ten titles and huffily tendered his resignation as general editor.³ He was placated and the Grattan commitment honored, but a certain chastening of his first optimism and enthusiasm resulted. The chastening was continued by the reception of the first two titles in April. Forsythe's *Pierre*, whose introduction challenged some theories of Lewis Mumford's about Melville, he had hoped would precipitate a critical controversy. It was born dead. And Meine's *Tall Tales of the Southwest*, for all its reprinting of the first known publication of Mark Twain, its vigorous preface by DeVoto, and its indisputable importance as a piece of Americana, did little better. In May, Miss Manley Aaron of Knopf wrote DeVoto advising him not to hold his breath until the book passed the twenty-five-hundred-copy mark, at which point it would earn him a doubled fee. *Tall Tales* at that point had just passed five hundred copies, and its daily sales were all but invisible.⁴

Furness' collection from the ladies' books, called *The Genteel Female*, did no better. The Depression hit the book business almost as soon and as hard as it hit the stock market and the banks. In May 1931, Knopf reported to DeVoto that the first three titles in Americana Deserta had cost him two thousand dollars and he was disinclined to lose any more than the other, already-contracted-for titles would certainly lose. DeVoto's *Beckwourth* appeared that month, Mencken's edition of Cooper's *The American Democrat* was scheduled for autumn 1931, Grattan's Timothy Flint would appear in spring 1932, and Carl Bridenbaugh's *Partisan Leader* in fall 1932. And that would be it. Instead of a shelf of important books, a library that would be indispensable to every student of America, there would be seven random titles, each useful in its way, but collectively nothing like what DeVoto had dreamed of.⁵

"Certain moments in history," he wrote much later, about much more important moments, "are like a man waking at night and counting the strokes wrong when he hears a clock strike."⁶ Americana Deserta's brief career was such a moment. Every book published in it, and nearly every book whose incorporation into it was discussed through two years and more, was a book useful to American-literature scholars and potentially interesting to American readers. The study of American literature and history was unquestionably due for a great enlargement and expansion. Publishers would unquestionably make money, and editors would make scholary reputations, from books exactly like those proposed for Americana Deserta, and since the 1930s they have. But DeVoto had counted the strokes wrong. He had mistaken his own intense interest, and the interest of a few friends, for a popular demand that in fact did not yet exist. And there was no way in which he could have predicted the Depression.

Well before the last volume in the series made its obscure debut in the fall of 1932, he knew the whole thing was a bust, another disappointment. Everything now rode on the Mark Twain book, tentatively scheduled for the fall of 1932.

Meantime, more personal matters occupied him, among them two deaths.

One of the casualties was Gordon King, his old friend of Harvard undergraduate days, the man who had once said DeVoto had "the most extraordinary case of ambition I've ever bumped into." As literary as DeVoto, he had introduced DeVoto to Copey's Monday Evenings. In the decade since their graduation he had written assiduously, at home and abroad, and had produced articles, plays, one novel, a child's history of Rome—but without marked success. If there is a real pain in the loss of a friend and contemporary, a person in whom something of one's younger self has remained alive, there is also a guilty comfort in being a survivor, talented enough to succeed where the friend has not, tough enough to endure where the friend has succumbed.[7] In pity and humility DeVoto named his first son, born on August 7, 1930, Gordon King DeVoto.

The second casualty, also in the winter of 1929–30, was Byron Hurlbut, one of his three Harvard champions. DeVoto wrote a touched and respectful obituary for the *Harvard Graduates' Magazine*, praising Hurlbut as one of the great teachers of writing, one of those who taught by delight rather than by the rules of scholarship and gave of themselves as freely as they gave of their wisdom. As it happened, Hurlbut's death affected him in another way than loss. In July 1930, DeVoto had fled to Conway to escape the heat, which was somehow associated with his nervous symptoms and affected him drastically. He had left Avis and Betty White inhabiting 10 Mason Street and reading books of arctic exploration to keep cool. When DeVoto was called back at the beginning of August by the imminence of fatherhood, he found that Hurlbut had left him an inheritance. He was asked to take over English 31, Hurlbut's writing course.

And one further development. At the same time he resumed teaching and moved from the anonymity of a tutor's office to a classroom podium, he assumed the editorship of the *Harvard Graduates' Magazine*, "a dignified little old lady of a periodical," as Mattingly calls it, "designed to gather dust in Harvard Clubs and to share an occasional living room table with the *Atlantic Monthly* and the Boston *Evening Transcript*."[8]

It was more than that to DeVoto, for as its editor he was not merely an obscure member of the Harvard family, minimally certified and approved, but a man with a forum and an audience. However inattentive it had been in the past, he intended to arouse that audience to attention. A residual Mencken still dwelt in him. He was the sort of Harry Pollett, who, as soon as he got to Heaven, would organize the angels and bring them out on strike. Readers of the *Graduates' Magazine* who were used to glancing through it and tossing it aside were going to read it from here on, some of them in dismay and fury.

He announced his accession mildly enough in the editorial column, "From a Graduate's Window." The former editor, Arthur S. Pier, had left to become a master at St. Paul's. The magazine had been near death but was temporarily resuscitated by gifts. It had two thousand subscribers and needed another thousand if it was to survive and pay its way. Though its new editor did not say so, he had insured harmony on the staff by inducing friends to serve—Kenneth Murdock as University Editor, and one issue later, his tutee George Homans as Undergraduate Editor. The policy of the magazine, as always, would be to provide a window on Harvard interests and accomplishments and a forum for Harvard men's "enthusiasms and resentments."[9]

The last word was significant. In an essay entitled "Literary Censorship in Boston" the new editor illustrated what he meant by it and forecast the tone of his editorship.[10] He leveled pointblank against one of Boston's untouchable institutions, the Watch and Ward Society, and pulled the lanyard.

The occasion was the arrest and conviction of the proprietor of the Dunster House Bookshop, James A. ("Al") DeLacey, for selling a copy of *Lady Chatterley's Lover*. Defending the novel's strong language as a sincere if unsuccessful attempt to "purify the language of love" by frankness, DeVoto attacked the statute under which the arrest was made, which forbade the sale of books containing obscene language or any matter tending to corrupt the morals of youth. Since there was no criterion by which corrupting matter could be judged, it generally turned out to be anything that had sexually excited some member of Watch and Ward, for whom morality was always sexual. He charged that DeLacey, a fastidious man, had actually been incited to sell the book by the snoops who had managed the banning of seventy-three other books in Boston in recent years, and that his eight-hundred-dollar fine and four months in jail were a grotesque distortion of justice and a monument to Boston's hatred of literature. In their "benignantly strabismatic innocence" the reformers had achieved another result, unlooked for: some of their own directors had resigned in embarrassment, and the whole of the Boston intellectual community was divided between indignation and laughter.

That stoutly civil-libertarian essay, which launched DeVoto on a career of resistance to censorship and censors of all kinds, would have found few objectors among the alumni who read the *Graduates' Magazine*. But in the December issue the editor turned his guns on Harvard itself, or rather on the *Alumni Bulletin*, which had suggested some "mature" adviser to curb expressions of undergraduate opinion: the *Crimson* had gone out of bounds in an editorial against the American Legion. The ex-chaplain of Herman Baker Post did not defend the Legion; he defended the *Crimson's* right to say what it thought of it. He wanted no censors, self-appointed or Harvard-appointed. "Alas, freedom of speech implies freedom of bad taste." One of President Eliot's greatest glories, he suggested, had been his consistent championing of freedom of speech and opinion, and he ended his editorial on tiptoe, spread-eagled against a text from *Areopagitica:* "Possessing that freedom and a few men to exercise it, Harvard would still be rich, though some depression annihilated its funds tomorrow. Lacking it, we should be poverty-stricken, though undreamed-of prosperity laid its increase at our feet."[11]

This sort of thing was exhilarating or in questionable taste or tainted with a dangerous radicalism, depending on which reader of the *Graduates' Magazine* you happened to be. In any case it was a pronounced change from what the magazine had contained before September 1929. And it continued. In his person as The Graduate—an insider, observe—DeVoto damned the building boom that was erecting new freshman dorms, creating payrolls, and desecrating the charm of the Yard. He publicly doubted the necessity of the proposed memorial chapel. He applied to Harvard the findings of Abraham Flexner's *Universities: American, British, German* and found Harvard guilty of becoming an adjunct of the plutocracy. He thought the new House Plan would freeze out the poor student unless it was accompanied by an enlarged program of scholarships. He championed the outsiders and the non-resident students, the neglected ones for whom Harvard was a streetcar college. He thought Harvard should stop building for a while and devote its resources to students and junior faculty caught by hard times. He proposed, as a fundamental element of the House system, a Thoreau House, where plain living, high thinking, and minimal costs would be the standards. The ideal, he said, was Pareto's "free circulation of the elite." Harvard's obligation was to renounce its affiliations with the plutocracy and devote itself to creating and sustaining an aristocracy of the mind.[12]

His editorials involved him in debate with readers, some of them hot readers against whom he had to defend even the principle of expressed editorial opinions. Dissent did not deter him; he took it as a sign that the moribund *Graduates' Magazine* had begun to stir. When he could find no lively material with which to fill the magazine, he wrote it himself, either inserting whole essays or stretching the Graduate's Window to fill unoccupied space. Three essays— "We Brighter People," in the spring 1931 issue, "Mark Twain and the Genteel Tradition," in winter 1931, and "Grace Before Teaching," in March 1932[13]—gave his obscure little forum a literary and intellectual distinction such as it had never had and would never have again. Any of the three essays, he could have sold to *Harper's* or the *Mercury*. All of them are significant in the development of his ideas, as he himself acknowledged by incorporating the Mark Twain essay into *Mark Twain's America* and including both the others in the first collection of essays that he liked well enough to reprint in book form. The last of the three to be published we may consider first, since it was an extension, in one way a reversal, of some of his earlier opinions on the teaching of literature. In form a letter to a prospective Ph.D., it was indulgently contemptuous of the methodology of graduate training and the "guild of nincompoops with degrees" under whose domination literature atrophied. It was true that the Professors sometimes knew what they were talking about, as the Young Intellectuals rarely did; but their increasing insistence on methodology was deadly. Literature "ceases to be an art, it ceases to have any bearing on human life, and becomes only a despised corpse, a cadaver without worth except as material for the practice of a barren but technically expert dissection."[14]

To that judgment, any lover of literature who has ever suffered through graduate school is likely to say amen. The New Humanists were in the same years attacking literary scholarship on similar, if more academic, grounds. Twenty-five years after DeVoto gave his advice to an unknown Ph.D.—incidentally justifying his own failure to pursue literature through that maze—the *Harvard Report on General Education* was making the same plea for education *through* literature rather than *in* it, and nearly forty years afterward, Saul Bellow managed to annoy both the Professors of literature and the Young Intellectuals, who by that time had merged into a single, formidable critical Establishment, with almost identical sentiments.

In 1932 the system had not yet metamorphosed, or even cracked its pupal case. DeVoto's dissenting opinion was relatively new to the public prints, though not new to him. He had from the beginning resisted the standard forms of dissection, as he had resisted the classical bias and the academic decorousness of the New Humanists and the vaudeville tactics of teachers avid for student approval. He had gravitated to those teachers who taught literature from the creative end, he had always been suspicious of theory and systematic analysis, he referred himself to facts and *ad hoc* situations. If you were going to teach literature—and "in this forbidding world we are everywhere surrounded by mystery, which wraps us in the cloak of our own ignorance, and any genuine solving of any genuine part of it is good"—teach it to undergraduates and teach it by being true to literature, not to pedantry or method. "I do not mean that a teacher of literature is, rightly, a man who would be a poet if only he could write poetry. I mean that the communication of literature to students is a form of the imaginative expression of experience, and is subject to the principles of creation, not to those of dissection."

"Be humble!" he adjured his young Ph.D. And also, "Be proud!" Like the West, which was a great place but was lousy with Westerners, the teaching profession was a high calling but was lousy with pedagogues. Dean Briggs, who had objected to the Mencken tone of some of the earlier essays, could have read this one with satisfaction, for it not only expressed some of his own convictions about literature and teaching, but expressed them with force and eloquence.

"We Brighter People" was more deliberately contentious. Even its title was a sneer. An attack on the Young Intellectuals—Van Wyck Brooks, Lewis Mumford, Waldo Frank, Harold Stearns, the whole *Seven Arts, Golden Day, America's Coming-of-Age* group—the essay represented DeVoto's matured but not necessarily mellowed judgment of ideas and tendencies that had infuriated him even as an undergraduate. It was also the first salvo of a bombardment that would go on for two decades and breed great bitterness and cause many great wounds, of the least of which an emir would have died. During the five years he had been working on the Mark Twain book, DeVoto had been steadfastly bent upon refuting the ideas of Van Wyck Brooks about Mark Twain and the frontier that had bred him. Those ideas had been profoundly influential. They were likewise widespread—were not only held by the Brooks coterie and those whom it had influenced, but were assumed to be true for a whole culture, not simply for Mark Twain.

Characteristically, DeVoto opened up firing by battery. The Young Intellectuals, he said, held their ideas in ready-made sets. Their idiocies began with Brooks's *America's Coming-of-Age,* "one of the decennial abstracts of Emerson's 'American Scholar,'" but did not achieve complete expression until *The Ordeal of Mark Twain.* The YI's spurned the "puritanism" and commercialism of America without having read enough history to know they were distorting it. Where facts conflicted with their a priori theories, facts were ignored. They canonized Melville and Emily Dickinson as symbols of the Artist crushed by materialist America. Having Freud ready to their hands (often confused with Adler, Jung, and J. B. Watson), they felt free to psychoanalyze writers, especially dead writers, and to find in them what they had gone looking for. Brooks said that Mark Twain had had the Artist in him crushed by frontier buffoonery and Calvinism, and had been combed all to thunder and effectively gelded by his mother and his wife. It was a nice theory, but it wasn't true. Very little of what the YI's said was true. Of all the books written about America by the YI's, Gilbert Seldes' *The Stammering Century* was the only one that did not misrepresent it.

To the YI, moreover, literature was seldom an art, any more than it was to the pedagogue. It was a means to reform according to a blueprint conceived without reference to life, history, or human nature. And it rarely meant what it said; it contrived to mean obliquely, symbolically, metaphysically. In contrast with physicists, say, who really knew something, but were very cautious about asserting it, the YI's knew nothing about fact or history, yet were constantly vulgarizing ideas and bending truth by asserting certainty.[15]

We have heard that dissenting opinion as early as 1922, when DeVoto rebuked Melville Smith for knocking America as a kill-joy civilization. We have heard something related to it even earlier, when he wrote Smith from Ogden announcing his resolution to spend his productive years comprehending the true history and spirit of America, not in Brooks or Mumford terms, not hearing the fiddles tuning up for any Golden Day, but realistically. Since he had read *America's Coming-of-Age* in the year of his graduation, he had worked more than ten years, interruptedly but with a singular persistence, to achieve that comprehension. It was finally coming to a head in his Mark Twain book, not yet ready for the press but getting there.

A modified chapter from that book, combining the theme of Mark Twain with the theme of censorship, was the last-but-one of the essays DeVoto published in the *Graduates' Magazine*.[16] It is not the whole story—it concerns primarily the contacts between Mark Twain and the genteel tradition—and it takes the rather mild position, unexpected in the light of DeVoto's belligerent antagonism to all censorship, that the combing over that Mark Twain got from the genteel, including his wife, Howells, and Richard Watson Gilder, did him less harm than the Brooks contingent seemed to think. Mark Twain's relation to the genteel tradition was the western relation: "He came East and he accepted tuition." The cleaning-up impoverished literature very little, and he submitted to it without complaint and without the collapse of artistic integrity that had been asserted. In the same way that he submitted to Clara's and Howells' editing, he allowed Gilder to bowdlerize *Huckleberry Finn* in the pages of the *Century*. A tradition enforced conformity on an alien, because the folkways of gentility would not then accept a realism rougher than that of Howells or James. Unfortunate, yes; seriously damaging, no. Not unless you were constructing a theory from it.

Having fired the opening salvos (the artillery metaphors are all but inescapable), DeVoto kept up a rolling barrage looking forward to the time when his book should come off the press and the attack should be made in force. In January 1932 he reviewed Clara Clemens Gabrilowitsch's *My Father, Mark Twain*, a collection of love letters from Mark Twain to his wife.[17] "This unneeded book," selected with a taste that was "really dreadful," could have been, he said, something notably more important. It could have contained all the letters to Howells that had been returned to the Mark Twain Estate when A. B. Paine was writing his biography. It could have drawn on the vast body of manuscripts and correspondence locked up in a New York warehouse and available only to Mrs. Gabrilowitsch and Paine. Mrs. Gabrilowitsch's principal purpose, to protect her mother's memory from the aspersions of Van Wyck Brooks, was hardly justification for a book. Nobody took those aspersions seriously anyway.

It seems impossible to come at the details of DeVoto's leaving the *Harvard Graduates' Magazine*, which he did with the issue of June 1932. The *Graduates'* last editorial reviews his two years and takes some pride in his several campaigns; it commiserates with his unknown successor; it praises George Homans' "unawed intelligence" as Undergraduate Editor. Also, it excoriates the "personified flaccidity" known as the Alumni of Harvard College—the *Graduates'* subscribers—thereby suggesting that his attempts to liven up the magazine had been resisted and that he was leaving by request.[18]

Whether that was true or not, he had left a mark. His files for a year or two afterward show letters from alumni regretting the end of his editorship and thanking him for his contributions. Beyond any question, DeVoto himself regretted the closing of that forum, for he was, then and always, a man in search of an audience. Many of the qualities of his later career as an editor and commentator are already here: the personal tone, the dissenting opinions, the impetuous rhetoric, the direct talk to readers, the willingness to do battle in attack or defense, the impatience with hypocrisy or nonsense, the championing of civil liberties and various kinds of underdogs, the bluntness that is close to insult. In later and more effective forums he would demonstrate that there was a vigorous editor in him, along with the novelist, the critic, the historian, and the pamphleteer, but that the editor could not operate except as a crusader and that every page of a magazine he edited would be an editorial page. Anyone who desires to experience the general tone and pace of a DeVoto-edited periodical can get it by going to the puppet shows of Palermo, especially in those moments when Orlando or Oliver seizes his sword, when the stamping begins and the dust rises and the blows rattle off the armor and the Saracen heads roll.

3 · New England: There She Stands

"An apprentice New Englander,"[1] DeVoto liked to call himself. Many things combined to make him one. His abiding vision of America as a new, emerging, ultimately hopeful civilizaton was one of them: in New England a marked and generally admirable variety of native America had already perfected itself. His persistent intellectualism was another: New England had been and at least in his eyes remained the model and schoolroom of the American mind. But personal insecurity and acute ambition had likewise helped fasten him like a limpet to the New England rock. Having repudiated Utah as deficient and stultifying, having rejected his mother's Mormon tradition and his father's irritable, dislocated intellectual snobbery, he was in the market for a new place and culture to belong in. America as a generalized nation provided it in some degree; but generalized America was large and diverse, and his attachment was primarily to its past and its process. New England gave him a second belonging-place.

Probably he was trying to replace an unsatisfying home, which he felt had rejected him and laughed at his literary ambitions, with a place that would satisfy his need for accomplishment, drama, recognition, and the companionship of true minds. But if that were all, Northwestern should have answered his needs better than it did. Maybe, as one of his analysts later suggested to him,[2] he was searching eastward for a father, determined to demonstrate his ability to prosper in an intellectual climate from which his father had been a dropout and a failure. Whatever psychoanalytic explanation he or his analysts might propose, he was never in the slightest doubt, from the time he arrived at Harvard as a brash sophomore transfer to the day of his death forty years later, that New England was the region he loved and respected, the best of all places to live and work. Next to the West, it is the most frequent subject of his writing over a period of twenty-five years; but unlike the West, it generally comes out smelling like a rose. He never said of New England that it was a fine place but lousy with New Englanders.

By 1931 he had had four years of it superimposed on his three undergraduate years. He had some experience not only of Cambridge, Boston, and their environs, but of the countryside. One summer on the Cape, one divided between Bob Bailey's farmhouse and the Almy place at Hix Bridge, and parts of two others near Conway, New Hampshire, had let him sample three varieties of New England landscape and three subspecies of New Englander. He had put Bailey over a good many miles of rural Massachusetts hunting down utopian colonies and New Jerusalems during the distracted summer of 1928, and since acquiring a car of his own he had gone back to his old Ogden habit of driving off the shakes, anxieties, and horrors by getting behind the wheel.

An apprentice New Englander. His son had been born in New

England, and though he probably would have subscribed to the Vermonter's laconics—"Cat kin have kittens in the oven but that don't make 'em biscuit"—he was closer to being biscuit after four years in New England than he would have been after a lifetime in Evanston. Then, in the summer of 1931, he discovered Vermont, and what had been respect and liking turned into a love affair. He fell for Vermont with the same headlong ardency that had marked his attachments to the brewer's daughter, Mattie, Skinny, Helen Avis MacVicar, and Harvard College.

Again it was a Cambridge friend who provided opportunity. His old teacher L. J. Henderson, famous for his research into the chemistry of the blood and a formidable gourmet, misogynist, and intellectual, was leaving with his wife to spend a sabbatical year in California. His summer place at Morgan Center, ten miles below the Quebec border, was available to the DeVotos, their ten-month-old child, and any friends they might choose to ask up.[3] Done, on the instant. On June 13, they drove up and took possession.

That quiet, green village looking southward across Lake Seymour to the peaks that walled Lake Willoughby could provide out of its own resources none of the intellectual stimulation that was the greatest charm of Cambridge. But it could provide everything else. It was New England to the seventh power. Its fields, hewn out of the forest just after the Revolution and maintained with stubborn labor since, were hedged with mossy stone walls and bounded with dense wild woods of maple, birch, beech, hemlock, spruce, white cedar, balsam, tamarack, white pine, ash, elm, ironwood, butternut and cherry. Its houses and their furniture and a lot of its wagons and farm equipment had been made out of those woods, and so had the character of the Vermonters. Every quality of independence, self-reliance, laboriousness, ingenuity, stubbornness, endurance, and hard-mouthed integrity that DeVoto admired in the New England character were here undiluted. Town-meeting democracy, democratic self-respect, an essential conservatism that went all the way from frugality in making things do, and do again, and do over, to a skeptical and humorous political view were demonstrated to him twenty times a day. He admired the Vermonters' uncomplaining adaptations to a hard climate and thin soil, he liked their jack-of-all-trades skill, he liked their humor, he liked their finished physical type. Something both explicit and implicit to the American gospels had here been allowed to grow and develop in relative isolation, back in a corner where boosters had found no reason to go and where the phony had no acceptance. Needs had been reduced to a minimum, adaptive skill was at a maximum. A Vermont farm family with a garden, a cow, a woodlot, and a sugarbush could get along in the Depression year 1931 on three hundred dollars cash a year and never lose one grain or scintilla of its independence and self-respect. Though he does not seem to have said it anywhere, in so many words, what he found exhilarating in Vermont was an extension into contemporary times of everything that he admired about the frontier, as well as much that he had been familiar with from childhood in the laborious mores of the Mormons,[4] many of whom, including both Joseph Smith and Brigham Young, were born in Vermont.

The Henderson place, composed of several cottages scattered through the edge of the woods along the lake shore, had every advantage. DeVoto could remove himself from the household during writing hours, and there were separate quarters for the students and Cambridge friends and New York editors who dropped in and created an intermittent but enthusiastic version of the DeVoto Academy. They dropped in in some numbers, and some of them returned several times, for Morgan Center was only ten miles from Canada, and just across the line, in the town of Rock Island, was a provincial bottle shop full of such things as Americans had not seen for years, or had seen only in cut and adulterated forms or at exorbitant prices.

The summer of 1931 was one long, bibulous picnic, either legitimate, on the Canadian shore of Lake Memphremagog, or bootlegged, on the shore of Lake Seymour. To one born in the West, where grass does not make a turf except in high mountain meadows, the cropped sward of a Vermont or Quebec pasture has a touch of the paradisaical about it as well as a reminder of boyhood trips into the wilderness. Though rains are frequent and often torrential in that country, which lies under the St. Lawrence storm track, the good days are like the good days in the western mountains. The light is intense, the deep sky is crossed by navies of fair-weather, strato-cumulus clouds, the horizons are cut with a diamond, the air has never before been breathed. And those days come so infrequently, between days of cloud and rain and violent thunderstorms, and are spaced through such a brief and fragile summer, that a man believes he deserves them and has a right, because of what else he has put up with, to enjoy them utterly.

All together, it was a difficult place to be a compulsive worker, and the anxiety that so much of the time accompanied DeVoto's industry was absent. "A magnificent summer of work and play," he reported it later.[5] He quit Mark Twain, or Americana Deserta, or the current potboiler, when weather or the spirit or the presence of friends moved him, and he spent many an afternoon trying to sample every sort and kind and vintage on the bottle shop's shelves. An education that had been aborted by Prohibition had to be crammed into a very short time; an affectation of a masculine, rip-roaring, frontier familiarity with firewater got a chance to edge closer to reality and true *afición*. The biographer who watches DeVoto acquire the expertise of an accomplished drinker is irresistibly reminded of a photograph in his files showing Benny with several companions in the uniform of the Ogden High School ROTC, sitting around a table on which are bottles and glasses. On their faces, especially on the round, smooth face of young Benny DeVoto, is the clear and aggressive intimation that the contents of the bottles and glasses are straight alcohol cut with a little branch water and flavored with plug tobacco and are never taken in smaller quantities than three fingers, tossed down the hatch with a curt "Here's how."

Their bootlegging activities, at first limited to the bringing back of bottles wired under the chassis or concealed in the toolbox or under the seats, acquired finesse and the possibility of continuance.[6] A Vermont farmer, whom in several Easy Chairs DeVoto later made into a shrewd rustic philosopher called Eli Potter, had a farm in Derby Line, right on the border. His sugarbush merged with Canadian woods a long way from the road and the customs officers. In his many-pocketed canvas hunting coat Eli could carry fourteen forty-ounce imperial quarts, the equivalent of nearly two cases of U.S. fifths. During the summer, he made a good many trips on behalf of the DeVoto establishment, and before they returned to Cambridge they made arrangements to have him make as many more as their needs required. A letter to Eli, a short wait while he made his little journey, a notification in code to Cambridge, and the Quebec and Southeast Transportation Company, composed usually of DeVoto and either George Homans or Emery Trott,[7] would drive up and assume proprietorship of what Eli had gathered together.

If he had calculated it, which he surely did not, DeVoto could have found no quicker way to certain Harvard hearts. Whenever he made a trip to Vermont, the word got around and he had more friends than Mayor Curley on the day after election. And he was generous; he gave of his substance and of Eli's dependable services. A man with access to good, inexpensive liquor was a natural aristocrat, attended by the warmest and most admiring vibrations. quence. He made and inspired lively talk; he dispensed with a free Drama and mystery were his companions, good cheer his conse-

hand. *þæt wæs god cyning.* He was as visible as a pillar of fire, and like a pillar of fire he came by night. Arthur Schlesinger, Jr., who would later be a favorite student of DeVoto's and later still one of his most active allies and admirers and coadjutors, was in the fall of 1931 a high school boy of fourteen. He first saw DeVoto when on several occasions through that fall and the ensuing winter he brought packages to the door. Young Schlesinger thought for a good while that he was the family bootlegger.

One further consequence of the summer in Morgan Center remained to be completed after DeVoto's return. It was an essay that was less essay than hymn, its subject New England and New Englanders, especially Vermont and Vermonters. It appeared in *Harper's* in March 1932, under the title "New England: There She Stands,"[8] and it did DeVoto's growing reputation no harm in Cambridge and Boston. What was perhaps more important, it caught the eye of Robert Frost, who found in it some of his own response to New England, and who particularly liked DeVoto's celebration of the independent farmer, above welfare and the dole and government programs, keeping his family and his self-respect on three hundred hard-earned dollars a year.

That was Frost's first awareness of Bernard DeVoto. Their meeting, several years later, would lead to a quick and intense friendship, mutual admiration, an alliance of two notable dissenters against the welfare world. The friendship would end in a bitter and destructive quarrel.

When "New England: There She Stands" appeared, DeVoto's first meeting with Frost was still three years away. DeVoto did not need Frost to confirm his addiction. The summer of 1932, he and his family again spent in Vermont, this time in Peacham, and he closed out the summer with two weeks at the Bread Loaf Writers' Conference, up the mountain from Middlebury. While he was still teaching there, Avis took young Gordon and went down-country to supervise the moving of their effects from 10 Mason Street to a big old house on Weston Road, in Lincoln. An eclipse of the sun accompanied the move—an omen that Benny, accustomed from a Utah boyhood to the importance of signs and wonders, might have made something dreadful of. He would have been wrong. There was never a more misleading omen. Lincoln brought the DeVotos to the realization of something long dreamed of.

They arrived in the new house at almost the exact moment when *Mark Twain's America* appeared in the bookstores: that is to say, they achieved the perfect place to live at precisely the moment when DeVoto finally broke through the literary barriers into a state of importance. His book, which was in many ways an amplified and documented version of his attack on the Young Intellectuals (though it was much more), was challenging, even truculent. It aroused an anticipated amount of indignation in the rooms where it had been wired to go off. But it aroused also real admiration, respectful discussion, serious consideration, frequent enthusiasm. He had struck out by himself, against the fashionable currents, and he had found an audience waiting.

For him or against him, people did not ignore this one. They paid attention to it as they had paid attention to none of his novels.

4 · *Bernardo Furioso*

From Hell to Nome the blow went home where the cockroach
    struck his foe,
From Nome to Hell the mongeese yell as they see the black blood
    flow;
The hawsers snort from the firing port as the conning chains give
    way
And the chukkers roar till they rouse the boar on the hills of
    Mandalay;—
And the cockroach said as he tilted his head: Now luff, you
    beggars, luff!
Begod, says he, it's easy to see ye cannot swallow my duff!
I have tickled ye, I have pickled ye, I have scotched your mizzen
    brace,
And the charnel shark in the outer dark shall strip the nose from
    your face—
Begod, says he, it's easy to see that the Narrow Seas are mine,
So creep ye home to your lair at Nome and patch your guts with
    twine!
Begod (says he) it's easy to see who rules this bloody bight—
So come ye again, my merry men, whenever ye thirst for fight.
                    Don Marquis, *The Hero Cockroach*

To the skeptical eye of hindsight, much of what are called "critical opinion" and the history of ideas are records of fad and fashion. Intellectuals have a distressing tendency to run in pack like other mortals. Strange manias and fevers, caught sometimes from men of genius, sometimes from charlatans and mountebanks, infect them and are spread by them to the outermost edges of the society. And what arrives at their door humble often goes forth proud; what is caught as German measles is communicated as *rubella*, a disease to be treated with greater respect because the elite have dignified it with their infection and their terminology.

Schools of thought can be as unanimous, and in their way as impressive, as schools of herring. Perhaps it is a demonstration of the open mind that the history of so many fads—phrenology, utopianism, Technocracy, the Back to Nature movement, ecology—so often begins with the conversion of an elite. Perhaps it was open-mindedness that drove Katherine Mansfield to Gurdjieff and the salutary exhalations of cows. Perhaps it is the open mind that welcomes onto contemporary college campuses and among the literary every sort of eccentricity from the New Left to glossolalia, from Encounter techniques to macrobiotic diets, from Skinner to Reich, from Ayn Rand to occultism. The observable fact is that the cultivated catch these drifting contagions about as readily as do the unlearned, whose open-mindedness is known among the intellectuals as gullibility.

Which should not surprise us. Like the rest of us, intellectuals and literary people desire to be in, and being more aware than most, they have a lively eye for what it means to be in, and whom it is desirable to be in *with*. Sometimes, as among contemporary New York critical cliques, the motive is frankly the search for power and influence—"making it," in the phrase of one of them. Sometimes it is a wistful search for conviction, certainty, and the security of an accepted system of belief. In either case, the seekers generally fasten upon a leader who is a system maker, and create a coterie around him. He is often a man of stature, larger than his followers, less doctrinaire, more flexible, but eventually he is likely to suffer from the reaction of those who rebel against the excesses of his followers. Robert Frost used to joke that he could stand the big Kittredge but not all the little ca'tridges. But the little ca'tridges cannot be dismissed without damaging the big Kittredge, for it is his convictions, reduced to absurdity or distorted out of proportion or clung to after he himself has outgrown them, that give the coterie and the movement its character.

Van Wyck Brooks was that kind of intellectual leader. Though throughout his life he demonstrated an admirable capacity to learn and grow, a true open-mindedness that steadily enlarged his books and his opinions, it was his early, passionate, oversimplified and underdocumented convictions about America that created his following and made him an influence. He taught the young intellectuals of a whole generation not only that Puritanism and Commercialism had combined to degrade American aspiration and thwart American artists, but that critics with a message, leaders of thought, could halt or reverse that trend. In particular, the "great gas-lighted barbarity" that Baudelaire thought had killed Poe was very real to the early Brooks. In his view, it had killed many more than Poe; it had killed virtually everyone who had tried to be an artist in America.

Neither in its view of the past nor in its view of the future, its confirmed distaste nor its implicit perfectionism, was the idea new. It is absolutely central to Tocqueville's report on *La Démocratie en Amérique*. It fills the pages of a whole library of British travelers in America. From the Revolution onward, statesmen, critics, and apologists saw America devoting itself to the practical business of investing a new continent, and necessarily neglecting the arts.[1]

What Brooks and his followers added, or emphasized, was that this neglect, often excused as temporary and necessary, was in fact the failure of a civilization, and that only leadership by the high-minded and culturally mature could save it. The American Dream thus far had been shoddy and a fake; we needed to redream democracy in more elevated forms. "It is nothing less than the effort to conceive a new world," says Lewis Mumford at the end of *The Golden Day*. "Allons! the road is before us!"[2] Meanwhile, looking backward, the Young Intellectuals were saddened by the stream of American artists maimed or thwarted or only half fulfilled, victims of a society without soul or spiritual aspiration and of a country with a distressing lack of cathedrals.

The thesis of America's previous social, cultural, and even political inadequacy had already been developed in *America's Coming-of-Age* (1915) and *Letters and Leadership* (1918), and had been enthusiastically overstated in Waldo Frank's *Our America* (1919), before Brooks undertook to psychoanalyze Mark Twain in search of the source of the black pessimism, the "deep malady of the soul . . . a malady common to many Americans," that surfaced in his later years. Brooks felt that there was "a reason for that chagrin, that fear of solitude, that tortured conscience, those fantastic self-accusations, that indubitable self-contempt." He thought it was "an established fact . . . that these morbid feelings of sin, which have no evident cause, are the result of having transgressed some inalienable life-demand peculiar to one's nature," and that "that bitterness of his was the effect of a certain miscarriage in his creative life, a balked personality, an arrested development of which he was himself almost wholly unaware, but which for him destroyed the meaning of life."³

Hunting the root cause, Brooks found Jane Clemens. "Had she been catholic in her sympathies, in her understanding of life, then, no matter how more than maternal her attachment to her son was, she might have placed before him and encouraged him to pursue interests and activities amid which he could eventually have recovered his balance."⁴ But instead, because she was "the embodiment of that old-fashioned, cast-iron Calvinism which had proved so favorable to the life of enterprising action," she looked upon his mischievousness, imagination, and love of adventure (his creative nature) as manifestations of "sin."⁵ And she put them all down firmly when, after the death of Sam's father, she led the boy in beside his father's coffin and in a dreadful, tearful scene made him promise to be a good boy. Then, having marked his soul, she apprenticed him to Ament, the printer, and started him on the road to conformity and mediocrity.

For a brief while in Sam's young manhood, the Brooks thesis went, he was whole, for his career as river pilot was an expression of his artistic aspiration of which, in that society, he need not be ashamed. But the division that Jane Clemens had started in him was widened by the experiences of Virginia City and San Francisco, where he was first lured to a frantic and vulgar scramble to get rich and was later reduced to taking a shameful job as newspaper reporter and frontier funny man.⁶ Then, having made his mark with a "barbarous backwoods anecdote," he came East, and Olivia Langdon, William Dean Howells, Richard Watson Gilder, and the genteel conventionalities of Hartford completed what his mother and the frontier had made inevitable. Meekly he yielded up his artistic integrity (if Brooks had been just a little more Freudian he would have said his testicles); meekly he submitted to the cleaning up of his language and his ideas. He became the sort of success his mother could approve, and not the artist he had been meant to be. His bewildered soul was crucified between two thieves, Puritan frontier vulgarity and eastern gentility. Even his literary name, "Mark Twain," in pilot's language meant "safe water."

This capitalist and playboy of letters, this desperate amateur, never rose to the conception of literature "as a great impersonal social instrument." His social indignation, evading American realities, was profitably diverted to safe targets—monarchy, seventh-century England, medieval France—or spent itself in silly attacks on the Presbyterian Sunday School, or emerged as the sophomoric pessimism of "What Is Man?" an exposure of something already well exposed. Only when he found his way back to the river of his childhood, and could escape to that boyhood idyl, was he anything close to what he should have been.

Thus Van Wyck Brooks, applying to America's greatest writer the thesis developed by the Young Intellectuals in the years preceding World War I and made compulsory after the war, when, as Malcolm Cowley says, they seized power in the literary world precisely as the Bolsheviks had seized it in Russia.[7]

Bernard DeVoto had been aware of that thesis throughout his thinking life—*America's Coming-of-Age* had coincided with his transfer to Harvard College, and *The Ordeal of Mark Twain* had coincided with his graduation—and he had watched it through the war years, when its socialist and pacifist bias got it into trouble, and on into the postwar years, when it merged with and to some extent directed a many-sided revolt. Child of his times, DeVoto had been part of that revolt, had been as rabid a spurner of the soulless village, the W.C.T.U., the repression, conservatism, and censorship in American life as any Young Intellectual. His difference was that his rebellion was selective. He was truly a dissenter; he did not run in pack, even in revolt. He had the instincts of a middle linebacker who loves contact, and he had certain abiding convictions of his own. One was that the literary critics deluded themselves when they thought they could direct social change. They could only report it, and they had better learn to report more than the literary aspects of society if they wanted to avoid absurdity. Another of his convictions he had learned from Pareto: that any society exhibited continuities, which Pareto called "residues," and that it was extremely easy to confuse a temporary modification or rationalization of one of these—a "derivation" in the Pareto jargon—with true change.

The more society changed, in fact, the more it was the same thing. DeVoto saw the perfectionism and reformist zeal of the Brooks group as simply another variant of the old American search for New Jerusalem and the perfected society. Perhaps he had already learned from his friend Hans Zinsser to look upon it as a sort of disease as well, a contagion shifting from endemic to epidemic in response to some change in the personal relations between infectious agent and host.[8]

In any event, he had never believed a word of it. He thought its devotees ideologues imprisoned in their system of assumptions and deductions, and blind to plain facts, especially the facts of history. The moment he found himself with a forum in the *Harvard*

Graduates' Magazine, he used it to attack the Young Intellectuals as lustily as he attacked the dinosaurs of Watch and Ward. He disagreed violently with all systematizing, all a priori thinking, all deductive logic, all New Jerusalem fervors whether religious, political, economic, or literary. He asserted—with passion—fact and the inductive method which built on it. Orthodoxies, which blinded people to facts, maddened him as the sight of a uniform used to madden a poolroom tough I knew in Salt Lake City. The minute a fight started, he looked around for the nearest soldier or policeman.

It is also true that DeVoto looked upon the Young Intellectuals as the "in" crowd, the aesthetes, the expatriates, the ambulance drivers, the effete Easterners. "The boys," he liked to call them in disdain, a phrase that he later applied just as disdainfully to the proletarians, the Marxists, the academic historians, the teachers of English, and the spokesmen for western cattlemen. It meant "those with whom I disagree." But when he disagreed with anybody, he made use of more than logic or rhetoric or his genius for rambunctious dissent. A journalist, he called himself, and he prided himself on looking up the facts. Generally he had.

He had been born in the West in the twilight between barbarism and vulgarity, or if you want, between the fading of New Jerusalem and the commercial present. He had been studying the frontier intensively for a decade, and had published three novels and many essays about it. He knew about the perfected society—he had been born in one, and learned skepticism therein. And though his own flight from Ogden might seem to cast doubt on his profrontier position, in *Mark Twain's America* it was actually not damaging to his present argument, for the Ogden he had fled from had only residual resemblances to the frontier that in Brooks's view had maimed Mark Twain; and neither he nor Mark Twain had sustained the specific damages that Brooks said the frontier inflicted. Above all, the West was DeVoto's country, especially the frontier West. When anyone from outside, anyone condescending and uninformed, challenged it, he was tempermentally bound to mount a counterattack.

Mark Twain's America was dedicated to Robert S. Forsythe, his old Northwestern colleague, one of the Americana Deserta editors, and author of the first and at that time the only critical appraisal of Bernard DeVoto. In his foreword, addressed to Forsythe, DeVoto took occasion to spank A. B. Paine for refusing him assistance and declaring that nothing more needed to be written about Mark Twain.[9] He offered his services to the Mark Twain

Estate for the editing of the manuscripts that Paine kept locked up (an irony, but a prophetic one). And he went to some pains to describe and justify his book. It was not literary criticism, nor was it biography, nor was it what Arthur Schlesinger suggested, the social history of Mark Twain. It was "an essay in the correction of ideas," though he was not naïve enough to suppose that literary ideas were really susceptible to correction. So call it simply "the kind of book I have wanted to write about Mark Twain." Actually he could have relied on his title, which was precise. The book is about Mark Twain's America, especially the America he knew before he came East and accepted instruction: the America that had formed him, the Mississippi River and the Sierra Nevada and San Francisco.

That frontier America, DeVoto said, had been misrepresented by "the lay popes of our thinking," and so had Mark Twain. "The criticism of literature in America is so frail, so capricious, so immature a force, that discussion has moved away from what a great man wrote, to what he was or was not, what he should have been, what America failed to be, and what the reformation of society might achieve if the world were amenable to pretty thoughts." And finally, "I have no theory about Mark Twain. It is harder to conform one's book to ascertainable facts than to ignore them. In literature, beautiful simplicities usually result from the easier method."[10]

The stance is absolutely characteristic, a stance he adopted at the beginning of his career and maintained to the end. Facts. The *ad hoc* approach. Suspicion of theories, of systems, of absolutes, of beautiful thinking and beautiful simplicities. Having stated his intentions, he set out to demolish *The Ordeal of Mark Twain* as a theory based on false facts, inadequate facts, misunderstood facts, and sometimes no facts at all.

No purpose would be served by a point-for-point discussion of that demolishment. It is a landmark of sorts in the history of intellectual controversy in America. The books exist, and may be read, and Mark Twain scholars as well as American social historians have read them. Most have elected to follow DeVoto most of the way. For though he was guilty of overstatement in asserting that Brooks knew no American history, was helpless to deal with humor, and was ignorant of the frontier, the most superficial reading of the two books makes it clear that Brooks knew less about all three than his corrector did. Clearly he had, as DeVoto charged, discovered some of his conclusions before he had assembled his evidence. His Puritanical and vulgar frontier society without art or folklore or aspiration was a straw man, his notion of the "artist" that was thwarted in Mark Twain was the figment of an eastern and European-oriented and overliterary imagination; his psychoanalytic portrait based on literary evidence was a caricature.

Step by step, DeVoto traced Mark Twain through the societies and the influences that had shaped him. In place of Brooks's theoretical Hannibal, created mainly out of a selective reading of Paine's biography and Mark Twain's late (and unreliable) reminiscences, he substituted the few sure facts then known about Sam Clemens' boyhood and youth, pointing out, among other things, that the apprenticing to Ament came not immediately after the death of Sam's father, but fifteen months after; that Sam's boyhood was not inhibited by Calvinist rigors, but marvelously free; that his imagination was not constricted, but enlarged by the violence, turmoil, and change of his boyhood town; that the superstitions of slaves and the humor of frontier newspapers were shaping forces to which he responded with awe and delight, and by which he was exhilarated and emancipated. What emerged from the crude but in certain ways idyllic society of the Mississippi Valley and the Pacific slope was not a maimed artist, a man devoured by inward guilts and shames, but the first truly American writer, precisely what Emerson's "American Scholar" had called for, but in a form so new that the literary did not recognize him for what he was. The literary tradition he represented was native, as was the tradition of humor that he practiced. He raised both to the level of art. He was actually the triumphant climax of a native subliterary tradition, and not the frustrated end of an imported one.

In 1973 these opinions are commonplaces; in 1932 they were a striking refutation of accepted literary opinion. Subsequent scholars have opened and cultivated the territory of the tall tale and newspaper humor that DeVoto, Franklin Meine, Walter Blair, and Constance Rourke explored at the beginning of the 1930s. The reputation of Mark Twain, who had always been read but seldom taken with full seriousness, has undergone a shift and an enlargement in conformity with the figure that emerged at the end of *Mark Twain's America:* a figure often called for, often heralded, a form of the creature Crèvecoeur had in mind when he asked, "Who is this new man, the American?"[11] What emerged was the American as artist, the development that Brooks and the literary Sanhedrin had denied and gone on calling for. Around him was the America that had created him without being understood or much investigated: the forming society given its native quality and its extravagant and exhilarating energy, as well as its idyllic freedom, by the fact of the frontier, which the Brooks view held to be deadly to art.

To get this said, DeVoto attacked Brooks frontally and by name as the most intelligent and influential of the Young Intellectuals. He went for the quarterback, and he was not gentle. Brooks was upset; his friends were furious; several reviewers, including Mark Van Doren in *The Nation*,[12] objected to DeVoto's "anger" and "loudness"; Lewis Mumford privately planned to give DeVoto "a few medicinal pellets" and wrote Brooks asking for a list of DeVoto's errors.[13] Though the reviews in many quarters were enthusiastic, even jubilant, the hives of the Young Intellectuals hummed as angrily as Utah had hummed when it opened *The American Mercury* for March 1926. The Mark Twain Estate hummed too. A. B. Paine was annoyed to find himself represented in the Foreword as a dog in the manger, and wrote, both personally and through the estate lawyer, Charles Tressler Lark, to complain and threaten suit.[14] Growing more truculent on being reproached, DeVoto said in reply that if Paine felt wronged, DeVoto was willing in the next edition to print the relevant passages from Paine's letter refusing his co-operation. Having deliberately set out to stir up the lions, he took some pleasure in their roaring.

Many years later Lawrence Kubie, the distinguished analyst who for a time had DeVoto as a patient, told him that his method of argument was too vituperative. "When you get roused to written argument, when you hear the clarion call of your own words, there is often a touch of the fishwife about your argufying. It is a curious thing, Benny, that this is never true of you in face-to-face argument; or at least I have never seen it. It discolors your argument when you are hurling words from a distance. Then it is as if you were jumping up and down with glee on the prostrate form of the opponent with whom you are disagreeing, not trying to find a common ground, but rather enjoying the opportunity to use a divergence of viewpoints to point out what a damn fool the other man is."[15]

Beyond any question, there is that tone in *Mark Twain's America* and in a good many of DeVoto's subsequent writings. Though he objected to being called the "volcanic" Mr. DeVoto by *Time-Life* journalists, volcanism was a habit that he either cultivated or could not avoid. Personal malice was not a significant part of it; he did not know Brooks personally, nor many of the other Young

Intellectuals. He took them simply as representative of ideas to which he strongly objected, and ideas that struck him as false or misguided raised his blood pressure and reddened his eye. Often, he seems to have been surprised when people he lambasted took the attack personally instead of assuming it to be all in the heat of controversy,[16] to be reconciled with a convivial postgame drink in the locker room.

Nevertheless, Brooks and his friends were aggrieved and offended, for what they thought more than adequate cause. DeVoto himself, perhaps instructed by reviewers who intensely admired *Mark Twain's America* but regretted its frequently railing tone,[17] came very shortly to feel that he had been too vehement. His facts alone, it was clear, would have demolished Brooks's theory. Within months of the publication of his book, he was planning a new edition that would reduce and moderate the attacks on Brooks. That edition did not become a fact until 1951, and then it had no corrections or changes, which was something of a pity, for revisions might have effected a reconciliation between men who had much to learn from one another. What DeVoto did not know was that Brooks, too, was planning a revision—had done a good deal of it before *Mark Twain's America* appeared—and that this revision would take care of a good many of the errors of fact or judgment that DeVoto charged against him. Brooks admitted to Mumford, while still smarting over the tongue-lashing he had taken, that he had benefited from DeVoto's book to the extent of "about a dozen corrections" that he had not already made.[18]

But in so far as literary ideas are ever corrected, the ordeal of Mark Twain was a discredited theory as soon as *Mark Twain's America* appeared, and no amount of revision and modification could fully reinstate it. America was at least partially vindicated; the great gas-lighted barbarity was demonstrated to have been a bogey to scare children and console the unrobust. As for Bernard DeVoto, he had become someone of importance, almost a personage, by his singlehanded raid against the intellectuals. And the public image of him was ambivalent, as he was himself. He was not simply a red Indian dancing the scalp dance and striking the pole and boasting of his exploits against the effete. He was a sort of champion of the West, a yea sayer where there had previously been a chorus of scornful nays. Fully as much as "New England: There She Stands," *Mark Twain's America* was a hymn of praise, not only a corrective report on the West and the frontier, but a celebration. And that was prophetic.

5·*On Bread Loaf Mountain*

I never see a dinosaur
So patient and so mute
But that a song of pity springs
Unbidden to my lute—
He stayed a lizard, but he wished
To be a bird, poor brute.
Don Marquis, *Reverie*

With the publication of *Mark Twain's America* DeVoto completed a decade of scrambling and climbing. He had made it from deprivation to a sort of fulfillment, had established himself in the place and among the people he most desired to be part of, had stated many of his major themes, had acquired a degree of authority over an area of knowledge that was distinctly his own. A compulsive self-tester, he had tried out his ability to support himself by writing, and found that he could do it. This Sir Gareth from the Utah backlands had won his way from the scullery to the fellowship of the Table Round. He had challenged the dragon Error and come home with one of its heads. He held a guest card in the Harvard community, and with many of its finest minds he was on terms of intimacy and mutual respect. Through George Homans and Charles Curtis[1] he was even welcomed at the thawed edges of Boston's frozen and wellborn center. That he was a stimulating teacher, many students attested. That he was a provocative and challenging mind, informed, quick in comprehension, tenacious in his grasp of fact, tough in controversy, his Mark Twain book had made plain. That he sometimes overstated himself, and that he made his living as a hack writer of slick magazine stories, were eccentricities that Cambridge could indulge with a smile.

Nevertheless, almost at home, almost secure, a roaring mouse somewhere in the walls of that quaint city, he needed something more than Cambridge could give him. Cambridge was Academia. He could still look upon it with an outsider's eye, and he knew that though it might be the hub of the universe and the intellectual engine room of America, it was not any longer the center of America's literary life or of the American publishing business. And he was a pro. If he had followed the path beaten by hundreds of his contemporaries, he would have headed toward New York, driven by the sheer economics of his profession. Instead, he got most of what he needed of New York at the Bread Loaf Writers' Conference, and he got much else besides.

On July 14, 1949, debating in his mind whether or not to accept Theodore Morrison's invitation to be once again a member of the Conference staff, DeVoto expressed himself with vehement ambivalence to William Sloane:

It is still an absolutely dead sure thing that I will not go but other pressures as powerful as yours are being applied to me. . . . Probably I will still be unalterably refusing to go when I drive into the yard of Treman and start bellyaching about Fletcher's martinis. . . . The truth is I mortally hate the place, its hysterias, its psychoses, its doublebitted axes, its miasmas, blights, poisons, obsessions, shuck mattresses, dining room regulations, Ophelias, Lady Macbeths . . . Pistols, Olsens, Johnsons, somnambulists, insomniacs, and most of all, by Christ, its glee-clubbers. The truth is, further, that it terrifies me and infects me with manias, depressions, and blue funks. Beyond that is the further truth that there are increasingly acute reasons why I should not come, and beyond that is the concentric truth that I always have the best time of the year when I am there.[2]

The visit that in the summer of 1949 he dreaded, resisted, and eventually made was his twelfth tour of duty at Bread Loaf. It was his last as a regular staff member. Through the 1940s his relations with some of the regulars, especially Robert Frost, had been growing increasingly acrid and uncomfortable. His last stay on the mountain, when he stole two days from an automobile tour designed to produce travel articles for *Holiday* and *Ford Times*, occurred in August 1955, and it was bitter with ill health, fatigue, and old quarrels. Nevertheless, from 1932 until the haunted weekend a few months before his death, Bread Loaf was something special in DeVoto's life—a focus, a trying-ground for ideas, a vacation, a reunion, an annual renewal of acquaintance and energy. No other places except Ogden, which shaped him, Cambridge, which he often affected to loathe but refused to leave, and the office of *Harper's Magazine* at 49 East 33rd Street, which gave him loyalty, affection, and a national forum during his last twenty years, had a comparable influence on his life.

Though the fee it paid him was minuscule to begin with and never got much better, he could justify the loss of two weeks of writing time as a sort of working vacation, the Sunday rodeo of a weekday cowhand. The fact that the Conference was held in Vermont had a lot to do with its continued attraction. As a bonus, during the first four years, when he was still teaching at Harvard, he found it useful to be forced to boil down his lecture notes to fit the demonic concentration of Bread Loaf, for often these boiled-down notes could be thriftily published as essays. And finally, as important as any of these, after his departure from Harvard in 1936 the Conference permitted a satisfying annual return to the teaching platform from which he had been untimely ripped. Professional writer he might be, but teacher he could not help being also.

In September 1947, after what he thought an especially successful Bread Loaf session, he wrote his impressions to Mark Saxton, once his student at Harvard, the son of his friend Eugene Saxton at Harper's, and later a colleague on the mountain:

When you come to write that obit for Fred Melcher,* recollect that one of the biggest of the conflicts that have made my inner life as picturesque as the Valley of Dry Bones is the one between teaching and writing. Jim Conant, who resolved it without solving it, sacrificed the useful part of me and certainly did nothing for beautiful letters. . . . Bread Loaf, as may have occurred to you, is the damnedest place. My own hangover has persisted up to now. The bloody membrane of personalities . . . oppressed me there and does still. I went only under duress and it about used up my margin of safety. At the same time, the experience of working with friends at a common job is damn near inestimable. . . . A man who is at once bright enough and ass enough to be a writer is also sensitive enough about his personal deficiencies to long for functional justification as part of an institution. I suppose that's why so uncomfortable, vexatious, and emotionally exhausting a place as Bread Loaf becomes so memorable to us as an experience looked back on.[3]

In several essays, columns, and Easy Chairs, DeVoto testified that the teaching that went on at Bread Loaf was the best he had ever observed or taken part in, far better than any English department in the country could provide.[4] The pros, he said, *do* do it best. But there were other reasons, more personal and compulsive, why he went to Bread Loaf every summer when his affairs permitted—went often at the sacrifice of something important to him.

Bread Loaf on its green plateau was in some ways a suburb of Cambridge, for many inheritors of the Wendell-Briggs-Copeland-Hurlbut tradition of the teaching of writing practiced there: Morrison, Robert Hillyer, Archibald MacLeish, Edward Weeks, and others. But scattered through this core group were writers from many other places, and always a salting of the editors, agents, and

* Editor of *Publisher's Weekly*.

publishers, mainly from New York, whom it was DeVoto's professional necessity to know and deal with. As much as any of the hopefuls who came there to break in, he benefited from the Bread Loaf associations, and he found them easy to make because he himself never had to break in. From the first, because of his Cambridge connections, he was an insider.[5]

Through the rest of his life, his closest friends and literary associates were likely to have at least a remote Bread Loaf connection. They were there when he came, or they came in later years by the natural processes of recruitment, or he met and liked them elsewhere and exerted himself to get them invited to the Conference. Certain Fellows about whom he was enthusiastic, especially Catherine Drinker Bowen,[6] Josephine Johnson,[7] and Fletcher Pratt,[8] got asked back as staff members in later years, and it was of the essence of Morrison's low-keyed administration of the place that people who worked well together and fitted in with what came to be called the "team" were repeatedly asked back. Instead of bringing together celebrities who might pull in customers, he chose people who had proved themselves willing and able to teach the customers something.

Of the team of fiction teachers, DeVoto was both strategist and field captain. By influencing the selection of the fiction staff and by further influencing the attack it made upon teaching problems, he steered the fiction program in directions congenial to himself. Those he could not influence, he accepted or worked around. In fact, he was far more tolerant of differences when the opposition was a colleague on the mountain than he would have been in Cambridge or in print. Thus with Gorham Munson, who as a little-magazine critic, a founder of *Secession*, an advocate of Social Credit, and the author of a book on Waldo Frank[9] could hardly have been farther from DeVoto's corner, he shared Treman Cottage for many summers without friction and with a good deal of conviviality. Occasionally a fastidious nature found the DeVoto bumptiousness offensive, as did Gladys Hasty Carroll in 1935. She complained about him to the management as vulgar and uncouth and given to profane revelry.[10] But it was DeVoto, not Miss Carroll, who returned in 1936 and subsequent summers.

Once in a while DeVoto took direct action against someone. For instance Raymond Everitt, who in 1934, at Bread Loaf, became DeVoto's agent, and later on, as vice-president of Little, Brown, became his publisher. What began as a warm friendship cooled somewhat. Before too many years DeVoto was thinking of Everitt as a mildly insufferable Yale boy, though he liked

Everitt's wife, Helen, and found her a solid member of the fiction team. As publications adviser to the Conference, Raymond Everitt had somewhat less to do than the active teachers on the mountain, and more time to play tennis. His game was precise and contolled, full of tricky drops shots, a lollipop game in DeVoto's view. Unfortunately, Benny's thunderous and muscle-bound power game did not always defeat it—and anyway, DeVoto had all but given up tennis. So he got Ted Morrison to import as a Fellow, in the summer of 1936, his first Cambridge friend, Robeson Bailey. Though as a former president of the *Advocate* and assistant editor of the *Harvard Graduates' Magazine* and as author of some sporting articles and stories Bailey had the qualifications to be a Fellow, he swears that the only reason he was brought to Bread Loaf was to defeat Raymond Everitt in tennis. For Bailey had played on the Harvard tennis team and was possessed of a severe service, sound ground strokes, and a habit of bouncing smashes over twenty-foot back fences. For a good many summers after that first one as Fellow, he returned to Bread Loaf in the role of Administrative Assistant and performed his solemn duty on the tennis court while DeVoto watched.[11]

That was a characteristic Bread Loaf situation, one expression of the irritable intensifications that the Conference produced in personal relations. Much more important were the relations with the fiction team, which, though it changed somewhat over the years, was remarkably consistent both in its personnel and in its approach. One perennial member was Edith Mirrielees, of Stanford, a maiden lady as gentle as DeVoto was bumptious, as natural-born a teacher as he was himself, and as acute a critic of a manuscript. They became, improbably, the closest of friends.[12] Another was Helen Everitt,[13] who besides being a member of the short story team, helped DeVoto plot the *Collier's* serials that, beginning with 1936, he ground out in a mist of migraine and fury when his money needs grew too acute. Another was William Sloane,[14] who first appeared on the mountain as an editor for Holt, Robert Frost's publisher, and returned year after year to become one of DeVoto's closest friends and coadjutors. Still another was Mark Saxton,[15] his former student who was first associated with William Sloane Associates and later with the Harvard University Press.

For three years in the 1930s Julia Peterkin[16] was a member of the team; for a while, Hervey Allen[17] was; now and again I was; at least once, though not when DeVoto was there, John Marquand[18] was. For a couple of years at the end of the 1930s, Herschel Brickell,[19] professional book reviewer and editor of the

O. Henry Memorial Awards short-story volume, fitted in. In the 1940s came A. B. Guthrie[20] and Joseph Kinsey Howard,[21] both Westerners and both close to DeVoto. With occasional short-term substitutions, those made up what might be called the working staff. In and around and through them, for a week or a week-end or the whole session, came a succession of publishers and agents: John Farrar, Everitt, Edward Weeks of the *Atlantic*, Lovell Thompson of Houghton Mifflin, Marshall Best of Viking, Alan Collins of the Curtis Brown agency, Herbert Agar of the Louisville *Courier-Journal*. At frequent intervals, to solace the customers for the unrelieved meat-and-potatoes diet provided by the team, celebrities added dessert, including some meringue.

This was fiction's single ring in a multi-ringed circus. Around it, running their own rings during business hours and contributing their own forms of intensification to Treman Cottage during hours of relaxation, were the poets: Morrison, Frost, Hillyer, MacLeish, Louis Untermeyer, once William Carlos Williams, once John Crowe Ransom, later John Ciardi, who would eventually, in 1955, succeed Morrison as director. Drama was handled by John Mason Brown, Walter Prichard Eaton, John Gassner, in the main; and non-fiction by Gorham Munson, Fletcher Pratt, Bailey, Catherine Drinker Bowen, and others. Some of these unquestionably influenced DeVoto—Edith Mirrielees, for instance—though by the variant of the second law of thermodynamics that makes powerful and highly charged natures flow outward to fill in areas of lesser potential, the influence was more often the other way. But all of them, even some he didn't much like, enlisted his loyalty because of the shared experience of the place. If DeVoto ever in his life had an intense loyalty to an idea and a group, he had it to Bread Loaf.[22]

Bread Loaf was summer's climax, discovered in 1932 and returned to in 1933, 1934, 1935, 1936, 1937, 1938, 1939, 1941, 1947, 1948, and 1949.[23] Like the annual rendezvous of the fur brigades in the 1830s and 1840s, which had always heated his imagination to incandescence, which had been the subject of his earliest western essays, and out of which he would make robust poetry in *Across the Wide Missouri*, this literary assemblage in greener and tamer mountains produced in him and many others among its participants a kind of frenzy, a heightening of every perception, capacity, and emotion. It combined a frantic amount of business with an equally frantic amount of fraternizing, revel, and emotional release. For two weeks DeVoto could divert the fatigue and anxiety of hack work, the belligerence of controversy, and the drive of ambition.

Diving into Bread Loaf was a little like overcoming the fear of drowning by deliberately going over Niagara Falls.

It was frenziedly, manically literary. It involved daily lectures, workshops, "clinics," symposia, conferences, mountains of manuscript. It called for strategy meetings of the fiction, poetry, drama, and non-fiction teams after breakfast to work out the best way to tell the customers the most in the shortest period of time with the greatest lasting effect.[24] It was argument, gossip, news, getting acquainted with newcomers to the staff and with the new batch of talented youngsters who came as Fellows. Between Bread Loaf Mountain's cold August rains it was hikes on the Long Trail, which crossed the road at Middlebury Gap, or swims in the marble basins of Texas Falls, or square dances to the fiddling and calling of the Dragon brothers in Ripton. Day in, day out, whenever the weather permitted, it was furiously competitive tennis, though by the time I reached Bread Loaf, in 1938, DeVoto himself had almost given up the game and had long since imported his ringer to whip Raymond Everitt. For some (not for the DeVoto crowd) it was a two-week-long croquet tournament dominated by Walter Prichard Eaton; for all, after about 1940, it involved an annual softball game down at Robert Frost's Ripton farm. And—what sometimes aroused disapproval or envy among the customers and even within the staff—it was a lot of not-uncompetitive drinking. Since DeVoto began his Bread Loaf career in the year that saw the repeal of Prohibition, he needed to exploit his Vermont border connections and double as Conference bootlegger only for a year or two, until state liquor stores opened and acquired adequate supplies. But he did his share in consumption.

Noons were mild; you had time only for a quick drink between the end of classes and the dining-hall bugle. Evenings were something else. I remember them as they were from 1938 on; they could not have been much different earlier.

At five o'clock Fletcher Pratt, that odd, brilliant little man, self-made historian and naval expert given to red-plaid wool shirts and pink-plaid ties, who hated breakfast and couldn't eat eggs without anchovy paste on them, appeared mysteriously in the kitchen door of Treman Cottage waving a pitcher of arsenical martinis and twitching his wispy beard. (The beard came later, during the war, but let it pass; it completed Fletcher in his character as Merlin, and we all remember him better with it than without it.) His hoarse *introit*, "Come out, come out, wherever you are!" brought forth staff and Fellows, bedraggled by the day's work or already slicked up for dinner. Many of the ladies, adding a touch of grace to chaos, would have put on long dresses.

The gathering in Treman before dinner was one version of the Hour on which DeVoto was to compose some of his most heart-felt lines. He loved that pause "when evening quickens in the street," the time of day that "marks the lifeward turn." Then, he felt, "the heart wakens from its coma and its dyspnea ends. Its strengthening pulse is to cross over into campground, to believe that the world has not been altogether lost, or, if lost, then not altogether in vain." Lengthened by loving preparations, the pause extends itself. The ear is soothed by soft voices, musical tinklings of ice and glass; the eyes are soothed by soft light. Then the glass comes dewed and icy into the hand, the head inclines, lips tenta-tively touch the rim. Magic. "The rat stops gnawing in the wood, the dungeon walls withdraw, the weight is lifted. Nerve ends that stuck through your skin like bristles when you blotted the last line or shut the office door behind you have withdrawn into their sheaths. Your pulse steadies and the sun has found your heart. You were wrong about the day, you did more admirably than you believed, you did well enough, you did well."[25]

Treman's noisy, crowded Hour was not the ideal. The ideal, DeVoto says in his dithyramb to Mother Alcohol, is no more than a handful, two or three friends, a charming woman, a quiet room, an unhurried foreplay of measuring and stirring. Like some other Bread Loaf experiences, its preprandial rituals, though he partici-pated in them with devotion, were rough drafts only, approxima-tions that often made the true believer wince. There is some reason to believe that the most blatant imperfection of the Treman Hour, the martinis of Fletcher Pratt, led DeVoto over several years to develop his personal theory of the martini, according to which the marriage of gin and vermouth is consummated in a proportion of 3.7 to 1 at a temperature of absolute zero. "Half genius and half rodent," he called Fletcher, and loved him as well as he ever loved anybody. But not even love could stomach Fletcher's martinis, and not even the affection and security of friends in a known and loved place could disguise the fact that the Ideal was unattainable even here, that the Hour at Bread Loaf was sixty minutes of bed-lam.

Evenings were a fitting completion of the days. If there was an evening lecture, either by a regular or a visitor, most attended, if not out of interest then out of sheer solidarity. But afterward they found themselves again sprawling in Treman's worn wicker argu-ing the lecturer's points or rehashing theory or trading notes on the

Conference madwoman (there was always one), or with astonishing generosity and unselfishness promoting some newly discovered talent among the Fellows or the customers. Or they played poker, or made a game of throwing ice picks at the pocked kitchen door, or settled down to soul-searching with highballs in hand. I can remember vignettes from those evenings as clearly as I remember anything: Eudora Welty sitting worshipfully at the feet of Katherine Anne Porter after a reading, Truman Capote holding himself conspicuously aloof from Louis Untermeyer after Untermeyer had lectured on contemporary poetry and called T. S. Eliot a writer of society verse, Carson McCullers in her starched, white boys' shirt deep in talk with W. H. Auden—and deep in my last bottle of bourbon, which I had been saving for Sunday, when the liquor store in Brandon would be closed. I can remember the night one of the Fellows, a boy just invalided out of the Royal Air Force after forty-seven bombing missions, lifted somebody else's bottle and hid it under his coat and took it to his room and went to bed with it, and to sleep; and how one of the staff, keeping an eye on him, went quietly over after a while and rescued the bottle and pulled the blankets up over the kid and tiptoed out.

That sort of evening. Sometimes, while the conscientious tried to read manuscripts in their rooms upstairs, to which every word and laugh penetrated, and while the snakebit lay down to recover, others stood with their arms around one another in the hall and sang barbershop under the baton of Louis Untermeyer, dominated always by the beautiful *basso cantante* of Colonel Joe Greene, editor of the *Infantry Journal*, and at least once with the assistance of the black soprano Dorothy Maynor and her accompanist, Arpad Sandor. I do not take seriously DeVoto's complaint about the glee-clubbers. Often I was one of them, and they were magnificent.

But exhausting, to themselves and their auditors. At least during the 1930s and 1940s, everything ran at such a pace, everyone worked so hard and played so hard and went to bed so late, that only will power held them together till the end. People of less than heroic fiber got sick, caught colds, got hung over, had accidents, sprained their ankles, ran into doors and blacked their eyes, fell in love, had quarrels, developed phobias and paranoias, so that every morning it was harder to get up and go forth to teach when duty's bugle blew. More than one staff member, trying to see clearly enough to pack his bag on the last morning, blessed fate and the management that the Conference lasted only two weeks. One added day would have left staff, Fellows, and customers only quivering puddles of protoplasm.

Nevertheless, from this combination of Plato's Academy and Walpurgisnacht the customers more often than not went home thrilled and stimulated and overflowing with ambition and ideas; the Fellows left knowing what they needed to do to get a start on their careers, and knowing some people who were ready, willing, and strategically placed to help them; the professionals went back to their offices purged and refreshed, perhaps with a new novelist or two on their string; and the staff members who were college teachers dispersed to their several campuses full of readiness for the autumnal renewal under the elms.[26]

That was when there were still elms. That was when the world was young. It was never younger for Benny DeVoto than during the last two weeks of August in the 1930s and early 1940s, when he was doing what he liked to do and did well, among people he liked to work with, in a place that he liked. It was as close as he ever got to being an insider, a leader with a constituency that he could have confidence in, a teacher who instructed not only his students but his colleagues. If it was Theodore Morrison and his wife, Kathleen, who were primarily responsible for pulling the Conference together and holding it together against all the multiple strains of Depression, war, talent, genius, temperament, neurosis, and propinquity, DeVoto helped define it, and it helped define him. Probably he never thought in such terms, but it was totally appropriate that this belligerently American intelligence should have been influential in the creation of the writers' conference, an institution as native to America as Rotary or universal free education.

Joseph Battell, a shrewd and successful Vermont Yankee, died of a cerebral hemorrhage on February 23, 1915. When his will was published in the *Middlebury Register*, which he owned, Middlebury College found itself endowed with thirty-one thousand acres of the Green Mountains, together with an inn and its numerous cottages and outbuildings three miles east of Ripton, below Middlebury Gap.[27] After five years of trying unsuccessfully to make the inn pay as a summer hotel, the trustees voted to put it up for sale. But, during those same five years, the college had been developing its summer language schools, imaginative enclaves of German, French, and Spanish (with Italian, Russian, and Chinese to follow later on) in the pleasant summer atmosphere of rural Vermont. With those as a model, and the unused Bread Loaf Inn as a base, a group of Middlebury professors proposed and got approved a Bread Loaf School of English, designed for teachers working toward the M.A. It opened its doors in the summer of 1920, an educational innovation that returned learning to the country at the precise time when the literary, including Bernard DeVoto, were fleeing the village in fits of the dry horrors and rural America was thought to be accurately pictured in *Winesburg, Ohio* and *Main Street*.

Six years later, largely through the efforts of President Paul Moody and John Farrar, who had been teaching at the English School, the innovation begot a secondary innovation, the Short Session for Students in Creative Writing, to follow immediately after the English School and run for ten days or two weeks. Farrar, then editor of *The Bookman*, soon to become a partner in the new publishing house of Farrar & Rinehart, was a literary professional, not an academic. His bulletin for the session of 1927 states an intention which has not substantially changed in nearly half a century and which has provided the rubric for every writers' conference since that first one: "The program will consist of background lectures on the writing of short stories, novels, articles, and poems, with practical suggestions on developing a prose style and the preparation and placement of manuscripts. Informal discussions on both the artistic and practical problems of creative writing, and group and individual conferences on manuscripts brought by the students, will furnish opportunity for professional criticism that should result in marketable writing."[28]

The emphasis was practical and professional—by some standards, crass. But the auspices were academic, and so, through the years, has been part of the staff. The combination has proved better than either of its components. What in other circumstances might have developed into something narrowly and even cynically commercial, a sort of Famous Writers school exploiting the yearnings of the untalented, was born with a conscience that was essentially academic —which is to say, disinterested, and at least in principle devoted to the impartial promotion of excellence.

Other possible developments—classes of amateurs under amateur professors, an arty mutual-admiration society of the pathetically ungifted, or a sort of Yaddo or MacDowell Colony where creators could take shelter while they created—were made unlikely by the continuing presence of people for whom literature was both an art and a business. What took shape, after some cloudy beginnings, was a literary teaching institution with a respect for the art, but with the practical perception that art must make its way with some reasonably representative audience if it is to be anything but a pleasant self-indulgence. Some, including DeVoto, insisted that until communication between writer and reader had been established, no art in fact existed. It was the writer's first obligation, by skill and cunning, to make contact with an audience. The level at which he established and maintained that contact was an index to his honesty and credibility as a writer.

John Farrar ran the Conference through 1928. His announced successor in 1929 was Robert Frost, who from the beginning had taken an interest in the English School and hoped to turn it toward creative purposes. ("We aren't getting enough American literature out of our colleges to pay for the hard teaching that goes into them.") But Frost had not got on well with Farrar, and he did not succeed Farrar as director, either, despite the announcement; apparently President Paul Moody of Middlebury feared putting so jealous and disruptive a personality into an administrative position.[29] Though Frost delivered an annual lecture at the English School almost every year from its opening until his death in 1963, he withdrew himself from the Writers' Conference, of which he has sometimes been erroneously called the founder,[30] and did not come back to it until 1936. The actual director in 1929 and in the two succeeding years was Robert Gay, the Simmons College professor who also directed the English School from 1930 to 1936. In 1932, finding the double directorship too burdensome, Gay turned over the Writers' Conference to Theodore Morrison.

Morrison gave coherence and direction to what had previously been somewhat haphazard and improvised. A Harvard graduate and native New Englander, he was heir to the Wendell-Briggs-Copeland-Hurlbut tradition of the teaching of composition, which was the best such tradition in the country. As poet, teacher, and former assistant editor of the *Atlantic*, he combined the qualifications that Bread Loaf uniquely required, and he was in touch with others who combined them. One of these was his closest friend and, since 1931, next-door neighbor in Cambridge. When he took over the Conference, his first move was to get in touch with DeVoto, summering seventy miles northeast of Bread Loaf, in Peacham, and bind him to the new enterprise. He had a great admiration for DeVoto's unconventional vigor of mind, and in the two years they had lived next door to one another they had become very close. It is appropriate that the span of years from 1932 to 1955, during which DeVoto participated in the Conference, exactly corresponded to Morrison's term as director. Bread Loaf as it developed was more the creation of those two than of any others.

It would be as unfair to judge DeVoto's literary theories by his Bread Loaf utterances as to judge a historian by his class notes. He was talking, after all, to an audience of whom the best were Not-

Yets and the rest were Never-Would-Bes. The coherent theory of fiction that he elaborated first in the series of columns called "English 37" in *The Saturday Review of Literature*,[31] and in 1951 published at full length as *The World of Fiction*,[32] leaked through only in simplified form into his Bread Loaf lectures and clinics. What he taught there was mainly practice, or at most the theory that derived from experience. The skeptic in him said that all theory was likely to be the rationalization of practice; here as elsewhere he was suspicious of a priori generalizations and abstractions. The pro in him, who seemed to stalk around inside cowing with a club the artist who now and then ventured a peep, said that any writer is to some extent a purveyor of what the audience, through its editors, wants and will accept. We may leave till later the discussion not only of his theory of fiction but the extent to which it was itself a rationalization of his own neurosis and his commercial necessities. The Bread Loaf teaching was a how-to course—how to do, how to avoid. Inevitably it reflected his personal attitudes, and it helped to establish Bread Loaf as a hardheaded, commonsensical, practical academy, anti-faddist, anti-modernist, anti-Bohemian, anti-Marxist, anti-coterie (or at least *non* all of these), closer to the middle class than to the proletariat either *Lumpen* or intellectual, closer to America than to Europe, closer to *Harper's*, *Atlantic*, and *The Saturday Review of Literature* than to *The New Masses*, *New Republic*, or *The Nation*, more inclined to stress the traditional than the experimental or revolutionary. And, DeVoto might have added, more inclined to think than to throb, more inclined to consult fact and experience than wishful theory, more interested in communication than in self-expression, exhibitionism, or public confession.

That was the essential teaching bias, but one of the triumphs of Morrison's administration was his practice of keeping the instruction practical, traditional, and consistent while opening the Conference to every sort of literary influence. Fellows were selected for their talent, not for their conformity to Bread Loaf principles, and often their opinions contributed stimulating clashes to clinics and round tables. The Fellows, over the years of DeVoto's service, included many names that became well known: Josephine Johnson, Catherine Drinker Bowen, Carson McCullers, Eudora Welty, Truman Capote, John Ciardi, Theodore Roethke, Eugene Burdick, William Lederer, and more. Likewise the staff and visiting lecturers, who during the Morrison and Ciardi administrations, in addition to those I have listed as the regulars, included writers as various as James T. Farrell and Katherine Anne Porter, Sinclair Lewis and

Hervey Allen, Dorothy Canfield Fisher and Joseph Wood Krutch, W. H. Auden and Merrill Moore, Nancy Hale and Dudley Fitts, Saul Bellow and Richard Wilbur, Eunice Blake and Jessamyn West. A full roster of the ships would include virtually every tendency apparent in the national letters. It is well to have a pedagogical orthodoxy of a conservative tinge; it is likewise well to have it constantly challenged.

Conservative or not, Bread Loaf's teaching was probably less calcified than it would have been under any variety of the revolutionary. Unlike the marriage of gin and vermouth, the intimate relations between writing instructor and potential talent took place according to no formula, and at a temperature closer to the boiling point of lead than to absolute zero. Everything in that relationship, as in every other context where the mind and spirit tried to make sense of experience, was *ad hoc*. There were no fixed rules, no abstract principles. DeVoto was not one of those who ask with a weary or superior smile if writing can be taught. He never tried to teach writing in that sense; he tried only to help young writers to an understanding of what writing was and what it entailed, and to set them on a path where their own capacities and necessities could become productive. Form and method were the resultants of the impact of the mysterious individuality of talent, intelligence, and passion upon the intractability of experience. Anything the material demanded was justified, anything you could get away with was legitimate. But make sure you were getting away with it, and try to make it worth getting away with. Before plunging into a story, ask if you had anything to say besides yourself; before adopting an experimental way out of a difficulty, inquire whether your new way was necessary or whether it was merely indulgence of personal cleverness. The chances were better than 3.7 to 1 that tried methods would work better. Experiments were best made by people who knew how.

It is possible that DeVoto's Bread Loaf instruction is not preserved even in students' notebooks, for Ted Morrison specifically discouraged the note-taking that was the first impulse of the eager and dutiful seeking the Way. The class topics listed in the Conference news sheet, *The Crumb*,[33] show rubric and content changing from year to year, splintering and re-forming against the *ad hoc* realities of new contributors, new manuscripts, new individual problems, and the slight annual changes in the staff. But some pragmatic rules of thumb have persisted and acquired the compactness of aphorism, and are probably still quoted on the mountain every August. It is ironic that DeVoto, who desired above all things to be a serious novelist, should be remembered by his friends and students not for any fictions of his own but for a handful of obiter dicta about the writing of fiction; and that the sworn enemy of critical theory and other forms of "beautiful thinking" should have ended his lifelong preoccupation with fiction with a book examining its psychological bases. At Bread Loaf he put his rules of thumb as bluntly as possible. They have the same relation to his theories as *The New England Carpenter*, say, has to the notebooks of Sir Christopher Wren.[34]

The one indispensable of fiction was movement. "A novel is always story," he said, and he defined the short story as "a narrative hurrying toward its end." If fiction did not move, it was nothing, and to move, it must present living people in action. But fiction was also illusion—reality transformed and made coherent, or fantasy given such form that it could be shared and utilized by readers. That did not mean that the writer was a mere enzyme or catalyst, any more than it meant that he was the helpless vehicle for his own efforts at equilibrium. "Art is man determined to die sane," he said; but he insisted that the artist was in part the creator of his own sanity, with a considerable degree of autonomy and control. On that point he argued heatedly with the Freudian critics and especially with Lawrence Kubie, who he said confused literary creation with self-therapy, and the creator either with a helplessly self-protective censor or an equally helpless self-purger.[35] Literature was no drifting lifeboat, said DeVoto in effect, but a craft under power, and with a steersman.

Being a maker, and in at least partial control of his fantasies, the writer had the obligation to be skillful, which meant submitting to a long apprenticeship in technique. "Write for the reader, never for yourself," he said over and over, in lectures, clinics, conversations, and arguments. Writing for the reader meant creating an illusion in which, at least for the time of reading, he could believe. The necessity for a created and maintained illusion in turn involved certain technical necessities, or near necessities. One was a point of view that let the reader know whether he was inside or outside the action, participant or observer, and that point of view could not be slack or inconsistent without risk to the illusion. Likewise, dramatic propriety, the fitting of style and tone to character, the consistency of a character with himself and his created world, was a doctrine not to be violated with impunity. Likewise style, which must submit itself to the fiction and not try to dominate it. If you found yourself inordinately admiring your own prose, suspect it. If there was doubt about a passage or a phrase, there was no doubt. "Murder your darlings!" the exhortation went, and in clinics and round tables the staff, working over the manuscript of some cringing victim, often wielded the knife like First and Second Murderers.

"Throw away the first five chapters," DeVoto liked to tell beginning novelists, meaning that too often those first chapters were written not for the reader and not in answer to the inner necessities of the story but for the clarification of the novelist's own mind. They were too often part of the preliminary gestative process carried over into the book, a sort of caul or afterbirth. They were likely to contain material that the novelist needed to know but that, once he knew it, he could trust the reader to pick up along the way. "In narrative, fewest is best," DeVoto advised Garrett Mattingly when Mattingly was struggling with the story of the Armada. "If anybody is with you at all, he is probably half a yard ahead of you."[36]

As for revision, which separated the men from the boys, he had a phrase for that too. "It's all right for a first draft," he told Kitty Bowen after slashing to pieces a manuscript she had worked over twenty times; and handing it back to her with a smile he added, "Just run it through your typewriter again."[37]

Run it through your typewriter again. There was nothing new about that advice. Horace nearly twenty centuries before had advised poets to polish their poems to the fingernail and then put them away for nine years to cure. There was nothing new about other elements of the Bread Loaf doctrine, either—about movement and the elimination of slow expository beginnings (who said begin *in medias res?*); about drama's being men in action (same old Aristotelian gospel); about economy (from Poe through Maupassant and Chekhov to Joyce and the moderns, that has been the essence of short-story effectiveness); about point of view (Henry James, whom DeVoto did not otherwise admire, had taught everybody about that one).

Nothing new. Standard fare, about equally compounded of the traditional and the inductively pragmatic. None of it encouraged self-indulgence, artiness, or the ineffable. There wasn't a heartthrob or a swoon or a social theory or a mystique in any of it. Compulsive public confession got the horse laugh, narcissistic autobiographical revelations drew anything but cries of admiration. In the phrase DeVoto later pinned on the greatest autobiographizer of them all, Thomas Wolfe, "genius is not enough."[38] You took what genius you had and you disciplined it—which was exactly what the New Humanists said, though DeVoto would not have relished the association.

One principal reason for the success of this body of doctrine—for it was a doctrine of sorts, and it did have perennial success—was that it was presented to the uninitiated by people who had proved themselves, in various ways and at various levels of excellence, able to practice what they preached. Because of the peculiar solidarity of the fiction team, the customers found themselves ganged up on, snowed under, forced to consider and take stock. I doubt that attendance at Bread Loaf convinced every young writer of the infallibility of those who instructed him in discipline, technique, and the primacy of perspiration over inspiration. But it cured a good many of the half-baked aestheticism that so often accompanies talent, and it made better writers of some, and it probably harmed or discouraged only a few. Most went away with something. They even went away more stimulated and determined to excel than if the Conference had set out on the dubious adventure of trying to "enthuse" them.

Yet even at Bread Loaf, where his friends were most numerous and most tested, where his authority was most respected and submitted to, where he was no Johnny-come-lately trying to break in but one of the inner group of regulars, DeVoto's abrasive temperament sometimes offended people, and their resentment brought him back to the old, unsleeping suspicion that there were "DeVoto-haters" around. Edith Mirrielees could cut away literary gangrene, or put a deformed story out of its misery, so gently that the victim did not even know he bled, and kissed the knife that ventilated him. DeVoto in private, or in a letter, or to anyone about whom he felt protective, could do the same—could deal with the sad incongruity between ambition and talent with a surprising understanding and gentleness. The respect for him that many Fellows and Conference members carried away with them was close to reverence. But when he stood before an audience he had to impress it. As Kubie told him, he heard the bugles of his own rhetoric and sniffed dust and gunpowder. He could not resist making a phrase, and when he was warmed up there was no such phrasemaker in the United States unless perhaps Mencken. The implacable show-off in him stamped and thundered, he lacked the internal governor that would have told him when enough was enough. In chasing foolishness and pretension through Bread Loaf's auditorium with his bloody hatchet, he sometimes forgot that pretension and foolishness had people wrapped around them and that these people could bleed.

For several years beginning with 1938, *The Crumb*'s final issue, called *The Last Crumb*, contained a portfolio of caricatures by Inga Pratt, Fletcher's wife. They are amused and amusing, witty, done with affectionate malice whose intent was to rib, not to wound. Yet in DeVoto's case they may have unintentionally wounded. For one thing, no one could caricature DeVoto's face without drawing attention to features about which he was sensitive. For another, those cartoons inevitably emphasized and exaggerated the vehemence of his public image. In one he steams and erupts and throws up rocks as "the only live volcano in Vermont."[39] In another he glowers from a pile of bones as "Ferocious Utah mountain lion, 'Ad Hoc,' tearing an author to bits."[40]

The role was one he rather cultivated, but he really, as often as not, felt friendly toward those he destroyed. It was only ideas that aroused his rage, and his public rage was therefore half theatrical, a show to make the safe and uninjured and even some of the victims twitter with half-scared pleasure. He expected his hearers to observe the heart of gold the ogre had sewn on his sleeve. Sometimes they did not. Occasional clients left the mountain full of bitterness, destroyed in their self-love and nursing a grudge at some staff member, more often than not DeVoto. There were the occasional Gladys Hasty Carrolls, who looked with distaste upon his Beowulfian revelry. And when these could not be observed, they could be imagined. In his down periods there were always DeVoto-haters off in the penumbra where he could not quite see. In the 1940s, when his friendship with Frost deteriorated into grievance and suspicion, "the bloody membrane of personalities" became so unbearable to him that from 1942 to 1946 he did not go at all.

In his way, he had tried to make Bread Loaf into a literary New Jerusalem, a perfected society of writers and teachers, with appropriate numbers of admirers and learners, and like other New Jerusalems it fell short of the dream. The admiration and applause of the great majority of the customers, and the consistent loyalty of the fiction team, could not quite drown out the hiss of someone's hurt feelings or the heard or suspected mutter of malice in some corner where he had expected a friend. Nor could it drown out the weary, honest inward voice that told him he was himself sometimes to blame. Without intending to, he went on alienating people. Myself am hell. He brought the worm with him to the Bread Loaf Eden, hidden in the apple—the same old troubling, troubled worm.

But disenchantment was a long way in the future, not even dreamed of or feared, during the years from 1932 to 1936, when DeVoto, from his three New England bases, in Lincoln, Cambridge, and Bread Loaf, was harrying the retreating literary faddists of the twenties, assaulting the literary and political faddists of the thirties head on, and trying to teach the Americans something about America.

6·*Lincoln, Mass.*

In *We Accept with Pleasure*, DeVoto has his character Ted Grayson, an assistant professor of American history at Northwestern, rage against the shabby Evanston flat entered by way of the kitchen, the meals out of tin cans, the threadbare clothes, the absence of any gaiety and diversion in the life he is able to offer his wife, Libby. Since the Graysons are in some ways closely modeled on the young Bernard DeVotos, that discontent with shabbiness, that wistful envy of colleagues who have private incomes or more secure jobs, whose wives wear silk and new warm coats, and whose houses contain paneled studies lined with books and equipped with cabinets stocked with good bourbon and distinguished brandy, may be taken as a reasonably precise statement of the DeVoto state of mind during his midwestern years. But when DeVoto had written Hurlbut in 1922, expressing his hope that someday he would be able to live and write in a small New England community, he had had in mind no such place as the house in Lincoln. A fairy godmother could not have provided better.

It had exactly the right combination of amplitude and casualness; living in it, DeVoto could feel like a country squire, prominent, openhanded, a good provider, capable of hospitality, without the least necessity for side. A great, white, green-shuttered square with seventeen rooms, five bathrooms, eight fireplaces, two great living rooms, a study as large as either, a huge kitchen with a maid's sitting room off it, an acre of land with fruit trees, a huge barn, and a little concrete swimming pool, it sat across the street from the Pierce House, now a National Landmark—a contemporary copy of the Longfellow House in Cambridge. On every side were open fields, lanes, stone walls, space; right next door was a toboggan hill; all winter the snow stayed white, all summer they had openness, fresh air, the coolness of lawns and swimming pool. There was no longer the need for a summer escape to the country: they lived in the midst of escape.

Almost without their perceiving it, a degree of affluence had sneaked up on them. Because the bad summer of 1929 had used up their only securities, the stock market crash meant little to them except that the cost of living dropped and kept dropping. DeVoto had established dependable markets and a high pay scale, and he had no trouble writing enough to keep them in comparative luxury. Their house cost one hundred dollars a month—a single *Post* story would pay the rent for more than a year.[1] In the best tradition of the Yankee squire, they had an Irish maid and a man who came every week to keep up the yard and fruit trees and vegetable gardens. Though he was not, and never had been, a man of hobbies and handicrafts, DeVoto in his euphoria generated a desire for the hobbies appropriate to his condition, with results that might have been foretold. The personal garden that he planted and cultivated and guarded from the woodchucks with a .22 grew some radishes that he allowed no one to pick until they were woody and inedible. The raccoons got the sweet corn, the cutworms enjoyed the carrots. No matter. Pleasure is not measured by its edible fruits. Similarly the workbench in the basement (he had a carpenter come in and build it) was there not for the construction of bookcases and end tables but for the contentment of *having* it there.

His real work, as always, was done in the study. His relaxation came not from any craftsy hobby (though he became a proficient photographer) but from a social life that was various and incessant.

Their Lincoln neighbors tended toward aloofness and Republicanism, but their Cambridge friends made neighbors unnecessary. They came out by the carload—Ted and Kay Morrison, Robert and Dorothy Hillyer, Kenneth and Laurette Murdock, Hans and Ruby Zinsser (Zinsser sometimes rode over on a retired circus horse), MacLeish, Charles Curtis, the Schlesingers, once in a while Henderson. Students and ex-students made the place a country headquarters and refuge. George Homans, Bob Bailey, aspiring writers, *Advocate* and Signet boys, student historians, gravitated to this newest version of the DeVoto Academy, so much ampler and gayer than ever before. Henry Reck, whose sister had been Avis' friend back in Michigan and whose brother had married Sarah Margaret Brown of the Northwestern crowd, came down often from Dartmouth, where he was an undergraduate.

Because there was a child in the house, their entertainment ran sometimes to blowing soap bubbles, roasting marshmallows and chestnuts in the fireplaces, and parlor tricks like trying to sit on a milk bottle. Often when Gordon was handed over to Hannah, the maid, they sang around the grand piano that someone had loaned Avis. Ballads, Gilbert and Sullivan, Tin Pan Alley, they sang their heads off, even Benny, who was tone deaf and hesitant about raising his voice in a crowd unless there was someone in it with a voice like George Homans' that drowned out all harmony and disharmony together. If they sang too late or drank too much, there were plenty of bedrooms. And if argument sometimes ran hot among them, so did friendliness and generosity. Henry Reck remembers a time when some lady guest unhappily knocked over and broke an expensive glass. She hardly had time to protest her chagrin before DeVoto threw his own glass down on the floor beside hers, mingling their fragments and absolving her sin.[2] What a gesture! said awed young Reck.

He would have opportunity to witness others, and to know the DeVotos more intimately than even their closest friends knew them. A house made for a large family is a self-fulfilling prophecy. It asks to be filled as naturally as water seeks its own level or freeways generate traffic. Florian DeVoto, sick, old, and alone, looked after by a housekeeper who he swore robbed him blind, had been a financial and emotional drain on them for several years. In the summer of 1933 they brought him east to Lincoln, and he lived with them until he died,[3] generous, implacably contrary, likable in spite of himself, complaining all the time that the Ogden hospital had given him diabetes but refusing to stay on any diet, going around in coat and scarf in the hottest weather and wandering outside in his shirt sleeves in blizzards, refusing to shave for days and then suddenly wanting to be taken in to the barber, insisting crabbedly that his body had special properties, and that if he fell into the swimming pool he would sink like a stone. He was a handful, and wistful, and they felt he was often lonely, and so the next summer, when Henry Reck graduated from Dartmouth and found mid-Depression America bare of jobs, he too came to live with the DeVotos, acting as typist, driver, general factotum, and male nurse. Until Florian DeVoto's death, on September 30, 1935, Reck conducted a running feud with the old man about baths, which he detested. Once, having got him down to his long underwear, drawn the bath, and shut the bathroom door on him, Reck listened outside to the obedient sounds of splashing until, growing suspicious, he opened the door again and found his patient, gimlet-eyed, truculent, and dourly amused, sitting on the edge of the tub, still in his underwear, paddling one hand in the water with intent to deceive.

An active household. "Goodness, we had fun!" says Avis, remembering Lincoln as the best years of her life. And goodness they worked, and read, and talked. DeVoto's enthusiasms and antipathies dominated them. He was no Socrates, slyly evoking error and fallacy in order to direct discussion to ultimate truth. He steered them, especially the young and impressionable among them, toward the matters that preoccupied him and the intellectual attitudes natural to him: toward realism, skepticism, and the inductive method, and the books and writers who were realistic, skeptical, and inductive; toward American social history, frontier folkways, the continental energies of the westward movement; toward Pareto, on whom L. J. Henderson that winter began leading a seminar that lasted for two years, and that included, of the Lincoln regulars, DeVoto, Zinsser, Homans, and Curtis. Not even DeVoto challenged Henderson, whose prejudices were untouchable; but anyone else who came at DeVoto smelling of intellectual systems, a priori conclusions, aestheticism, proletarianism, literary Marxism, or the deductive certainties of the Young Intellectuals got his feet knocked from under him.

As usual, he wrote, most of the time with confidence, a good part of the time for money, a certain amount of the time for the purpose of proving up on areas he had already homesteaded. Between the publication of *Mark Twain's America* and September 1936, when his life turned an abrupt corner, he produced eighteen stories, all but three for the *Post* and *Collier's*, and one ten-part *Collier's* serial. For purposes other than money he wrote one serious novel, eighteen serious articles and one story for *Harper's*, plus three essays for other magazines, and seventeen reviews, most of them on books central to his interests.[4] Not an inordinately productive four years, as DeVoto years went. He was teaching half time (the second semester of 1935–36 full time) and giving a chunk of every summer to Bread Loaf. Besides, he was diverted in a hundred ways by the seethe of the Harvard mind and the bubble of Harvard gossip, and he was living the good life in Lincoln. Such as they are—and they would have strained most full-time writers—the productions of those years express him. They were a part, some of them an important part, of his consolidation of personality and field and status and place.

The popular fiction we may ignore, as he did himself except when belligerently asserting the legitimacy of professionalism. But several aspects of his activity during those four years are worth at least a brief look. These were his flirtation with Pareto, his related ruminations about the West, his novel *We Accept with Pleasure*, and the beginning of his correspondence with Kate Sterne.

7·*Seminar on Pareto*

As early as March 1928 DeVoto was expressing enthusiasm for Vilfredo Pareto's *Traité de Sociologie Générale*, "the hardest boiled book I have ever read." "Three times, since I passed my puberty, has my mind been made over. Once by a nexus of which Henry Adams was the center, once by a matrix of which Frazer burned brightest, and once by a long study of genetics and evolution. Pareto is doing the job a fourth time, and far more vitally than any of the others."[1]

It is not clear just where or when he discovered Pareto, but in view of L. J. Henderson's later prominence in the Pareto group at Harvard, it is a fair guess that DeVoto either encountered him in Henderson's history-of-science course in 1919–20 or was encouraged to read him by Henderson after the DeVotos moved to Cambridge in the fall of 1927. The French version of the *Trattato*, the only really available edition until the English translation by Andrew Bongiorno and Arthur Livingston was published in 1935,[2] appeared in 1917, and so could have been an item on Henderson's reading list. But the freshness of DeVoto's enthusiasm in the spring of 1928 ("Pareto *is doing* the job a fourth time") makes it seem likely that he had then just recently come across him. It does not matter. Whoever introduced him to Pareto was pander to an intellectual crush that burned hotly for several years, at least until late in 1934, before it moderated into an influence. In the Italian engineer-turned-economist-turned-sociologist, DeVoto thought he found a method that did not war with common sense and that allowed a degree of scientific precision in the study of society. He never called it a gospel; it was a method only, a tool, and it resulted not in ultimate truths but in approximations subject to correction. That was precisely the reason for its persuasiveness. It avoided the ex-cathedra certainties that he objected to in the Young Intellectuals. It made the Marxists look like children fascinated by shadows and ignorant of what cast them. When applied to the study of American history it clarified many things and reconciled apparent contradictions.

It might not be a gospel—it was an enthusiasm in the direction of skepticism rather than in the direction of belief—but he felt about it the zeal of a discoverer. It is permissible to guess that he was drawn to it all the more strongly because the literary had

neglected it—it came from the scientific line, not the literary—
and because it confuted them. He did his best to compensate for
others' neglect: he urged Pareto upon his Harvard tutees and
promoted him among his friends. He wrote labeled Paretian doctrines into *Mark Twain's America*, asserting frontier America as a
dynamic equilibrium among complex energies including such irrational energies as Manifest Destiny; and he found in Brooks's
yearning for a perfected cultural life only an old American lust
for perfection rationalized and given a different terminology—a
"residue," as Pareto would have called it, rationalized into a "derivation."

It was probably Henderson who suggested the Pareto seminar
that began in the fall of 1932 and ran for two academic years.[3]
Certainly it was he who organized and dominated it. But it was
DeVoto's immediate circle that provided many of its participants
and much of its enthusiasm. Zinsser, Homans, and Curtis were
close friends and members of the DeVoto Academy—a bacteriologist, a sociologist, and a lawyer temporarily lecturing on sociology
at Harvard. In addition, the group that met every week in the
Common Room of Winthrop House included Crane Brinton, another historian friend of DeVoto's; Elton Mayo, then a professor in
the business school; Talcott Parsons, then an instructor in sociology; Robert Merton, then a graduate student, later, like Parsons,
a distinguished professor of social science; and Joseph Schumpeter,
then newly transplanted to the Harvard Economics Department
from the University of Bonn.

They were a bunch of Harvard professors playing, out of working hours, a characteristic Cambridge intellectual game. But they
played it with more than casual interest and persistence; these were,
we should remember, Depression years, and every thinking mind
from Harvard professors such as these to the "bughouse intellectuals" of the blue-shirted classes was in the library reading books
and trying to determine what had happened to America. On many
members of the seminar Pareto exercised an enduring influence.
Talcott Parsons' career as a sociologist took direction from those
meetings, in which Henderson, pink-bearded, weak-chinned,
reedy-voiced, and strong-minded, expounded sections of Pareto's
vast treatise, and the group discussed them. In 1934 Curtis and
Homans published an *Introduction to Pareto*, dedicated to Henderson.[4] Henderson himself, a year later, produced *Pareto's General
Sociology*.[5] And DeVoto, beginning with the April 22, 1933, issue of *The Saturday Review of Literature*, flung Pareto as a challenge into the teeth of the New York intellectuals, many of them

criers of doomsday, some of them New Dealers frantically tinkering with the social and economic machinery to make it run, some of
them Depression Marxists clamoring for thoroughgoing change
and denying that it could be achieved through democratic means.

As usual, DeVoto could not defend without attacking; he could
not celebrate Pareto without denouncing those who were ignorant
of him or resisted his teachings. It seemed odd, he told the opposition in that first article,[6] that when everybody was busy remaking
society nobody bothered to examine the only study of society that
made any sense, the one that superseded Marx and all other social
thinkers. Nobody except himself and Henderson, DeVoto said, had
mentioned in print this book that Henderson as a historian of
science called one of the most important books of the twentieth
century. No one read the book that did for sociology what
Newton's *Principia* had done for mechanics. Sociologists rejected
Pareto's work because it invalidated most sociology that preceded
it. Marxists and others with a cause could not read it at all, because to Pareto's cool view society was not an imperfect approximation on its inevitable way to becoming the classless society, or
the New Jerusalem, or the Community of Just Men Made Perfect,
but an unstable equilibrium among ignorance, prejudice, protective
thinking, inertia, fear, habit, innovation that was as likely as not
something old under a new label, and a thousand other energies,
most of them irrational, an overwhelming proportion of them
persistent, and almost none of them susceptible to the revisionism
of idealists and do-gooders.

He got a good deal of irritated response to that article, some of
it from leftist writers who called Pareto "the Karl Marx of
Fascism"[7] and cited his influence on Mussolini and his acceptance
of an award from Il Duce; some of it from Lewis Mumford, who
caught him in a factual slip or two and used these errors to de-
preciate his attacks on Van Wyck Brooks[8]; and some of it from
within the seminar itself.[9] Having, as he admitted to Mattingly,
written his piece before he was really ready,[10] he had no alternatives but to back off or go forward. Characteristically, he went
forward. He could explain Pareto's acceptance of an award from
Mussolini as the act of an old man living under Fascism who had
no options, and he could easily enough dispose of the notion of
blaming Pareto for the uses Mussolini had put his analysis to—you
did not blame the inventor of gunpowder for the World War. But
he could not excuse his oversimplification of Pareto's thought, nor
his implication that Pareto was totally unknown in the United
States. He was a man who prided himself on working from facts.

Now that he had, through haste and enthusiasm, embarrassed himself in public, he got back on the horse that had piled him and wrote a second, more considered explication of Pareto's sociology, which *Harper's* published in October 1933.[11]

This is not the place to explicate Pareto, even if one could. As several of his disciples, including DeVoto, have testified, it is difficult to summarize him without distorting him into simplicity, and simple he is not. A horseback definition of his method, about as accurate as the horseback version of the second law of thermodynamics—"Anything left to itself deteriorates"—is perhaps as good as one can do. The following summary is not guaranteed against defects, and should be kept out of the hands of children.

Basic to Pareto's method is the analysis of society through its non-rational "residues," which are persistent and unquestioned social habits, beliefs, and assumptions, and its "derivations," which are the explanations, justifications, and rationalizations we make of them. One of the commonest errors of social thinkers is to assume rationality and logic in social attitudes and structures; another is to confuse residues and derivations. Pareto, seeking to approach society inductively, looked first for the fundamental, non-rational actions of men. Next he looked for uniformities by which these could be arranged in classes, for classification is "a halfway house between the immediate concreteness of the individual thing and the complete abstraction of mathematical notions."[12] By classification we approach scientific "laws." Classification, generalization, hypothesis, and testing give us a means of describing or explaining the relations of men in society in approximately the way we understand the relations of particles and electrical charges in physics. But in society cause and effect are delusory; we must search instead for ways of interdependency among many variables, the machinery of dynamic equilibrium.

Residues are the *sentiments* out of which social actions arise. The six tentative classes into which Pareto divides them provide a way of seeing the discrepancy between actions and the reasons that are commonly given for those actions, which often express a sentiment not related to the act. The art of government, says Pareto, consists not in altering residues, which are often astonishingly persistent over centuries of apparent change, and which stubbornly resist alteration, but in manipulating derivations, finding new ways of rationalizing actions that are totally non-rational and non-experimental. We do not take action to defend our class, or promote egalitarianism, or defend underdogs, or cry for law and order, because we think. We are compelled to these actions and attitudes by persistent residues. None of these actions is the observable effect of an observed cause; all are the product of "an intricate interdependence of phenomena." Nevertheless we characteristically try to develop rational reasons for them, derivations in Pareto's terms, of which he finds four types: affirmation, reference to authority, accord with sentiments or "principles," and verbal proof. If we call for avoidance of entangling alliances, we are making an affirmation based on nothing we are able to verify. If we quote Edmund Burke, we are passing on to him the burden of proof for an action taken more often than not without reference to any rational or experimental process.

Habit, in fact, is for Pareto far more significant in social organization than experiment or logic. He does not denigrate the sentiments and folkways underlying our actions, and here he diverges dramatically from all revolutionaries, reformers, and uplifters. Folkways he sees as the cement of society; the only way to eradicate them is to exterminate all people who conform to them. They are absolutely essential for social stability. "No one can think experimentally in every department of life. A skilled workman, and in a greater or lesser degree everyone else, thinks experimentally within the limits of his job, but outside that is guided by a non-logical discipline, by the uniformities of action inculcated by society. If he were required to use his own unaided logic over a wider field of action, he would be at a loss and become panic-stricken. Indeed, there is reason to believe that people cannot develop an adequate logic even within a limited field unless they are subject to the wider, non-logical, social discipline."[13] Whitehead says, "Unless society is permeated, through and through, with routine, civilization vanishes."

No doctrine could be more stiffly set against Perfectibility, unless Perfection is conceived as the end product of millenniums of evolution, mainly non-rational and non-experimental. To a Paretian, blueprints for perfection, whether those of Joseph Smith, Karl Marx, Van Wyck Brooks, or any other, ignore the absolutely fundamental fact of all society, its predominantly non-rational basis. An impartial scientist, Pareto takes no side, he is neither for nor against reform. He grants the value, indeed the necessity, of innovation and experiment, for to subside upon the residues means acceptance of an insect society or one frozen in a rigid elitism, and "history is the graveyard of aristocracies."[14] The ideal society, one with the possibilities of liveliness and growth in it, is one in a state of dynamic equilibrium between change, which constantly challenges the static non-rational, and conservative resistance, which constantly tries to bring the society back to balance whenever change disrupts it. Residues act as counterweights to innovation and experiment. People who do not acknowledge that fact, who look upon society as indefinitely manipulable and perfectible, often produce by their well-intentioned reforms consequences that astound them, as when the Prohibitionists, by passage of the Volstead Act, vastly increased drunkenness and crime.

Thus the Henderson seminar, and especially DeVoto, on the Paretian teachings. They reinforced his proscientific bias, his skepticism, his faith in facts and common sense, his suspicion of the theoretical and the ideal, his interest in folkways, even his ingrained belief in human irrationality and cussedness and the persistence in the world of some principle of evil or imperfection. He had never expected too much of people, governments, or movements of reform, and Pareto, whose cool impartiality reminded him of Machiavelli's, gave intellectual support to his skepticism. When he defended the democracy, as he was always inclined to do, he acknowledged its violence, credulity, and frequent lapses from taste and decorum. He acknowledged the adamantine resistance it offered to change, the glacial slowness with which it was modified, the mulish persistence with which it clung to beliefs and sentiments indefensible by any reasonable standard. And when he defended his own role as gadfly to that society, he did not assume that he could sting it into sweet reason, much less perfection. A little; that was all, that was the hope. He was one member of the freely circulating elite that Pareto thought salutary. He did not despise the democracy when he stung it; it was as essential to him as a horse is to a horsefly, and he respected it. He always had; he had represented it, even, in the halls of effete learning. The democracy was a fact, a complex fact, and you did not despise facts. He came closer to despising "the idea boys." But whatever he attacked—professors of education, the Harvard House System, the intellectuals, the Marxists, the Ogden Chamber of Commerce— he was part of an essential counterpoise of social and intellectual forces.

The period of his addiction to Pareto lasted from 1928 to 1934. By the time he wrote his *Harper's* article he was already warning against the adoption of Pareto's thought as gospel, and he admitted to Mattingly that his interest had waned. He was not by nature susceptible to the jargon that sociologists have thought necessary for rigorous thought, the aseptic vocabulary as meticulously denotative as mathematical symbols; and Pareto's vocabulary must have put strains on his patience, for his own habit in language was metaphorical to a degree. He thought by trope and analogy.

Pareto had been a handy stick to beat the intellectuals with, and he had used it. The response of the intellectuals had been to call both him and Pareto Fascists, thereby (said DeVoto) demonstrating their willingness to leap to push-button conclusions about things they had not even read. But Pareto had also been involved with DeVoto's full acceptance in Cambridge. The seminar had provided, as much as any other single association, the fellowship of stimulating minds that had always been his need and his ambition. After the seminar ceased to meet, his interest in Pareto per se waned. But he never repudiated what the *Trattato* had taught him. It conditioned and confirmed his view of society as a nexus of energies in uneasy balance, and confirmed his view of American history as the working out of persistent drives that shifted and changed and took on different colorations and terminologies and explained themselves differently and sought different ends, but that worked almost like Fate toward large resolutions demanded by the unconscious, irrational national will. Only the surface changed; the residues did not change and were not susceptible to manipulation.

When Mattingly wrote him that American history was history in transition from an Atlantic to a Pacific phase,[15] DeVoto seized upon the phrase as the expression of something he had long been groping for. It was the Paretian in him, as well as the student of westward expansion, who found the phrase meaningful.

8 · *The Literary and the Left*

As we have plentifully observed, DeVoto had had it in for the ideas of the Young Intellectuals ever since he had begun to think, and had achieved a sort of manhood status by taking a scalp or two from their camp. He was not one to sit at home among the women, rusting on his laurels. From time to time, during the four years in Lincoln, he prayed and fasted and sang his medicine song and tied up his scalp lock and painted himself for war and slipped out on raids. To Brooks and his friends, the persistence of his antagonism must have looked obsessive, a persecution. To DeVoto it probably seemed a form of knight-errantry. But the literary critics were not the only enemies he elected.

As the Depression stretched out in bread lines, and Fascism

fastened itself on Italy and Nazism on Germany, and many Americans began to say that American democracy was done for and that the country must choose between Right and Left, he had other doctrinaires to make war on, and he made it the more willingly because many of the aesthetes and expatriates, returning in some disarray and disillusion, had embraced the Left. So far as DeVoto was concerned, they displayed all the gullibility, susceptibility to dogma, insulation from history, and coterie solidarity that had annoyed him when they were exclusively literary. So, though he might as of old go out hunting Assiniboin scalps, he had no objection to picking up a little Shoshone hair along the way, and perhaps a few Arapaho horses.

In that spirit he reviewed Malcolm Cowley's *Exile's Return.*[1] It was not, he said, the history of a generation that it purported to be; it was "the apologia of a coterie." On the one hand it assumed that a small group of expatriates represented American writers of the period, and on the other it repeated Van Wyck Brooks's error of overestimating the importance of literary people and literary ideas. What Cowley thought was the voice of the nation was only the manifesto of a house organ. DeVoto did not believe any generation had been lost, and he offered to explain this small group's uprooting in terms of the castration complex and to equate its flight with fugue. Even if one read Cowley's book with a sociological rather than a psychological bias, the facts were wrong. Assaying literature in terms of the belly and members—something he had learned from Mark Twain—he said this group was neither representative nor important. Its members had "escaped," and some of them had broken down or perished, and some of them had returned to make themselves whole by alliance with, generally, the workers and the Marxists. Meantime, other writers, who had not conceived themselves to be lost and so had not needed to escape (we are to imagine the figure of Bernard DeVoto among them), stayed home and wrote their books without agitating themselves about the religion of art. And while they were doing their job, laboratory scientists and politicians and other people with real power to affect the social equilibrium were doing work that (he suggested) was infinitely more important than that of any writer.

There was the anti-literary stance that Van Wyck Brooks had already noted.[2] Amplified and documented, it would crop up again in *The Literary Fallacy*, a decade later. In a way it was a foreshadowing of C. P. Snow's celebrated 1959 lecture "The Two Cultures," for it pinned a "vocational neurosis" on the literary, while observing that "the actual possessors of power show no sense of frustration." It is a puzzling state of mind for a man whose earliest aptitudes and inclinations had been literary, who still yearned above all else to be a serious novelist, and whose career as a novelist had been a sequence of frustrations. At the same time, the respect for science and fact and history and the experimental method were just as real a part of his God-awful emulsion; and as his hopes of being recognized as a major novelist waned, these scientific leanings, augmented by Pareto, increasingly dominated his thought. He became not merely antagonistic to coteries and dogmas, but actively anti-literary. To the literary, that translated as "philistine."

In "The Skeptical Biographer," in January 1933,[3] he had suggested that the literary be prevented from writing biography. "The literary mind may be adequately described as the mind least adapted to the utilization of fact," and literary criticism was "an activity in which uncontrolled speculation is virtuous and responsibility is almost impossible." The strengths of the literary—intuitiveness, sensibility, imagination, the sense of wonder—disqualified them from biography, whose purpose was to report what had actually occurred in a man's life. The recent tricks developed by literary biographers, the psychoanalysis, exegesis, incorporation of documentary materials as if they were dialogue or introspection, and the invention of whole scenes and conversations, might be brilliant but were not biography, and it was as reprehensible to call their product biography as to mislabel packaged foods. "Biography," DeVoto said, "is the wrong field for the mystical, and for the wishful, the tender-minded, the hopeful, and the passionate. It enforces an unremitting skepticism—toward its material, toward the subject, most of all toward the biographer. He cannot permit himself one guess or one moment of credulity, no matter how brilliantly it may illuminate the darkness he deals with or how much it may solace his ignorance."

That was hard doctrine, which his own practice had sometimes transgressed. But he left it as a challenging moccasin track where the Brooks tribe would find it (they did) and went on to other things. A year later he was on the warpath again. In "How Not to Write History,"[4] he took after those who attempted history without either the tools or the responsibilities of the historian. Appealing to sentiments and preconceptions instead of facts, he said, they generalized and then personified such large, yeasty notions as "the American mind," and "the frontier," which, once created, could be treated as substantive.[5] The Brooks crowd, as usual, was guilty, but not alone. The poetic and the mystical were also guilty, as when Mary Austin found in the Gettysburg Address the rhythm of a man walking through woods with an axe on his shoulder, and so derived a theory of how the land and its occupants spoke through the man. Why the axe? DeVoto asked, more or less in the spirit of Bob Ingersoll. Where did one feel it in the rhythm? And why through woods? Was the rhythm of walking through woods different from the rhythm of other walking? And why should the rail-splitting portion of Lincoln's life have affected that speech? Why not his experience as a flatboatman or soldier? Also, had Mrs. Austin tried to walk that rhythm she had arrived at by breaking up the Gettysburg Address into blank-verse lines? It couldn't be walked. And finally, why did she twice have to misquote the speech, including the most famous sentence ever written by an American?

She did so because she was literary. For the same reason, Lewis Mumford selected the boundaries of his Golden Day to match his preconceptions. Others, with different preconceptions, outlined other Golden Days. For the same reason, Ludwig Lewisohn chased the Puritan through all American experience and found him behind every tree and in every buffalo wallow. For the same reason, V. F. Calverton had recently hunted the Class Struggle through the same territory, and found it as infallibly. None of them had been right about the American past, because they simplified it, nor about the frontier, because instead of being the personified thing they said it was, it had been forty different frontiers spread across three centuries and inhabited by hundreds of different kinds of people, with different levels of education and culture and with contradictory aims and impulses. "The past of America," said DeVoto, "is immensely complex and immensely at war with itself. No unity exists in it. Its discords and contradictions cannot be harmonized. It cannot be made simple. No one can form it into a system, and any formula that explains it is an hallucination."

Those opinions, perhaps Paretian as to source, would seem to raise impossible difficulties in the path of the historian. If you cannot reduce historical events to some kind of system or order, how do you write about them? You cannot have a bag of marbles without a bag. And you cannot handle them loose. In his later historical works, DeVoto struggled with the difficulty of representing complex and interrelated variables in an effort to approximate the complexity of truth. He had already experimented with the method he called "history by synecdoche" in "Footnote on the West" and in the opening chapter of *Mark Twain's America*, utilizing symbolic unifications and conducting narratives meant to appear simultaneous. He would try something of the same sort in the novel *We Accept with Pleasure*.

But full achievement of history by synecdoche and the method of multiple focus was still in the future. During the Lincoln years he contented himself with announcing what biography and history should *not* be, with denouncing those who he thought approached them irresponsibly, and with praising a few books (Schlesinger's *The Rise of the City*, Constance Rourke's *American Humor*, Forsythe on Melville, C. Hartley Grattan on Henry James, and surprisingly, F. O. Matthiessen on Sarah Orne Jewett) that he thought gave historical facts and historical personages the respect they deserved. In his review of Schlesinger[6] as well as in a *Forum* essay called "The Rocking Chair in History and Criticism,"[7] he applauded the patient devotion to facts that marked the best historians, and cheered the social historians' recognition of the interdependence of forces, the interpenetration of change and stability.

Complexity, he kept saying. Facts. Relationships. Hypotheses. Contradictions. Tentative synthesis kept open to modification or reversal. Not the honeypots of assumption and doctrine. Not "must have been," but "was."

While he was asserting, perhaps more stringently than he himself was prepared to follow them, the general principles of the historian's creed, he was busy examining the complexities of the West that he had known. He did this, during the Lincoln period, in three principal essays: "Jonathan Dyer, Frontiersman,"[8] "The West: A Plundered Province,"[9] and "Fossil Remnants of the Frontier."[10] Recapitulations and reconsiderations of material that he had written in acid in his first published essays, they are of a different tone and a higher stature than those early efforts. They have lost the compulsion to get even with his birthplace for personal humiliations. If they contain corrections about western stereotypes, they make them without rancor. If they stress the complexity, diversity, and contradictions of frontier society, they do so without the need to ridicule the ignorant. If they involve DeVoto himself, as two of them do, they do so without bitterness or self-assertion, and they make his personal experience brilliantly illuminate the ways in which a place and a society, even a half-formed one, can influence and mold individuals.

Of those three essays, the first is an affectionate and respectful biography of his Mormon grandfather, Samuel Dye, under the pseudonym of Jonathan Dyer. The second is an economic analysis of the West as a colonial dependency of the East. The third is an examination of residual frontier influences in DeVoto's boyhood surroundings. Together, they do in non-fictional (and much more persuasive) terms the portrait of Ogden that he attempted fictionally in *The Crooked Mile* and *The House of Sun-Goes-Down*. They point out how much co-operation was absolutely necessary for survival in the arid West that the stereotype called ruggedly individualistic, how much curious learning lay around in any frontier and postfrontier community, how the frontier that convention called a safety valve was actually the source of much American radicalism and unrest, how it was not to be considered separately from the civilization whose fringe it was, because it *was* that heterogeneous civilization randomly transported to the wilderness. Those essays are eloquent, persuasive, and good-humored. In them, more than in his fiction, DeVoto went home again and made his peace.

Closely examined, he was not unlike the aesthetes and exiles of whom Malcolm Cowley wrote. Though he had not overtly espoused the religion of art, he had harbored an acute literary ambition. If he had not escaped from America, he had surely escaped from Ogden, and not without the castration complex and fugue that he attributed to the aesthetes. If he hadn't hunted the ampler life in Paris, he had hunted and found it in Cambridge. He had achieved his stability, such as it was, by the same means he had called attention to in his review of Cowley: by a spiritual return to the place fled from, and by affiliation with a group. In DeVoto's case it was neither the workers nor the Communist Party that gave him sanctuary and security. It was the American system, including the American past, seen as steadily and whole as he could see it. The affiliation would condition all his future writing. The four essays in which he indirectly announced it, essays as good as anything he ever wrote, were an index of his growing security in Cambridge as well as of the maturing of his mind.

9·*Pen Pal*

In the summer of 1933, just before the Bread Loaf Writers' Conference, the mail brought DeVoto a fan letter praising one of his potboilers, "The Home Town Mind," in the April *Post*, a story about a newspaper reporter in a western town. The lady who praised it had until recently been writing art criticism for the New York *Times*, and she thought she could spot a real newspaperman when she read about one.

Ordinarily DeVoto would have acknowledged the communication with a polite, humorous note. He always acknowledged such letters, all his life, even when they came in at the rate of a dozen or two a day. This time, because the Katharine Sterne who liked his story introduced herself as a tuberculosis patient in a Saranac sanitarium, he answered with one of the impulsive generous gestures that trouble so often evoked from him. From Bread Loaf, on August 23, he sent her a copy of *Mark Twain's America*, saying she was entitled, if she was going to read him, to read his best instead of his *Post* stories. She read the book promptly and wrote him about it. He replied from Lincoln on September 7. She replied to his reply the day she received it. Before their correspondence was over, something more than six hundred letters would pass between them.[1]

Everything about her as she revealed herself in her letters, attracted him. For one thing, she was young—only twenty-five. For another, she was desperately ill. For still another, she fronted her illness and its gloomy prospects and all the grisly details of the Saranac hospital with a spirit that was bright, gay, playful, humorous, and unfailingly intelligent. She was a Wellesley graduate, she had had some years in New York galleries and magazines and on the *Times*, she was a city girl but she had spent winters in Phoenix as a child. She was Catholic and had attended a nuns' school. She was sophisticated, irreverent, plain-spoken, modern, a nice girl who was nice out of character and not out of ignorance. Though she never said so in her letters, she sounded pretty; a homely girl could not have written that way.

And she was imprisoned, seriously ill, starved for talk. She adopted him, expressed an interest in his writings and his friends and his reputation. She wondered why John Chamberlain, a friend of hers, should have compared him with Gustavus Myers,[2] and DeVoto replied, with a sardonic glance at his public reputation as an ogre, that Myers' book on the great American fortunes "would have been so much better if I'd done it, for Myers suffers from chronic indignation and sometimes the facts don't come through the blood pressure."[3] He sent her a copy of MacLeish's *Frescoes for Mr. Rockefeller's City;* he took her advice about what artists to look at, and where to catch an exhibit of the photographs of Paul Strand. When she asked him why he had been kicked out of Northwestern, as she had heard, he said he had not been kicked out, he had been appalled out, and went into detail,[4] thus beginning the habit of autobiographical narrative that runs through the letters of the next eleven years.

Up to that point, their correspondence was still casual and

amused, like the conversation of a couple of people thrown together at a cocktail party, and might have been broken off by any slight event or by the pressures of a busy schedule. But in mid-October Kate Sterne wrote him a letter from the depths,[5] a letter full of dissatisfaction with herself for her "intellectual floppiness" and for a character that had been misformed by unmarried aunts, her father's indifference to her, the lesbian atmosphere of a Catholic girls' school, the aggressive broad-mindedness of her father's mistress. Into the chatty inconsequentiality of their correspondence, that confessional, self-critical letter intruded like a cry. It obviously embarrassed its writer, who at the end scrawled an apology and an explanation: she was going to New York in the morning to have eleven ribs cut out and a lung collapsed.

His response was immediate, and of a delicacy that would have been unbelievable to readers of the bellicose DeVoto. He sat down and wrote her a long letter, many pages.[6] It did not mention her operation, in which the chances of death were high. It did not buck her up or express any of the banalities of cheer and comfort. It talked about the madnesses of Cambridge, which in its way was worse than Greenwich Village. It discussed at length the Kaufman and Hart show *Let 'Em Eat Cake*, which had just opened in Boston and which he said would get brickbats in New York because it kidded the revolutionaries, a sacred cow. He told her about the novel he had just begun, his first gesture in that direction in five years, and remarked on what advance he had requested from Little, Brown, and what revisions the *Post* had suggested for his last story. Pages of soothing shoptalk, gossip, chatter. But reassuringly prompt, and skillfully calculated to divert Kate Sterne's mind from pain and the danger of death.

The moment he heard that personal, lonely cry from out of a sick girl's trouble, he was hooked. At a distance, by remote control as it were, he found himself in the relationship that fantasy had long wanted. By the time the long crisis in New York's Mount Sinai Hospital was over and Kate had been sent to the Bowne Hospital in Poughkeepsie, they were on a basis that was father-daughter, that was Leatherstocking and the Colonel's daughters, that was Prince and peasant girl. At her request he wrote her long fragments of his autobiography, and both fantasy and the desire to entertain had a part in the ornamentation that he put in. He was her guide to books, her teacher and adviser, her confessor, sometimes her gossip, sometimes her analyst. She was the beautiful and fragile and perhaps doomed girl (she said she had gone into Mount Sinai looking like a slightly desiccated Hepburn and come out looking like Mae West) who looked up to him as wise and wonderful and to whom he could occasionally come for comfort when his own hide was smarting from the world's nettles. Absolutely chaste and safe, their friendship could play (because it *was* safe) along the edge of sexuality. The jokes they wrote each other were not always the kind you would tell your Sunday-school teacher. But what most shows in DeVoto's letters to Kate Sterne is protectiveness. Here was Skinny all over again; here was the mutual dependence of two people who liked and respected each other and asked of each other nothing but friendship. In DeVoto's life he had often felt the need of someone who admired him uncritically, someone to whom he could appear the confident man he had always wished he was.

To Kate Sterne he was kindness itself, generosity personified, thoughtfulness incarnate. He was the best thing in her doomed life, and the long midnight letters he wrote her came to have an importance that nothing in her imprisoned sickness approached. She lived in his world more than in Bowne Hospital, but she was by no means inert or helpless. She could not have been better for the role she played in DeVoto's imagination if he had invented her. She was daughter, mistress, sister, child bride, and the Virgin. She was the emancipated, scrappy, good-sport flapper who answered to the need he had once thought Skinny served. In fact, it was in several of his long autobiographical letters that he told Kate the story of Skinny—and perhaps invented it.[7]

If there is truth in the notion that men who remarry tend to marry the same woman over again, there is probably truth in the corollary that when men fantasize about women they create versions of the same image. The image, for DeVoto, was always younger than he, but outwardly undeferential, sassy, competitive, bright, uninhibited in talk but fastidious and even chaste in action and idea. And capable of the deepest and most self-sacrificing devotion, which she characteristically covered up with flippancy and the comedy of insult. This coltish creature had her pretenses and her ways of protecting herself, but when the chips were down she gave her trust absolutely to the DeVoto figure. She submitted to being instructed, guided, informed, adored, and above all protected. When DeVoto described Skinny to Kate Sterne, he might just as well have been describing Avis or a half dozen of his fictional heroines. Or he might have been suggesting the role Kate might play, the character she might assume.

If that was it, he succeeded. The whole friendship was astonishingly safe from any shattering realities; it could not be soured by the all-too-human consequences of propinquity. Both recognized it very early for what it was, and understood the conditions. In the letters of the first year DeVoto suggested several times that when he was passing through Poughkeepsie on his way to or from some lecture or other, he might pay her a visit. Kate Sterne did not encourage that visit. When it seemed imminent, she asked him not to come, pleading that she had been particularly unwell, with hemorrhaging, and was too emaciated to be seen. She never sent him any picture of herself except one, and that was a picture taken when she was a child; but she did send him, at least twice, pictures of other women, clipped from magazines or newspapers, with the note, "This is what people say I look like."

Before long, he quit offering to come by. What both pretended to desire, neither quite dared. They went on writing one another for eleven years, until Kate Sterne, without ever having been released from her hospital room, finally died, on August 31, 1944. During those years DeVoto did not much talk about her or about their correspondence. He kept her private, in her niche, and once or twice a week, generally at the midnight end of a long day, he sat down and wrote her his full mind and full feelings, let down his hair, expressed himself more intimately than in any other writings.[8]

Kate Sterne was probably DeVoto's best fiction as well as his most personal correspondent. She gave him the titles for two of his books,[9] and he tried for many years, unsuccessfully, to write one of them, a novel, which he had promised to dedicate to her. She was dead before he finally succeeded in writing it, but in the meantime he had kept his promise of a dedication by substituting another book. When he sent her, at the beginning of 1943, the galley proofs for *The Year of Decision: 1846*, he sent her also a paragraph he had written expressly for her:

Dear Kate:
    While I was writing this book you sometimes asked me what it was about. Reading it now, you will see that, though it is about a good many things, one theme that recurs is the basic courage and honor in the face of adversity which we call gallantry. It is always good to remember human gallantry, and it is especially good in times like the present. So I want to dedicate a book about the American past written in a time of national danger to a very gallant woman.[10]

10 · *We Accept with Pleasure*

Near the beginning of his epistolary friendship with Kate Sterne, DeVoto mentioned that he was at work on a novel, tentatively

called *Second Gentleman*. Perhaps influenced by his own exhorta-
tions to the hopeful, he began it immediately after returning from
Bread Loaf, at the beginning of September, 1933. By the Yale game,
at the end of October, he had written a hundred thousand words.
"I had forgotten," he told Kate Sterne, "that it's fun to write fiction."[1] A month later, he was already circulating a partial manuscript among Hans Zinsser, Don Born, Edith Mirrielees, and Arthur D. Hill, the Back Bay lawyer who had been one of the defense
team for Sacco and Vanzetti, and he promised to send it to Kate as
soon as the typist got up to page 200. He said he could afford to
give the book only six months (one sees him calculating how much
of this unprofitable diversion the budget will stand). Since it would
have to appear practically in first draft, he wanted criticism as he
went.

He sent Kate the two hundred pages around Christmas, as promised, but she did not see the second half until the following June.
One reason for the delay was that he had to turn aside to write
some magazine pieces; another was that he had got involved in *Second Gentleman*, it had begun to matter to him, and as soon as it
did he was unable to grind it out like a serial. Two functions and
two personalities were at work in him. Just here, when he dared
once more to take himself seriously as a novelist, he divided himself
formally in two. Hereafter, most of the slick fiction appears under
the pseudonym "John August," the name he had invented for
Mencken to disguise the author of the never-published article on
sex and the co-ed. Hereafter Bernard DeVoto, Harvard lecturer
and man of letters, will not have to be embarrassed by what John
August does for a living.[2]

Not all the people to whom he showed the novel encouraged
him. At the beginning of July, after a visit to Henderson in Morgan
Center, he dropped by Barnard, Vermont, to see Sinclair Lewis,
and in exchange for reading Lewis' play *Brother Burdett*, got
Lewis to sample a chapter of *Second Gentleman*. Boozy, vehement, and incessant, Lewis spent the evening and the next morning
telling DeVoto that he was the greatest critic in America but
should not try to write novels.[3]

That was not what DeVoto wanted to hear. He was as avid for
approval as any Bread Loaf amateur, and as willing to take any
criticism that did not seriously question his book's matter or manner. Kate Sterne told him he had a tendency to be obscure and that
he had an addiction to the words "slumbrous," "almost," and "utterly." He denied the obscurity—his version was that he was so
afraid of obscurity he was overexplicit[4]—but he granted her verbal

objections. Hastily, as he wrote her, he struck out a thousand "almost's" and two gross of "slumbrouses" and sent the book to press.

He would have done well to listen to her hesitant comment. For what he did have was such a horror of seeming dull that he was constantly tempted to make his characters too clever, his dialogue too allusive, his sentences too elliptical. Like his personal relations, his fiction had a certain defensiveness and bravado in it.

Second Gentleman, which made the bookstores under the title *We Accept with Pleasure,* came closer than any previous DeVoto novel to distinction. It is the story of a group of people, New Englanders and Midwesterners, over whom broods the figure of a brilliant friend untimely dead—a man on whom each of several other characters has conferred, each in his own way, unlimited possibility. The relations among these people are as complex as even Pareto might have prescribed if Pareto had prescribed for fiction. Attraction and repulsion, the threads of blood and passion that bind these people together and the forces of personality, opportunity, and history that drive them apart, are intricately conceived and elaborated. Isolated and analyzed, individual after individual is a persuasive portrait. The social and intellectual fabric is dense, the long scene of Boston on the night of the Sacco-Vanzetti execution is a virtuoso set piece. All through the novel are the stigmata of a major intelligence, a major organizing capacity, an acute observation of social and psychological detail.

But it just misses. Virtuosity often encumbers the style, the compulsion to be clever blurs portraits otherwise cleanly drawn. Remembering DeVoto's habit of writing his histories three times, working first through the organization and interrelation of parts and then combing and carding the text for proportion and style, one is tempted to guess that if he hadn't hurried *We Accept with Pleasure,* if he had not been looking over his shoulder at the needs of the budget, if professionalism had not given him the habit of tossing off his fiction, if he had been willing to write as hard on it as he had written on *Mark Twain's America* and would write on all the later histories, he might have made it into the book he hoped it was. The Bernard DeVoto who thrilled and scared Bread Loaf virgins could have told him what to do: Run it through the typewriter again.

But it is interesting to the biographer, for though modification, control, and disguise are everywhere apparent, the materials themselves are personal to Bernard DeVoto, many of the events parallel events in his own life, many of the people are drawn from people close to him.

Here is Ted Grayson, a young teacher at Northwestern University, a school at which his author also taught. His field is American history, in which his author had an interest. His rank is assistant professor, presumably because even in a disguised semi-portrait DeVoto could not bear to put himself as low on the academic totem pole as he had actually been. Grayson is interested in folksongs, as his creator was. He is a natural musician and sings to the guitar, as his creator would have liked to do if he could have carried a tune. His wife is his former student, whom he first noticed in the front row of a freshman class, and she has the honesty, forthrightness, resilience, and commonsensical loyalty of Helen Avis MacVicar. This Ted Grayson is subject to spells of neurotic dread, when he cannot cross a street, doesn't dare go outside. In class he locks his legs around the legs of his chair so that he can't flee in panic. He is not well liked by his superiors, some of whom he despises and who think him a dangerous radical. His apartment is on Orrington Avenue, the street where for a time the Bernard DeVotos lived. When he is fired because of a presumed (and quite false) sympathy for pacifism, Grayson is rescued by some former Harvard friends and carried off to Boston, where they can look after him. In Boston and at Harvard Ted and Libby Grayson experience the friendship, the decency, the intellectual stimulation, and the enlargement of life that were missing in Evanston, Illinois.

What is more, Ted Grayson and his friends Loring Gale, Jonathan Gale, and Ric Barreda have had a brilliant friend, Julian Gale, who died of an obscure sort of polio just after the war and whose loss has affected all of them, and some of their women as well, in profound ways. He was in their opinion the best man among them; they are all haunted by his life-hungry ghost. Loring Gale is editing Julian's war letters as an act of memorial friendship, just as Bernard DeVoto once set out to edit the war letters of a similarly brilliant dead friend, Kent Hagler. Loring, in fact, is one side of Bernard DeVoto, as Ted Grayson is another. He has an ambition to write the story of undiscovered America, and in preparation for this has knocked around the West through long *Wanderjahre*. He had also put in a term of exile as a liberal Chicago editor, and thus has the continental perspective.

There are other parallels too. Unflattering portraits of Bernard DeVoto's favorite enemies at Northwestern need not be identified, but the bacteriologist Gage Ewing, intricately related by blood and affection to the several Gales, who are in turn related to John Gale, the historical *raisonneur* of *The Crooked Mile* and *The House of Sun-Goes-Down*, is a composite based partly on Hans Zinsser and partly on Arthur Hill,[5] whose Sacco-Vanzetti role is, however, here transferred to Jonathan Gale.

A *roman à clef*, or nearly. During the heat of the writing, other things were poured in: Harvard memories, echoes of Kent Hagler's war experiences, even the ersatz sheepskin of Harvard diplomas, even the characteristic DeVoto suspicion of self-conscious nobility and idealism. "It's a toxin," says cynical Gage Ewing, walking through Boston on the execution night and observing the self-immolating hysteria of one kind of Sacco-Vanzetti sympathizer. "It's a toxin, and there's no vaccine." Various kinds of do-gooders move through the novel, the most extreme of them a deluded seeker after obscure martyrdoms, fighter of lost causes, modern descendant of the nineteenth-century men who had eaten Graham's bread in a dozen consociate families or climbed the hills to await the Last Days.

But an interesting thing has happened to Julian Gale, the dead friend based upon Kent Hagler and remembered in complex but powerful ways by so many people. The necessities of the story, and the shift in DeVoto's values from earlier idealism to later skepticism, warp him into a facsimile of those devotees of the religion of art whom DeVoto despised. In his lust to encompass all experience, his Faustian (and too calculating) embracing of all heroism and all evil and all wonder as literary material, this Julian reveals himself to his cousin and chronicler Loring as a sort of monster. Among other things, it turns out that he has deliberately sought for and obtained command of a firing squad to execute a deserter. For the experience. The legend that has dominated the minds of all his living friends turns out to be tainted and obscene.

We Accept with Pleasure came partly from the spirit's subbasement. It was inextricably mixed with DeVoto's persistent effort to define himself in relation to other people, to America, to Boston. While he was writing it, he wrote for Kate Sterne a long, semifictionalized draft of the Kent Hagler story and sent her extended character studies of Northwestern and Boston characters, most of whom can be recognized in the novel.[6]

It would be a mistake to read *We Accept with Pleasure* as autobiography. But it would not do to overlook the personal elements in it, either. Fiction for DeVoto, whether serious or popular, was always going to be linked in some Rube Goldberg way with the author's fantasies. "Art is man determined to die sane." To write his anxiety neurosis into Ted Grayson was in some degree to control it. To chronicle the Graysons' acceptance by Boston (however unworthy Ted Grayson turned out in the end) was in some sense to assert a place that his author had won.

But note that Grayson, like his dead friend Julian, does *not* turn out to be very admirable. He is spoiled by the success his wife and friends help him win. He is not the image of his author's self-satisfaction or self-justification, no matter how closely his nervous troubles may resemble his author's, or his wife resemble his author's wife.

Fiction was not public confession or exhibitionism. Control was of the essence. It was basic to the doctrines DeVoto expounded at Bread Loaf; it underlay all his objections to Thomas Wolfe, which he consolidated in the essay "Genius Is Not Enough," a review of Wolfe's *Story of a Novel*, in the April 25, 1936, issue of the *Saturday Review*. He felt it necessary to reject the raw autobiographical method of Wolfe—to Kate Sterne he commented sourly that Wolfe's fiction was a sort of chyme, neither food nor feces.[7] Without pressing that metaphor too far, we may remark that the subject was much on his mind, and that writing *We Accept with Pleasure* crystallized it. In the July 1936 *Harper's* he published, anonymously, his own story of a novel, and it is not the story Wolfe told.[8]

Novels, he said, are written to find out what novel one is writing. Every novel is in that sense a mystery story. It has its own inevitabilities; yet if a character "runs away" with a scene or a book, his author is a bad novelist. A real novelist writes in "full, if unconscious understanding" of the novel's internal demands. In the "imposed honesty of the desk" he understands that a novel exists in its own right and that "the novelist is committed to an endeavor whose issue is predetermined." The process "has no more doubt or chance in it than a chemical reaction has," though there may be almost interminable experimentation before the writer uncovers those inevitabilities. Moreover, no novel is personal history, even if its author attempts to make it so, and psychoanalysis is most unlikely to come at the "true" bases, whether the psychoanalysis is amateur or professional. The amateurs write bunk and the professionals do not understand the nature of fiction. For any novelist must make free-will judgments and choices; he is not the helpless stylus of his unconscious. He must select among alternatives, he must ask how each such choice serves the inevitability toward which he gropes. The resolution of apparent contradictions between inevitability and choice, the fabrication of the "wire" that communicates an imaginary world to readers, is enforced at the desk. That is what art is, and no good novelist will falsify or pervert that process, either for profit or for praise.

On the other hand, no good novel is planned; no good novel is *about* anything—about the class struggle or the westward movement or anything else. It is only about people and their relationships. "How men and women grow up and adapt themselves to themselves, to one another, and to the conditions of their lives. How they fail to grow up and adapt themselves. How they learn, or fail to learn, from what happens to them. How they deal with experience and how it deals with them. How desire and disaster and the death of friends affect them. How they are entangled with the world. Above all, the friendships they form, the love that racks them, the marriages they make. What happens in the caverns of the soul."

It is the sort of doctrine one would expect from an anti-doctrinaire—tentative, exploratory, inductive, dead set against simplification, Paretian in its emphasis upon the dynamic equilibrium of many variables. And it describes with considerable accuracy the kind of novel *We Accept with Pleasure* is, a human maze whose exploration works "toward the dissipation of mystery."

But this after-the-fact explanation or apologia was not written in the warm haze of triumph or addressed to an audience of admirers. It was written out of a bruised sense of renewed failure. Before the novel had appeared, DeVoto had been, against his will and despite the caution generated by previous diappointments, seduced into hope. Little, Brown was convinced he had hit it this time; there was the possibility of a book-club choice.[9] When he sent Kate Sterne a prepublication copy at the beginning of September 1934, DeVoto's depreciative noises did not conceal his euphoria. He reported in amusement that Zinsser did not like the bacteriologist some people thought resembled him. Though his own language was salty, he thought DeVoto had subtracted dignity from Gage Ewing by putting profanity in his mouth, and he somewhat grimly offered to infect DeVoto with *Spirochaeta pallida* so that next time he wrote about bacteriologists who caught their own diseases in their own labs he would know what he was talking about.[10] That demurrer was amusing, not ominous—Zinsser's belligerent tone was precisely the tone that DeVoto himself used upon the ignorant and the literary.

The novel was published on September 21. On that day DeVoto wrote in good spirits that he was going down to the Square and pick up some magazines and see what the boys had done to him. What they did to him was to respect the organization and complexity of his novel, grant the validity of his characters and the reality of his episodes, and conclude that none of this involved them very much except those parts of the story that dealt with Ted and Libby Grayson. Alvah Bessie, in the *Saturday Review*,[11] said it for most of them: "Yet he [the reader] can witness the dramatic events with equanimity; he can contemplate the petty mishaps, misunderstandings, jealousies, and passions of them all without sharing in them more than intellectually. They are all fatally intelligent; they are all witty and wide-awake (so much so that at times their conversation becomes almost interchangeable); they are all in motion, but they do not move." Novels are what happens in the caverns of the soul, yes; but the novelist has to be a successful spelunker.

It did not take long. Two months after publication, DeVoto could remark ruefully to Kate Sterne that his "fifth flop" had been "decently interred."[12] By December, when the reviews cast their eyes back over the season, *We Accept with Pleasure* could be nominated for Disappointment of the Year.

11 · Editorial Temptations

From 1931 onward, DeVoto had been denying to his old associates at Northwestern that his position on the Harvard faculty was more than temporary.[1] He affected to be still disaffected with teaching; he said he taught at all only because people at Harvard kept urging him. But he accepted whatever teaching Harvard offered him—first some tutees; then Hurlbut's English 31; then a course in contemporary literature, English 95—and he liked it all. For several years, his half-time status was exactly what he wanted. Being a sort of utility infielder to the Harvard English Department left him time to write but at the same time gave him a certain security and the institutional affiliation he craved.

English 95, which he took on in the spring of 1935 in place of his writing course, began a new phase in his teaching. With the disaster of an empty mind constantly threatening, he read frantically to keep ahead of his students. Often he organized his lectures in the car, driving in from Lincoln, and finished the hour with his last note used up.[2] But he liked it, and so did his students. When it seemed undesirable to give up his writing course for a second year in a row, he agreed to teach both it and contemporary literature. That would put him back in full-time teaching. There is no evidence that he looked forward to the spring of 1936 with anything but pleasure. He expected to get a book of some sort out of the course.

Teaching may have looked more interesting because of his deteriorating position in the fiction market. For a year or more the *Post* had expressed dissatisfaction with some of his stories. Some had been sent back for revision, some rejected cold.³ In the spring of 1935 he felt that a change of editors had closed the *Post* to him completely. At once his nervous symptoms recurred. His eyes gave him trouble, the insomnia and migraines returned, he was haunted by the fear that other magazines, too, would find his work unacceptable and that the flow of his prosperity would be cut off as if by the closing of a tap. Henry Reck recalls times when, sitting at the table or lounging on the porch, DeVoto would break out into an instant, profuse sweat, throw a stricken look at Avis, and vanish, to reappear a few hours or a day or two days later, pale, quiet, and drained.⁴ Avis herself remembers the last year of Lincoln as uneasy and tense.

It was in those circumstances that he agreed to go on full-time teaching the following year. And he made another move to shore up his economic and psychological defenses. His long association with *Harper's* had made him virtually a member of the editorial staff. About the beginning of June 1935, Lee Hartman proposed that he make the alliance official by taking over the department called The Editor's Easy Chair, currently conducted by the eighty-year-old Edward S. Martin. As a counterproposal DeVoto suggested that Mencken be recruited for the Easy Chair and that he himself undertake the Books and Otherwise department of Harry Hansen. He said he did not want to be a public thinker, he wanted to be a literary critic. He wanted to give the country the unprecedented opportunity of a book section that every month would review an important book by an important writer, at length and in the context of his other work and from a consistent point of view.⁵

Mencken proved unavailable, Hartman persisted in wanting DeVoto. At the end of July, still hopeful of Books and Otherwise but ready to accept the Easy Chair if he must, "for I'd rather have that forum than no forum,"⁶ DeVoto went to New York for discussions. When he returned, he had signed up to conduct the oldest feature in American journalism, begun in 1850 in *Harper's New Monthly Magazine* by Donald G. Mitchell, shared from 1852 to 1859 by Mitchell and George William Curtis, written singly by Curtis until his death in 1892, picked up again in 1900 by William D. Howells, and taken over from Howells by Edward S. Martin in 1920. Though it was not a book section, it was a department of the highest prestige, in a magazine with the most intelligent lay audience in America.[7]

His pay for those brief essays, rigidly limited to 2,650 words, would be only two hundred dollars apiece, twenty-four hundred dollars a year, and the prospect of getting one out every month, year after year, through sickness, crisis, and the pressures of other work, would have appalled anyone less fecund in ideas or less bent on airing a point of view or less eager for some economic security. Once he had agreed to take it, he had a piece of everything he wanted: a public forum, an affiliation with Harvard, some (more or less hypothetical) time for his own writing, and two small salaries that would keep him, meagerly, if the bottom fell entirely out of the slick-magazine market.

Bread Loaf that year provided the usual frenzy of lectures and manuscripts, the usual hectic stimulation, the usual Conference madwoman, the usual bruised feelings, the usual Treman drinking, the usual clashes of temperament (that was the year that Gladys Hasty Carroll protested about DeVoto, Munson, and Everitt as roisterers). But it also held, unspoken, a further possibility for DeVoto's future. One of the staff that summer was George Stevens, the managing editor of *The Saturday Review of Literature*, and the Bread Loaf friendship would prove to be important in the selection of the *Review*'s next editor.[8] Henry Seidel Canby, the former Yale professor who had founded the *Saturday Review* in 1924 and had edited it ever since, was giving part of his time to his much more profitable preoccupation the Book of the Month Club. He had not said that he wanted to retire, but it seemed likely he soon would. The magazine was struggling—had never done anything *but* struggle—and if Canby retired it could obviously use a vigorous editor, a change of emphasis, a face-lift. Looking back years later Canby himself reflected, "It needed a mind seeking conflicts rather than trying to reconcile them; a younger mind with no compelling memories of an age of confidence."[9]

No one in search of a mind that liked conflict need look beyond Bernard Augustine DeVoto. During the fall, Stevens wrote a report on DeVoto for Noble Cathcart, the *Review*'s publisher, who with Thomas Lamont, the financial angel, had decided to start a search for an editor to replace Canby.[10] At that point the proceedings were so confidential that Stevens typed his report at the Harvard Club to escape the attention of people in the office. His report was persuasive. In November he came to Cambridge, ostensibly for the

Harvard-Yale game, and while there he sounded out DeVoto about his interest in the editorship of the *Saturday Review*. "How far the *Harvard Graduates' Magazine* shines in a naughty world!"[11] said DeVoto, completely aware of what they hoped for out of him.

It was a job that would have solved his security problem, enhanced his image in some ways, and increased his public. But by then he was firmly settled into the Easy Chair (his first essay was in the November *Harper's*, then on the newsstands) and had all the forum he wanted. He had contracted to teach full time, and presumably could continue to do so. But more important, he had solved the problem of the slick-magazine market. Before going to Bread Loaf, John August had written four sample installments of a serial for *Collier's*, and *Collier's* had subsequently bought it for twenty thousand dollars.[12] "If some of those bastards now clamorous for my personal charm and dignity had made me offers say last June, when any maidenhood of mine could have been had for a nickel, & that mortgaged, I wouldn't have had to write the damned thing," he grumbled to Kate Sterne.[13] But he had written it, or John August had, and *Cosmopolitan* had also bought a story for a high price. The divorce from the *Post* was no longer scary. DeVoto pondered Stevens' inquiry only briefly, and indicated that he was not interested.

But there was no reason not to let Harvard know he was wanted elsewhere. Before he went off on a lecture tour that would take him to Chicago, Evanston, Columbia, Missouri, and St. Louis, he passed on word of the offer, without indicating that he had refused it, to George D. Birkhoff, the Dean of the Faculty, and James B. Munn, Chairman of the English Department. He let them know that he thought an appropriate answer to the *Saturday Review*'s bid would be a Harvard appointment that had the assurance of permanence—say an associate professorship at six thousand dollars.[14]

He reckoned without several things. One was the determination of President James Bryant Conant to pare away all but the absolutely essential faculty positions. To people in the humanities, most of whom had backed Kenneth Murdock for the presidency against Conant, it seemed that he was particularly bent on paring away jobs in their area, for which it was widely believed he had little sympathy. Another was the inferior status that orthodox academicians, and in this case pretty surely President Conant too, granted creative writing as an academic discipline. Another was the fact that DeVoto's other field, American literature, was already staffed to the maximum number of people Mr. Conant seemed ready to allow, with Kenneth Murdock in the primary professorship and Perry Miller coming up, and F. O. Matthiessen established in the single slot in History and Literature. Finally, there was the dislike DeVoto had generated, to various degrees and for various causes, in some of his colleagues. One of these last was Matthiessen; another appears to have been Dean Birkhoff. Mr. Conant's own feelings about DeVoto, if he had any at all, were inscrutable.[15] In any event, when DeVoto returned from St. Louis in mid-December, he found an apologetic letter from Munn, passing on the word from the President's office: Mr. Conant would approve Mr. DeVoto's appointment for three years as a lecturer at an annual salary of four thousand dollars. He would not approve his appointment as an associate professor at six thousand dollars, nor as an assistant professor at four thousand dollars.[16] That was to say, DeVoto was not to be admitted to the permanent faculty or put on the promotion ladder that might lead to permanence.

DeVoto's first impulse was indignation. He burned up the wires to New York and found out from Stevens that the *Saturday Review* job was still open.[17] But then, as he talked the situation over with Murdock and his other friends, it seemed that the rejection might not be final, that some quiet inside work might produce a better offer from Harvard. So he turned away from the *Saturday Review* possibility for the second time and put his future in the hands of his friends. In his correspondence and conversation he treated the whole affair as an entangled bureaucratic joke.[18] But a finger had been pointed at him. He stood revealed as no true member of the club, an outsider without proper qualifications, a mere journalist, unwanted where he most wanted to belong.

That was where matters stood when he went off to Cincinnati in the week between Christmas and New Year's to tell the Modern Language Association what was wrong with all the systematic critical approaches to Mark Twain.[19] They still stood there on January 9, when he left to lecture at the University of Miami's Winter Institute of Literature. It was a sort of southern Bread Loaf, and even contained one old Bread Loaf companion, in the person of Hervey Allen, who had plowed some of the take from *Anthony Adverse* into an expansive place at Coconut Grove, nearby. And on the evening of January 16, another man associated with Bread Loaf knocked on DeVoto's door. This was one who was fated to be one of the strong influences, admirations, and emotional disturbances of his life: Robert Frost.[20]

12·*"Keep Your Self-Respect"*

Frost, who was also lecturing at the Institute, was on an errand unusual for him—to praise another man's work. He must, in fact, already have praised it in their previous meetings. Four years be-fore, he had read "New England: There She Stands" and liked it for its celebration of the Vermont farmers who, on less than three hundred dollars cash a year, were making it through the De-pression without government handouts and without self-pity, a sense of grievance, or loss of pride. In *Harper's* for December he could have had his memory of that essay refreshed by a second on the same theme—DeVoto's second Easy Chair, called "Solidarity at Alexandria," praising a New Hampshire town that had rejected federal rehabilitation and relocation and stuck to its homes and its threadbare pride.

As Lawrance Thompson has pointed out, Frost and DeVoto shared a maverick political position in a time when fashionable literary opinion was stampeding to the Left. They shared a con-tempt for doctrinaires and joiners; they found the tough-minded independence of New England countrymen admirable; they nursed a certain suspicion of Roosevelt, the New Deal, welfare, all "help" and those who cried for it.[1] Frost, fond of announcing his "God-given right to be good for nothing," was equally fond of re-marking about Henry Wallace, whom he personally liked, "Henry will reform you whether you want to be reformed or not." He was more conservative by far than DeVoto, but not more in-dependent. It was exactly in Frost's spirit that DeVoto deplored the Federal Writers' Project and other artistic boondoggles.[2] It was exactly in that spirit that he refused all his life to apply for a Guggenheim or any other fellowship, though he willingly wrote letters of recommendation for others. He preferred to earn his own way; it was part of the testing he set himself. The citizens of Alexandria, New Hampshire, refusing to be thrown on relief "so we can buy radios," spoke a language his spirit applauded. He accepted the credo he took out of, or put into, the mouth of a housewife, that "it was good to respect yourself, to keep out of debt, to stay off relief, to expect that anything you got would have to be paid for, to hold onto what you were sure of, and not to mistake either a vision or a promise for a fact."[3] That second Easy

Chair might have been read as a gloss on Frost's remark that, if we ever got a benevolent dictatorship in the United States, he could stand the dictatorship easier than the benevolence.[4]

The friendship between these two recalcitrants had been instantaneous; their mutual perception of shared opinions and shared antipathies was like a joyful shout. "You and I," Frost wrote DeVoto somewhat later, "without collusion have arrived at so nearly the same conclusions about life and America that I can't seem to figure out how we came to vote different tickets at the last election."[5] And in the same letter: "I can't get over my not having realized you were on earth. You don't know your own power. No one else has your natural sensible and at the same time embracing thoughts about life and America. And the way you lay into the writing with your whole body like an archer rather than a pistol man. Neither perverse precious nor international. I wasn't marked off from the other children as a literary sissy like Yeats and Masters. Maybe that's what's the matter with me. There's consolation in the thought that you weren't marked off either."[6]

If Frost's admiration for DeVoto was uncharacteristically open and generous, that of DeVoto for Frost was close to worship. To Kate Sterne he wrote that the one good thing about Florida was that he had "spent at least five hours a day with the greatest living American. And the more I see of Frost the more I'm convinced he's just that. I go tearful whenever I talk about him. . . . He talks along, moderately, aimlessly, quietly, rather slowly, and you listen and pretty soon you notice some sparks, then a glow, then a blaze, then the incandescence of the interior of a new star. He is the quintessence of everything I respect and even love in the American heritage. . . . I am not an inordinately silent man, dear, but I hold my peace so long as Robert Frost is willing to so much as grunt. . . . One of my lectures was on Red Lewis. It griped Frost so hard that he couldn't sleep for the ensuing eighteen hours and was constantly driving over or phoning over to make new rebuttals. He was like the sound of a horseshoe on iron. He was superb. And I got the lead I've been half-consciously looking for into my chapter on Frost when, if ever, I turn my English 70 notes into a book. Just this: Lewis, the Sauk Center boy, in flight to the metropolitan point of view, turning on Sauk Center the lens of his own insufficiencies and finding Main Street—and Frost, the San Francisco boy retiring of his own will to Salem Depot, New Hampshire, and finding—North of Boston. I can drive that point pretty deep into the literature of our times, or I'm not half so hot as I pretend to be.'"[7]

In one particular, at least, they were unlike: Frost had trouble brooking rivals or equals; DeVoto had a capacity for a filial reverence in the presence of minds he greatly respected. L. J. Henderson had been one of those. "So goes another of my fathers," he remarked when Henderson died, in 1942.[8] But of all the intellectual fathers he adopted during his lifetime, Frost came closest to being a crush. When DeVoto found that Frost was to deliver the Charles Eliot Norton Lectures at Harvard beginning March 1, 1936, he eagerly offered his services, promised to find the Frosts a house, and said he would act as their agent and information bureau and handyman.

He did find them a house, at 56 Fayerweather Street, and he did appoint himself publicity man, greeter, and *chef de protocol* for the lectures. Since his own house in Lincoln was too far out to be convenient, he asked Ted and Kay Morrison to hold a small reception at 8 Mason Street after each talk.[9] It was a gesture that would be full of consequences for all of them. Though the Morrisons had met Frost at the Bread Loaf School of English, and Kay had been one of a committee of undergraduates who had brought him to Bryn Mawr in 1920, DeVoto's arrangement of those postlecture receptions was Frost's reintroduction to the two people who after the death of Elinor Frost would become the intimate focus of his life.

The Norton Lectures were in some ways a confrontation between Frost and his poetic enemies. His new volume, *A Further Range,* in which he had vented some political spleen and expressed some political views infuriating to the Left, had been greeted by bitterly negative reviews. Horace Gregory, Rolfe Humphries, Newton Arvin, R. P. Blackmur, Granville Hicks—the chorus had been all but unanimous. The selection of the volume by the Book of the Month Club only confirmed the opinion of the Left that it was reactionary capitalist garbage. There was, furthermore, a modernist, Eliot-Pound coterie at Harvard that thought Frost's selection as Norton Lecturer a disgrace.[10] But the coteries turned out to be no match for Frost's gift of taking poetry to people. From the minute he came down the aisle of New Lecture Hall, flanked by DeVoto and John Livingston Lowes, he turned the lectures into a personal triumph. What might almost have been called the Bread Loaf point of view got expounded to capacity houses, and Frost's poems got read to encore after encore. With that triumph DeVoto was closely associated from the beginning;

in the confounding of the men of Gath he took a pleasure as great as Frost's own. And his association with Frost made him even more visible in the Harvard community, and his uncertain status more a topic of conversation.

He still did not know where he stood. The *Saturday Review* was still available, Henry Canby was still unaware of the planning that had been going on around him. The Harvard friends had generated nothing new. On February 11 DeVoto had written Kate Sterne in a mood of assumed amusement and indifference: "My recent maneuvers with Harvard did not quite reach a full stop, and I've been living in an atmosphere of sustained comedy. Or farce. . . . Not the least fantastic, nor the most, is a phone call from the President of Harvard, not knowing all the circumstances, to the editor whose job I was being offered, who did not know of the offer, to find out what an outside opinion of me might be. So far as I can see I, having refused the editorship, am now committed to leave Harvard at the end of next year, and Harvard being committed to a forthright rejection of my services, is now fully resolved that I shall not leave. It will probably work out as all Harvard revolutions do: in a change of names and the status quo." He said he was half tempted to take the editorship just for the chance to break some heads.[11]

Not that he withheld his club from deserving heads while he waited. Circumstances that might have immobilized some men with uncertainty simply galvanized him. In his December Easy Chair he had ridiculed the Absolute by pursuing its logic toward the perfect automobile.[12] In January he compared the doomsday cries of Marxists and New Dealers with the jitters of the 1830s, when the world was also coming to an end and the Millerites were scampering up the hill to be ready for it.[13] In February he defended the folk mind against those who said it had made a demigod of Abraham Lincoln: the folk mind was saner and more humorous than its critics.[14] In March he doubled back and confused pursuit by asserting the legitimate, if limited, functions of little midwestern sectarian colleges. They might not be quite educational institutions, but, like Rotary, the Loyal Order of Moose, Sigma Chi, and the Browning Society, they helped people in a half-formed culture to find the place that Europeans knew by inheritance and habit.[15] In April he took scalps from both the educators and the proletarians in a raid on Black Mountain College, the haven of the consociate mind in the Blue Ridge.[16] And in the same month he finally published, in the *Saturday Review*, the long-contemplated essay on Thomas Wolfe, who, he said, tried to get by on genius alone and sinned against the art of literature by publishing raw or half-digested stuff, scenes of the greatest evocativeness mixed with "long, whirling discharges of words . . . raw gobs of emotion, aimless and quite meaningless jabber, claptrap, belches, grunts, and Tarzan-like screams."[17]

Those forays, plus the Frost association during the same period, kept him fairly spectacularly in the public eye while Harvard discussed his future. On March 22, while admitting that Conant was scaring everybody at Harvard stiff, he said he approved of that way of running the university even if it worked out badly for himself.[18] But within a week he contradicted his overgenerous judgment by remarking with glee that Harvard's attempt to woo the scientific great had come to nothing: Niels Bohr and Werner Heisenberg had both refused the chair of physics Mr. Conant had offered them.[19]

His future was on his mind, but so was much else. He spent a lot of time with Frost, drove him up to Derry to visit the old Frost farm, talked, consulted, argued, listened. He taught his writing class and read his papers and lectured three times a week in English 70. He wrote reviews, essays, Easy Chairs, long letters to Kate Sterne. He conducted a stiff and bristling correspondence with Lewis Gannett, who had accused him of boorishness in his Black Mountain article and challenged his information on millennial sects.[20] He set his secretary and research helper, Rosamond Chapman, to getting together a collection of his essays for book publication. He read for the frontier book that had been in his mind for several years; he made notes for a novel and accepted Kate Sterne's suggestion for a title: *Mountain Time*.[21]

If Harvard should let him go, it would not be for colorlessness or inertia. Nevertheless Harvard did let him go, and in the end he went bitterly.

There are all sorts of rumors, still remembered, about DeVoto's leaving Harvard, and several explanations of why the university made a decision that on its face was close to incredible. Though he had asked James Munn to try for an associate professorship at six thousand dollars, DeVoto would have accepted an assistant professorship at less. What he was after was a place on the road that led to permanence. He thought he had the qualifications. In mere length of bibliography he would probably have lapped anyone on the Harvard faculty, for in the spring of 1936 his magazine publications alone, including book reviews, numbered more than 230.[22] If asked for more solid accomplishments, he could have cited four novels (dubious, perhaps even damaging in some Harvard eyes), the textbook that he and Arthur Nethercot had revised (acceptable but minor), the editorship of the *Harvard Graduates' Magazine* (controversial), the general editorship of Americana Deserta and the personal editing of Jim Beckwourth (definitely a plus), the volume of essays to be brought out in the fall by Little, Brown (some quite solid things in that),[23] and *Mark Twain's America*. This last was a book that had already begun to revolutionize thinking about one of the greatest, and certainly the most American, of American writers. By itself it was a contribution as great as some professors made in a lifetime, and DeVoto and his Americanist friends knew it if Dean Birkhoff and President Conant did not.

Ironically, that single seminal book might have impressed some Cambridge minds more if it had been more lonely, if it had not been surrounded by so many potboilers, reviews, and ephemera. Such diverse energy was not quite decorous. No wonder someone was rumored to have told President Conant that DeVoto's scholarship wasn't sound.[24] A man who wrote so much about so many things must be shallow. And he did not, of course, have the Ph.D., he was not academically trained. Finally, though he had made firm friends, he had also made enemies—by his profanity, by his jeering attacks on Sacred Ideas, by his maverick intractability.

In the end it was almost certainly the freezing of faculty positions—which was in turn a consequence of the Depression—that ruled DeVoto out. The English Department itself seems to have been divided, and even those who were his supporters were helpless. On May 2, Professor Lowes, whom DeVoto had asked to exert his influence on President Conant, wrote back saying that he did not feel he should offer advice to the President unless the President asked for it. He would like to serve DeVoto but could see no way.[25] Four days later, after DeVoto had gone to President Conant himself, Mr. Conant put an end to the case in a letter that became famous.

It was not a brusque or unkind letter. It was polite; it praised DeVoto's services to Harvard. But it reiterated the decision previously communicated to Mr. DeVoto, that though the university would be glad to continue him as a lecturer, it could not look forward giving him a permanent appointment at full salary. That meant he could stay on in a low-status position or on part time. But then came the touch for which Mr. Conant became famous, the all-but-infallible gift for the wrong emphasis, the wrong phrase, certain to madden someone like DeVoto, whose worth had been slighted and whose life was being uprooted from the place where with great difficulty and long labor he had established himself. "In view of this fact," said President Conant at the conclusion of his note, "I feel that I must urge you strongly to accept the position which you said had been offered to you."[26]

"Which you *said* had been offered to you." Hell and damnation, was the man accusing DeVoto of faking an offer in order to extort a raise? Later, DeVoto got it into his head that Dean Birkhoff had never believed the *Saturday Review* offer was real,[27] and had told President Conant so. It does not seem to have occurred to him that Henry Canby might have been asked about the offer, and, knowing nothing about the negotiations for his successor, might have said that no such offer had been made. Whatever inspired it, whether his famous ineptitude at letter writing or his real doubt of the authenticity of the offer, the final sentence of Mr. Conant's letter, repeated with all the shadings from mirth to disbelief to indignation, went through Cambridge like cholera through a western wagon train. And it acquired an addendum, an artistic touch, perhaps contributed by DeVoto himself, perhaps a slip of the tongue made by Mr. Conant in conversation, to complete and cap it. The way Cambridge heard the letter reported, it said, "the position which you said had been offered to you by *The Saturday Evening Post*." It was a shrewd addendum, whoever made it, for it confirmed a widespread feeling among antagonists of the President that Mr. Conant knew nothing whatever about the humanities, including their slick fringes, and cared less. He couldn't tell the *difference* between *The Saturday Review of Literature* and *The Saturday Evening Post*.

During the time of waiting, DeVoto had taken his problem to several of his close friends. He took it, for example, to Zinsser, and that manic, intense, fierce, tormented man, who fouled his own scientific nest as DeVoto fouled his literary nest, told him to get out of Harvard before he got institutionalized. His job was to interpret the West, as essayist and controversialist, not to fiddle around in classrooms, and not to write novels. He took it to Henderson, who thought he had been wise in not inviting a *Saturday Review* offer.[28] He took it to Kate Sterne, throwing himself on her distant but partial judgment. If he took the *Saturday Review* it would probably mean the "dictatorship of literary opinion in the U.S. for the next ten years." But it would mean the loss of Harvard, and it would mean he would write no more history and probably no more novels. He knew he wrote novels badly, knew he wrote things like the Tom Wolfe essay easily; but he hated the literary life, disliked criticism, and both despised

New York and was afraid of it. On the other hand, "decent people need a spokesman," and he was a competent controversialist. There was also the fact that he couldn't go on spending 60 per cent of his time on the teaching that provided only 20 per cent of his income. He intimated, not quite accurately, that if he didn't accept the editorship, George Stevens would probably leave, and the one literary magazine that was inclined to support the middle against both ends would probably fold.[29]

Jitters, backings and fillings, changes of mind, decisions and revisions. Between the decision and the act falls the shadow. He took his dilemma to Robert Frost, and Frost gave him an answer as hoarse as the cawing of a crow. Resign, Frost said. Keep your self-respect.[30]

13 · A Hazard of New Fortunes

There were certain proprieties, reticences, and delays. Henry Canby, for example, must not be told of the November and January negotiations, and must be led to think of DeVoto as his own discovery. That would take a little time. The change of editors would not be announced till June and would not take effect until September. There was the whole summer, which at first looked like an opportunity for some serious writing and for the locating of a country place in Vermont, accessible from either New York or Boston, which the DeVotos might buy with the money from the serial he started even before his last classes ended at Harvard. He was also expanding "The Centennial of Mormonism" from the essay length of the *Mercury* version, and that stretched and stretched until he wondered if it, too, wanted to be a book.[1] And he had dug *Mountain Time* out of the desk, anticipating three months of happy productivity before he was led off in chains to New York.

His last act at Harvard was, oddly, that of a peacemaker. Frost, who was scheduled to deliver the Phi Beta Kappa poem in June and a tercentenary address in September, threatened to abort both, because no one had officially thanked him for the Norton Lectures. DeVoto extracted a letter of thanks from the Secretary of the Corporation and mollified him.[2]

But the summer was feckless, nothing went well. Their drives around Vermont and upper New York State gratified nostalgia but located no convenient country place that they wanted. Then the serial that was to supply the purchase price refused to go. From early June until after the middle of July he fought it, and it retaliated with insomnia and migraines. On July 17 he blew up and threw it away. The insomnia and migraines went away, but he was left rueful and bruised, and the loss of the anticipated country place troubled him. "I am the boy who apprenticed himself to a Yankee and didn't make good."³ He turned to *Mountain Time*, and that wouldn't go either. Nothing to show for the whole summer except Easy Chairs and the revised "Centennial of Mormonism."

One small success he managed: he persuaded Rosamond Chapman to go to New York as his secretary on the *Review*.

Aware of himself as he was, DeVoto could not have missed the parallels between himself and William Dean Howells. Like Howells, he was a product and a defender of the natively American. Like Howells, he was a country boy who had brought the vigor of the hinterlands to the houses of the cultivated; like Howells, though less uncomplicatedly, he enormously admired the aristocracy of brains to which he aspired to belong. Without believing in local color as Howells had, he believed in the sections as the roots and tendrils of quintessential America growing into a continental plant, elements of the extravagant variety of the American experience. He accepted the *e pluribus unum* of the motto. In tone and style his writing was as unlike that of Howells as it could well be, and he had no sympathy for the squeamishness and gentlemanly reticence of Howells' selective realism; but at the same time, he acknowledged the centrality of Howells' vision, the influence of his example and teaching, and the precision and flexibility of his prose. He would have agreed with Frost: "We are eight or ten men already and one of them is Howells."⁴

"Nothing that God has made is contemptible," Howells had said.⁵ In something like the same spirit, DeVoto had interested himself in the plain habits of plain lives, the social history of a crude, vigorous people on their way West. And if he did not accept Howells' notion that the introduction of a dark, Dostoevskian note into American literature would be a false and mistaken act and that American writers should occupy themselves with "the more smiling aspects of life, which are the more American," still, in his own way, he asserted the native, the common, and the hopeful. He and Frost were on Howells' side when they resisted the growing influence of the international and modernist strain, especially those aspects of it which presented American traditions as contemptible. It was not darkness DeVoto objected to—he believed in that as a condition of life—but a belittling theory; and he was very close to Howells when he demanded that pictures of American life be grounded in observation and fact, not in literary fashions made abroad.

Quite as truly as Howells, DeVoto had found an intellectual and spiritual home in Boston and Cambridge. If he had not won the eminence that Howells had, he had at least dug out a foothold, and he wanted no other. His expatriation stopped at the Charles; his Left Bank extended only from MIT to Waltham, his France no farther than from Cape Cod to Bread Loaf Mountain. And finally, like Howells, DeVoto passed on from Boston to New York in pursuit of influence and distinction; he went, in fact, to occupy the same Easy Chair that Howells had occupied from 1900 to 1920.

But there the comparison ends, for Howells went by choice, making his hazard of new fortunes, perceiving that New York had overtaken Boston as the place where ideas, books, power, and influence were generated. DeVoto went hating what he went to and determined to fight it, consumed by nostalgia for what he left behind.

His thirteenth Easy Chair, which appeared in November after he had been editor of the *Saturday Review* for two months, expressed him fully, at the usual 200 per cent of parity. "Good-by to the Pops, to the worst newspapers and the best libraries in America, to twisting alleys and soft voices, to bad manners full of kindness, to a formalized ineptitude that thinks itself courtliness, to Adam paneling and Phyfe tables in the offices of executives. . . . Good-by to privacy, to suburbs of wide lawns and tall hedges within twenty minutes from Park Street, to family dinners and the last homes in the East. Good-by to the Athenaeum's calfbound eighteenth-century books and the hidebound eighteenth-century people who read them. Good-by to all that is left of the eighteenth century, its last shimmer above the horizon of thought, its last habit and color maintaining the village still in the midst of the city. Good-by to simple dignity and simple quiet. . . ."[6]

New York he saw as an enormous con game and side show, its first citizen P. T. Barnum. He supposed he could learn to live in it—he had managed to live in Chicago. But ah, the sentimental tug, the snapped connections, the dissolving friendships! "And good-by to Harvard. To L.J. and Hans, to Ted and George, to Kenneth and Perry, to Arthur and Fred, to the college that conscripts your energy and writes you doubtful letters, to the republic that no one knows except those who have held its citizenship, to the dedication admitted only with a jeer but never betrayed. . . . September, 1915, and the east wind bringing the sun-dazzle over the South Station; September, 1936, and tourists in the Yard and someone nods to me and when I see Harvard again I shall have no privilege there. Twenty-one years. No one, not President nor Dean nor department head, says, 'Thanks, sorry you're going, you did a pretty good job.' Why should they? They are Bostonians and don't know how. They are Harvard and take good jobs for granted. It was a long way, in 1915, from Utah to Harvard Square, but it's a longer one, in 1936, from Harvard Square to New York."

That was a very different farewell to pedagogy than the one with which he had left Northwestern. He had left Northwestern expecting never to return; he left Cambridge hoping to be gone at most a few years. Meantime he took as much of the old life with him as he could arrange to. He had enlisted his friends to contribute essays, poems, and reviews to his journal. One principal way of enlivening the *Saturday Review* would be to give it a shot of Harvard. But he also took along a resolution that seemed as much from his western and midwestern experience as from Cambridge: Remember to keep the wires open beyond the Hudson. Never make the New Yorker's mistake of taking New York for America.

The literary, he believed, were more or less synonymous with the New Yorkers, and they were "annoyed by the Americans, a vigorous people, and terrified by their country."[7] He had long considered it his public duty to enlighten them, if necessary with a club, and to challenge their assumptions about America that were based on ignorance. He never learned to enjoy New York, he never thought Gotham for Cambridge was a fair exchange, his favorite New York hangout was the Harvard Club, he was exasperated by New Yorkers and daily offended by the literary Left, which extended from *Anvil*, the *Daily Worker*, and *New Masses* through *Partisan Review* to *The Nation* and the *New Republic*, and which in 1936 spoke with the confidence of a combine that has cornered the market.

Before he ever loaded his last luggage and his son into the Buick, he knew that he had powerful weapons with which to fight them. He was no longer a maverick Harvard camp follower. He had in his hands a popular literary weekly that, though struggling, was at least as influential as any of the journals of the Left, and he had instructions to welcome controversy. At the same time, he occupied the oldest department in American journalism, in the most widely respected monthly magazine of opinion. Between them, *Harper's* and the *Saturday Review* gave him power such as no other editor in the country possessed.

So he set out to use it. The hope of being eventually restored to Harvard was still alive in him; the will to demonstrate President Conant's blunder was a hot coal in his breast. And all the old whipping boys, all those whose ideas and ways of thinking he had been resisting since he was a schoolboy, were there before him in New York, stooped over, hands grasping ankles, backsides enticingly bared.

Hervey Allen and Bernard DeVoto in Coral Gables.

Bernard DeVoto, approximately 1934.

The DeVotos at Bread Loaf in the 1930s.

Victoria Lincoln and John Mason Brown at Bread Loaf in 1935.

Bread Loaf, 1935. Top row: Gorham Munson, John Crowe Ransom, George Stevens, Ted Morrison, John Mason Brown; middle row: William Harris, Victor Lowe, Victoria Lincoln Lowe, (unidentified), Avis DeVoto, Julia Peterkin, Catherine Brown, Bernard DeVoto, Raymond Everitt, Helen Everitt; bottom row: Mrs. Gorham Munson, Isabel Wilder, Shirley Barker, Gladys Hasty Carroll, Kay Morrison.

Bread Loaf. Kay Morrison.

Perry Miller (wearing glasses) and Kenneth Murdock visiting DeVotos at Walpole, New Hampshire, summer 1938.

Bread Loaf. Fletcher Pratt, Edith Mirrielees, Kathleen Morrison, Avis De-Voto, Lovell Thompson.

Bread Loaf. Margaret Farrar,
John Farrar, Alec Laing.

Bread Loaf, 1938. Avis DeVoto and Robert Frost.

Bread Loaf. Edith Mirrielees and Wyman Parker.

IV

THE MANHATTAN CAPTIVITY

a lightning bug got
in here the other night a
regular hick from
the real country he was
awful proud of himself you
city insects may think
you are some punkins
but i dont see any
of you flashing in the dark
like we do in
the country all right go
to it says i mehitabel the
cat and that green
spider who lives in your locker
and two or three cockroach
friends of mine and a
friendly rat all gathered
around him and urged him on
and he lightened and
lightened and lightened you
dont see anything like this
in town often he says go to it
we told him it is a
real treat to us and

we nicknamed him broadway
which pleased him
this is the life
he said all i
need is a harbor
under me to be a
statue of liberty and
he got so vain of
himself i had to take
him down a peg youve
made lightning for two hours
little bug i told him
but i dont hear
any claps of thunder
yet there are some men
like that when he wore
himself out mehitabel
the cat ate him

Don Marquis, *archy
and mehitabel*

1 · *On Moving to New York*

Before he ever approached DeVoto, George Stevens had studied the *Harvard Graduates' Magazine*. He knew pretty accurately what sort of editor he was wooing: one who liked a fight, one who would impose his own tone, personality, and opinions upon any magazine he edited, one who would be more of a writing editor than a procuring one. He thought—and after a long dinner session at the Parker House, Noble Cathcart also came to believe—that the *Saturday Review*, struggling in the Depression doldrums, running deep in the red, grown somewhat dowdy and out of fashion, shouted down by the confident Left, needed just this vigorous personality in the editorial chair.[1]

As it turned out, the *Review* needed something more, but the vigorous editor looked for a time like the answer. During the sixteen months of his effective editorship, DeVoto wrote for it eleven essays, twenty-five reviews, sixty-four editorials, and eleven serial installments of a book on the psychology of fiction. He gave the magazine all the writing energy that did not go into the Easy Chair. *Mountain Time*, which had grated to a dead stop anyway, went into the drawer. The only significant serious essay outside of those for the *Saturday Review* was "A Sagebrush Bookshelf,"[2] which was a continuation of the autobiographical fit that Kate Sterne had stimulated during the spring.

But if he wrote for it incessantly, he did not take the *Review* apart and put it back together in new patterns. It was nearly a year before he made any substantial changes in the departmental content, and he never did get to the point of redesigning or face-lifting the magazine. What he did was simply to take the old bottle and pour his own wine into it. *The Saturday Review of Literature* had always been what its name indicated, a literary journal. De-Voto did not alter its general direction, but because he himself was addicted to history, he broadened the word "literature" to include history, and such history as most interested himself. The Civil War, the westward movement, the frontier took precedence over other aspects of American history, and American history took decided preference over all others. The Harvard group of historians, especially Samuel Eliot Morison, Schlesinger, Buck, and Brinton, became members of the *Saturday Review* reviewing team.

The war party that he brought with him into enemy country was, as a matter of fact, composed almost exclusively of his Harvard and Bread Loaf friends. He had little to lure them with except a forum for their ideas, for he could do nothing with the *Review*'s traditional, even notorious, practice of paying almost nothing for reviews and delaying the payment of even that pittance interminably.[3] DeVoto's reviewers reviewed for love, mainly, and the love was partly for DeVoto and partly for the value system whose spokesman he was. Essentially, the DeVoto team shook up the reviewing practice and gave more assertive expression to attitudes not too different from those of the pre-DeVoto *Saturday Review*. His historian team attacked historians of other tendencies, his reviewers of popular fiction (especially Frances Prentice, who had wandered into his ken at Bread Loaf along with Kitty Bowen, and who had recently married Charles Curtis) continued in the *Review*'s columns the sort of discussion that was standard on Bread Loaf Mountain. Judgment of books with a legal content fell to Curtis, Felix Frankfurter, Thomas Reed Powell, and other graduates or faculty of the Harvard Law School. Political commentary came from such people as Elmer Davis, who as novelist, journalist, drinker, and believer in the middle class even though he saw it through a screen of skepticism, was a man after DeVoto's own heart. The *Saturday Review*'s favorite poets and reviewers of poetry were friends from Cambridge or Bread Loaf: Hillyer, MacLeish, Josephine Johnson, Frost, Ted Morrison.

There is no question that the infusion of these people into the *Review* enlivened it. But DeVoto did not depend entirely on his friends. He imported his enemies as well. In his essays, reviews, and editorials he attacked all the old adversaries: the censors, the education-school pedagogues, the jargoneers, the historical establishment which ignored social historians, the English departments which deadened literature, the Pulitzer Prize Committee and its juries, most of all the Young Intellectuals and the literary Marxists. Having dependable allies in history, he could delegate chastisement there. When he dealt with the literary in any form he most often pulled on the gloves himself, and he exhilarated a good many people unaccustomed to seeing their ideas represented in a literary periodical. A month after he took over, Elmer Davis wrote him, "One gets used to the eternal spectacle of Truth on the scaffold and Wrong on the throne, but without liking it much; and it looks to me as if you might make a large contribution toward reversing their positions."[4]

That, in so far as DeVoto had an editorial policy, was precisely what he wanted to do. By February 1937, when he had been editor for four months, even an unfriendly critic, Edmund Wilson, admitted in print, "Mr. DeVoto has already succeeded in making *The Saturday Review* quite interesting. The whole magazine is coming to bear the stamp of the new editor's point of view and special interests, with the result that it is acquiring a force and a definite personality which it never had before."[5]

He came, as he admitted privately to Kate Sterne, hunting scalps.[6] But that was nothing new; he had never scrubbed off the war paint since his earliest articles for Mencken. Before he ever landed in New York, his July Easy Chair[7] announced him. It was a sardonic piece of advice to the proletarian critics, telling them how to achieve the classless Millennium: 1) Quit calling everyone who dislikes a proletarian book a Fascist. 2) Confine wish fulfillment to poetry and drama and let criticism deal with facts. 3) Get rid of the neomaniacs. "Every literary movement that ever existed has been infested with such vegetarians, dew-walkers, numerologists, and swamis. They will get off anyway as soon as wave-mechanics or Zoroastrianism has provided a clue to the next fashion." 4) Come to grips with the fact that every movement is conditioned by its opposition and may not expect the achievement of absolutes. The Marxists, he said, were too smug. They hailed every Guggenheim Fellowship as a step toward a total victory;

they reveled in the cumulative triumph over what they conceived as the demo-plutocratic conspiracy against them. There was, in fact, no conspiracy, but just as soon as the Marxists became a real threat rather than a noisy nuisance the opposition *would* organize against them and either put them down or buy them out. And even if prophecy should be fulfilled and Marxist literature become dominant, the Millennium would not be at hand, for then the young and ambitious would have to attack the proletarians as the establishment, since that would be the way to notice.

That Easy Chair repeats DeVoto's old warning about theorizers, in the terms of Paretian skepticism. "Too much [of the Marxist critical system] is settled in advance of the facts, organized and elaborated in alien places in earlier times, separated from the phenomena it is asked to work with, in part prophetic and in greater part deductive, not easily adjustable and not willingly adjusted." Those were fatal weaknesses. "For the decisive force in any revolution is not the theory of revolution but the social institutions along whose channels revolution must move. . . . If proletarian criticism is to do its job it must go native." And going native, which meant acknowledging the basic irrationality and persistence of social structures, admitting the force of American habits and "residues," would destroy the party line.[8]

Good-natured as that was, it was a challenge. It appeared just a month after the announcement of his taking on the editorship of the *Review*, and it said, "Don't forget about me, I'm on the way."

But not happily. The move was more like disorderly flight than a war party. Bread Loaf was a series of colds, accidents, personality clashes, and what in the folklore of the place were referred to as Incidents.[9] Immediately after the Conference ended, he had to go through the distress of turning over the Lincoln house, which he loved, to Dumas Malone of the Harvard University Press, whom he did not. Because he had promised Samuel Morison to write up the celebration in an Easy Chair,[10] he had to sit through the Harvard Tercentenary, at which his old companion Melville Smith played the organ and President Emeritus A. Lawrence Lowell twice quoted Pareto, and everything on every side, through every minute, reminded him of the three-hundred-year-long tradition from which he was now ejected.[11] He drove down to White Plains, where Avis had gone to prepare the house, with a miserable nostalgia riding in the seat behind, and in the seat beside him his son, Gordon, obviously coming down with a cold. In White Plains the furniture had not arrived, but the cold, complete with fever and vomiting, had, as also had urgent communications from the

Saturday Review reminding him that he was to write the leader for his first issue. He sat down to write it, without books or a desk, and in the midst of his labors the maid who had replaced their much-loved Hannah turned up with a positive Wassermann.

The hypochondriac and the spoiled M.D. in DeVoto erupted like Old Faithful: there was a frenzy of tests for the family. The furniture arrived, there were five or six thousand books to be shelved, the lights burned very late at 333 Ridgeway, migraines and eyestrain perched on the plate rail and watched the quivering carcass. Out of all this, little by little, emerged a degree of order, a degree of health, the blessing of negative Wassermanns for all three of them, and the leader for the September 26 issue of *The Saturday Review of Literature*.[12]

"A Generation Beside the Limpopo"[13] he called it, and he told Kate Sterne that it was an Easy Chair that had been rejected as too rough.[14] It may be read either as a continuation of *Mark Twain's America* or as a forecast of *The Literary Fallacy*. Read either way, it is consistent with his many-times-stated convictions about the literary and the Left. Ostensibly a review of Carl Van Doren's autobiography, *Three Worlds*, it took the self-appraisals of a self-conscious literary generation and used them as the excuse for a minority report.

He said (again) that the literary rebels of the twentieth century had not known American experience and had misrepresented American society. They had admired abroad what they despised at home. They could not see America for their literary and cultural preconceptions. The period in which they throve, up to 1929 or some other arbitrary date, was indeed an interesting one; with a few absolutely first-rate figures, it had had a broader excellence than any other in our history, and it had brought American writing for the first time to international pre-eminence. But about America these literary rebels were always wrong, and some had by now begun to admit their error, as when Van Wyck Brooks, the finest critic among them, pointed out in *The Flowering of New England* things about the American past that in earlier books he had said did not exist there. Also, while these writers were denouncing and fleeing from the "puritan" and philistine America that destroyed its artists, America had been supporting its artists better than any civilization had ever done, to the extent that a lot of them had lost money in the stock-market crash.

Nothing is so marked in that essay as its anti-literary tone. Writing to Mumford about *Mark Twain's America*, Van Wyck Brooks had noted that it was not simply *The Ordeal of Mark*

Twain that DeVoto objected to, it was the whole literary idea. He was right. Ostensibly a literary man, upholder of the literary mind in thunderous arguments with Hans Zinsser (who was a scientist with literary temptations), DeVoto had felt little grief at parting from the Harvard English Department, much at being torn from his historical and scientific friends.[15] His mind had been hardened, and perhaps bent, by L. J. Henderson, a man of great brilliance, much assertion of objectivity, and inflexible prejudices. A romantic and most literary sensibility had had to digest the fact that it was never fiction, but essays and history, that brought notice and distinction to the DeVoto door. His own partial failures as a novelist were certainly involved in his attacks on the literary, and perhaps gave them some of their virulence.

Which does not alter the fact that his intelligence was acutely aware of literary pretensions, even when his sensibility might sometimes be tempted. "Since 1912," he said in his opening blast as editor, "it has always been 11:59 in America, and only a few heroic literary folk to fend doom away." Their posturing was ridiculous; they attacked shadows and defended mist. While they complained about monotony and stereotype in American life, all around them lay bewildering variety, "a chaos of races, cultures, creeds, traditions, philosophies, political and economic systems that had only once or twice been a nation and then only in periods of danger." Consistently wrong through much of its productive life, this generation had finally, by 1936, begun to circle back to the position "from which Robert Frost started in 1913." Meanwhile the new literary generation substituted economic and political golden calves for cultural. Disenchanted with democracy, taught to condemn America, they yearned for the Utopia along the Neva and the Volga. Somebody needed to remind them that the cemeteries of Russia and Germany were full of the bodies of aesthetes and intellectuals who had tried to lead the intellectual life against *real* opposition.

Raging champion of the real, passionate advocate of common sense, incautious preacher of skeptical caution, rationalist historian of the irrationality and imperfection of all human society, he jumped into midtown Manhattan, threw his coonskin on the ground, jumped on it, leaped into the air and cracked his heels together three times, and announced himself half horse, half alligator, ready to take on not only moderates like Van Doren but all the literary aesthetes and political idealists of a quarter century: Brooks again, Mumford again, Stearns and Frank again, Pound, Eliot, *Seven Arts* and the *Dial* and the old and new *Masses,*

Malcolm Cowley and Edmund Wilson and Granville Hicks, Emma
Goldman and Mike Gold and all the faithful to leftward, poeticules
and expatriates and theoreticians and fellow travelers. As usual, his
challenge escaped into overstatement: it is hard to see where he
got the notion, for instance, that Eliot, Lewis, Dreiser, Anderson,
and their younger compatriots Hemingway, Fitzgerald, and Wescott knew neither the Middle West nor the middle class. But his
essay contained a legitimate corrective of much excess on the other
side, and in 1936 it was exhilaratingly bold. He crawled into a
cave packed with bears, and shined his insolent flashlight around,
and growled.

2 · Beside the Limpopo

A rousing leader, an auspicious beginning for the "new" *Saturday
Review*—an announcement of its willingness to open its columns
to controversy, an invitation to readers who liked to hear the
victimized and scorned middle defended against both ends. But
the challenge was not immediately taken up, and for a time the
campaign was mild for lack of visible and newsworthy antagonists.
Still, DeVoto continued to send out probing patrols from both his
outposts. The October Easy Chair[1] called into question the Marxist
assumption of the class structure of society. In America, DeVoto
said, the sections were far more potent than the classes: a New
Hampshire mill worker had more in common with a New Hampshire banker than he did with a mill worker from Carolina or
Indiana. Simultaneously, a *Saturday Review* editorial[2] scoffed at
the notion that New York was America or could adequately
represent it, and offered the *Review*'s columns to outlanders who
felt that their views were unexpressed in so-called "national" magazines. In the same issue, DeVoto reviewed with enthusiasm Gilbert
Seldes' *Mainland*, which he took as a healthy refutation of the
literary people who had been wrong about America for so long—
"not wrong in part, in occasional detail . . . but always wrong
about everything."[3]

When those patrols stirred up nothing beyond the barbed wire,
he called on his artillery and dumped a barrage on quite another
sector. It could have been predicted that a chorus of national self-
congratulation over the award of the Nobel prize to Eugene
O'Neill would stir him to bilious dissent, but he had another
reason than mere captiousness or resistance to a coterie. He had

been teaching O'Neill, and he thought him not a great dramatist but a master of tricks and devices whose significances, when he called on us to observe them, turned out to be trivial or stereotyped. His intentions were cosmic, but his results rudimentary. So, why the Nobel prize to this "Model T Euripides"? And while he was at it, DeVoto dropped a few rounds on the theater as a literary art form. It had, he said, its inescapable limitations, "especially the necessary conditions of people meeting together as an audience, the lowered intelligence, the lulled critical faculty, the enhanced emotionalism and suggestibility of a group, the substitution of emotional accord for the desire to experience and understand that is fed by other forms of literature."[4]

Spoken like a true maverick, anti-urban and a non-joiner, and within blocks of the heart of show business, into the teeth of the New York theater audience that had made O'Neill and was now cheering his prize. It made the *Saturday Review* very visible, especially since that November 21 issue scooped the world with Henry Canby's review of T. E. Lawrence's *The Mint*, a book published in an edition of twelve copies at a price of five hundred thousand dollars per copy.[5] But apart from some enthusiastic letters such as that of Elmer Davis, no immediate results that could be capitalized were produced by even so lively an issue.

The December 5 issue of the *Saturday Review* contained his essay on the Christmas that the Lewis and Clark expedition observed in 1804, far up the Missouri, lost in Mandan country, deep in the central reaches of unknown Louisiana on its way to Oregon and a United States that stretched from sea to sea.[6] (His account of the gift of weasel tails that Sacajawea gave William Clark set one of DeVoto's Rocky Mountain admirers to combing the Wasatch for a duplicate set, to be presented to her favorite editor.) DeVoto wrote that essay to please himself, and because another contributor had failed to come through with a promised article. It is an index of how hand to mouth his procurement of articles was likely to be, and also an index of how completely, when he found himself unprovided at deadline, he turned the magazine in the direction of his own preoccupations. Not everyone on the *Saturday Review* staff thought it appropriate—George Stevens, for one, thought it got too far afield from the proper material of a literary review—but if Stevens had looked closely he would have seen that "Passage to India" essay as simply a positive manifestation of the American gospels whose negative statements lashed the intellectuals as with nettles. He could not have DeVoto as editor unless he had him whole.[7]

All together, a lively three months, the last three months of
1936, but they brought no immediate improvement in the *Review*'s
fortunes. The letters that came in were both enthusiastic and angry;
certain telephone calls suggested, anonymously, that DeVoto was
about to have his hide nailed to the barn door.⁸ December and
January went by with nothing more controversial than a rebuke to
the Salt Lake City librarians who had put the works of Vardis
Fisher, a novelist whom DeVoto deplored, on the restricted shelf.⁹
But then, in the *New Republic* for February 3, Edmund Wilson
picked up the gauntlet that DeVoto had flung in "A Generation
Beside the Limpopo." In "Complaints: II. Bernard DeVoto,"¹⁰
after acknowledging DeVoto's vigor, style, and independence of
mind, and praising the new life he had brought to the *Review*, he
asked him to "stand and unfold himself." Why was he so angry?
What, exactly, was he objecting to? What general philosophy or
system of ideas did he operate from? He sounded as if he must
have some such system, but reading him failed to make it clear.
"This indignation at other people's errors which seems to prevent
him from stating his own case, this continual boiling up about
other people's wild statements which stimulates him to even wilder
statements of his own, have been characteristic of all his criticism."
He seemed to be a supercilious academic lambasting the non-
academics of literature, a professional Westerner accusing all others
of ignorance about the West, a follower of Pareto who simply
threw the name Pareto at his readers' heads without explicating
him, a champion of "fact" who accused whole generations of the
most various people of "misrepresentation" and "fantasy," a critic
of psychoanalytic biography who did not hesitate to use psychoanalysis himself when it was convenient, a damner of utopian and
idealistic and progressive thought who did not say how he expected
society ever to be improved and appeared not to believe it could
be. What did he want? He was obviously intelligent and articulate
and well read. If he would state himself clearly, he would have an
attentive audience.

That was by no means the nailing to the barn door that DeVoto
had been expecting. Wilson's tone, puzzled, skeptical, judicious,
mildly remonstrative, even respectful, did not warrant a slam-bang
reply. But the article provided the opportunity for public debate
that DeVoto had been waiting for. He answered Wilson on February 13 in a double-length editorial.¹¹

Not even his most uncritical advocate could pretend, on the
basis of this editorial, that DeVoto adequately answered Wilson's
demand to know why he was so angry. That was a question he

probably could not have answered if he had tried. Indignation was his style, and the style was the man. There was no more moderation in him than there is in gunpowder. But other parts of Wilson's inquiry he replied to with relish, and some part of the answer, as he wrote to Kate Sterne,[12] came out of the self-examination that she had stimulated the year before.

Modestly he denied being an academic, pointing out his lack of degrees and his lack of a university job. Modestly he denied being an expert on Pareto, referring Wilson to Henderson and the other authorities and to the new English translation of the *Trattato*. He said that Wilson had appeared to misunderstand some of his writings, and to have ignored others. Gently he chided Wilson for taking seriously some things that had been meant as jokes. But he pounced on the demand for an articulated system of ideas by which he could be explained. "For, you see, this is a demand for a gospel, and I have been acquainted with it since my earliest days. I was brought up in a religion which taught me that man was imperfect but might expect God's mercy—but I was surrounded by a revealed religion founded by a prophet of God, composed of people on the way to perfection, and possessed of an everlasting gospel. I early acquired a notion that all gospels were false and all my experience since then has confirmed it. . . . I distrust absolutes. Rather, I long ago passed from distrust of them to opposition. And with them let me include prophecy, simplification, generalization, abstract logic, and especially the habit of mind which consults theory first and experience only afterward."

If labels were needed, then he would describe himself as "a pluralist, a relativist, an empiricist." He rested not upon a gospel but upon a method, the inductive method of science. If he objected to a great many kinds of people, he objected because they exemplified a particular way of thinking which most of them consistently pretended was something else. "As for America, let us go slowly. Many men are confident that they can sum up a nation and a people in one manuscript page; but I must refuse to try. I have no formula to explain the American past or present, still less the future; I have no logically articulated system of conceptions that will make all clear. The fault I find with the literary is precisely that they have such formulas and systems. . . ."

An impartial critic might find in DeVoto's characterization of "the literary" something interestingly close to the generalization he objected to in them. Pressed, he would have had to exempt many individuals from his indictment, and he would have had to retreat from some categorical absolutism of phrasing. But the generation beside the Limpopo had demonstrated, as a pervasive coloration of mind, as a dominant tendency, much of what he accused it of categorically. Before too many years, he would have so unlikely a convert to his essential position as Van Wyck Brooks himself.[13] But that would be a wartime flurry, an aberration brought on by crisis. Brooks's premises were never DeVoto's; they never ceased to be literary and elitist, they never quit assuming the essential importance of the intellectuals as a force. And neither DeVoto, nor Brooks, nor Archibald MacLeish,[14] nor any of the patriots of the 1940s much altered the course of literary ideas. If DeVoto were alive in 1973, he would find another whole generation beside the Limpopo, yearning toward the perfected society that the history of Mormonism had taught him to treat with skepticism and scorn.

The little public debate with the champion chosen (as he thought) by the opposition flared and waned. He was on record, the battle was joined, there was sniping from editorial offices on the Left, but there seemed to have been little or no immediate benefit to the *Review*. Meanwhile, he was chained to his guns, and no amount of irritable wanting to write his own books made him find the time to write them. He went on as he had begun.

Thus when Harold Stearns, in *America, A Reappraisal*, reversed the opinions he had expressed in *America and the Young Intellectual* and illustrated in his symposium *Civilization in the United States*, DeVoto could dance on Stearns's repentant body in an editorial.[15] When Judge Curran dismissed the obscenity charges that John S. Sumner had brought against Farrell's *A World I Never Made*, DeVoto could repeat his confidence in the free forum of ideas and reassert the right of people to select their own reading without help from self-appointed censors.[16] When the League of American Writers issued a call to a congress that would discuss literary matters and especially how literature could encourage a healthy culture, DeVoto could comment with a Bronx cheer. "We like writers, but we like them writing, not making speeches and adopting resolutions." And when Burton Rascoe's autobiography and Malcolm Cowley's anthology *After the Genteel Tradition* came out more or less simultaneously, DeVoto could use Rascoe's comfortable nostalgias as a stick to beat Cowley with, and use the Cowley book as the text for a sermon on the tendency of the literary Left to find in American life and literature whatever it had previously hidden there. "*Plus Ce Change*," he called that review when he collected it in *Minority Report*. He did not regard it as a personal attack on Cowley. It was an attack upon a set of ideas, one more blow against the Saracen holders of a desecrated Holy Sepulcher, the monkeys who had inherited Angkor Wat.

3 · "You're There to Lick 'Em for Us"

He conceived his crusade to be against ideas, not against individuals, though in the heat of battle he often attacked *ad hominem* and though his opponents, under a hail of blows, could hardly be blamed for failing to understand that the lumps they received were impersonally intended. To the Left, he seemed a reactionary, perhaps a Fascist; even Wilson had suggested that he came close to being that rare thing, a spokesman for the literary Right.[1] (By the same principle under which everything east of Cheyenne is "back East" to an Ogden boy, everything to the right of Norman Thomas was "reactionary" to the *New Republic* and "Fascist" to the *New Masses*.) Whatever they called him, his genius for hyperbolic scorn and superheated invective had made him cordially hated in leftist quarters by the time he left New York early in June to receive an honorary degree from Middlebury College (an honor that Frost had arranged with Middlebury's President Paul Moody)[2] and to spend the summer in the Shingled Cottage on the Bennington College campus (a house that Frost had helped obtain for him). Impersonally meant or not, his controversies inevitably involved the personal element, and it was increased by his alliance with Frost, a good hater and a canny manipulator of his friends in behalf of his reputation.

For more than a year DeVoto had been itching to take on Frost's critics, especially those of the Left who had universally disparaged *A Further Range* when it appeared in the spring of 1936. Rolfe Humphries, Newton Arvin, Horace Gregory, Granville Hicks, and R. P. Blackmur, in series and in parallel, had found the book poetically wanting and politically offensive, and neither its selection as Book of the Month nor its winning the Pulitzer prize could salve for DeVoto—and Frost—the cuts of these notices. In the fall of 1936, DeVoto had lectured at Amherst on Frost's invitation and had begged Frost for the chance to reply to the critics. He could do it better from the *Saturday Review*, a literary journal, than from the Easy Chair, where he was expected to be a public thinker rather than a literary critic. Throughout the winter, which Frost spent in San Antonio, DeVoto kept renewing this offer, until Frost agreed to "let you strike that blow for me." Then the debate with Wilson broke out, and Frost backed away, unwilling to get drawn into a controversy that had nothing to do with his own poetry.[3]

Later still, he was again persuaded, but the article was delayed, partly by DeVoto's other work and the illnesses that kept recurring like psychosomatic warnings, partly for lack of the precisely right occasion. In May 1937, just before DeVoto left New York for Middlebury and Bennington, Frost was clearly counting on the article and clearly a little afraid that DeVoto would leave the *Saturday Review* in disgust before it got written. "I hope I haven't made you too unhappy by having thrown my weight into your decision to leave teaching," he wrote. "Nothing is momentous. Nothing is final. You can always go back if back is where you can best strike from. Some like a spear, some like a dirk. The dirk is the close-in weapon of city streets. Anybody can take his choice of weapons for all of me. I suspect you're an all round handiman of the armory. I had no idea of sacrificing you to the job down there—or letting you sacrifice yourself. You're there to lick em for us. To Hell with their thinking. That's all I say. I wish I were any good. I'd go up to the front with you. As it is—as I am—I must be content to sick you on. Results is all I ask."[4]

Given his filial and reverential feeling toward Frost, DeVoto needed no sicking. They held many enemies as well as ideas in common. But there was still not the proper occasion that would give the blow news value. That came, finally, in October 1937, brought about partly through another admirer of Frost's, another Pulitzer-prize poet, another Harvard colleague, another Bread Loaf regular, Robert Hillyer.

In the *Atlantic Monthly* for August 1936, Hillyer had published a two-hundred-line "A Letter to Robert Frost," an excessively adulatory poem in rhymed couplets.[5] At Bread Loaf, toward the end of the month, he showed parts of a second poem to DeVoto. DeVoto asked for it for the *Review*, only asking that its title be changed from "A Letter to Bernard DeVoto" to something else. In early October he published it as "A Letter to the Editor."[6] Its change of title did not alter its personal tone or its assumption of shared antipathies, for it began, "Time brings us, Benny, to our middle years," and it went on to paraphrase Caligula in wishing that the symbolists, the proletarians, the literary illiterates, the pretentious, the commercial, and the publicity-seeking had only one neck among them, and he or Benny a sword.

The poem released the acids in Granville Hicks, who promptly

sent in to the *Saturday Review* a parody "Letter to Robert Hillyer," in which he took skin off not only Hillyer but also Frost and
especially DeVoto:

> The Eliots and Cranes you damn in toto
> But speak with vast respect of one DeVoto
> The Howells of our age—God save the mark!
> Who's bid his sad farewell to Durgin Park,
> To swanboats, Pops, and other Boston joys,
> And now laments the humbug and the noise
> Of Mannahatta, though there's some suspicion
> He's well equipped to furnish competition.
> He's versatile at least, and swiftly shuttles
> From co-ed tales to forays and rebuttals.
> (His forays fill the women's clubs with awe,
> And his rebuttals slaughter men of straw.)

Cagily, not to expose himself to a *New Masses* blast, DeVoto
neither quite accepted nor quite rejected Hicks's contribution. He
said it was not good enough poetry to be accepted for the regular
columns of the magazine, but that he would print it on the Letters
page if Hicks would cut it down somewhat.[7] Hicks chose not to
do anything more at the time, but a year later, when Hillyer's poem
was published in a volume along with similar letters to Frost, James
B. Munn, Charles Townsend Copeland, and others, he sent his
anti-Hillyer parody to the *New Republic*, which printed the less
abusive part on October 20.[8]

The Hillyer-Hicks exchange restored Frost to the limelight as a
figure of controversy without any overt move of his own or of
DeVoto's. Very shortly, Holt brought out Richard Thornton's
Recognition of Robert Frost, a retrospective anthology of critical
praise, and that provided the immediate occasion DeVoto had
been waiting for. Just after Christmas 1937 he sent to Frost in
Florida the proofs of his long-planned article, written as a review
of the Thornton book, and scheduled for the issue of January 1.[9]

It was DeVoto at his most vehement. Though the second part
of the essay was an exposition of Frost's qualities as a poet and an
examination of the reasons why critics had so often misunderstood
him, he did not reach that part of the discussion until he had kicked
all the chairs out of the way—and the critics in them—to clear the
place for action. Thornton's book, the ostensible excuse for the
essay, was hardly mentioned. The real excuse, the unfriendly
critics, brought on some of the most violently vituperative para-
graphs DeVoto ever wrote.

From the beginning, he said, Frost had been victimized by critics who couldn't read him. Amy Lowell's review of *North of Boston,* for example, was "screamingly silly." Nothing even came close to it for idiocy until Newton Arvin and Horace Gregory reviewed *A Further Range.* But even those were outdone by R. P. Blackmur's review of the same book in *The Nation.* That "may not be quite the most idiotic review our generation has produced, but in twenty years of reading criticism—oh, the hell with scholarly reservations, Mr. Blackmur's is the most idiotic of our time. It is one of the most idiotic reviews since the invention of movable type. The monkeys would have to tap typewriters throughout eternity to surpass it."

Wiping his hands, he finally got around to the reasons why Frost's poetry was so often misunderstood and underestimated. His comic spirit, for one thing, his playfulness with word and idea, his "antic willingness to make jokes about the verities," his belief that poetry was a game played between poet and reader, that it involved deliberate obscurings and false leads, that the poet should "always keep one step ahead of his own sincerity," had always offended the solemn, and bewildered them. DeVoto linked Frost with Mark Twain, who had a similar effect on the solemn, and who like Frost was more truly a "proletarian" than any of the fashionable Marxist intellectuals, since he wrote out of an identification with working people, and in their native vernacular and rhythms.

The review delighted Frost. If Lawrance Thompson is to be believed, and the letters between Frost and DeVoto can hardly be interpreted otherwise, this was precisely what Frost had been grooming DeVoto for.[10] Most of Frost's friends were likewise delighted. Ridgely Torrence thought those particular critics would "never get up off the slaughterhouse floor." Some others, among them Ted Morrison, though completely sympathetic to Frost and DeVoto, thought the attack too abusive and insufficiently judicial. As for the opposition, it was predictably furious. One of them, F. O. Matthiessen, wrote in to defend Blackmur's review as a serious attempt to come to grips with Frost's excursion into political poetry, and objected to DeVoto's "tub-thumping and windy declarations."[11]

Up to that time, DeVoto and Matthiessen had been polite acquaintances, though too many temperamental and intellectual differences existed between them for friendship. After the Frost episode, Matthiessen was an enemy—an enemy, moreover, in the place where DeVoto least wanted to cultivate enemies, and at a time when enemies in that place would have the power to do him ill.

4 · *"An Incumbrance for His Lively Spirit"*

For months it had been clear that the *Saturday Review* was not rallying financially under DeVoto's editorship. Though it had achieved some improvement in circulation (15 per cent, according to his own statement) it was a long way from edging into the black. Staff morale was not good and was probably not improved by DeVoto's announcement when he left for Vermont in June 1937 that next year Christopher Morley's The Bowling Green, Amy Loveman's Clearing House, Carl Purington Rollins' The Compleat Collector, and George Jean Nathan's nighttime column would all be eliminated. He may himself have offered at that point to resign.[1] Whether he did or did not, he left New York to stew in its summer heat and escaped to Vermont, where he intended to write three short stories for money. To keep the editorial presence apparent, he left behind him, to be run serially through the summer, his articulated class lectures on the art of fiction, to be entitled "English 37."[2]

But once he settled down in Bennington, the will and capacity to work were not in him. His Harvard friends, visiting, brought him tales of dissension and unrest and resistance to President Conant, tales that half distressed and half gratified him. But when Mr. Conant invited him to deliver three lectures, at some time convenient to him during the next academic year, on some subject related to American literature and American history, he accepted with almost precipitate promptness.[3]

Stories would not come; his days were unproductive and his nights restless. He tried tennis, he tried his old therapy of motoring through the countryside, he tried girl-watching, for Bennington was conducting a dance school and the place was full of leotards. Nothing availed. A tentative proposal that he become editor of the *American Mercury* reminded him of the uncertainty and unsatisfactoriness of his condition.[4] From her imprisonment in Poughkeepsie, which had now stretched out through three and a half years, Kate Sterne wrote him miserably, apologizing for the dull poverty of her letters and telling him not to let *noblesse oblige* keep him answering them.[5] Uncharacteristically, he responded with a letter as gloomy as her own:

You certainly know by this time that writing to you and hearing from you are indispensable to my spiritual equilibrium. You know too that it doesn't much matter what either half of the correspondence says, and that I squirm with the frequent knowledge that what I write to you is dull as clabber in an August drouth. But you will have to be patient. . . . It develops that, after all, I am forty and have driven myself harder than I should have for more years than seem reasonable, and I've run into a streak—I trust not a long one—of paying for it.[6]

His spirits were low, his health uncertain, his confidence shaky. Of the three stories he had projected for the summer, he would be lucky to finish one, and would end the year fifteen hundred dollars in the red. "In short my soul is becalmed in the shallows and seaweed beyond Sargasso."

That was on July 16. He had a month of the doldrums before Bread Loaf and Edith Mirrielees rescued him—and how could that gentle, inexperienced, Victorian maiden lady ever have developed the understanding she had of the black caves of the spirit? Yet she had, she *knew*. Bread Loaf itself, "the best club I've ever belonged to,"[7] was a good session, without Episodes or Incidents or hysterics, and he left it refreshed, to give his spirit a final buffing on the beaches of Martha's Vineyard. From there, improved in everything but his eyes, which had been bad all summer, he returned to New York on September 13 to find the morale of the *Review* office lower than ever. The place reeked of failure and imminent collapse, the air was thick with blame. Conversations, it seemed to him, stopped when he entered a room. It seemed that he was the goat—he had gone off for three full months, letting the magazine down, not carrying out his proper duties, not even writing regular editorials, but leaving the *Review* to groan under eleven dull installments of the art of fiction, leftovers from the classroom.[8]

His feeling that they blamed him begot in him a defensive sense of grievance. He thought that when he took the editorship the *Review* had agreed to three conditions: that he would have his summers off, that there would be a promotional campaign, and that he would be given three years to get the magazine on its feet. But those terms had never been written down, and now it developed that others did not remember them as he did.[9] Neither Stevens nor Cathcart had heard of any three-year trial; in fact, Stevens had gathered from remarks of the DeVotos themselves, when they first moved down, that they expected to stay only a year or two. The promotional campaign appeared to have been the sort of soothing assurance one makes to a man he is attempting to hire; even if it had been promised, there were not resources to carry it out. As for the summers off, that expectation might have arisen out of a casual remark of Cathcart's that nothing much went on during the summer months.[10]

No matter whose memory was correct, and even if all memories were wrong, some of the staff thought DeVoto might have slowed or reversed the *Review*'s decline if he had stayed on the job. There was a fundamental difference in the way they looked upon the magazine. To the staff, many of whom had been there from the beginning, it was the life job, the career, an entity made up of shared experience, responsibility, dependence, and affection. To DeVoto it was, subconsciously or consciously, an interlude—as Canby puts it in his memoirs, "an incumbrance for his lively spirit."[11] He had married it on the bounce. Given his choice, he would have chosen Harvard. Untroubled by the problem of money, he would have preferred writing.

And yet his obscure desire for some institutional justification would feel the loss of the *Review* if he did lose it. And he did not relish the notion of having failed at it. His sensitive and hypochondriacal spirit resented the fact that others seemed to blame him. For his own part, he blamed the Depression and the business office, in that order, for the *Review*'s troubles. The Depression no one could help, but an efficient business office might have made it possible for the magazine to survive it. Instead, in DeVoto's view, it was a department of utter confusion, without an ABC rating, without an advertising rating, without a rate card, without a circulation manager. Its payment to reviewers was meager and always slow. Its subscription list was so full of deadheads and lapsed subscribers that if it were closely examined its announced twenty-six thousand might shrink to as few as sixteen thousand. And no promotional campaign, no move to take advantage of the publicity his forays and rebuttals had generated.[12]

I have found no documentary evidence from Cathcart's side of the affair, but it seems clear that he felt himself every bit as much on trial as DeVoto, and was badly shattered by his failure to pull the *Saturday Review* out. In retrospect, the Depression seems the villain, not any individual's shortcomings.

Shortly after his return in September, DeVoto seems to have once again offered to resign. If he did, he was dissuaded. In mid-November Thomas Lamont summoned the staff to a luncheon and told them that he could no longer absorb the losses. The *Saturday Review* would have to close. But during the talk that followed, there was so much real regret, the affection and loyalty of the staff were so apparent, that Lamont eventually said he would underwrite one third of the deficit for another year if a buyer could be found who would take over the magazine and renovate it.

Under the circumstances, renovation suggested a housecleaning that would include the present editor. During the last weeks of 1937 and the first weeks of 1938, while Harry Scherman of the Book of the Month Club toyed with the idea of putting money into the magazine, there were rumors that he was sounding out several potential replacements for DeVoto: Elmer Davis,[13] Frederick Lewis Allen of *Harper's*, Clifton Fadiman.

During those weeks DeVoto was doing his best to make the *Saturday Review* a lively magazine, partly for the sake of his pride, partly perhaps because a good magazine might sell more readily and he be rid of it faster. He was also conducting his own conversations outside. Harper & Brothers, as Mark Twain's publishers, were hinting that he might be asked to replace Albert Bigelow Paine, recently dead, as curator of the Mark Twain papers, and some Cambridge friends, anticipating DeVoto's week of lectures in December, wrote confidentially asking for a statement covering the circumstances of his leaving Harvard, to be used as data in a move to get him restored there.[14] With that hope revived in him, he worked hard over his three lectures and over the address he was to give the Modern Language Association in Chicago between Christmas and New Year's.

That is to say, even when he poured his energetic efforts into the *Saturday Review*, he was still divided. He ended the year more an academic than an editor, following the Harvard week with a lecture at Connecticut College for Women and taking off for Chicago immediately after Christmas. He left with his hopes enhanced for a Harvard appointment. For even though Murdock, Schlesinger, Frankfurter, William Scott Ferguson, and Ralph Barton Perry were all on the Committee of Nine and hence inhibited from becoming his overt champions, they were all working for him behind the scenes, and apparently getting somewhere. While DeVoto was lecturing at Harvard, President Conant, who in the past had demonstrated himself something less than graceful in his handling of distinguished visitors, went out of his way to invite him to tea and to converse amiably for three quarters of an hour. Thus encouraged, DeVoto went to Chicago and gave the MLA a talk that left their ears buzzing, and returned to New York glum about the *Saturday Review* but with hopes of an escape from it and back to the more privileged earth of Cambridge.[15]

Others were more cheerful too. One afternoon in January the staff sat around the office and told each other that the magazine was the best it had ever been. A week or so later Lamont summoned them to another business meal. The negotiations with Scherman had come to nothing. DeVoto should consider himself on three months' notice and free to look for another job. For the time being, and on the desperate outside chance that a buyer might still be found, Noble Cathcart and George Stevens would run the magazine with the help of Mary Ellen Whelpley, once Devoto's secretary on the *Harvard Graduates' Magazine*, who had replaced Rosamond Chapman in March 1937. Anything DeVoto wrote for the *Review* after April 1 would be paid for at space rates, $4.50 a column.[16]

That was the way his editorship of the *Saturday Review* ended—definitely not with a bang.

5 · *Cambridge Regained*

Of the several proposals made to him after word of the *Saturday Review*'s troubles got around, only two interested him. As he had written to Copey in January, he was "fed up with editing, with New York, and especially with writing about books instead of writing books,"[1] but he listened with attention to the tentative proposal about the Mark Twain papers. In fact, he coveted the job. Another Harper's suggestion, that he take over the *Harper's* book section, he did not covet but found hard to refuse.[2] It was what he had asked of Lee Hartman when the Easy Chair was offered him, on the grounds that he preferred being a book critic to being a public thinker. Now the criticism business had left scars on him, and he had found public thinking sometimes exhilarating, and so he stalled Hartman without saying either yes or no, while he waited for word from his friends at Harvard and for the decision of Clara Gabrilowitsch, whose edition of her father's letters he had panned, and Charles Lark, the lawyer for the Mark Twain Estate, who had not much liked his comments on the unhelpfulness of Albert Bigelow Paine.

Even if they overcame their dislike and agreed with Harper's that he was better qualified than anyone else to edit the papers, he would have solved none of his financial problems. He had set a fee of one thousand dollars for reading and evaluating the manuscripts. There would be nothing else in the curatorship for him except secretarial help and perhaps some fees or royalties from the purely hypothetical books he might assemble from the papers. His income had shrunk to the twenty-four hundred dollars from the Easy Chair. Characteristically, he did not apply for help to any foundation or fellowship; he was used to paying his own way. And though he might get out and dust off the failed novel *Mountain Time* and the notes for the frontier book, those were not what he could expect to earn a living from. They demanded a subvention: teaching, editing, or the assistance of Mr. John August, or since he was who he was, perhaps all three.

The day after the Lamont decision, he wrote Kenneth Murdock, then Master of Leverett House, one of his closest friends at Harvard and certainly the most powerful. He had been the Dean of the Faculty, he had been Mr. Conant's chief rival for the presidency when A. Lawrence Lowell retired, and he was the champion of the humanities which the Murdock faction felt Mr. Conant had systematically undersupported. There were those who insisted that the only sensible decisions Mr. Conant had made as president had been made at the urging of Murdock. DeVoto felt that it was Murdock who had made the strongest effort to keep him at Harvard, and that it was Murdock, along with Henderson, Zinsser, and the American historians, who was most anxious to bring him back. Trying to give him information to work with, DeVoto put his desire bluntly:

My feeling is that the case for me at Harvard is simple. I am a fairly prominent man of letters who happens to be a proved scholar and a proved teacher. The conspiracy cannot, of course, let it go at that. It will be necessary to list assets and arguments in detail. For all my reputation, I hate both bragging and the appearance of bragging, but I'm not going to pull a bushel over myself at the decisive crisis. I'd rather teach at Harvard than do anything else on earth. So, when the time comes, I'm going to draw up a brief for you. It will not be modest.[3]

The brief was on Murdock's desk within ten days, and it was what its author had promised. If, as rumor said, Mr. Conant had been told DeVoto's scholarship was deficient, then rumor had to be spiked. He did not have the orthodox academic degrees, but he had competences that were his alone, or nearly alone. One recent development was in his favor. The program in American Civilization that had been planned in many conversations among DeVoto,

Murdock, Samuel Morison, Schlesinger, Frederick Merk, and Perry Miller had been formally announced in April 1937, and DeVoto had written a strongly favorable editorial about it in the *Saturday Review*.[4] DeVoto hoped that under its rubric some special position could be created for him, some roving professorship out of the jealous departmental winds. In his brief he listed his total qualifications, just in case.

What was he qualified to teach? Composition? He thought he was probably the best teacher of composition that Harvard had had since Copey. Contemporary literature? The success of his English 70 could be ascertained from students. Moreover, a year and a half as editor of the *Saturday Review* had vastly increased his competence in that area. He planned a book about the whole poetic outburst after 1912, using Frost as a focus, that he was sure would force a revision of much critical opinion. "I know something about modern poetry that no one has bothered to put into print." Mark Twain? "I'm the authority." American humor? "Franklin Meine knows more about the field than I do and Walter Blair knows fully as much . . . but I know of no one else who is as well qualified as I am." Frontier literature? "So far as I can learn there has been only one course in the American colleges on frontier literature· it consisted of my Mark Twain book, Meine's book, and Constance Rourke's. . . . This is, of course, my culminating field. . . ."

Hope wrote the brief, and hope waited out the results. But not long. Murdock and Henderson both talked with President Conant and got nowhere. DeVoto heard that Murdock, pressing too hard, had received a "ferocious" rebuff. The "red bible" which had formalized Mr. Conant's policy of fixed faculty positions was hard to crack, and some of DeVoto's strongest supporters were in the awkward position of having helped write it. None of them in the circumstances was likely to be particularly effective in getting a variance in DeVoto's behalf. Murdock had been a rival and in some ways a leader of the opposition. Zinsser, a maverick, was not *persona grata*. Cambridge rumor, as indefatigable as a ferret in a maze of rat holes, said that once in a committee meeting he had shouted at Conant, "For God's sake, forget for a minute that you're President of Harvard College!" All felt that too strong advocacy, unless their advice was asked for, might do more harm than good.[5]

The departments were locked into their budgets and their grid of fixed appointments. English as well as History and Literature contained some DeVoto enemies, especially F. O. Matthiessen.

History, when Zinsser suggested that it appoint DeVoto, had no overt enemies but no open positions, either.

Eventually, Cambridge being Cambridge, rumor got around to the *Crimson*, which with the usual undergraduate willingness to embarrass the administration began a campaign for DeVoto's return that Murdock made an effort to squash, explaining to DeVoto that he feared it would harden the opposition irremediably.

For so skinless a man, DeVoto had shown singularly little rancor against the university that had rejected him. He had written a hymn to its community of free minds in his Tercentenary Easy Chair,[6] had editorialized in praise of the American Civilization program, had celebrated Boston as a living place and the New Englander as a human type, and had come back eagerly for the three lectures in December. He now suggested to Murdock that if, as seemed likely, he was put in charge of the Mark Twain papers, he would ask that they be deposited in Widener Library.[7]

Nothing availed. Harvard was as impregnable as Machu Picchu; it had no more use for a maverick than the New York literary world had had. It had made its feelings clear by March. The next month, it underlined them in red by appointing Granville Hicks, the exemplar of every intellectual affiliation that DeVoto despised, as a one-year Fellow of United States History and assigning him to Adams House, the house of the Boylston Professor of Rhetoric, DeVoto's ally Robert Hillyer.

That indeed looked like the work of a conspiracy, or like a deliberate attempt to humiliate the DeVoto-Hillyer faction. Hillyer thought so and was furious.[8] The *Crimson* somewhere dug up the unpublished and more destructive portions of Hicks's "Letter to Robert Hillyer" and printed them, either in pure enjoyment of the squabble or out of some obscure desire to take sides in it.

But the Hicks appointment had been too humiliating to DeVoto; it had made too plain what his friends were up against. Quietly he called them off, withdrew his claim, swallowed the pill that had been handed him, and gave up forever the hope, and at least outwardly the desire, of being a part of Harvard.

Elinor Frost died in Florida on March 20—one more reason that the year 1938 gave for gloom. When he went to Amherst for the memorial service, on April 22, DeVoto had an odd reminder of how commonly academic institutions undervalued their employees if the employees were outspoken non-conformists. One of the honorary pallbearers,[9] along with DeVoto, Morrison, Hillyer, Untermeyer, David McCord, and others of the Cambridge-Bread Loaf fellowship, was Wilbert Snow, of Connecticut Wesleyan, the same Wilbert Snow who in 1915 had been fired from the University of Utah and whose firing had precipitated Bernard DeVoto out of Utah and into Harvard. They shared a sense of injustice, but there was a difference, too. Snow had benefited, rather than suffered, from being let go; the University of Utah had done the suffering. But Harvard, at least in DeVoto's view, was a university from which all roads led down, and its prestige and self-esteem were proof against admission or correction of error. The only courses open to an ousted teacher were to go elsewhere and eat his heart out for lost beatitude, or stay on in the Harvard community without affiliation or status. He had already determined on the second. He would take his affiliation and status with him, as curator of the Mark Twain papers.

By the time of the Elinor Frost service he was already free of the *Saturday Review* and at work on the papers in the law offices of Charles Lark.[10] From weeks of immersion in them he emerged with the conviction that Paine had taken more liberties as an editor than could be condoned, and that at least three books were visible among the manuscripts that Paine had rejected or suppressed. He agreed to assemble a volume of sketches, a volume of autobiography, and a volume of letters, and to edit and publish these for a fee of five hundred dollars each, without any participation in royalties, and he persuaded Lark to ship the papers to Widener Library at Harvard, where a secretary-typist under DeVoto's supervision would put them in order.[11]

The agreement was signed on May 31. By that date the DeVotos had located a house on Coolidge Hill Road, in Cambridge, close to the Shady Hill School. On June 12, just before they were to start for a summer in the country at Walpole, New Hampshire, *Collier's* bought the serial he had begun working on before he was even quite clear of the *Review*. They wanted it, naturally, to be completed within a month. On June 14, suddenly solvent but weighted down as usual with work, DeVoto left New York. His sentiments upon leaving, which he expressed in the August Easy Chair, were not calculated to endear him to the New Yorkers. He pitied them. He thought they lived a life of unbelievable artificiality, like the highly bred dogs they led around muzzled, or turned loose for a little exercise with a rubber rat on the greasy grass of Central Park.

Theology tells us that sin sunk to acceptance is depravity, and psychiatry tells us that even a psychosis is an adaptation, a way of staying alive, and four million people are adapted to living with the aorta tied off. . . . But I no longer have to live under that ligature. . . . I'm moving away. . . . I'm getting out. I'm going back to America, to civilization. . . . I had my rubber rat: I came here to write about other men's books, and that gives the measure of this maniac town. In this air it seems sensible, it has the town's logic—and it is quite as functional as any dog stretching his legs on a treadmill in a steam-heated room.[12]

New Hampshire for the summer, Cambridge in prospect. After what he had been through, and even without a Harvard connection, it sounded like Beulah Land.

First he gave defeat the satisfaction of the last word by writing his Easy Chair "On Moving from New York." Then he dug in and finished the serial. Then he wrote the introduction he had promised to write for *Hired Man on Horseback*,[13] the biography of Eugene Manlove Rhodes by his widow; and with the generosity that was his frequent impulse, because he knew she was in need, he directed Houghton Mifflin to send his fee to May Rhodes. Finally, his immediate jobs done, his spirits high and going higher, the summer tidied up and the temptations of the road upon him, he yielded to Avis' desire to revisit her home town of Houghton, Michigan, which she had not seen in fifteen years. On the way, he made his wife's nostalgia pay research dividends by routing them through the Oneida Colony and past the Hill Cumorah, where the Angel of the Lord had directed young Joseph Smith to dig up the Golden Plates.

By August 9 they were back in the God's country of the Connecticut Valley, with just enough time for an Easy Chair before Bread Loaf and "the best time of the year." This time it would not be unalloyed pleasure. The session of 1938 would see the beginning of his filial quarrel with Robert Frost.

6 · *An Incident on Bread Loaf Mountain*

DeVoto was a Bread Loaf regular of six years' standing, but Frost's association with both the place and the idea had been much longer. He had been dreaming about some sort of literary farm with himself as its focus as early as 1915,[1] when he was just back from the stimulating companionship of Edward Thomas and

Lascelles Abercrombie in the English countryside, and when De-Voto was a raw sophomore transfer student at Harvard. When the School of English was created to make use of the Bread Loaf Inn in 1920, Frost had immediately written to Wilfred Davidson and offered to participate. He had been at the English School nearly every year since 1921, and had become the *genius loci*, shedding his light around and getting back worshipful reflections. It was the place, above all others, where he went to shine and be admired.

His relations with the Writers' Conference, though its program interested him more, had been less congenial. He participated in 1926, its first year, but thereafter, because of disagreement with some of John Farrar's policies, he held aloof. In 1929, when Farrar was to be replaced, Frost was announced as the new direc-tor, but someone—Thompson thinks President Paul Moody of Middlebury College—vetoed that, and after serving through the 1929 session Frost did not return again until Morrison and DeVoto, during the intimate Cambridge winter of the Norton Lectures, persuaded him to come in the summer of 1936. He came again in 1937, and would be there in 1938.

But 1938 was the year of his disaster. With his wife's death, his life had been cracked like a dropped cup. He suffered not only from her loss but from his children's resentment and their feeling that he had always neglected his family for his poetry. His own profound guilts gnawed at him, his dependence of many years left him fearing the future without her companionship and sup-port. "She could always be present to govern my loneliness with-out making me feel less alone," he had written DeVoto in April. "It is now running into more than a week longer than I was ever away from her since June 1895." In the time of loss he did not trust himself. "I expect to have to go depths below depths in thinking before I catch myself and can say what I want to be while I last. I shall be all right in public, but I can't tell you how I am going to behave when I am alone."[2]

For a time it seemed that he was right about being "all right in public." Once past the illness that made him delegate his wife's cremation to their daughter Lesley, he rallied. The memorial serv-ice at Amherst on April 22 went so well that DeVoto reported it as more like a reunion of old friends than a funeral.[3] When it was over, Frost cleared his future by resigning his Amherst professor-ship, to which he had never paid more than minimal attention, and selling his house back to the college. He got through a painful visit to the Derry farm, where Elinor had wanted her ashes scattered along Hyla Brook, and when he found the farm in the possession of unfeeling strangers, he made the difficult decision, with his children's concurrence, that it was best not to carry out her wish. He came to Bread Loaf in mid-August, direct from Shaftsbury, where he had been staying with his son Carol, and only the ashes of his wife, which he kept in a jar in his room, knew how he behaved when alone.

But shortly most of Bread Loaf knew how he behaved in public.

Hindsight, reviewing Frost's behavior during the year or two following Elinor's death, concludes that during that time, and erratically and at intervals for a good while afterward, he was not quite sane. That is the belief of some who knew him best. Nothing entirely new and aberrant marked his actions. But during the time when he was, as he put it, "living with his dead," he simply gave way with less provocation to the vanity, pettishness, and malice that had always been mingled with greatness in his nature.

Lawrance Thompson's superb biography demonstrates, in a hundred contexts, how much irritable self-love lay beneath the rumpled white thatch and the rumpled clothes, behind the piercing blue eyes, back of the teasing smile. It suited Frost to wear in public the mask of the humorous sage, to speak in jokes and riddles and eclogues, to talk his poetry and poeticize his talk, to probe and ruminate as if artlessly, to touch off, as one admirer put it, "a slow fuse of wit"; and yet he never failed to give the true impression of being deeper than he seemed, deeper than almost anybody else, saner, wiser.

That was the Frost whom the Bread Loaf patrons had always known. In 1938 he came back to them apparently unchanged, except that his stoical bearing and their pity for his loss gave his wit a sharper poignancy and his wisdom the depth of sadness. And yet all his friends knew that he had much of his father's brutality in him, that he tolerated rivals badly, that he was a prima donna who was never content to share the center of the stage. His self-love demanded admiration and demanded it undiluted and unqualified; and when his self-love was wounded he struck back like a child in a tantrum. He would permit his worshipers no other gods, and he had knives in his tongue and thunderbolts in his rages. Louis Untermeyer, who knew him as well as anyone, referred to him privately as Jahweh.

A jealous god. But a god. No one was in his presence for five minutes without feeling his voltage. He enforced the admiration he fed on, and many a person who had been whipped with his wit, and suffered from his jokes that drew blood, put away anger because the man who wounded him was so clearly a great man and a great poet.

Add that he could be cruel to people he loved, and even especially to these. That he could punish family and friends for his own pain. That his malice was at least as notable as his wisdom. That he could speak out of six sides of his mouth at once, and mean everything he said from every side, and not quite mean any of it. That he profoundly understood the human heart, including his own. What he did in petty anger or jealousy or injured vanity he could comprehend with the coldest sort of self-knowledge, and then as often as not hide the knowledge from himself. Better than others did, he knew his own desert places, and sometimes scared himself with them, and sometimes acted as if he were rather proud of them. Public or private, in his poetry or in his personal relations, he looked simple and was in fact a demon of complexity. While she was alive, Elinor Frost had guided and to some extent controlled or concealed the vanity and malice in him. Without her—and with the bosom serpent of her bleak and speechless death devouring him internally—he began to dismay his friends with his petulance. On the night of August 27 he dismayed half of Bread Loaf, and in particular DeVoto, not so much because of what he did as because what he did was so far beneath the greatness in him.

One of the more formal aspects of the Conference was the evening lectures by staff members and visitors. Frost had opened the series with a talk and reading on August 18. He had sat in the Inn parlor with people at his feet, and had autographed books and dispensed authentic wisdom. He had even attended some of the lectures of others, and had followed the crowd over to Treman Cottage afterward, and talked away two or three hours, always at the center of an attentive group; and as often as not he had ended the evening by picking out some awed young writer to walk and talk and count stars with him along the midnight road to Middlebury Gap. More than one Fellow or junior staff member crawled into bed at two or three o'clock after such an expedition, his mind dizzy with the altitudes it had been in and every cell in his body convinced that Robert Frost was the wisest and sanest man alive.

Then, on August 27, Archibald MacLeish came visiting, and that evening read from his poems. Once one of the expatriates, he had gone through a conversion to the notion of poetry as urgent public speech. He had a political intensity and a humanitarian social conscience that were attractive to many who in 1938 had suffered eight years of Depression and were now confronted with Hitler's campaign against the Sudetenland and Czechoslovakia and God knew what more. Most of his hearers at Bread Loaf had read his "sound-track" called *America Was Promises*, most had listened respectfully to his anti-Fascist radio play *The Fall of the City*. He was a friend of most of the staff, an old Bread Loafer, and warmly welcomed. Of all the poets who had been on the mountain that summer, he was the only one who could have been said to rival Frost, though neither he nor his most fanatical admirers would have made any such claim. But without intending to, he dimmed the local sun, and the dimming was less tolerable because Mac-Leish's politics, though definitely opposed to those who said Comrade, seemed to Frost mawkish with New Deal welfare sentiments.

At MacLeish's reading, Frost sat near the back. Early in the proceedings he found some mimeographed notices on a nearby chair and sat rolling and folding them in his hands. Now and again he raised the roll of paper, or an eyebrow, calling the attention of his seat mates to some phrase or image. He seemed to listen with an impartial, if skeptical, judiciousness. About halfway through the reading he leaned over and said in a carrying whisper, "Archie's poems all have the same *tune*." As the reading went on, to the obvious pleasure of the audience, he grew restive. The fumbling and rustling of the papers in his hands became disturbing. Finally MacLeish announced, "You, Andrew Marvell," a tour de force that makes a complete thirty-six-line poem out of a single sentence. It was a favorite. Murmurs of approval, intent receptive faces. The poet began. Then an exclamation, a flurry in the rear of the hall. The reading paused, heads turned. Robert Frost, playing around like an idle, inattentive boy in a classroom, had somehow contrived to strike a match and set fire to his handful of papers and was busy beating them out and waving away the smoke.[4]

Those who knew Frost of old laughed and shook their heads over him. Those who did not know him that well thought his bonfire the comic accident he made it seem. But later, over in Treman, a circle of people gathered around MacLeish and persuaded him to read his new radio play, *Air Raid*. There he was, still on center stage, and there was Frost again in the audience, on the periphery—a thing he could not stand.

In *Air Raid* the announcer, waiting with the inhabitants of a nameless town for the coming of the planes, repeats several times the dry refrain, "We have seen nothing and heard nothing." Some of the people in Treman Cottage that night, not paying much attention or not comprehending, could have made a similar report. One was myself. Another was Charles Curtis, gifted with an enviable capacity for enjoying a party, who went smiling around through the whole evening remarking on how wonderful Bread Loaf was, what good talk, wonderful people, wholehearted good times. But others, including DeVoto, interpreted every rattle of ice in a glass, every cough and murmur, as sight or sound of war.

For Frost was quite deliberately trying to break up the reading. His comments from the floor, at first friendly and wisecracking, became steadily harsher and more barbed. He interrupted, he commented, he took exception. What began as the ordinary give and take of literary conversation turned into a clear intention of frustrating and humiliating Archie MacLeish, and the situation became increasingly painful to those who comprehended it. Once, DeVoto got up and went outside and walked around the house to get over his agitation. When he came back, the inquisition was still going on, MacLeish patiently going ahead, Frost nipping and snapping around his heels, and now and then sinking his teeth in with a savage quick bite that looked playful and was not. People sat where they had been trapped, and looked into their drained glasses and did not quite dare look around.

Eventually DeVoto, who more or less agreed with Frost's opinion of the play, but who completely sympathized with MacLeish, being systematically humiliated by a man he enormously respected and would not reply to, said something. No one who was there seems to remember exactly what he said something like "For God's sake, Robert, let him read!" Hardly more than that— not enough to catch the attention of the ones like Charles Curtis who were enjoying the literary evening. But a rebuke, and one did not rebuke Jahweh.[5]

It does not appear that Frost replied at once, or directly. But shortly he elected to take offense at something—DeVoto remembered it as his taking personally a derogatory remark that was meant for Stephen Spender. He said something savage, got up and went out on the arm of the cheerfully oblivious Charles Curtis. The reading went on, lamely but with relief, to its end, and people escaped to their rooms.

But the incident was not over. Frost apparently steamed all night with fury, envy, shame, whatever it was that fueled his agitation. The first thing in the morning, he summoned Herschel Brickell and asked to be driven over to Concord Corners, a hundred miles to the east, near the New Hampshire line, where he had recently bought a house in which his daughter Irma was living with her family. Brickell drove him over, left him there, and returned to a Bread Loaf buzzing with rumors and replays of the night before. It was said that, either after he left Treman Cottage with Curtis, or on the way over to Concord Corners, Frost had deliberately *eaten* a cigarette. Why? To make himself sick and pitiable? To punish himself for his childish ill temper? It was anybody's guess. By the following morning, rumor had something else to dissect and distort. Frost had telephoned Brickell to come and get him. Brickell did. It seemed that Irma had infuriated her father by putting him in a bedroom that had no way in or out except through the bedroom of her and her husband, and had told him that she would keep him but would receive none of his friends. To a man who had recently lost his wife, who felt the spoken and unspoken blame of his children, who blamed himself and had just made an unmannerly fool of himself, there was no escape except from the intolerable into the humiliating. He came back to Bread Loaf and the subdued greetings of his friends. Maybe it was on the way back that he ate the cigarette—by this time, rumor and the distortions of memory have made nearly everything obscure.[6]

An Incident, one of those Bread Loaf incidents common enough toward the end of the session, when propinquity and intense stimulation and fatigue combined to produce explosions of temperament. It didn't actually amount to much. But Noah had appeared drunk and naked before his sons, and one of the sons took it very seriously indeed. The only thing worse than being a parent, DeVoto used to say, is being a child.

Whatever form it took, a clash between those two was inevitable. They were both strong personalities, both prima donnas, both touchy. No such enthusiastic friendship as had developed between them in Florida in 1936 could possibly have lasted unchanged. Some people did worship Robert Frost all their lives, but they were more submissive people than Bernard DeVoto. Sooner or later Frost was bound to scoff at DeVoto's desperate dependence on psychoanalysis, thinking it a failure of common sense and self-reliance. Sooner or later DeVoto was sure to resent what he felt was Frost's malice, whether aimed at him or whether expressed in sly diminishments of other poets, or in the mocking anti-Semitic remarks he consistently made to Louis Untermeyer, or in an outrageous copperheadism in politics that went beyond DeVoto's toleration. And sooner or later DeVoto's most central admiration, his conviction that Frost demonstrated the highest poetry to be compatible with complete sanity, was bound to encounter one of Frost's irrational and petulant outbursts, and be disillusioned. Nothing that ever happened between them diminished DeVoto's opinion of the poetry; it was the man who shrank. Instead of confirming his Miltonic belief that a man who would write a great poem must first himself be a great poem, the incident in Treman brought DeVoto to the distasteful notion advanced by Oscar Wilde: the fact that a man is a poisoner has nothing to do with his prose. That is an altogether less comforting idea.

There were more than temperamental causes for friction, too. DeVoto's closest friends were the Morrisons. Together they had shaped and steered the Conference, they were rack and pinion in the Bread Loaf machinery. Now Frost's bereavement and his search for some anchor to replace Elinor had thrown him upon the Morrisons, especially upon Kay, who shortly after the Conference agreed to act as his secretary, and DeVoto felt that the responsibility Frost enforced upon them wedged them away from him. He was sensitive to apparent slights; he was always detecting in others the symptoms of cooling friendship. It is possible, also, that he had begun to feel—as he certainly felt later—that Frost had used him in the battle against the leftist critics, and that the hardening of the "conspiracy" which had shut him out of Harvard and installed Granville Hicks in Adams House was in some sense Frost's fault. And it is further possible that his agitation and his rebuke were caused by sincere generosity of spirit. He was too magnanimous himself to sit quiet while the man he worshiped picked on a man he liked.

That is all speculation. But the rift was not, in DeVoto's mind, a minor or temporary one, for according to Thompson he repeated his rebuke when they shook hands at the end of the Bread Loaf session. "You're a good poet, Robert," Thompson reports him as saying, "but you're a bad man.[7]

Writing about all this to Kate Sterne a few days afterward,[8] DeVoto guessed that the demon in Frost had always been controlled by Elinor, and that no one now, not even Kay Morrison, who handled him better than anyone, could fully control it. He admitted that the whole thing was shattering to him, for he had once thought Frost living proof that genius could be sane. He had been living in a blind migraine ever since that night in Treman. There would be hell to pay—hurt feelings, bruised sensibilities. Things would never be again as they once were.

But if DeVoto thought of the break as final, Frost evidently did not. Within a week he got the DeVotos to go over to Concord Corners with him to look at houses. They had been trying for two years to buy a place in Vermont. Here was a whole village for

sale. They could take their pick. They could get a few friends to
buy in with them; the village could be made over into a literary
summer colony, a Bread Loaf closer to the heart's desire. The outburst on the mountain might never have happened. Frost showed
them around with the greatest friendliness, he urged Concord
Corners upon them with eloquence, he estimated the authentic
age of his own house by the pine wainscot, one single board four
feet wide. In New England there had not been such a tree as
would make that board for a hundred and fifty years.

But DeVoto was dubious. He and Avis had thought Peacham
too far north to be convenient, and Concord Corners was farther
yet, and not half so attractive. It was a dying village—no real
village at all, only a cluster of survivors, poor whites, a Vermont
Tobacco Road. And he did not now trust Frost, in whom he felt
an ill-concealed desire to bind them to his future and use them.
That came out, Avis says, before they parted in St. Johnsbury. He
offered to buy the DeVotos a house in Cambridge if they would
maintain a room or two for the old poet when loneliness got too
much for him, or when he needed a moment to reflect.[9]

A month earlier, the request would have touched them, would
have seemed a privilege of friendship. In September it found them
suspicious, reluctant, in the end unwilling. They told him no, and
returned to Walpole, where the celebrated 1938 hurricane ma-
rooned them for three days. On September 23, after the flooded
Connecticut had receded and the roads somewhat cleared, they
made their delayed way across lots and down back roads through
the wreckage of century-old elms—as if New England itself had
thrown a tantrum—to the house which, whatever its limitations, at least gave them sovereignty in their own place. Somewhat
later, Kay Morrison found Frost an apartment on Mount Vernon
Street in Boston, opposite Louisburg Square.

It is probable that Frost's effort to ally them with him, either in
Concord Corners or in Cambridge, was his way of making amends
for his behavior at Bread Loaf, a way of indicating that he did
not desire a break in their friendship, a way in fact of suggesting
how real was his need of friends. Their evasion of his offers may
have given him the idea that the trouble was more serious than he
had thought, for in October, from Columbus, Ohio, he wrote
DeVoto a letter that returned them to the moment of their parting
after Bread Loaf, the moment of DeVoto's reproachful, "You're a
good poet, Robert, but you're a bad man." In one sense the letter
was an apology, in another an effort to joke away their difference,
in still another a suggestion—or a warning—that he must be taken

as he was, with all his faults about him. Like the birthmark on Hawthorne's Georgiana, his faults were too entangled in the sources of his life to be tampered with. The letter *asserted* Frost's badness, but whether as joke or brag, or even a sham demand for pity for what the loss of Elinor had done to him, only Frost himself could have told:

. . . it wouldn't be fair to my flesh and temper to say that I am always tiresomely the same frost I was when winter came on last year. You must have marked changes coming over me this summer. Who cares whether they were for the worse or not. You may as a serious student of my works. But Avis and I don't give a sigh. One of the greatest changes my nature has undergone is of record in To Earthward and indeed elsewhere for the discerning. In my school days I simply could not go on and do the best I could with a copy book I had once blotted. I began life wanting perfection and determined to have it. I got so I ceased to expect it and could do without it. Now I find I actually crave the flaws of human handiwork. I gloat over imperfection. Look out for me. You as critic and psychoanalyst [observe the half-hidden mockery] will know how to do that. Nevertheless I'm telling you something in a self conscious moment that may throw light on every page of my writing for what it is worth. I mean I am a bad bad man

But yours R.F.[10]

V

"PERIODIC ASSISTANCE FROM MR. JOHN AUGUST"

1 · Mostly Waste Motion

To move from the *Saturday Review* office into 98 Widener Library was to go underground. Here was no public place crowded with people making, dispensing, and resisting public opinion. It was a scholar's cell deep in the stacks, as remote as a Pharaoh's tomb in the heart of a pyramid. The furnishings were a desk, a type-writer, a couple of chairs, bookshelves, and three steel filing cabinets. The people who worked in it, besides DeVoto, were Rosamond Chapman, the perfect research assistant happily re-gained, and Henry Reck, rescued from an unproductive two years at the Divinity School.

They were in the office a good deal more than DeVoto himself was, for not even the *Saturday Review* had cured him of working at home; one of the complaints against him had been that he was not around the office enough. But he raided Widener's rich col-lection of western Americana, which was one of the attractions that had brought him back to Cambridge in 1927 and brought him back again now. As voraciously as Wolfe's Young Faustus, in *Of Time and the River* (a novel DeVoto deplored), he set out to read his way through it. Single volumes and whole sets, Park-man's histories and Mormon diaries, British travelers, the memoirs of mule skinners and traders and Mexican War officers and pioneer wives, biographies of generals and religious leaders,

Dickens and Mrs. Trollope and George Frederick Ruxton, *Wah-To-Yah* and Ashley and Jed Smith and *The Commerce of the Prairies*, Susan Magoffin and Tamsen Donner, Thoreau and Alcott and Brownson, Thwaites's *Western Travels* and *The Jesuit Relations*, the papers of James K. Polk and *The Journal History of the Mormon Church*—he carried out and read and digested and returned. He wanted everything that had occurred in, or foreshadowed, or resulted from, or in any way cast light upon, the year 1846, which was going to be the focus of his many-times-put-off book on the frontier.

"The apparent diversity of my interests," he had written to Kenneth Murdock in February, when there was still hope of a Harvard appointment, "is in fact a fully worked out set of objectives which support one another."[1] Now, relieved of all obligations except scholarship and subsistence, he expected to devote a good part of his enormous capacity for work to the historical study that had had only fitful attention since *Mark Twain's America*. To be sure, he had to do a monthly Easy Chair. To be sure, his scholarship would be split between the frontier book and the Mark Twain manuscripts. To be sure, he still took on reviews and other literary jobs. But to one who had characteristically led a most frantic and disunited literary life, it seemed he had come into the cool quiet of woods after a run across a hot meadow.

Both controversy and popular fiction he put aside. The *Collier's* serial *Troubled Star*[2] had temporarily solved his financial problems. There was no need to write slick stories about young love in the city, young love at summer resorts, or young love in college, with plots that would offend no one by their relation to life, and no more sex than could be consummated by implication offstage, and with a touch of nakedness somewhere to give the illustrator a chance. The more he knew about those salable formulas the less he wanted to write them, at least in small and relatively unprofitable pieces. A John August serial every year or so would do it. He relaxed upon opulence, bought a new Buick and an expensive record player and piles of records, established Gordon in Shady Hill School, cobbled up a darkroom and renewed his vows to photography, and left open the door of his house (which he disliked and called a hencoop) for the friends who from Mason Street and Francis Avenue, from Lincoln and Concord, from the North Shore, from over on Chestnut Street and Joy Street and Louisburg Square, found their way quickly back to the old De-Voto Academy.[3]

He had no gift for living small or living dull. When he came out of his study he liked friends around him, and he liked the Cambridge gossip as a grayling likes fast water. It was his drama, his delight, his anxiety, his amusement, his consolation. It brought him confirmation of his belief that Harvard, a carbuncle of cabals and cliques, was deteriorating. Having had the chance to get both Frost and MacLeish (and for that matter DeVoto), it had fumbled them away. It was torn by dissension over the Walsh-Sweezy firings and their consequences. It backbit and conspired. A kind friend informed DeVoto that Murdock and Miller, supposedly his friends, had actually engineered his departure from Harvard and prevented his return. As he wrote Kate Sterne, you didn't believe rumors like that, but they gave you an idea of what blew around in the Cambridge air.

MacLeish's *Air Raid*, which had caused all the trouble at Bread Loaf, was broadcast and stimulated a lot of cocktail-hour talk. Hans Zinsser turned out to have leukemia, and it broke your heart to see how considerate and gentle he had become. And Frost was coming home from his lecture tour, and DeVoto would bet a month's earnings that the attempt to anneal the DeVotos to him would not be remitted, that the notion of a Frost biography by DeVoto was going to be renewed, and that the first step would be to have DeVoto in some way destroy Robert Newdick, the authorized biographer at Ohio State University, with whom Frost had become dissatisfied.[4]

The Cambridge talk came through his house and was passed on to Kate Sterne, who, in her sixth year of imprisonment, reduced to eighty-five pounds, made use of it to compensate for a bitter birthday and a desolate Christmas and a hopeless New Year's. She lived in Cambridge, through DeVoto's letters, as surely as he did, and she shared the uneasy fluctuations of his relationship with Frost. After one five-hour evening with the poet, DeVoto wondered, not for the first time, if he was quite sane. For he confided in DeVoto more than in anyone, it seemed, and then hated him for it. He kept making offers equivalent to that house in Cambridge—the latest was an invitation to go to Laramie, Wyoming, with him in April—that DeVoto could not help seeing as subtle traps. He thought that Frost had solved his ambivalence, the clash of liking and rejection in himself, by concluding that DeVoto's fiction was no good, and hence no threat, but that his essays were the best of their time, and hence effective for fighting Frost's battles or writing his biography.[5]

From the complication of complexity trying to psychoanalyze complexity, the wise biographer had better keep aloof. No formula can explain the emotional relationship between those two; any explanation would be too simple. But the biographer may note a fact or two, if only to express DeVoto's own explanation of himself.

When Florian DeVoto died, on September 30, 1935, after a life of persistent and as if deliberate failure, DeVoto had written to Kate Sterne about the mixed feelings induced in a son by the death of his father. From early in his career he had mythologized his pilgrimage eastward as a quest or trial, a journey designed to let him prove himself in the intellectual East from which his father had dropped out. He had proved himself after a fashion, and grown by the proving; but when his father died the son had a qualm of guilt for knowing himself the better man.

And meantime he had adopted other fathers, looking for one with the authority he craved and without the weaknesses visible in Florian DeVoto. L. J. Henderson, Mark Twain, Frost, had all played that role. Now, in the fall of 1938, stimulated by Frost's return and by the renewal of their emotional struggle for dominance, DeVoto was swiftly chased out of historical scholarship and back to the manuscript of *Mountain Time*. He sent the first fifty pages of it to Kate Sterne just after Christmas, with the note that it was "about the death of the Old Man" as much as anything.[6]

The oblique glance at Frost was not accidental; and it expressed a determination rather than a fact. He had already told Kate that Frost was bent upon dominating him, that anyone he could not dominate he tried to break, and that DeVoto always felt that he was battling for his identity when he was with Frost. The Old Man was not really dead. He was very much alive, and must be resisted. In that way he was different from the other surrogate fathers. Mark Twain had been primarily a challenging example—Henry Reck reports a time when DeVoto came out of a spell of analysis in Lincoln feeling relaxed and writing better "now that I'm no longer trying to be Mark Twain."[7] And L. J. Henderson, as dominant and impressive intellectually as anyone in DeVoto's experience, had so many preposterous prejudices that DeVoto ended by feeling protective about him. Frost was something else. The novel that DeVoto now tried to write involved him in devious and shape-shifting ways. It was, he told Kate, "markedly obsessional" and "full of symbols straight out of my Id."[8]

Writing to Kate Sterne later, after the intimate excitement of creation had subsided, DeVoto wished that some good psychologist with literary taste, maybe Lawrence Kubie, would sometime analyze a novel from its first conception to its final typescript. "It would be something to follow ma and pa through all those dissolves, yes, and Mattie Guernsey too, and the Brewer's Daughter, and Skinny. . . ."[9] Fiction, like psychosis itself, was for him a psychological adaptation, "a means whereby its author adjusts the world as he must feel about it to the world as he is forced to think about it."[10] Its sources were the sources of dreams, its methods were the metaphor and metonymy and synecdoche of dreams. What one heard in art and literature was the tolling of bells from the sea-sunk Lyonesse of the soul.

That theory of fiction DeVoto had been elaborating and polishing ever since he left the eleven installments of "English 37" for George Stevens to run during the summer of 1937. He was publishing essays that dealt with it during the fall of 1938, and his interest had been immensely stimulated by the discovery of the "Great Dark" manuscripts among the Mark Twain papers. At exactly the time when he was beginning to rework *Mountain Time*, during the fall of 1938, DeVoto was discussing these manuscripts avidly with his former analyst William Barrett, and was developing the hypothesis that the several broken fragments of those manuscripts, with their false starts and their shifting images of desolation, were Mark Twain's attempt to write his way out of despair following the collapse of his fortunes, the epilepsy of his daughter Jean, the invalidism of his wife, and the death of his favorite daughter, Susy.[11] They were the attempt, that is, to make despair itself serve a saving adaptation, and in the end, the theory went, they came to a late, autumnal consummation in *The Mysterious Stranger*. There is no reason to examine the theory or the manuscripts here, except to note that they were on DeVoto's desk while he "fought for his identity" with Frost, and very much on his mind as he tried to work his own emotional entanglements into the order and safety of art.

He abused Van Wyck Brooks for attempting to psychoanalyze Mark Twain, and he himself should not be subjected to the analysis of amateurs. The excuse here is that one is taking the analysis from the subject's own mouth. He was electrically aware of the complicated things he was braiding or unbraiding—aware not in the way of an analyst but in the way of a writer. (He said a writer who tried to write like an analyst was like a man carrying his bicycle on his back.) DeVoto was trying to ride it. With a seriousness that, always quick with the memory of his own nervous troubles, was never far from desperation, he was struggling with "what happens in the caverns of the soul." The irrational had its profound importance in human experience, and must be coped with somehow. Freud, Pareto, and his struggle with neurotic dread had taught him that. But Pareto's lesson was cold, Freud's infused with emotion. "There is a noble and tragic poetry in his vision of man's journey deathward from childhood, beset by terrors whose shape and import are disguised from him, striving to discipline a primitive inheritance of delusion and rebellion into a livable accord with reality, striving to establish mastery over disruptive instincts, striving to achieve a social adaptation of anarchic drives."[12] And, he might have added, striving to reconcile respect for a father with the father's weaknessess, love for a father with the father's harshness, imitation of a father with the impulse of rebellion.

Art, he said, is man determined to die sane. In *Mountain Time*, picked up again during his trouble with Frost, DeVoto was wrestling with his paternal angel, or believed he was, as surely as Mark Twain in the Great Dark manuscripts had been wrestling with despair.

And like the Mark Twain of his theory, he was defeated, he couldn't write it. The novel had balked him during the summer of 1936 and it balked him again, though he was some time in admitting failure. On January 20, 1939, with sixty thousand words written, he was cautiously optimistic. A month later, offering to send the completed Part I to Kate Sterne if she wanted to see it, he was listless and halfhearted. By the end of March he had given it up. Though all his novels had been, below the literary camouflage, intensely personal, this one was too close to his obsessive and affectional life. Its wires were tangled, it shorted out.

A wasted six months. Within a short time it developed that the whole year had been wasted, except for the efforts of John August. On March 10 DeVoto had taken to Charles Lark the completed manuscript of *Letters from the Earth*, consisting of the manuscript by that name plus the related "Papers of the Adam Family" and "Letter to the Earth," plus a second section of miscellaneous essays including the Great Dark fragments. Paine had withheld much of this material from publication, because it continued Mark Twain's quarrel with the Christian God or expressed unflattering opinions of certain sects and public figures. Shortly it turned out that Clara Gabrilowitsch agreed with Paine. She thought her father might be accused of anti-Semitism on the strength of some passages, and she thought it unfair to his memory to renew, in times of crisis, that quarrel with God. She particularly wanted the essay "Letters from the Earth" deleted.

DeVoto protested that to remove that essay would gut the book.

Clara held firm. Under pressure from Harper's, DeVoto agreed to some small deletions, but he would not agree to eliminate "Letters from the Earth."[13] By May 14 it was clear that Harper's would not back him against Clara, and *Letters from the Earth* was as dead as *Mountain Time*. To cap his disgust, in the midst of the argument Mrs. Gabrilowitsch discovered in her house a box containing more than six thousand pages of additional Mark Twain papers and manuscripts, so that not even the careful cataloguing of Rosy Chapman and Henry Reck would stand. The entire body of papers would have to be reorganized and reindexed to include the new find.

From March until well into July DeVoto was in New York much of the time, trying to straighten out the difficulties. Frustrated, angry, living at the Harvard Club and lunching at the Century, hating the city and the city's heat, walking as empty and artificial as any leashed greyhound on the streets he did not respond to, killing evenings at the World's Fair, he felt that New York had released him only to imprison him again. His fiction was aborted and his scholarship had come to nothing.

Nothing but irritations and humiliations attended his stay. For a good while, ever since he had carefully split his personality, he had written no popular fiction under his own name, preferring to let John August take the onus. Now *Cosmopolitan* announced that it was finally publishing a story it had bought from him years before, and it would appear signed "Bernard DeVoto," as if DeVoto valued it or didn't care what he signed his name to.[14] Then Eugene Saxton dropped him from the committee of judges for the Harper Nobel Prize because he had said in an Easy Chair that no one would ever write a good novel about the Mormons, and now it appeared that Vardis Fisher's *Children of God* was a strong contender for the prize.[15] DeVoto grumbled that no matter what he had said in print, he could be as objective about a Mormon novel as the next man, and was a hell of a sight better qualified to read it than most. But Saxton, afraid of an appearance of prejudgment, did not reinstate him. Then Allan Nevins published in *Gateway to History* a story about the biographer of John Reed who had suppressed some letters Reed had written from Russia shortly before his death expressing disillusionment in the Revolution. Nevins in a footnote specifically said he did not refer to Hicks and Stuart's *John Reed*, but there was no other biographer he could have referred to, and he had cited the story as an example of intellectual dishonesty. Granville Hicks, sleuthing around, got a hint that the story had come from DeVoto, as indeed it had—or rather, it had come from one of the Harvard historians and DeVoto had told it at a cocktail party. Challenged to produce proof, he could not do so, nor would he pass the buck back to the story's source. So he ate crow in the *New Republic,* a meal that did not improve his mood, for it was the second time he had lost to Hicks within the year.[16]

Nevertheless, since the menu seemed to be crow, he took a second helping. He reviewed Fisher's *Children of God* for the *Saturday Review* and praised it as the good novel he had said would never be written about the Mormons.

After that, he wrote Kate Sterne a little grimly, he was about ready to get back to Cambridge and return to the offensive.

2 · Certain Satisfactions

Grumpy, irritable with the sense of lost effort and lost time, damning the city of New York and the Mark Twain Company, he returned to Cambridge on July 13 determined to work on the volume of Mark Twain autobiography, write an introduction to the Limited Editions Club *Tom Sawyer,* and really settle into the frontier book. But his mouth was still tainted with New York, and his mind was sore. In Cambridge, hot and nearly deserted, no one but him seemed to be doing any work. Avis was pregnant, expenses went on, the money from *Troubled Star* was dwindling, John August would soon have to be called on again. But first a little interlude, some summer puttering, the pretense of life without pressures, a time to drink beer with Hillyer and play fist ball and badminton with George Stout of the Fogg Museum.[1]

Almost by accident, in a mood of irony, he found himself a consumers' advocate.

Back during his editorship of the *Saturday Review,* Kate Sterne's difficulties with books too heavy for her frail strength had led him into a brief campaign for small, light volumes fitted to people's hands and pockets.[2] He was a long way, in 1937, from bringing on the paperback revolution; that would await the end of a war that had not yet begun. In the end he solved Kate's problem not by reforming publishing practices, but by sending her the unbound sheets of books that came in for review.

Nevertheless, their correspondence about books and binding led them into the questioning of other industrial products. Her leaky and undependable fountain pen brought from him the confession that he himself had never found one that suited him—he used a penholder and the Estabrook ⅍313 nib, which he bought by the gross. From that repudiation he was led on into consumer skepticism over a broad front, and in April 1939 his Easy Chair, "The Paring Knife at the Crossroads,"³ had aired some of the findings. Of standard typewriters, he said, he had had many models of many makes and had never had a bad one. Of portables, he had had as many of as many makes, and never had a good one. What was the matter with the most industrialized economy in the world, the inventor of the system of mass production with interchangeable parts, that it couldn't build a decent portable tyepwriter? Fountain pens, as aforesaid, were universally worthless, as were mechanical pencils. Plumbing fixtures were reasonably dependable, but the water closet had not had its valve system improved in a hundred years. Household hardware was bad and getting worse, quality going down with price. Automobiles, on the other hand, were better built than almost anything Americans used. Automobile manufacturers could make a door handle that did not come off, electric switches that did not wear out. Why couldn't the building trades? As for kitchen gadgets, those were cynically bad. Stainless-steel knives wouldn't take or hold an edge, can openers wouldn't open cans, labor-saving devices created rather than saved labor, or were so flimsy they came apart in the hands. In the tradition of liberal economics, he assumed that makers of shoddy goods would eventually be caught up with, but meantime he had a fear that Harry Hopkins might enter the knife factory and put it under federal controls before the factory got around to improving its product.

Through the whole spring and summer, mail kept coming in in response to that complaint. The housewife elected him her champion by acclamation.

Cheered on from all sides, DeVoto returned to the subject in July. The American housewife was not happy with the products offered her, and the only response of manufacturers seemed to be the soothing syrup of public relations. But you did not improve a bad can opener by painting the handle green or hiring a new advertising man, and you did not make up for a knife that would not cut by pointing out how shiny it was and how expensive chromium was. There shouldn't *be* any chromium in a knife—knives were for cutting, not shining. What went for gadgets went for many foods, especially processed cheese, "unfit even to bait mice with." It looked and tasted like laundry soap, but was no good for washing clothes. Presliced bread had the women hunting for little bakeries where they could get an honest, unadulterated, unlaborsaving loaf. He hoped they would go on hunting, and leave food processors to consume their own products.

He enjoyed that foray. It was invigorating, like his old forays against the literary, but the target was new and there was a strong intimation of a supportive public. Also, the response amused him. Kraft-Phenix Cheese Company wrote in in great pain and some rage; there were mutterings about a suit. Knife manufacturers sent him samples, and wistfully explained that too little chrome left a supposedly stainless knife subject to stain, and too much made it difficult—though not impossible, they said—to sharpen. They instructed him in sharpening techniques, which he tested and found inadequate.[4]

Four years in the Easy Chair, a post he had taken with some unwillingness, had proved in fact to be a satisfying experience, and had led him to develop public attitudes on several favorite themes. When he had been autobiographizing for Mattingly in 1936, he had told Kate Sterne, with surprise, that his first Easy Chairs were written for the *Harvard Graduates' Magazine*. It was a form ideally suited to him; its very brevity made his commentary pungent and pointed; its continuity allowed him to return over and over to a subject that proved important. His defense of the consumer was not going to end with a discussion of kitchen knives and processed cheese, nor was his attack on censorship going to stop with a slap on the wrist of Boston booksellers and the Watch and Ward Society. He would continue to praise science, fact, and the inductive method, continue to object to a priori thinking and the literary fallacy, continue to celebrate American history and the democratic gospels, continue to thump ignorance, stupidity, and the venality of public officials, continue to appoint himself supervisor over the self-appointed. His habits of mind would change no more than his favorite subject matters, and he would lay himself open, more than once, by his vehemence. As his student and friend Arthur Schlesinger, Jr., told him, he often by a single overstatement, the sort of thing his friends characteristically overlooked or discounted, gave an enemy the handle by which he was able to win or draw a debate without ever actually refuting DeVoto's solider arguments.

But that habit, like Robert Frost's "badness," was not to be disentangled from his vigor and his common sense. His four years in the Easy Chair had given him a national following—while it was making him some enemies. Even in 1939 he was probably better known through those monthly essays than by all his fiction, both slick and serious, and all his historical work up to that time. His emotional life had failed to find an adequate artistic transformation, but his intellectual life had discovered both a forum and an effective form.

With the new year, about to become a father for the second time and ready to take to his bed with couvade, he consulted his financial necessities and recalled John August from retirement. The child, a second boy, whom they named Mark Bernard (if it had been a girl, DeVoto had half planned to name it Katherine, for Kate Sterne), was born on January 11. For the next two months, the serial went forward through a confusion of nurses, illnesses, postparturitive transfusions, and efforts to spare Gordon the pains of sibling rivalry. For the moment, Frost was not a trouble to DeVoto's mind: he was in the hospital "resting on his laurels," as he said, after a fistula operation that DeVoto could not help describing as piles. It was a good, distracted, domestic time, toward the end of which he wrote to Kate Sterne in a mood of humility and gratitude, "It is hard to realize that we know so many people who so honestly wish us well."[5]

In literary ways, too, his second year away from the *Saturday Review* was far more satisfying than his first. The Limited Editions Club *Tom Sawyer*, with illustrations by Thomas Hart Benton, came off the press in time to be sent to Kate Sterne for Christmas.[6] Rosy Chapman was putting together Easy Chairs and *Saturday Review* pieces for a second volume of essays, for which Kate would shortly suggest the title *Minority Report*.[7] The autobiographical manuscripts that they were calling *Mark Twain in Eruption* would—Harper's and Clara Gabrilowitsch consenting—be another book.[8] John August's newest subsidy, *Rain Before Seven,* was within a few installments of its end.[9] The scholar, the publicist, and the hack would all be represented in print in 1940. In March, DeVoto was scheduled to deliver the William Vaughn Moody Lecture at the University of Chicago, and that discussion of the Great Dark manuscripts, together with the introductions to *Tom Sawyer* and *Huckleberry Finn,* would eventually make still another book, *Mark Twain at Work.*[10]

Satisfactions. Before he left Cambridge for Chicago he had two others, both of a soul-warming kind.

One was the publication of "Anabasis in Buckskin,"[11] the story of the march of the 1st Missouri Volunteers, under Kearny and Doniphan, in the Mexican War. It was a preview of the frontier book, an episode from the year 1846, and the enthusiasm of his historian friends was immediate. For gusto, narrative drive, evocativeness, and the sense of participation, it was a kind of history all too few historians were equipped to write. The approval of Morison, Merk, and others convinced him that now, finally, he should make the last big effort and write the whole book about 1846.

The second satisfaction, expressed in the Easy Chair of the same issue,[12] was of a more personal kind. The Hitler-Stalin pact had been a blow that no American Communist could take without reeling; some of the more idealistic could not take it at all. A general confusion, a caving-in of the party line, tension among the professors of the Left, were followed by a series of recantations, notable among which was that of Granville Hicks, ex-editor of the *New Masses*, author of a Marxist interpretation of American literature, and once Fellow of United States History at Harvard. The breast-beating and the *mea culpas*, the mourner's bench and the repentant tears (the metaphors were inevitable for one raised, as DeVoto had been, on the pentecostal faiths) were grimly amusing to those who had consistently fought the Marxists and resisted their ideas. But amid the general satisfaction that they had at last seen the light, there was an odd tendency to honor the recanters, and on the part of the recanters themselves an assumption of special virtue for having been through the fire and having emerged scarred but safe into democratic territory. That somewhat smug stance infuriated DeVoto more than militant Marxism ever had. Let there be rejoicing in Heaven over the sinner saved, yes. But that did not qualify the sinner to put on airs.

When, he asked, had these converts begun to be wrong? And when had those who had been saying for years exactly what these penitents were saying now begun to be right? Did the Hitler-Stalin pact make the ex-Reds wrong, or hadn't they been wrong all along, supporting "a brave and wholly literary rebellion on inherited incomes"? Where did they acquire the right to be listened to with special attention? What gave them their current authority? Their previous gullibility and capacity for making intellectual mistakes? It would make more sense to listen to people who had never had to hit the sawdust trail, who had never *been* gullible. And though the psychic homelessness of these people was often pathetic, and shattered faith was nothing to laugh at, yet it had to be remembered that many of these same people who had just lost Communism had previously suffered the loss of Art, and before that of God. He suggested unfeelingly that for their next devotion they take to drink, for "Drink may make you an involuntary drunkard but it won't make you a voluntary damned fool."

On that note he went off to Chicago. When he came back he swiftly finished the serial, got *Mark Twain in Eruption* off to Harper's and Lark—and, astonishingly, had it promptly approved—and completed the last little jobs. On May 19 he climbed into his Buick along with Arthur Schlesinger, Jr., and started for a motor trip through the West, which he had not seen since the summer of 1925.

3 · *America Revisited*

His immediate purpose was historical research, a refreshment of his somewhat faded familiarity with the West at large and a personal look at the Santa Fe Trail, along which so many of the events of 1846 had moved, and which he had not previously seen. But it was no serene scholarly journey, for Germany had invaded the Low Countries only nine days before the two left Cambridge, and as they drove West the car radio reported successive, stunning disasters: the fall of Rotterdam, the fall of Brussels, the advance of the panzers to the Channel, the desperate evacuation from Dunkerque, the capture of Paris, the fall of France, the first flurries of the Battle of Britain. Tracing the history of the small, almost lighthearted war of 1846, DeVoto kept hearing like the strokes of doom the defeats of a war that might end civilization.

In the terminology of the 1960s, he would have been called a hawk; he had been convinced it was America's war since the invasion of Poland, or before. He offended St. Louis newspapermen by crying fire into their untroubled midwestern isolation. On May 16 he and Schlesinger stopped outside of Trinidad, Colorado, to listen to Franklin D. Roosevelt on the car radio, with a group of silent Hispanos leaning to listen too, and heard the President ask for a preparedness program to cost two and a half billions, and agreed that that settled it: sooner or later we would be in.

It was hard for him to stay with the functions of his trip; the 1918 patriot in him kept urging him to go back and enlist in something. But he stuck, partly because Avis on the telephone said he would be a fool not to, and when he was through with Santa Fe (it was not *his* West, and he felt no affinity for it, however well he knew its history) she and Gordon joined him in Ogden, having left the baby on Coolidge Hill Road with a trained nurse. They had a queer, half-lyrical, half-fearful vacation in Jackson

Hole, struggling with bad radio reception to get the reports that harrowed up their souls, before they drove back through Montana and the northern Plains, on along the shore of Lake Superior and down the St. Lawrence into Quebec, and thence, through New England, home. In the next months, according to his habit of making Easy Chairs out of what happened around him, DeVoto wrote four of them about the western trip, plus a full-length *Harper's* article.[1] Representing as they do both reiterations and reappraisals, they are worth a look.

Anxiety had made a patriot of him; going home after long absence had kindled both nostalgia and the perception of change. He found it a better West than he had known. Perhaps remembering MacLeish's *Air Raid*, and certainly oppressed by the war news, he was almost offended by how *safe* the continental interior felt, how snug and secure behind its lawns and banks of flowers, how hopeful in the midst of the New Deal's windbreaks and reservoirs. There were better schools than he remembered. The population was relaxed and good-humored, and offered the traveling historians not a single instance of discourtesy or rudeness. The pioneering that he had honored in his grandfather Dye had gone farther, there was noticeable progress away from barbarism and vulgarity toward "clean and garnished towns." The earlier and more commonplace war of 1846 had won it, American effort had improved it. Now, how much of hard-won America would have to be sacrificed in order to preserve the rest? One thing was certain: Whatever of America could be saved was worth fighting for.

Crisis, plus nostalgia, plus perhaps a degree of wishful thinking, made him deny in these Easy Chairs much that he had previously said about the West. Thus in the bars that had replaced the saloons of an earlier time he found barmaids of a YWCA rectitude who worked trigonometry problems or read Thornton Wilder in their off minutes. He found town matrons dropping in for a beer, and turning loose their toddlers to play among the tables as in an Old World ordinary, and he reassured America that it need not fear any resurgence of Prohibition from the prairies. He found foods better and tastier than he remembered them, the salad had spread, domestic-science courses had taught a lot of girls about nutrition. He inspected with interest the new caravanserais, the motel strips, whose food he found calamitous, and he recommended instead the corner drugstore of any town, which at least understood how to make a sandwich. He dismissed the folklore that said any truck stop was a place where the food could be depended on. He praised the roads and the highway commissions in general, and the Michigan roadsides and the Montana historical markers in particular. He found the western drivers fast and dangerous, thereby demonstrating that in fifteen years he had ceased to be a Westerner and had lost his casualness about speed and distance. He found roadside garagemen skillful but of dubious morality, and he praised the American automobile and damned the automobile tire, which wore out after sixty-five hundred miles. He warned the Middle West about its smugness and isolationism. He thought it was calm out of hysterical panic, whereas it was probably demonstrating something he had long believed in, sometimes denounced, and occasionally praised: the continental mind. It did not listen as De-Voto went through crying that its house was on fire and its children would burn, it did not believe him when he said that the bombs falling on Dover were destroying its house, its future, its children's school, its peace of mind. Sleep in times like these, cried the Easy Chair, is death. All that exhortation, replied the Middle West editorially and by letter, is hysteria.

But on one issue DeVoto and the Middle West met with a gladness that had not always marked their contacts. In November 1940, *Harper's* published the culminating report of his western trip, the essay called "Main Street Twenty Years After." In it he said what the Middle West had always believed, or wanted to believe, about itself. He reported again the clean, flowery towns with self-respecting houses and wide lawns. He said that in Great Bend, Kansas, there were now no farmers, or at least no farmers' wives, according to the specifications standard among literary people. No yokels, no frumps, no drabs. Farmers' wives in Great Bend looked like the club women of Great Bend, who in turn looked like the women you saw on Madison Avenue or Boylston Street. The show windows of Great Bend contained most of the consumer goods that all Americans wanted. If America was promises, as a MacLeish poem declared, then some of the promises had been kept. "The economic system in the years of its collapse has somehow contrived to distribute goods more variously and more deeply than it ever did in the years of its greatest vigor."

He needed and wanted no vision of the classless or perfected society. The American approximation was as good as an imperfect world was likely to provide. Standardization, which scared people when it threatened thought, had actually meant pride and self-respect to the farmer's daughter. The "spongy decay" of the small towns, about which literature had been bitter in the 1920s, had been arrested and the trend reversed: now it was megalopolis, not the villages, that declined. In the backlands, radio had compensated for bad newspaper coverage and emancipated country kitchens from isolation and loneliness. WPA and other agencies had created parks and built swimming pools in rural places. Good music came over the airwaves. Without a Five Year Plan or a Ten Year Plan or a Twenty Year Plan, our small towns had been transformed since Carol Kennicott had walked in dismay down Main Street in Gopher Prairie. The American heartland had a well-informed, confident, and increasingly cultivated public now. In Council Grove, Iowa, where once the fleeing Mormons had died of the bloody flux, DeVoto and Schlesinger had heard teen-agers at a soda fountain discuss Brahms. Why hadn't literature been as assiduous to report that transformation as it had been to report the village virus?

As a matter of fact, it had begun to. In "A Generation Beside the Limpopo" DeVoto had remarked that some of the literary intellectuals were finally arriving in 1936 at the position from which Robert Frost had started in 1913, and he might have adduced as evidence more than Harold Stearns and Van Wyck Brooks. Ever since *Nearer the Grass Roots*, in 1929, Sherwood Anderson had been heard saying over and over, "It really is a democracy, it really is," and he said it again in *Home Town* the year DeVoto went West. After dropping his blockbusters on Gopher Prairie and Zenith and the state of Winnemac, Sinclair Lewis had come full circle to the last democratic bastion, a Vermont village, in *It Can't Happen Here*, and had made his peace with the middle-class family in *The Prodigal Parents* in 1938. In the crisis last years of the 1930s it was beginning to be a bandwagon.

But if it was a bandwagon, DeVoto could at least say with truth that he had been on it early, and had preached the American gospels when they were far less popular. It undoubtedly gave him a certain satisfaction when in the fall of that same pivotal year 1940, shortly after DeVoto had returned from his restorative trip westward, Granville Hicks published a utopian romance called *The First to Awaken*.[2] For who was the hero of that book by the ex-editor of the *New Masses?* The same that Sinclair Lewis had found in *It Can't Happen Here*, and Bernard DeVoto in "Main Street Twenty Years after": village democracy.

4 · Keeping Promises

At some point or other, DeVoto had offered to resign from every position he had ever held except his teaching job at Harvard.

Americana Deserta, the *Harvard Graduates' Magazine*, the *Saturday Review* had all brought him to the point of high-minded and hot-tempered withdrawal. Now, when he returned in early July 1940, he found that *Mark Twain in Eruption*, approved in May, had generated in Clara Gabrilowitsch the same qualms she had felt over *Letters from the Earth*, and that Harper's had yielded to her objections and modified the text. In a fury he told them to cross him off as editor, throw away the introduction, and make a public statement, first submitting it to him for approval, canceling any publicity that had linked him with the book.[1]

Harper's, pinched between door and jamb, made mollifying sounds.[2] Charles Lark tried to persuade Mrs. Gabrilowitsch that her fears were excessive, and DeVoto that a few changes wouldn't be too damaging. DeVoto insisted that there was no reason to soften remarks Mark Twain had written for publication. But he did not have much hope that arguments would avail with Mark Twain's daughter. He said to Lark that no sound book could come out of the papers as long as she was alive. He said he would finish arranging the papers, since he had begun the job, but he wanted the book withdrawn.

Lark did not, Harper's did not. In the end Mrs. Gabrilowitsch did not, and neither did DeVoto. As a last concession he softened some remarks about Bret Harte and about Thomas Bailey Aldrich's daughter, and removed a libelous reference to Judge Landis, and excised an anti-God passage, and that did it.[3] By late September the book was in press, by November it was out, the first and so far only fruit of two and a half years as curator of the Mark Twain papers.

There remained, of the three books that DeVoto had agreed to do, the volume of letters. But two stiff battles with Mrs. Gabrilowitsch had diminished his enthusiasm, and even without the threat of Mrs. Gabrilowitsch, two other matters would have taken precedence over Mark Twain at that point. One was the frontier book, the other was the war. He would gladly have postponed the first to serve in the second; but as it turned out, he worked on both simultaneously.

Before going West he had put his name in with several agencies that might have a use for him. No call was made on him during his trip, none after his return. He kept waiting for the Army Air Corps to "command his pen,"[4] but it never did. After a month of waiting, in self-defense he sat down and wrote by hand the first page of "Empire" and put it in the mail to Kate Sterne as a token or promise.[5] He said he could write on it with only Easy Chair interruptions until about February, when he would have to lay it aside to give John August his turn.

Once he had started it, the book went fast. He had been preparing for it for a long time, it was ready to spill over. Complicated as its structure was, with dozens of lines of development and the obligation to present as if simultaneously the events of a whole continent during a critical time, it seemed to write itself. "We think we can weave," DeVoto confessed to Garrett Mattingly; "maybe we can only sew."[6] Yet, weaving or sewing, he wrote forty-five thousand words in less than two months, and that despite insomnia, war anxieties, migraines, and a weekend visit to Bread Loaf that renewed his gloomy antagonism to Frost and convinced him that Frost was breaking apart all the bonds of fellowship and trust and shared effort that had made the place DeVoto's favorite club and the staff his surest friends.[7]

Despite all that, despite the reading glasses that told his hypochondriac mind that he had passed a climacteric and that from here it was all downhill, the book wrote itself steadily from day to day. It went on writing itself through the newest of Frost's domestic disasters, the suicide of his son Carol in October. Pitying and apart, DeVoto watched the repercussions of that, but he did not forgive. That odd little incident at Bread Loaf in the summer of 1938 had shown him God acting like a malignant and sadistic boy, and he was implacable. "The friendship that was pretty fervent between us for some years went out like a light in three or four days two years ago, since when he has hated me with an appalling violence as a man whom he could not consume and whom in the process of trying to consume he has opened himself to far more than the demon in him could ever bear to remember."[8]

Hallucinatory or not, excessive and paranoid or not, his sense of Frost's evil and destructive side, and his resistance to what he thought Frost's domination, put him under additional emotional strain, for which the cure, as usual, was work. Work got him past the Frost crisis and past the divorces of two of the couples with whom the DeVotos were closest in Cambridge; and when work on "Empire" stopped according to schedule in February, what took its place was alternative work—a spy thriller that made its way into Vermont from Canada along routes that DeVoto, Homans, Eli Potter, and Emery Trott had pioneered for the transportation of alcoholic beverages a decade before. *Collier's* bought it with enthusiasm in April.[9] Security achieved. Back to work.

By now there was no question in his mind or Avis' where they would live the rest of their lives. They had found that membership in the Cambridge community did not depend on affiliation with Harvard; their removal from the faculty even gave them a spectatorial and ironic distance without in any way inhibiting their participation. So in May DeVoto made an offer on the William Roscoe Thayer house at 8 Berkeley Street—a big, old, three-story ultra-Cambridge house in an ultra-Cambridge neighborhood only a short walk from the Yard, the Square, and the Common. By a quirk of circumstance its former owner had been an editor of the *Harvard Graduates' Magazine* and a historian whom Harvard had seen fit to let go. The estate was eager to settle. Before the end of the month they found themselves owners and had conferred upon them a sort of instant gentility.

It was as a place to work, as much as anything, that 8 Berkeley Street pleased DeVoto. The double parlors to the right of the entrance hall were matched by double library rooms to the left. Sliding doors could be opened to create a vast study with room to spread out all his jobs at once, or closed to shut away sight of what he didn't want to work on. There were bookshelves for a library of ten thousand volumes. But also the house had an uppercase address and a shabby, Cantabridgian dignity. One of its near neighbors was Craigie House. The Episcopal Theological Seminary shared (and coveted) its drive, so that DeVoto was warned to post it once a year as private property, to thwart the seminary's designs. Antique neighbors gave a cautious, polite sanction to the new owner—said to be a literary man—and a surviving lady relative of the Thayers, Mrs. Thayer's sister, unable to bear the thought of selling off all the furnishings or giving them to Morgan Memorial, sent her chauffeur to pick some of them up and carry them off to the warehouse, where she had already stored the furniture of two or three other family houses. One evening in the dusk they found her, an Emily Dickinson figure, with the help of her chauffeur digging up a white lilac in the yard.[10]

The house needed extensive modernization, and they would not move in until September. But in June DeVoto had a gratification at least as ego-enhancing as being a Cambridge property owner. That was the day when, as Phi Beta Kappa orator, he sat on the stage in Sanders Theater beside President James Bryant Conant and heard himself introduced as a distinguished scholar and man of letters and a great teacher in the tradition of Barrett Wendell and Dean Briggs.[11]

Days later, when the Germans invaded Russia, it was sardonic joy to watch the flip-flops of the remaining Communist intellectuals as they converted party-line pacifism and neutrality into the United

Front. For lack of any more heroic duty, he was keeping track of things like that in the Easy Chair. And he would not have been Bernard DeVoto if he hadn't been gratified by an invitation to deliver the annual lectures at the Lowell Institute in the fall. He would kill the usual two birds with one stone by telling the Lowell audience about the year 1846, which Paul Buck was urging him to call The Year of Decision.[12]

But the interruption while John August fattened the bank account, plus the distractions of the Easy Chair, the Phi Beta Kappa address, and the purchase of the house, had cost him his momentum on the history book. The summer of 1941 seemed to him wasted in random lectures, time lost consulting the newly discovered Oregon Trail diaries of Francis Parkman,[13] consultations with Walter Wanger and Jesse L. Lasky about movies that never came off, trips to New York that produced nothing. In August Ted Morrison induced him to return to Bread Loaf, but the strain of his relations with Frost, who had bought the Homer Noble farm in Ripton and had more than ever established himself as the *genius loci*, made an otherwise good session half unpleasant.

In September, just after his return to Cambridge, Lee Hartman died,[14] and that was a second climacteric. Zinsser was already gone; now he lost the editor who had made him welcome at *Harper's* for fifteen years. Both had been people whose intelligence, realism, and toughness of mind he had greatly respected and whose friendship had warmed his life.

Work, therefore. In October a series of lectures in Ames, Iowa, gave him a fresh admiration for the democratic heartland. It took the war too lightly, but in every other way Ames cheered him up: it was prosperous, healthy, self-confident, alert, and its students kept him on his toes, he said, more than Harvard's ever had.

Perhaps. When he had a point to make, he usually made it at a good, hearty markup, and in those months he was diligent to unearth evidences of the strength of democracy.

The oncoming of the Lowell Lectures returned him perforce to "Empire," from which the lectures would be taken. He was in the midst of delivering them to the modest audience of academics, antiquarians, and bums come in off Park Street to keep warm when Pearl Harbor all but blew him out of his mind.

He had an extraordinary capacity, or weakness: war news hit him as personally as if bombs had landed on the roof of 8 Berkeley Street and put the names of his family and friends on the casualty lists. A setback to the British could keep him sleepless, the defeat of the *Graf Spee* stirred him to resolution and heroic thoughts, the long retreat of the Russians before Hitler's armies was a doom that he endured with anguish. Pearl Harbor, precipitating the United States into the war he had always thought she belonged in, but in a way that no variant of the DeVoto war plan had suggested, galvanized him with new impulses toward duty and self-sacrifice. There had still been no call for his services, Washington remained mute, Archie MacLeish at the Library of Congress did not pick up the telephone. There remained the sort of humble but not inglorious service that had had all Cambridge laughing when T. S. Eliot, not with a whimper but a bang, put on steel helmet and gas mask during the Battle of Britain. DeVoto's Phi Beta Kappa address in June had opened with that irony, as one more demonstration of how wrong literary opinion could be. Now he joined up as an air-raid warden, enlisted in a first-aid course, and accepted assignments as a four-minute morale speaker at bond rallies and in Army training camps.

And hurried with the writing of "Empire," "shoveling on the coal," as he wrote Kate Sterne, in order to free himself for whatever war service he could perform. On February 15, 1942, a couple of months after Pearl Harbor, he copied off the final page, which reported the discovery that Henry Bigler and some other disbanded members of the Mormon Battalion made at a millrace they were digging for John Augustus Sutter on the South Fork of the American River in January 1848. Their discovery was a postscript, actually. The dull gleaming that they saw in the millrace when they turned the water out of it, together with all the intricately interrelated events of the year 1846 that had started Henry Bigler and his companions toward that piney place on the Pacific slope, made it inevitable that the South was not going to win the appeal to arms when it came in 1861, that the forces of disunion were not going to shape the future or Balkanize the United States, that the American nation would be one nation from sea to sea. Full of the uncertainties of present crisis, he copied out the episode that had confirmed the nation's direction in another crisis nearly a century earlier, and then he had John Dos Passos and others who had gathered for a drink at 8 Berkeley Street sign it before he put it in an envelope for Kate Sterne, a redemption of the pledge he had sent her on August 5, 1940.

He had written the book out of his own internal necessities and his own understanding of American history, but he had also written it as a declaration of national unity in time of crisis, and finally, he had written it as a gift for a girl he had never met, but to whom he had once said he would dedicate a novel that he had proved unable to complete. He was a man who valued friends and tried to keep his promises.

5 · War Effort

It is hard to understand why, during years when hundreds of writers and professors were being enlisted to promote the war effort through the Office of Facts and Figures, Writers' War Board, the Office of War Information, half a hundred agencies of the proliferating wartime bureaucracy, Bernard DeVoto, who yearned like an ardent boy for that opportunity, never had his name called until late in the conflict, and then in a way that he could not, finally, respond to.

For a while he had hopes of Archibald MacLeish, who as a sometime speech writer for FDR, as Librarian of Congress, and as head of the OFF, was a man of power and could summon men to their duty. He did not summon DeVoto; instead, he summoned Malcolm Cowley and some of the poets—almost as personal a rebuke as Harvard's appointment of Granville Hicks to be Fellow of American History. It apparently did not occur to DeVoto that his Phi Beta Kappa speech, which had taken specific issue with the literary idealism of MacLeish's *The Irresponsibles*, might have hurt MacLeish's feelings. But he disagreed with his ideas, which he thought not too far from the unreconstructed literary-ness of the other expatriates, and he had said so very publicly. Whether or not MacLeish was offended, he never called on DeVoto to come to Washington and write the war. Neither, later, did DeVoto's even closer friend Elmer Davis, when he became head of OWI, though the two did collaborate in an effort to get war information more freely released, and DeVoto did air in the Easy Chair some opinions that Davis was officially prohibited from airing or operating by.[1] For a while in 1943 the Army proposed to use DeVoto to teach teachers how to teach American history. Later there was a project for a nationwide lecture tour for the Army. Still later, in late 1943 and early 1944, DeVoto spent a couple of fruitless months in Washington discussing with the Secretary of War and others the writing of the history of certain campaigns: first North Africa, later Guadalcanal, finally (and lamely) Attu.[2] The negotiations went so far that DeVoto had all his shots and kept a bag packed, subject to call. In the end, when it turned out that he would be expected to write military history without being given access to battle reports and other confidential papers, Avis looked at him and burst into tears and said, "Don't go," and he didn't. Sam Morison, an expert in such matters, had given him the same advice: Don't go unless they will open it all up for you.[3]

That was the closest Benny DeVoto ever got to serving officially in World War II; it was the closest he ever got to leaving the North American continent. World War II left unhealed, actually abraded, the scars of 1918, when the Armistice had left him stranded—shoulder bars, Sam Browne belt, leather puttees, overseas cap, and Expert Marksman medal—in Camp Lee, Virginia.

All around him, Cambridge thinned out as students and younger faculty went into uniform and older faculty taught Army Specialized Training Program courses or drained off toward Washington. Henry Reck was off to the Navy. President Conant had disappeared on some unspecified assignment and DeVoto's friend Paul Buck ran Harvard. Radcliffe, "the Annex," was admitted to full partnership over the dissent of certain alumni and of a few faculty men whose salaries were more than thirteen thousand dollars.[4] Gas rationing mired Cambridge in its own steaming rumors. The harbor was full of British warships, and Cambridge parties were full of British naval officers. Submarines were daily sighted off Ipswich, mysterious rubber rafts brought saboteurs ashore through the murk of imagination and boredom, as if in imitation of a John August serial. Inept, well-meaning people met two evenings a week to listen to inept, well-meaning lecturers discuss what to do in an air raid or how to splint a broken limb, and those with some medical training or medical imagination went home praising God that no real emergency had yet occurred, for the victims would never survive the assistance.

Dull non-combatant, fumbler on the home front, listener to the gossip of British officers and the inside dope of experts such as Davis and Fletcher Pratt, huddler over short-wave broadcasts from England and Germany, guesser and worrier, projector of luminous war plans and of prophecies based on false rumors or misleading communiqués, DeVoto had only two channels for the patriotism that melted and flowed in him. One was to do whatever humble job was handed him, however futile for any but morale purposes. The other was to warn and advise and thunder from the Easy Chair. Public thinker, historian, student of American life, defender of the democratic system, a man with a captive audience, he need not depend on calls from Washington. He could fight his war in the monthly dispatches he sent down to 49 East 33rd Street.[5]

Of the thirty Easy Chairs that he wrote during 1941, 1942, and the first half of 1943, by which time the suspense about the war's outcome had given way to the less crucial suspense about how long victory would be delayed, twenty-five either dealt directly with the war or reflected upon conditions of American life that the war modified, threatened, or confirmed. Some expounded historical parallels, some were concerned to make plain the stern inevitability of the war (and this even before Pearl Harbor) and the rightness of the cause. To the young men who asked, "Would you send us out to die?" he answered, "Yes, when the time comes."[6] There were times when sacrifice was not only heroic but necessary. *Dulce et decorum est;* the country one offered to die for was the source of all the freedoms one had grown up taking for granted. Including the right to bellyache. Including the right to full and honest and even disastrous information. Including the right to take a little refreshment and pleasure as one could, even in wartime.

Publication of Dixon Wecter's *The Hero in America* led him to evoke the mythic figures in whom the democratic nation had embodied its best impulses and highest aspirations. Dorothy Thompson's denunciation of American materialism and fat pay envelopes brought him forth protesting.[7] It did not become Dorothy to condemn the materialist industrial economy for Americans while holding it up as the hope of the undeveloped world. And it was absurd of her to say she was going to sell her luxurious possessions and turn them into war bonds. The poor could not afford such gestures and should not be urged to make them. Their morale, moreover, was going to be higher for the occasional steak, the little gas wasted on a Sunday drive. Mr. Ickes had forgotten that, and had lost his chance to be effective. Trust the people.

But several Easy Chairs, including the ominous "Toward Chancellorsville,"[8] drew lessons from the Civil War and warned against the isolationist complacency of the Middle West. Would we, DeVoto asked, have to go through Fredericksburg, Second Bull Run, and even Chancellorsville before we buckled down? Would it take an army at the edge of Washington, or bombs on Chicago and Gary, before the Middle West would admit the fact of salt water, the reality of foreign aggression? On the other hand, how could the government expect full public support for its policies when it withheld vital information, doctored news of casualties and ship losses, turned catastrophes into cautious victories, and issued "preliminary reports" that were plain lies? He denounced Army, Navy, and the President for their failure to trust the American people with their own vital business. He said out loud that no war in our history had been so misreported and so unreported, and as a consequence was given opportunity to be for a time political adviser to Wendell Willkie, who found that sort of historical information useful on the campaign trail.[9]

He did not run a hate campaign, he did not, like some columnists, cry to Europe-bound troops, "Kill some for me!" He asserted the American gospels and the duty and privilege of defending them. Indignant, hortatory, sometimes inspiring, always protective of the right of citizens to know, he fought his war from The Easy Chair, and he probably did the war effort at least as much good as he would have done if he had joined the other frustrated writers in the OWI.[10] Perhaps, in the process, he did himself some harm. In his tart rebuke to Dorothy Thompson he cast some bread upon the waters that Dorothy Thompson's husband would return to him a hundredfold. And in dedicating himself to patriotic public speech for the duration, he suspended for the duration the kind of public speech at which he was better than anybody else. All during the war he was an unpaid and independent propagandist, not a writer operating with a free mind. Crisis dominated his thinking, he put aside "Lycidas" and *Paradise Lost* to be Latin Secretary.

Fair enough. That was what the times demanded, that was the only wartime service that circumstance let him perform. He accepted the duty and the consequences. But when he finally collected a third volume of essays,[11] in the last year of his life, he did not include in the book a single one of the Easy Chairs he had written between the end of 1940 and the end of the war.

6 · History as Synecdoche: The Year of Decision: 1846

The Year of Decision: 1846 was completed on February 15, 1942, and delivered to Little, Brown the next day, along with its dedication to Kate Sterne and two pages of acknowledgments of the help various people had given in the book's preparation. The last name on the list was the most important. "Finally," DeVoto wrote, "I acknowledge that I could not possibly have written the book if I had not had periodic assistance from Mr. John August."

Those who knew both DeVoto and August knew how real was the debt thus humorously admitted. *The Year of Decision: 1846* had been gestating since at least as early as 1933, and had been DeVoto's main preoccupation since 1938. John August, invented in 1926 to disguise the authorship of "Sex and the Co-Ed" and resurrected in 1934 to assume responsibility for the *Collier's* serials, had supported DeVoto's serious work ever since. There was not an artistic bone in August's body, not a single aesthetic corpuscle in his blood. He was all pro, and he provided the security that other historians got from academic tenure and other novelists from foundation grants. *Troubled Star*, *Rain Before Seven*, and *Advance Agent* had each brought in twenty thousand dollars or more as serials, and each had been made into a book that outsold any novel signed by Bernard DeVoto. August was even beginning to have a reputation in England, where DeVoto had never had a book published. After receiving his public thanks in the front pages of *The Year of Decision: 1846*, he would be called on once more, and would respond with a fourth serial, *The Woman in the Picture*, in 1944. Three years after that, he and DeVoto would dispute authorship of a fifth, *Mountain Time*, and August would lose. After that, partly because Sinclair Lewis would publicly expose his identity, partly because he would have served his purpose, he would quietly disappear.

But even in 1942 it had begun to seem that his creator might soon be self-supporting. History signed by Bernard DeVoto demonstrated itself more profitable than fiction by the same hand, and almost as profitable as fiction by John August.

A pleasant though not overwhelming benefit came when the *Atlantic* bought *The Year of Decision: 1846* as a five-part serial.[1] The first installment was on the stands in July, when Henry Canby's judges picked the book as a Book of the Month. Their act, DeVoto wrote Canby, was the biggest break he had ever had; but to Avis, when the news came, he reacted almost with panic. Oh God, he said, now I suppose something will happen to one of the kids.

His reputation took a leap, along with his bank account. *The Year of Decision: 1846* settled territory that *Mark Twain's America* had pioneered. It made DeVoto the most conspicuous interpreter of the West, and though some "objective" historians such as his old friend Arthur Schlesinger, Senior, declared that the book wasn't history, and some old Harvard enemies were reported to be "raging" ("Why? I'm not a candidate for promotion"),[2] many who up to that time had considered him a picturesque or insufferable wild man useful at best for stirring up excitement at the annual meetings of the American Historical Association found this new book important and praiseworthy. It also enlarged him in the opinion of the literate public that had known him theretofore primarily through the *Saturday Review*, the Easy Chair, and the controversial essays.

Delayed by the book-club choice, *The Year of Decision: 1846* was not published in book form until March 1943. Its reception was almost unqualified praise. Book pages featured it, *Time* gave it two very respectful pages, historians as eminent as Frederick L. Paxson, Ralph Gabriel, Richard Hofstadter, and Henry Nash Smith reviewed it with respect or admiration or both.[3] On one thing, the professional and the lay reviewers were agreed. If this was history at all, it was a new kind of history, infinitely complex, intricately organized, extremely detailed where it chose to be and willing to ignore entirely what did not serve its purposes. On a close look, what seemed merely colorful narrative proved to be full of provocative generalizations. The bold portraits and dramatic scenes led to uncompromising judgments of men and events. Though DeVoto's strategy of keeping many stories advancing simultaneously through the year meant jumping from story to story and place to place, most readers survived the somewhat bewildering first chapter[4] and were hooked. Almost every reviewer testified to the book's extraordinary impression of seething human activity, all of it bearing westward, all of it expressing the impulse that was not quite formal national policy (that in fact violated such specific elements of policy as the segregation and protection of the Indian Territory), and not quite even idea, but an urge below the level of consciousness, moving a people westward as inevitably as the sun compels the face of a sunflower.

Manifest Destiny was what *The Year of Decision* was about, Manifest Destiny conceived as geopolitical inevitability. It was also "the story of some people who went West in 1846," a frankly literary attempt "to realize the pre-Civil War, Far Western frontier as personal experience."[5] It was both intensive and extensive. From the Invocation in which Henry David Thoreau confessed that "Eastward I go only by force; but westward I go free. . . . I must walk toward Oregon and not toward Europe," to the final page, about the discovery of gold at Sutter's mill, the book was a thesis developed and demonstrated by scores of individual examples. The thesis was that the year 1846, which fought a war with Mexico and barely evaded one with England, which confirmed Oregon and added California and the Southwest to the United States, which watched a growing file of wagons labor up the Platte Valley and over the mountains and deserts to Oregon and California, which

opened the Santa Fe Trail to trade and empire, which saw the
Mormons evicted from their City Beautiful on the Mississippi and
driven into the wilderness on their dolorous way to the settlement
of the Rocky Mountain West, which gave most of the men who
would be Northern or Southern generals in the Civil War their
baptism of fire at Palo Alto or Matamoros or Chapultepec, which
produced the Wilmot Proviso banning the spread of slavery into
the new territories—that this year 1846 made the Civil War inevitable and at the same time made certain that the Union would
win it.

It was a thesis that not all historians were willing to accept. *A
year of decision*, yes. A very important year. But other years just
as crucial in our history might have been picked; any year closely
scrutinized becomes a year of decision. Nevertheless, it was this
thesis which held together the complex narratives of the book,
and in fact justified their selection. It provided the bag that made
manageable all the loose marbles of events during that chosen year.

Some professional historians complained about a principle of
selection that gave the mountain man James Clyman more space
than Senator Thomas Hart Benton, the very trumpet of Manifest
Destiny, and the Donner Party's anthropophagous ordeal more
space than any other happening of 1846. Almost all objected
mildly to some of DeVoto's inevitabilities. Henry Nash Smith,
while generally admiring, thought that by accepting geopolitical
inevitability DeVoto had shut his eyes to the moral dubieties of the
Mexican War—and, he might have added, to the moral dubieties
of our extirpation of the Indian cultures as well. Schlesinger, defending the objectivity of history, protested his unqualified judgments, his willingness to call Frémont a popinjay and Zachary
Taylor a lucky fool. Paxson evaded the issue of historical objectivity by describing the book as "a brilliant job on the borderland
common to the historian, the essayist, and the analyst." Hofstadter,
while not accepting the central thesis without qualification, thought
DeVoto had not meant it to be taken too seriously. "Had he set out
to prove it, he would have written an analytical history of an epoch,
not the narrative history of a year."

Perhaps. An orthodox historian would certainly have done it
that way. But DeVoto was an unorthodox historian, at odds with
the monographic mentality. If he had a model, it was Francis Parkman, who dealt with sweeping events in which a continent was at
stake and re-created them as vividly as fiction. In this very book,
he did object to Parkman as a Brahmin snob who missed the
greatest opportunity offered to a historian since Xenophon, for

Parkman was out on the Oregon Trail in 1846 and failed to see the significance of the crude Mormon and Oregon pioneers he met on Laramie Creek and elsewhere. But an objection to Parkman's snobbery did not prevent him from adopting Parkman's methods. *The Year of Decision: 1846* is romantic history conceived in literary terms—and that statement implies something about form and organization as well as about narrative style.

It implies that the form of this history is not chronological or topical form, but artistic form.[6] It implies that proportion, relationship of parts, emphasis, and the evocation of a personal response are all part of the conception, to be reconciled in any way possible with the facts of history. Response, not mere comprehension, is the goal, and this means that the sort of selection practiced will have more in mind than the accurate reproduction of events. It means that big scenes and colorful characters will be as important to this kind of historian as they were to Walter Scott, and will be exploited by every fictional device. "When you get a scene, play it!" DeVoto advised Garrett Mattingly.[7] He did not mean distort it. He meant take advantage of drama when history offers it. A historian, he said, should not stop at second simply because some taboo of his trade said that historians did not hit home runs. Go for the fences.

The grisly ordeal of the Donner-Reed party and the hardships of the Mormons driven from Nauvoo by mobs were stories of human agony too strong to be omitted or played down, part of the action on the far-western frontier that was realizable as personal experience. Possibly the space given them might have been devoted to Congressional debates or the private correspondence of Thomas Hart Benton, but that was not the kind of history DeVoto was writing. His kind of history not only permitted the selection and dramatization of striking actions, it also allowed the historian to pass judgment on both events and people, and it permitted the elaboration of large, umbrella theses to contain and explain events, so long as the theses were developed inductively and not imposed from without. Furthermore it permitted symbolic selection—history by synecdoche, the illumination of whole areas and periods through concentration upon one brief time, one single sequence, a few representative characters. DeVoto's concentration upon the year 1846, his "narrative history of a year," was not an attempt to limit consideration to that small, focused set of actions. Quite the opposite. It was an attempt to use the part for the whole, the less for the more inclusive; to make the chosen events of that single year illuminate all the years leading up to the Civil War and the triumph of Union and the continental nation.

It was a method he had experimented with as early as the 1927 essay "The Great Medicine Road," but its rationale he almost certainly got from Robert Frost, who was calling himself a synecdochist in poetry when others were calling themselves vorticists or imagists, and who on occasion saw the world almost as emblematically as Emerson or Hawthorne. DeVoto did not go so far toward transcendentalism, and as in so many matters, he had arrived at his opinions independently and had only had them corroborated by Frost. Nevertheless, with his knack for aphorism, Frost might have been writing a commandment for DeVoto's historical method when he said, "All that an artist needs is samples."[8]

The swarming individuals, the multiple continued narratives of *The Year of Decision: 1846* were samples selected out of an otherwise unmanageable variety. The events that in the gestative process had given rise to a thesis were then used to demonstrate, illustrate, and symbolize it, and so carried more than their own weight in the narrative. A reviewer who objected to the space given James Clyman was not reading DeVoto as DeVoto asked to be read. Clyman is in the book not because he was personally so important, but because he was incredibly representative, and touched the energies of his time at many points. Ten years before *The Year of Decision: 1846* was published, DeVoto had assigned him a significant place in a book that was as yet only dimly conceived. As he wrote to Mattingly,

I've found a culture hero. Look at his career—and it's history, not my invention. Born on Washington's land in Fauquier County. Met the Gen'l in person. Down the Ohio in time to be present at Tippecanoe. Militiaman in 1812–14. Helped Alex. Hamilton's son survey national lands in Indiana and Illinois. Got to St. Louis in time to join the 2nd Ashley expedition, which opened up the Interior basin. On the party that found South Pass. One of the four who explored Great Salt Lake in a skin boat. Five years as a fur trapper. Present at practically everything that happened in those years. Then back to Illinois, where he bought land. In Abe Lincoln's company in the Black Hawk War. Pioneered in lumber & then in farming in Wisconsin. The milksop Winnebagos shot him twice—& he'd fought Blackfeet. Got asthma & went west to cure it. To Oregon in the great 1844 emigration. In Oregon, was with the Applegate party that blazed the trail to California. Bear Flag revolt as an associate of Fremont. Helped Hastings make his cut off, quarreled with Hastings about its safety, & denounced H's book. Met Lillburn Boggs & turned him from Cal to Oregon. Met the Donner party & advised them not to take the road they did. Met the Mormons. Came back to Wisconsin & was employed by the Mecomb party to guide them to Calif. Got to Sutter's in time to see the first gold. Married one of the Mecomb girls, bought a ranch at Napa, and lived halfway through the administration of Rutherford B. Hayes. Think that career over—and I didn't invent a comma of it. . . .⁹

The historical monographer might assume half contemptuously that DeVoto was dressing up his narrative by exploiting a see-all character, a sort of historical Lanny Budd who initiated no events and affected nothing importantly, whose only importance was that, like a television commentator, he was *there*. That was precisely his function and precisely his usefulness to a historian who thought like a novelist. Sample. Symbol. Culture hero. A part that might be taken for the whole, an individual in whose experience was subsumed a whole folk-wandering.

In the 1936 essay "On Beginning to Write a Novel," DeVoto had spoken of the fictional process as the trial and error through which the novelist groped toward the inevitabilities inherent in his material. Now it turned out that, for him, history was the same process. History, too, was people in action through times and places, and it did not exclude what went on in the caverns of the soul. But there was one difference, one that was perhaps never fully clear to him.

In his Bread Loaf lectures he had always been something of a strict constructionist with regard to fictional point of view. He believed that a writer of fiction could not shift his point of view, once he had established it, without risking the illusion he was trying to create. He believed the fiction writer should be invisible and not call attention to himself by authorial comment. The first person singular never appealed to him; he thought it too easy, too likely to be verbose, too subject to the intrusions of self-love, exhibitionism, and public confession—everything that gagged him in the novels of Thomas Wolfe. In his own fictions he preferred the strategy of objectivity, or that variant of it which permits the reader to see with the eyes of a single character, and to know only what he knows. That method enforced a degree of identification while still violating none of the rules of objective reporting. In a novel, with due precautions, the point of view might be shifted, preferably at a chapter break or other mechanical division that acted like a theater curtain, from one character to another. But there was no place in his kind of novel where an author could stand and make judgments, nor could the author speak in any but the ventriloquisms of his characters. In short, the judgmental author was as out of place in

DeVoto's kind of fiction as he was in Arthur Schlesinger, Senior's kind of history.

A weakness in DeVoto as a novelist was that he never mastered ventriloquism. Comparing his fictions with his histories, one is led to wonder if the tentative, brittle unsatisfactoriness of the one and the lusty authority of the other do not stem from that fundamental problem of approach. DeVoto was a man full of opinions. He marshaled facts with great swiftness and made them into generalizations, and he discriminated among ideas with the positiveness of one discriminating between sound and rotten oranges. The iconic and hesitant representation of ideas as people was not enough for him. When he couldn't judge and comment, he was inhibited; when he couldn't speak in his own voice, he was constrained, as Tom Wolfe would have been constrained in fiction by the same limitation.

Which is to say exactly what Frost, Lewis, and many others had said to him: he was an intellectual, a man of ideas, not a novelist. For half a lifetime he had stubbornly misread his gifts, and even after *The Year of Decision: 1846* demonstrated what he was best at, he would make periodic efforts to be what he was not. It would take him nearly another decade to persuade himself finally that he was not at home among the puppeteers. He was more truly at home among scientists, historians, and reporters. The pretenses, disguises, and self-effacements of the objective fiction he favored kept him from being himself, and his belligerently anti-literary pretenses were probably an acknowledgment of his dissatisfaction with his own performance.

But history-ward he walked free, and there is a paradox in the way the writing of history emancipated him. History did not ask the historian to disappear; it only asked him to be objective. In history the word "objective" did not mean "invisible"; it only meant "impartial." But to ask impartiality of Bernard DeVoto was as bad as asking him to efface himself; it was like asking docility of a wolverine. So he challenged the historiographical fashion that said a historian must be cautious in his judgments, and by doing so he acquired a freedom within the historian's mystery that he had never enjoyed in the related mystery of the novelist. In fact, he introduced into history his controversialist habit of foray and rebuttal. He not only asked his representation of the pre-Civil War farwestern frontier to be accurate as history and as vivid as a novel, he asked it to be as challenging as an Easy Chair.

One might select dozens of passages that would illustrate both the vigor and the disconcertingly judgmental character of his

method. Take one from the early part of the book, a thumbnail
profile of the President who, "carrying twin torches through a
powder magazine," led the nation into and out of 1846:

"Who is James K. Polk?" The Whigs promptly began campaigning on
that derision, and there were Democrats who repeated it with a sick
concern. The question eventually got an unequivocal answer. Polk
had come up the ladder, he was an orthodox party Democrat. He had
been Jackson's mouthpiece and floor leader in the House of Representatives, had managed the anti-Bank legislation, had risen to the
Speakership, had been Governor of Tennessee. But sometimes the belt
line shapes an instrument of use and precision. Polk's mind was rigid,
narrow, obstinate, far from first rate. He sincerely believed that only
Democrats were truly American, Whigs being either the dupes or the
pensioners of England—more, that not only wisdom and patriotism
were Democratic monopolies but honor and breeding as well. "Although a Whig he seems a gentleman" is a not uncommon characterization in his diary. He was pompous, suspicious, and secretive; he had
no humor; he could be vindictive; and he saw spooks and villains. He
was a representative Southern politician of the second or indeterminate
period (which expired with his Presidency), when the decline but not
the disintegration had begun.
But if his mind was narrow it was also powerful, and he had guts. If
he was orthodox, his integrity was absolute and he could not be scared,
manipulated, or brought to heel. No one bluffed him, no one moved
him with direct or oblique pressure. Furthermore, he knew how to
get things done, which is the first necessity of government, and he
knew what he wanted done, which is the second. He came into office
with clear ideas and a fixed determination and he was to stand by them
through as strenuous an administration as any before Lincoln's. Congress had governed the United States for eight years before him and,
after a fashion, was to govern it for the next twelve years after him.
But Polk was to govern the United States from 1845 to 1849. He was
to be the only "strong" President between Jackson and Lincoln. He
was to fix the mold of the future in America down to 1860, and therefore for a long time afterward. That is who James K. Polk was.[10]

Examine that passage in any way you wish, for its organization
(as firm as the octave and sestet of a sonnet), for the crispness of
its unequivocating judgments, for its generalizations about American politics across a span of years, for the rawhide flexibility of its
prose, for the way it states in small a theme that the book which
follows will state in large, and you must admit to being in an unmistakable presence, listening to an unmistakable voice. Even some
monographers who deplored the method had to admire the result.
When DeVoto re-created past events as personal experience he

was carrying on, as we have observed, from the great romantic historians, especially Parkman. When he retained and even accentuated the presence of the historian, he was challenging the dominant historiographical school stemming from Ranke. What is more, the historical presence that he asserted was not an impartial judge, but a maverick of the Henderson-Zinsser kind, a man in a state of deadlock between scientific principle and personal prejudice, who stated his inductive conclusions with passion. That was striking enough. But when he converted chronology into simultaneity (what Paxson called a "chronological symphony"), and when by synecdoche and other devices he gave to history a form almost as intricate and almost as impressionistic as Faulkner's *The Sound and the Fury*, then he was doing something no American historian had done.

He had learned, with others of his generation, the trick of telling stories in a few bright, quick scenes. He had discovered the benefits to be had from turning chronology on its head or playing games with it. He had grown used to asking more and more alertness and participation from his readers,[11] he had adjured many a Bread Loaf audience to show, not to tell. When he applied the methods of impressionistic fiction to history, mounting upon the scrupulous gatherer of facts the storyteller skilled in mass entertainment; and when he mounted upon those, like an acrobat on the shoulders of two fellow acrobats, the social analyst and controversialist and editorial thinker of The Easy Chair, he had a combination that might look unstable and even self-contradictory, but that worked. Those who read *The Year of Decision: 1846* knew they were hearing a new voice, and many suspected that the voice was major. It was the voice of Bernard DeVoto, unmasked by the ventriloquisms that properly should have accompanied his impressionism. Like its author, the book had the capacity to wake up any room it entered. As the Mormon historian Dale L. Morgan wrote,[12] the only real mistake in the whole book was the title, which threw the emphasis on a doubtful generalization and diverted attention from the brilliant re-creation of individual people and events.

V I

BLOWS GIVEN AND TAKEN

---

1 · "So Goes Another of My Fathers"

During March 1943, just when *The Year of Decision: 1846* was being reviewed, DeVoto delivered the Patten Lectures at the University of Indiana.[1] His month in Bloomington was not the love feast he had enjoyed at Ames in the fall of 1941. It seemed to him that his lectures went badly and that the audiences were either unfriendly or inert: "It's like talking into a featherbed." He was exasperated by what he felt to be a prevailing midwestern complacency about the war. He grew tired of Hoosier jokes and the provincial smugness from which it seemed to him they derived. Depressed by his failure to catch and hold his hosts and hearers, he committed some social gaucheries that he regretted. Though he found a few kindred spirits such as R. C. Buley, the historian, he felt generally disliked and ignored, and he wrote Kate Sterne that he could hardly wait until Robert Frost, who was coming to Indiana during DeVoto's last week there, tried to work his usual crowd magic on those people.

But he did not mean he could hardly wait. He meant he dreaded Frost's coming, for as parallel attractions they would be thrown much together, and even (he does not say this) put into a kind of competition for attention, a competition that in the circumstances DeVoto was sure to lose.

As during all their contacts since the night in Treman Cottage in the summer of 1938, the suspicion and resistance seemed to be all DeVoto's. Frost sought his company and talked as freely as ever, with the autobiographical openness that had once been so flattering and that now filled DeVoto with suspicion and alarm. Frost was living with his dead, and gnawing the choices that seemed to compose his future. For three consecutive nights, according to DeVoto's account, he delivered himself of a monologue whose intimacy fascinated and repelled his onetime friend. More strongly than ever, he felt that Frost must be a little mad. More than ever, he feared that Frost was trying to "ingest" him, that he had to defend his integrity against a kind of incubus. And yet he was baffled to find a motive either for the intimacy that Frost assumed or for the malice that he thought it concealed.

It was possible that all the revealing talk might be part of a renewed, indirect campaign to get DeVoto to write the biography that they had apparently discussed in Florida in 1936, for Newdick, once approved as official biographer, had died, and his tentative successor, Lawrance Thompson of Princeton, had recently published a critical book, *Fire and Ice,* with which Frost was not fully satisfied. But if there was any such intention in Frost's mind, it was not an intention that he had shared with any of his intimates or, apparently, with his publisher.[2] So far as anyone knew, Thompson was the biographer, and there had never been any suggestion that he would be replaced. DeVoto had told Kenneth Murdock, when his friends were trying to get him invited back to Harvard, that he planned a book on the poetic outburst from 1912 onward, with Frost as its unifying figure; but in 1943 that, too, had long since been put aside. The 1938 incident at Bread Loaf had completely soured him, and there was neither forgiveness nor friendliness in him. He listened, wary and uneasy, while Frost assumed the old intimacy, or pretended to, and wondered what sly purpose, what masked and destructive design impelled him.

He did not believe at all in Frost's apparent friendship. He thought it hatred. He feared being sucked like an orange and thrown away an empty rind. From every walk, for those three consecutive nights, he went home and made incredulous, nearly horrified notes on what Frost had said. He had no way of telling how much of it was true, how much false, for if part of it was lies, they were "the lies of genius."

One hesitates to accept more than partially DeVoto's interpretation of that brief overlapping in Bloomington. It is possible that what Frost offered him was indeed the old friendship, and that the personal exposures Frost made came out of his loneliness, sorrow, and sense of guilt—wrenched out of him, as it were, by the savagery of his own conflicting impulses. DeVoto, moreover, had a history of anxiety and formless fears, and a further history of attachment to and resistance against a series of surrogate fathers. He could have imagined Frost's emotional excitement, which to DeVoto seemed almost diabolic, and his will to dominate or destroy. He could (though this is less likely) have been envious, for they were celebrities in something like competition, and Frost was far more successful with the Bloomington audience than DeVoto had been and was lionized where DeVoto had felt half ignored. All those speculations about Frost's desire to secure him as his biographer were speculations only; and though there is no way of knowing what the two may have said to one another on that subject during their seven-year acquaintance, one remembers that DeVoto's version of the *Saturday Review* agreement did not match the version of a perfectly friendly participant, George Stevens.

He did not *want* to hear revelations of Robert Frost's emotional life. He did not *want* to feel compelled, as by some Ancient Mariner, to listen for hours to confidences whose purpose he suspected. The moment his lecture obligations were over, he got away and returned to Cambridge—though that was not exactly sanctuary from what he feared, for as if to indicate that you did not cast off a father that easily, Frost had bought a house on Brewster Street, a five-minute walk from 8 Berkeley Street, and showed every sign of settling down as a permanent neighbor. Moreover, DeVoto had been home only a little while when a letter from Bloomington confirmed his feeling that underneath all of Frost's behavior there had been some obscure destructive intent. Frost was reported as having said at a faculty dinner, "DeVoto, you know, has been under the care of a psychiatrist, who has told him that I am not good for him, that if he is ever to succeed, he must not cultivate my company; I am too strong for him, and have a bad effect upon him."

If DeVoto had taken Frost's friendliness with an almost paranoid suspicion, he took this overt jibe even harder, because it seemed a knife-thrust at the very vitals of his shaky security. He was not under a psychiatrist's care, even for supportive therapy, and had not been since he left New York and Lawrence Kubie in 1938. He thought Frost knew that. Then, how should his remark be taken? Was it Frost trying to get even, backhandedly, for DeVoto's obviously cooled friendship? Was it simply one of his usual digs at psychiatry and those who were enslaved by it? Or was it (DeVoto thought it was) a destructive, devious, hurtful diminishment of a sort of son by a sort of father who could not tolerate independence?

Cambridge gossip had brought to DeVoto's ears rumors of similar remarks by Frost in other places and at other times. He brooded about what sort of reply to make, how to confront and challenge him. He talked to Kay Morrison and to Lawrance Thompson, then just about to go to sea as a Navy lieutenant, but it was early June before he finally wrote Frost a letter. Delay had not lessened his sense of injury. He quoted the story that had come to him, from two sources, out of Bloomington. He said he did not like it, and had not liked others of the same kind that had come back to him in the recent past:

The statement is altogether false. . . . I think you know that. What satisfaction you get from circulating a false and damaging statement about me I don't know or care, but I have made no earlier protest out of respect to years of friendship with you. I have decided, however, that I no longer care to submit to it. I do not want to hear of your making that statement again in public or in private. Please see to it that I do not have to act any farther in the matter than thus calling it to your attention.[3]

As blunt as a blow, that letter announced the end of all friendship between them, and perhaps of all association. There went another of his fathers, the biggest one. But Frost did not accept DeVoto's note as a termination, and he did not reply to anger with anger. In his version, that dinner-table remark was a joke. But he was incapable of direct and forthright apology, even if he regretted the remark. Among his papers at Dartmouth College is the undated draft of his reply, as ambiguous and confusing as the motivation of his original jibe:

Benny Benny!
The first thing Kay did when she got here was to give me what you in your unconventional Western way would call Hell for talking about you too much in company. (She did not say in public.) And now comes your letter to give me more Hell for the same thing. I feel injured and misunderstood. You bring up an evening in Bloomington when the conversation not unnaturally got round more than once to your lectures there and to your latest book. In any "faithful" report of that evening I should have ranked second to none in praise of both the lectures and the book. When never mind who said the book might be something better than history but it wasn't history I asked if he meant in the sense that Herodotus Plutarch and Tacitus weren't history or had he in mind the sense in which Frude [sic] didn't seem history to the partisans of Freeman. When somebody else said he had

stayed away from your lectures because in your book you hadn't found anything nice to say about life on the Mississippi I answered neither had Mark Twain himself. I said I had to laugh at your being shunned as a disparager of anything American: my admiration for you had begun in an article you wrote in admiration of life on submarginal Vermont farms where the cash income was something like three hundred dollars a year. What was more your lectures had been one hammering denunciation of disparagers in general. I never speak of you but to praise. I have been mentioning you for membership in the Academy. I have predicted that you would have to be called back to Harvard. But I am nobody's propagandist. You know my danger. I am prone to think more things are funny than you would. I suppose it may have been in self defense but the disappointed novelist pent up in me started to play with the idea the minute I heard that your doctor had advised you not to associate with me. You say the story isn't true and I take your word for it but I had it on the best authority and your attitude toward me for the last two years had tended to make it seem plausible. I don't see why you want to spoil it. By changing your name to John August you can write a twenty thousand dollar novel for Collier's any time you please. An Italian Catholic English Mormon blend in birth you are neither a Catholic nor a Mormon in religion but a Freudian in philosophy. I don't think these facts take away from your greatness as a writer. They do add to your interest as a character. Just so with this story you so much object to. I wouldn't have thought it hurt either of us and it makes us both more amusing. Get it straight from me though. I forever played up the absurdity of your letting extraneous analysts come between us to tell you I was too strong for you. A gentle versifier like me too strong for a powerful prose man like you? Rah. But true or not true I wouldn't for the world go on repeating the story if it bothers you or anybody else. Now lets forget all this and get something written. You want to be friends, I could tell by your manner in Bloomington. I want to be friends as you can tell by my manner in this letter. . . .[4]

The draft ends in crossed-out, repetitious adjurations: you want to be friends, let's forget all this and get back to work. But whether to take the letter at its face value, there was the rub for DeVoto. Whether this was sane Hamlet, or mad Hamlet, or mad Hamlet in a sane moment, or sane Hamlet mad only north-northwest; whether it was as close as Frost could come to frank apology or whether it was an attempt to deny the unfriendliness of what DeVoto considered a clearly malicious piece of gossip; whether it concealed the fixed egotistic purpose of coercing talents he admired toward the writing of a biography that would insure him immortality; whether it was all a complicated jeer—who could tell? Whom was Frost deriding in that remark about "a gentle versifier like me too strong for a powerful prose man like you"? Was he kidding the analyst who could suggest such an absurdity, or the powerful prose man who let himself be confused by witch doctors? Or was he slyly asserting that he *was* too strong for DeVoto?

DeVoto thought he knew, and his resentment and estrangement were too strong and of too long duration to be cured by an ambiguous letter. If he wanted to be friends, as Frost said, then it seems clear he didn't dare—a fact that suggests some truth in the notion of Frost's dominance. So as surely as Thomas Wolfe cast off Maxwell Perkins, DeVoto cast off Frost. Simple disillusionment in the sanity and magnanimity of genius was not enough to explain the emotional intensity of the repudiation. A remark at a dinner party, malicious or otherwise, did not explain it. An alarming autobiographical frankness which to DeVoto's ears revealed a monstrous egotism and ruthlessness did not explain it. Rightly or wrongly, he felt endangered, he feared being devoured, and those feelings had been with him for nearly five years. Whether he was right about Frost's dominating malice, or whether he misread a humorous poet as badly as he had said the Marxist critics did, or whether the hypothetical psychoanalyst (if anybody ever made that remark to DeVoto it had to be either William Barrett or Lawrence Kubie, and either might have) was right, and DeVoto *couldn't* stand association with a father figure so potent as Frost, DeVoto himself insisted on the break. He made it, hardened himself to it, suffered from it, and out of resentment or in self-defense made it permanent.

Once already he had attempted to write his complicated filial feelings into a novel: with him, serious fiction was always to some degree thaumaturgy and exorcism. The overt break with Frost insured that sometime he would have to try to exorcise his demon again. For it was a demon; if it hadn't been, he would not have felt so strong a need to put it down. What he felt on breaking off relations with Frost was perhaps not unlike the panic he had felt on the Union Pacific train headed East from Ogden in 1922, when as a shaky young man of twenty-five, fearful that he would never get off the train alive, he had written his name and his father's address on a card and put the card in the side pocket of his coat, where it would be easily found.

2 · *"Fools, Liars, and Mr. DeVoto."*

When Frost called DeVoto's Indiana lectures "one hammering denunciation of disparagers in general," he meant the literary disparagers on whom the two had long before agreed. The Patten Lectures were an amplified final statement of his argument against the Young Intellectuals and the literary Marxists and all the other divisions of the "superior caste" who had scorned, condemned, and despaired of the American people and American democracy. They were the testament of a cultural patriot, an indignant one, and it should not be forgotten that they were made in wartime.

DeVoto's attention had been drawn back to the subject even before America became involved in the fighting. Crisis, culminating in the fall of France and the desperate Battle of Britain, had brought many a former expatriate to some sober second thoughts. In the spring of 1941 one of them, Archibald MacLeish, had published an essay, "The Irresponsibles," in which he blamed the writers of his time, including himself, for having been too "objective," for having failed to fulfill the writer's true "office," which was to be a priest of democracy, and for having by these delinquencies contributed to democracy's dark time. DeVoto had begun his Phi Beta Kappa address of June 1941 with a discussion of MacLeish's essay, which he thought an expression of crisis patriotism, and his address had scorched the crisis patriots and deathbed converts almost as hotly as "A Generation Beside the Limpopo" had scorched the same people before national emergency or the United Front had brought them to the defense of their country and culture.

Their trouble was not, he had said to the Sanders Theater audience on the day before graduation day 1941, that they had been too objective or had failed to live up to the mystical obligations of their priestly calling. Their trouble was what he had been telling them it was since the end of the twenties. It was that, pretending to describe American life, they had persistently misrepresented it.

In Bloomington, in the spring of 1943, he set out to document that thesis once and for all. It was not a simple thesis, and he granted many exceptions, and began by admitting the absurdity of trying to characterize a whole generation of writers in an hour, or even in six. He deplored the simplifications forced upon him by circumstance. Nevertheless it was the simplifications that most of his hearers heard, partly because DeVoto's gift for phrasemaking in the heat of combat made his castigation of the literature approved by the intellectual critics sound like an indictment of the entire literature of the period. For another thing, he perhaps underestimated the extent to which the "approved" literature had consolidated its position within such academies as the University of Indiana —the extent to which the academy and the Young Intellectuals had fused. The tradition had already set and hardened, and it resounded with the solidity of stone when he attacked it. His hearers thought him, not without reason, anti-literary, and many resented his vehemence. They had not learned the trick of discounting him 20 per cent for rhetoric; they did not hear the qualifications, because they were all but drowned out in the impetuousness of attack. Both in the Phi Beta Kappa address and in the Patten Lectures, DeVoto thought he was speaking of the fashionable or accepted literature, that which the critics had granted validity for its time. What he said, more often than not, was "the literature of the nineteen twenties."

The literature of the nineteen twenties [he had said in the Phi Beta Kappa address] was rooted in ignorance and contempt. It did not challenge or summon. It asserted that the bud had been winterkilled, that the planting was unworthy and there could be no harvest, that the people had no greatness. . . . But we may remember that while literature repudiated America as the waste land, the American mind pushed back the limits of the unknown, advanced the frontiers of knowledge, carried science and invention farther than they had ever gone before, tremendously extended and improved the educational system, grappled with the problems of a postwar world, made over transportation and communication, made over commerce and manufacture and distribution and finance, remade the face of the continent, progressively, even in depression, raised the living standards of the American people, educated them, lengthened their span of life, increased their health, refined their taste, and filled the world with a plenitude of goods never dreamed of in all history before. Here at least was a spectacle. But what literature saw in it was the waste land, peopled by the contemptible typist home at teatime and the young man carbuncular.[1]

Back in the time of the Battle of Britain, when the author of the typist home at teatime and the young man carbuncular had put on the steel helmet of an air-raid warden, all Cambridge had smiled. The world was not ending with a whimper as literary prediction had specified. And that, said DeVoto, was because literary prediction was based upon literary description, which in so far as it referred to America had been spectacularly wrong through most of the twentieth century. It had taken soundings on the literary side and found America shallow, whereas all it had had to do was to throw the lead over the other side and find depth. The prodigals had squandered their substance abroad, living on remittances from America until they wore out their funds and their welcome, and then they came home and were greeted with fatted calves, and developed stern, resolute feelings about the old farm. DeVoto's feelings toward them were not warm, and never had been. He rewrote the story of the Prodigal Son from the viewpoint of the son for whom no fatted calves had ever been slaughtered, the one who had been stuck in a furrow while his brother played expatriate.

In Bloomington he expanded the unpublished Phi Beta Kappa talk into six lectures, pouring in as documentation much material from the English 70 notes that he had once planned to utilize in a book with Robert Frost at its center. To those six lectures illustrating how some of the most talented men of their time had gone wrong about their country because they took too narrowly literary a view of it, he appended a chapter on two non-literary Americans who by simple devotion and integrity in their work had affected American life in ways the literary might envy. One was John Wesley Powell, explorer of the Colorado River and founder of the United States Geological Survey, the Bureau of American Ethnology, and the Bureau of Reclamation. The other was Dr. Robert H. Aldrich, the Boston physician who had played skeptical instructor to DeVoto's comic-opera first-aid class in Cambridge and who was the developer of the gentian-violet treatment of burns. The America which by literary appraisal was enfeebled, stereotyped, vulgarized, insensitive, puritanical, and philistine had produced hundreds and thousands of such men, whom the literary had never heard of. Forget to be literary for one moment and America revealed itself as one of the most vigorous civilizations mankind had ever evolved. Not flawless. Vigorous. Creative. Ready. Hopeful. And capable of meeting such a crisis as Hitler's war with cheerfulness, humor, and confidence.

Once, years before, defending his overstated essay on the co-ed as the hope of liberal education, DeVoto had said to William Sloane, "Well, I made my point. Women have minds." Here, too, he made his point, and overmade it: a non-literary activity may be important, and a civilization may as properly be judged by its science as by its literature. But he made his point at the expense of the profession of letters, the profession to which he had given twenty-five years of his life, the profession his hearers had come to hear explicated and praised. Not everyone in the Bloomington audience listened with a calm mind, and that surprised DeVoto and threw him on the defensive. He had thought that crisis patriotism, and the conversion of such people as MacLeish and Van Wyck Brooks,[2] would have produced some support for his position. Instead, he encountered resentful silence, all the stronger and more widespread because, in hunting major adversaries through the smoke of battle, he had again come upon Saladin. A good part of the Patten Lectures came down to another repudiation of the early ideas of Van Wyck Brooks, not because DeVoto hated Brooks or wished to persecute him, but because he found him, as before, the most eloquent and influential champion of literary ideas with which he disagreed.

He went home from Bloomington feeling that the lectures had been a disaster. Shortly he had to fight out his crepuscular battle with Frost, and there was always the Easy Chair to consume the best part of a week out of every month, and the war to worry about, and the way in which his favorite country managed war information. The vortical suction of his own energy drew him into other matters, including other controversies more rewarding than his warmed-over irritation at the literary. But with a certain defiance, confidently expecting to see the reviewers illustrate the very attitudes he described, he revised the Patten Lectures into a book and called it *The Literary Fallacy*. Simultaneously with its publication, in April 1944, the *Saturday Review* ran a part of the final chapter under the title "They Turned Their Backs on America."

This time the lectures got more than the damnation of minimum and chilly applause. One week after his essay appeared in the *Saturday Review*, one of the novelists whose work DeVoto had used to illustrate the endemic literary disparagement of America erupted into reply. He was a Nobel prize winner and a sort of friend; in the early twenties DeVoto had thought him the most significant American novelist. He was also the husband of Dorothy Thompson, whom DeVoto had publicly spanked in the Easy Chair for December 1942. And he was a close friend of Van Wyck Brooks, who had recently, and not for the first time, been taken to the hospital suffering from nervous collapse. If DeVoto had deliberately set out to stir up an antagonist with a personal grievance and with powers of vituperation equal to his own, he could hardly have done better than Sinclair Lewis.

In literary treatises [began Mr. Lewis] it has not been customary to make one's points by yelling "Fool" and "Liar," but perhaps we have all been wrong. In his new volume *The Literary Fallacy*, my old friend Mr. Bernard DeVoto . . . has this pronouncement:
"Writers must be content to hold their peace until they know what they are talking about. Readers must be willing to hold them to the job if they refuse to hold themselves. An uninstructed gentleness toward writers has been the mistake of readers of our time. Words like 'fool' and 'liar' might profitably come back to use. . . . If literature is to be serious, then it cannot be permitted folly and lying, and when they appear in it, then they must be labeled and denounced."

Very well. I denounce Mr. Bernard DeVoto as a fool and a tedious and egotistical fool, as a liar and a pompous and boresome liar.[3]

That sort of journalism had hardly been seen in America since the Gold Rush. It went beyond insult; it resorted to horsewhip, derringer, biting, gouging, and kneeing in the groin. The rules of debate which DeVoto thought he had followed in the lectures, the statement of the opposition case and a systematic refutation of it, here went out the window. Lewis stated the DeVoto thesis as baldly as possible, with none of its qualifications and exemptions, only to denounce and ridicule it, and he pounced upon the renewed dispute with Van Wyck Brooks. The real thesis of *The Literary Fallacy*, Lewis said, was "merely that Mr. DeVoto is an incalculably wiser and nobler man than Mr. Van Wyck Brooks," and the real impetus behind the book was DeVoto's brattish, febrile necessity to show off in public.

Lewis used more terms than "fool" and "liar." He found such epithets as "yahoo." He called scornful attention to the slick fiction of John August, whose serial *The Woman in the Picture* was then running in *Collier's*. He quoted some John August dialogue as an example of the serious literature that DeVoto wrote while belittling the fiction of Hemingway, Fitzgerald, and Wolfe. With approval he quoted *The Literary Fallacy* to the effect that when writers chance to be frivolous or silly their books will correspond. He described his early encounters with DeVoto, his "screaming, his bumptiousness, his conviction that he was a combination of Walter Winchell and Erasmus." He made venomous reference to "that froglike face."

The savagery of the attack brought a kind of appalled stillness into the literary world, followed by a boil of discussion both happy and indignant. DeVoto's enemies wrote letters to the *Saturday Review*, saying in effect how gratified they were to see a man who had gone around twisting donkeys' tails finally lay hands on a mule. His friends were filled with an embarrassed anger that inhibited them from entering a quarrel already so painful. Many felt that the low blows, the personal vilification and ridicule, the unforgivable reference to DeVoto's looks, could simply not be replied to, though Dixon Wecter, Ted Morrison, and Kitty Bowen all wrote the *Saturday Review* protesting its publication of personal scurrilities.

This last was DeVoto's own attitude. He was as furious with Norman Cousins for printing Lewis' piece as with Lewis for writing it. He said that if he had still been editor he would never have printed such an attack on anyone until the personal vilification was removed from it. Argument he had expected; disagreement was his native atmosphere. But he insisted that he had vilified no one in *The Literary Fallacy*, had been contemptuous of no one and angry at no one, and had imputed bad motives to no one. He had attacked certain ideas and a certain way of thinking, and he had expected that anyone replying would feel bound by the ordinary rules of decency. When Cousins permitted the continuing publication of letters and doggerel containing personal slurs on DeVoto, he wrote Cousins a sizzling cold letter demanding that he make correspondents confine themselves to the ideas and leave personalities alone. They were indefensible either as literary discussion or as journalism.[4]

By May 8, when that protest was registered, it had been a month since publication of the excerpt that had started all the controversy. By then the talk had begun to die down. DeVoto's failure to reply to Lewis publicly starved the fire. But there was one unexpected and positive result brought about by the squabble. Malcolm Cowley, who was about to review *The Literary Fallacy* for the *New Republic* when Lewis' blast appeared, wrote to DeVoto to dissociate himself from the virulence of the Lewis essay. Cowley, too, was a close friend of Brooks's, and like Lewis he did not think much of *The Literary Fallacy*. But he wanted DeVoto to know that his forthcoming unfavorable review was not motivated by personal rancor. He thought that DeVoto's apparent ill will toward some of the writers he discussed had provoked similar feelings in some readers, and he did not think DeVoto understood the period from 1905 to 1920, when the ideas he disliked had been germinating. Brooks, he said, had probably not understood it fully either, but he had *described* it exactly. After his first breakdown he had become more scholarly and more cautious in judgment (as DeVoto had admitted); he had grown from a prophetic Emerson into a sort of Prescott-cum-Holmes. And through all his development, Cowley said, Brooks had remained one of the finest and gentlest of men.[5]

Cowley's letter contained an implicit rebuke, but its frankness and honesty blunted the DeVoto stinger. Cowley was one of the Young Intellectuals—once a Harvard aesthete, then an ambulance driver, then an expatriate, then a literary Marxist—precisely the kind whom DeVoto habitually deplored and disagreed with. But he showed himself reasonable and friendly, and his openness turned away wrath. DeVoto replied to his letter with a completely reasonable and friendly letter of his own. By one of those accidents that provide seasoning to literary controversies, he made his most explicit and revealing statement on the long disagreement with Brooks to one of the opposition, one of Brooks's closest friends.

It seems to me, and this is the point of my book, that the writers I was talking about sank their shafts in too small, too restricted, and too unrepresentative an area. Certainly the plumbing industry thinks that bathtubs are the measure of civilization, which leaves criticism the duty of pointing out that they really aren't. So I point out that literary experience isn't the measure, either.

I owe you a considerable debt for stating in public what the book is about. So far, in the stuff that has come in, only Harry Hansen, apart from you, has done that. . . . It's only silly of, for instance, Gannet to maintain that when I talk about Powell, medicine, and the like I'm showing off how much I know and calling people's attention to the fact that so-and-so knows less than I do. What I'm saying is, look, this kind of experience is one of many good kinds that the boys failed altogether to sink their shafts into, and until they take this and other vital kinds of experience into account, what they say is necessarily wrong. That's my thesis.

Now consider this, and don't think I'm kidding. I honestly think the book is good-natured and soft-spoken. I intended everything I said about individual writers to be considered in the light of the reservations and qualifications which I thought were made sufficiently clear in the opening statement. . . . However, all I want to say now is that I don't think I'm strident, angry, or unjust. . . .

I did know about Brooks's breakdown. I faced that question long ago. I had written about half of my first Mark Twain book when I learned about it. Nothing in the world appeals so directly to my emotions as nervous trouble. I scouted around and found that Hans Zinsser was an intimate friend of Brooks's. I went to him and said, look here, I'm writing such and such a book, saying such and such things—told him the whole argument and all the points I intended to make, reading him some of the passages I had written. I offered to do either of two things, drop the book entirely or rewrite it centering the argument on someone else and leaving Brooks entirely unmentioned, if he thought that it would have a bad effect on Brooks, wound him personally, or affect his future. It was the first time I had met Hans, and one of the most profound friendships of my life began that day. Hans first said that he did not think my book would have a bad effect on Brooks, that if it had any effect at all he thought it would be a good one. Then he turned to and preached. He said, you damned young fool, this is your book isn't it? you mean and believe what you say don't you? then what in hell do you mean by taking into account anything except what you conceive to be the truth? He laid into me as few ever have, and I went away and took up my stand at the passages of Jordan. Ever since then I have tried to concentrate on the idea, whether Brooks's or anyone else's, and to disregard the personality of its begetter, along with its psychological origins. . . .[6]

That friendly, confidential, and healing conversation with a member of the enemy camp was probably the best thing that came out of the furor over *The Literary Fallacy*. It demonstrated something about DeVoto, too: know him a little, learn to discount him a little, meet him on some sort of personal basis, and the belligerence and contentiousness dropped away, leaving exposed what all his friends knew—a man who had much to say, even if he did always oversay it, and a man, moreover, of principle, kindness, and generosity of spirit. It might have astonished Sinclair Lewis to see what the dropped guard revealed, though he was himself, with emotional difficulties that made DeVoto's look minor, a man whose essential spirit was both kind and generous.

3 · *Strange Fruit*

Lillian Smith's *Strange Fruit*, a novel on the theme of miscegenation, was published by Reynal & Hitchcock on February 29, 1944. It showed every sign of climbing rapidly up the best-seller lists, and sold freely in Atlanta, Birmingham, and many cities that in 1944 might have been expected to suppress it because of its subject matter. On March 17 its sale was stopped in Boston and Cambridge on the ground that it was obscene.

It was not stopped by legal proceedings. The Massachusetts obscenity statute forbade the sale of materials tending to corrupt the morals of youth, but no one made a complaint to the police that *Strange Fruit* was contributing to juvenile corruption. The book was closed out of Boston and Cambridge bookstores by action of the Board of Trade of the Boston Book Merchants, which for a good while had been preventing legal actions under the obscenity statutes by killing doubtful books in advance—opening their own veins in order not to be bled. A bookseller who violated the ban of the association would not be defended by the association if a criminal complaint was brought against him. Needless to say, the association got most of its confidential clues about books that might cause trouble from the Watch and Ward Society.

This preventive censorship operated by caprice, whim, timidity, and premonition. Books had been known to be untouched in their original editions and then banned in reprint. On occasion, publishers faced with the likelihood of Watch and Ward blacklisting had agreed not to ship any more books after those already in the stores were sold. This meant that a title could become obscene on a deadline, or when purchased directly from the publisher, but be without spot if purchased before a certain date or from a jobber who had made no promises to Watch and Ward. Sometimes booksellers afraid of snoops and plain-clothes men simply sent back questionable books rather than take the risk. And nobody knew what was supposed to corrupt youth, though Bernard DeVoto's early guess in the *Harvard Graduates' Magazine* was as good as any: anything that sexually excited a member of Watch and Ward was corrupting. In the case of *Strange Fruit*, the offense was a single word, twice repeated. Richard Fuller, owner of the Old Corner Bookshop and head of the booksellers' association, admitted, in a tone almost aggrieved, that the excision of a couple of short passages would have made the novel entirely acceptable, since aside from those passages the Watch and Ward had given it a clean bill of health.[1]

The Civil Liberties Union of Massachusetts (CLUM) had long desired a test case in order to get a legal definition of obscenity and to bring the Massachusetts regulation into line with recent court decisions in other states. This could be done only by forcing censorship into the open, which meant into the hands of the police. *Strange Fruit*, a serious novel on a serious theme, and written moreover by a southern lady of unimpeachable gentility, seemed a good vehicle for such a case. After consultation with the publishers, the CLUM decided to precipitate an arrest by staging a carefully publicized sale of the book.

The Harvard Coop, approached, shrank away. So did other prominent bookstores. Eventually the Harvard Liberal Union located a bookseller who was willing to put himself in jeopardy. He was Abraham Isenstadt, operator of the University Law Book Exchange, on Harvard Square. The man who bought the book was Bernard DeVoto, chairman of the censorship committee of CLUM—a committee that included his old enemy F. O. Matthiessen, now quaintly become his ally.

Propped conveniently around the crowded little bookstall on April 4 (this was virtually the very hour when the *Saturday Review*, carrying an excerpt from *The Literary Fallacy*, arrived on the stands, and a week before Sinclair Lewis' retort incourteous rattled the windows), were reporters and news cameramen, four Cambridge policemen, Frank Taylor of Reynal & Hitchcock, Matthiessen, a Civil Liberties attorney named Anthony Brayton, and A. Sprague Coolidge of the Harvard Chemistry Department, who was there to discuss bail as a member of CLUM. DeVoto asked for the book, Isenstadt produced it, DeVoto handed him a five-dollar bill and received, as witnesses solemnly attested later, $2.25 in change. Sergeant Breen then stepped forward and arrested DeVoto and Isenstadt and confiscated the book. As he was doing so, a copy of May's *Criminal Law* fell off a shelf onto the head of one of the witnesses.[2]

On April 12, after a brief hearing, Judge Arthur P. Stone of the district court postponed proceedings for two weeks while he read the offending novel. On April 26 he ruled *Strange Fruit* obscene under the statute. Though he thought it "a story that might be told," he found scattered through it "indecencies" that had been lugged in for the apparent purpose of selling the book, and these in his opinion tended to corrupt the morals of youth. He fined Isenstadt two hundred dollars and gave him a suspended jail sentence. The charges against DeVoto he dismissed, since there was no law against buying an obscene book, only against selling it.

Within a few days of Judge Stone's decision, and basing their action upon it, several other Massachusetts towns banned *Strange Fruit*. On May 15 the Post Office Department, acting on the same decision and perhaps under pressure from Watch and Ward and the Society for the Suppression of Vice, prohibited its distribution through the mails, and warned newspapers and magazines not to accept advertisements for it, under threat of prosecution. Within hours, under counterpressure from the literary and publishing world, it lifted the ban, saying somewhat lamely that *Strange Fruit* could be accepted for mailing "at the publisher's risk." Presumably the final action of the Post Office would depend upon the decision of the Supreme Court of Massachusetts when CLUM's appeal finally reached it.

Reynal & Hitchcock announced that it would take the risk, admitting with few evidences of sorrow that since its publication only a month and a half before, the novel had sold two hundred thousand copies, quite a few of them (though it did not say so) probably attributable to the Massachusetts censorship. Norman Cousins of the *Saturday Review* suspended his epistolary dispute with Bernard DeVoto over the Lewis article long enough to announce that he would defy any ban against advertisements for *Strange Fruit*. He said he would accept them until the Post Office Department's order had been backed by due process of law. So he, like Matthiessen, found himself simultaneously at war with DeVoto and allied with him. Dorothy Thompson and others had already joined up as signatories of a protesting letter from the American Center of the P.E.N. to the Boston booksellers, and so there they were too, intimately associated with the anti-literary philistine in the defense of literature.

Between the uproar over his own book and his much-publicized activity in the *Strange Fruit* case, DeVoto could hardly have been more in the public eye if he had assaulted President James Bryant Conant in the Yard. Plenty of people had been lying in wait to fill him with arrows, and some did; but some, like Matthiessen, were partly disarmed. Rather than divide allies in a cause he thought worthy, Matthiessen withdrew his request to review *The Literary Fallacy* for the *Saturday Review*. And Malcolm Cowley, though his unfavorable review appeared as scheduled,[3] went out of his way to remark in it how friendly a man DeVoto was "when not at his typewriter," and to praise his generous help to "neglected scholars and persecuted books." The fact was, the man whom many of the literary Left had called a Fascist showed himself more ready to fight for civil liberties than almost any of the Left except Matthiessen. The radical in him, the western Populist who had been submerged during his long struggle for recognition and his long war with the literary fashionables came out again, not cautiously like a groundhog scared of his shadow, but boldly, even truculently. It was as if writing *The Literary Fallacy* had permitted the healing of an old, infected wound. Just as his desire to write fiction would ultimately be cauterized by public neglect, his parallel impulses toward literary criticism were here brought to an end by the revelation of how little agreement he evoked from the guild. For better or worse, he was a total maverick, and the truth was, he did not enjoy the role nearly as much as he appeared to. Whatever he might pretend, he did not enjoy feeling that his ideas, which were as honest as they were positive, were being met with cold or angry hostility.

Good-by to literary criticism, then. The noise about his little book died down quickly. The struggle against censorship, a struggle in which he enlisted the support and approval of even his enemies, was a longer and more rewarding fight. It would go on until his death.

Delayed by the slowness of the courts, but given a persistent interest because of its possible effect on the whole field of civil liberties, the *Strange Fruit* case dragged on for a year and a half, until on September 17, 1945, the Massachusetts Supreme Court upheld the lower court's decision and declared the novel to be finally and incontrovertibly and legally obscene. Strange as that opinion must seem now, and misguided as it seemed to many then, it was not unexpected, and it had its compensations. The case had brought about a movement for revision of the Massachusetts obscenity law, for one thing; for another, it had given a man with an established pulpit repeated opportunities to preach civil liberties to a national audience.

DeVoto let the American public in on the development and implications of the *Strange Fruit* case in three separate Easy Chairs (May and July 1944 and February 1945), as well as in numerous lectures and letters to the press, and he summarized it finally in a long article, originally planned as a pamphlet, that he published in the *New England Quarterly* in June 1946. For more than two years, he kept the Boston booksellers and their Watch and Ward ringmasters exposed to a publicity they did not want and a ridicule they could not reply to. He threw down and tramped on the notion, widely believed in intellectual Cambridge, that it was exclusively Catholic bigotry that motivated and supported Boston's censorship. The Catholic Church might support it, he pointed out, but so did plenty of Protestants. Bigotry was not so narrowly denominational as it was held to be, and censorship could never have fastened itself upon the community without the tacit support of rich, wellborn, indifferent, lazy citizens of all religious varieties inured to the "comfortable acceptance of the intolerable."

Losing all the battles, he and CLUM won the war. The new obscenity statute that the legislature passed in May 1945 was no great improvement on the old one, but by the time it passed, the booksellers were far less likely to collaborate in its enforcement. And though the Supreme Court had upheld the lower court's decision, the dissenting opinion of Judge Lummus was so eloquent a civil-liberties document that the Easy Chair was overjoyed to publicize and praise it while lambasting the majority opinion. When correspondents rebuked the Easy Chair, saying that opinions of the high court were above public criticism, the Easy Chair had its friend Charles Curtis dig out a whole series of cases demonstrating that high-court decisions were no such thing.

Strange Fruit was not one of the great landmark cases by which literature was progressively emancipated from the interference of snoops, prudes, and psychopaths. It lost all along the line. But neither was it a mere side show, like Henry Mencken's vaudeville defense of "Hatrack" and the *American Mercury*'s mailing privileges in 1926—that famous couple of days when Mencken, equipped with a peddler's license, stood on Brimstone Corner and sold a copy of the *Mercury* to T. Frank Chase, the head of Watch and Ward, and, clowning for the news cameras, bit the fifty-cent piece that Chase handed him. In the long run, though he saved the *Mercury* from postal suppression, Mencken probably did little for freedom of the press and civil liberties in general. The *Strange Fruit* case did.

Far more publicly than DeVoto's obscure protest in the *Harvard Graduates' Magazine* against the prosecution of Al DeLacey and the Dunster House Bookshop, it challenged Watch and Ward and the booksellers who submitted to its domination. It helped make the phrase "Banned in Boston" in a term of ridicule and contempt. Even while going down to defeat, it weakened the control of the narrow and censorious over literature and ideas. It began to put the censors slowly to death by shutting off public acceptance of their role.

It also established Bernard DeVoto more firmly than ever as a public defender, champion of the consumer, asserter of the people's right to know and to make free choices. If Edmund Wilson in 1944 or 1945 had still been curious to know what "body of ideas" DeVoto lived by, he could easily have found out. DeVoto had more and more plainly stood and unfolded himself. In 1937 he had told Wilson that he operated *ad hoc*, but he had read too much Pareto even then to believe that any man's whole life could be lived experimentally. He should have said that he operated *ad hoc* the way a spider does. He might spring into the air, or hang by a thread, or turn handsprings while assaulting a fly, but he kept his web under him or attached to him, and he retreated to it when he felt endangered. Whitehead had said, "Unless society is permeated, through and through, with routine, civilization vanishes." The routine that DeVoto counted on, spoke for, defended against its enemies, was the routine of the Bill of Rights. He was a very American intelligence, and in nothing was he more American than this.

4 · *"The Job I'm Eyeing Is Lewis and Clark"*

John August opened 1944 with his fifth and last serial, *The Woman in the Picture,* which ran in *Collier's* from January 6 to January 29. As an omen of the year to come, it could have been better, for in the belief that DeVoto would at any moment be on his way to Africa for the Army, *Collier's* had not called on him for the revisions it thought necessary, but had had them made by the staff.[1] Somebody had rewritten the first third of the story, and thus had exposed DeVoto, even more than John August's workmanlike prose would have exposed him, to Sinclair Lewis' sneer about "serious literature." It had not been a good story before *Collier's* mangled it. Melodramatic and implausible, a combination of cops-and-robbers and *It Can't Happen Here*, it was the least defensible of August's efforts, despite its author's attempt to give it verisimilitude by writing into it much of the itinerary of his last trip West and by endowing its hero with Bernard DeVoto's well-observed migraines. From its opening page it was a horse made by contrivance. *Collier's*, introducing the committee principle, brought it into the semblance of a camel, and it was still a camel when Little, Brown published it in March, on the eve of the *Strange Fruit* and *Literary Fallacy* fights.

Throughout the spring, with both disputes going, DeVoto was also involved in a continuing protest against the suppression and distortion of war news, a subject with which his fruitless negotiations with the War Department and his close friendship with Elmer Davis had given him some familiarity. That protest had led him to the edge of politics, for when Wendell Willkie, campaigning for the Republican presidential nomination, picked up one of the Easy Chairs saying that the government's management of war news was more arbitrary and more stringent than in any previous American war, DeVoto laid aside everything else and at Willkie's request documented the statement out of the Spanish American and Civil wars. As he wrote Davis, "If Willkie says we know less about this war than about any previous war we've fought, that's me speaking. By the book."[2] But Willkie withdrew after the Wisconsin primary in April, somewhat to DeVoto's regret. He would not likely have voted for him, but he liked Willkie's honesty, he was fed up with the New Deal, and he hated to see good historical research go to waste. Clearly it would have gratified him to be close to the engine room of politics, advising a man of power.

During that same spring of 1944 he was in continuous conflict with the Mark Twain Estate. Late in 1943 Clara Gabrilowitsch had deposed Charles Lark, a friend of her father's and a man whom DeVoto had come to respect highly, and replaced him with a somewhat fussy, meticulous, unliterary maritime lawyer named Thomas Chamberlain. Knowing nothing about his job, he set out to learn it. He wanted lists, inventories, abstracts. He liked things in tripli-

cate. He wanted to make the smallest decisions, down to the repair of the typewriter in the Widener office. In particular, he
caused DeVoto endless trouble by his unwillingness to accept the
usual procedures for copyrighting materials out of the Mark Twain
papers which were to be published in magazines. Instead of allow-
ing them to be copyrighted along with the total contents of the
magazine, and having the copyright later assigned to the Mark
Twain Company, he demanded the much more cumbersome, indeed almost impossible, procedure of copyrighting them in advance
so that the magazine which printed them could then credit them to
the Mark Twain Company. And he was slow and cautious about
everything, so that opportunities for publicity profitable to the
Mark Twain interests were lost.[3]

His stubbornness on the copyright issue, plus his habit of procrastination, plus his apparent belief that DeVoto was some kind
of salaried underling whose time was always at the Estate's command, plus his unwillingness to let DeVoto make editorial or other
decisions, led to a series of irritations and eventually to DeVoto's
attempt to resign. He made the offer informally in December
1943, when Chamberlain was taking over from Lark, and he made
it again, formally and forcefully, on May 27, 1944, remarking that
he got neither pay nor status from the job, that it burdened him
with correspondence of many kinds, that he was constantly being
called upon for inventories, that he was given no editorial discretion, not even the discretion to say what scholars should be allowed
to use the papers, and that his right to publish anything he wanted
from the papers, never questioned until now, seemed to have become a matter of petition and permission. At a luncheon meeting
with Chamberlain and representatives of Harper & Brothers at the
Century on June 5, he passionately asked to be released, but was
soothed and persuaded to remain. He did refuse to gratify Chamberlain by coming down from his summer hideout on the Ames
Estate in Annisquam to supervise the new inventory that Chamberlain wanted made.

The fact was, he had lost interest in the Mark Twain papers,
and he had written most of what he wanted to say about Mark
Twain. That interest seems to have failed along with his general
interest in literary criticism. Though he could have finished in a
short time the volume of letters that he had three-quarters assembled, he made no move to do so. After the summer of 1944 his
curatorship of the Mark Twain papers was nominal, a token position which he was ready at any time to unload and which he left

almost entirely to Elaine Breed, Rosamond Chapman's successor as secretary.

He had a tendency to consume things, to need new fuel. As he told the literary wars good-by with *The Literary Fallacy*, and as his interest in Mark Twain cooled, he felt the oncoming of another book, the quickening of a new excitement. Over a period of years, ever since he had inserted into the *Saturday Review* the story of Lewis and Clark's Christmas among the Mandans, he had been periodically tempted toward a history of their expedition. There, and in Jefferson's purchase of Louisiana, was the match that had touched off the long running fire of the westward expansion. Following his habit of going to the experts for advice, he had talked about such a book with Mattingly, Paul Buck, and other historians. On April 30, 1944, at the hottest time in *The Literary Fallacy* and *Strange Fruit* fights and at the height of his irritation with Chamberlain and the Mark Twain Estate, he accosted Henry Steele Commager:

Dear Henry:

As the man who discovered I'm a bum novelist before Red Lewis did, you've got certain obligations. The one you're held to at the moment is to give me advice. I'm playing with the notion of getting to work—in a minor way since I won't be able to go all out on it for some months—on a historical job. . . .

The job I'm eyeing is Lewis and Clark. . . . I propose to draw on the narrative talent that is denied me in the current reviews and write a narrative history of the expedition. That's that, but naturally I want the book to be as complete, as understanding, and as widely useful and applicable as it can be made without breaking up the narrative. I want to learn as much as I can. I also want to shorten the learning process as much as possible. . . .

You see, I'm taking a backward leap into a field where I'm virginal, bucolic, naive, wide-eyed, trustful, and practically as ignorant as Red Lewis. So, the idea is, you take me by my little hand and lead me in.

I want to know about Louisiana. I want to know how the sense of that vast, unknown area began to penetrate the American consciousness, in what form, with what speed. I want to know how people thought about it—and how to find out what they believed about it and what they knew about it. . . . The idea of Louisiana before we got it. And, as a lead out of that, how much can I get in Jefferson and how do I go about looking for it?

That's the heaviest job. But I also want to master the purchase itself and to do so with as little waste motion as possible. I want to master the essentials on the spot and at the sources, French and American—and Spanish too, if they're essential, and I'm too damn dumb to know—and also in the judgment of modern historians. . . .

I think I can get the Indians for myself. Some time ago I got an urge to read more about them and so I've been laying down something that turns out to be useful. But if you have any notions, just run them in.

And General Remarks. You're Old Killbuck in person and here I am, a greenhorn, a mangeur de lard, just starting off into the hills for the first time. With a horn or two of Monongahely under your belt you're feeling genial and you decide to prepare me as well as you can for the first sight of the buffalo and the Blackfeet. You think it's a shame that as nice a guy as me should enter the wilderness so poorly equipped. You're going to give me all the general advice that occurs to you, in the pious hope that I'll be able to save my scalp.

Sure, I know this is unconscionable and you have more to do than you'll ever get done and who the hell am I to bust in on a busy man, and all that. On the other hand, you've got a stern obligation to your profession, and if amateurs will insist on trying to practise it, you've got to do what you can to keep the resulting damage at a minimum.[4]

That was where his wandering glance was falling at the end of April 1944. That was what, out of a whirlwind of intellectual warfare and a daily life tense with crises and deadlines, his extraordinary energy suggested to him. It began to feel as if all the varieties of literary and historical experience to which he had exposed himself had been leading up to this. The program that he had announced to Melville Smith from the middle of his breakdown in Ogden in 1920 had been headed steadily, by whatever detours and deviations, this way. The continental vision that he had then merely glimpsed was coming into focus. Now he was looking back 140 years to the time when the Lewis and Clark party was gathering at the mouth of the Missouri with the intention of dissipating mystery and finding the way to the Great South Sea, and with the less-than-half-comprehended further intention of creating a United States that was one country from the Atlantic to the Pacific.

But even now he could give it only a glance. There was always the Easy Chair, as demanding as a bright child and as unshakable as an albatross. There was the twice-failed novel *Mountain Time*, which he had dug out again while hanging around in Washington hotel rooms waiting for the Army to make up its mind to something. And there was also a historical interruption, a completely unexpected diversion of his interest and energy: On the way back to 1804 he got hung up in the 1830s. As if following his own historical practice of simultaneity, these matters all demanded to be dealt with, and were dealt with, at the same time. But they are best treated one by one.

5 · *Historian by Serendipity*

Sometime near the beginning of 1944, about three months before the publication of *The Literary Fallacy* and the comic-opera sale of a copy of *Strange Fruit* in the crowded little University Law Book Exchange, there came into the Houghton Mifflin office at 2 Park Street, Boston, a gentleman named Emery Reves.[1] He had in his briefcase the rough outline of a book and a bundle of more than one hundred watercolors of the western plains and mountains painted in 1837 by a Baltimore artist, Alfred Jacob Miller. These belonged to a Mrs. Clyde Porter of Missouri. She had run into them in the Peale Museum in Philadelphia, had recognized them as a unique record of the mountain fur trade, and had succeeded in buying them.

Reves, already known to Houghton Mifflin, was a Hungarian émigré, an enigmatic and fascinating figure like one of those historical people DeVoto was fond of pulling out of the past to illuminate a moment when the energies of a man or a nation were about to enter a new phase. A friend of Winston Churchill and other international politicians, he had made a living in Paris before the outbreak of war by copyrighting the League of Nations speeches of his acquaintances and selling them to the news media, splitting the take with the authors. Later, after coming to America, he had written a book called *The Anatomy of Peace*, and as agent or representative of the author Jan Karski had brought out an account of Poland under the Nazis called *The Story of a Secret State*, which had been a Book of the Month Club choice. Two years hence, in 1946, he would serve as the intermediary who enabled Houghton Mifflin to buy book rights to Churchill's memoirs for three hundred thousand dollars. He was an operator, and one with authentic connections. Now, in early 1944, he was the owner of Hyperion Press, which was actually defunct and existed only as a name; and he wanted to publish, in some sort of collaboration with Houghton Mifflin, these Miller watercolors of the West, with an introductory essay by their owner and discoverer, Mrs. Porter. He wanted some competent western historian to write about twenty thousand words of captions, for a fee. Various people including Dixon Wecter, then director of the Huntington Library, had suggested that DeVoto was his man.

Houghton Mifflin agreed that DeVoto was his man, though it foresaw a possible difficulty. DeVoto was a Little, Brown author. He might be borrowed for a caption job without serious difficulty, but it was Houghton Mifflin's opinion that twenty thousand words of captions would not do justice to the Miller pictures, or make an adequate book. Clearly the watercolors and the captions would *be* the book, since Mrs. Porter's introductory essay was not conceived as anything more than that. The tentative title, *The Stewart-Miller Expedition*, suggested a full account of the western journeys of William Drummond Stewart, the Scottish baronet who had spent parts of seven years in the West at the very climax of the fur trade and had taken Miller into the wilderness with him in 1837 to paint and draw it. Houghton Mifflin guessed that what Reves ought to ask of DeVoto was more like forty thousand words than twenty thousand, and that would be a book, to write which DeVoto would have to get a release from Little, Brown.

The release turned out to be the smallest of the problems connected with Reves's proposal. And if it had been forty times as difficult as it turned out to be, DeVoto would somehow have arranged it. One look at the pictures, which he knew were the first ever painted of many of the places they reproduced, and some of which were drawn from such real-life models as Jim Bridger, told him that he must do those captions at all costs.

Houghton Mifflin let him take the pictures home to study, and on February 15, 1944, he reported on them to Reves. Two, perhaps more, had been previously published, but most were new and of inestimable historical importance. He thought the book's title should be changed, since the expedition on which Stewart took Miller was in no sense a joint effort. It was Stewart's expedition; Miller was along as a paid artist. Moreover, if they went through with the book as proposed, DeVoto's contribution and Mrs. Porter's would have to be separately signed. The "research" notes that she had given Reves, on which her introduction would presumably be based, were in DeVoto's opinion totally inadequate and were full of historical errors.

By March 13, when he again wrote to Reves about errors in Mrs. Porter's notes and proposed the terms on which he would undertake to write the captions, he indicated that he was finally free of all military-history projects and ready to go to work. He stated the terms on which he would do the job, but he did not suggest that he would back out if his terms were not met. The Miller pictures had captivated him completely; he was willing to ally himself with someone he thought an incompetent amateur in order to get a chance at them. This was at the time when he had already begun to contemplate Lewis and Clark. Clearly he thought of the captions as an interesting but not-too-demanding preamble.

Within a week he was in correspondence with Charles Camp, Dale Morgan, the Missouri Historical Society, and other informed sources,[2] asking questions about Stewart's years in the mountains, about possible connections between Miller's pictures and the characters Killbuck and Labonté in Ruxton's *Life in the Far West*, and about the implications of specific pictures, including one showing Jim Bridger in armor. As yet he had no commitment either to Reves or to Houghton Mifflin.

On May 11 he sent back the contract that Reves offered, objecting that it did not bind Reves to publish within a specific time and that it said nothing about the return of the manuscript in case Reves failed to perform. Clearly he mistrusted Reves and found his Hyperion Press a dubious publishing house. But on May 27, those minor details having been satisfied, he sent back the signed agreement. The very next day, as we have seen, he tried to resign from the curatorship of the Mark Twain papers, as if clearing away other obligations to permit the pouring of his energies into western history.

But though he might sign the agreement, he remained uneasy about both Reves and Mrs. Porter. He did not trust the one; he thought the other incompetent. Shortly it became evident that Reves did not trust him either, for on June 11 Reves protested DeVoto's writing directly to Mrs. Porter—all communications should come to him as her agent. DeVoto replied that Reves could see his letters to Mrs. Porter for all of him. He had no ill feeling toward her, or toward Reves. He simply did not trust her research and had been trying to straighten out her history. "She confuses wish and guess with fact, as all amateurs do, and I begin by doubting everything, as a historian must." At that point he indicated that he was about ready to begin writing. The job, he estimated, would take four to six weeks, but he did not want to begin until he had seen a fairly finished draft of Mrs. Porter's contribution.

Thus lightly, in approximately the way he would have approached the writing of a magazine article, he set out into the fur trade. But his June 11 letter to Reves accepted the role of historian, and a historian's need for accuracy and thoroughness was already working in him. Having left Stewart's personal history to Mrs. Porter, he kept writing to her trying to get firm facts about the dates of Stewart's expeditions, the fur brigades he traveled with, his relationships with certain famous partisans such as Bridger, Thomas

Fitzpatrick, and Lucien Fontanelle. She could tell him little that he trusted.

But he trusted Reves even less. On September 9, just returned from a working summer on the shore at Annisquam, he wrote Mrs. Porter in frank misgiving. Exactly what was her relation with Reves? DeVoto had no guarantee that Reves would publish the book, and the more the material worked upon him the less willing he was to undertake it until certain details were clearer. So far as DeVoto could tell, Reves had published no books and had no facilities for doing so. Hyperion Press was only a name, and a dead name at that. Reves had approached Houghton Mifflin in the first place as an agent, no more. Just exactly what was he, agent or publisher? What sort of agreement did Mrs. Porter have with him?

DeVoto was still talking about thirty thousand to forty thousand words of captions. Up to now his research had been directed toward locating each picture in time and place, identifying landscapes and possible historical figures and incidents, and relating these sketches from life to the known movements of actual fur brigades during those years in the mountains. But the deeper he went into the pictures, the clearer it became that here in a capsule was the entire mountain fur trade. Here were the great partisans, the competing companies, the native tribes, the repercussions produced by confrontations between the Americans working up the Missouri and across South Pass and the British working up the Columbia and the Snake from the Pacific Northwest. Here were the skills, the way of life, the costumes, stories, legendry, the savage color of the heroic age that had always fired his imagination. Stewart in his baronial wanderings had touched it all. His expeditions were the perfect synecdoche, a part that could be used to illuminate the whole. The plainer that became, the more DeVoto wanted to do it right, and the more uneasy he became about the obscure and unsatisfactory four-way deal among Houghton Mifflin, Reves, Mrs. Porter, and himself.

On September 22 he wrote Mrs. Porter again, laboriously recapitulating the entangled negotiation from the beginning, cautioning her about publishing practices, and saying that in his opinion they ought to talk again and clarify the contract. He also said something else, something significant: that Houghton Mifflin was willing to publish the book even if the caption text ran to twice forty thousand words—if, in fact, the book was converted into something quite different from its previous intention and made into a history "which would indicate the larger outline of the trade, fill in the outline with enough details to make it intelligible to a contem-

Bread Loaf, 1938. Top row: Raymond Everitt, Robeson Bailey, Herbert Agar, Herschel Brickell, Wallace Stegner, Fletcher Pratt; middle row: Gorham Munson, Bernard DeVoto, Theodore Morrison, Robert Frost, John Gassner; bottom row: Mary Stegner, Helen Everitt, Kay Morrison, Eleanor Chilton (Mrs. Herbert Agar).

Archibald MacLeish, Bread Loaf, 1938.

George Homans visiting DeVotos in Walpole, New Hampshire, 1938.

Bernard and Avis DeVoto in 1930s.

Avis DeVoto, Mark and Gordon DeVoto, 1940.

Bread Loaf, with Mr. and Mrs. Mark Saxton.

Bread Loaf. Fletcher Pratt, Bernard DeVoto, William Upson.

Bread Loaf. A. B. Guthrie, Jr., and Bernard DeVoto.

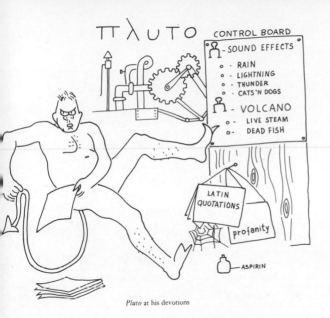

ΠλUTO

CONTROL BOARD

♁ -SOUND EFFECTS
○ - RAIN
○ - LIGHTNING
○ - THUNDER
○ - CATS 'N DOGS

♁ - VOLCANO
○ - LIVE STEAM
○ - DEAD FISH

LATIN QUOTATIONS

profanity

—ASPIRIN

Pluto at his devotions

Two cartoons by Inga Pratt, 1941 and 1947.

To our left we have *Mount DeVoto*, sometimes slurred by the local patois into Mon'deVocal, only active volcano in Vermont. In a recent eruption 43,022 children perished, and several libraries were swallowed up in the crevasses.

Next, distinguished by the revolving air beacon, is *Mount Dean Pratt*, characterized by unusual and complex formations which scientists have been able to study only from the air. Tricky bogs at its foot have trapped many earthbound historians. The middle slopes are infested with snails.

DeVotos home on Berkeley Street, where they moved in 1941.

porary reader, and relate the parts to one another and especially to westward expansion as a whole."

Lovell Thompson and Paul Brooks of Houghton Mifflin were DeVoto's good friends and hearty admirers. From the beginning, they had not wanted to see him held down to twenty thousand words of captions. And now serendipity had worked on him, opportunity had intersected with personal inclination and accumulated capacity. Both DeVoto and Houghton Mifflin wanted that book at its maximum, not at its minimum, and they did not want it inhibited by a dubious collaboration and uncertain publishing arrangements. Though Thompson never shared DeVoto's ill opinion of Reves and thought him simply unacquainted with American publishing practices, he and Brooks agreed that the contract should be discussed and clarified.

On October 15, after conversations with Thompson and with George Stevens, his old *Saturday Review* colleague now with Lippincott, DeVoto wrote Mrs. Porter that they all thought the contractual terms she apparently had with Reves were unfair both to her and to DeVoto. They now proposed a new contract, under which Reves would get 15 per cent of gross and DeVoto 5 per cent of gross and Mrs. Porter 5 per cent of net out of Reves's share. For his function as agent and go-between, those terms were more than generous. If he would not accept them, DeVoto would withdraw.

On October 31 he proposed the new terms to Reves, indicating that Houghton Mifflin would pull out rather than proceed on the old basis. He took a big-money tone: he wanted to begin writing in about six weeks, as soon as he finished a serial (that was *Mountain Time*, and it would be a lot longer than six weeks before he finished it), and he could not afford to put his high-priced time into the Miller book without a new agreement.

Writing privately to Charles Curtis,[3] who was both his lawyer and Houghton Mifflin's, DeVoto denounced Reves as a crook who was trying to cut himself in for a publisher's share, an agent's share, and an author's share, and profit three ways from a transaction in which his contribution had only been to bring the real contributors together. He said he was checking the contract he had made with Reves with the Authors Guild, to whose board DeVoto had recently been appointed, and he wanted Curtis to determine if he and Mrs. Porter were legally obligated to Reves.

Curtis replied[4] that they were legally bound only if Reves had a legal contract with Mrs. Porter, which from her description did not seem to be the case. With that reassurance, DeVoto undertook to bring Reves into line. His letters for the next month were icy and cutting to Reves, encouraging to the bewildered Mrs. Porter. Hang on, he told her; we have Reves where we want him. But it was not a book about the Miller-Stewart Expedition that he was now talking about, and it was not a little caption job added onto Mrs. Porter's amateur essay. What he wrote her on November 16 was that if Reves caved in, he expected to use Sir William Drummond Stewart "only as a line to hang the whole fur trade on."

By the purest accident, he had arrived at a book he had been unconsciously preparing himself for twenty years to write. He could finally, if Reves did cave in and perhaps even if he didn't, express at full length, but within the metaphorical form that best suited him, the enthusiasm he had felt for the mountain men since he was a romantic boy in Ogden Canyon walking dust that had been trod by the moccasins of heroes. He could describe and celebrate skills that he had always admired and sometimes imitated. He could tie this job, which had begun as some casual captions, into the grand theme of the development of the continental nation. Here was the Manifest Destiny of *The Year of Decision* before it had ever been formulated as a conscious idea. Here was one of the first and most direct consequences of Lewis and Clark, whose decisive explorations he had barely begun to study. A Hungarian-émigré promoter and a women's-club amateur had opened a door and released him into the large freedom of the mountain past. There was something almost ruthless in the way he responded to that accidental opportunity, something like manifest destiny in the way he made the book his own.

It still took some doing, however. Reves resisted and declared himself wronged, and did not finally sign the new contract until February 1945, more than a year after the negotiations had begun. Mrs. Porter's contribution remained unsatisfactory to DeVoto, and DeVoto's taking over of a book she had thought of as her own was unsatisfactory to Mrs. Porter. She intimated, in some women's-club talks after the publication of the book, that DeVoto had merely "recast" and "written up" her historical notes, and Houghton Mifflin felt obliged to ask her not to make such statements.[5] Actually DeVoto had either corrected or thrown out those notes in the first weeks, when the captions had begun to twist in his hands and become a narrative history of the fur trade during its climactic years. It was a long way from being Mrs. Porter's book by the time he was through with it, for both in subject matter and in the quality of the writing it went far beyond her competence. It was written with all of DeVoto's passion for the geography, climate, and history of his native region, and with all the tricks of the novelist's trade that never quite worked for him in fiction but worked superbly when he applied them to historical people, real geography, and real events.

God was very good to give him Sir William Drummond Stewart as a line to hang the fur trade on, though one suspects that, once galvanized as he had been by the Miller watercolors, he would have found some other line if Stewart had not been available. His mind demanded such culture heroes as James Clyman, whom he had used in *The Year of Decision: 1846;* and in fact he did make use in the fur-trade book of Joe Meek, another of Clyman's breed, to dramatize a moment, at the end of August 1839, when the first Oregon-bound wagon train met one of the last free trappers in "a splendid transit of past and future."

Joe Meek, the bear killer, a Carson man, a Bridger man, an RMF Company man, a Company man—Joe Meek, free trapper, raised his hand and rode off toward Fort Davy Crockett. And the three greenhorns, authentic settlers, and their Snake guide took the trail again, toward the Columbia.[6]

On that symbolic meeting between the dying fur trade and the first of the wagon trains, *Across the Wide Missouri* finally ended, more than two years after the completion of the publishing arrangements and more than three after their beginning, when Emery Reves first brought the Miller pictures into Houghton Mifflin's office for a quick caption job. The job turned out to be not 20,000 words, nor even 40,000, but something closer to 170,000. The whole of the vast, panoramic narrative—and much of the mountain fur trade—occurs between the year 1833, when four "Flatheads" (Nez Percés) appeared in St. Louis seeking teachers in the religion that Lewis and Clark had told them of, and the day in 1839 when Joe Meek encountered three Oregon pioneers on the Bear River.

As in *The Year of Decision: 1846,* recognized and recurring figures braid through the narrative, encounters in the wilderness open up unforeseen consequences and suggest remote, imperial rivalries. The Oregon question that will be settled in 1846 moves up the Columbia and the Snake with Ogden and Ross; the Spanish Southwest whose future will be settled in the same year has its contacts with the Wyoming wilderness along the trail from Bent's Fort to Fort Laramie. Counterespionage or its probability drifts in and out with the ambiguous figure of Captain Benjamin Louis Eulalie de Bonneville, as bald as if scalped and playing the fur-trade game so improvidently that he *must* have had other and more im-

portant things on his mind.[7] If Bonneville's fur trading may have
been a cover, that of Nathaniel Wyeth was not, and Yankee ambition challenges the great fur companies in his person. The partisans
lead their brigades through the most romantic wilderness ever
known or imagined, performing prodigies of skill, endurance, and
war. The Scottish baronet and his party touch here, touch there,
live with Indians, hunt buffalo and grizzly, make the rendezvous,
know familiarly the men in dirty buckskins who are as heroic as
anything in Homer and who sit by their fires smelling of bear's
grease and singing Injun while their squaws gnaw green hides or
pound service berries or embroider deerskin moccasins with beads
and porcupine quills. The artist is always around too, making
his quick sketches of things that no pencil or brush has ever re-
corded or will ever record again with such primal purity.

In 1837 the fur trade might have been dying, but the life it enforced showed no signs of weariness or decay. It might have been a
form of slavery, trappers the bond servants of the Company, never
out of debt, always in danger of losing furs or life, but the trappers
themselves did not know it—or, knowing it, still chose that life
above all others. They knew their life to be as free as the wind or
the wandering herds of the buffalo, as savage and free as the tribes
from whom they took squaws and with whom they felt more at
home than among whites.

This was the life that DeVoto set out in his third book about the
West to render as personal experience. In June 1944 he referred
to it as "a small job on the fur trade."[8] A year later he was so involved in it that he canceled the trip West that he had been planning for several years. No finger and no dike could have held back
the flood that wanted to pour out onto paper. Being an apprentice
Vermonter, he knew about Runaway Pond, not too far from
Morgan Center, where nineteenth-century farmers had dug a little
diversion ditch to get water from the lake and seen the whole lake
rush out the gap they started. That was the way *Across the Wide
Missouri* wrote itself once it started to flow.

On every page, we hear the sound that history makes when it is
written by a spoiled novelist in love with what he writes about:

Something moves in the willows and the Manton is cocked and Sir
William stands up in his stirrups—Ephraim is there, Old Caleb, the
white bear of the mountains, so terrible that to kill one is a coup as
glorious as striking with your bare hand an enemy in his own tipi.
For half a mile mules and wagons are stretched out in flat light, dust
above the caravan like an opening umbrella, emptiness everywhere, the
earth flowing like water at its edges, a false lake hung with groves that

have no reality. Here are the braves riding in from the hunt; their faces are like a sorcerer's mask, they are naked to a g-string, the blood of buffalo has soaked their moccasins and dyed their forearms and calves, the squaws wait for them with basins of clear cold water from the Siskadee. . . .[9]

A romantic wrote that, the same romantic who took long, solitary hikes armed with a .32 automatic or a .22 rifle in the Wasatch back of his home town, imagining dangers and driving himself to great endurances and playing survival in a world gone tame. The same romantic who climbed Mount Ogden to look over the salt lake that Jim Bridger and his companions had explored in a bullboat, the same who slept outside the window of an Ogden girl with a string tied from his finger to hers, and at first light pulled the string to awaken her to shared sunrise. He could not have written as he did of the fur trade, of the dreams that pulled westward all sorts of men as various as James Dickson and Jedediah Smith and Henry Harmon Spalding, of the intimate contents of the "possible sack" that every trapper carried, of the campfires and the rendez-vous, of the lore and gear of beaver trapping, of the hunting of buffalo and the stealing of horses, of the sudden raids and the long pursuits, if he had not dreamed those dreams himself and imagined those hardships and those freedoms with himself in the hero's role —if he had not waked many times in the same mountain light to the blue wetness on the grass and the smell of a cold campfire, if he had not seen through the Freudian notch-and-tower of his sights targets that imagination could transform into Old Caleb or a dodging Blackfoot, to be brought down while dependent and trustful female eyes watched.

Is it literary extravagance to believe that some of the silliest, most half-baked experiences of an adolescent full of hormones and wish fulfillment may on occasion find an ultimate expression that proves them both true and profound, and that links their victim/author with the imaginary fulfillments of a race, a place, and a time?

Sure you're romantic about American history [he wrote to Kitty Bowen while *Across the Wide Missouri* was still in his typewriter]. What your professor left out of account was the fact that it's the most romantic of all histories. It began in myth and has developed through three centuries of fairy stories. Whatever the time is in America it is always, at every moment, the mad and wayward hour when the prince is finding the little foot that alone fits into the slipper of glass. It is a little hard to know what romantic means to those who use the word umbrageously. But if the mad, impossible voyage of Columbus or Cartier or LaSalle or Coronado or John Ledyard is not romantic, if the stars did not dance in the sky when the Constitutional Convention met, if Atlantis has any landscape stranger or the other side of the moon any lights or colors or shapes more unearthly than the customary homespun of Lincoln or the morning coat of Jackson, well, I don't know what romance is. Ours is a story mad with the impossible, it is by chaos out of dream, it began as dream and it has continued as dream down to the last headline you read in a newspaper, and of our dreams there are two things above all others to be said, that only madmen could have dreamed them or would have dared to—and that we have shown a considerable faculty for making them come true. The simplest truth you can ever write about our history will be charged and surcharged with romanticism, and if you are afraid of the word you had better start practicing seriously on your fiddle.[10]

In his preface to *Across the Wide Missouri* he denies any intention of writing a comprehensive history.

. . . Instead I have tried to describe the mountain fur trade as a business and as a way of life: what its characteristic experiences were, what conditions governed them, how it helped to shape our heritage, what its relation was to the western expansion of the United States, most of all how the mountain men lived. . . . I shall have succeeded if the reader gets from the book a sense of time hurrying on while between the Missouri and the Pacific a thousand or so men of no moment whatever are living an exciting and singularly uncertain life, hurrying one era of our history to a close, and thereby making possible another one, one which began with the almost seismic enlargement of our boundaries and consciousness of which I have written elsewhere.[11]

Had written of elsewhere and would write of again, approaching it at its beginning, with the Louisiana Purchase and the expedition of Lewis and Clark, to complete a trilogy of histories of which *Across the Wide Missouri* was the middle one. In the opinion of most lay readers and of those historians who can accept his method as legitimate history, the middle book is the best, a re-creation that turns an intimately known historical period into fable and the heart's desire. It brought the Pulitzer prize into his trophy case, and at ten dollars a copy, a very high price in 1947, it sold thirteen thousand copies in its first year and a half and has gone on selling steadily since.[12] It is a standard work, as essential to an understanding of the fur trade as Chittenden, and a great deal more exciting to read. The Miller watercolors and the care that Houghton Mifflin lavished on its production made it one of the handsomest books of 1947 or any other year, and the Appendix called "The First Illustrators of the West" was an excursion into an important area that few professional historians had ever touched.

It was a pity that his loyal audience in Bowne Hospital in Poughkeepsie died when he was just beginning to think about it. She
would have responded to the romantic richness that he hung on the
line of Stewart's western expeditions. It is not out of the question
to think of her as another girl with a string tied to her finger, waiting to be awakened to wonder. She would have been useful to
DeVoto too, for in the unfamiliar territory of art and art history
she would have functioned as a guide and might have saved him
much wasted motion as well as some disputes with art critics.

It says something about a career which has crested and is running
at the flood that Kate Sterne's death, though it deprived him of one
of his closest and warmest friendships and dried up one of the
springs of his fantasy life, probably did not slow him down by
more than one sad evening. One thing, however, it did do. It insured that the novel he had begun away back in the spring of 1936
when he was being repudiated by Harvard, the novel he had begun
with the intention of dedicating it to Kate, the novel whose title she
had given him, the novel he had wrestled with twice and twice been
thrown by, would have to be finished somehow. It was a promise
he had made her and not kept. All the time he was writing *Across
the Wide Missouri* he was also trying to make that novel *Mountain
Time* come around.

6 · *Dog to His Vomit*

Nobody is entitled to call himself a novelist until he has written five
novels, DeVoto was accustomed to say at Bread Loaf. There was a
certain amount of self-encouragement in the remark, whether he
conceived of himself as Bernard DeVoto, who had published four
novels up to 1934, or as John August, who had published four
since.[1] Either way, that fifth one was hard to come by. There was
evidence, too, that he didn't quite know which writer he was.
Siamese twins, August and DeVoto walked webbed together, and
sometimes one answered to the other's name.

When he resumed work on the shelved manuscript of *Mountain
Time*, near the end of 1943, he did so mainly out of boredom, to
give his mind something to do while he waited for the Army to de-
cide whether or not it wanted him to write up any part of the war.
But he had been thinking about it ever since the brush with Frost in
Bloomington, and the outright break a few months later had con-

vinced him that he now knew where the novel wanted to go. From its beginning, it had had in it both the struggle against a father (brought to a head by the death of Florian DeVoto, in the fall of 1935), and the fantasies clustered around the Skinny figure, whom he had been remembering and half inventing for Kate Sterne. It had also contained, in ways that he could not quite tie down, the West-East conflict, the problems of Westerners who came East toward enlargement and opportunity and were never quite satisfied, were always eaten by the desire to return.

The break with Frost crystallized at least the father conflict for him, and he very quickly rewrote Part I of *Mountain Time*, and sent it off to Kate Sterne for an opinion in early March 1944. In that section Cy Kinsman, a young surgeon from the West, a man with gifted hands and a talent for offending people with his bluntness and honesty, declares his independence from his medical superior Dr. McAllister, an older surgeon who "thinks with his fingers" and combines enormous skill with a certain ruthlessness and a strong instinct for the grandstand. Kate Sterne would know that she was supposed to substitute literature for medicine, that for Dr. McAllister she was supposed to read Robert Frost, and for Cy Kinsman Bernard DeVoto. She would also know how to read symbolically Cy Kinsman's decision to go back West, where he came from, and sort out his life.[2]

Many things combined to slow and hinder the completion of the novel: the time-consuming controversies of the spring of 1944, the housebound, gasolineless summer at Annisquam, the complicated negotiations that would lead eventually to *Across the Wide Missouri*, his inability to say no when Irita Van Doren asked him to take over Lewis Gannet's daily book column in the New York *Herald Tribune* during October, and not least, the pleasures of research on both Lewis and Clark and the fur trade. Through the summer he could give the novel only now-and-then effort. But it is also clear that he did not know quite what to do with it; the fight with Frost that had carried him in one burst through Part I would not carry him further.

At the end of August Kate Sterne died, and her death both relieved him of an obligation and permitted him an evasion. He put on his false face and walked past himself unrecognized. Just after Christmas, he decided that *Mountain Time* was not a serious novel, or at least that he could not write it in those terms, and that the only way he could salvage all the work he had put into it was to turn it into a *Collier's* serial. Its title became *Everybody Got to Walk*, and its author was said to be John August. Its purpose became not the cauterizing of emotional wounds and the exploration of what happened in the caves of the soul, but the fattening of the bank account in order to subsidize what promised to be a long period of unprofitable historical research.

On the day after Christmas, he sent in his proposal to *Collier's*, along with sample installments from Part I. He said he wanted to get it out of the way in a hurry to free himself for Lewis and Clark (nothing said about the fur trade, which was still no more than hypothetical captions). On February 5, 1945, *Collier's* bought *Everybody Got to Walk* as a four-part serial.

But DeVoto did not finish it promptly, as he had intended. The serial gave him as much trouble as the novel had. He simply could not sit down, grit his teeth, and grind it out. Whatever he said to himself and to *Collier's*, it was still fretting him as a book that was very personal to himself, and hence difficult. He remarked to Garrett Mattingly that he would have to tack a bitter ending on it, to make it respectable, before he sent it to Alfred McIntyre at Little, Brown for publication.[3] And as if unwilling to face it fully, as if wanting to evade and delay it, he kept filling his days with other activities. He signed up for a fall lecture tour with a New York agent, Charles Pearson. Though in March 1945 he said he was still working on "a serial and a history,"[4] he should have said that history had all but crowded the serial out, for by that time the negotiations that led to *Across the Wide Missouri* had been completed, and without quite giving up Lewis and Clark he was deep in the fur trade.

By June, when he again retreated to Annisquam to escape the summer heat, he was still not done with *Everybody Got to Walk*. By the time he returned to Cambridge, in September, he had added to his job list the *Viking Portable Mark Twain*, whose text and introduction he delivered in December.[5] November was killed by his lecture tour, December by his participation in "Invitation to Learning" and other New York radio shows. He was during the same months conducting a campaign among the magazine editors, seeking assignments that would pay his expenses West along the Lewis and Clark route the following summer. It was not until December 1945, almost exactly a year after he had sent in his hurry-up prospectus to *Collier's*, that he could tell Mattingly, "John August has written something like a novel." *Collier's* ran it between February 2 and March 2, 1946.

But at the last minute an odd transformation occurred. Though it was as *Everybody Got to Walk* that he had finished the book at last, it appeared in *Collier's* with its old title, *Mountain Time*, restored, and almost as if in defiance he had signed it not "John August" but "Bernard DeVoto."

Moreover, he was still not through with it. Through the early months of 1946, between attacks on the revisionist historians of the Civil War,[6] bursts of extraordinary productiveness on the fur-trade book, and correspondence with magazines, federal bureaus, and western friends setting up his coming trip, he was still tinkering with the manuscript in an attempt to improve it for book publication—that is, to completely reconvert John August into DeVoto. His always oversubscribed time had to be stretched for discussions with the promoters of the new History Book Club, which wanted him to act as chairman of its panel of judges. When he finally, reluctantly, let go of the manuscript of *Mountain Time*, finishing it in a dead heat with *Across the Wide Missouri*, he was on the eve of departing for the West. Little, Brown did not publish the novel until January 1947, almost a year after its appearance as a *Collier's* serial and eleven years after Kate Sterne had given it a title.

Wait for the book, he kept telling correspondents who wrote in after reading *Collier's*. Don't judge it by the serial version. He anticipated the critical and popular response with an anxiety that he could not disguise. To Kitty Bowen he wrote that "the boys" would think it was *Arrowsmith*, Little, Brown would advertise it as *Arrowsmith*, and the reviewers would review *The Literary Fallacy*.[7] But when the book appeared, and the reviewers did not like it, he felt a frustration and exasperation that emerged often in his correspondence as defensiveness.

To those friends who loyally said they liked it—a handful including the Mattinglys and Anne Barrett, the former wife of his former analyst, he felt almost unduly grateful, admitting, *"Mountain Time* means a good deal more to me psychologically than as a novel," because "it was the one that threw me twice, the one I couldn't write."[8] Against those who did not like it—Avis, Josephine Johnson, the dedicatee Ted Morrison, his Ogden librarian friend Madeline McQuown, Fletcher Pratt who asked plaintively why it was written in shorthand—he defended it with a stubbornness that gave away how deep his psychological involvement was. The fact that the novel sold better than any of his earlier ones he realistically attributed to his expanded reputation and not to any special popularity of the book. But the fact that so many reviewers and so many friends found it opaque and unsatisfying puzzled and troubled him. As he wrote to Madeline McQuown:

There are things I'm interested in doing in fiction. There is a part of me that finds expression in fiction and can't find it in anything else. There are things I think I know about life and reality for which fiction is the only possible vehicle. . . . The things I set out to do in history are enormously, almost incomparably, easier than the things I try to do in novels. . . . As a writer of fiction I am interested only in the subtleties, ambiguities, and colorations of personal relationships, of love and marriage and friendship. . . . My dissatisfaction with *Mountain Time* . . . is confined mostly to the conclusion I've reached reluctantly, that I made the ellipses and lacunae rather greater than was right, even in the terms I'd set myself. Only about one percent of the book is printed on the page; I calculated wrong, I ought to have made it, maybe, one and a half percent.[9]

That self-judgment is not entirely inadequate, however exaggerated the percentages. He did expect too much of his readers, he did compress too much, he did demand that readers retain the most casual hints and most disguised forecasts and signposts, sometimes for two or three hundred pages, until another bare hint should illuminate them. Concentrating on the subtleties and ambiguities, he often neglected to draw in the obvious. But what is much more damaging, he failed to endow his obscurities with ultimate importance; he didn't succeed in making the characters who mattered so much to himself matter that much to his readers.

Cy Kinsman might misunderstand himself through 357 pages, might fail to comprehend that he loves the version of Skinny who in the novel is named Josephine. He might not fully understand that his quarrel with Dr. McAllister is simply another round with his actual father, Old Doc Kinsman, and that his return to the West is an attempt "to face and fight his [dead] father in his father's home town."[10] He might scorn the literary deviousness and dishonesty in Josephine's divorced husband without recognizing similar deviousnesses in himself. He might in the end come to the glad realization that it was Josephine all along whom he wanted and Old Doc Kinsman whom he was fighting ("I was afraid of Old Doc Kinsman. I didn't dare to be the better man.")[11] Those realizations, so important to their author, strike the reader as just a shade obvious, the realizations of a John August serial. Their author presses too much, and at the same time he hides too much. His aim seems less fiction than self-therapy, and less self-therapy than a *formula* of self-therapy—precisely the thing he accused Lawrence Kubie of wanting fiction to be, precisely the thing DeVoto denied it should be.

The biographer, confused by what his subject seems to take so seriously, hunts for evidence in DeVoto's life that Florian DeVoto was as important and as dominating as his son seems to think, and cannot find it. To the outside eye, *Mountain Time* looks more like an assertion of self-understanding than like understanding itself. It reads like an elaborate charade, the attempt of a literary analyst to find an acceptable caption for his own emotional troubles. And that uncomfortable impression occurs whether one reads *Mountain Time* as a self-revelation or as a novel. One feels the artificer bending people and events toward some tolerable conclusion. At the end, when Cy and Josephine cement their affection beside a mountain stream, up one of the canyons of their shared youth, one hears the sort of fantasy that sounded in the Skinny story as told by Bernard DeVoto to Kate Sterne.

Once, DeVoto had expressed to Kate the wish that some good analyst, perhaps Kubie, would analyze a novel from its inception to its final period.[12] Writing to Kubie on January 16, 1947, just after the book publication of *Mountain Time*, he confessed that he was "crazy to know" what questions and theories Kubie had about the book, and he explained that it should be read as the middle volume of a trilogy that had been planned to carry Cy Kinsman out of his native West to the East Coast, then back to fight his dead father in his father's home town, and then back East again, not as his father's rival, a doctor, but as a physiologist, something related but different, and hence non-competitive. He did not want Kubie to think he had advocated flight back westward as the solution of anything —that would have been Harold Bell Wright.

The whole job was conceived and I'd bogged down in the writing of it once before the fall of 1935, when I first became intimate with Frost, so the inner block was not Frost—at first, anyway. I bogged down again in 1939 when, you may remember, I was in a post-analytical storm. I wouldn't question that Frost has something to do with that. . . . I was never able to get farther than the middle of the present book, where the two of them leave New York, till I broke whatever the dam was. The second half of *Mountain Time*, that is, wasn't written on either of my first two attempts, though clearly in mind. . . . I orginally conceived the book as the converse of *We Accept with Pleasure*. That one dealt with people making terms with personal defeat, this one was to deal with people triumphing over what threatened from within to destroy them. It was going to be me being positive about life. . . . I'd say that the emotional genesis of the relationship between Cy and Josephine was me and Skinny . . . and that there is a hell of a lot more phantasy than fact in what I remember about Skinny and me. But also, the second time I tried and also the third time, I was aware that I was writing straight toward that penultimate scene in the mountains where they finally sleep together. That would appear to be important as hell, but it wasn't in the first conception. There's a job for you: why was it so damn important? Unless as a symbol of the impotence proved on me when I couldn't write the novel.

One does not inquire of a man's analyst why, or if, he thinks a scene in his patient's novel particularly significant in the patient's emotional life. But like so many of the tormented and intricate questions woven into *Mountain Time*, it is at once insoluble and subject to an explanation too simple for DeVoto himself to believe. The consummation of the unfulfilled fantasy of Skinny, rich, beautiful, game, friendly, adoring, daughterly, and afflicted with the horrors (Josephine in this novel has just such horrors, and Cy Kinsman deals with them by just such medico-parental understanding as young DeVoto dreamed of employing with Skinny, and the older DeVoto actually did employ with Kate Sterne and a whole series of emotionally troubled women friends and with several men friends as well) appears from outside to have been much more important to the author of *Mountain Time* than any struggle against a dominant father. One has trouble seeing Bernard DeVoto as Franz Kafka. John August sneaked into this novel when Bernard DeVoto wasn't looking. At its heart is not an oedipal struggle but a romantic daydream, nourished now for a quarter of a century and brought to a new vividness, a compulsive recapitulation, by Kate Sterne.

Some of DeVoto's inordinate ambition and focused energy probably did derive from the effort to prove himself in the intellectual East from which his father, brilliantly equipped, had dropped out. Some of it may have derived from the need of a provincial Dick Whittington to rise to be Lord Mayor of London, the urge of a Rocky Mountain Jack to climb the beanstalk and come back with tales and treasure. But it is hard to avoid the conclusion that a large part of it was the uncured and incurable need of a poor, gifted boy, an outsider in the town he was born in, to show off before the girls and win them, or one of them, to adoration.

Almost every time he touched fiction, that compulsion revealed itself. Almost every time his fantasy life intruded into his fiction, something self-conscious and mawkish showed through the story fabric. He could deal with everybody but himself, and himself was what he most needed to deal with, surmount, justify, and assuage.

When he finished *Mountain Time*, he apparently intended to write another novel, in which he would bring Cy Kinsman triumphantly East as a whole man, no longer at war with his father and no longer blind to himself. That novel he does not seem ever to have begun. Instead, he began quite another, one set in the intellectual community of Cambridge.[13] It was never published or submitted for publication, and it was the last attempt at a novel that DeVoto ever made. The need to fantasize remained strong in him, but successive failures eventually persuaded him that he lacked some essential gift. Though he went on working on the manuscript of the Cambridge novel practically until his death, he admitted early that it would probably come to nothing. The man who had started as a belligerent pro came finally to the status of amateur, writing privately, almost secretly, a fiction that he would show to no one. The dominant father figure is still in it, and so is the adoring, gravely protected female, evidence that whatever haunted DeVoto's private life had not been exorcised by thirty years of literary effort.

But the temptation to clothe that incubus in fictional forms for public consumption did die. Even so stubborn a spirit as DeVoto's had to admit that he was best at history and controversy. As he had worn out other preoccupations, especially literary criticism, he eventually wore out fiction. *Mountain Time* was his last public try at it, and his farewell. Inexorably, experience was scrubbing away the literary overlay, correcting DeVoto's long misreading of his own talents, and leaving the historian and the polemicist and the public defender unencumbered by a mistaken self-image.

VII

FULL CAREER

1 · *"The Best Thing I Ever Did in My Life"*

Bernard DeVoto was forty-nine on January 11, 1946. After almost
a quarter of a century of intense writing activity, he was identified
with the Rocky Mountain West in the mind of every reader who
knew his name at all. He had celebrated its scenery, defined its
geographical and cultural and mythic boundaries, scorned its
limitations, criticized its state of mind, re-created its history, and
interpreted its legends, folklore, and emerging literature. The book-
review editors who in 1925 had type-cast him as a western authority had either been extraordinarily prescient or had exerted the
strongest sort of influence on his development.

But the fact was, his extensive knowledge of the West was more
from books than from personal experience. The only part of even
the Rocky Mountain West that he knew intimately was the narrow
Wasatch front, and only the northern end of that. He had traveled
the Union Pacific to and from Utah several times, and there is a
story, unconfirmed and by now probably unconfirmable, that as a
boy he went with his father to Mexico. After he settled in the
East, lectures had taken him to Kansas and Nebraska as well as to
the gateway city of St. Louis—all of this "back East" to his Ogden
consciousness. In 1940 he had followed the Santa Fe Trail into
New Mexico and Colorado and come home by way of Utah,
Wyoming, Montana, and North Dakota. He was one who prepared

for travel with maps and books, and he learned as he went. Nevertheless it is true that even of the country he had visited, he had up to 1946 only the briefest firsthand acquaintance, and there were whole regions of the West that he did not know at all. He had apparently never visited the Northwest, California, Nevada, Texas, or Oklahoma; and he knew southern Utah and Arizona only casually, and no part of Idaho except the southern edge. By 1946 he had lived more years in Cambridge than in Utah. Westward he walked free, like Thoreau, but he did so largely in Thoreau's fashion—in books and in imagination, from a narrow New England base.

This acknowledged authority on the West was just completing a book on the fur trade without ever having set eyes on much of the country over which the fur trade had operated. Not from choice: he had been held down by lack of money, by the Depression, by the demands of a furious work schedule and the needs of a number of dependents. His 1940 tour, the first in many years, had whetted his appetite and led him to project another, for the summer of 1941. Anxiety about the war, as much as anything else, had killed that, and Pearl Harbor and gasoline rationing insured that it would not be revived until the war was over.

When chance threw the fur trade into his lap, he was able to write about it with all the vividness of personal knowledge only because he was an avid and intuitive reader of maps, because he was familiar with an extensive literature, and because he had a novelist's visualizing imagination and the gift of synecdoche. As he was fond of saying with cynical emphasis, he could make a fact go a long way. For however limited his western experience was, it was deep. What he did know, he knew in his bones and skin and eyeballs and emotions as well as in his head. He could re-create a rendezvous on Horse Creek or in Pierre's Hole from knowing Ogden's Hole and Cache Valley. He could imagine the Absarokas or the Wind Rivers from knowing the Wasatch. He could find words for mountain weather, mountain light, mountain water, because they lived in him, his most authentic inheritance.

Those qualifications would not be enough for the job he was now embarked on. To present as personal experience the adventure of discovery, to trace the opening of Upper Louisiana and the groping out of a Northwest Passage up the Missouri and across the Stony Mountains and down the Oregon to the Great South Sea demanded detailed knowledge of a lot of country that he knew only from books. Before he could discover the West with Lewis and Clark, he had to discover it for himself. In the summer of 1946 his personal inclinations, the end of wartime travel restrictions, and the completion of his other writing jobs coincided to send him out after the geographical expertise that most of his readers assumed he already possessed.

As we have seen, he was busy all through the winter and spring at a dozen different jobs. He conducted a calculated raid, in two successive Easy Chairs, against the revisionist Civil War historians J. G. Randall and Avery Craven; he argued with Clara Gabrilowitsch, now Clara Samoussoud, over her stubborn opposition to *Letters from the Earth* and with Thomas Chamberlain over his slowness in permitting little actions with regard to the Mark Twain papers; he advised Alfred Knopf on the possibilities of a new series of western books of the Americana Deserta kind; he negotiated with the History Book Club about his possible participation in its selective process; he finished up *Across the Wide Missouri* and *Mountain Time*. But all the time he was giving thought to his coming expedition. It had to be self-supporting, and he had an incurable unwillingness to ask help from the foundations. Magazine commissions, therefore; and since he had long since given up his connection with the Curtis Brown agency, he had to negotiate the commissions himself.

A good journalist with a historian's conscience, he prepared his sources through an extensive correspondence with Newton Drury, director of the National Park Service, with Walt Dutton, Chief Forester of the National Forest Service, and with friends and informants, official and unofficial, scattered over the whole West. A worrier and hypochondriac, he fretted about such things as Rocky Mountain fever, and whether the family should be inoculated. An anxious father, he enlisted Stewart Holbrook and a flock of forest supervisors to find a summer job in the woods for Gordon, now seventeen, and consulted other friends in the attempt to locate a mountain ranch or camp where Mark could be left for at least part of the summer. Jittery as the greenest tourist about hazards, discomforts, and the lack of civilized facilities, he badgered correspondents for the names of decent hotels and restaurants, and for several months he had half the *Time-Life-Fortune* staff working to get him a Ford or Mercury station wagon as soon as the assembly lines newly converted to peace should turn one out. No 1846 pioneer outfitting at Independence in anticipation of Pawnees, Sioux, flooded rivers, poison water, and the terrors of a desert crossing could have been more concerned.

Or excited. Or willing to share his preparations with anyone who would listen. The Personal and Otherwise column in the April *Harper's* gave a report of his activities, including his plans for a three-month western tour that would be paid for, he said, by articles in *Harper's* and "less exalted journals." These, as things finally developed, were *Life, Fortune,* and *Woman's Day,* the A&P magazine which under the editorship of Mabel Hill Souvaine was becoming his most dependable meal ticket, open to practically anything he chose to send it.

In the July Easy Chair,[1] written before he left, he took the public into his confidence and announced himself prepared to test and rate the goods and services offered the American tourist in the first postwar summer. He could not report on the new station wagon, because it had not come off the assembly line, but he could announce in advance that the eighteen-dollar fountain pen he had bought for the trip was worthless, and that when he had shopped for new pants he had found everything so shoddy and overpriced that he was going in his old ones.

On June 5, the old Buick loaded like a pack horse, Mark developing hysterical vomiting spells, Avis "determined to shame" her husband by wearing long shorts,[2] they got the doors closed upon themselves and started out of Cambridge.

Their itinerary took them to Buffalo, by boat to Detroit, across the south peninsula of Michigan, and by boat again from Ludington to Manitowoc, and across Wisconsin and Minnesota to Pierre, South Dakota, the site of old Fort Pierre, built in 1832 as a bastion of the Sioux trade. There they made rendezvous with a *Life* photographer, Wallace Kirkland, who had been working upriver from St. Louis shooting Lewis and Clark and fur-trade sites set up for him in advance by DeVoto. As a team, they went on up the Missouri to Fort Clark, sixty miles above Bismarck, North Dakota, where they found the boom precipitated by the Garrison Dam submerging a place whose history should have exempted it from progress. Thence on to old Fort Union, at the mouth of the Yellowstone, which for some years had been the uppermost reach of the river fur trade. DeVoto had prowled it in the books while writing *Across the Wide Missouri,* had lived inside its palisades with the naturalists Townsend and Nuttall and the titled amateur Maximilian of Wied-Neuwied, and with Maximilian had watched a battle between Assiniboins and Blackfeet outside the walls. Now he could prowl it on foot and in fact and in the reduced present.

From Fort Union, going backward up Clark's return route of

1806, they went up the Yellowstone, past the mouths of the muddy, swinging rivers—the Powder, the Tongue, the Bighorn—also reduced in the present and busy pouring Wyoming and Montana toward the Gulf of Mexico. At Billings they turned northward to Great Falls and Fort Benton, and then on through Helena, Three Forks, Dillon, and over the Lemhi Pass to Salmon, Idaho, where DeVoto took a look at the Salmon River and scribbled a postcard to Carvel Collins, a friend back in Cambridge, instructing him not to try it in his foldboat. North again into Montana, down the Bitterroot Valley to Missoula, over the Lolo Pass that had so punished Lewis and Clark, and on to Lewiston, the Whitman Mission at Waiilatpu, and at last to the Columbia, whose lower reaches they got to in time for a Portland Fourth of July.[3]

Every stage of that journey to the Pacific was familiar from books; nearly every stage was as new to DeVoto's eyes as it had been to the eyes of Lewis and Clark. It was the part of his summer journeying that interested him most and that would be most immediately useful, not only for the writing of the Lewis and Clark book but for the improvement, in galley proofs, of *Across the Wide Missouri*. But there were whole empires of the West still to be seen, and what would have been pure pleasure was made, as usual, compulsive by the obligations he had assumed in order to pay the expenses of historical research. Some of his articles could be generated out of the daily adventures of the road, but the *Fortune* article demanded fresh impressions of six or eight national parks, only two of which he had ever visited.

From Portland, on July 6, they drove south to Crater Lake, and on to San Francisco, and on again to Yosemite. Because he had no choice, DeVoto drove like a tourist trying to set mileage records for a short vacation, but he worked very hard en route with his boxed library of books and maps, fitting each new valley, mountain range, desert sink, and town into his mental relief map of the continental geography and his outline of the history of exploration and settlement. All this was new to him. Having left Kirkland on the Columbia, and Gordon in his forest job, they were less encumbered, and in spite of their haste could relax and enjoy what came toward them up the road. They took turns driving, changing every fifty or one hundred miles, so that each could get a chance to look. The desert in particular, that gray-green sagebrush waste rising in long alluvial skirts to the worn ranges, all that emptiness domed with the big sky full of strato-cumulus clouds that quenched and darkened the light one moment, and the next let the intolerable brightness flood across great hammocked valleys and the twisted, tormented, worn, and furrowed mountains—the desert all but shocked them with its beauty, and when they drove across it at night to Salt Lake City, and watched dawn come on, and then sunrise, DeVoto had one of his articles instantly in hand. "Night Crossing," he called it when he published it in *Woman's Day*.[4] It was from the heart, a hymn, a poem. And the freshness with which the desert came to him is an index of how little familiar he had been, up to that time, with his chosen country, even the Great Basin desert which had been his boyhood's front yard. As usual, it was coming back that opened his eyes to it, half in recognition, half in sharpened perception.

Dispelling his private ignorances and confirming his book knowledge were among the purposes of this trip, and he dispelled and confirmed at a gallop. Pausing in Utah only long enough to buy a new set of tires and to say hello to a few friends, including Chet Olsen in the regional Forest Service office in Ogden, they went northward again to Grand Teton and Yellowstone, gave those a brief inspection, talked with National Park Service people, and went on out the east entrance to deposit young Mark at a ranch camp near Cody, in the Sunlight Basin.

Now south to Rocky Mountain National Park, in Colorado, for another fast look and some talk with Park Service people; and after a couple of days they made a U turn and went straight back the way they had come. South Pass, the gateway both for the mountain fur trade and for the wagon trains that followed it, was something DeVoto had to see.

Off the main road now, and not often visited, South Pass is one of the most deceptive and impressive places in the West. Stop there and watch the cloud shadows go over, and see the white rumps of antelope move among the sage, and study the deep, braiding ruts that the wagons made as they fanned out and came down the long, even slope from Pacific Spring, on the western slope at last—stop there off the road (Wyoming 28), with your motor shut off, and listen to the wind, which breathes history through dry grass and stiff sage, and smell dust and distance, and look eastward over the gentle rise to where you know the Sweetwater and Devil's Gate and Independence Rock and the last crossing of the Platte recede on backward toward the United States, and then turn and look west, down the long, easy slope toward the Green, and you can believe you understand something about the spirit of the *Völkerwanderung* that moved America westward. It was DeVoto's major theme, and he wanted South Pass to speak to him. But they turned east from Farson in a dreary rain. The

gray slope rising eastward was dim; the unpaved road was slick
and soapy. The magic that he had hoped for, and that he might
have found on a better day, was not there: he could not visualize
the toiling wagons coming over that rise and heading downhill
toward Oregon, California, the Zion in the valleys of the mountains. He couldn't imagine Old Gabe and Black Harris squatting
by a campfire on this sagebrush slope and discussing with Brigham
Young and his counselors the possibilities of settlement in the
Great Basin.

So they turned away, heading north and west toward Thermop-
olis, Three Forks, Helena, finally Glacier National Park, clear up
against the Canadian border. From Glacier he wrote to Bob Bailey
and Garrett Mattingly, calling this western tour the best thing he
had ever done in his life.[5] He wished he had been born in Montana instead of in "the scurvy little Mormon-Catholic dump that
created all my neuroses." That sidelong disparagement of Ogden
was reflex, a joke, a piece of role playing, not the expression of
a renewed hatred of his home town. As a matter of fact, coming
back to him on this euphoric tour of all the country he had
dreamed of and made himself an expert on, his home town looked
a good deal better than it ever had before; and though he had
fallen in love with Montana, he had all but forgiven Utah by the
time he came across the salt desert into a Utah sunrise.

From Glacier the DeVotos dropped down again to Yellowstone, picked up Mark from his ranch near Cody, and made a
great bend to the west, clear out into the Sawtooth Range in
Idaho, where in a Forest Supervisor's cabin at the end of thirty-
nine miles of frightful mountain road they rested ten days while
DeVoto straightened out his notes, caught up with his correspondence, and wrote a couple of Easy Chairs. On September 12 they
were back in Cambridge, greatly enlarged.

Out of that hectic, zigzagging loop of 13,580 miles, DeVoto
emerged with a firm sense of the outlines and relationships of
western geography, a heightened feeling of how the wilderness
had worked on the American consciousness, and an increased confidence about the geopolitical implications of the expedition whose
story he had set out to tell. The travel book that he had half
planned to write about the trip never got written, nor did the
anthology of western writing that he had promised Alfred McIntyre ever get assembled. The *Life* articles somehow fell through
the crack and were never published, though according to Avis'
recollection he was paid for three and had his expenses compensated besides. Nevertheless, spread over the next twelve months,

there were substantial written consequences of the trip: five Easy Chairs, two full-length *Harper's* articles, three articles in *Woman's Day,* and the text that accompanied a dozen pages of Ansel Adams's National Park pictures in *Fortune.*[6] The bulk of those pieces were the work of the journalist who had taken over from John August as provider. A few were serious and provocative studies produced as the weapons of controversy—a controversy that did not flicker out as the *Literary Fallacy* dispute did, but went on, hardly interrupted, for the rest of DeVoto's life. The summer of 1946 turned him into a conservationist, one of the most effective in our history. When he finally came West in person, he came like Lancelot.

The ephemeral writings repeat the conclusions and exhibit the habit of rather glib generalization that had been apparent in "Main Street Twenty Years After" and other reports on his 1940 tour. DeVoto the journalist was most interesting when he was reporting personal experiences or the visible social phenomena of western towns, most tedious when he was counting up how many synthetic tires, spark plugs, and quarts of oil his Buick had consumed. (He conceived these facts to be part of his duty to the traveling public, and an impulse related to the one that made him interested in the clothes and traps and skills and "possibles" of the mountain men made him mount his platform and instruct a public more knowing than he gave it credit for being on How to Travel in the West.) He was least persuasive when he generalized about regional attitudes and about such abstractions as the western character.

His commentary on the new motel civilization of the western roadside was sharpened by the fact that he had been away all through the time when it was developing, and he could see it as what it was: a swift, sensible adaptation to American habits and the conditions of the automotive age. His advice to car manufacturers about the sunshades, double glass, air conditioning, and heavy-duty springs and shock absorbers needed on cars built for western driving was sound—a generation or more later another consumer advocate, Ralph Nader, would make similar suggestions a whole lot more urgently—though DeVoto's list of necessities romanticized the difficulty of western roads. Some of his complaints, especially about the chambers of commerce that used historical sites as tourist come-ons but did nothing to preserve or maintain them, were well taken. The Whitman Mission, Fort Clatsop, and other key points on his tour had turned out to be neglected, litter-strewn shacks and rural slums, and his protests had a good deal to do with their later rehabilitation.

Other complaints—bad service on the ferries, the absence of

Wisconsin cheese in Wisconsin restaurants—were predictable and fairly trivial. His general demand that roadside entrepreneurs exploiting the renewed floods of travelers start offering decent service and fair prices undoubtedly earned him the gratitude of disgruntled tourists. But some of his confident generalizations about western character and attitudes are worthy of a congressman's book about Red China.

Back in 1936, reprinting some of his articles on education in *Forays and Rebuttals,* DeVoto had admitted that he got his reputation as an authority on education simply by assuming it. Up to 1946, some part of his reputation as an authority on the West was similarly open to suspicion. His generalizations were sometimes challengeable, and even some of his "facts" were the flash impressions of a book-learned reporter willing to show off his expertise.

One comprehensive western tour could not cure him of old habits. Thus he found western speech less marked by local variations than the speech of any other American region (true), but thought the *au* sound gave it away. Maybe. Most Westerners say *dawg* and some say *Gawd.* But they say many other things, too. Cache Valley, Utah, an authentic western community within fifty miles of DeVoto's home town, could have taught him a local dialect clearly distinguishable from most western speech; and his friend Edith Mirrielees, born in Big Timber, Montana, within sight of the Crazy Mountains and the Absarokas, enunciated as pure a *dahg* and *Gahd* as if she had taught all her life in the schools of Massachusetts.

DeVoto thought western humor self-depreciatory, as if reflecting "an inner chagrin." Yet his own humor, developed in the West from western models, was of a very different kind from that, and so was the humor of the Virginian and Lin McLean, and so was that of the celebrated Mormon preacher J. Golden Kimball, and so was that of the ex-river pilot whom DeVoto had once defended against the "chagrin" theory of Van Wyck Brooks.

Somewhat blithely, he declared that all Westerners ate steak and fried potatoes for breakfast, probably because he himself, in certain circumstances and mainly in Montana, did so. He found Westerners "passionate eaters," and all overweight, though from his letters it seems that he himself was the one who went wild on western beef after the wartime shortages of Cambridge and the horsemeat steaks of the Harvard Faculty Club.[7] He told his Easy Chair readers that Westerners rode horses naturally, which was unreliable information on the face of it: he forgot that the West is

an oasis (which is to say a primarily urban) civilization, in much
of which horses are about as common as they are in Scarsdale;
and he forgot the deficiencies in the riding line of that well-known
Westerner Bernard DeVoto. He said Westerners accepted too
many of the myths and fantasies deriving from the cattle kingdom—a generally valid judgment in which he should have included himself, for many of his ineradicable attitudes were the
result of his adoption of the outdoor-Westerner role. He thought
the West's single contribution to architecture was the mountain
cabin of shellacked logs, a contention which seemed to forget the
Swedes of Delaware, who had naturalized the log cabin long before the West was ever dreamed of; and which seemed also to make
shellac a function of architecture.

And so on. He was not an infallibly reliable witness. Writers
whom he had scolded for generalizing about the frontier, for making a unity out of a loose collection of variables, would have been
justified in suggesting that he listen to his own warnings. The
West was no more a unit than the frontier ever was, and only
his own enthusiasm could make it so. As young Arthur Schlesinger
once told him, he sometimes, by a single outrageous statement,
gave an opponent the handle by which to pull down an otherwise sound argument. Exaggerations and horseback judgments that
DeVoto's friends understood and discounted as mere exuberance
and phrasemaking sometimes got frozen into print and made him
look as if he knew less than he did.

Nevertheless, at the end of the summer of 1946 he knew far
more about the West, past and present, from books and in person,
than his roadside journalism suggested. Some of what he knew
emerged with the clarity of revelation and withstood not only his
own second thoughts but repeated angry challenges from without.
When he thought he detected in many areas of western life an
internal stress that sprang from economic and cultural colonialism,
he put his finger on something elusive but real. And when he
moved into the subject of western land and resource use, historical
and contemporary, he was talking about something he knew and
understood and could prove. In that area he was entirely disinterested and impartial, and he had read Powell and Walter Webb and
had grown up along his grandfather Dye's irrigation ditches under
the Wasatch watershed.

Throughout the states where the Public Domain was a large
factor, which meant wherever aridity had balked the land-dis-
posal laws of the United States, which meant the whole West with
the exception of Texas and parts of the Pacific Coast, he heard in

1946 a tune he had heard all his life: the ambivalent clamor for more federal subsidies and federal aid discordantly fused with complaints about absentee federal landlordism. In his understanding of the importance of aridity in the West, DeVoto followed Powell, to whom he had devoted part of a chapter in *The Literay Fallacy*, and Walter Webb, whose *The Great Plains* was a basic book about the lands west of the ninety-eighth meridian. He understood the West's vulnerability, the dangers of overgrazing and the logging of watersheds in a dry land. He knew exactly what it meant when he saw the Powder, the Tongue, and the Bighorn pouring their silt into the clear Yellowstone. He knew—and on his 1946 trip he had it constantly forced on his attention—the pressures that miners, loggers, dam builders, and stockmen put upon the federal bureaus entrusted with the management of the Public Domain. From his Cambridge sideline he had watched Senator Pat McCarran of Nevada geld the Grazing Service and turn it into the impotent Bureau of Land Management, perennially underbudgeted and too weak to manage anything. His close friends in the National Forest Service had kept him informed about the hostility of stock interests to range regulation.

Now in Boise, toward the end of his western tour, he was intercepted by his friend Chet Olsen from the regional Forest Service office in Ogden. Olson brought word of discussions held between committees of the American Livestock Association and the National Woolgrowers' Association in Salt Lake City, and he had copies of the resolutions they had passed. He put them into DeVoto's hands, because he hoped that an airing in the Easy Chair might forestall the designs the stockmen had against the grazing division of the National Forest Service.[8]

Olsen did better than he knew. He did more than ignite an Easy Chair. He ignited a whole string of Easy Chairs, articles, speeches, and political maneuvers. He lit a pilot light that burned steadily through the rest of DeVoto's life and exploded into hot action at every new injection of fuel. He handed DeVoto the cause and the controversy that took precedence over all the other causes and controversies of his contentious career, the one that most enlisted his heart, conscience, and knowledge.

DeVoto went West in 1946 a historian and tourist. He came back an embattled conservationist, one whose activities would eventually entitle him to be ranked with George Perkins Marsh, Powell, Karl Schurz, Pinchot, and Roosevelt. Appropriately, his strength was the strength of words. His platform was more often than not the Easy Chair, which through the eleven years of his incumbency had developed a loyal and influential group of readers.

He had never ceased to be a Populist radical, a small-d democrat of a recognizably western kind, but for a decade or more, during the 1930s, he had been moved (largely because of the extravagances of the literary Left) to damn all crusaders and reformers as the dupes of abstract thinking. By 1946 his Paretian skepticism and his nearly fatalistic acceptance of a marred world—an attitude probably borrowed from L. J. Henderson—had passed.[9] He was ready to grant that a reformer could sometimes be as pragmatic as old Ad Hoc himself. His intensified, firsthand contact with the West and western problems in the 1940s, and his informed awareness of the more or less concerted campaign against the resources of the Public Domain, insured that during the rest of his life DeVoto would himself be a crusader, and not a tame one.

2 · *A Function of Journalism*

For years after he ceased to be an academic, DeVoto's life ran by the academic calendar. About the time of the autumnal equinox, when the trees began to pull in their chlorophyll and the lilacs fattened their winter buds and the leaves changed, long habit told him it was time to return to town, tie up the loose ends of summer, renew acquaintance with friends and colleagues, listen to the latest gossip, visit the Harvard Coop in search of supplies, put a new ribbon in the typewriter and lay in a few of the ledgers in which he wrote his longhand first drafts, and dig in for the winter. That was his program when he got back from the West in September 1946, and he had his usual multiplicity of jobs to dig into.

In the Cambridge novel which was one of those jobs and which he kept on trying to write long after the reception of *Mountain Time* told him all over again that he was not a novelist, the principal male character is a compulsive worker. At one point in the narrative another character says of him, ". . . a necessity so powerful, a need to work so monstrous . . . must spring from something terrible within."[1] It is quite likely that DeVoto was commenting on himself, and yet one must be cautious in accepting the comment as an unqualified truth. For one thing, he was a most gregarious man outside of working hours. His friends knew him as a man who, in Ted Morrison's words, "laughed his head off" about all sorts of things,[2] who loved a drink and the gathering of friends in the "violet hour" after five or six o'clock, who loved Cambridge gossip and off-color stories, who would go to any length to help a friend in trouble. Maybe there was "something terrible" within him, but his daily life did not show it, and there is no evidence, from the word of his friends or from his letters, that he found his incessant work a burden.

As a matter of fact, he loved work; he could not have existed without it; and though he sometimes complained about it, that was standard bellyaching, part of the pleasure. "Go ahead and holler," he advised the American people during the war, resisting the frequent and somewhat Calvinistic call for a sterner self-sacrifice.[3] Hollering was healthy. So was work. Later on, in the 1950s, when he found himself unexpectedly with all his books written while his lifelong habit of work went on demanding exercise like a beaver's growing teeth, he would discover that work without a believed-in objective could bring on both panic and depression. But it never became less than necessary to him, and so long as he had projects that absorbed him—and in 1946 he had several—he was a contented beaver with a dam to build, a lodge to make, and countless cottonwood trees to fell for bark. To say nothing of his need to gather each afternoon around six with other beavers and rechew the day's chips.

There were all those articles to be put together out of his notes. There was the steady reading in sources, the steady correspondence with scholars, libraries, historical societies, newspaper morgues, and local enthusiasts in the long preparation for writing about Lewis and Clark. There was the continuing war over literary censorship; he was no sooner home than he was involved in another Massachusetts suppression, this time of *Forever Amber*, a book he called cheap and vulgar and privately thought obscene but insisted should be freely chosen or rejected by readers, not pulled off the shelves by censors.[4]

There was the frustrating relationship with the Mark Twain Estate, with which after more than eight years he was completely disgusted and which, if the truth were told, was not too delighted with him. On October 4 he told Chamberlain that he would stay on until he had finished the volume of letters, but no longer. Less than a week later, having tasted freedom in anticipation and found it good, he began to urge that Dixon Wecter, who was writing a biography of Mark Twain and had worked extensively with the papers, should be made the new curator and take over the volume of letters.⁵ The papers themselves, he said, ought to be moved to the Huntington Library, of which Wecter was then the head.

It took him some time to get the succession approved, not because Clara Samoussoud was unwilling to be rid of DeVoto but because the biography on which Wecter was working was committed to Houghton Mifflin, and Harper's was reluctant to have a curator whose Mark Twain books would not be on its list. But by the end of November Wecter was approved, the Huntington was approved, and DeVoto had extracted a legal receipt and quit-claim, carefully prepared by Charles Curtis, to insure that he would retain the right to publish things from the papers and that he would not be subject to the niggling of Mr. Chamberlain.⁶ Before 1946 ended, he was free of the job he had been so eager to obtain in 1938, when he had lost both Harvard and the *Saturday Review* and needed the reassurance of a formal institutional place.

Characteristically, he had no sooner cut himself free of the Mark Twain affiliation than he undertook another. The two bad years after his resignation from Northwestern had taught him about the anxieties of total independence. He had come to realize, as he would write Mark Saxton the next summer, that "a man who is at once bright enough and ass enough to be a writer is also sensitive enough about his personal deficiencies to long for functional justification as part of an institution." Northwestern, Harvard, the Easy Chair, Bread Loaf, the *Saturday Review*, and the Mark Twain papers had all provided him with corners into which he could back like a crab to protect his flanks and rear. Circumstances had forced him out of all of them except the Easy Chair. Now he gave up the Mark Twain papers without regret, because another institution was ready to make him a new place.

He had gone West in June half committed to the History Book Club, which was being organized by a group of businessmen with advice from the bookseller Charles Everitt, Raymond's father. On October 1 there was a meeting in New York, from which DeVoto emerged as chairman of the book club's panel of judges. These included, besides DeVoto, Randolph Adams, Frank Dobie, Stewart Holbrook, and Arthur Schlesinger, Jr. Their duty was to select a monthly History Book Club choice and an occasional dividend book. More than the modest retaining fee motivated the judges. Their hope was that they might invigorate the writing of American history and widen its audience.⁷ Thanks in part to the influence of DeVoto and Everitt, the club, though a business venture, was also a campaign against the academic monographers. It promoted the kind of narrative history that the judges themselves, especially DeVoto, wrote and admired. Like every other editorial venture with which DeVoto affiliated himself during his lifetime, the club took a position (his) and vigorously promoted it. As one of the earliest come-ons in the drive for members, De-Voto dug out of his file and turned over to the advertising director the letter he had written to Kitty Bowen: "Sure you're romantic about American history. It's the most romantic of all histories. . . ."

Being a history judge involved reading virtually every book in the field of American history that appeared. It also involved a constant correspondence with the club's New York office as well as with the other judges, scattered from Cambridge to Chicago, Texas, and Oregon.[8] But it still did not quite fill up the cracks in a workday that he seemed determined to make seamless and uninterrupted from breakfast time till bed. He still found time for the crusade he had brought back from the West.

He did not hurry; he preferred to pick his own time and occasion for battle. As early as August 3, from Bozeman, Montana, he had written Arthur Schlesinger, Jr., that he intended to do something about the "western hogs" whose mentality was "straight out of the cabinet of Ulysses S. Grant," but he indicated that he wanted to time his blow so as to do maximum harm to the legislative program that he and his Forest Service friends expected the stockmen to introduce. Throughout the fall, he quietly prepared and orchestrated his effects. He stated the theme, but obscurely and without specifics—a sort of brief horn solo—in "The Anxious West" in the December *Harper's*, amplifying and updating the generalizations of the much earlier "Footnote on the West" and "The West: A Plundered Province." Then, in the issue of January 1947, which appeared a couple of weeks before Congress reconvened, he let go with full brass and percussion. Having been for eleven years the magazine's most dependable and provocative contributor, he demanded and got double space. He presented the case against the stockmen, and exposed their intentions, in "The West Against Itself," a full-length article; and in the Easy Chair of the same issue he gave historical perspective to the stockmen by comparing them with the Mesta, whose grazing practices had turned Spain into a semi-desert, and in whose history he had been instructed by Garrett Mattingly.[9]

From a purely Populist recapitulation of the West's economic history—the raids against furs, metals, timber, grass, gas, and oil—and the psychology and economics of liquidation that these raids had demonstrated, he went on to a discussion of the high interest rates, short-haul freight rates, and other methods by which eastern capital had kept the West an economic fief. He noted the federal reclamation and power projects and the war-stimulated industry that in recent years had given the West the beginning, or the hope, of a self-sufficient and home-owned economy. He paraphrased the curious response of western interests to the federal government: "Get out and give us more money." He observed that many well-intentioned Westerners had been duped into taking the side of the resource raiders against themselves. And this brought him to the calculated attack that those interests were now preparing against the federal bureaus, especially against the Forest Service, whose management of western resources was the West's best safeguard.

All the resource-liquidating interests were behind the moves that had been planned in Salt Lake City, he said, but the stockmen were for the moment carrying the ball. They were bent upon converting their privilege of cheap-permit grazing on Taylor Act and Forest Service lands into a vested right, and eventually into outright ownership. They wanted the Taylor Act grazing lands removed from the Bureau of Land Management and distributed to the states for next to nothing: the Salt Lake City meeting had suggested prices as low as ten cents an acre. They wanted Forest Service lands reclassified and all the grazing lands within them, which meant most of the endangered watersheds, transferred to the states along with the Taylor Act lands. They wanted these lands of both kinds, once transferred, sold into private ownership, which meant to the present permit holders; and they wanted the Forest Service deprived of its regulatory power over grazing and limited to the management of pure timberland. In other words, they wanted to liquidate the Bureau of Land Management and emasculate the Forest Service and gain ownership of a princely but fragile domain that now belonged to all Americans.

Having outlined the strategy, he outlined the bills, old and new, by which the stock interests had tried and would try to gain their ends. In particular, and in detail, he warned against the Robertson bill, S. 1945, introduced in the previous session and due to be reintroduced in the coming one. It would empower the transfer of all unappropriated and unreserved lands, including the minerals in them, to thirteen western states, with the right to dispose of them as they saw fit; and it would create a commission, easily packed by western politicians friendly to the stock interests, to re-examine all federal reservations with a view to transferring out of them such lands as were more useful for grazing than for other purposes. This commission, DeVoto said, would "re-think the justifications" of all federal reserves, with the transparent object of getting large parts of the Public Domain into state ownership so that timber, grazing, and mining interests, always able to dominate a state as they could not dominate a federal bureau, could open a new day in the economics of liquidation.

Landgrab, DeVoto called it, the biggest landgrab in our history if it realized its intentions. Passage of the legislation it proposed would bring enormous profits to a few, and return the West "to the processes of geology."

There you have it. A few groups of Western interests, so small numerically as to constitute a minute fraction of the West, are hellbent on destroying the West. They are stronger than they would otherwise be because they are skillfully manipulating in their support sentiments that have always been powerful in the West—the home rule which means basically that we want federal help without federal regulation, the "individualism" that has always made the small Western operator a handy tool of the big one, and the wild myth that stockgrowers constitute an aristocracy in which all Westerners somehow share. . . . To a historian it has the beauty of any historical continuity. . . . But if it has this beauty it also has an almost cosmic irony, in that fulfillment of the great dream of the West, mature economic development and local ownership and control, has been made possible by the developments of our age at exactly the same time. That dream envisions the establishment of an economy on the natural resources of the West, developed and integrated to produce a steady, sustained, permanent yield. While the West moves to build that kind of economy, a part of the West is simultaneously moving to destroy the natural resources forever.

That was for openers, and it committed him. Between January 1947 and his death, nearly nine years later, DeVoto wrote more than forty more articles about the West. All but three or four of them are conservationist polemics, most of them aimed against the same interests and many of the same individuals that he named in "The West Against Itself." They were the same interests that had almost got away with the Public Domain during the administration of Herbert Hoover and his Secretary of the Interior, Ray Lyman Wilbur, the same interests that Theodore Roosevelt and Gifford Pinchot had fought in the early years of the century, the same that Major John Wesley Powell had challenged and lost out to in the 1890s.[10] There are clarifications as well as discouragements in the study of history. It demonstrates with precision who the adversaries are. Always are.

DeVoto opened fire on them so unexpectedly—dry-gulched

them, according to their way of thinking—that the stockmen were at first disorganized and could do no more than reply with some personal disparagements in *The Stockman* and other controlled papers. Conservationists and bureaucrats, on the other hand, were delighted. The conservation organizations, far weaker in 1946 than they were even a few years later, distributed offprints of his articles to every member of Congress and filled DeVoto's mailbox with enthusiastic letters. At the end of March, when he suspended his other jobs long enough to go to Washington for more ammunition, he was assured by his Forest Service friend Walt Dutton and by Secretary of Agriculture Clinton Anderson that he, a disinterested private citizen, had singlehandedly stopped the landgrab cold.[11]

Neither part of that judgment was quite sound. He had not done it alone: allies had been quick to rally around him, because they had been dug in and fighting all the time. And the landgrab was not quite stopped. The forces behind it had money, influence, organization, a potent lobby, and their own natural allies in the meat-packing industry and the United States Chamber of Commerce. Though discretion suggested to these forces that the Robertson bill should not be pushed, there were other ways. Congressman Barrett of Wyoming brought before the House his annual bill to turn over to the Forest Service (and hence expose to envelopment by the larger attack against that bureau) parts of the Jackson Hole National Monument, old ranching country which had been bought up a ranch at a time by the Rockefellers and presented to the National Parks system. The perennial effort to whittle away a portion of Olympic National Park so that its valuable timber could be logged was still being pressed. And on April 17, 1947, when the stockmen had had time to regroup, Congressman Barrett got through H.R. 93, authorizing the Subcommittee on Public Lands, of which he was chairman, to hold public hearings on the grazing policies of the Forest Service.

During the hearings on the Jackson Hole National Monument bill, the stockmen's witnesses had found it expedient to praise the Forest Service to which they wanted parts of the Monument transferred, but their clear intention in the August-to-October hearings on Forest Service grazing practices was not praise of the Forest Service. They were going for the jugular.

In an effort to restore ranges damaged by years of overgrazing, the Forest Service had been making small reductions in the numbers of cattle and sheep permitted on specific National Forest ranges. Without any question, the reductions worked a hardship upon individual ranchers who held permits in the National Forests; equally without question, the reductions were essential for the health of the ranges. Stockmen to whom their permits had always seemed a right, and especially the organizations which represented the stockmen politically, were bent on eliminating the control exercised over the ranges by the Forest Service, and for that purpose they went to Washington, where the power resided.

In June, their political representatives proposed deep cuts in the budgets of both Agriculture and Interior, following a strategy of demolishment that Senator McCarran had used on the Taylor Grazing Service.[12] The demand for slashes in the budget was an open invitation to the stockmen who would testify at Billings, Rawlins, Grand Junction, Salt Lake City, Redding, and Ely to destroy the credibility and morale of the Forest Service as a bureau. Congressman Barrett's friendly chairmanship insured the advantage of the stockmen's witnesses: he would systematically limit the time of anti-landgrab witnesses, keep their testimony off the record by setting it aside for the written report, encourage the airing of stockmen's grievances, and permit stacked audiences to heckle and drown out witnesses friendly to the Forest Service.[13]

But in the event, his chairmanship was too friendly, and the effort to produce a pro-stockmen report boomeranged, partly because DeVoto and his conservationist allies kept the light turned brightly on the meetings. In Billings, several stockmen defended the Forest Service against their own associations. In Rawlins and Grand Junction, Congressman Barrett so far ignored the pretense of impartiality that newspapers, including the influential Denver *Post*, began to denounce the methods of "Congressman Barrett's Wild West Show." A hearing scheduled for Phoenix was hastily canceled, presumably because it appeared in advance that the opposition would make a strong showing. By the time of the last meeting, in Ely, Nevada, an aroused public and press had organized so effectively that the Barrett subcommittee went home in disarray.

During the whole effort against Barrett and the stockmen, DeVoto was intensely busy, both in writing and in organizing the opposition. In the June Easy Chair he brought his public up to date on what he had warned it about in January and reminded readers that they, too, had representatives in the Congress and they, too, could afford a stamp. Once the hearings began in August, and he found himself unable to obtain transcripts from the unco-operative subcommittee, he enlisted western correspondents including Struthers Burt of Jackson Hole and Charles Moore of Dubois, both prominent in the Dude Ranchers' Association and both anti-landgrab. In several of the hearings, especially the one at Rawlins, DeVoto and a *Collier's* writer named Velie had been considerably vilified, probably because their articles unfriendly to the stockmen's associations had appeared in magazines of large circulation and influence, and hence had been more damaging than those by Arthur Carhart, Kenneth Reid, and others, which had appeared in conservation journals for an audience of the already converted. Without a transcript, DeVoto had been unable to counter the slurs of the subcommittee or publicize its methods, but by the end of the year he had the published *Report*, eight volumes of it, and in the Easy Chair for January 1948 he could summarize the whole sorry spectacle, and with considerable satisfaction make it clear how thoroughly the subcommittee that had set out to discredit the Forest Service had discredited itself. None of the legislation designed to achieve the stockmen's aims had passed; none now seemed likely to.

A good year's work, and one that DeVoto took pride in. All his talent for controversy, all his radical Populism, all his knowledge of the West, all his skill in the gathering of information, came to focus in it. Knight-errantry was congenial to him; and if, in this contest with the cowboys, he shows some resemblance to the Lone Ranger discomfiting the gang of the crooked sheriff, why, so be it. He was both a professional Westerner and a romantic, as a lot of the cowboys themselves were. But he demonstrated, as they did not, that the self-conscious western role is not incompatible with disinterested public spirit.

Coming as it did in conjunction with the publication of *Across the Wide Missouri*, which appeared on October 27 to praise that was fervent and nearly unanimous, the landgrab fight gave DeVoto much publicity, and he was not averse to publicity. His career, in fact, was cresting. After much trial and error, he had found his proper functions in history and controversy, both focused on the West. In December he was elected to the National Institute of Arts and Letters and thus achieved certification among the literary, whom he had so consistently and compulsively disparaged and whose territory he had abandoned after the failure of *Mountain Time*. In January 1948, Secretary of the Interior Julius Krug, impressed by his *Fortune* piece on the national parks and his stoutly conservationist campaign against the stockmen, appointed him to the Advisory Board for National Parks, Historical Sites, Buildings, and Monuments,[14] a congressionally authorized civilian group charged with advising the Secretary on conservation matters.

Membership on that board, with its twice-a-year meetings in Washington and its occasional inspection tours of national-park areas, gave DeVoto confidential contact with new sources of information and allied him with the National Park Service almost as firmly as he had always been allied with the Forest Service. He was not the paid mouthpiece of the federal bureaus that some stockmen charged him with being, but he was certainly of the federal bureaus' party, and an insider at that.

More recognition was to come: in May the Pulitzer prize for history, in June an honorary degree from the University of Colorado, which gratified him exceedingly, for it honored his conservation activities and it came from the West, where so many prominent people so prominently hated the sound of his name.[15] In July he received the Bancroft prize, which with the Pulitzer gave *Across the Wide Missouri* a sweep. Whatever his pretenses, he valued these honors. "I find the indignity singularly easy to bear" was his standard response to congratulations. In the spring and summer of 1948, when praise and blame whirled around him like fighting birds, he was exhilarated by the sense of being the acknowledged champion of justice, sanity, conservation, and the public interest against the "Two-Gun Desmonds"; and the persistence and effectiveness of the stockmen, who were a long way from admitting defeat, stimulated all his capacities as a tactician and pamphleteer.

He made Cambridge the center of an information network, with confidential informants in Washington and in the regional bureau offices, and with friends in the West such as A. B. Guthrie and Joseph Kinsey Howard in Montana, Struthers Burt and Charles Moore in Wyoming, Stewart Holbrook in Oregon, Frank Dobie in Texas, and Arthur Carhart in Denver. He worked closely with the Izaak Walton League and the Wilderness Society, and he could count on influential friends among the columnists—Elmer Davis, Marquis Childs, his old student Joe Alsop—to back up the Easy Chair or even front for it. By letter and by telephone he was in touch with nearly the entire conservation movement as it then existed, and he encouraged Carhart and Olaus Murie of the Wilderness Society to make an up-to-date list of "hot spots" that were likely to need concerted attention.[16] He also knew an increasing number of senators and congressmen, whom he influenced both privately and through his writings.

Harper's was a most effective way of reaching Congress, but he wanted to reach a wide public, too, especially after the stockmen's lobby began to plant articles of its own in the magazines. Unfortunately, most magazines of large circulation were wary of controversy, and all DeVoto's vehemence and eloquence could not turn them into vehicles for his cause. He did write an article on the national forests for *Collier's*, but it got sidetracked like his earlier articles for *Life*, probably because the editors felt he took too belligerent a stand. The same thing happened to an article he wrote for *Look* about the rehabilitation of watersheds in the Wasatch National Forest, Chet Olsen's bailiwick, under the somewhat surprising leadership of the Kiwanis Club of Ogden. He succeeded in planting conservation articles by Arthur Carhart in the *Atlantic* and in the *Pacific Spectator*,[17] the quarterly edited at Stanford by his friend Edith Mirrielees.

Anticipating a Republican victory in the November elections, he kept his eye on Dewey, Stassen, and other potential candidates, and collected dossiers on people they were likely to appoint to the key secretaryships of Interior and Agriculture. The prospects were depressing; he tried in advance to build an organized opposition to the worst of them.[18]

Like all who elect to be hammers, he found himself now and then an anvil. A small factual blunder in the Easy Chair for January 1948, in which he attributed to Congressman Barrett an Alaskan statehood bill authored by Congressman Bartlett, forced him to publish a correction in a letter to the editor. The opposition, which had been trying to discredit his facts for a long time, was pleased. It took a big man, the stockmen said, to admit an error like that. They looked forward to his admitting a lot more.[19]

The spokesmen for the stockgrowers—Norman Winder, J. Elmer Brock, Farrington Carpenter, and others—were experienced lobbyists and public-relations men, and worthy antagonists. But it would have been discreet of them not to twist the mule's tail, for DeVoto was a controversialist whose voltage increased when he was chastised or humiliated. In March 1948, more than a year after his first attack on the stockmen, he wrote to Struthers Burt, who was riding out the tail end of winter in the Wirt Hotel, in Jackson, Wyoming:

If you listen late at night—in that springtime wonderland of yours where doubtless the cottonwoods are budding and you've cut your first alfalfa, whereas we are at this moment finishing our eleventh foot of snow of this winter—you will hear an odd, steady sound. That is me boiling. I don't know when I came to a boil or just why but I suddenly realized that it had happened. I've just been knocking up practice flies in this game so far. Now I'm coming up to bat. Give me some offstage noises for I'm in the saddle again, off the reservation, and out for blood. Somehow I seem to have got mad.

Having got mad, he stayed mad. Let the Cheyenne *Eagle* suggest that he had spoken untruths about Barrett's subcommittee hearings, let Congressman Ellsworth of Oregon intimate that the Forest Service paid him to defend its policies, and he came back with bristling demands for retractions, and persisted till he got them. Let someone publish a book useful to the conservation movement and he reviewed it, bought copies for congressmen and columnists, plugged it in speeches, articles, and letters, and replied to anyone who reviewed it unfavorably. He was a one-man publicity department for Gifford Pinchot's reissued autobiography, *Breaking New Ground*, for Richard Lillard's book *The Great Forest*, and especially for William Vogt's *The Road to Survival*. When he went to Boulder in June to receive his honorary degree from the University of Colorado, he turned his speech into an environmental warning, which Arthur Carhart promptly reproduced and distributed to schools, politicians, and organizations all over the state.[20]

Let a politician make a speech adopting the stockmen's line, as Harold Stassen did while wooing western support for his candidacy, and he was at once accosted, by letter and in the public prints, by this angry watchdog DeVoto. If there is such a disease as infectious high blood pressure, he had it, and communicated it. He had Avis lying awake nights over the sinking water table and prepared at any time to start saving nightsoil. On May 8 he wrote William Sloane that there were now only three kinds of Harvard professors: those who had enlisted in Avis' conservation crusade, the dead, and those in headlong flight.

In July he made a second demand on *Harper's* for double space. In an article, "Sacred Cows and Public Lands," and simultaneously in an Easy Chair, "Statesmen on the Lam," he laid out in detail the continuing efforts of the landgrab forces and the fatal errors of Congressman Barrett's Wild West Show. When the stockmen wrote Frederick Lewis Allen, the *Harper's* editor, trying to close *Harper's* to him, Allen rebuffed the demand. When they wanted space to answer DeVoto in, DeVoto pointed out in advance so many provable distortions of fact in their answer that *Harper's* rejected it. When the stockmen did succeed in stating their position in *Liberty*, the *Farm Journal*, and even in *Consumer's Guide*,[21] which swallowed the line that Forest Service grazing restrictions were forcing up meat prices, DeVoto refuted the position point by point and cross-examined the editors, who, he told them bluntly, had been played for suckers.

Shortly after July's double-barreled blast, Allen somewhat wistfully suggested to DeVoto that *Harper's* could not go on turning itself into an embattled propaganda sheet. DeVoto replied that the issue was of the first importance and insisted that at least the Easy Chair should be open to conservation whenever the occasion demanded. But he did not again ask for double space; he was in complete agreement with Allen that *Harper's* held its position as the leading magazine of opinion precisely because it was independent of outside controls.[22] And once, when the campaign against the stockmen had been devouring all his time and attention and Allen had to send back an Easy Chair as inadequate, DeVoto promptly and humbly accepted correction.[23] That was the first and only Easy Chair that ever came back, and the rejection hurt his professional pride. He was like a sheep dog whistled back to his duties from a wild chase after a jack rabbit. He admitted the weakness of the piece and in twenty-four hours produced another: a piece on the Welsh Indians, cannibalized out of the Lewis and Clark research.

In September, after a miserable Bread Loaf session complete with a Frost crisis, he went back out to Denver as an official delegate to the Denver Inter-American Conference on Conservation of Renewable Natural Resources. The chairman of the conference, his ally-by-mail William Vogt, he did not meet, because Vogt went to the hospital for an emergency appendectomy just before the meeting convened; but he spread the gospel and consolidated his influence among the delegates from the United States, who included the Secretary of State, the Undersecretary of the Interior, Senator Young of North Dakota, Congressman Hope of Iowa, the Chief of the Forest Service, and the Director of the National Park Service, Newton Drury.

On October 11 the New York *Herald Tribune* published his Denver speech and a week later printed the extended statement on the public lands, prepared for the *Herald Tribune*'s annual forum, in which he debated with the stockmen's public-relations man Farrington Carpenter. A fortnight after that, Truman's unexpected victory over Dewey relieved for the time his fear of a Republican giveaway of the Public Domain, and as one of its side effects retired from office some of the more prominent stockmen, including Senator Robertson of Wyoming. DeVoto's journalistic war against the landgrab could not be said to have had any substantial effect on the election, but it had played a large part in stalling the stockmen's legislative program until other, larger events changed the political situation and reduced the danger.

3 · *Crusader*

Though 1948 ended with a victory, it did not bring demobiliza-
tion. What had begun as pitched battle against the landgrab continued as public education. *The Land* reprinted DeVoto's *Herald
Tribune* Forum statement, along with Farrington Carpenter's, in
January 1949. In that same month DeVoto combined public education with gainful employment and told his housewife readers in
Woman's Day that "Water Runs Downhill," a fact which has
consequences in floods, erosion, and other matters ignored by people intent only on cutting off the timber and grazing off the grass.
The Easy Chair for March turned from the public-lands controversy to another aspect of conservation and reported the perilous
state of the National Park Service, underbudgeted, understaffed, its
facilities run down from years of wartime neglect and its public
pleasuring grounds exposed to a vastly increased postwar visitation
that it had neither the men nor the means to cope with. The May
Easy Chair stoutly rebuked *Time* for pooh-poohing the desert
challenge and the Malthusian threat that were the theme of Vogt's
The Road to Survival. *Time*'s contemptuous advice to Americans
to "eat hearty," DeVoto said, was in the circumstances not only
insanity, but criminal insanity, and ignorant besides. For months
after that angry flurry against the American gospel of plenty he
was advising correspondents to quit reading *Time* and take up
Newsweek.

Finally, having no more immediate dangers to publicize, he ended
1949 on a positive note, and a profitable one. *Reader's Digest* had
commissioned, and assigned for first publication to the Phi Beta
Kappa magazine *The American Scholar*, an article on how the
Forest Service, with CCC labor, had rehabilitated part of the
Wasatch watershed.[1] The summer cloudbursts of 1949 had made
the rehabilitated slopes a bright demonstration of the effects of
good range management, for during those cloudbursts the creeks
from the rescued slopes had run barely turbid while all up and
down the range the denuded and unreclaimed canyons had run
mud, boulders, and destructive floods. The moral was very clear,
and DeVoto made it: restrain the economics of raid and liquidation,
and put the vital watersheds of the West into the hands of the
bureau that knew how to protect them.

He had been trying for a long time to get *The Saturday Evening Post*, with its large circulation and popular influence, to take a conservation piece. In the spring of 1950 he finally succeeded, and for the purpose of collecting information he allied himself with a flamboyant ex-Bread Loaf Fellow, Commander William Lederer, a Navy public-relations officer with ambitions to be a writer. At Bread Loaf the summer before, Lederer had met another Bread Loaf Fellow as flamboyant as himself, Eugene Burdick, and begun the friendship that would come to a sort of fizzing climax in *The Ugly American* some years later. In 1950 Bill Lederer was unknown as a writer but widely known in the Navy as the damnedest promoter alive—an engaging, fuzzy-haired, fast-talking con man with a genius for publicity and for getting others to co-operate in anything he wanted. It took him a good many weeks to bring off the informational trip West that he and DeVoto coveted, but when he finally brought it off he brought it off with class.

On May 2, 1950, an Air Force plane with a pair of Air Force pilots picked up DeVoto and Lederer at Bolling Field, hopped them across country to Plattsmouth, where the Platte meets the Missouri, and then took them, low level, crisscrossing, and returning on their tracks, up the Platte Valley along the Oregon Trail. They crossed South Pass, which in 1946 DeVoto had been prevented from seeing by the rain, so low they could see the whites of the antelopes' eyes. It was laid out there in relief, like a triumphant equation summing up the historical movement that so fascinated DeVoto. He got the pilots to turn around and fly over it again, just to imprint it on his mind, all that country from the last crossing of the Platte to the Green River, with the Wind Rivers to northward, the Uintas to the south and west, the characterless sagebrush pass bulging up from the Sweetwater toward the drainage of the Green. When he had it by heart, they turned northward and flew up along the Wind Rivers to where the Wind and the Popo Agie join to form the Bighorn, and then on to Great Falls, where they were met by A. B. "Bud" Guthrie, recently a Nieman Fellow at Harvard, a friend and intense admirer of DeVoto's. In Great Falls the three, by prearrangement of Bill Lederer, put themselves into the hospitable hands of the Corps of Engineers, who were to display to them their plans for the controlling of the Missouri River.

The Engineers, as DeVoto said in several places, were "not simple virgins." They knew who their guest was and what his opinions were likely to be. Also they understood how to put on a PR tour, and they were excellent company, most especially Brigadier General S. G. Sturgis, who acknowledged DeVoto's potency as a publicist by personally directing their three-week inspection. He showed them the Missouri from headwaters to mouth, by air, by boat, and by car, and he even acceded to their Tom Sawyer side by turning them loose on the river for three days in a small boat. General Sturgis understood early that he and DeVoto had a fundamental disagreement on the subject of main-stem dams, but he remained affable to the end and sent them home unpersuaded about the control of the Missouri but personally very friendly. On their way back, there was a "carefully unrehearsed moment" when DeVoto and Guthrie threw the publicity-conscious Lederer into the Platte for the benefit of some opportune photographers, and then they flew back to Boston to find their moment made immortal in the Boston *Globe*—another authentic Lederer miracle.

DeVoto was never quite sure how Bill Lederer had managed to hit the Boston papers so fast, from so far out in the sticks, but Lederer's next move made his previous accomplishments look like child's play. During their trip he had heard a good deal about the Nieman Fellowships from Bud Guthrie and had decided he would like one. Upon inquiry he found that, not being a working newspaperman, he was not eligible; but Louis Lyons, the Nieman Foundation director, finally agreed that he might participate as an auditor, without stipend. Then Lederer applied to the Navy and got himself assigned for duty to Harvard, at commanders' pay. Filled with admiration, DeVoto remembered the time he and Guthrie had ducked Lederer in the Platte, and wished that they had done it from an airplane.[2]

Out of the Missouri junket came more than the unlikely friendship with General Sturgis, an improved notion of the South Pass section of the Oregon Trail, an enhanced appreciation of what Lewis and Clark had seen while moving steadily upriver through the greening bottoms, and an admiration for Bill Lederer's promotional talents. The principal conviction that DeVoto brought back with him was an opposition to the Pick-Sloan Plan for the Missouri, and indeed for any variety of Missouri Valley Authority. He expressed his opposition in the Easy Chairs for July and August, and in the *Saturday Evening Post* for July 22[3] he challenged the Corps of Engineers and the Bureau of Reclamation, both dam-building bureaus and both politically potent, as the greatest enemies of the National Parks.

The National Park Act of 1916 specified that the park areas were to be set aside in perpetuity for "use without impairment." But the Engineers and the Bureau of Reclamation had on their drawing boards plans for dams in Glacier, in Grand Canyon, in Dinosaur National Monument, in Yellowstone. He accused them of deliberately trying to get one such dam built in order to set a precedent that would open the way to others. Once the protection of the National Park Act was proved ineffective, the parks would be exposed to flooding whenever one of the dam-building bureaus found a canyon it wanted to plug and a local citizenry that was interested in a boondoggle. He challenged the cost-benefit figures of the bureaus, which he said were always deceptive; he disputed the rosy expectation of many Westerners that dams would actually create water. His principal target was the Colorado River Storage Project of the Bureau of Reclamation, his bull's-eye the Echo Park dam proposed at the junction of the Green and the Yampa, in the heart of Dinosaur National Monument. That is to say, he made public, very public, the anxieties that had been troubling the meetings of the National Parks Advisory Board for more than a year. When the *Reader's Digest* reprinted the *Post* article in November, many million people were made aware of a threat to something most of them instinctively or out of personal experience valued highly.

Several consequences ensued from DeVoto's attack on the dam builders. For one thing, Ben Hibbs, the *Post*'s editor, got so much pressure from western lobbies and from the bureaus themselves that he closed the door to DeVoto's pamphleteering and never reopened it. For another, the public controversy over the Dinosaur dams, a controversy that would give conservationists one of their most complete victories, was opened with the precise arguments that would finally win it: that dams within a national park area would constitute an "impairment" of the kind specifically forbidden by the National Park Act, and that the cost-benefit figures of the bureaus, the economic justifications of main-stem dams, were open to the gravest doubt. The Sierra Club and other conservation organizations would finally bring those arguments home to the public, and thence to Congress, five years after DeVoto aired them in the *Post*.[4] And for still another, that article made the name DeVoto more hated than ever in Utah, which had counted on the boondoggle of the Echo Park dam and had generated a good deal of unrealistic expectation with regard to new water on its dry eastern edge. First, said apoplectic Utahns, this fellow smears his home state with a lot of lies, now he tries to prevent the building of Utah's last water hole. In their rage, they demonstrated the truth of some of the things he had said in "The West Against Itself."

It did not surprise him that he made enemies of many people in the West that he kept trying to rescue from its own folly. He had elected them enemies before they elected him. The stockmen and lumbermen exerted their steady political influence against both Forest Service and National Park Service; the Corps of Engineers and the Bureau of Reclamation, each in its own behalf, leaned against the Washington structure of power with the force of a prevailing wind; and the West, with the shortsightedness that De-Voto had more than once noted, took up arms against itself, and hence against him.

His inclination to fight them was hampered by the long, drawn-out labor on Lewis and Clark, or what had started out to be Lewis and Clark, as well as by a growing anxiety about his health and an increasing need for money as his historical research dragged on and on. His last institutional affiliation, together with its small stipend, had gone when he resigned from the History Book Club, after a year and a half of trying, in March 1948.[5] This time, he had not hastened to replace that small security with another, and he suffered psychologically from the lack. Moreover, he found it increasingly difficult to combine money-making with propaganda for conservation. Magazines began to steer clear of him, because his articles were so often polemics. Both Fred Allen and John Fischer of *Harper's* had indicated a wish that he wouldn't harp on the same old issue all the time.[6] But that, DeVoto told them, was exactly the point. You didn't mount the barricades until noon and then go out for a three-hour lunch.

The intensely concentrated job of writing *The Course of Empire* occupied the whole of 1951. He found time for only one more warning against the renewed activity of the stockmen's lobby, in the Easy Chair for March. There was no Bread Loaf for him that year—had not been since 1949 and would never be again—but something like nostalgia for the good old summers, some need to feel again the reassurance of working with friends in a joint effort, led him to accept an invitation to Joseph Kinsey Howard's writing conference at the University of Montana. There, besides Howard, he was working with Helen Everitt and A. B. Guthrie. They turned the Missoula meetings into a "Bread Loaf, Montana," and, like Syracusans writing back to Corinth or Athens, sent long messages of report and humorous adjuration to their mother institution in Vermont. Discreet parts of those letters were read aloud in Treman Cottage,[7] and those of us who heard them read found in them, despite the confident assertion of western superiorities, a note of homesickness for the place he could now neither stand nor stand to miss.

In Missoula his friends from the Region One office of the Forest Service put a parachute on him and sent him out with their fire-fighting crews to a number of forest fires. He loved it; it satisfied a desire for danger and adventure that had lain in him ever since the anticlimactic ending of his Army service. Characteristically, he turned it at once into words, and wrote for the November *Harper's* an article, "The Smoke Jumpers," that managed to speak to the conservation issue without giving Fred Allen a chance to complain. Ostensibly a journalistic report on an exciting and dangerous job, "The Smoke Jumpers" was in fact a shrewd defense of the Forest Service against its enemies, for in the course of dramatizing the techniques of fire fighting by air, DeVoto resurrected most of the general article on the national forests that *Collier's* had commissioned and then killed in 1948. With that article he ended five years of service in the conservation wars. To that point, he had acted as a private citizen and as a journalist. With the beginning of 1952, his Lewis and Clark book at last off his back and his temporarily unfocused energies in need of new occupation, he would take the action onto the center court and go political.

From the beginning, the Easy Chair had been the expression of a political independent. DeVoto had given it his highly personal coloration, and though essentially a New Dealer, had attacked some New Deal measures and deplored the New Deal's political slipperiness and its suppression of war information. For the previous five years, DeVoto had used the Easy Chair to fight the land bills of the western lobby. He described himself to his public as one of the few surviving Populists and only a "55% or 60% New Dealer" —which meant a mugwump. In Massachusetts he usually but not always voted Republican, in national elections Democrat. He had never voted a straight ticket in his life, and though he said he was the only member of his generation who had never cast a vote for Eugene V. Debs, he had on many occasions come close to the position of Mattingly, who was a Norman Thomas socialist. After Wendell Willkie withdrew from the presidential primary race, in 1944, DeVoto declared that he would never have voted for him; yet he had enthusiastically helped Willkie's attempt to smoke out better war information, and by 1944 he was sufficiently jaundiced with some of Roosevelt's actions that he might in the pinch have gone for a Republican whom, like Willkie, he personally admired.

It was conservation, along with his rediscovery of the physical West, that returned him to his natural condition as a radical Populist in 1946, and it was conservation that made a thoroughgoing Democrat of him in 1952.

Early in that year, in late February or early March, he had a telephone call from his former Northwestern student George Ball, now a lawyer in the firm of Cleary, Gottlieb, Friendly & Ball, with offices in New York and Washington. Harry Truman had indicated his intention not to accept renomination by the Democratic Party, and Ball, a close friend of Governor Adlai Stevenson of Illinois, was quietly organizing a cabal to persuade Stevenson to run. He had heard from Arthur Schlesinger, Jr., that DeVoto might be willing to help, and he suggested a meeting in New York to talk the possibility over.[8]

In enlisting DeVoto's help, Ball was probably moved by several considerations, not least of which was DeVoto's influence, through his writings, and especially through the Easy Chair, upon liberal and independent voters. Another was his firsthand, intimate, and fighting knowledge of the conversation and public lands problems that would surely be an issue in the campaign. But also, he says, he remembered his old Freshman English instructor as an "exciting and glamorous figure" with a gift for words and for friendship, even friendship with sixteen-year-old freshmen. Personal liking as well as political considerations led him to make his call, and he was not disappointed when DeVoto came down and met him for a long talking lunch at the Harvard Club. It seemed to George Ball a classical illustration of how minds that truly met could continue almost in midsentence a conversation interrupted years before. Though he was a little puzzled about how he might help, DeVoto was sympathetic to what Ball told him about Stevenson, and he agreed to go out to Springfield with Ball to spend a few days with the Governor. It might be he would be called on to draft speeches, it might be he could help most with an article or articles introducing Stevenson to a national audience that had barely heard his name.

They went to Springfield together, and Ball left DeVoto there for several days. From Ball's account, it seems that Stevenson himself was somewhat puzzled about why DeVoto was there. But he liked him instantly, and was flattered by the attention and respect of a writer whom he had long admired. As for DeVoto, he returned home convinced that Stevenson was not only a superb candidate, but that Ball and others would be successful in persuading him to run. He had the word long before other journalists were as sure as he, and he loved a scoop—it was not often that the Easy Chair, which was written six weeks before publication, got a chance to scoop the dailies. His April Easy Chair, "Stevenson and the Independent Voter," made DeVoto an instant prophet. It also had a large influence in firming up Stevenson's emerging public image, and it succeeded in making him look, all at the same time, like a white hope, a dark horse, and a front-runner.

Like thousands who worked for Adlai Stevenson, DeVoto gave him support that was close to idolatry. *"Use* me," he said after the Democratic National Convention. He offered to write a brief for the conservation and public-lands planks in the platform, he offered to write speeches, he expected to travel as a sort of reporter/adviser with the candidate's campaign train.[9] It was a crush, like his crushes on Henderson, Zinsser, and Frost. In his enthusiasm he predicted that Stevenson would win in a walk.

It is not clear whether he did or did not write a brief for the conservation plank, though he must surely have influenced Stevenson's and hence the party's position. He did supply some speech material, not too much of which remained in the speeches as finally delivered. Once, he reported that "the first third of the St. Louis speech" was his, and he would obviously have been gratified if more had been used. But as Arthur Schlesinger, Jr., said,[10] DeVoto was too good a writer to be a good speech writer, and Stevenson himself once told me the same thing. The same inability that hampered him in fiction hampered him in political oratory: he could not sound like anyone but himself.

By September, though his enthusiasm for Stevenson was as great as ever, he had become somewhat frustrated in his desire to be of use, and his optimism had waned. He expected a Democratic defeat. The campaign train he was looking forward to, the personal participation in the greatest American game, kept being postponed and never did come off. And the willing suspension of his private concerns had kept him from putting money in his purse. At the end of September he grumbled to Mattingly that he had gone broke writing *The Course of Empire* and desperately needed to write something for money instead of warming the bench as a political relief pitcher.[11]

Despite Ball's hopes, and his own, and Stevenson's, he made relatively minor contributions, after that first introductory Easy Chair, to Stevenson's 1952 campaign. There was an August Easy Chair in which he discussed Utah's eroded watersheds and the need for rehabilitation efforts that were much more likely to be made by the Democrats than the Republicans, and an October Easy Chair in which he attacked General Pat Hurley's land-use plank in the Republican platform. Hurley, advocating a return to the "traditional Republican lands policy," sounded ominous indeed to DeVoto, for he did not suppose General Hurley meant a return to the traditional public-lands policy of Theodore Roosevelt, Gifford Pinchot, and W J McGee, the creators of the twentieth-century conservation movement now taken over by the Democrats. He supposed Hurley meant the traditional Republican land policy of Secretary of the Interior Ballinger, who had collaborated in the stealing of a lot of America's forests, or of Albert Fall, who had given us Teapot Dome, or of Herbert Hoover and Ray Lyman Wilbur, who had wanted to give away the Public Domain to the states in ways that would have pleased the Two-Gun Desmonds. If that was indeed what General Hurley's plank meant, DeVoto said, then the Desmonds had put one over on General Eisenhower, and what Eisenhower had innocently accepted was going to cost him votes.

Though he was frequently moved to prophecy, DeVoto was not a prophet with a high batting average. What Eisenhower had innocently accepted might have cost him votes, but not enough votes to affect his landslide victory, and that landslide brought the landgrab forces back into power precisely as Truman's 1948 victory had put them out. Congressman Barrett rode the Republican wave into the Senate. Soon it became clear that Eisenhower's choice as Secretary of the Interior would be Douglas McKay, an Oregon automobile dealer, and as Secretary of Agriculture, Ezra Taft Benson, an apostle of the Mormon Church. DeVoto threw up his hands: he was scared to death of them both.

But he did not subside in defeat. He and his allies were very busy, immediately after the election, in lining up opposition to expected land bills. His files are full of the letters he wrote to Senator Aiken of Vermont, Senator Metcalf of Montana, and many congressmen including Dodd of Connecticut, Eugene McCarthy of Minnesota, John Saylor of Pennsylvania, and John F. Kennedy of Massachusetts. He thought the Forest Service had some protection in the fact that the agriculture committees of both houses were made up mainly of Easterners and would not be susceptible to the western chant of "Get out and give us more money." But Interior, and especially the National Park Service, was wide open, for the public-lands subcommittees of the insular-and-interior-affairs committees of both houses were stacked with the cowboy clique, and the Bureau of Reclamation, by reason of its empire-building ambitions that fitted well with western inclinations toward the boondoggle and the economics of liquidation, was among the enemy. It was not clear how the Eisenhower ad-

ministration would treat either the Bureau of Reclamation or the
Corps of Engineers, since both were associated with public power,
and public power was not a Republican pet. But it did not seem
likely that either bureau would be controlled in the ways and for
the reasons that DeVoto would have liked. After November 1952
he expected a bad time for conservation, and got what he expected.

Dead journalism, like dead Congressional battles, makes fairly
dull reading. DeVoto's conservation journalism can still be read,
precisely because it *isn't* dead. The policy disagreement that it
reflects is as unresolved in 1973 as it was in 1952, and this despite
an exponential increase in the strength of the conservation movement. When he put together a group of his conservation essays
and published them in his last book, *The Easy Chair*, under the
title "Treatise on a Function of Journalism," DeVoto was in a
sense justifying, on more than temporary grounds, his sortie into
conservation politics. He was also writing a chapter of the history
of conservation, a subject that grows ominously in importance as
the twentieth century grinds and clanks on, and what he wrote
could well be instructive to people involved in succeeding chapters
of the same story.

Through 1953, swimming upstream, ironically an adviser to a
Secretary of the Interior with whom he would not even sit
down to lunch,[12] he helped his Congressional allies and an increasing number of conservation groups resist what he had correctly
foreseen. In that year he wrote four Easy Chairs on public-lands
problems,[13] in the last of which he shocked his readers with the
proposal that we close our National Parks and keep them closed
until Congress appropriated the money to run them properly. He
finally crowded *Collier's* into action with an article called "Our
Great West, Boom or Bust?" in the issue of December 1953. The
year 1954 produced three more conservation Easy Chairs,[14] a
Holiday article,[15] and a gloomy summary in *Harper's* called "Conservation—Down and on the Way Out."[16] In 1955, three years
deep in the Eisenhower administration and growing gloomier as he
went, he still had enough left to write two more public-lands
Easy Chairs,[17] besides two others that moved the conservation
battle into New England.[18]

He lived to see the conservationists lose the tidelands oil controversy. He lived to see Douglas McKay turn public power out
of the Snake River canyons and let the private Idaho Power
Company in—and then, apparently throwing a sop to the Bureau
of Reclamation, permit the dusting off of the Upper Colorado

River Storage Project that wanted to build a dam in Dinosaur National Monument. He did not live to see that project stopped by a massive uprising of conservation force, though he had started the uprising with his 1950 article in the *Post*.

There have been many developments, some of them deriving straight from fights he engaged in, that he did not live to see. He did not live to hail the Wilderness Act or any of the major conservation legislation of the Kennedy and Johnson administrations under the leadership of Secretary of the Interior Stewart Udall. Nor did he live to see his favorite bureau, the National Forest Service, embroiled in bureaucratic rivalry with the National Park Service, which was expanding mainly at the expense of Forest Service lands. He did not live to see conservation groups almost as harshly at war with the Forest Service as they have traditionally been with the Corps of Engineers and the Reclamation Bureau. But even though his career ended short of victory in a good many controversies, he still came close to being what Senator Neuberger of Oregon called him,[19] the greatest (if by greatest we mean "most effective") conservationist of the twentieth century.

The heated, repetitive struggles between exploitation and conservation are an aspect of life in America in the twentieth century that historians will have to deal with in general and in particular. Within a single generation the environmental sickness that Secretary Udall called "the quiet crisis" has revealed itself to be a threat as deadly as the Bomb. DeVoto did more than his share in building the public sentiment that climaxed in the Dinosaur National Monument struggle in 1955–56 and has since developed into something like a religion of Nature, shared by hippies, housewives, mountain climbers, river runners, fishermen, and many other kinds of Americans. The function of journalism that he served in his half a hundred articles and Easy Chairs was a function DeVoto was proud of. It validated him as a professional journalist and as a controversialist, and it gave his reforming impulse a purpose and a cause. His wars with the literary had been ambiguous and entangled, because he never freed his emotions from envying and desiring what he attacked. His conservation writings record a continuing controversy unmarred by any scramble for personal advantage or any impulse toward self-justification, a controversy in every way dignified by concern for the public good and for the future of the West from which he had exiled himself in anger as a young man.

His crusade had not pleased everybody in the West, not by a good deal, though he was always getting letters from people in Montana or Idaho or Colorado, letters almost tearful with gratitude that someone had finally said, powerfully and well, what these correspondents had always wanted to hear said. The state university of a state neighbor to his own might defy the anger of miners, stockmen, and resource exploiters at large and honor itself and him with a degree. People the length and breadth of the West, people in Congress, people in the Izaak Walton League and the Wilderness Society and the Sierra Club and the Audubon Society and the National Parks Association might trust him and depend on him as they depended on no other. The Sierra Club might make him an honorary life member for his services to conservation. But the fact remained that he had over and over again, and perhaps mortally, offended the powers of his native region.

He had begun his career by offending them, injudiciously and in exaggerated ways, and Utah has not even yet forgiven him. The most distinguished writer who ever came out of the state, he is not recognized in his own country. Dislike and mistrust have overgrown his name because of those early articles and because of his vigorous and persistent opposition to the exploiters; and ordinary people have not taken him up as a champion of their submerged interests, because he ridiculed the mythology by which many of them live. To many kinds of people in the West he has looked like a traitor to his home place, and there are ironies in that.

One irony is that this rationalist, this heated defender of common sense and the skeptical, *ad hoc* approach, should have ended his career as a crusader nearly as single-minded, if not so simple-minded, as the Boy Orator of the Platte, William Jennings Bryan. Another is that his crusade should have been made in behalf of the West, which he had done his best to scorn; not until he had cured himself of being literary could he give himself back to it. And still another is that the feeling against him in his native region should have demonstrated the truth of one of his earliest generalizations about the West, that the only true individualists there eventually found themselves on one end of a rope whose other end was in the hands of a bunch of vigilantes.

4 · *The Lost World of Fiction*

The temporary lull in the conservation wars that followed Truman's 1948 victory over Dewey brought DeVoto not relaxation but a letdown. It exposed him to himself, gave him time to work on the Cambridge novel and convince himself that he couldn't write it, and confirmed the death of John August. August had not published a short story since 1939, or a novel since *The Woman in the Picture*, in 1944, the one that had been ridiculed by Sinclair Lewis. After the 1946 western trip, August had worked at a new serial, sharing the desk with the novelist who struggled over the complicated wiring of the Cambridge novel, but that effort had gone dead in the typewriter. Doubly frustrated, physically and emotionally unwell, overtaken by the exhaustion of years of over-work, and no longer sustained by the excitement of the landgrab controversy, DeVoto wrote Struthers Burt in April 1949 that he was having "a dark queer time," and found it hard to leave familiar surroundings.

Part of the darkness and queerness was either cause or effect of his having come to his end as a writer of fiction—as a "writer" at all in the terms that he had spent so many years trying to be. His effort to come out of his depression now involved the effort to resolve in his mind the question of what fiction meant, both in general and to him personally.

A week after his confessional letter to Burt, he sent off to Garrett Mattingly, for comment, a bundle of his correspondence with Lawrence Kubie,[1] whose patient he had been during his months with the *Saturday Review* and whom he had found intelligent, provocative, and exasperating. He told Mattingly that ever since the September 1948 Easy Chair, called "Sigmund Freud and W. H. Auden," in which DeVoto had distinguished art from psychiatry, Kubie had been accusing him of "parricidal transferences." He said irritably that Kubie thought himself coextensive with psychiatry and felt that his views were objective truth and that all conflicting views were symptoms. In their long argument about art and literature, Kubie had seemed to DeVoto to support the notion that the emotions aroused by art in viewers or readers were ephemeral, a mere discharge, and that art and literature succeeded only in so far as they increased their creator's area of conscious control and decreased the area of unconscious control—that is, they succeeded only in so far as they were effective self-therapy.

In his state of dissatisfaction and failure, that was not a position with which DeVoto wanted to agree; to do him justice, he had never agreed with it. He did not write to heal himself, or did not admit that he did. He wrote to make emotional contact with an audience, and he could only justify his effort if he *did* make contact—as, from the evidence, it seemed he had not. So now, having wasted a year trying to write a serial and eighteen months

trying to write a novel, he found himself (he told Mattingly) involved in a book on the art of fiction. He was going to straighten
Kubie out (so goes another of my fathers). But there is a strong
implication in his letter to Mattingly that he needed to straighten
himself out as well. He had to find out, if possible, what fiction
was, now that it had become impossible for him. One guesses that
he had to find out that he was right about it, that it was *not* self-
therapy, for if it was self-therapy and he had failed at it, where
was he left?

Much of the book that rapidly took shape during the summer of
1949 had already been written as Harvard and Bread Loaf lectures, as Easy Chairs and random essays, and as "English 37" in
the *Saturday Review*.[2] Over the years, as he had written them out,
discussed them with Kubie and with Beata Rank (to whom he
would dedicate the book when it was finished), and elaborated
them in a hundred book reviews, his ideas had been refined but
had not substantially changed. Once begun, the book went fast;
he finished it by August. In September he described it to Mattingly
as "a purely therapeutic effort," thus accepting for criticism the
function that he denied to art. It was "a book about how to write
novels by a man who lately proved himself unable to write a novel."
He declared that, having used it to bring himself out of a tailspin,
he had already forgotten it.[3]

That statement was either not quite candid or was self-deceiving.
It was a statement of intention, not necessarily of fact. Though
he might embalm the body of what had been dear to him, and
bury it in his deepest basement, its ghost would walk now and
then and his floors would creak and his corridors breathe with its
troubling presence. One does not forget such a defeat as brought
on *The World of Fiction*, one only elects henceforth to ignore it.
And if the book was not quite effective exorcism, neither was it
quite a book about how to write novels. It was a book about *why*
people write novels and why other people read them. It was a
philosophical and psychological justification of fiction, not as the
novelist's self-therapy but as an art. *The World of Fiction* was "an
analysis of the relationship between the person who writes a
novel and the person who reads it."[4]

He said it was not reality that novelists reported in their fictions,
and not reality that readers sought in them. Novelists were seldom
good observers, because the reality that was before their eyes was
constantly being dissolved in reverie. "A stream of reverie flows
beside the main channel of consciousness and at all times floods
over into it. When psychologists speak of the stream of con-

sciousness, in fact, they mean the river in which the streams have joined. The Mississippi of the mind is always below the mouth of the Missouri."[5]

His very metaphor demonstrated the kind of merging that he asserted. And what floated on the river was not entirely helpless. It was to some small extent maneuverable, like a raft with a sweep oar. For though the pattern of a novelist's books was probably fixed in his childhood, and though each novelist probably had only one essential story to tell, the triumphant novel was not the one that went helplessly with the current but the one that navigated it and steered a way across or down it. True fiction, fiction at the level of art, was "a victory for the reality principle, for the faculty of control, for the human will."[6]

It was something that he desperately needed to believe. He had staked his life on it and used his faculty of control to keep desperation and panic at arm's length, and when he came to state the principle he perhaps overstated it. Part of the novelist's gift is surely the ability to direct fantasy and to order the disorderly. But his own experience as a novelist had demonstrated the inefficacy of the will in the absence of some vital and elusive knack. Or had it demonstrated the opposite? Several of his friends, at various times, told him that he didn't fantasize well; I have suggested that his fictions failed partly because he never got the hang of ventriloquism, of the disguising of his own voice. Either judgment would suggest that the failure lay not in the strength of his unconscious fantasies but in the aesthetic distance he was able to achieve. And if that is true, then his novels failed for a reason not unlike the reasons for Thomas Wolfe's partial failure.

That conclusion, though he would have found it unpalatable and perhaps infuriating, does not damage his point about the importance of the shaping will in literature, nor does it invalidate his further point about the reciprocity between writer and reader. "A reader always writes the greater part of any novel," he wrote; "the skill of the novelist is to make him write the novel intended."[7] (Frost had said it a little differently: A writer is entitled to anything the reader can find in him.) And since fiction was inescapably a collaboration, it could not be charged with telling lies—the most persuasive version of that charge having been made, as DeVoto pointed out, in a *roman à clef* by Plato, who was at the time invoking the aid of fiction to describe the Perfect State. The fear that readers might mistake fiction for reality was an empty fear, for fiction was a temporary relief that the reader always knew was temporary. In that sense, all novels were "escape" novels, open falsehoods that the reader accepted and participated in and that inoculated him against other and more private and more injurious fantasies. The point was crucial. Fiction was not a substitute for reality, either for writer or reader. It was a substitute for more dangerous fictions. Its virtue lay in the fact that it had been molded into order. If chaos was the law of nature, as Henry Adams said, and order the dream of man, then the dream expressed as literary art might persuade readers drowning in irrelevant experience that there was a meaning in their lives. The therapy involved in fiction was more for the reader than for the writer.

Once he has stated that theme, the rest of *The World of Fiction* is tactics. Since the basic fable is unconscious, fixed by temperament and experience, "the largest part of the creative process is the determination of necessity." But it is the novel that is determined, not the novelist. If the novelist does not efface himself, an essential transformation has been left incomplete, though it is sometimes possible, as in Mark Twain's "Great Dark" manuscripts, to see a deep personal trouble trying, through successive versions, to impose order and meaning on itself.[8] "Art is the terms of an armistice signed with fate"; but only when it transforms experience into symbols *appropriate to the fiction being attempted*, when it acknowledges the essential substance but exercises discretion and choice in the finding of means, is art true to itself or to life.

But if fiction is not unsteered compulsion, neither is it *exemplum*. It cannot be bent by its creator to demonstrate something and still remain itself. It is not "about" anything—the westward movement, the genetics of Lamarck, the oedipal relationship, anything. The novelist is neither the "spellbound" man of Kubie's heresy nor a man making fully logical choices and combinations and directing everything to an expository end. Fiction is not philosophy, uplift, reform, morality, or ideas of healing. It is art. It is people in action, a created illusion that a reader willingly accepts—for the time.

The people who read novels will continue to ask of fiction what they have always asked. They want for a moment to breach the walls of loneliness and look into other lives and find confirmations and perhaps some slight fulfillment of their own, some order and significance, something life has granted to these people that it has denied them. Beyond that there is the strangeness of things happening to others that becomes a strangeness to them. Still farther out are the edges of the dark, and the voices that whisper so terrifyingly there may be appeased or silenced—for a moment. There is the need that the knife be taken from one's hand and the much greater need that, even if only for a moment and even if only in imagination, one's life and destiny, and with them destiny itself, seem composed to an intelligible end.[9]

If the novelist is his own patient, he is also the reader's doctor—his position is in fact, though DeVoto does not say this, singularly like the relation that DeVoto himself had to all sorts of troubled friends. The novelist is in control, though the control is barely enough to keep him from collapse: He is like Frost's farmer mending wall and using a spell to keep his rocks balanced. "Stay where you are until our backs are turned."

"A purely therapeutic effort," he called *The World of Fiction*, and in making that remark he did not have in mind the effect of the book on readers. He was clearing his emotional house. The book was a compulsive act, begun in a fit of depression and concluded within a few weeks. It compensated for the double failure of Bernard DeVoto and John August to write their novels, even while it realistically admitted their defeat. Apologia and swan song were blended in it; the validity of art was asserted into the teeth of diminishment and reality. The novelist he had started out to be ended as a philosopher of fiction, an analyst of the creative process; and fiction turned out to be—had always been for him, and on re-examination looked more than ever to be—only one of several possible stays against chaos, loneliness, and fear.

Controversy had been one such stay; from his youth onward he had been toughened and given confidence by the act of giving and taking blows. Friendship had been a stay, he had valued his friends, and had a generous concern for them, and depended on them. Alcohol had been a stay, not alcohol as a crutch or an oblivion but alcohol as ritual, as Host in the absolving Eucharist of the Hour. And work had been a stay, the safest one of all. But neurosis, which might have been a temptation and which he had described as an adaptation permitting the daunted to stay alive, he had looked upon throughout his life as his own peculiar and malevolent enemy, not to be succumbed to, to be fought and evaded and exorcised. All the other stays had been marshaled against this most deadly one. Controversy, fiction, friendship, alcohol, work, even his need for institutional justification and affiliation, had all been invoked tactics in his effort to die sane. In the end, he could not bear to believe literature coterminous with neurosis, as uncontrollable and compulsive as his panics. He had to demonstrate, and if he found himself unable to demonstrate he had to assert, that fiction was creation, an act of control and will, not the compulsion of a sick soul to puke up its disease as words.

Asserting fiction in those terms, he abjured it once and for all. The moment he turned over the manuscript of *The World of Fiction* to Houghton Mifflin, he gave up literature as a house of safety. Years before, he had thought he could trace Mark Twain's transmutation of despair into the symbolic shape of *The Mysterious Stranger*. He had been wrong, or partly wrong, because he misread the internal evidence of the manuscripts and did not have all the external evidence that scholars would later find.[10] But he had not been wrong in seeing Mark Twain's lifelong habit of work as the road by which he reached safety. Mark Twain was a professional writer, which may be described as a body that will go on moving a pen even with its heart cut out. So was Bernard DeVoto. And because he was a pro, the mere act of finishing something, at a time when he had wondered if he would ever finish anything again, probably did as much to take him out of his depression as the resolution of his literary argument with Dr. Lawrence Kubie and his own soul.

But he had given up literature beyond recapture. In the last six years of his life only one short story, published under one of the pseudonyms that replaced John August, appears in his bibliography. Even articles about literature, even reviews of fiction and poetry, virtually disappear. From the time he threw away John August's last, unsatisfactory serial and put the several versions of Bernard DeVoto's last, unsatisfactory novel in the drawer, he was a writer of travel articles, a writer and reviewer of history, a pugnacious champion of conservation and civil liberties, and a continuing speculator about the nature and future of the West, but no novelist and no literary critic.

History waxed as fiction waned. One of the effects, though not necessarily one of the purposes, of his clearing the desk of all literary leftovers was that now he could no longer put off the book that he had announced in his letter to Henry Commager back in April 1944. Lewis and Clark, and all they implied about the pull of the continent upon the seaboard consciousness, and all they meant to the fabric of Bernard DeVoto's incorrigibly western ideas, were there before him. They had begun the discovery and consolidation of the nation that stretched beyond the Missouri to the western sea.

DeVoto's earliest and most effective defense against depression was work, and work was still to do. In August 1949 he posted off the manuscript of *The World of Fiction*[11] and cleared his life of literature and sat down to write the book which, if any book of his life was, was preordained for him.

5 · *The Course of Empire*

Preordained, but not yet clearly defined. He had started with the innocent intention of writing a narrative history of the Lewis and Clark expedition, something in the general vein of the Christmas feature he had published in the *Saturday Review* in 1936. His old Harvard companion John Bakeless had beaten him to it,[1] but he had already left that limited objective far behind before Bakeless' book appeared. With the cockiness that was the other side of his insecurity, he was confident he could outwrite Bakeless with one lobe tied off if he chose to. He didn't choose to. His subject had expanded on him, seeking its own dimensions. It reached outward in every direction, and especially it reached backward and backward and backward. In November 1948, DeVoto had complained to Mattingly about the endlessness of his research. For instance, he had had to spend months clearing up the explorations of Vérendrye, because he was uneasy with the accounts he found in the historians. From Vérendrye he had been led back to earlier explorers, and beyond those to still earlier ones. He had had to investigate, it seemed to him, all the native tribes of North America, even the mythical ones. The fabled Welsh Indians and their ramifying legendry had diverted him for many weeks, simply because the Mandans among whom Lewis and Clark spent their first expeditionary Christmas were held by some who did not know them to be descendants of the followers of Prince Madoc.

Do I think maybe I'm Francis Parkman? [he asked Mattingly rhetorically].
What do you do about geography? I mean, what do I do about it? Have I got to go up the Saskatchewan too? Or Lake Winnipeg? This guy Burpee appeared to know which peak was up but I got stalled when he had the Red River flowing both north and south in the same stretch. . . . Christ, Mat, I can't dig out the background of the background of the background. How the hell do I learn historical geography?
For that matter, why should I? What the hell am I doing farting around with Charlevoix and who was where in 1690 and was there anything in that yarn of Marquette's and if so what did it get bent into why? This was supposed to be about Sacajawea, wasn't it? I figure I can clean up the predecessors of L&C in 30 years more, oh, easy. I figure I can do the empires and the wars in less than ten years more and

the trans-Allegheny U.S., the state of scientific thought, symmetrical
geography, the diplomatics and American politics in another 10, and
maybe in 5 years I can get Napoleon and La. straightened out, though
not as easily as F. Pratt could in five minutes. . . . Well, God damn it,
twice now you've been able to tell me what book I was writing on the
basis of the first draft. We haven't got time for that sort of thing any
more. You damn well tell me pretty soon what I'm working toward
now or I'll get buried under it.[2]

Mattingly told him he suffered from the sin of pride:

Only God knows everything. And we neither of us started early
enough in our lives, or have worked single-mindedly enough since, to
be Francis Parkmans. . . . And even Francis Parkman didn't know
everything.
You've just got a light case of *regressus historicus*. I've seen some lulus.
Thirty years ago my colleague R. P. Evans decided that he couldn't
write about the 16th century German Sacramentarians without a little
background of medieval heresies. Now he despairs of really knowing
anything about the Albigenses without exploring the 11th century
Bogomils and the 9th century Paulicians, and behind them, he knows,
are Yezedees and Manichaeans and dark little twisty passageways leading off into Persia and Assyria and Egypt. Meanwhile he works away
doggedly at the connection between Peter Waldo and the Humiliati, at
Catherine and Potarini, half a continent and five hundred years from
his starting point, which by now he has practically forgotten. And he
hasn't written a line on his real job since Coolidge took the oath of
office. . . . There comes a point in writing history, as in every other
activity, where a conscience is just a God damned nuisance. You have
to kick it in the teeth and say, "Shut up and lie down and let me get
about my business."[3]

That good advice was easier to accept than to follow, for what
fascinated DeVoto in the early explorations was the gradual over-
taking of fable by fact, "the movement of these boys across a map
that is not the map they have in their mind."[4] And shortly, while
he made his exploration of the boundaries and nature of his subject,
his conception of it changed, as the conception of the continent
changed for the men who pushed into it. The Lewis and Clark
expedition became not simply an adventure in the wilderness but a
key action within a global context. Again it was Mattingly to
whom he tried, sputtering and apoplectic, to explain what his
book was doing to him:

In the odd moments during which my, shall we say, mind has been
working on the material for this ectoplasmic book, I have somehow
crossed the frontier into, shall we say, Historical Ideas. I say the hell

with them but there I am. . . . Being of the uncircumcised, I don't know how important they are—which is part of the impasse—but I do know that they're fairly sizable. I told you there has to be a third leg to Parkman's stool, which has just two. I seem to be swarming like bees around that third leg, and, as a case history in the vagaries of the psychopathic personality, I seem to have started swarming as far back as MT'sA, and to have been more or less working toward an eventual destination ever since, more or less the way you might go to Worcester from Boston by way of Key West, Rio, Nova Scotia, and Pittsfield. At any rate, the symptomology is that I'm running some ideas. And I just don't know enough and I just don't see how it's possible to learn enough in the remaining time. . . . It isn't a question of not knowing how Jefferson knew he was going to buy La. six months before he did know it—I'm perfectly willing to follow your theorem and tell the reader, look, I don't know. It's a question of an all-encompassing ignorance of the field in which alone the ideas I've spawned have any meaning at all and in which alone their validity can be tested. The L&C expedition was not primarily what Brebner, the best of the lot, wrote it off as, the beginning of a new era of exploration of the North American continent, the methodical, so to speak industrial-age era and no damn nonsense. It was, unless it was just some soldiers that Mr. Jefferson sent to find out how he could protect the sea otter trade from British sea power in case of war, it was a turning point in world history. And what the hell do I know about world history? . . .
There's no reason to write a book about how a well-conducted party got to the mouth of the Columbia and back. John Bakeless . . . has written it. There's no reason to produce a one-volume summary of Parkman or a modernization of Justin Winsor. . . . The only thing worth my writing or anyone's reading is a book that says, hey, this seems to have been left out of the picture. And before I write it, I'd like to know whether it's nonsense.
Diagnosis: intellectual palsy or elephantiasis of the ego. Prognosis: doubtful. Consultation requested.[5]

By the time DeVoto felt himself ready to start writing, in the fall of 1949, he was less terrified of the vastness of his subject than of withholding himself from it any longer. He was still making sour jokes about how, "properly speaking, Ch. 1 of this book would be about the last withdrawal of the ice cap and Ch. II would pick up with the Crusades," but he had brought himself to the point where he could shrug away the ignorances that he could now do nothing about, and, accepting his limitations, go ahead. And nothing, now that *The World of Fiction* was off to the printer and his fictional temptations shelved, could be used as an excuse. As he wrote Mattingly on September 11:

I still know as little as ever and I'm oppressed by it. But also I'm suddenly oppressed by how much I know, at least how much information
I have, and how hard it's going to be to impose form on it and make it
readable. I suppose there's a structure; I know it's going to be hell to
find it. This pre-delivery stage is always a holy horror and I wonder
anyone writes books. I've got some odds and ends to do and I hope also
to pick up a little cash from the journals of fashion and thought before
I begin. Then dip the pen and write, "Verrazano." Or maybe "Folsom
Man." . . . I'll write as far as I know, then stop and find out, then write
some more.[6]

The journals of fashion and thought, despite his need for money,
got only odd moments of his attention, and then as often as not
only if they welcomed something on the unceasing conservation
struggle. He dipped his pen and wrote the first word, took the first
paddle stroke toward the unimaginable Columbia, and he began
neither with Verrazano nor with Folsom Man but with Columbus'
letter to Ferdinand and Isabella announcing the discovery of the
New World. The first chapter went to Mattingly for comment in
early October. There followed a year of intense work, interrupted
only by Easy Chairs (including "Due Notice to the FBI" and "For
the Wayward and Beguiled," respectively the most salutary and
the most charming of that long, distinguished series),[7] by occasional reviews, by conservation forays, and by light essays on
many subjects, most of them in *Woman's Day* and most of them
signed by Cady Hewes, who had taken up with non-fiction the
slack left when John August retired from fiction.

In May 1950, he suspended the writing in order to examine
South Pass and the Missouri River, courtesy Bill Lederer, the Air
Force, and the Corps of Engineers. But immediately upon his return he plunged back into his history book, and he had been
writing on it pretty steadily for a year when he again blew up to
Mattingly about the impossibility of what he was doing. A year's
writing had turned everything that was solid in his temperament
into liquid, everything that was liquid into gas, which was escaping
from every petcock and threatening to blow the safety valves. "It
is entirely your fault," he told Mattingly, ". . . that I am embarked on the God-damnedest fool literary, or if it pleases you to
say so, historical enterprise this side of John Bakeless or the far
side of Bedlam."

I say you will fry your ass in hell forever, as I stew mine daily in the
dullest broth of watery, uremic, and flatulent prose ever compounded,
of which there is not only no end but not even a middle. Middle? hell,
there is not even an approach, there is not even a beginning. It takes

me thirty thousand words to draw even with where I was when I began them. To begin a chapter is enough to make sure that I will be farther from the end of the book when I finish it—farther by twice as many words and God knows how many years. I run furiously, at the extremity of my (waning) strength, and the sweat that pours off me is all words, words, words, words, words by the galley, words by the thousand, words by the dictionary, and I sink forever deeper in them. . . . And Jesus Christ, what words, shapeless, colorless, without sound or substance or taste or perfume or indeed existence, words of immense viscosity and no energy or luminescence whatsoever, words out of a lawyer's brief or a New Critic's essay on Truman Capote or the ghost who writes MacArthur's communiqués, words of unbaked dough, of glucose thinned with bilge, words less than a serum and somewhat more than an exudation, and in all the mess and mass of them not a God damned thought that would trouble the intelligence of Norman Cousins. . . .

I have, in nomine Patris et Filii, this day got the French out of North America. One year to the day, and three million words, after I began a book that had no intention of getting the French into North America. . . . And now I perceive an error in what I have set down here, an error which flows inevitably from my total incapacity to handle facts. It is not three million words I have written getting the French out of North America, it is thirteen million. Well, to be sure they compose, so far, what would be only a good fat third of a book for Jim Farrell or thirty-five books for Fletcher Pratt, and we may observe with interest that it took Francis Parkman, that elegant Brahmin who was plagiarizing me anticipatorily eighty years ago, nine books or eleven volumes to get as far as I have. So where are we? With thirteen million words written, or by our Lady some two score million, we have now accounted for 229 years that do not enter at all into my book, and have only forty more years to go, or say an even million words, if in the meantime I can learn something about concentration or alternatively get a tight cinch on my bowels, before we reach the beginning of my book and, with a sigh of infinite satisfaction and a suffusing glow of happy realization that only ten million words lie ahead, take up a blank, virgin sheet of paper and write at the top of it Page One.[8]

Mattingly was the only friend at once close enough to withstand these explosions and learned enough to be a *ficelle* for DeVoto's ideas as the book generated them. Loyally he read the chapters that came to him, loyally he approved them as history and praised them as prose. He cooled the spiritual waters set to boiling by the heat of creation. On December 4, 1950, he got another installment of Historical Ideas from DeVoto:

I put it up to you. It only hit me last week as an idea. If this stuff is five percent as good as you hold when drunk or five thousand percent bet-

ter than my more realistic intelligence judges it to be, then by the end
of page 2626 herewith something of an implicit point should have
made itself apparent to the reader's, if any, mind: that the land has by
now affected the shape of the consciousness (North American). I succeeded in writing the '46 thing without feeling I had to make the implicit explicit and I think that the reader, again if any, got there without my help. But I am not the gay young swaggerer I was in those days
and I no longer feel if the dumb son of a bitch won't work at this, so
much the worse for him. I'm not only grateful to him, I sympathize
with him very deeply. . . . It occurred to me that five to eight pages
might undertake to set down in words, the simplest ones possible, that
you learn to plant corn in hills, you then find you are making corn
shocks that are architecturally and functionally different from the way
they pile wheat in England, presently your house has the logs lengthwise instead of on end, by damn the helve of the axe you felled them
with has a curve in it as no axe did before, you think entail ought to be
abolished and by God of eternal and manifest right there must be no
limeys in San Francisco Bay where rolls the Oregon. . . . There it is as
a problem, and if anywhere, then at the end of the T. Jefferson chapter,
which is not T. J. really, but the Young Republic. And nice, too, for
Tom believed of 18th century right reason, and said so repeatedly in
pellucid prose, that of course this continent is so damn big and the
Pacific is so damn far away that the Young Republic won't get there
and what we got to work for is a free and independent Republic of the
Pacific, dowered with our own inspired political institutions, popu-
lated by manly freemen of American blood, and bound to us by ties of
friendship, philosophy, and the dollar balance. So he said of right good
reason. And nevertheless, beginning with the time when the Rev.
Maury was beating Greek verbs and the unity of continental geography into his head right on to L&C, he put on a perfectly straightfor-
ward, coherent, cumulative series of measures and deeds which would
prove to anybody who hadn't happen to hear him talk that by God
what had to get to the mouth of the Columbia was the United States.
I can now say clearly that the principal reason why I am disgusted with
this book is that it is a different *kind* of stuff from its predecessors and
I don't enjoy the dilemma, for if one is history the other isn't and who
am I.[9]

Again Mattingly had to play teacher. He approved the explicit
statement of the process by which Europeans were made over into
Americans. He gave at least tentative approval to the theory that
Jefferson had had conscious continental aims that contradicted
his public statements. And he reassured his floundering amateur
friend about the legitimacy of his present enterprise:

This is a different kind of history from anything you have written so
far, but it's been implicit (you know as well as I do) in practically

everything you've ever written, and you'd got to the point where it had to be explicit. For your temperament, or mine for that matter, striding across the centuries, hitting the high spots, isn't nearly so satisfactory as concentrating on a shorter time span. Hard as it is for anyone to know even a very little about North America in 1846 or Western Europe in 1588, it isn't downright impossible; but nobody can cover a line of development over two or three centuries . . . without feeling oppressed by the weight of his own ignorance and the absurdity of trying to write anything that makes sense, sounds like English, and tells approximately the truth. . . . But both kinds of work are history, both are necessary and each implies the other.[10]

Four months later, writing to Helen Everitt, Mattingly was more explicit. DeVoto's new book, he said,

gives linear historical narrative an extra dimension, and perspectives as wide as the continent. Every historian has to grapple with the problem that any significant action occurs in a frame of space, and that the more significant the action the more it is implicated with other actions, antecedent, contemporary, and subsequent. . . . Tackling anything like the L&C expedition in those terms (something I had no idea Benny meant to do when he started—I don't suppose he quite knew himself) is a pretty heroic enterprise. . . . After all, "long book" is the wrong term. It's a big book.[11]

Long or big, it tormented its author with problems he had had no experience in solving. Big or long, it deprived him of his favorite device of synecdoche, for how did you find a part that would represent so massive and multiple a whole? And it presented him with such an extended time span that he could not practice simultaneity, and could only rarely develop any scene at length and with novelistic vividness. By its size and scope, it limited his use of original sources and made him more dependent upon the historians, whom he did not always trust. It made him seem to plod, and he hated plodding. It raised questions of scale and proportion that his previous histories had avoided by being so consistently immediate. He worried about producing something in which "the birth of Christ got a dangling participle and Rome rose and fell in a paragraph."

"Okay, she's dull," he said resignedly in April 1951. But he was growing a little cocky, too, as he put the backgrounds behind him and advanced toward the climactic expedition. He thought he had made it forever impossible for historians to overlook the political and diplomatic implications of Lewis and Clark. He thought he had put into the book, here and there, some touches of original historical scholarship that would let him look the elder

Schlesinger in the eye and belch modestly behind a deprecative hand. Almost with astonishment, he noted that the book was going to peak right where he had guessed it might, all English, French, Spanish, and American exploration converging on the upper Missouri, ignorance and dream and fable and hearsay and growing knowledge coming together as if to await the two captains who would dissolve most of the fables, begin the substitution of systematic knowledge for ignorance, and start the American dominance that would succeed the free-for-all. He was heading into the stretch. "If she don't write herself from here in, I don't know how to write," he told Mattingly. "Downhill all the way."[12]

But if downhill, then down as long a hill as led Lewis and Clark to the Pacific from the crest of the Continental Divide. It took nearly another year.

Once he finally got Mr. Jefferson's ambiguous expedition afloat on the Missouri, on page 435 of his book, he could at least enjoy the trip more—could, in fact, write the last 120 pages in one sustained narrative burst. He moved his little company of Americans across the map that had been made of guess and wish and fable and the blankness of total ignorance, and beyond the last cleanly drawn lines of knowledge, and through the twilight zone of hearsay, and what they looked at as they passed became clear, as the world becomes clear when the oculist drops the right lens into the testing frame. The fuzzy and out-of-focus moved out ahead. The Welsh Indians, who for a time had seemed to DeVoto to be everywhere and account for everything (he wanted to run one for President), turned out not to be the Mandans, as rumored. The real Welsh Indians were farther on somewhere, like other fables, just beyond the range of vision, along with the water connection to the Saskatchewan for which they earnestly searched.

Past the Great Falls, through the Gates of the Mountains, up the diminishing streams until the streams gave out, the captains went expecting any day to be past the single range that they conceived the Rockies to be, and on their way down the easy slope to the Pacific via the Oregon, or the Multnomah, or the Buenaventura, or some other fabled river. When there was no water for the boats they went on foot until they encountered Sacajawea's relatives—that part of the real-life script was written by a historian even more romantic than Bernard DeVoto—and then on horseback over the Lolo Trail to the Clearwater, the Snake, and the Columbia, real rivers in a real and discovered geography. DeVoto followed them only as far as Fort Clatsop and Tillamook Head, where a party made salt at the place where the beach resort of

Seaside now offends the shore, and he left them with the inscription that Clark carved in a tree during the interminable winter rain: "William Clark. December 3rd 1805. By land from the U. States in 1804 & 1805." There was no need to follow them farther. They had completed what Columbus had announced in his letter to Ferdinand and Isabella, they had asserted history in its transition from an Atlantic to a Pacific phase, they had opened the Northwest Passage that had been the dream of navigators since the beginning of the sixteenth century.

Writing his response to the whole manuscript, in March 1952, Mattingly summed it up for him:

And so we come to the Pacific with a sense of having crossed a continent, and a foreknowledge of getting back again, and a premonition of the nation that would cross after us, and the feeling of history shaping us and being shaped by us and emerging from the fluidity of dream or myth into concrete, ineluctable reality. It was an exhilarating experience.[13]

So the reviewers found it when it was published in the fall. There would be a little carping in the quarterlies later, but the daily, weekly, and monthly reviewers reporting to the lay audience found *The Course of Empire* superb. Henry Steele Commager, who had had a glimpse of it when it was no bigger than a man's hand, thought it "the best book that has been written about the West since Webb's *The Great Plains*" and "the best written book about the West since Parkman."[14] He praised its feeling for western geography, accepted what he felt was an inescapable selectivity and a legitimate proportioning of its parts, admired the informed treatment of the Indians as members of different tribes, linguistic groups, and even cultures, and expressed, not for the first time, his respect for DeVoto's grasp of frontier social history and knowledge of frontier skills and occupations. Walter Webb, in the *Saturday Review*, went out of his way to join DeVoto in his quarrel with the academic historians who "tell their students, thereby taking away their courage, that no man should undertake a big task in history," and he found entirely legitimate DeVoto's way of selecting, suppressing, and emphasizing in order to make his point about the emergence of the West as a geographical reality and a force in world polity. Henry Nash Smith, in the New York *Times Book Review*, liked the *reach* of the history, the way in which American exploration was linked with the imperial quarrels of Europe, and the clear exposition of the impact of fact upon a fabric of legendry and the impact of a technological invasion upon the native tribes. He, too, found himself comparing DeVoto with Parkman in the breadth of his canvas, the romantic largeness of the chosen action, and the immediacy of the writing.

But if there was great satisfaction in having put between covers the body of human experience that he had always found most significant and moving to his western perceptions; and if there was a cumulative fulfillment in having completed, backward it was true, and half accidentally, but still in full measure, the trilogy of histories that expressed his continental vision, there was something obscurely and demoralizingly final about it, too. He had told an acquaintance in 1949 that once he put away fiction he had solved his life. As we have seen, that was a consummation more desired than achieved. Putting away fiction, he had to some degree impoverished himself. His right hand had failed him and he had cut it off, but that did not mean he was whole. During the hard three years when he was writing *The Course of Empire* he had not felt the lack of fiction in his life, for the history drew on all his capacities and kept his mind and imagination fully occupied. Then, for one year more, he could keep himself green by editing and shortening Lewis and Clark's *Journals*, a job made inevitable by *The Course of Empire*. And then he was done.

The Course of Empire brought him the National Book Award for history in 1953. He was now possessed of all the obvious medals of his borrowed trade—Pulitzer prize, Bancroft prize, National Book Award, membership in the National Institute of Arts and Letters and the American Academy of Arts and Sciences. And it began to dawn on him that the moment he wrote the last words of *The Course of Empire* he was as empty as a dry gourd. For the first time in his life he was without book, and for him that meant being without motivation, goal, safety, life. What promptly set in was panic, and it never fully went away.

6 · *The Perils of Paul Pro*

Virtually all the historians whom DeVoto knew, as well as a lot of the novelists, poets, conservationists, and civil libertarians, were subsidized by a job, more often than not in a university. Many of them were given periodic working time by sabbaticals or by the foundation grants that DeVoto's overdeveloped self-reliance forbade him to accept or seek. Since 1936, when Mr. Conant had failed to see a permanent place for him at Harvard, DeVoto had

had to subsidize all his serious work by journalism, and for ten years before that, beginning with his later years at Northwestern, the major part of his income had been produced by his free-lancing for the magazines. His 1927 brag to Byron Hurlbut, "I am getting near the place where I can sell everything I write," had not been idle, nor had he. He had worked like the pump of an oil well, and with predictable consequences.

More than occasionally, his need, his facility, and his capacity to sell whatever he wrote had led him to write what he could sell. This he justified as professionalism, and in the academic precincts that were inclined to look down on such professionalism he affected and perhaps felt a belligerent pride in it. He had elected independence, and independence had its necessities and professionalism its rules. You played the game within those rules and on the prescribed field. He never resented editorial suggestions as such; and even in his most serious work, where he might have felt he had no one to please but himself, he maintained an almost moral concern for the reader, who had to be interested and entertained and enlisted.

But there was a consequence, one he should have been able to anticipate from his study of the Public Domain and his knowledge of western history. A resource could be raided, depleted, liquidated; and for such resources as lay hidden in a free-lance historian and journalist there was no depletion allowance. There was only so much oil in the hole—or if you conceived these as renewable resources there was such a thing as overgrazing and clear-cutting what with decent conservation might have been made to go on healthily reproducing itself. He could take his choice among metaphors—dry hole or eroded watershed—but he could do nothing about the fact that he had applied the economics of liquidation to his own energies as surely as the cattlemen had applied them to the grass.

Fatigue, eyestrain, vague symptoms of physical and nervous distress were his constant companions through working days that started immediately after breakfast, halted for a weight-watching cheese-and-salad lunch and perhaps a walk to Harvard Square during the noon break, resumed until the clock told him it was virtuous to get out the martini pitcher and summon wife, secretary, friends, whoever was around, and resumed again after dinner to run until midnight, or, if he was sleepless, much later. The only one of his chronic ailments that he ever got over was his migraines, which he had eventually learned to forestall with ergotamine tartrate at the first symptoms, and which sometime in the 1940s simply stopped occurring. There was no room for migraines in his schedule.

The work that he took seriously—the late-lamented novels, the histories, the conservation and civil-liberties articles—had its intrinsic satisfactions, and could sometimes be combined with the need for making money. But for the strains and uncertainties and constantly renewed effort of his less vital journalism there was only the satisfaction of money and of demonstrated professional skill. No one who has not lived by it can imagine the nervous exhaustion that can come from having to make things in which one is only half interested bundle themselves neatly into beginning and ending, premise and conclusion. A professional writer cannot, like a teacher, be dull and be protected in his dullness. He must recapture his audience with every new start. He must be fascinating, bright, or pontifical, he must impress, charm, amuse, inform. No wonder that sometimes, when the pump sucked air, when the grazing mind found only shad scale and the unpalatable weeds that had replaced the grass, DeVoto felt dread, to which his only response could be redoubled effort, aggravated fatigue, and a more frantic depletion.

In September 1951, after two driving years, he had completed a rough first draft of *The Course of Empire* and was revising the manuscript, which he would deliver to Houghton Mifflin in March 1952. But his concentrated attention had been partially diverted as soon as he saw the end in sight. He was like William Clark at the mouth of the Columbia: "Ocian in view. O! the joy!" And with the traveling over for the time being, he turned his mind toward security. He started to build Fort Clatsop, he went to boil salt down toward Tillamook Head. For months he had been complaining to Mattingly that history had left him broke. The moment he foresaw the end of what had seemed endless, he told himself he had to make some money.

History got the blame for his flat purse, but more than history was responsible, and history was responsible in more than one way. From October 1, 1946, to the end of March 1948, the reading and correspondence demanded by the History Book Club had eaten out of every week time that he might have spent much more profitably writing for the magazines. Moreover, for the last ten months of his History Book Club service he had been the editor, in fact if not in name, of its little monthly publication *America in Books* and had written an editorial and one or more reviews for each issue. For all this his stipend had been little more than his stipend from the Easy Chair. And he had an expensive life style, with a big and hospitable house, a part-time secretary, two boys in private schools, considerable travel and research costs, and large medical bills. It was the need to put in his time more profitably, as well as exasperation with what he thought inefficiency and procrastination in the club's New York office, that led him to resign, in March 1948. As seemed expedient or necessary, he supplemented his income by lecturing, but the involvements of his life from 1947 on had limited that, too.

One of those involvements, the landgrab controversy, had in fact taken the bulk of his time from his opening move in January 1947 to the end of the 1948 election. Despite his strenuous efforts to do so, he had been unable to put many of his conservation articles into mass-circulation magazines, where they would at once educate more people and pay him more money. Most of them wound up in *Harper's*, either as Easy Chairs or articles, or in other magazines of small circulation and low fees. Part of 1949 had gone into the making of *The World of Fiction* and the decent interment of his fictional ambitions. Once past the depression that had initiated and accompanied that purgative act, he had dived into Lewis and Clark and the people and events that led backward from them toward Atlantis and the Ice Age.

None of that left him much time to write for pay, and because he had so little time, he couldn't afford to gamble; he had to be sure of his market. That was how he came to rely heavily on Mabel Hill Souvaine, of *Woman's Day*. She was a pleasant and intelligent woman, equally admiring of DeVoto's intellectual vigor and of his reliability as a contributor. The magazine she edited was owned by The Great Atlantic & Pacific Tea Company and distributed through A&P stores. It was read by women who picked it up at the checkout counter, who were more likely to be interested in the recipes, the advertisements, and the woman-oriented departments than in its text articles. Thus Mabel Souvaine found herself in the position that editors of women's fashion magazines sometimes enjoyed: she could put into her pages material that pleased herself, she could run a magazine with a higher IQ than she might have been supposed to be able to. Under her editorship, though *Woman's Day* was such a magazine as its name suggested, it did not devote itself exclusively to the domestic female mind. A good many of its articles on history, geography, and general ideas were by Bernard DeVoto. And also, once he found the formula and the tone, a good many of the articles that did cater to the domestic female mind were by Bernard DeVoto's alter ego Cady Hewes.[1]

Mrs. Souvaine could not pay what the big slicks paid. Her usual price for a DeVoto or Hewes piece was $750. But she loyally published practically everything that either one sent her, even conservation polemics; thus she singlehandedly financed a good part of *The Course of Empire*.

Until October 1951, when, with the book drafted and in process of revision, DeVoto set out to broaden his economic base and renew his status as a highly paid free lance. Long ago he had parted from Curtis Brown to act as his own agent, because so much of his stuff went into *Harper's* that there was no point in paying an agent 10 per cent for handling it. For a time he had had an informal arrangement with Rae Everitt, the daughter of Raymond and Helen, who worked with Music Corporation of America, but that had produced nothing except one commission from *Reader's Digest* and had been amicably ended. Now he felt the need of an agent who could rebuild his name in the editorial offices.

The National Parks Advisory Board was to meet at Mammoth Cave, Kentucky, on October 25 and 26. On the way to the meeting, DeVoto stopped off in New York for a conference with Carl Brandt, head of the Brandt & Brandt agency. He was broke and he was tired. One guesses that his failures with *Look, Life,* and *Collier's*, all of which had commissioned travel or conservation articles and then had not published them, were troubling to the pride of a self-proclaimed pro. His depression, deepest in 1949, was seeping back; he was half afraid he might be washed up.[2] He worried about old age and the security of his family, and he saw no more books ahead except the Lewis and Clark *Journals*, which would pay few bills. His overture to Brandt was rather like his old habit of taking jobs to hedge his troubling independence.

Brandt himself was an old pro, a storytelling, Coke-drinking, warmhearted regular who had been around the publishing world all his life. His brother and former partner Erdmann had left to become an editor of *The Saturday Evening Post*, but he still had in his office two people besides himself—his wife Carol and Bernice Baumgarten, the wife of James Gould Cozzens—who were as respected as anybody in the business. Brandt had friendly relations with editors at all levels, and he had as high-powered a stable of authors as any agency. He was always threatening to write his memoirs and call them *What I have Done for Ten Percent*. In 1951 he knew DeVoto only by reputation, but he liked him at once for his commonsensical attitude toward professional writing

and for the unexpected humility he discovered in the celebrated
human volcano. He had no doubt in the world that with a little
work DeVoto could be brought back as one of the highest-priced
names in the magazine world.

The Brandt & Brandt file on DeVoto,³ which covers the period
from their first conversation until DeVoto's death, is a short course
in the economics of authorship. It is also the record of a friendship
that was warm and constant. And it is finally, especially during
the first fifteen months, when Brandt was working very hard to
re-establish his client with the magazines and when nothing seemed
to avail, a sort of psychograph, an index of DeVoto's mental
state, a graph whose curve was steeply up and steeply down.

At the outset, Brandt had nothing to offer except a frivolous
little series in *This Week*, which would pay $250 for six-to-seven-
hundred-word essayettes called "Words to Live By," explicating
some notable quotation. There would be more and better things
as soon as editorial offices heard that DeVoto was again in the
market. Meantime DeVoto had a couple of suggestions of his own.
He thought that the whole Lewis and Clark section of *Across the
Wide Missouri* might make a serial for somebody, or that certain
chapters might be lifted out as articles; and he thought he might
capitalize on his intimacy with the National Park Service and the
scenic and historic areas it administered. He was prepared to do
travel-and-history articles on any number of places he thought too
little known: the Shenandoah Valley, the old forts around Washington and Richmond, Hopewell Village in Pennsylvania, Kitty
Hawk, the Cumberland Gap. He did not propose doing any fiction,⁴ nor did he suggest many western subjects. He seems to have
had the feeling that the West had been his specialty too long, and
that for commercial purposes he might have worn it out.

Hopefully and energetically, he entered into an arrangement
with Carl Brandt. On November 4, when he sent in outlines for
several proposed articles, he thought the auspices were all favorable. *The Hour*, his hymn to alcohol collected out of Easy Chairs
and other articles, was being published on the eleventh, and he
was to mix ceremonial martinis for the office staff at Houghton
Mifflin, with most of literary Boston and Cambridge standing in
line. That would start his new money-making career with a modest
clinking of the cash register.

From there on, it can be read like a malaria chart, with more
spells of chills than of fever, or like the record of a lot of fishing
with few fish.

At first there seemed to be numerous rises, and several strikes.

Holiday, though it found nothing in *The Course of Empire* to make into an article, was interested in a piece on the birch-bark canoe and the *voyageurs* who adopted it. Could DeVoto do it? He could. *Mademoiselle* took an article, "The Seventh Pocketbook," but that hardly counted, because it had been half commissioned before DeVoto went to Brandt. *This Week* approved, for its "Words to Live By" series, a gloss on Hamlet's words: "If it be now, 'tis not to come; if it be not to come, it will be now; if it be not now, yet it will come: the readiness is all." DeVoto said he thought the final phrase the greatest statement in English. And he was prepared to live by it. He was ready to do anything the editors of America could think up. While they were doing their thinking, maybe Brandt could sell the enclosed article, "Topic One," which he had written for Mabel Souvaine and which she had found a little sexy for her audience.

Two weeks later, hearing no good word from Brandt and growing anxious for one solid assignment to be done during the spring lecture tour he planned for the West Coast, he sent in a précis for a piece on Donner Pass, and a week after that he asked Brandt to try out the *Post* on an article blasting the Bureau of Reclamation's plans for the Green River. But the third month of Brandt's efforts went by with nothing to show except the canoe piece for *Holiday* and the "Words to Live By" squib for *This Week*, neither of which DeVoto had yet written. His situation was still that he had a sure-fire market at *Woman's Day* and practically no market anywhere else.

On January 30, 1952, Mabel Souvaine took "Women in the Military Services," paying him double her usual fee because he had put everything aside to write it for her in a hurry. Lewis and Clark, Donner Pass, the conservation piece, the travel articles, went begging through New York's editorial offices, but then on February 5 *American Magazine* bit on an essay celebrating the peace and solitude of the Rocky Mountain high country.

Not much, but something. DeVoto tore into the canoe article, finished it, and started on the high country, drawing solace for his fatigue and brainfag from the memory of Ogden's Hole and the mountain meadows in the Wind Rivers and Bitterroots. With that and the canoe article in the mail, he had nailed down $2,500, and on March 5 Mabel Souvaine, staunch as a paladin, bucked him up by taking with enthusiasm a Cady Hewes piece, "The Impatient Patient." Another $750. He was too much a pro to be discouraged by the continued rejections of Lewis and Clark and the others, though he was anxious for the fish to start biting.

Instead of biting, they sulked on the bottom. On March 10 *Holiday* sent back the canoe article, dissatisfied with its lead. He bowed his neck and revised it, barely looking up to observe that *Look* and other places had said no to Donner Pass, and "Topic One" had bounced promptly from every office it had been sent to. But he did look up when *American* came back with four pages of suggestions and directives for the emasculation of "High Country." What they asked involved more than patience or a willingness to revise. It involved his professional pride.

Needy or not, he waited hardly long enough to finish reading *American*'s letter before he fired back his reply: "No doubt there are writers who would be willing to attempt the piece you outline, but I am not one of them." To sympathetic Carl Brandt he blew sky high:

Go easy about sleeping on the ground—Jesus Christ! Don't mention the fact that the slopes are steep, if you're writing about mountain climbing; don't mention the fact that you sometimes sweat, if you're writing about playing tennis. "Alluring vacation resort"—God damn! I'm telling them what this country is like. Give us some gemütlich family stuff. Don't say I don't fish—presumably some trout-hunter's feelings will be riled, or those of an advertiser who makes fishing rods. And as the ultimate payoff, maybe I'd be bright to stop off and refresh my memory when I go west in April. There will be thirty feet of snow on every inch of the country I'm talking about in April. . . . Why doesn't the crazy bastard get some copywriter from his advertising department to write the piece he wants? It would cost a hell of a lot less than a thousand dollars, and the advertising manager could sit by the boy's shoulder and see that he worked in a lot of trade names that would bring in some nice ads.

As if disgust had overwhelmed him, DeVoto that same day refused a travel-article request from the New York *Times Magazine* on the ground that the price, two hundred dollars, would be "an eighty percent discount from my usual fee." Better to rise stark naked than fall in calico.

On March 24 Mabel Souvaine, the old reliable, fell heir to "High Country," unbowdlerized. But also on March 24, Carl Brandt discovered that the canoe article, which *Holiday* now liked, was going to be used as a front-of-the-book piece, for which the price was only five hundred dollars, not the fifteen hundred he and DeVoto had expected. In great distress Brandt wrote Ted Patrick, *Holiday*'s editor, taking the blame for the misunderstanding and asking if, in this single instance, the price could not be raised. It couldn't. So Brandt wrote a shamed letter to DeVoto advising him to accept *Holiday*'s terms and take out the difference in kicks at his agent's backside.

Depressed and overworked, DeVoto accepted; he had no other option. But this disappointment, added to the *American* fiasco, left him with only one fifth of the money he had counted on. He thought he might have to cancel his trip West, which involved a lot of travel, long stopovers, and no high fees. And he was gloomy about his prospects:

What about it, Carl? I can't write for magazines like the *American*. I can't seem to impress Patrick. The *Post* isn't much interested. What's your honest opinion? . . . Are there enough places and chances for the kind of stuff I write to make it sensible to try, or should I stick to books? Don't spare my feelings.

That was mid-March 1952. They had then been playing the magazine market hard for six months. Apart from the *Mademoiselle* article and several to *Woman's Day*, which had not been Carl Brandt's doing, their success amounted to one cut-rate *Holiday* article, one *American* article that Mabel Souvaine had taken on the bounce, and the squib for *This Week* that even yet DeVoto had not got around to writing.

Scribbling on a yellow pad, at home in his apartment on a Sunday, Brandt replied that he couldn't be pessimistic but didn't want to be unrealistic either. DeVoto had been out of the market a long time. Magazines and editors had changed. But DeVoto was a fine and wonderful and respected name, and sooner or later the magazines would want him, if only for his "g.d. circulation value." The problem was simply to find the subjects that would make them jump up and down. He blamed himself for not yet finding them, but he did not despair.

All right, then. Forward. Plug the old ideas and peddle the unwanted articles and try to find the topics for new ones better fitted to the demand. While Brandt worked at it, DeVoto went off on his lecture tour to Oregon, California, Utah, and Colorado, and when he got back he went to the hospital for tests to determine the causes for his fatigue, depression, and gastric discomfort. The tests were inconclusive. Gloomily he came out and went to work on the Lewis and Clark *Journals*.

That was in June. Through the summer, Brandt worked doggedly, trying to sell DeVoto's articles and ideas and especially to establish him solidly in certain places, especially *Holiday* and *Reader's Digest*, while DeVoto fought the conservation wars and worked for Stevenson and kept one eye on the possibilities of money-making. It began to be a year since Brandt had confidently started to re-establish DeVoto as a big magazine name. None of DeVoto's ideas for pieces on conservation, scenery, historic sites, forest fires, and the national forests had been picked up. Lewis and Clark had gone begging, though DeVoto had himself put a piece of it into *Harper's*. "Topic One" had been rejected by everybody between 33rd and 60th streets, and had finally gone back to Mabel Souvaine, who had turned it down in the first place. This time she took it, and she also took the Donner Pass article that no one else wanted, and asked for two more. She was, as before, his one, lonely market. In desperation he had even turned back to fiction and written a story called "The Link," which he sent out under the name of Frank Gilbert, because both Bernard DeVoto and John August had foresworn fiction. Nobody wanted that either, apparently.

By October, DeVoto was discouraged enough about his future as a magazine free lance to let Brandt start negotiating a lecture contract with the W. Colston Leigh agency. He refused to let Brandt get him into writing on speculation for the *Reader's Digest*, for, as he said, the deal was always a big fee if they used it and $250 if they didn't, and the fee always turned out to be $250. But he offered to do a monthly column for the *Digest*, either on books or on slang, gobbledegook, jargon, and the vagaries of language.

And just then the luck began to change. *Ford Times* wanted an article on Ogden as a boyhood home (and there he went back to his starting point, in nostalgia instead of in derision). Fred Ware Smith, the editor, was so delighted to catch DeVoto that he listened when DeVoto, through Brandt, proposed writing him four to six articles in exchange for a Ford station wagon in which to make a trip West. On November 17 *True*, acknowledging De-Voto's bartending reputation, asked for an article on the martini, for a fee of $750. Three days later, DeWitt Wallace of *Reader's Digest* rejected DeVoto's ideas for monthly columns, but com-missioned a one-shot piece on Indian contributions to the Ameri-can language, guaranteeing one thousand dollars whether he used it or not, and more if he did. About the same time, DeVoto finally wrote his "Words to Live By" theme for *This Week*. And just after mid-December, when *Ford Times* had him out to Dear-born, Michigan, to do an article on Henry Ford's home town, the love feast with Fred Ware Smith was consummated and the sta-tion wagon assured. To pay for it, DeVoto would do, in addition to the Dearborn article, the article on Ogden as a boyhood home, an article on the Great Lakes ore boats, and one other. And just after Christmas, Carl Brandt wrote that *Collier's*, to commemorate the 150th anniversary of the Louisiana Purchase, wanted a long article on the purchase and the historical events that led up to it, for which it would pay at least twenty-five hundred dollars, and perhaps twice that much.

On the next to last day of 1952, after fifteen months of difficulty and recurrent disappointment, Brandt was finally able to feel that his efforts had brought results. Acknowledging on that day the receipt of the Dearborn article, he reminded DeVoto of his pending chores: revision of the *Reader's Digest* article on Indian words, the writing of the big Louisiana Purchase essay, an Easy Chair, the martini piece for *True*, two articles immediately and one somewhat later for *Ford Times*, and one more for Mabel Souvaine. "You have quite a little spate of work for the minute, haven't you, my friend?" he said, with some satisfaction.

Quite a spate of work. None of it, apart from the Louisiana Purchase article, which derived from his research for *The Course of Empire*, was work that he particularly wanted to do. But all of it was work that he had been able, with great effort and many disappointments, to sell.

7·Collection of Clowns and Cowards

No one of DeVoto's temperament and beliefs could have inhabited the Easy Chair through the late 1940s and early 1950s without using it to denounce the witch hunts of the time. His entrance into those battles was progressive; he became more active as the atmosphere of fear and repression thickened. The enemies he challenged, in the order of their appearance if not of their importance, were the book censors both private and public; the security policies of the United States as interpreted, administered, or initiated by the FBI; and the politics of thought control and character assassination as practiced by the House Un-American Activities Committee, the Reece Committee, the Gathings Committee, and most spectacularly Senator Joseph McCarthy of Wisconsin.

In a time when a humiliatingly small number of intellectual and political leaders dared openly to defy the inquisition, the Easy Chair spoke out loud, blunt, and often. DeVoto was no more ready to think America in need of police-state methods at mid-century than he had been to think it must go either right or left in the 1930s. He would have concurred with Robert Frost's judgment. Just before he went to Russia with Stewart Udall in 1962, I asked Frost what he was going to say to Khrushchev. He said, "I'm going to tell him America has a ramshackle government. The harder you ram it, the firmer it shackles." That was DeVoto's faith, too. His knowledge of history gave him a perspective on crises that in their time had seemed fatal but that had somehow been survived. Though his temperament made him suffer more from crisis than most, he had a basic confidence that no matter how long it took in the ramshackle democratic system to get a wrong righted or an ill amended, in the end the worst wrongs and the most drastic ills got dealt with. It took a long time for a demagogue to hang himself, but history showed him no demagogue who had not wound up on the end of the rope the system gave him. He loathed, and spoke contemptuously of, the "unspeakable" McCarthy, but from the beginning he insisted that the junior Senator from Wisconsin was bush league, and would not last. Would not last, that is, if the country was kept open to the oxygen of discussion and dissent. The germs of McCarthyism, like those of botulism, are anaerobic.

For such a purpose as the defense of traditional American liberties, the Easy Chair was made to order. By the mid-1940s it was an opinion-making column of the first importance. When it defended civil liberties, its motives could not be seriously impugned or its loyalty seriously questioned, and neither could the motives and the loyalty of the magazine in which it appeared. *Harper's* had no compulsion, like that, say, of the Democratic Party, to be hard on communism in order to prove it had never been soft on it; and DeVoto himself had earned a reputation not unlike the one he had read from history's tea leaves when writing up James K. Polk in *The Year of Decision: 1846*. He might have certain limitations, but he could not be scared, manipulated, or brought to heel. During the time when the novelist in him was going down for the last time, and when the historian in him was writing his way through his one great theme, the controversialist in him remained unmodified and undiminished, a live wire, almost a short circuit, of pugnacious principle.

He had used the Easy Chair repeatedly to publicize the *Strange Fruit* case. Coming back from his western tour in the fall of 1946, he was drawn into the defense of Kathleen Winsor's *Forever Amber*, and within a few months also found himself publicly on the side of Edmund Wilson's novel *Memoirs of Hecate County*, against which the Hearst press was fulminating and which was eventually declared obscene in New York and Los Angeles, though San Francisco gave it a clean bill of health. While that harassment of Wilson was in progress, the New York Board of Education withdrew from circulation among high school students one of Howard Fast's novels, and so there were three books to fight the censors about.

Though he thought *Forever Amber* vulgar trash, though Wilson was one of the literary intellectuals and an old antagonist, and though Fast's books ran down the party line as if magnetized to the rails, DeVoto, unsympathetic to all three, insisted that suggestive vulgarity, literary arrogance, and party-line Stalinism all had the right to go as far as they could go in the free market of ideas. "The place to fight censorship is whatever place it appears in," he said; for "anyone who denies us access to error by that act denies us access to truth as well."[1]

When Judge Frank J. Donahue ruled that *Forever Amber* was not obscene, DeVoto was so jubilant he asked the judge to dinner. In the Easy Chair for May 1947, he called Donahue's decision "the first civilized judicial judgment in Massachusetts in fifty years"—the sort of decision which, if it held up on appeal, could make even a bad statute into a good one. He cheered the admission of literary and psychiatric testimony, and Donahue's firm declaration that behavior, not provocation, must be the basis for any finding of corruption by books. He could not resist needling the Boston bluestockings with the fact that Donahue was a Catholic, a member of the church supposed to have been almost solely responsible for Boston censorship. And he noted the irony the case left behind it: *Forever Amber*, a silly and suggestive novel, could now be sold in Massachusetts, but *Strange Fruit*, a fine and serious one, could not.

Irony or no irony, a great step had been taken. Two years later, in the Easy Chair for July 1949, he could report others that seemed to take literature almost into the clear. Judge Donahue's decision on *Forever Amber* had been upheld by the Massachusetts Supreme Court, and on the strength of that sustaining vote Judge Fairhurst had thrown out obscenity charges against James M. Cain's *Serenade* and Erskine Caldwell's *God's Little Acre*. In discussing the Donahue decision, DeVoto had praised a Catholic for making a liberal and civilized judgment; in discussing this, he praised Judge Fairhurst for saying that no book was obscene simply because it was offensive to Catholics, and for warning against the censorious and repressive tendencies of racial and religious minorities. On that last point he grew more concerned as he grew older, characteristically assuming a position that would offend the embattled of all colorations. "We will have solved the racial problem," he said toward the end of his life, "when, if a Negro is a son of a bitch, I can call him one."[2] In the 1970s it does not sound like the formula for peace, and it needs to be stated in reverse as well—something DeVoto would have done willingly. But it states a principle: the crucial matter is being a son of a bitch, not what color son of a bitch you are.

The Easy Chair backed the principle, not the party, and so it was again elated when Judge Curtis Bok, in the Court of the Quarter Sessions in Philadelphia, cleared nine books that had been gang-swept from the bookstore shelves by the police. Judge Bok's decision, said the same Easy Chair, of July 1949, was worthy to stand beside the great opinions on *Ulysses* by Judge John M. Woolsey and Judge Learned Hand, for it asserted the "unpardonable error and arbitrariness" of all definitions of obscenity. "We are so fearful for other people's morals," Judge Bok had said. "They so seldom have the courage of our own convictions." When DeVoto, down in Philadelphia in November to make a speech and to hunt out Lewis and Clark materials in the American Philosophical Society, was asked to dinner by Judge Bok through the good offices of their mutual friend Kitty Bowen, DeVoto told Mrs. Bowen that he felt like one of the elect.

But if writers had been liberated to speak frankly, and overfrankly, on some matters hitherto called obscene, there was no such loosening of political restraints. Thought control was no fading adversary, especially after Joseph McCarthy was elected to the Senate in 1948, when the brief openness of American-Russian relations had already hardened into the cold war.

One of Benny DeVoto's most conspicuous gifts was viewing with alarm. A watchdog, he barked at burglars, murderers, Peeping Toms, voices, shadows, and ghosts. Sometimes he created an uproar when there was little to warrant it, and there were impatient neighbors who said he kept them awake all night with his yapping. But when a real threat developed, he was there on the porch to meet it, growling and showing his teeth. He had been growling at landgrabbers and censors for a long time, and he was in good voice when Chairman Wood of the House Un-American Activities Committee, during Commencement Week, 1949, sent out letters to seventy colleges and universities with government research contracts, requesting the reading lists for their courses in sociology, geography, economics, government, philosophy, history, political science, and Amerian literature.

A few colleges co-operated, some ignored the request, some indicated their intention to resist it publicly. Under pressure from some members of his own committee, Chairman Wood sent a second letter, assuring the colleges that he had in mind no censorship of their curricula. Nevertheless, said the Easy Chair[3] in a voice that carried across the country, that was exactly what he did have in mind, and he had been put up to it by the Sons of the American Revolution. In asking for the lists, Wood had assumed authority that he did not have; and in co-operating with the request, some colleges had half acceded to thought control. Behind Wood's letter, DeVoto smelled the generals, and he feared the increasing leverage of federal research grants on academic freedom—an issue that would become explosive twenty years later. And if the colleges declared that they would not admit known Communists to their faculties, then they had already given up most of their fighting room, for determining who was Communist and who not would involve investigations that would in themselves be intolerable. Before long, the FBI would be passing on all appointments. A Communist or two on any faculty constituted a far smaller danger than the procedures that would be necessary to keep them off.

This was the DeVoto whom the leftist intellectuals had been calling a Fascist in 1936. Most of them had by now retreated from their pro-Communist sympathies, either by conversion or out of caution. Few were anxious to have their past associations publicized, and hence few were eager to defend too vigorously the civil liberties of former comrades. Their experience with Stalinism had been shattering to some,[4] and they had moved closer to the middle, where for years DeVoto had been taking on all comers. Or they had quietly blended with the liberals—though it became clearer every day that there was little more safety there than on the Left. Now the old Left found a champion in its former opponent.

People who have the same enemies do not necessarily believe alike, but it is fairly easy for their enemies to make it appear they do. Inevitably DeVoto got smeared. From 1949 on (in that year, he attacked the House Un-American Activities Committee, the FBI, the censors of various colorations, the western stockgrowers' associations, the United States Chamber of Commerce, *Time*, the Bureau of Reclamation, and the Corps of Engineers, as well as sundry individuals), he was called a Red by some authoritative-sounding patriots, including Congressmen Kearns and Ellsworth, Senator McCarthy, and a spokeswoman for the Daughters of the American Revolution. He did not accept either charge or innuendo tamely, but made bristling demands for retractions, and at least in the Kearns affair he tried to force Kearns to publish a retraction in the Congressional Record, where he had made his charges. He took some pleasure in quoting an article in *Pravda* that had attacked him as a reactionary. When the Daughters of the American Revolution wanted a public airing of their differences of opinion, he refused to debate with them, saying that he had as little as possible to do with subversive societies, of which he considered the DAR one of the worst.[5]

He was neither a Fascist nor a Communist, but something perhaps even more disliked by the Inquisition—a bona fide liberal, a small-d democrat who truly believed in the Bill of Rights even when it protected and was abused by his antagonists. His experience had taught him that "the right to speak out and act freely is always at a minimum in the area of the fighting faiths,"[6] and in making a fighting faith of the right to speak out, he understood that he fought with one hand tied behind him, for he guaranteed his opponents the protection of the civil liberties they were determined to subvert. But when the witch hunts began to seem so ominous that, to use his own words, "we have to begin to make scenes," he waded in, for in his view the only safety lay in freedom of inquiry, thought, and expression, complete and passionately defended. "There is no such thing as a partial virgin."

When he took on the House Un-American Activities Committee, in September 1949, he had just written his swan song as a novelist and had just said a final farewell to Bread Loaf, that best of all possible clubs, with everything that it had once meant in acceptance, friendship, and security. His emotions and his eyes were bothering him, not for the first time. He felt "winter in the air" as his inordinate energy began to run down and his maligned but quite remarkable health began to fail. The signs said to slow down—he was fifty-two and had been living on his reserves for a long time. So, being who he was, he licked the envelope that contained his attack on the House Un-American Activities Committee, sent off the manuscript of *The World of Fiction*, wrote the first few pages of *The Course of Empire*, and rushed out, growling, upon J. Edgar Hoover and the FBI.

For months, Cambridge gossip had been full of security checks that for unstated reasons were being made upon all sorts of people: potential federal appointees, putative saboteurs, people mistrusted by some congressman. The well-groomed, Ivy League young men who appeared at doors and flipped their credential-bearing wallets and came inside and asked questions and made notes and went away were sometimes seen going straight next door to the house of the most notorious gossip on the block, or of one's worst enemy, and imagination suggested very plausibly that the subject of inter-rogation might have changed, and that one was now under discus-sion over there, and that notes were being made, and would be carefully filed, for uses that the imagination boggled at, especially after Senator McCarthy introduced into the Coplon trial material from such a raw file, supposed to be available to no one except the FBI itself. It was DeVoto personally and Cambridge collectively that erupted into protest in the Easy Chair—but it was DeVoto who signed the complaint, personally.

In "Due Notice to the FBI," the Easy Chair for October 1949, he described the characteristic security investigation, the sorts of questions asked, the ways in which gossip, malice, paranoia, and worse got lumped with valid data in the raw files; and the way the raw files, in mysterious ways, sometimes fell into the hands of people who used them for character assassination. He said we were in danger of becoming "a nation of common informers." He said he could see only one way of determining what elements of any such investigation were legitimate and of forcing the investigators to act responsibly. From here on he intended to take it.

Representatives of the FBI and other official investigating bodies have questioned me, in the past, about a number of people and I have an-swered their questions. That's over. From now on any representative of the government, properly identified, can count on a drink and per-haps informed talk about the Red (but non-communist) Sox at my house. But if he wants information from me about anyone whomso-ever, no soap. If it is my duty as a citizen to tell what I know about someone, I will perform that duty under subpoena, in open court, be-fore that person and his attorney. . . . I will not discuss it in private with any government investigator.

I like a country where it's nobody's damned business what magazines anyone reads, what he thinks, whom he has cocktails with. I like a country where we do not have to stuff the chimney against listening ears and where what we say does not go into the FBI files along with a note from S-17 that I may have another wife in California. I like a country where no college-trained flatfeet collect memoranda about us and ask judicial protection for them, where when someone makes statements about us to officials he can be held to account. We had that kind of country only a little while ago and I'm for getting it back.

It was a stout cudgeling, and though it brought some happy cheers from some Cambridge acquaintances and from correspondents all over America, it also scared some of DeVoto's friends badly. They feared both for him and for themselves by association. And the mail brought poison pen letters, anonymous denunciations, and earnest arguments from people who wanted to know how else we were to be protected against subversion, conspiracy, and the Communist threat. For months he was "fighting bees," as he said, over that essay, and for weeks he was trying to smoke out J. Edgar Hoover into a public discussion of the charges the essay had made.

But Mr. Hoover was cagy—or perhaps he chose to take the line that DeVoto had taken with the DAR. He did not choose to dignify by denial, and he would not write to DeVoto directly, though, as DeVoto said, he was noble and lofty, "by the stickful" on every front page in the United States. The closest he came to answering DeVoto's charges was to deny in a letter to *Harper's*[7] that DeVoto's information was true and accurate and that investigators asked such questions as DeVoto asserted they asked. Hoover also wrote to Daniel Mebane of the *New Republic* denying that his operatives asked their informants if the person being investigated read, subscribed to, or quoted from the *New Republic*. Using Mebane as go-between, DeVoto offered to debate Hoover anywhere, in print or in person, and he encouraged friends at the Yale Law School to offer the two of them a forum. (Mr. Hoover did not choose to debate.) DeVoto even said he would write for the *New Republic* if Hoover would meet him in its columns—but he would debate only if the FBI would make public, as an exhibit and a reassurance and a testimonial to the purity of its methods, one single raw file, perhaps the Coplon file, which Senator McCarthy had already publicly quoted from and which he had obtained, by means as yet mysterious, from the FBI.

But he never got J. Edgar Hoover into the ring, and in the end he had to be content with a restatement of his own position in a letter to the editor in the December *Harper's*. He said that Mr. Hoover was simply not truthful in denying that his operatives asked the questions DeVoto said they asked. He had a questionnaire form on his desk and could get others. He denied that FBI security checks deserved the confidentiality of a grand-jury report, to which Hoover had compared them. A grand jury was an impaneled group of citizens; the FBI was a secret police force.

Inquiries which I know the FBI has made and others which have been plentifully published in the press have suggested to me that it invades areas of thought and behavior which are entirely improper for it to inquire into, that it has great power to injure the reputations of innocent people without being held to account, and that it holds ideas about what constitutes dangerous or subversive activity that are unacceptable in our form of government. That is what my piece was about.

Challenge offered, challenge evaded or ignored. His foray endeared him to anxious liberals and made him for the moment an ally of the *New Republic* and *The Nation*, magazines which in the months of his Manhattan captivity he had scorned and ridiculed and which had united in deploring his maverick intransigence. But the alliance was uneasy, more on their part than on his, and he did not welcome it. Some months following the appearance of "Due Notice to the FBI," Carey McWilliams of *The Nation* asked DeVoto's support for the Hollywood Ten. He would join nothing until he had the names of those he would be associated with, and he commented tartly that in the past *The Nation* had never mentioned him except as a Fascist or a fool. Why did they want his help now?[8]

He professed to be more amused than annoyed by Hoover's refusal to reply to specific charges, but he was not truly amused. His essay had been generated by moral and political indignation and the will to correct what struck him as a manifest tyranny. But, in something like the way the times were against him when he resisted the leftward stampede in the 1930s, they were against him now, when he resisted the stampede into repression on the one side and fear on the other. Circumstances outside his control combined to weaken his effort. The Alger Hiss trial, and the verdict against Hiss that followed soon after DeVoto's sally against the FBI, convinced DeVoto that the activities of the snoop organizations would grow more virulent, not less, and that the secret-police methods of the FBI would seem to many people to be warranted by clear and present danger. Not very optimistically, he went on fighting them.

He was a middlist, or an equilibrist. He suspected extremes, and he had a passionate faith in common sense. If his mental life was a tripod composed of a radical leg, a conservative leg, and a common-sense leg, then the common-sense leg was elongated like a rake handle, and dominated the others. He was neither a push-button liberal nor a knee-jerk conservative. Thus, when a correspondent lugubriously doubted that the American system could last, feared that you could not give the people any policy-making power and still survive, doubted that Congress could do anything right, and guessed that government would have to be handed over to experts, DeVoto reacted by defending Congress —a position as outwardly unlikely and as inwardly logical as his alliance with the *New Republic* against the FBI.

Congress, he said, was representative of the people, so truly representative that the associated garden clubs could sometimes scare a congressman into defying the power lobby. Congress *was* the people, and the people were ourselves. And—his old refrain—we should not expect perfection, knowing the fallible material out of which democracy was made. "Sure the people are stupid: the human race is stupid. Sure Congress is an inefficient instrument of government. But the people are not stupid enough to abandon representative government for any other kind, including government by the man who knows." Experts, he said further, were useful employees, disastrous masters. Like any other elite given power, they ended up with a machine gun in their hands, imposing their higher wisdom on the unenlightened.

It must have surprised readers who had heard him express opinions of congressmen not too distant from those of Mark Twain, who referred to them as a "criminal class." But it shouldn't have surprised anyone who knew DeVoto. Like an anti-clerical Catholic, he could believe in the cloth without necessarily believing in the men who wore it. When he made his defense of the Congress, in November 1950, his mood was still relatively sanguine, or at least resolute. He thought that the erosions of American liberty could be halted, and would be. Eventually the people, through their representatives, would produce some sort of Soil Conservation Service of the spirit that would restore, not fully but enough, the gullied and wind-blown guarantees by which the republic lived.

He was still in a relatively confident mood when, in the *Atlantic* for February 1951, he returned to his old theme of the ex-Communists, some of whom had recently, like Whittaker Chambers, been testifying against what they had once supported, and acting as if they were the only people who understood democracy, having for so long been deluded into subverting it. DeVoto thought they were, as a class, people who found freedom intolerable—panacea hunters, true believers whose self-righteousness had not been cured by conversion but only redirected. He thought them not dangerous but ridiculous:

With ideas, empirical demonstration is the payoff, and serves as at least a rough measure of intelligence. If the side of a cube is twelve inches square the man who measures it and says it is twelve inches square is right. A man who for some time maintains that it is a half gallon in the key of C-sharp and blue at that is not displaying conspicuously penetrating intelligence when he finally picks up a ruler.[9]

It was the tune he had been singing all his life, the same tune he had sung when going to war against the literary intellectuals and their successors the literary Marxists: in lusting after the impossible, they misread and undervalued the possible. In giving away their hearts to perfection, they gave away their minds.

It is difficult even for people who lived through it to bring back the atmosphere of oppression, fear, and silence that hung over the McCarthy period. But it was real and frightening and bewildering at the time, a smog that tainted all American life. Simply by asserting the American gospels when so many were publicly attacking them and so many were privately doubting them, DeVoto heartened his Easy Chair readers. Attacked in two speeches by McCarthy,[10] he was disturbed, angered, and sickened, and Avis remembers his walking the floor, scowling and upset, saying that he could take a lot, but there came a time when he had to speak up if it meant he would lose his markets and never hold a job again. There was a sorry sort of amusement in the typical McCarthy blunder—in the first speech, the man attacked was called "Richard" DeVoto—and even a sort of protection in it, for a man who could not correctly name the people he attacked could hardly be trusted to know their politics. Nevertheless he did not underrate McCarthy's power to poison; he knew some of the victims: Owen Lattimore had been a Bread Loaf staff member; the son of his friend Dr. Jacob Fine had been entangled in an Army loyalty hearing. No Cambridge cocktail party, no gathering of the DeVoto Sunday evening group, failed to bring up new instances.

Despite his basic confidence in democracy's capacity to correct its imbalances, he had long since begun to wonder if this demagogue McCarthy was as bush league as he had once thought. He wondered where the public's nerve was. Too few had the courage to fight back and call McCarthy the liar he was. The President sat on his hands, the Congress did nothing to control the member whom many of them deplored and despised. The public, for all one could tell, was apathetic, scared, or actively behind the witch hunt. And one of the uncomfortable facts about a ramshackle government was that Congressional committees were exempt from the usual forms of legal redress. To fight them, too often meant the swift termination of one's public character and perhaps of one's job. At the same time, if one were Bernard DeVoto, one did not rush to the unqualified defense of everyone whom the witch-hunters attacked. Witness his refusal to sign a declaration in defense of the Hollywood Ten until he knew the people with whom he would be associated. That was not fear of McCarthy. That was, from his point of view, only a reasonable concern for his intellectual self-respect and a caution about being manipulated.

By April 1953, when the Easy Chair returned to the Congressional investigations in "The Case of the Censorious Congressman," DeVoto had lost a good deal of his optimism. Stevenson had been badly defeated, the raiders were in the saddle in the West and in Washington, the attrition of civil liberties had proceeded alarmingly, the fungus of suspicion and fear had spread. So, though the Gathings Committee, of which he wrote in this Easy Chair, had only wanted to censor cheap comic books and paperbacks, he took it with the greatest seriousness. For this represented, in his view, the spread of an infection. This was an attack on the right to read, and it was made not by village snoops or the Watch and Ward, but by Congress. This was official, and because of its auspices it had to be considered along with Congressman Wood's attempt against college reading lists. The Gathings Committee report, on the surface, did no worse than degrade Congress to the level of any police-court snooper. What it did less obviously was pound another nail into the coffin of traditional American freedoms. For what could be censored in paperback could be censored in royal octavo boards; what Congress could suppress as pornography it could as easily suppress as heresy or un-American activity.

The accuracy of the Easy Chair's analysis was promptly attested when one of the members of the Gathings Committee, Representative Kearns of Pennsylvania, called his criticism pro-Communist. He entered in the Congressional Record a statement about "activities" of DeVoto's which, he said, "spoke for themselves." DeVoto had signed a New York *Times* advertisement urging the abolition of the Wood-Rankin Committee. He was on the council of the Society for the Prevention of World War III, "headed by Rex Stout, former editor of the *New Masses*." He had published in *Harper's* an article, "Due Notice to the FBI," which the *New Masses* had quoted with approval. The *Daily Worker* reported that he had been among those opposing a move to outlaw the Communist Party. The *People's Daily Worker* said he had denounced an action of the House Un-American Activities Committee.

Absurd, predictable, symptomatic, and scary, that sort of generalized smear had already destroyed too many people, and had to be replied to. DeVoto replied in the Easy Chair for August 1953, and incidentally told the story of his unsuccessful attempt to force a retraction from Representative Kearns in the Congressional Record. (Representatives Celler of New York and Eugene McCarthy of Minnesota, and Senator Neuberger of Oregon had all assisted him in that effort, but without success.) Since Kearns elected to be a "hit and run defamer," DeVoto said, he would use him as an instance of the technique of defamation. He pointed out that every major newspaper in the United States, as well as the *New Masses,* had commented on and quoted from "Due Notice to the FBI." Dozens of papers besides the *Daily Worker* had reported his distaste for the Un-American Activities Committee and his considered opposition to the outlawing of the Communist Party. His attitude toward communism could have been ascertained by fifteen minutes in any library. Rex Stout was not, and never had been, editor of the *New Masses,* and prevention of World War III was not exactly a sly Communist maneuver. All of this, Representative Kearns could have determined or have had a staff member determine. Instead, he chose to make an official smear and then hide behind Congressional immunity.

Being who he was, with a gift for controversy and a forum from which to practice it, he effectively shut Kearns's mouth and calmed the pulse of anyone who for the moment might have feared that the Easy Chair was fellow traveling. But not everyone had such skill in self-defense, and the technique of smear that was ridiculous when applied to someone who could fight back was fatal to the many who could not.

Call them liars, he had kept saying, and they will back down. But by the beginning of 1954, what had at first galvanized him with indignation had begun to sicken him. In February he wrote Mattingly, abroad on a Guggenheim Fellowship, asking not quite humorously where he could find sanctuary from the American scene. It seemed to him that we had come out of the war the strongest and most confident nation on earth, grown-up, civilized, and powerful, and that in less than ten years we had become "the sorriest collection of clowns and cowards in the contemporary world."[11] During the years when he had been writing *The Course of Empire* he had been working against difficulties that half maddened him, and yet he had felt, too, "like a lover imagining the young girlhood of his bride." That bride had become something that made him turn his back. All the exhilaration that American

institutions had always stimulated in him was gone; his robust confidence in the country and the system had weakened, along with
the depletion of his energies and the decline of his health. On
every side, he saw Americans collaborating in the destruction of
their freedoms, as the people of the West had consistently collaborated in the rape of their natural resources. Ignorance, greed, suspicion, cowardice, cynicism looked at him out of every morning's
New York *Times*. America was potentially a great place, but it
was lousy with Americans.

It demoralized him to see a whole nation afraid—demoralized
him so utterly that he read the Army hearings in the summer of
1954 as a McCarthy triumph, whereas in fact the ramshackle
system had been shackling to its belated firmness. The tears of a
hardboiled lawyer, seen by millions on television, and one outraged cry, "Senator McCarthy, have you no shame?" were like
an alarm clock waking a sleeper from an ugly dream. From that
point on, the system went quietly on with the job of adjusting
the noose around McCarthy's neck that DeVoto had predicted
four years before.

Demoralized or not, gloomy or not, DeVoto never stopped
fighting what he hated. The Easy Chair was never more serious,
more public-spirited, or more effective than during 1954 and 1955,
when out of twenty-three issues thirteen dealt either with environmental problems or the ordeal of civil liberties. In April 1954,
with acrid distaste, he discussed the activities of the Veterans of
Foreign Wars and the American Legion in collecting lists of
"proved" Communists, "suspected" Communists, and fellow travelers. In May the Red-baiting attacks on Chief Justice Warren and
the episode in which some Puerto Rican militants fired into the
House of Representatives had him shooting back from the middle
at both sides. He did not blame the Puerto Ricans for their anger,
but he was appalled at their way of expressing it; it sickened him
to see Congress fired upon, but he had to believe also that "the
most dangerous subversives operating in the United States today
are in Congress." As vividly as he hated the cowardice that dared
not fight back against the tyranny of the witch-hunters, he hated
the timidity that was afraid to impose law and order lest revolution
follow.

Yet even then he had, or declared, a hope. Sooner or later
the country would call a halt. Sooner or later it would get pushed
so far that it would start resisting, and would deny that discussion and dissent were treason. Sooner or later we would restore
the Bill of Rights to operation, without fear of being "wasted at

noonday." Not forever would we be subjected to the spectacle of Mike Fink becoming Caspar Milquetoast, the eagle-screamers becoming poltroons, the tradition of popular freedom becoming "a box of sawdust for Joe McCarthy to spit in."

He had never feared the Communist revolution even when it was being confidently announced. All around the Communist intellectuals, while they passed their resolutions and wrote their editorials and slanted their book reviews and bored from within into liberal organizations, the real revolution of the New Deal had been going on—an American-style revolution-by-reform, which worked within the social and political habits of the American people. By 1955 not even McCarthy was convincing many people that the country was riddled with Communist conspirators. His capacity to terrify began to shrink after the Army hearings, and before long, taintedly, he would be dead.

DeVoto lived to see only the beginning of the change. In his lifetime there was no legitimate reason to relax. In April 1955 the Easy Chair hit the mind-hating Reece Committee and its investigation of the tax-exempt foundations, in "Guilt by Distinction." In July, reviewing Murray Kempton's *Part of Our Time*, a study of communism among the intellectuals, DeVoto noted for the hundreth time how futile had been the whole movement. "Peter and Wendy in the Revolution," he called that contemptuous Easy Chair. The Communists would have got only a footnote in history, like the Millerites, if for reasons of political power seeking the 1950s had not chosen to make into bogeymen this "heterogeneous miscellany of unworldly dreamers, flawed ascetics, officious nonentities, arrogant neurotics, followers of a dime-store grail, and intellectual gossips and stumblebums." Now ballyhooed as a dangerous gang, they had always been about as socially dangerous as the Jehovah's Witnesses. The Reds had never been cause for alarm; only the Red-baiters were.

In August he wrote his last installment on that theme when he attacked the Public Health Service for withholding research funds from projects conducted by anyone against whom "derogatory information" had been alleged. The Public Health Service, he said, wanted to be "clean" in the eyes of Congressional committees, and avoid trouble. Result: medical research got shorted, responsible scientists such as John Edsall of Harvard announced they would accept nothing with loyalty strings attached, and the system sank deeper into its hysterical restrictiveness. The Public Health Service, with important public duties to perform, opened its veins for fear of the knife, like the Boston booksellers intimidated by Watch and Ward.

In the summer of 1955, when he wrote that Easy Chair, DeVoto was fifty-eight, and sick, and tired, and gloomy in his mind. No one would have known it from reading the column he had now written in *Harper's* for nearly twenty years. His pieces still had their old muzzle velocity, and he was still a deadly shot. Tired he might be, and afflicted with ailments whose precise nature he could not define, but he was more than ever a man of principle, and he was still a warrior. The first role that he had adopted had proved one of the most durable.

8 · *"May Six O'clock Never Find You Alone."*

In the fall of 1920, yearning outward from his exile or refuge in deepest Ogden, DeVoto had written to Melville Smith that he wanted to spend his vigorous years in "creative criticism of America." He wanted to pour his "God-awful emulsion" into the examination of whether, or how, the nation would make the turn from adolescence into adulthood, from exuberance and confusion into a greatness commensurate with its expressed ideals and the inspiring vastness and variety of its geography. His motives in 1920 had been mixed. Even then he was a cultural patriot, though a critical one; and even then, in the midst of his first and most helpless breakdown, he had seized upon work, the more ambitious the better, as the surest safety. Ambition was a trapeze on which he swung high above everything he despised and feared, but in his cunning he hung the habit of work beneath him like a net. Part of his panic in 1920 had been brought on by an inability to work. He had fallen, and fallen hard. Part of his recovery had involved rigging the safety net so that he could force the coward within to get up on the rings.

Except for brief periods, he had kept the interior coward too busy to become that afraid again, and whenever he had fallen, work had saved him. "The bravest damn man I even knew," Avis called him, knowing what the effort cost. Others, seeing what he produced, thought him the most compulsive worker alive, and that impression grew stronger, not weaker, upon close acquaintance, for only his close acquaintances knew the enormous correspondence that flowed in and out of his study each week. Four fifths of his productive iceberg was under water. He was a public man, with public mail: fan letters and their polite acknowledgment, argument and its rebuttal, inquiries and information, all the questions and answers of research, all the continuations in private of controversies begun in public. He had had careers for three men, and he had subsidiary correspondence for them all;[1] but everything including the correspondence tended to focus on the creative criticism of America that he had set himself when barely out of college.

Except for his bootlegging excursions into Quebec, a couple of drives across Ontario, a hypothetical trip to Mexico as a boy, and a brief trip to the Canadian Rockies with Gregory Rochlin, one of his psychiatrist friends, he had never been outside the United States, yet his view was wide, not provincial. The perspective that others got by looking back from Europe (as *John Brown's Body* and *Look Homeward Angel* had come out of a European homesickness) he got by looking West from Cambridge, or back from the present into the past, or forward from the past into the present. There have been few American writers whose work is more of a piece, or whose "vigorous years" produced more illumination of the country and culture that produced them. The brattish boy from Ogden taught his contemporaries something, even those who thought him an angry barbarian.

Much of the light, as well as some of the incidental heat, came from his maverick unwillingness to run with the herd—any herd—or to accept the standard varieties of intellectual fashion that his times offered him. "There are no new ways to be new," his father and adversary Robert Frost used to remark. As with so many of Frost's wisdoms, that was something DeVoto knew without being told. He had chosen not to be new but to be himself, not to be *in* but to be at liberty, with consequences to his reputation, both during his life and since, that have been more damaging than otherwise. The man who walks by himself has no gang or coterie, and in the profession of words it is coteries that more often than not determine reputations, at least in the short run.

In forcing the inward coward to productive effort, DeVoto had involved himself in a series of free-for-alls with a variety of systems and cliques and beliefs, and had made himself more enemies than he needed to; and yet despite his vehemence he had managed to wring from his often reluctant contemporaries most of the rewards the profession had to offer. Loved by a small circle, he was respected a long way outside it, and disliked and feared by many with whom he had found himself in conflict. But by the early 1950s, as we have seen, he had kept himself so harshly at the desk that most of his projected jobs were either done, or were abandoned as beyond his powers. What succeeded was a restlessness without definable cause, a hunger without ascertainable origin, a pain that was less pain than emptiness, a discontent that groped for its own stimuli, a busy-ness without enough real satisfaction. Once he had finished editing the Lewis and Clark *Journals*, in 1952, his only solid intellectual gratification came from the forays against the thought police and the enemies of conservation, and even those were often tainted by his feeling that they were rear-guard actions without much hope in them. His energies, which even in their exhausted state were formidable, were too much applied to turning wheels that he had to think unimportant, however economically necessary. Because he took pride in being a pro, he wrote his best in the travel articles for *Holiday*, *Ford Times*, *The Lamp*, and other magazines with which Carl Brandt eventually allied him. But because he had been ambitious and the reverse of humble—"My mind is as good as there is"—he often chafed for work that demanded his full powers.

From the time of his 1946 western tour he had projected a book about the modern West,[2] but it came off only piecemeal, as essays, and when he tried to bend those into a coherent argument he found himself betrayed into the generalizations that had made challenging journalism but looked dubious in the soberer context of a book. One feels that this book (its working title was *Western Paradox*) seemed to him a logical necessity, the completion of his long study of the West, and yet he found it very difficult. The chapters that he was sending down to Carl Brandt during 1955 did not please him; he thought they had no shine or brightness, they were chapters in a book he was writing because he was determined to have a book to write, not chapters of something that demanded powerfully to be said. In the end they wound up among his papers like the Cambridge novel *Assorted Canapés*, unpublished and unpublishable except for one Easy Chair, "Birth of an Art," which examined *The Virginian* and all subsequent horse opera against the real-life background of the Johnson County War, the cowboy myth against cattle-kingdom realities.

The house at 8 Berkeley Street, which had been sanctuary and workshop since 1941, was still the place to which he repaired for both work and healing, but the necessities of his life forced him out of it constantly on lecture tours, business trips to New York or Washington, and excursions to the West. The Lewis and Clark route that he had first traveled in 1946 had introduced him to his favorite country, and he returned again and again to the forested mountains around Missoula. In 1951 he had transferred his Bread Loaf affiliation to Joseph Kinsey Howard's "Bread Loaf, Montana," and had barely missed being present for Howard's fatal heart attack a few weeks after the conference. Missoula had also become the demonstration area, even more than Chet Olsen's region based on Ogden, of the Forest Service's watershed and timber preservation; he had friends in the Region One office from stenographers to regional foresters. In 1954 they happily collaborated with him in his last and in many ways most satisfying expedition. What made it especially satisfying was two companions, one of them Adlai Stevenson, the other the young man who since 1952 had been DeVoto's physician, Dr. Herbert Scheinberg.[3]

Their intimacy was new but intense. Scheinberg had finished up a junior fellowship at Harvard in 1950, and, uncertain whether he wanted to practice or teach, had settled for the time being on both. He hung out his shingle on an old house on Story Street in Cambridge and saw a limited number of patients while continuing to do research at the Children's Hospital and teaching at Peter Bent Brigham. He had always been interested in psychoanalysis, and had many friends among the psychiatrists of Boston. One was Gregory Rochlin, also a close friend of the DeVotos'. When DeVoto, suffering from his vague uncomfortable symptoms and a persistent cancerophobia, indicated that he was unsatisfied with his current doctor, Rochlin sent him to Scheinberg for an examination.

It was clear that DeVoto thought Scheinberg too young to be his physician, but when he returned from his western lecture tour, in June 1952, with all his symptoms intact, he went back to him, and Scheinberg put him in Peter Bent Brigham for exhaustive tests, primarily aimed at looking into his high blood pressure. He did not tell DeVoto what he was worried about, because he did not want to add another worry to his patient's hypochondria. And anyway he found no kidney, heart, or brain difficulties that might have been anticipated, and concluded that DeVoto's hypertension might continue for years to be asymptomatic, without serious consequences.

That fall, Scheinberg was in Geneva editing a book for the World Health Organization and combining that chore with a honeymoon. On his return, in October, he again saw DeVoto, and from that point their intimacy grew swiftly. Scheinberg's father had been killed when he was six; he had always, he says, been unconsciously hunting for a father. As for DeVoto, father hunting had been almost a career for him. This time, father and son got

curiously mixed, for though Scheinberg was almost young enough
to be DeVoto's son, he was a doctor, a member of a profession
for which DeVoto had always had reverence, and was in charge of
DeVoto's health, and so in a way became father to the man he
himself looked upon as a father.

The two families were very close friends by the time Scheinberg's young wife gave birth to a child, in the spring of 1953. A
little while later, only a few days after they had been together at
one of the DeVoto Sunday Evenings, Mrs. Scheinberg died of a
brain hemorrhage. The next time Benny DeVoto and his doctor
met, DeVoto broke down in tears.

Shortly afterward, Dr. Scheinberg moved from Cambridge to
the Albert Einstein College of Medicine, in New York, and their
friendship was interrupted. But on his frequent trips to New York,
DeVoto made it a point to see his medical father, and their correspondence was constant. When Scheinberg suggested to DeVoto
that they go together, in June 1954, to see the total eclipse of
the sun in Minnesota, DeVoto said he wasn't very interested in
that, but why didn't Scheinberg come along with him in August
and help him teach Adlai Stevenson all about the problems of the
West.

He had made a standing offer to Stevenson that, at Stevenson's
convenience, and no matter what else he himself was doing, he
would undertake that instruction. He and Arthur Schlesinger, Jr.,
had discussed the development of a strong conservation plank in
the Democratic platform for 1956, when Stevenson would surely
run again, and they had also had conversations about a possible
conservation congress, to be held in the West, to revise and renew
what the Roosevelt-Pinchot Conservation Congress of 1906 had
done.[4] The congress never came off, but the instruction in western problems did.[5] Stevenson and William Blair and a small
group would be coming back from Alaska and would meet De-
Voto in Missoula. There DeVoto's friends in the Region One
office of the Forest Service would take over.

It was an interlude that Stevenson, Scheinberg, and DeVoto
himself remembered as pure pleasure. The camping trip itself was
enough to ask; to DeVoto the companionship of good friends, the
presence of two people whom he loved and respected and whom
he could also instruct, the sense of being schoolmaster on important matters to the politically important, was even more. The
junket was arranged and carried out with a minimum of publicity,
though when the Stevenson plane was struck by lightning on the
way home they got a little more attention focused on the where-

abouts of the candidate than they had wanted. DeVoto was in
Missoula, at the Florence Hotel, which he called the best hotel in
the West, two days before Scheinberg and two and a half before
the Stevenson party. The Forest Service, not wanting to get embroiled in political accusations, had been discreet. The party slipped
out of town and into the mountains for two days of what the
White House correspondents have taught us to call working vacation. The movie film shot by Dr. Herb Scheinberg shows them
to have been a jovial and relaxed party. Stevenson impressed both
Scheinberg and the Forest Service with his quickness in catching
on to both the environmental and the political aspects of the
National Forests, and he indicated a subtle deference to the much-
publicized alcoholic prejudices of his mentor DeVoto when
somebody offered him scotch. "I believe in free trade," he said,
"but I would not go *that* far. Bourbon, please."[6]

Stevenson got the fishing on the Lochsa that he had been looking
forward to, and after two days he left refreshed and instructed—
the instruction was rubbed in a little later when DeVoto sent him
six single-spaced pages of notes entitled "Remember About the
West"[7]—while the Forest Service drove DeVoto and Scheinberg
down to Ogden. There one evening in the Weber Club, the only
place they could find to have a drink, DeVoto told Scheinberg,
his medical father-son, all about Robert Frost, his poetic father.
"Kronos," he called him, and surprised Scheinberg with the depth
of bitterness and hatred he revealed. He also told Scheinberg he
would never write another novel—told him and repeated it several times, though in his desk at 8 Berkeley Street a drawer contained several tries at the Cambridge novel, which dealt with
one of the avatars of Kronos and which he would go on tinkering
with in private until he died.

Walking one morning on the Union Pacific tracks near the farm
of DeVoto's grandfather Dye, DeVoto and Scheinberg were passed
by one of the last steam locomotives on the line, a survival, and in
the passing of its smoke and steam and churning drivers, Scheinberg, an eastern city boy and a Jew, felt a curiously emotional
tension. The Dye farm was gone, unrecognizable, its orchards long
since cut down to make way for a fox farm that had long since
failed. All the painful labor that the immigrant English mechanic
had expended in clearing sage, building ditches, planting and
pruning and harvesting, extending little by little his small oasis of
productive green in the Weber bottoms, had been obliterated, and
the suburbs were spreading like a skin disease outward from Ogden. And as the engine of a past time chuffed and churned by

—"To Avis and Bernard Florian Augustine, Elmer Davis, 10 February 1942."

Bernard DeVoto raising a Colt .45, a publicity photo taken in the 1940s.

Laurette Murdock, Kay Thompson (Mrs. Lovell), Bernard DeVoto, and Avis DeVoto.

Bernard DeVoto.

Bernard DeVoto and students at Radcliffe Publishing Procedures class, summer 1950.

Meeting of Advisory board, National Parks, Historic Sites, Buildings, and Monuments, Mammoth Cave National Park, Kentucky. October 26, 1951. Alfred Knopf is just behind Bernard DeVoto.

President Stearns of the University of Colorado and Bernard DeVoto.

"A gathering of characters at Erickson's Saloon." Portland, Oregon, January 12, 1954. Bernard DeVoto and Stewart Holbrook.

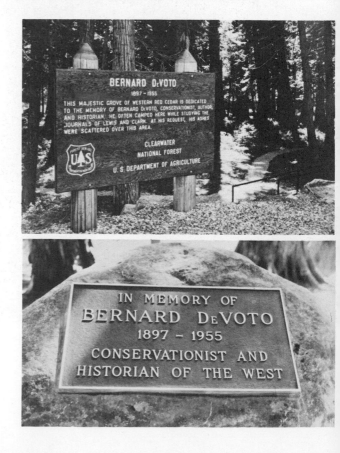

them, it seemed to Scheinberg that he had a glimpse of what it might have been like to grow up in that canyon mouth terraced by the fossil beaches of a dead lake, with the mountains behind, high and protective against the east, and the flats spreading westward to the dead salt sea. New Jerusalem, asserted and declared and chanted, and Bernard DeVoto not of it, suspicious of it, scornful of it. And yet the mountain light lay over the lucerne fields and the scattered roofs, and the protective loom of the mountains was gentle, and the gateway canyon led eastward through the mountain wall toward adventure, accomplishment, and the anguishes of maturity. Dr. Herbert Scheinberg was a sensitive and understanding man. He thought he could feel, a little, how it had been for the man beside him when he had been a boy there half a century before.

One more excursion remained. From Ogden the two hired a car and drove down to Salt Lake City—DeVoto said he wouldn't drive *into* Ogden but he didn't mind driving out, thereby declaring his undying feud even while nostalgia was at work in him—and from Salt Lake City Chet Olsen in a Forest Service car drove them over into Colorado, to the Manitou Experimental Forest, near Pike's Peak. There they met Alfred Knopf, once DeVoto's publisher when they expected Americana Deserta to sweep the country, later DeVoto's pupil in matters western.[8] Knopf, however western he might have become under DeVoto's tutelage, remained himself. He had brought with him a case of carefully selected wine, and he had arranged a dinner at the Manitou Ranger Station that made their eyes bulge. They ended on that high note, and Scheinberg hurried off to Denver and back to his duties and his daughter, left with relatives, while DeVoto came home on the train,[9] and on the way felt the euphoria of the excursion seep out of him and the vague, unplaceable symptoms of malaise reveal themselves still there, unassuaged.

Other trips were bad both going and coming, as desolate as the circuits of a traveling salesman. His lecture tours of 1953 and 1954 were an agony to him. The Leigh agency consistently overlooked his requirements, booked him for three weeks or more instead of the two that had been agreed upon, scheduled lectures during the periods that he had specified must be kept open for the writing of the Easy Chair, and scheduled him, after two or three warnings, during times when the National Parks Advisory Board was meeting. It also objected, as if to a breach of contract, when he accepted an honorific and unremunerative lecture invitation from the American Philosophical Society.[10] The lecture contract was the only ill turn that Carl Brandt had ever done him, and he had done it out of the best of motives, when it seemed he would never be able to restore him to a profitable place in the magazine market.

He was a pro. He grumbled, but he carried out the schedules the agency arranged, at a cost to his health and his peace of mind, as well as to his other work, that he ultimately found himself unwilling to pay. The long journeys, the lonesome hotel rooms, the strangers whose hospitality was either too eager or too dutiful, the waiting in airports and stations when he wanted more than anything else to be back in his study at 8 Berkeley Street or in his own living room with a handful of friends, eventually wore his patience completely out, and he begged Brandt to get him out of the contract. Brandt finally did, and none too soon. DeVoto did not like speaking before universities and women's clubs, and he felt, often correctly, that he did not thrill them. Some of the Indiana apathy seemed always present in the groups he faced—apathy or an angry repudiation of his ideas. He was not a good speaker except in indignation or before an audience he knew and trusted; and indignation was hard to sustain through many repetitions of the same written-out lectures. Even read as essays, the lectures he gave for Leigh[11] are seldom comparable in challenge and gusto with the things he wrote monthly for the Easy Chair.

And they took him from where he wanted to be; they exposed him to a loneliness that was increasingly harder on his spirit. "May six o'clock never find you alone," he says in *The Hour*. He says it humorously, but like much else in that little book, it is meant. Sometimes a joke, glancing off the unspeakable, speaks it more plainly than seriousness could. A marksman, DeVoto understood the principle. If it breaks the edge, it's a bull's-eye.

The Hour, put together out of three genial Easy Chairs and an *Atlantic* essay signed "Fairley Blake,"[12] had gone into a lot of Christmas stockings and delighted a lot of readers in the Christmas season of 1951. A mock-heroic hymn to alcohol, it is a long way from being a funny book in praise of drunkenness. In an indirect way it is a piece of American social history, part of the celebration of American folkways that was DeVoto's abiding obligation. He was not entirely joking when he said,

In the heroic age our forefathers invented self-government, the Constitution, and bourbon, and on the way to them they invented rye. . . . Our political institutions were shaped by our whiskeys, would be inconceivable without them, and share their nature. They are distilled not only from our native grains but from our native vigor, suavity, generosity, peacefulness, and love of accord. Whoever goes looking for us will find us there. . . .
The roads ran out in dust or windswept grass and we went on, we

came to a river no one had crossed and we forded it, the land angled upward and we climbed to the ridge and exulted, the desert stretched ahead and we plunged into it—and always the honeybee flew ahead of us and there was a hooker of the real stuff at day's end and one for the road tomorrow. Nothing stopped us from sea to shining sea, nothing could stop us, the jug was plugged tight with a corncob, and we built new commonwealths and constitutions and distilleries as we travelled, the world gaped, and destiny said here's how.[13]

But *The Hour* is not simply a piece of humorous cultural patriotism either. It is a manual of witchcraft, a book of spells and observances. If it makes jokes, it makes them to mislead and confuse the desperate necessities from which the Hour is the surest and sometimes the only escape. Epicurus was the remote ancestor of these rituals; nobody ever understood better that the justification for our brief and precious pleasures is the abiding certainty of pain.

All sorts of things, in DeVoto's view, were important in the rituals of drinking. The place, for instance—best of all, the home; next best, a good, quiet, restful bar with low lights and low voices. The liquor? Rye or bourbon, honest American whiskey with honest branch water, and for special occasions and purposes the martini, made according to the mystic formulas and with a regard for the proprieties. No bargain brands—"Cheap liquor is grudge liquor"—and none of the sickening concoctions, reversions to the soda fountains of childhood, that hostesses commonly called cocktails. And the people? Friends, no more than a handful, including an attractive woman or two. As for the preparations, especially the preparation of the martini, those were distillations of witchcraft feasible only to the properly purified soul.

You began by selecting, through long experiment, a gin and a vermouth that were compatible with each other and with your taste, and having found them, you stuck with them. You proceeded with an accumulation of ice—five hundred pounds of ice. When you mixed, you measured, 3.7 to 1, for the martinis should not vary from round to round. You mixed quickly but not hastily, and you mixed only what you would immediately pour. When you mixed again, you dumped the dregs and renewed the ice and started from scratch.

The goal is purification and that will begin after the first round has been poured, so I see no need for preliminary spiritual exercises. But it is best approached with a tranquil mind, lest the necessary speed become haste. Tranquility ought normally to come with sight of the familiar bottles. If it doesn't, feel free to hum a simple tune as you go about your preparations; it should be nostalgic but not sentimental, neither barbershop nor jazz, between the choir and the glee club. Do not whistle, for your companions are sinking into the quiet of expectation. And you need not sing, for presently there will be singing in your heart.[14]

The thaumaturge of *The Hour* was himself a more complex and difficult mixture than the potion whose secrets he revealed. Essences and elixirs of many kinds had gone into him: flavors from Mark Twain and H. L. Mencken, extracts squeezed from Sinclair Lewis in a manic and verbose mood, tinctures from Mormon preachers and frontier Methodist spellbinders, pauses and hyperboles caught from rivermen and mule skinners and tellers of tall yarns. What he produced was a most American performance, unmistakable and tall. And under it, through it, behind it, forcing its creation and threatening every minute to interrupt or destroy it, was the panic from which in his whole life DeVoto never escaped for long.

May six o'clock never find you alone, for late afternoon finds all of us "with all lost but courage, fighting honor's rear-guard action without hope. . . . That last shuddering half hour!—the soul shredded to excelsior, the heart deaf and blind, the nerves carrying the overload that will burn out the last fuse. . . ." And then the escape, the jaws that snap shut just as we go out the door, and the sudden sanctuary, the promise of peace, the nerves quivering into quiet. For

This is the violet hour, the hour of hush and wonder, when the affections glow and valor is reborn, when the shadows deepen magically along the edge of the forest and we believe that, if we watch carefully, at any moment we may see the unicorn. . . .[15]

The Giant Killer, Ernest Hemingway called liquor, and in regard to it, as in regard to so much else in his life, he practiced rituals, observances, offices, skills, charms, magic formulas that are so close to the compulsions of a terrified and propitiatory child that psychologically there is probably no difference. He was a Catholic convert, DeVoto an apostate Catholic. Both found identical uses for identical magics.

> Like one that on a lonesome road
> Doth walk in fear and dread,
> And having once turned round, walks on
> And turns no more his head;
> Because he knows a fearful fiend
> Doth close behind him tread,

DeVoto went through a strenuous, productive, socially useful, sometimes heroic life working his head off so as not to notice what

lurked just behind him. When he looked up as dusk gathered in the
street, he went straight across the hall from the double study to
the double parlor, from books to bottles. Writing humorous essays
about it did not remove the necessity or quiet the inner trembling
more than temporarily. That was why he so liked the company of
friends, why his house had always been a hospitable house. That
was why, through all the later years of his life, he and Avis
designed and then found themselves dependent upon the Sunday
Evening Hour.

Expressing him, the Sunday Evenings sustained him. The participants changed over the years as young faculty friends were not
promoted or moved away or took other jobs, as people faded from
close friendship or were divided by divorce, as new Harvard or
Boston or Cambridge members of the elect appeared and were
confirmed, as old friends happened through town. The group was
never large—rarely more than four or five couples, often fewer.
Across the years, DeVoto had much to do with psychoanalysts,
and though the strategy of the profession prohibited social relationships between the patient and his healer, there were other members of the profession whose friendship was not thus inhibited, and
once analysis had been terminated, so-called "supportive treatment"
did not call for social separateness. So there was generally an
analyst in the inner circle—for a while William Barrett, during
the Annisquam summers Beata Rank, still later Gregory Rochlin.
DeVoto's secretaries, too, became friends, handmaidens, admirers,
dependents, and if not so often present at the more ritualistic
Sunday Evenings, were almost always part of the similar gathering
at the end of a working day. Rosie Chapman, Elaine Breed, Parian
Temple, Julie Jeppson (who after DeVoto's death married his
last analyst, Alfred Ludwig), all moved as inevitably as DeVoto
himself from study to parlor when the clock struck the hour.
Mollie Brazier, an English physiologist who had been stranded in
Boston by the war, was a regular. So, after her divorce, was Anne
Barrett. So was Elizabeth Kennedy, who lived just through the
lot, and less often her husband Sargent Kennedy, the Harvard
registrar. Old Harvard friends like the Paul Bucks and the Murdocks, newer Harvard friends like John Kenneth Galbraith and his
wife, old students like Arthur Schlesinger, Jr., literary friends like
Walter D. Edmonds, made up a circle that was singularly regular
and faithful.[16]

These were the people who saw Benny DeVoto with the masks
off and the guard down. This was the time when he was at his best
as a storyteller, an argufier, a laugher at the absurdities of the
world or of some acquaintance or himself. He was never more

earnest than when talking with this close group of friends about things that troubled or excited him. He was never less inhibited in expressing himself than after six on Sundays, unless perhaps in his letters to Kate Sterne. Sometimes he overspoke, sometimes his old habit of never knowing when enough was enough led him to say what one of his women friends referred to as "skunky things." She forgave him, as others did, because in the whole scale of friendship the mouthiness of a moment, especially after two or three martinis, did not weigh heavily. In a way, that sort of remark revealed his own insecurity and made people protective about him, as he had once felt protective about the implacable prejudices of L. J. Henderson.

In the later stages of the Sunday Evening development the regulars were the Kennedys, Rochlins, Galbraiths, and Schlesingers. A good deal of the political discussion and speculation that developed into Americans for Democratic Action and was a force in the two Stevenson campaigns and finally rode into Washington to usher in the new Augustan Age of John F. Kennedy was initiated in the double parlors at 8 Berkeley Street. The old DeVoto Academy eventually came to include some major intellectual movers and shakers, and all of them felt his influence, some very strongly. But it is not likely that he would have gone to Washington with the rest of Cambridge if he had lived to see Kennedy elected. For one thing, the close association of Robert Frost with the Kennedy victory would have been uncomfortable for him. For another, he never shared the admiration of his friends for John F. Kennedy, whom he knew primarily as his congressman.[17]

Political, inevitably, the Sunday Evenings sometimes were. But the principal reason for the gatherings at 8 Berkeley Street, which usually ended with Avis getting together a supper for eight or ten people, was the same that had led the DeVotos to fill their Evanston apartment with the bright boys and pretty girls of Northwestern University thirty years before; the same that had led DeVoto to issue an invitation that was almost but not quite an appeal to an unknown Harvard undergraduate named Robeson Bailey; the same that had turned the Lincoln house into a weekend potlatch of friends—Bucks and Murdocks and Morrisons and, Zinssers, and always a changing stream of the young, and always a troubled neighbor, a blocked writer, a woman in emotional or nervous trouble, who had adopted DeVoto as father and lay psychiatrist, and by whom, in helping, he was helped.

Once he had written about Sigmund Freud, "There is a noble and tragic poetry in his vision of man's journey deathward from childhood, beset by terrors whose shape and import are disguised from him, striving to discipline a primitive inheritance of delusion and rebellion into a livable accord with reality, striving to establish mastery over disruptive instincts, striving to achieve a social adaptation of anarchic drives."[18] In writing that, he might have been writing a rubric for his life. Friendship and alcohol, like art, like work, were part of his effort to die sane. He was a long way from being an alcoholic, though he used alcohol regularly and largely. For reasons inextricable from his sense of where safety lay, he was the absolute opposite of a solitary drinker.

May six o'clock never find you alone.

9 · *Deathward from Childhood*

Ognuno sta solo sul cuor della terra
trafitto da un raggio di sole:
ed è subito sera.
                              Salvatore Quasimodo

And suddenly it is evening.

Fighting his wars, earning his living, worrying about the future and his health, pushing himself beyond his endurance and his rallying capacity, finding his safety in rituals of a King's X hour and in friends whom he sometimes insulted even though he loved them, or perhaps *because* he did, he came finally to the place where neither body nor mind would quite obey his will. He sickened, and could not tell where, nor whether mind or body had sickened first. But he thought that the physiological ailments were the horse, and his anxieties the cart, rather than the other way around, when he allowed Herbert Scheinberg to hospitalize him for tests, in June 1952.

Actually Scheinberg was not too worried about the symptoms that DeVoto described: an "empty soreness or sore emptiness" in the viscera, a general, undifferentiated, unfocused discomfort that might well have been only an expression of his hypochondria but that he was irritated to hear called a "nervous stomach." Scheinberg, aware of his history of nervous trouble, thought his anxiety probably out of proportion to his symptoms, but he wanted to evaluate the hypertension that his medical record showed to be of long standing. Tests showed the hypertension to be consistent but asymptomatic. There was nothing wrong with his heart, kidneys, brain. There was nothing at all, in fact, except a smoker's cough, not surprising in a man who smoked two packs a day, and a small hard spot on the prostate that X rays suggested did not mean anything.[1]

Anxiety was the horse, then; the sensation of emptiness might come from the cavity where a new book should be. He began therapy sessions with Dr. Alfred "Dutch" Ludwig, complaining all the time about not being able to work and turning out work enough for four. Nothing assuaged the gnawing in him, not the Stevenson campaign, not the conservation and civil-liberties battles, not the satisfaction of winning the National Book Award for *The Course of Empire*. He was one of those whom the Buddha described, one of those who strive always toward fulfillment, and in fulfillment yearn to feel desire. The spoiled M.D. and the psychoanalyst manqué who were part of him quarreled about his symptoms. There was a time when he was dismayed to find his beard perceptibly less heavy than it formerly was. He went to Boston doctors, but he fully trusted only Scheinberg, who was father and son as well as healer but who now lived in New York. A letter he wrote Scheinberg on May 5, 1954, is typical:

Whenever I haven't anything better to do I think up a hypochondria. I've thought up another one. Ludwig says so and I agree with him. It's all mixed up with a recent exposure to a father image who had almost had lung cancer, with various other episodes in my incredible psychic life, and, so Ludwig says, to some extent with you. Anyway, besides my normal cigarette cough I've been having vague and quite indefinable, mild, changeable, and perhaps imaginary sensations here and there in my chest. On Ludwig's word, not heart symptoms, not lung cancer symptoms, symptoms he gets three times a day from his couch. . . . but sometimes they are unmistakably carcinoma of the lungs and I was buried several weeks ago. Apparently Ludwig is in process of chasing them to their lair but since I'm going to be in New York anyway, he says, why not reassure myself with the chest x-ray you didn't take last time.[2]

Scheinberg took the chest X ray, which showed no carcinoma, but DeVoto was not reassured. He came back from New York still gnawed by nameless symptoms. In July, Dr. Richard Muellner, in Boston, took a closer look at the prostate and concluded that there was nothing there but a benign hypertrophy. He did not want to bring on a new wave of anxiety by proposing a biopsy, which in any case did not seem to be indicated. He assured Scheinberg that he would keep an eye on it. In August DeVoto took

Scheinberg West with him, and during the two weeks of travel, during which he had all the pleasures of a paternal, filial, or magisterial demonstration of the West as it really was, he had no symptoms. But they returned as *he* returned, and by Christmas the sore emptiness or the empty soreness was with him steadily, and did not go away. He experimented with diet. Sourly, he even contemplated going on the wagon. As Cambridge emerged out of winter and the crocuses popped up through the blackened and sooty lawns on Berkeley Street, there was no ease in his body or peace in his mind. As before, he went on turning out work. He even seriously began the book he tentatively called *Western Paradox*.

Carl Brandt by that time had him solidly lined up with editors who valued his contributions. His problem was not now to sell what he wrote but to write what he had already sold. Much of the summer of 1955 he spent driving around New England gathering material for travel articles, but even driving country roads in the region he loved, dining in good inns and filling his eyes with the evidence of a formed and shapely American civilization, could not relieve his symptoms or lift his depression. His visit to Bread Loaf in August was, for him at least, bleak. He knew he would not listen to Ted Morrison's urging that he return as a staff member and do for non-fiction what he had used to do for fiction. In Treman's crowded parlor there were too many strange faces; in the cold mountain dusk he could smell the oncoming of winter.[3]

He gave his lecture, aware that many in the audience had come to hear the volcano erupt and the ogre roar. But he couldn't erupt and roar for them. He gave them a talk that he himself thought lame, though Bill Sloane remembers it as a splendid exposition of the technique of synecdoche—how one might write a social history of New England through consideration of a single town[4]—and Ted Morrison recalls it as "impressive to the point of brilliance."[5] But DeVoto thought it lame, and went lamely off toward Maine, where the vacationland blight so offended him that he did erupt. He belched up an Easy Chair, "Outdoor Metropolis," in which he described the tourist promotions that had turned coastal Maine, and southern New Hampshire as well, into a "jerry-built, neon-lighted, overpopulated slum." That Easy Chair in turn so offended the Maine Tourist Bureau that its director angrily announced the withdrawal of all Maine advertising from *Harper's*. Harper's then responded angrily to the boycott of a free and independent press, and demanded and extracted an apology from Governor Muskie for his subordinate's words, and a restoration of the withdrawn advertising.

A characteristic DeVoto performance. His exposure of an environmental disease and his recommendation for its cure—state controls over the spread of the resort business, controls as strict as those of the National Park Service if necessary—was reprinted with approval in Florida and California and Vermont. Editorials and letters cried, "Sic 'em, Tige!" to the Easy Chair. The old watchdog was still on the job. It might have occurred to some that "Easy Chair" was the wrong label for that column. "Fire Alarm" might have suited it better.

Nevertheless, it was as *The Easy Chair* that DeVoto's third collection of essays, all culled from that misnamed department, was published, in the first week of November 1955. It represented him, it contained all his causes and enthusiasms and angers, it summed him up, and he began to get early and prompt response from readers even before the book was officially out. He had spoken the minds of a lot of people who did not dare speak their own. Their communications touched him, as did the publication parties: the little incidental book was something of an event, a milestone. Unknown to him, *Harper's* had conspired with Louis Lyons, the bellwether of the Nieman Fellows who conducted a news-commentary program called "Backgrounds" on WGBH-TV, to present to Benny DeVoto over the air a bound volume of the November *Harper's* containing the twentieth anniversary essay ("Number 241") and an inscription from the editors. The inscription read:

To Bernard DeVoto, seasoned practitioner of the journalistic craft, widely ranging in competence and punctual in deadlines, as resolute in his approvals as in his dislikes, partisan of sound sense and adversary of cant, friend of the public lands and enemy of the lukewarm martini, who in the twenty years he has occupied the Easy Chair has never learned to write a dull sentence.

On November 13 he was supposed to be in New York to appear on the CBS show "Adventure," a series in which he functioned as an authority and commentator on the West. As had become his habit, he had arranged to have dinner after the show with Herb Scheinberg and one or two other friends. But DeVoto's heart was not in the trip. On November 3 he wrote Scheinberg:

I've had a note from Shelby Gordon saying they'll want me in N Y the 12th. So dinner is O K, and very swell. That is, provided.
The real question is whether I can bring myself to go on down to Washington for a week, the next day, Monday I mean. The shabby

truth is that either my gut or my neurosis has been giving me hell all
fall, and is giving me particular hell now, & is building up a fine case
why I shouldn't go to Washington or for that matter anywhere. My
drive is to run out on everything, including the Democratic Party &
our old travelling companion.

I've been to see Wessler. He says it's just more of the same. That
doesn't ease the drive.

I don't know how I'll work it out. Humiliatingly, no doubt. But I'll let
you know. And so far I can contemplate New York without going
nuts.

He nerved himself up to make the trip, and appeared as scheduled
on "Adventure" at 3:30 P.M., Sunday, November 13. The stimulation of the show was good for him. He enjoyed it and was in
cheerful spirits when he walked back to his room at the Gotham
with Scheinberg, who had attended the show. They sat on the
bed and talked a while.

And so six o'clock did not find him alone.

Because not even close and filial friendship canceled the medical necessities and professional obligations, Scheinberg's notes, dictated the next day, reported the evening in detail.

11/13/55

About 6 P.M., while half-lying-half-sitting on a bed and talking quietly,
this 58 year old writer suddenly began to have epigastric pain. This
was pressure which was below xiphoid and did not radiate to chest,
back, arms, neck, or legs. He defecated and began to sweat pro-
fusely with pallor, pulse unobtainable and continued pain. Over the
next half hour the pain moved down to halfway between umbilicus and
xiphoid. There was vomiting and diarrhea and continued diaphoresis.
About 40 minutes after onset he complained that his right foot was going to sleep and then of pain in the right foot, then calf and then thigh.
Pallor and sweating continued and the abdominal and thigh pain remained severe enough to require morphine.

The patient has had hypertension of about 200–230/110–130 for an unknown number of years. There has been no evidence of cardiac, renal,
or cerebral complications, but his aortic shadow has shown widening
in x-rays taken over past three years. He has never been known to
fibrillate.

P.E.: Sweating, cold. Heart slow and regular. Abdomen soft. No right
dorsalis pedis, posterior tibial, femoral or radial pulses felt. Left good.

Impression: Dissecting aneurysm of aorta.

Course: Patient was given 15 mgs. of morphine sulphate before being
taken by ambulance to Presbyterian Hospital. Abdominal pain continued severe, although his leg got better. At Presbyterian he was given
10 mgs. of morphine sulphate at 8:15 P.M. and was taken from the ad-

mitting floor to a room. His blood pressure was taken by me in the left arm and was 190/110. He asked what this meant and about a minute thereafter gasped and was unconscious. No heart or pulse beat could be obtained and a needle containing adrenalin was introduced left of the sternum. No blood was obtained, but either by the stimulus of the needle or for some other reason the heart began to beat again. Limb leads of the EKG taken at this time were normal in rhythm and shape. He began to breathe, having stopped briefly, opened his eyes and looked around momentarily. He then again became unconscious and soon thereafter his heart beat became disorganized electrocardiographically and he died.

Those almost grimly medical notes say nothing of Scheinberg's feelings when in the room at the Gotham, feeling the pulse changes that in 1955 indicated a condition 100 per cent fatal, he heard Benny DeVoto say, "It's bad, isn't it?" and could only answer, "I don't know, but I think we'd better get you over to the hospital." Nothing of the excruciating slow ambulance ride through dense evening traffic, with an ambulance driver who would not use his siren. Nothing of the desperation of the effort to save a man he knew was already dead.

DeVoto died in good hands, in spite of quick, efficient, trained, and most personal efforts of a most trusted friend to keep him alive. If he was going to have a heart attack instead of the lung cancers and stomach cancers of his anxiety, he couldn't have arranged to have it at a better place or time, when he was having a quiet drink and talk with his friend and doctor. And he was perhaps lucky, too, that Dr. Scheinberg's care did not pull him through. For as if to illustrate the inescapable justifications for human anxiety, the autopsy revealed that the apparently benign hard spot on the prostate was a well-developed adenocarcinoma that would have killed him far more painfully within a year or two.

So the humorous tribute that the editors of *Harper's* had written in the presentation copy containing the 241st Easy Chair was read over the air not as a living accolade but as an obituary. As a matter of fact, DeVoto had written a form of his own obituary in that essay that summed up his twenty years of monthly journalism and his career as gadfly and public thinker. His journalism, he said, had been personal, because it had seemed to want to be that way. It had taken on all sorts of jobs from the trivial to the urgent—a lot of them because no one else seemed likely to do them and they must not be left undone.

My job is to write about anything in American life that may interest me, but it is also to arrive at judgments under my own steam. . . . With some judgments that is the end of the line; express them and you have nothing more to do. But there are also judgments that require you to commit yourself, to stick your neck out. Expressing them in print obliges you to go on to advocacy. They get home to people's beliefs and feelings about important things, and that makes them inflammable.

If he were to put a single label on what he had written in the Easy Chair, he said, he would call it "cultural criticism," and the buried Howells in him rose to the surface when he insisted that "no manifestation of American life is trivial to the critic of culture." Something else rose—pride—in his final paragraph:

I hope that what I have said has been said gracefully and that sometimes it has been amusing, or informative, or useful. No one has got me to say anything I did not want to say and no one has prevented me from saying anything I wanted to. The Easy Chair has given me a place in the journalism of my time. No one knows better than a journalist that his work is ephemeral. As I have said in my preface, it is not important, it is only indispensable. The life or the half life of an issue of *Harper's* has never been calculated; the magazine has durable covers but even the copies kept in doctors' waiting rooms wear out and are dumped in the bay or ground up for pulp. But a historian knows that a lot of writing which has no caste mark on its forehead gets dumped in the bay too, and that he can count on finding bound files of *Harper's* in library stacks. He has to use them; he cannot write history without them.

The historian has to use Bernard DeVoto, too; he cannot write the history of his times without him, though some of the parties and coteries he was at war with have tried.

In the days following his death, that fact was not unapparent. He was a force that had passed, a wind that had suddenly died and left a stillness. Eric Severeid, Alistair Cooke, Senators Neuberger and Metcalf, editorial writers and politicians and conservationists memorialized him and regretted his passing and wondered who would do his work.[6] They were agreed it would take three men. (If they looked back from 1973 they would have to agree it has not been done.) They called him hardheaded and softhearted, the nation's environmental conscience and liberty's watchdog, the West's most comprehensive historian and most affectionate spokesman and most acid critic.

On November 15, at 2 P.M., in Christ Church, Cambridge, where the DeVotos' musically gifted son, Mark, had been a choir boy and was now a bell ringer, DeVoto's old Harvard companion Melville Smith, Director of the Longy School of Music, played Bach and César Franck for his memorial service and the congregation was made up of friends gathered from Cambridge, Boston, New York, Washington. If he had been alive, he might have remarked humbly how many people sincerely grieved for his loss. The ushers were long-time members of the inner circle of the DeVoto Academy: Sargent Kennedy, Mark Saxton, Lovell Thompson, Kenneth Murdock, Theodore Morrison, Arthur Schlesinger, Jr., Walter Edmonds.[7] The pews were filled with former students, old Harvard colleagues, writers and publishers and editors, people who had learned from him and liked him and been offended by him and had come out on the affectionate side of exasperation into wholehearted respect. He had made heavy demands on all who knew him well, but he had paid back, often in advance and almost always with interest, the drafts he had made on their friendship. And he had made even heavier demands on himself. One test of that was the way in which they remembered him: not haunted, not anxious, not distraught or gloomy, though inside himself he had been all of those much of the time. They remembered the pleasure and excitement they had derived from his company and his talk and his crackle of ideas. As Samuel Eliot Morison wrote Avis shortly after DeVoto's death, "Benny's conversation was sparkling; his writings, whether essays or history, were lively and vivid; his erudition in western history and American literature was amazing; his friendship warm and responsive."[8]

And how, said Mrs. Howard Mumford Jones, how he could wake up a room!

One final detail. In mid-April of the following year Avis heard from Chet Olsen, who had been entrusted with a friend's duty. Benny DeVoto had wanted his ashes scattered over one of the national forests, and James Vessey, one of his close Forest Service friends, had suggested the Lochsa. He had sent Olsen a map showing the approximate spot where Benny used to sit on a rock beside the stream and make remarks about anyone who would rather be riding a goddam horse. Olsen sent the map now to Avis, showing the spot on the Lochsa River between the Powell Ranger Station and Lolo Pass where Operation Lochsa had just been completed by him personally, in a plane rented from the Johnson Flying Service of Missoula. It was a beautiful day, Olsen said, the first good day of spring. The area was covered with an unusual depth of snow. He had seen not a person, a smoke, or a wild creature as he and the pilot made their pass.

That was the end of Benny DeVoto's journey deathward from childhood. He sifted down as a handful of light ash—and probably illegal at that—over a forest wilderness he had loved. In twisting the arm of his inward coward, and in achieving mastery over his anarchic drives and bending his disruptive instincts to socially useful ends, he had first had to teach himself courage and then make himself live by it.

He never expected perfection, and even his most fitting memorial did not achieve it. When, some years after his death, Chet Olsen and James Vessey, with Gregory Rochlin, Senator Metcalf, and others organized a memorial for him on the Lochsa, they debated between an inscribed granite boulder and a bronze plaque, and decided on the plaque. As Vessey said, either stone or bronze was sure to be mutilated eventually—he was a man who had dealt with the traveling and vacationing public, and knew—but a plaque could be renewed from time to time, whereas a carved boulder, once defaced, would have to remain in its spoiled condition forever.

The reasoning would have pleased DeVoto. It acknowledged the principle of destructiveness and evil in the universe and especially in the damned human race, which sooner or later defaces everything, even what it reveres. But it asserted as well the capacity for renewal and repair that inheres in the human will. It said that you *can* exert sense and foresight and wisdom and care in this lamentable world, and that you should expect to have to.

At first they planned to fasten his plaque on a four hundred year-old western red cedar, a tree fifty inches through at breast height, in a grove that he had several times admired. In the end they fastened it to a boulder, as more lasting, and then dedicated the whole grove to him in another sign. There tourists who probably never heard his name, but should have, can read a sentence or two about him, there in the state where he wished he had been born, on a stream that he loved, at the side of a historic trail that he had followed from end to end with the excitement of discovery.

Notes

Most of Bernard DeVoto's papers, manuscripts, correspondence, and memorabilia, as well as his extensive personal library, are at Stanford University. Small collections of letters are among the Henry L. Mencken papers at the New York Public Library, the Robert Frost papers at the Dartmouth College Library, and the Alfred Knopf papers, destined for the University of Texas Library but quoted here directly from a Xerox copy of the files provided me by Mr. Knopf before the transfer to Austin. A body of youthful letters dating from 1919 to 1921 is in the possession of Mrs. Arthur Perkins of Ogden, Utah; and I have been privileged to see and quote from a folder of late, revealing letters written to Dr. Herbert Scheinberg of New York City. Numerous random items, as well as the complete correspondence between DeVoto and his last literary agent, Carl Brandt, are in my own files. These will shortly find their way into the DeVoto archive at Stanford. Files turned over to me by Arthur Schlesinger, Jr., Kenneth Murdock, Dr. Lawrence Kubie, and Robert Stearns have already found their way there.

When previously unpublished items are quoted, the sources are indicated by the following abbreviations. If no designation appears, the item is in my own possession, which means, shortly, Stanford's.

BB—Brandt & Brandt
DCL—Dartmouth College Library
NYPL—New York Public Library
KBP—Katharine Becker Perkins
SUL—Stanford University Library
AAK—Alfred A. Knopf
HS—Herbert Scheinberg

When the source of any fact or quotation is identified adequately in the text, I have not bothered to duplicate the identification in the notes; and I have not appended a bibliography, because that of Julius Barclay, in *Four Portraits and One Subject: Bernard DeVoto*, Houghton Mifflin, 1963, is virtually complete on DeVoto's own writings and is readily available. It is from DeVoto's own writings, more than from any other source, that this biography has been made. The life of a man who wrote so much, and so directly out of his own thought, experience, and feeling, demands to be considered as a sort of annotated bibliography.

I THE AMNIOTIC HOME

Chapter 1 ·

1. BDV to Melville Smith, July 8, 1920. SUL

Chapter 2 ·

1. Despite frequent assertions throughout his life that he hated Ogden and all it stood for, DeVoto gave just as frequent evidence that its physical setting remained vivid in his memory. He wrote the Wasatch and its canyons into his earliest novels as well as into his last one, *Mountain Time*, and always in celebratory terms. In the last year of his life he wrote his most nostalgic description of the canyons and their influence on his boyhood, and specifically took back much of what he had previously said about Ogden as a living-place. See "Good Place to Grow In," *Lincoln-Mercury Times* VIII (March–April), 1956, pp. 1–3.

2. In an autobiographizing fit inspired by his invalid pen pal Kate Sterne, DeVoto in the mid-1930s produced a number of essays dealing with the historical, social, and intellectual, as opposed to the geographical, aspects of the Ogden of his boyhood. See especially "Jonathan Dyer, Frontiersman," *Harper's* CLXVII (September 1933), pp. 491–501 (reprinted in *Forays and Rebuttals* as "The Life of Jonathan Dyer"), and "Fossil Remnants of the Frontier: Notes on a Utah Boyhood," *Harper's* CLXX (April 1935), pp. 590–600. The tone of these, as well as the later "A Sagebrush Bookshelf," *Harper's* CLXXV (October 1937), pp. 488–96, is notably mellower than that of his earlier essays about Utah. Both the personal grudge and the literary convention of revolt from the village have passed with the 1920s.

3. BDV to Robert S. Forsythe, October 6, 1927. SUL. In this letter DeVoto provides a brief family history, along with thumbnail sketches of his parents and both his grandfathers, as a basis for the biographical and critical booklet that Forsythe was preparing for Macmillan. At the age of thirty, DeVoto still speaks of his father as "the finest mind I have ever known," a statement that tells as much about his own capacity for hyperbolic intellectual admiration as about his father's intellectual attainments.

4. Family tradition may well have been helped along by Bernard's imagination. In 1926, in response to a query from his son, Florian DeVoto made certain corrections: "As to your reading Pope, I can not say where you first got it. While Alice, Edith and Rhoda studied their

lessons at the table, you in your high chair attempted to grab their books. I then got the magazines for you and you thumbed the advertisements. Your first impressions of form, however, were from the paper on the ceiling and I told your mother then that they were interesting you—so when you got the magazines you soon distinguished between the letters, the kids, mother, and myself telling you. You learned the alphabet long before you began to talk. When you did talk, you went forward rapidly. Your first recital was the Three Little Kittens and their mittens. Mother had been reading it to you sometime and you memorized it. Hiawatha was the first book you mastered, then Poe's poems. I think Pope came next, tho you were still in dresses. . . ." Florian DeVoto to BDV, July 29, 1926. SUL.

5. BDV to Robert S. Forsythe, October 6, 1927. SUL.

6. Glenway Wescott, *Good-bye, Wisconsin*, Harper & Brothers, 1928, p. 39.

7. Her distaste, though in keeping with the sentiments of many people in Ogden, was perhaps excessive, since she had had two close relatives to protect from the contamination of DeVoto's company; her younger brother, who was an early friend of BDV's, and her son, who was later a pupil of his at North Junior High School. But the resentment and dislike that his name brought up in her existed to some degree in most good Mormon families with whom he had contact. He threatened what they wished to preserve.

8. His "autobiographizing" letters to Kate Sterne indicate that at various times during his youth he worked on the Salt Lake and Ogden Railroad as expressman, ticket seller, bookkeeper, brakeman, and general factotum (BDV to Kate Sterne, June 27, 1934. SUL); and that he worked on a road-building gang and as a cowboy in the Raft River Valley; and that he wrote in several capacities and at several times for the Ogden *Standard-Examiner*. To other correspondents he confided that he had worked cattle on the Platte and had mucked in a mine, location not specified. Some of this seems the innocent prevarication and exaggeration of a boy desperate to shine, though the stories persist well into his maturity. The summer on the Salt Lake and Ogden, the stints with the *Standard-Examiner*, and the (very brief) cowboy episode on the Raft River are corroborated by other evidence. The other experiences may be either imaginary or exaggerated.

9. He discusses his early experiences with books in "A Sagebrush Bookshelf," *Harper's* CLXXV (October 1937), pp. 488–96.

Chapter 3 ·

1. There are twelve letters and five poems, dated from October 3, 1915, shortly after BDV arrived at Harvard, to October 24, 1916. Two were written from Ogden in the summer of 1916. SUL.

2. His Harvard transcript shows a grade of B in History 2 and in History 32a and 32b, and an A in History of Science (with Henderson).

3. BDV to Harvard College, November 25, 1915. Personnel File, Registrar's Office, Harvard University.

4. Garrett Mattingly, *Bernard DeVoto, a Preliminary Appraisal*, Little, Brown, 1938, p. 19.

5. Bernard DeVoto, "The Maturity of American Literature," *Saturday Review of Literature* XXVII (August 5, 1944), pp. 14–18.

6. Ibid. But this somewhat captious judgment is contradicted by DeVoto's respectful memorial to Hurlbut in *Harvard Graduates' Magazine* XXXVIII (March 1930), pp. 302–7, and by his respectful, even reverential friendship for Dean Briggs.

7. BDV to Kate Sterne, "The Kent Potter Story," first installment, p. 2. SUL. This is a fictionalized account of the Hagler story, written for the entertainment of DeVoto's invalid friend Kate Sterne. It is filed as a separate manuscript with the DeVoto Papers at Stanford and is a useful, though not always reliable, fragment of autobiography. Since all the Sterne correspondence is in the Stanford Library safe, it will not hereafter be identified by library in the notes.

8. Ibid. These same Harvard years are recollected in Malcolm Cowley, *Exile's Return*.

9. Malcolm Cowley, *Exile's Return*, Viking (Compass Books), p. 38.

10. "Exiles from Reality," *Saturday Review of Literature* X (June 2, 1934), pp. 721–22.

11. BDV to Kate Sterne, "The Kent Potter Story," first installment, p. 4.

Chapter 4·

1. Ricardo Quintana to WS, July 1971. Tape.

2. There are eighteen of these, dated from May 11 to October 7, 1918. SUL.

3. BDV to Mother and Dad, June 15, 1918. SUL.

4. BDV to Mother and Dad, June 23, 1918. SUL.

5. BDV to Mother and Dad, June 30, 1918. SUL.

6. BDV to Mother and Dad, undated, but from context early July 1918. SUL.

7. Personnel File, Harvard Appointment Office, Harvard University.

Chapter 5·

1. BDV to the Secretary of Harvard College, January 8, 1919. Personnel File, Harvard University Registrar's Office.

2. BDV to Robert S. Forsythe, October 6, 1927. SUL.

3. Katharine Becker, the girl with whom DeVoto was infatuated from 1919 to 1921, eventually married his first Harvard roommate, Arthur Perkins, and in the summer of 1973 was still living in Ogden. The original letters, still in her possession, were transcribed for possible publication by Constance O. Bunnell, a friend. It is this transcription from which, through Mrs. Bunnell's kindness and with Mrs. Perkins' permission, I have quoted.

4. BDV to Kate Sterne, "The Kent Potter Story," second installment, p. 2. SUL.

5. In conversation. Considering that for many years, from Harvard on, he and his friends lost a good deal of skin in BDV's attacks on the literary and the Left, Mr. Cowley shows a generous and understanding spirit in his recollections. As in many other of his persistent quarrels, DeVoto's objections to Cowley were intellectual and not personal; he in fact often seemed to avoid personal contact with those he attacked, for fear his intellectual disagreement would be softened by liking. The rift between him and Cowley was at least partially healed in 1944 by Cowley's temperance on the issue of DeVoto's book *The Literary Fallacy* and by their alliance on the question of book censorship, specifically the *Strange Fruit* case. See Section VI, Chapter 2, "Fools, Liars, and Mr. DeVoto."

6. Ricardo Quintana to WS, July 1971. Tape.

7. BDV to Kate Sterne, "The Kent Potter Story," second installment, p. 2.

8. Mattingly, *Bernard DeVoto*, p. 11.

9. Ibid., p. 10.

10. This is an inference from BDV to Byron Hurlbut, Sept. 15, 1920, SUL, in which BDV tells the story of the acceptance and then rejection of his editorial on Senator Reed Smoot. I find no references to any other "liberal weekly" in the early correspondence.

11. In "The Kent Potter Story" BDV told Kate Sterne that he refused the Belgian fellowship that Dean Briggs and Henderson "threw his way." But a letter from Dean Briggs (Briggs to BDV, May 14, 1920, SUL) indicates that DeVoto was not recommended for the fellowship. Briggs says that if the recipient chooses not to accept, DeVoto might have a good chance as an alternate.

12. BDV never liked his Aunt Rose, who was pious and who was, he thought, inordinately severe with her daughters. One of these, Rose (Mrs. Jean-Marie Guislain), BDV did like, and in later years he went out of his way to assist her husband, an artist and writer. During the Harvard years and the years immediately following, Florian DeVoto's letters to his son scold him for not writing to his aunt, and for disregarding her religious suggestions. See, for example, Florian DeVoto

to BDV, September 3, no year, and Florian DeVoto to BDV, September 23, 1927. SUL.

13. Mattingly, *Bernard DeVoto*, pp. 10–11.

Chapter 6

1. BDV to Melville Smith, August 4, 1920. SUL.

2. BDV to Melville Smith, undated but from context late August or early September 1920. SUL.

3. BDV to Byron Hurlbut, September 15, 1920. SUL.

4. BDV to Melville Smith, October 22, 1920. SUL.

5. BDV to Melville Smith, November 9, 1920. SUL.

6. Martha Guernsey, one of the recurrent figures of BDV's amatory fantasies.

7. BDV to Melville Smith, November 9, 1920. SUL.

8. BDV to Melville Smith, December 17, 1920. SUL.

9. The letters from Clarissa Hagler to BDV, dated from November 8, 1920 to December 3, 1921 (SUL), report the facts and guesses of the case as they came to her, and also much else: details of Kent Hagler's life and military record, earnest assurances that she will follow BDV's advice and try to be "Kent's kind of woman," and comments on BDV's manuscript novel. The relationship is fairly intense on both sides. What marks BDV's part in it is his protectiveness and his profound sympathy with trouble.

10. These were never published, and it seems impossible now to tell how far BDV got with their editing. Among the BDV papers at Stanford is a duplicate notebook of his queries about Kent's letters, addressed to Clarissa from May 3, 1921, to October 20, 1921. There is no correspondence indicating that he ever submitted Kent's letters for publication.

11. Most of what he did uncover is contained in Melville Smith to BDV, November 28, 1920. SUL.

12. "The Kent Potter Story," which remained unfinished, with the note "More, but not more than 2 pages more." BDV summarized his theories of the mystery in BDV to Melville Smith, February 10, 1921. On that same day, he wrote a somewhat disinfected version to Clarissa, and kept a copy in his file—perhaps as something useful for the proposed edition of Kent's letters, perhaps for his own still-undefined fictional purposes. Six months later he recapitulated it for Clarissa in six typed pages. BDV to Clarissa Hagler (carbon), November 12, 1921. SUL.

13. BDV to Melville Smith, February 10, 1921. SUL.

14. BDV to Melville Smith, September 26, 1921. SUL.

15. According to a genealogy that BDV with the help of his Aunt

Grace prepared for Kate Sterne in the spring of 1936, several members of his mother's family suffered from nervous disorders not unlike his own. Genealogical Notes, Dye Family, filed as a separate manuscript with the DeVoto Papers. SUL.

16. BDV to Kate Sterne, "The Kent Potter Story," fourth installment, p. 2.

17. Ibid.

18. Describing Skinny to Kate Sterne, BDV said that "except for the one I did marry, [she] was the only woman I tried to marry" (BDV to Kate Sterne, November 2, 1934), and that Skinny gave "a sort of sachet of bergamot or mignonette to the whole period." This burst of nostalgic reminiscence had been called up by the latest book of Phyllis McGinley, one of Skinny's old Ogden crowd. That generation of emergent flappers, DeVoto felt, were "the first females who had been human beings since 1870." The short stories and novels are full of the "Skinny" figure. See, for example, "Front Page Ellen," *Redbook* L (November 1927), pp. 32–37, or the character Libby Grayson (a composite of Skinny and Avis DeVoto) in *We Accept with Pleasure*, or the character Josephine Willard in *Mountain Time*.

19. BDV to Kate Sterne, "The Kent Potter Story," fourth installment, p. 3.

20. BDV to L. B. R. Briggs, February 1, 1922. Personnel File, Harvard Registrar's Office. Briggs had evidently suggested possible openings at Syracuse and some midwestern university, and also the possibility of an assistantship or part-time job at Harvard. In reply DeVoto wrote: "I don't want to apply to either the midwest university or Syracuse so long as there is a fair chance of getting in at Harvard. . . . It isn't a question of going where I can make the most money, for the traditional crust and garret—provided the garret is equipped with a cold shower—will do amply for me, but of getting back to the United States first and foremost, and second of getting to the more privileged earth. The Yard and the Square are the most congenial places in the world, and I should rather be there than anywhere else for the year or two of trial, error, and investigation necessary to determine which particular tassel of the literary fringe I am [to] get attached to. Any place east of Utah is good, and I should happily, even joyfully, accept an appointment from a Methodist seminary with compulsory chapel, a ten o'clock rule, and an index expurgatorius, for it would be better than a Mormon community which doesn't need the ten o'clock rule and has no books at all." In applying to the Harvard Appointment Office on March 26, he appended a note to the forms, saying that he was not interested in any job in the Intermountain country or in the

South. "Anywhere east of the Rockies and north of Mason's and Dixon's line." Personnel folder, Harvard Appointment Office.

21. BDV to Kate Sterne, "The Kent Potter Story," fourth install-ment, p. 2. "Skinny," presented with BDV's fantasizings about her, re-membered their friendship as real and warm but without any of the romantic trimmings. She did not remember that they were two neu-rotics holding each other up, though she admitted having been ill and having appreciated BDV's understanding and sympathy. It had never even occurred to her that *he* was ill, and the elopement story made her laugh. She wore his fraternity pin for a while on the understanding that it meant no formal engagement. EBM (Skinny) to WS, January 9, 1972.

22.   In response to a letter from Clarence Budington Kelland saying that DeVoto knew nothing about the cattle industry and should stick to asphalt, where he was at home. BDV to Kelland, February 21, 1947. SUL.

23. Once, commenting on the clumsiness of his son Gordon, he confessed to Kate Sterne that he had himself never been any handier than Gordon was now. BDV to Kate Sterne, December 7, 1934.

24. BDV to Kate Sterne, "The Kent Potter Story," fourth install-ment, p. 3.

25. Since the Kent Potter story is fictionalized, though lightly, and since the autobiographical elements in it involve some showing off be-fore Kate Sterne, one must admit the possibility that his abrupt de-parture from the Hagler family was not fear of Clarissa's too-clinging adoration or of her mother's willingness to promote a match, but some social inadequacy or outright gaffe of his own. Viewed objectively he would not seem, apart from his friendship with Kent, a suitor whom the Haglers would have found irresistible, being nameless, penniless, and unwell.

26. BDV to Byron Hurlbut, undated, but from context December 1922. SUL.

II NORTHWESTERN

Chapter 1 ·

1. Betty White, *I Lived This Story*, Doubleday, Doran & Company, 1930. The novel was written mainly in the DeVoto household during the summers of 1928 and 1929, and was dedicated to DeVoto.

2. Helen Howe, *We Happy Few*, Simon & Schuster, 1946.

3. Fred Bissell to WS, October 28, 1971. He adds that he has no proof she ever did say it to President Lowell, or that President Lowell

would have understood her if she had. It is a characterization that Avis DeVoto repudiates with dismay now, but the story is an only moderately extreme form of the legendry she has sometimes inspired. Leave it that she was outspoken.

Bissell took DeVoto's full-year course in writing during his senior year, 1930–31, a class that included Joseph Alsop and Russell Maloney. Later he was a graduate student and teaching assistant in history and literature, from 1932 to 1936, and to some extent a member of the DeVoto "crowd," though not so intimate a member that DeVoto couldn't confuse him with his brother Richard when Richard Bissell published, and DeVoto reviewed, *A Stretch on the River*, in 1950.

4. Always ostentatiously susceptible to feminine charms, BDV made much of the short skirts and rolled stockings of his students. His hyperbolic tribute to the girl college student, "The Co-Ed, the Hope of Liberal Education," *Harper's* CLV (September 1927), pp. 452–59, begins with a tribute to the legs in the front row.

5. This is Avis' recollection of how BDV first noticed her. "My legs were never that good."

6. Fred Bissell to WS, October 28, 1971.

7. Betty White, *I Lived This Story*, p. 48.

8. George Ball to WS, August 25, 1971. Ball's older brother Stewart was a classmate of Avis MacVicar's, and one of BDV's favorites. He typed the manuscript of DeVoto's first published novel, *The Crooked Mile*, and often played tennis and boxed with DeVoto. It was perhaps through his doing that his brother George landed in DeVoto's advanced section of Freshman English when he came to Northwestern in 1926. When DeVoto resigned and did not return the next fall, George Ball was handed on to DeVoto's close friend Garrett Mattingly, who had not yet switched from English to History.

9. BDV's caustic opinion of Northwestern was expressed, after he left there, in "Farewell to Pedagogy," *Harper's* CLVI (January 1928), pp. 182–90, and in "Northwestern," *College Humor* (January 1929), pp. 24–25. It was also apparent that in other essays on education he kept Northwestern in mind as a horrible example, and even in the stories that he wrote about "Morrison" and "Olympus" universities for *Redbook* and the *Post* during the late 1920s, it is plainly Northwestern that is the model. At least in his early years as a writer, DeVoto had a mountain man's dislike for the Middle West and a Harvard man's contempt for the middle western mind.

10. The anecdote is told in "Farewell to Pedagogy," and a fictional situation that closely resembles BDV's clash with President Scott is used in *We Accept with Pleasure*.

11. George Ball to WS, August 25, 1971.

12. Miss Brown, now Mrs. William C. Boyden, besides reminiscing for me on tape, in person, and in many letters, dug out a batch of her old Northwestern English papers, with BDV's comments on them. These corroborate the pedagogical thoroughness that is evident in his comments on the papers of Helen Avis MacVicar preserved among the DeVoto papers at SUL, and Mrs. Boyden's recollections of those Northwestern years amplify and corroborate the recollections of Avis DeVoto, George and Stewart Ball, Henry Reck, and DeVoto's English Department colleague Arthur Nethercot.

13. BDV to Melville Smith, October 22, 1920. SUL.

14. BDV to Byron Hurlbut, undated, but from context late May 1923. SUL.

15. Washington Island I have reconstructed from DeVoto's letters, Avis DeVoto's recollections, the essay "Vestige of a Nordic Arcady," *American Mercury* IX (November 1926), pp. 327–32, and the short story "Front Page Ellen," *Redbook* L (November 1927), pp. 32–37.

16. BDV to Kate Sterne, "The Kent Potter Story," fourth installment, p. 3.

17. *The Crooked Mile*, Minton, Balch & Company, 1924. The title, like so many of DeVoto's titles, was the product of somewhat desperate collaboration between author and publisher.

Chapter 2 ·

1. This is the opinion of Sarah Margaret Brown, who as a Chicago newspaperwoman was familiar with the literary scene there from the time of her Northwestern apprenticeship onward. Her impression is borne out by Avis, who remembers the Chicago years as poverty-stricken, restricted, and half frantic with ambition and hard work. There is preserved no correspondence between BDV and Chicago writers, editors, and reviewers of the time, and he did not meet Fanny Butcher, of the Chicago *Tribune*, until she joined the Bread Loaf staff in the summer of 1934.

2. E. H. Balch to BDV, January 21, 1923. SUL. Subsequent letters in the same file trace the course of the negotiations. Balch to BDV, April 18, 1923, lists the revisions requested when the novel was finally accepted for publication: they amount to the cutting of John Gale's conversations, analyses, and quotations, the softening of some sexy passages, and the reduction of redundant description. Later letters report on reviews, sales, movie bites, etc.

3. Catherine Drinker Bowen, *Biography: the Craft and the Calling*, Little, Brown, 1969, p. 98.

4. This was on his mind from the beginning, evidence of BDV's determination to write his way out of the poverty and drudgery of

teaching. The ambition to live well had never been dim in him. The original of "Skinny" says that once, surveying her father's luxurious house, he confided that this was the way he wanted to live. EBM to WS, January 9, 1972. Balch, predictably, replied to his young author's anxious query that he had no objection whatever to his getting rich off the *Post*.

5. See "Writing for Money," *Saturday Review of Literature* XVI (October 9, 1937), pp. 2–4.

6. "I think you are a little hipped on the subject of your own physiognomy," Balch said, bluntly and accurately. Balch to BDV, July 21, 1923. SUL.

7. The *Transcript* reviewed him on October 4, 1924.

8. On October 5, 1924.

9. On November 15, 1924.

10. Llewellyn Jones, "Extry! All about the Diaspora!" Review of Bernard DeVoto, *The Crooked Mile*, Chicago *Evening Post* Literary Review, October 24, 1924.

Chapter 3 ·

1. "Lesion," *The Guardian* I (December 1924), pp. 4–7.

2. "America by the Frontier Formula," Chicago *Evening Post* Literary Review, December 26, 1923, and "An American Tragedy," *Saturday Review of Literature* I (December 27, 1923), p. 412.

3. To the correspondents who accused him of caricaturing Joseph Smith and the Mormons he replied uniformly that the character of Ohio Boggs was a composite figure based mainly on Peter Cartwright. But the "mobbings" and the pitched warfare against a frontier sect and the eviction of Boggs's followers from the settlements have close parallels in the history of Mormonism, and the death of Boggs is clearly modeled on that of the Mormon Apostle Parley P. Pratt.

4. Duncan Aikman to BDV, January 7, 1925. SUL.

5. "Ogden: The Underwriters of Salvation," in Duncan Aikman, ed., *The Taming of the Frontier*, Minton, Balch & Co., 1925, pp. 25–60.

6. See Julius P. Barclay, "A Bibliography of the Writings of Bernard DeVoto," in Bowen, Mirrielees, Schlesinger, and Stegner, *Four Portraits and One Subject: Bernard DeVoto*, Houghton Mifflin, 1963. Though it needs a few small corrections and the addition of some items that have come to light since its publication, the Barclay bibliography has been indispensable in the making of this book.

7. E. H. Balch to BDV, February 12, 1925. SUL.

8. This visit to Utah is very thinly represented in the correspondence. It is alluded to in some of the letters from Florian DeVoto to his

son, but for detail I have depended almost entirely on the recollections of Avis DeVoto.

9. If the article was designed to make the state of Utah aware of its rebellious son, it could hardly have been more successful. My own experience (I was then a resident of Utah) was perhaps not unrepresentative. Appearing for an early-morning class in the old L Building of the University of Utah, I came up the stairs just as the office door at the end of the hall opened and a magazine came skidding down the slick battleship linoleum. The door slammed—it belonged to George Emory Fellowes, a professor of history who had once been president of the University of Maine—and I picked up the magazine. It was the *American Mercury,* of which I had vaguely heard. In it, as I thumbed through looking for the cause of Professor Fellowes' wrath, I found an article entitled "Utah," by—as unfriendly publicists of any faith are likely to say in such circumstances—"one Bernard DeVoto."

10. In 1926 he was still romantic about the cowboys. Later he became one of the bitterest critics of the cattle kingdom's history, economics, politics, and assumptions.

11. The Mutual Improvement Association, known as the MIA or "Mutual," is a Mormon institution built into every ward house in Zion. It incorporates the Beehive Girls, Boy Scouts, and other youth groups, and publishes a magazine, *The Improvement Era.* It is the youth arm of Mormon orthodoxy and neighborly helpfulness and personal wholesomeness, much scorned by the rebels and probably as responsible as any other element of the Mormon system for the stability of Mormon society. In the amusement hall of every ward it sponsors dances, athletic leagues, amateur theatricals, movies, and much else. Every Mormon child, and many a Gentile child as well, is likely to be found at Mutual on Tuesday nights. In DeVoto's mouth, in 1926, it is a term of contempt, the epitome of everything pious, middle-class, and dull.

12. BDV reports it as fact in "Farewell to Pedagogy" and also in a letter, BDV to Paul Ferris, July 15, 1926. SUL.

13. BDV to Melville Smith, September 25, 1922. SUL. "Do not persuade yourself that art is greater than life," he told Smith in a tone that would become familiar to a whole generation of the literary—"that the greatest art is as worthy as the meanest life. Gravest of all, do not think that art can be separated from life for one second's existence in itself. Make music. Make music of the elevated, of the billboards, of the vaudeville, of the baseball games, of the gasoline air, of the river stinks, of the garbage cans, the slums, of every blatant and vulgar monstrosity of this civilization. Incredibly vulgar it may be, offensive, repellent, hideous, intolerable. Nevertheless, it is alive; and while it is, your duty is to make art of it."

"This," he added in a spasm of self-awareness, "is almost worthy of immortalization on Christmas cards." He might also have said that he probably wouldn't have been talking that way if Carl Sandburg's *Chicago Poems*, published a half dozen years before, had not taught him how. He meant it, nevertheless. He meant it then and all the rest of his life. "America, alive, is the future." But, for the moment, in the first flush of being a published writer, and in the scornful sense of having proved himself to Ogden, Utah, he talked out of the other side of his mouth.

14. Florian DeVoto to BDV, June 6, 1926. SUL.

15. This recantation, first written as a letter to Jarvis Thurston on May 14, 1943 (SUL), was published in *The Rocky Mountain Review* X (Autumn 1945), pp. 7–11, and reprinted in *The Improvement Era* 49 (March 1946), p. 154. There is a discussion of DeVoto's changing attitudes toward Mormonism in Leland Fetzer, "Bernard DeVoto and the Mormon Tradition," *Dialogue* VI (Autumn–Winter 1971), pp. 23–38.

Chapter 4·

1. To numerous correspondents, over the span of a good many years, he asserted that he took up the theme of the continentalizing of the American nation because he was afraid to tackle the Civil War, the single most important event in American history.

2. Florian DeVoto's research on behalf of his son is reported in many letters: Florian DeVoto to BDV, January 18, 1926; February 8, 1926; February 24, 1926; undated, 1926; March 11, 1926; and September 3, no year. SUL.

3. BDV to H. L. Mencken, February 7, 1926. NYPL.

4. Mencken to BDV, February 4, 1926. SUL.

5. Mencken to BDV, February 13, 1926. SUL.

6. Mencken to BDV, March 4, 1926. SUL.

7. Mencken to BDV, March 8, 1926. SUL.

8. Never published, apparently never written, though "Farewell to Pedagogy" contains some ridicule of the education schools.

9. Mencken to BDV, March 20, 1926. SUL.

10. Mencken to BDV, April 15, 1926. SUL. Here, perhaps, is the model for DeVoto's later campaigns against the Watch and Ward and other proponents of literary censorship. On April 5, ten days before writing DeVoto that "Sex and the Co-Ed" was being pulled from the May issue, Mencken had gone to Boston, obtained a peddler's license, and publicly sold a copy of the warned-against April issue to T. Frank Chase, the President of the Watch and Ward Society, on Brimstone Corner. He was arrested and brought to trial, but the

charges against him were dismissed by Judge Parmenter. After his acquittal, the April issue of the *Mercury* was banned from the mails ex post facto, though it had already been mailed. It was this situation that led Mencken to pull "Sex and the Co-Ed," for fear of provoking more trouble. Years later, when writing autobiographical notes to go into the New York Public Library with his papers, Mencken wrote DeVoto asking if he had ever published the essay anywhere. He hadn't. See Mencken to BDV, September 20, 1937, SUL, and BDV to Mencken, September 22, 1937, NYPL. The "Hatrack" case is summarized in Edgar Kemler, *The Irreverent Mr. Mencken*, Little, Brown, 1950, pp. 191–216.

11. W. F. Bryan, Arthur H. Nethercot, and Bernard DeVoto, *The Writer's Handbook*, Macmillan, 1928.

12. Bernard DeVoto, *The Chariot of Fire*, Macmillan, 1926.

13. "Vestige of a Nordic Arcady," *American Mercury* IX (November 1926), pp. 327–32.

14. "Saving the Sophomore," by Richard Dye. *American Mercury* IX (November 1926) pp. 288–94.

15. "The Mountain Men," *American Mercury* IX (December 1926) pp. 472–79.

16. "College and the Exceptional Man," *Harper's* CLIV (January 1927), pp. 253–60.

17. BDV to Byron Hurlbut, December 29, 1926. SUL. The hunt for a suitable Cape Cod boardinghouse is reported in L. B. R. Briggs to BDV, February 16, February 19, February 27, March 20, and April 16, 1927. SUL.

18. Briggs to BDV, November 20, 1926. SUL.

19. Briggs to BDV, October 6, 1924. SUL. "At least to a person somewhat old-fashioned like myself, your method seems mistaken, next that I do not for a moment question your sincerity, next that though I question your wisdom in directing your power I do not question the power, and lastly that I am always yours with warm regard."

20. Briggs to BDV, November 20, 1926. SUL. The doubt of DeVoto's powers as a novelist, expressed early by the writing teacher whom he most respected, was repeated over the years by many people both friendly and unfriendly. Though DeVoto was never until late in his life completely discouraged from writing fiction even though he officially renounced it in 1949 (see Section VII, Chapter 4, "The Lost World of Fiction"), Briggs's judgment seems to me a sound one. DeVoto expressed himself better in history and in his controversial essays than in any of his fictions.

21. Briggs to BDV, October 30, 1926. SUL.

22. BDV to Paul Ferris, December 14, 1925. SUL.

23. DeVoto's letter is not preserved in its entirety. A piece cut from it is folded in with Briggs to BDV, April 6, 1927. SUL.

24. H. S. Latham to BDV, no date, but, from context, spring 1927. SUL.

25. "The Great Medicine Road," *American Mercury* XI (May 1927), pp. 104–12.

26. Briggs to BDV, April 30, 1927. SUL.

27. "The Co-Ed: The Hope of Liberal Education," *Harper's* CLV (September 1927), pp. 452–59.

28. "In Search of Bergamot," *Harper's* CLV (August 1927), pp. 302–12.

Chapter 5 ·

1. "Footnote on the West," *Harper's* CLV (November 1927), pp. 713–22.

2. "Front Page Ellen," *Redbook* L (November 1927), pp. 32–37, and "Sleeping Dogs," *Saturday Evening Post* CC (November 19, 1927), pp. 18–19.

3. BDV to Byron Hurlbut, September 1, 1927. SUL. His announced intention was to work on the Mark Twain book and on a "leisurely study of the brave old days of the West"—presumably either a collection of essays such as "The Mountain Men" and "The Great Medicine Road" or an articulated book in the same vein—while supporting himself by writing magazine fiction. He supported himself in the way he proposed to, and he worked on the Mark Twain book as he proposed to. But his "leisurely study of the brave old days of the West," by diversions and torques that all writers will recognize, became something else—became most importantly the trilogy of histories *The Year of Decision: 1846, Across the Wide Missouri,* and *The Course of Empire,* which, among them, won him the Bancroft prize, the Pulitzer prize, and the National Book Award.

III MORE PRIVILEGED EARTH

Chapter 1 ·

1. Robeson Bailey to WS, November 9, 1968.

2. "Farewell to Pedagogy," *Harper's* CLVI (January 1928), pp. 182–90.

3. "This Must Not Get Out," *Redbook* L (January 1928), pp. 68–73.

4. "English A," *American Mercury* XIII (February 1928), pp. 204–12.

5. Fred Bissell indicates that even four or five years after DeVoto's return to Cambridge he was "regarded by the literary faculty as a kind of wild man from the West, Utah, and probably had a lot of Mormon wives," and that he "met the sneers" at his *Saturday Evening Post* writing "by letting checks be seen from the Curtis Publishing Co., when he would blow his nose." And "in 1930," Mr. Bissell remarks, "S.E.P. writers were the highest paid writers in the universe." Fred Bissell to WS, October 28, 1971.

6. In the early 1940s Miss Howe spent part of a summer near the DeVotos at Annisquam, on Cape Anne; her impressions apparently come from that contact. Her portrait of A. R. Boyer, who has some of DeVoto's qualities, is a portrait done with an axe. The psychological obsessions with which Miss Howe endows him may have stemmed from the presence on Cape Anne, in that same summer, of Beata Rank, with whom DeVoto loved to discuss the psychological bases of fiction and to whom he later dedicated *The World of Fiction*. After publication of the novel *We Happy Few*, relations between Miss Howe and the DeVotos were somewhat strained. Richard Scowcroft tells of entertaining both shortly after the book appeared, and reports a general ice storm. On the other hand, DeVoto reviewed *We Happy Few* ("When the Goths Took Harvard," New York *Herald Tribune* Books XXII (June 30, 1946), with what seemed enthusiasm: "Miss Howe is a better novelist here than she was in 'The Whole Heart.' Though there is less feeling in this book, its content is harder and firmer and her skill has greatly increased. She does not ask why academic life—for what she complains of is not a Harvard monopoly—erodes courage and integrity, but she is excellent and sometimes magnificent in rendering the surfaces of that erosion."

7. New, that is, as a field of concentration and serious study. At the end of the 1920s very few courses in American literature were yet offered in American colleges, and it was more or less standard to obtain a degree in English without ever having taken a single American-literature course.

8. "Sitting a Little Apprehensively on 'The World,'" *Harvard Advocate* CXIV, No. 8 (May 1928), pp. 23–27.

9. Cora Wilkenning acted as DeVoto's agent from sometime in 1927 until October 1934, when he became dissatisfied with her and signed up with Raymond and Helen Everitt, of Curtis Brown. A further inducement to change was that the Everitts promised to work him into the serial game, which offered an easier and more lucrative living than short stories. After Raymond Everitt became an editor at Little, Brown, Helen continued to work with DeVoto on his *Collier's* serials.

10. During 1928, four appeared in *Redbook*, three in the *Post*, one in *Harper's*. See the Barclay bibliography, pp. 147–48.

11. "Northwestern," *College Humor* (January 1929), pp. 24–25.

12. BDV to Harold Latham, December 20, 1927. SUL.

13. Robert S. Forsythe, *Bernard DeVoto, A New Force in American Letters*, Macmillan, 1928. One of DeVoto's closest friends at Northwestern, Forsythe had gone on to an unsatisfactory job at the University of North Dakota. In 1929 DeVoto brought him into the Americana Deserta series to edit Melville's *Pierre*. Later he went to the Newberry Library, in Chicago.

14. It did. The letter, BDV to a Mr. Collier, March 15, 1928 (SUL), was shortly incorporated into an essay, "Tools for the Intellectual Life," *Harper's* CLVII (October 1928), pp. 602–9. The tools he recommends are languages, mathematics, and science. He disparages the formal study of literature and the "pseudo-sciences" of psychology, anthropology, and sociology. History he ignores, for some reason; and he indicates that all instruction ought to be tutorial. The colleges justify themselves mainly as places where one can learn the tools for continuing self-education.

15. Reviews of *The House of Sun-Goes-Down* appeared in the New York *Times*, May 13, 1928, p. 8; the Boston *Transcript*, May 29, 1928, p. 2; the Chicago *Tribune*, June 9, 1928, p. 15; and New York *Herald Tribune* Books, July 29, 1928, p. 14.

16. BDV to Paul Ferris, July 10, 1928, Labor Day 1928, and September 25, 1928. SUL.

17. Robeson Bailey to WS, November 19, 1968. SUL.

18. Including two unpaid articles in the *Harvard Advocate* not listed in the Barclay bibliography. These were "Sitting a Little Apprehensively on 'The World,'" already cited, and "The Bloody Shirt, World War Model," *Harvard Advocate* CXV (November 1928), pp. 9–19, an inflated and bombastic account of his political shenanigans as chaplain of Herman Baker Post of the American Legion, and signed Richard L. Caxton.

19. Plus two more unpaid *Harvard Advocate* items not in the Barclay bibliography: "Toward Another War," *Harvard Advocate* CXV (April 1929), pp. 9–19, and "Remarks at the New York Dinner," *Harvard Advocate* CXV (May 1929), p. 7.

20. Throughout his life he had periodically to seek psychiatric help, and for a number of reasons he moved from healer to healer. His first Boston analyst, Dr. William Herman, died in the winter of 1934–35. His second, William Barrett, referred him to Lawrence Kubie when the DeVotos moved from Cambridge to New York. Later, after their return to Cambridge, DeVoto did not go back into analysis with

Barrett, but saw him often in a "supportive" capacity until Barrett's divorce and removal to California. In the early 1940s DeVoto saw a good deal of Beata Rank, but though they had many discussions about the relation between literature and psychiatry, it is uncertain whether or not he was ever her patient. Neither was he ever a patient of Dr. Gregory Rochlin, though Rochlin was one of his closest friends during the 1950s. His last psychiatrist was Dr. Alfred O. Ludwig, of Boston, who later married DeVoto's secretary Julie Jeppson. The sessions with Ludwig lasted from late 1951 or early 1952 until DeVoto's death, in November 1955.

21. The original proposal, with an extensive list of possible titles, is contained in BDV to H. C. Block, January 27, 1929. AAK. After several letters of elaboration and clarification, and one trip to New York, DeVoto received the formal agreement for signature on April 25. He and Alfred Knopf did not meet at that time and did not become close friends until quite a number of years later, though as an owner of the *American Mercury* Knopf would have known DeVoto's name and work as early as 1926.

22. Block to BDV, May 22, 1929. AAK.

23. As with later books that involved much reading and research, DeVoto was jumpy and nervous about beginning, exaggerated the difficulties, feared the likelihood of failure, and made humorous game of the way the book had expanded from something called a "Preface," calculated to take six months in the doing, into something that had already taken four years and would have to be followed fifteen years later by a more ponderous work. BDV to Paul Ferris, March 26, 1929. SUL.

24. "Brave Days in Washoe," *American Mercury* XVIII (June 1929), pp. 228–37. This comprises pages 115–33 of *Mark Twain's America*.

25. BDV to Byron Hurlbut, July 2, 1929. SUL.

26. "The Penalties of Wisdom," *Redbook* LIII (September 1929), pp. 52–55.

27. Meine to BDV, July 21, 1929. SUL. Meine found the sketch in *The Carpetbag* for May 1, 1852, an issue that also contained a John Phoenix drawing, and type for which was partially set by Artemus Ward. Meine, a non-academic but encyclopedic folklorist and biblio-phile, was managing director of Chicago Book and Art Auctions.

28. This move brought on a notable and important friendship. Their neighbors at 8 Mason Street were Theodore and Kathleen Morrison. Morrison, a poet and tennis player, had recently left the *Atlantic* to teach writing at Harvard. A little later (in 1932), he became director of the Bread Loaf Writers' Conference and brought DeVoto

into the warmest literary association he was ever to enjoy. DeVoto, in turn, brought Robert Frost into the lives of the Morrisons, where he stayed.

29. Published in *American Mercury* XIX (January 1930), pp. 1–13, and reprinted in considerably expanded form in *Forays and Rebuttals*, pp. 71–137.

30. The records show that in 1929–30 his duties were entirely tutorial. The next year, he took over Hurlbut's writing class, English 31, and taught it through the academic year 1933–34. In the spring term of 1933–34 he gave up the writing course temporarily in favor of English 95, a course in contemporary American literature. In the spring term of 1935–36 he taught both English 31, renumbered English 3-A, and English 95, renumbered English 70. Class records, Harvard Registrar's Office.

31. BDV to Melville Smith, July 8, 1920. SUL.

32. BDV to L. B. R. Briggs, February 4, 1922. Personnel Folder, Harvard Registrar's Office.

Chapter 2 ·

1. "The Real Frontier: A Preface to Mark Twain," *Harper's* CLXIII (June 1931), pp. 60–71; "The Matrix of Mark Twain's Humour," *Bookman* LXXIV (October 1931), pp. 172–78; "Mark Twain and the Genteel Tradition," *Harvard Graduates' Magazine* XL (December 1931), pp. 155–63; and "Tom, Huck, and America," *Saturday Review of Literature* IX (August 13, 1932), pp. 37–39.

2. "College Education for the Intelligent Few," *Current History* XXXV (March 1932), pp. 792–98; Anonymous, "Grace Before Teaching, a Letter to a Young Doctor of Literature," *Harvard Graduates' Magazine* XL (March 1932), pp. 261–75.

3. BDV to Knopf, January 22, 1930. AAK.

4. Manley Aaron to BDV, May 6, 1930. AAK.

5. Knopf to BDV, May 28, 1931. AAK.

6. *Across the Wide Missouri*, Houghton Mifflin, 1947, p. 272.

7. The collection of long, intimate letters from King to DeVoto (SUL) expresses King's steadily growing frustration at his failure to do anything substantial as a writer, though as an advertising executive he was both successful and prosperous.

8. Mattingly, *Bernard DeVoto*, p. 22.

9. "From a Graduate's Window," *Harvard Graduates' Magazine* XXXIX (September 1930), pp. 47–50.

10. "Literary Censorship in Boston," *Harvard Graduates' Magazine* XXXIX (September 1930), pp. 30–42.

11. "From a Graduate's Window," *Harvard Graduates' Magazine* XXXIX (December 1930), pp. 176–79.

12. These matters run serially and largely through the editorials of the four 1931 issues.

13. "We Brighter People," *Harvard Graduates' Magazine* XXXIX (March 1931), pp. 323–37. For "Mark Twain and the Genteel Tradition" and "Grace before Teaching" see notes 1 and 2, above.

14. "Grace Before Teaching."

15. DeVoto believed with some justice that his outbursts in print were directed against ideas, not against individuals. But for reasons geographical as well as reasons temperamental he often sounded more personal than he intended. Of Brooks he did not always speak respectfully, but he meant to: he thought him the best and brightest exemplar of a way of thinking with which he profoundly disagreed. On Mumford he looked with dislike, on Ludwig Lewisohn and Waldo Frank with contempt. Some inhibition against personal contumely in print kept his published opinions somewhere within bounds—though those he attacked were unlikely to notice the inhibition. But in conversation and in letters he was not inhibited in the least, and his gift for vituperation often led him into extravaganzas of disagreement that ended by becoming humorous. As a single example, here is a comment on Waldo Frank, taken from a letter to Kate Sterne on December 26, 1934: "It is the rock on which my church stands that, for instance, Waldo Frank can't be right about anything, that Waldo Frank's odor of sanctity is ipso facto hydrogen sulphide, that when Waldo Frank sees God, necessarily his vision, like Moses's, is confined to the hinder parts, that any opinion ever held by Waldo Frank in any circumstances about anything is axiomatically blithering nonsense and can no more be accepted by any intelligence, however limited, than Joseph Smith Jun. could consecrate the Eucharist. And when the to-do about this new book [about Stieglitz] started I got out the god-damnedest silliest book ever written by anyone not a Christian Scientist, I refer unabashed to *Our America*, and read what Waldo wrote about Stieglitz in 1919, while, here and there, a faintly comprehensible meaning was still left in his cirro-cumulus style. And I don't know, Kate, I don't know." That is a fair example of his gift for hyperbole, "the Mencken tone." It is also a sufficient explanation of why the Kate Sterne letters, his most uninhibited outpourings, are in the Stanford University Library's safe.

16. "Mark Twain and the Genteel Tradition."

17. Review of Clara Clemens, *My Father, Mark Twain, New England Quarterly* V (January 1932), pp. 169–71.

18. "The Graduate's Window," *Harvard Graduates' Magazine* XL (June 1932), pp. 408–13. He gave different explanations of his leaving

to different correspondents. To Wesley Stout of *The Saturday Evening Post* (BDV to Stout, April 15, 1932, SUL) he wrote that he was quitting. To Kate Sterne he declared, almost bragged, that he had been fired.

Chapter 3 ·

1. BDV to Kate Sterne, June (no day), 1936.

2. Or vice versa. He was at least as nimble in interpretations as any of his analysts. See his self-analysis of *Mountain Time*, Section VI, Chapter 6.

3. The invitation was reported, with obvious delight, in several letters, for example BDV to Paul Ferris, May 1, 1931, SUL, and BDV to Lee Hartman, May 15, 1931, SUL.

4. Joseph Smith was born in Sharon, Brigham Young in Whittingham, other leaders in St. Johnsbury, Danville, and other villages and towns in the Green Mountains and the Caledonian Hills. The cohesive Mormon social system was as much a product of New England village folkways as of divine revelation; Mormon virtues were about equally those of the frontier and those of upstate New York and Vermont. DeVoto admired in Vermonters precisely what he admired in some of his mother's family, and since it had nothing to do with his own experience or his own emotional life, and nothing to do with dogma, he could "return" to Vermont as he never could have to Ogden.

5. BDV to Rev. C. J. Armstrong, September 1, 1931. SUL.

6. Late in his career, DeVoto wrote up this episode in "My Career as a Lawbreaker," which his agent Carl Brandt tried vainly to sell to some magazine and which ended up as Easy Chair No. 219, *Harper's* CCVIII (January 1954), p. 8.

7. A friend during the Cambridge years, and, after the DeVotos' move to Lincoln, a country neighbor.

8. "New England: There She Stands," *Harper's* CLXXIV (March 1932), pp. 405–15. Frost's interest in the essay, and even more in the attitudes and moralities it explicitly applauded, is attested by Lawrance Thompson, *Robert Frost, The Years of Triumph*, Holt, Rinehart & Winston, 1970, p. 671, note, and also by Frost to BDV, ca. June 10, 1943, Thompson, *Selected Letters of Robert Frost*, Holt, Rinehart & Winston, 1964, pp. 509–10. See Section III, Chapter 12.

Chapter 4 ·

1. The inescapable ironies of a war that was supposed to save the world for democracy, and its aftermath in repression, anti-syndicalism laws, and such events as the Sacco-Vanzetti trial and execution, encouraged after the war the spread of what had been essentially a literary-coterie attitude before it. Thus a period of intense and brilliant

literary activity coincided with a period of literary contempt for the country and culture that produced it, and even with the common assertion that high creativity was impossible in America. For a single sample, related to the Brooks-Mumford doctrines but not immediately associated with that school, consider T. K. Whipple's *Spokesmen*, a series of literary essays celebrating American writers and simultaneously demonstrating how the gas-lighted barbarity had blighted their genius.

2. Lewis Mumford, *The Golden Day*, Beacon Press (first paperback edition) 1957, p. 144.

3. Van Wyck Brooks, *The Ordeal of Mark Twain*, E. P. Dutton, 1920, p. 14.

4. Ibid., p. 34.

5. Ibid., pp. 35–37.

6. Ibid., p. 84. The thesis that in becoming a funny man Mark Twain "felt that he was selling rather than fulfilling his own soul" is central to Brooks's "ordeal" theory. It was one of the targets over which DeVoto sent wave after wave of bombers.

7. Malcolm Cowley, ed., *After the Genteel Tradition*, Southern Illinois University Press, 1964, p. 184.

8. If he had not learned it in 1932, he learned it later. Zinsser's "biography" of typhus, *Rats, Lice, and History*, begins with arguments between Zinsser as scientist and a literary man who is Bernard DeVoto. The two were close friends until Zinsser's death; and they met when DeVoto took to Zinsser the manuscript of the first part of *Mark Twain's America* and asked Zinsser, a friend of Brooks's, if he should soften his attack on Brooks's ideas in consideration of Brooks's reported nervous illness. See Section VI, Chapter 2, "Fools, Liars, and Mr. DeVoto."

9. *Mark Twain's America*, Little, Brown, 1932, Foreword, pp. ix–xiii.

10. Ibid.

11. It should be pointed out that the American celebrated and represented by Mark Twain and assiduously prospected for by Henry James was a temporary synthesis only; he represented the culmination of a limited number of racial stocks and a limited number of cultural variants within the context of a continental nation expanding to its geopolitically logical limits. He might look a little out of place in contemporary New York or Detroit or San Francisco.

12. Mark Van Doren, review of *Mark Twain's America*, *The Nation* 135 (October 19, 1932), p. 370.

13. Robert E. Spiller, ed., *The Van Wyck Brooks-Lewis Mumford Letters. The Record of a Literary Friendship, 1921–1963*. E. P. Dutton, 1970. Mumford to Brooks, December 27, 1932, p. 84.

14. Paine's letter, though somewhat condescending (and hence irritating to DeVoto) had been kindly enough, though it refused access to the papers. Paine repeated the refusal on October 2, 1928, while giving DeVoto permission to quote from Paine's books, with credit, as much as he pleased. In that October 2 letter he justified his refusal of access to the papers on the ground that these papers were Mark Twain's "refuse," properly closed to everyone. Out of this refuse, since DeVoto's original request to see it, have been published not only DeVoto's *Mark Twain in Eruption*, parts of *Mark Twain at Work*, and *Letters from the Earth*, but several volumes edited by Dixon Wecter and Henry Nash Smith; and at the present time every word of the "refuse" is being scrupulously edited and published under the direction of Frederick Anderson of the University of California at Berkeley. This will run to fourteen to sixteen volumes.

So time has been on DeVoto's side in the disagreement about Mark Twain's unpublished manuscripts. Nevertheless his blunt assault on Paine in his Foreword brought indignant demands for an apology and threats of a court suit from Paine, who said DeVoto was guilty of something very close to libel or slander; and from Charles Lark, the lawyer for the Mark Twain Estate, a demand for a photostatic copy of the Paine letter that DeVoto said had said no more books about Mark Twain needed to be written. DeVoto refused Lark's demand, but a week later, he had either acknowledged his overstatements or Paine had cooled down. "Hell, let it go," he said. As for Charles Lark, he later became a close friend of DeVoto's, the one individual in the Mark Twain Company whom DeVoto thoroughly respected. See Paine to BDV, October 2, 1928, October 27, 1932, and November 4, 1932; BDV to Charles Lark, October 24, 1932; and BDV to Paine, November 1, 1932. SUL.

15. Lawrence Kubie to BDV, November 3, 1949. SUL.

16. Compare his reactions to the attacks on him by Sinclair Lewis and others after the publication of *The Literary Fallacy*. Section VI, Chapter 2, "Fools, Liars, and Mr. DeVoto."

17. See, for example, Henry Seidel Canby, review of *Mark Twain's America, Saturday Review of Literature* IX (October 8, 1932), p. 164.

18. Spiller, *The Van Wyck Brooks-Lewis Mumford Letters*, Brooks to Mumford, December 30, 1932, p. 85.

Chapter 5 ·

1. Homans, DeVoto's first Harvard tutee, became his intimate friend, as did Charles Curtis, a Boston lawyer and member of the Harvard Corporation. In his complicated way, DeVoto valued both of

them for their connections as well as for their intelligence and good company. Homans was the son of Henry Adams' favorite niece, and so as blue-blooded as the Back Bay produced. Curtis, later forced off the Corporation because of his divorce, was a bluestocking who became a victim of the bluenoses. Both Curtis and Homans were members of Henderson's Pareto seminar; in 1934 they collaborated in *An Introduction to Pareto*, the first extended study of Pareto's sociology in English. In 1936 Curtis married Frances Prentice, an ex-Fellow at Bread Loaf, a friend of Kitty Bowen's, and, like Mrs. Bowen, one of DeVoto's fervent admirers. Both Curtises were regular reviewers for *The Saturday Review of Literature* during DeVoto's editorship, she of popular fiction, he of books on sociology and the law. DeVoto and Charles Curtis were associated as members of the board of the Civil Liberties Union of Massachusetts, and in later years Curtis was not only DeVoto's lawyer but the attorney for his publishers, Houghton Mifflin. In 1947, as chief judge for the History Book Club, DeVoto helped pick Curtis' book on the Supreme Court, *The Lions Under the Throne*, as a History Book Club selection. George Homans is presently a professor of sociology at Harvard. Curtis died tragically in a house fire at Stonington, Connecticut, on December 23, 1959.

2. BDV to William Sloane, July 5, 1949. SUL.

3. BDV to Mark Saxton, September 18, 1947. SUL.

4. See especially the Easy Chair, *Harper's* CXCV (November 1947), pp. 434–37, a product of the same euphoria that provoked the letter to Mark Saxton quoted above, and "Bread Loaf, Vermont," *Ford Times* XLVIII (May 1956), pp. 2–6. Dozens of letters recommend Bread Loaf to aspiring writers.

5. "When we can barricade ourselves away from the customers we'll have a good time," he wrote Kate Sterne just before the beginning of his third Bread Loaf session. "At four P.M. on Thursday the entire gang will be in that pre-game jitters, deciding wholesale that it was a mistake to accept the appointment, quarreling with each other, and clamoring to poor Morrison for room transfers and transportation out, and drinking some lukewarm infusion of Hervey's [Hervey Allen's] made up of old tea, sweet vermouth, sugar syrup, Scotch, lemon peel, grenadine, cedar bark and table salt, and never wondering why they feel so bad. The bark of a Pontiac horn, a bellboy enters bearing ice, then silence and expectation for a space, and, the dust of Lincoln still on him, Benny is seen mixing martinis. At once she'll be driving six white horses and no one needs to tell me why I'm asked to Bread Loaf year after year." BDV to Kate Sterne, August 12, 1934.

6. Catherine Drinker Bowen, distinguished member of a distinguished family, was a protégée of DeVoto's from the time they met

at Bread Loaf in the summer of 1933. She had all the qualifications: she was acutely intelligent and greatly talented, she was a lady but by no means a stiff lady, she had a sense of humor, she admired him and valued his advice and took it. And her researches on Holmes and John Adams led her into American history, where they met on ground that both revered. DeVoto was instrumental in bringing her to Little, Brown, then his own publishers, and for years he acted as her patron, critic, and adviser.

7. Josephine Johnson, frail, pretty, poetic, and feminine, appeared at Bread Loaf as a Fellow, along with Frances Prentice, in the summer of 1934. She elicited from DeVoto a fury of admiration that lasted for several years. Her winning the Pulitzer prize for *Now in November* was a triumph that he predicted and enjoyed fully. As editor of *The Saturday Review of Literature* he published a number of her poems. His admiration did not go unnoted. On one occasion, a staff artist at *SRL* produced a DeVoto Map of the United States, which showed only Cambridge, Bread Loaf, Utah, and the routes of Lewis and Clark, Mark Twain, and Josephine Johnson.

8. Fletcher Pratt, author of *Ordeal by Fire, The Navy: A History, The Navy's War, Empire and the Sea,* and other books. His Bread Loaf career began when he came as a Fellow, in 1937, and continued until his death, in 1956.

9. Gorham Munson, an editor with several publishing houses, was the author of a number of books, including *Waldo Frank, a Study* (1923); *Robert Frost: A Study in Sense and Sensibility* (1928); and *The Dilemma of the Liberated* (1930). He died in 1969.

10. DeVoto alludes to Mrs. Carroll's objections, and suggests that she was a busybody and a gossip, in a letter defending the administration of Ted Morrison and offering suggestions about how Bread Loaf could be continued and bettered. BDV to President Paul Moody of Middlebury College, fall 1935. SUL.

11. Robeson Bailey to WS, November 9, 1968. Bailey's reward was a forty-ounce bottle of Hudson's Bay Scotch.

12. In 1902 Edith Mirrielees came to Stanford University from Big Timber, Montana, in much the same spirit that brought DeVoto to Harvard. She rarely left the Stanford campus except to make her summer trips to Bread Loaf, first to the English School and later to the Writers' Conference, though she did spend some years working with Indian schools in New Mexico. At Stanford her students included, among others, John Steinbeck, who continued to come and see her long after he had repudiated the rest of the university. Both at Stanford and at Bread Loaf she was sincerely loved by all sorts and conditions of people. Long after her retirement, in 1943, she was a

fixture on the Stanford campus, a bridge between the early days of the university and the present. When she was well past seventy, she edited *The Pacific Spectator* for several years, and when she was eighty, she wrote the history of the university that had enclosed her life.

13. Helen Everitt, first an agent with Curtis Brown, returned to the publishing business after the death of her husband, Raymond, in 1947. From 1947 to 1952 she was with Houghton Mifflin, in 1952 she became fiction editor of *The Ladies' Home Journal*, and in 1968 she joined Lovell Thompson and Mark Saxton in the new publishing firm Gambit. She died in 1971.

14. In 1946 Sloane left Henry Holt & Company to form his own firm, William Sloane Associates, which failed and was taken over, on July 1, 1952, by William Morrow. Since 1955 he has been director of the Rutgers University Press.

15. Presently an editor at Gambit. His father, Eugene Saxton, was an editor at Harper's and a friend of DeVoto's from the time of his earliest *Harper's* articles and stories.

16. Julia Peterkin, South Carolina writer best known for her novel *Scarlet Sister Mary*, which won the Pulitzer prize in 1928.

17. Hervey Allen wrote many things, including poetry and a biography of Edgar Allen Poe, but he will probably be remembered primarily for his phenomenally successful novel *Anthony Adverse* (1933).

18. John Marquand was several times a short-term visitor and lecturer at the Writers' Conference. He seems to have served as a full-time staff member only in 1940, a year DeVoto missed because of an extended trip West.

19. From a long career as a newspaperman and book columnist, Herschel Brickell had branched out into editing. He was editor of the O. Henry Memorial Award short-story volume during his Bread Loaf years.

20. A. B. ("Bud") Guthrie, author of *The Big Sky*, *The Way West*, *These Thousand Hills*, *The Blue Hen's Chick*, and *Arfive*, also began as a newspaperman. He was a Nieman Fellow at Harvard, working on *The Big Sky*, when he met DeVoto. Nieman dinners were not unlike sessions in Treman Cottage at Bread Loaf, and the effect was often the same: many people in both places came firmly and permanently under Benny DeVoto's influence.

21. An Alberta boy transplanted to Montana, Howard was the author of *Montana, High, Wide, and Handsome*, and *Strange Empire*, a history of the Canadian métis revolts. DeVoto did not meet him until his 1946 trip West, but in many letters of the late 1940s and early 1950s he describes Howard as "one of the two good writers in the

West." (The other was Thomas Hornsby Ferril, of Colorado.) In the summer of 1951 both DeVoto and Helen Everitt taught at Howard's Montana Writers' Conference, in Missoula. A few weeks after the conference, Howard died of a heart attack, and DeVoto subsequently finished up and wrote an introduction for *Strange Empire*. With a characteristic gesture, he sent his fee to Howard's mother.

22. He told Kate Sterne it was the only literary crowd he could even imagine spending two weeks with. BDV to Kate Sterne, August 12, 1934.

23. Official records of Bread Loaf, especially of the Writers' Conference, are meager, and I have been unable to locate any correspondence files. The years of DeVoto's service on the mountain are reconstructed from his personal letters, from the Middlebury College Catalogue and the annual Bread Loaf Bulletin, the Conference newspaper, *The Crumb*, and the reminiscences of Ted and Kay Morrison, William and Julie Sloane, Kitty Bowen, Robeson Bailey, and others. George K. Anderson, *Bread Loaf School of English: The First Fifty Years*, Middlebury College Press, 1969, contains a useful summary chapter on the Writers' Conference.

24. Compare BDV to William Sloane, July 14, 1947, SUL, working out in detail the assignments that each staff member will carry out.

25. *The Hour*, Houghton Mifflin, 1951, p. 83. The alcoholic rituals are discussed at greater length in Section VII, Chapter 8, "May Six O'clock Never Find You Alone."

26. This is how I saw it during my summers on the mountain, and see it now. On the other hand, it has been fairly easy for a certain kind of journalist to strike the body and count coup on it, as witness Rust Hills, "We Believe in the Maestro System: The Bread Loaf Process," *Audience*, Vol. 2, No. 8 (May–June 1972), pp. 90–108.

27. For the history of Bread Loaf, see Anderson, *Bread Loaf School of English*.

28. Ibid., pp. 136–37.

29. For an account of Robert Frost's relations with the Bread Loaf School of English and the Bread Loaf Writers' Conference from 1921 to 1936, see Lawrance Thompson, *Robert Frost, The Years of Triumph*, pp. 683–85.

30. *Who's Who in America* calls him "co-founder."

31. "English 37," *Saturday Review of Literature* XVI (June 26 through September 4, 1937).

32. *The World of Fiction*, Houghton Mifflin, 1951.

33. There is a complete file of *The Crumb* in the Wilfred Davidson Library, at Bread Loaf.

34. Variants of the Bread Loaf doctrine are remembered by Sarah

Margaret Brown Boyden, by Arthur Schlesinger, Jr., Mark Saxton, Fred Bissell, and others who took writing courses from DeVoto. Other variants are contained in the many long and singularly generous letters he wrote to those who asked advice or sent him, asked or unasked, their manuscripts. The ghost of DeVoto was very apparent even as late as the Bread Loaf session of 1972, when John Ciardi stepped down with a nostalgic farewell speech.

35. The argument with Dr. Kubie extended over a period of several years, incorporated into a dozen long letters each way, and in at least three magazine articles by each man. For a summary discussion, see Section VII, Chapter 4.

36. BDV to Garrett Mattingly, June 15, 1938. SUL.

37. Catherine Drinker Bowen, *Biography, the Craft and the Calling*, Little, Brown, 1969, p. x.

38. "Genius Is Not Enough," *Saturday Review of Literature* XIII (April 25, 1936), pp. 3–4.

39. "Bread Loaf Guidebook, 1947," *The Crumb*, August 27, 1947.

40. "Bread Loaf Circus," *The Crumb*, September 1, 1938.

Chapter 6 ·

1. Avis DeVoto to WS, February 2, 1972.

2. Henry Reck to WS, October 25, 1970. Tape.

3. Avis DeVoto to WS, October 8, 1968. Tape.

4. See the Barclay bibliography, pp. 151–55.

Chapter 7 ·

1. BDV to Paul Ferris, March 12, 1928. SUL.

2. *The Mind and Society* (Trattato di sociologia generale), by Vilfredo Pareto; edited by Arthur Livingston; translated by Andrew Bongiorno and Arthur Livingston, with the advice and active cooperation of James Harvey Rogers. Harcourt, Brace, 1935.

3. George Homans to WS, October 20, 1970; Talcott Parsons to WS, March 1, 1972.

4. Charles Curtis and George Homans, *An Introduction to Pareto*, Alfred A. Knopf, 1934.

5. L. J. Henderson, *Pareto's General Sociology, a physiologist's interpretation*. Harvard University Press, 1935.

6. "A Primer for Intellectuals," *Saturday Review of Literature* IX (April 22, 1933), pp. 545–46.

7. See Curtis and Homans, *An Introduction to Pareto*, Chapter 1.

8. DeVoto answered Mumford, humorously but not quite convincingly, in a letter to the *Saturday Review* Points of View column on May 20, 1933.

9. Robert K. Merton, also in the Points of View column for May 20, 1933, reminded DeVoto of some others who had heard of Pareto.

10. BVD to Mattingly, May 10, 1933. SUL. See also "DeVoto and Pareto," *Saturday Review of Literature* IX (May 30, 1933), p. 607; "Mr. DeVoto Wins," *Saturday Review of Literature* X (July 22, 1933), p. 4; and "Pareto and Bassett Jones," *Saturday Review of Literature* X (September 2, 1933), p. 80. These are all letters to the editor stemming out of the Pareto article.

11. "Sentiment and the Social Order; Introduction to the Teachings of Pareto," *Harper's* CLXVII (October 1933), pp. 569–81.

12. Curtis and Homans, *Introduction to Pareto*, p. 20.

13. Ibid., p. 236.

14. Ibid., p. 249.

15. The phrase is adopted in BDV to Mattingly, November 1, 1945 (SUL) as the key to his as-yet-unwritten book.

Chapter 8 ·

1. "Exiles from Reality," review of Malcolm Cowley's *Exile's Return, Saturday Review of Literature* X (June 2, 1934), pp. 721–22.

2. "He has tried to invalidate the literary and critical approach *as such.*" Spiller, *The Van Wyck Brooks-Lewis Mumford Letters.* Brooks to Mumford, December 3, 1932, p. 85.

3. "The Skeptical Biographer," *Harper's* CLXVI (January 1933), pp. 181–92.

4. "How Not to Write History," *Harper's* CLXVIII (January 1934), pp. 199–208.

5. Of this, too, DeVoto was himself sometimes guilty, as witness his common use of such phrases as "the continental mind." In practice, such generalizations are all but indispensable. The crucial matter is whether the historian begins with facts and arrives at his generalizations or whether he begins with the generalizations and selects his facts to prove them. DeVoto's generalizations are not as reprehensible as they are made out to be in Peter Skiles Pruessing, "Manifest Destiny and 'The Literary Fallacy,'" unpublished M.A. thesis, Iowa State University, Ames, 1968.

6. "American Life," review of Arthur M. Schlesinger, *The Rise of the City, Saturday Review of Literature* IX (March 4, 1933), p. 464.

7. "The Rocking Chair in History and Criticism," *Forum* LXXXIX (February 1933), pp. 104–7.

8. "Jonathan Dyer, Frontiersman: A Paragraph in the History of the West," *Harper's* CLXVII (September 1933), pp. 491–501.

9. "The West: A Plundered Province," *Harper's* CLXIX (August 1934), pp. 355–64.

10. "Fossil Remnants of the Frontier; Notes on a Utah Boyhood," *Harper's* CLXX (April 1935), pp. 590–600. As indicated earlier, both "Fossil Remnants" and "Jonathan Dyer," as well as the later "A Sagebrush Bookshelf," *Harper's* CLXXV (October 1937), pp. 488–96, were partly stimulated by Kate Sterne's questions about his background. He confessed that he had never autobiographized for anyone but her (BDV to Kate Sterne, February 25, 1935, SUL), and she in turn was "proud of [her] midwifery." But the autobiographizing served other and less personal ends, and some of its effects may be seen in DeVoto's reply to Edmund Wilson when Wilson challenged him to "stand up and reveal himself." See Section IV, Chapter 2.

Chapter 9·

1. The correspondence with Kate Sterne, in which DeVoto spoke his mind about issues and people with uninhibited vehemence, has been put in the Stanford University Library safe until the year 2000. But because as Avis DeVoto's vicar I myself put the file there, I have been privileged to read it, and I quote from it with Mrs. DeVoto's permission and with, I hope, discretion. I have suppressed nothing important to this biography, and in general have avoided only personal allusions that DeVoto himself would never have made publicly or in print.

2. Kate Sterne to BVD, October 17, 1933.

3. BVD to Kate Sterne, undated, but from context shortly after the above.

4. Ibid.

5. Kate Sterne to BDV, October (no day), 1933.

6. BDV to Kate Sterne, October 17, 1933.

7. BDV to Kate Sterne, "The Kent Potter Story," Installment 4.

8. His letters to Kate came back to DeVoto after Kate's death. There is evidence that he reread them and was struck by the fact that they added up to an intimate journal of a decade. Jottings in the margins indicate that he may have planned to use passages or whole letters, perhaps as elements in some fiction, perhaps as the basis for a diary of the depression and war years. It is not unlikely that he was kept from doing so by the same inhibitions that kept him from ever meeting Kate Sterne.

9. *Minority Report* and *Mountain Time*.

10. *The Year of Decision: 1846*, Little, Brown, 1943, dedication.

Chapter 10·

1. BDV to Kate Sterne, November 25, 1933.

2. Even before Sinclair Lewis commented scathingly on John

August's fiction in "Fools, Liars, and Mr. DeVoto" (see Section VI, Chapter 2), DeVoto had begun to feel that as an alias John August was too well known. Two years before the Lewis attack, the Boston *Globe* publicly challenged DeVoto to admit his identity with August (BDV to Kate Sterne, February 15, 1942). After Lewis' exposure, DeVoto did not use the pseudonym again, but instead substituted a series of others: Cady Hewes, Fairley Blake, Frank Gilbert. He wrote Kate Sterne (BDV to Kate Sterne, June 27, 1934), when he had just begun to make use of the August nom de plume, that he "refuse[d] to publish tripe" under his own name.

3. He told Kate Sterne about the episode in BDV to Kate Sterne, July 4, 1934.

4. BDV to Kate Sterne, June 27, 1934.

5. BDV to Kate Sterne, December 30, 1934.

6. BDV to Kate Sterne, shortly after October 10, 1933, while he was working on the manuscript of *We Accept with Pleasure*.

7. BDV to Kate Sterne, April 14, 1935.

8. Anonymous, "On Beginning to Write a Novel," *Harper's* CLXXIII (July 1936), pp. 179–88.

9. BDV to Kate Sterne, September(?) 1934.

10. BDV to Kate Sterne, September 16, 1934.

11. Alvah Bessie, "Bernard DeVoto's Novel of Character," review of *We Accept with Pleasure*, *Saturday Review of Literature XI* (September 22, 1934), p. 125.

12. BDV to Kate Sterne, November(?) 1934.

Chapter 11 ·

1. "A faculty appointment with full academic trappings has been offered to me every year since I came to Cambridge and will doubtless be offered to me every year I stay but I am not interested in it and will not take it. I am editing the *Harvard Graduates' Magazine*, and this year I am guest conductor of a composition course which was given for many years by Byron Hurlbut who was an old friend of mine and who died last year. . . . I may give the course next year. . . . Certainly I will not give it more than once more, and just as certainly I will not give any other courses or do any other teaching work." BDV to Ney McMinn, April 29, 1931. SUL. That was what he felt compelled to say to those who had heard the vehemence of his farewell to pedagogy. He may have been offered teaching positions at Harvard, as he said, but his disinclination was less than what he asserted. So far as one can tell, he accepted every teaching offer that Harvard made him in the next four years.

2. BDV to Kate Sterne, April 20, 1936.

3. Avis says, "First he found he couldn't sell them, then he found he couldn't write them." Avis DeVoto to WS, February 2, 1972.

4. Henry Reck to WS, October 25, 1970 (tape).

5. BDV described the negotiations to Kate Sterne as they developed. BDV to Kate Sterne, May 14, July 19, August 1, and August 7, 1935.

6. BDV to Kate Sterne, July 19, 1935.

7. The history of the Easy Chair, and DeVoto's intentions in writing it, are described in "Number 241," Easy Chair, *Harper's* CCXI (November 1955), pp. 10–17.

8. George Stevens to WS, March 6, 1972.

9. Henry Seidel Canby, *American Memoir*, Houghton Mifflin, 1947, p. 402.

10. George Stevens to WS, March 6, 1972.

11. BDV to Kate Sterne, November 26, 1935.

12. Originally entitled *Senior Spring*, it was published in ten installments as *Life Begins So Soon, Collier's* XCVII (February 1 to April 4, 1936).

13. BDV to Kate Sterne, November 26, 1935.

14. J. B. Munn to BDV, December 16, 1935. SUL.

15. Mr. Conant discusses his promotion policy, and the difficulties in which it involved him, in his autobiography, *My Several Lives*, Harper & Row, 1970. Though he spends some space on the case of Walsh and Sweezy, which roused wide-spread disaffection because of its political overtones, he does not mention DeVoto, whose crisis had come up the year before. Presumably Mr. Conant does not remember it as particularly significant. His subsequent behavior toward DeVoto suggests that he had no personal ill will toward him.

16. J. B. Munn to BDV, December 18, 1935. SUL.

17. As reported by BDV to Kate Sterne, December (no day), 1935, and corroborated by George Stevens to WS, March 6, 1972.

18. BDV to Kate Sterne, February 11, 1936, contains a long and perhaps heightened and dramatized account of the negotiations.

19. "Mark Twain and the Limits of Criticism," paper read before the American Literature section of the Modern Language Association, January 1, 1936. It was never published in a periodical, but was collected in *Forays and Rebuttals*, pp. 373–403.

20. Lawrance Thompson says that the meeting occurred on January 17, and implies that it was the first between the two men. (Lawrance Thompson, *Robert Frost, the Years of Triumph*, pp. 436–37, and p. 671.) I have taken the date January 16 from the notes that DeVoto made immediately after the meeting, which are among the DeVoto Papers at Stanford. The meeting was actually the

third between Frost and DeVoto. The first was at Bread Loaf, near the beginning of the Writers' Conference in August 1935. Evidently Frost, though he was not on the staff of the Conference, had stayed over from the English School. Two entries in Elinor Frost's engagement book, both in Robert Frost's hand, indicate a Bread Loaf speaking engagement for "Aug. 7 or 12," and later change the date to "July 16 or Aug. 9" (Frost Papers, DCL). But the Frosts must clearly have stayed on after the opening of the Conference on August 15, for in the Kate Sterne correspondence, which Mr. Thompson never saw, DeVoto refers to a photograph he took of Frost at Bread Loaf in the summer of 1935, and a letter, BDV to Kate Sterne, August 17, 1935, remarks in passing, "Robert Frost is not only the best poet in all U.S. lit., he is also the swellest gent that walks the earth." A later letter, BDV to Kate Sterne, November 4, 1935, alludes to an afternoon and evening spent with Frost at Amherst. So they were acquainted, and a mutual admiration was well under way, before the Miami encounter.

Chapter 12 ·

1. Compare Thompson, *Robert Frost, the Years of Triumph*, pp. 437–38.

2. "What is an unemployed writer?" he asked Kate Sterne scornfully. But he did value the WPA Guides to the several states—productions, as he pointed out, less of "unemployed" writers than of professionals brought in for the job. See "Unemployed Writers," *Saturday Review of Literature* XV (October 31, 1936), p. 8, and "The First WPA Guide," *Saturday Review of Literature* XV (February 27, 1937), p. 8.

3. "Solidarity at Alexandria," Easy Chair, *Harper's* CLXXI (November 1935), pp. 765–68.

4. Thompson, *Selected Letters of Robert Frost*. RF to BDV, November 1936, pp. 430–32.

5. Ibid.

6. Ibid.

7. BDV to Kate Sterne, January 29, 1936.

8. BDV to Kate Sterne, February 15, 1942.

9. Thompson, *Robert Frost, the Years of Triumph*, p. 445.

10. Ibid., p. 437. Also BDV to Kate Sterne, January 29, 1936.

11. BDV to Kate Sterne, February 11, 1936.

12. "The Absolute in the Machine Shop," Easy Chair, *Harper's*, CLXXII (December 1935), pp. 125–28.

13. "Memento for New Year's Day," Easy Chair, *Harper's* CLXXII (January 1936), pp. 253–56.

14. "The Folk Mind," Easy Chair, *Harper's* CLXXII (February 1936), pp. 381–84.

15. "Terwilliger in Plato's Dream," Easy Chair, *Harper's* CLXXII (March 1936), pp. 493–96.

16. "Another Consociate Family," Easy Chair, *Harper's* CLXXII (April 1936), pp. 605–8.

17. "Genius Is Not Enough," *Saturday Review of Literature* XIII (April 25, 1936), pp. 3–4.

18. BDV to Mattingly, March 22, 1936. SUL.

19. BDV to Kate Sterne, March 30, 1936.

20. See BDV to Gannett, March 29, 1936, and the undated note from Gannett to BDV in reply (SUL). Gannett (Gannett to BDV, April (no day), 1936, SUL) ended the dispute charmingly by saying he had assumed that DeVoto, a rough controversialist, would appreciate a similar roughness in others.

21. Kate Sterne to BDV, no date, but between March 3 and March 10, 1936.

22. This count is made from the Barclay bibliography, from which, as we have seen, a number of reviews and minor articles are omitted.

23. Published as *Forays and Rebuttals*, Little, Brown, 1936.

24. DeVoto thought that it was Dean Birkhoff and hinted that Birkhoff might have been poisoned by F. O. Matthiessen. BDV to Kate Sterne, May 1, 1936, and BDV to Mattingly, June 4, 1936. The guess about Matthiessen is given a certain credibility by a story from Mrs. Howard Mumford Jones. When Jones was being interviewed in the spring of 1936 in connection with his possible appointment at Harvard, Bessie Jones said aloud that she hoped her husband wasn't being sought as a replacement for Mr. DeVoto, whom she admired. Matthiessen, she says, asked rather coldly, "What's he done?"

25. J. L. Lowes to BDV, May 2, 1936. SUL.

26. J. B. Conant to BDV, May 6, 1936. SUL. But note that in accepting BDV's resignation (J. B. Conant to BDV, May 25, 1936, SUL), President Conant specifically regretted his inability to offer a permanent position, and thanked BDV again for his "distinguished service."

27. BDV to Mattingly, June 4, 1936; BDV to Kate Sterne, January 7, 1937.

28. The consultations with his friends are reported in BDV to Kate Sterne, May 1, 1936.

29. Ibid. He was in error about Stevens' plans. Stevens says he had no intention of leaving the *Saturday Review*, unless for a better job, in book publishing. This move he finally made, to Lippincott, after two years as editor of the *Saturday Review*. Stevens to WS, March 6, 1972.

30. Thompson, *Robert Frost, the Years of Triumph*, pp. 448–49.

Chapter 13 ·

1. The expanded version was published in *Minority Report*.

2. BDV to Kate Sterne, June (no day), 1936. His version is subject to some discount, being part of his confident front at a most uncon-fident time. Harvard seems to have been less at fault than DeVoto suggested. As Thompson points out, Frost reneged on his agreement with the university, which called for publication of the six Norton Lectures. Frost, who never wrote out his talks, first procrastinated, and then apparently destroyed the notes that John Livingston Lowes had had made. The lectures were never published. Thompson, *Frost, the Years of Triumph,* pp. 434–35, 674–75.

3. BDV to Kate Sterne, June (no day), 1936.

4. Thompson, *Selected Letters of Robert Frost,* p. 164, Frost to Hamlin Garland, February 4, 1921.

5. In *Criticism and Fiction*.

6. "On Moving to New York," Easy Chair, *Harper's* CLXXIII (November 1936), pp. 669–72. The piece became a favorite dramatic reading by Don Born, one of DeVoto's fervent admirers.

7. Ibid.

IV THE MANHATTAN CAPTIVITY

Chapter 1 ·

1. George Stevens to WS, June 16, 1971 (tape).

2. "A Sagebrush Bookshelf," *Harper's* CLXXV (October 1937), pp. 488–96.

3. BDV's hope was that he could first lure good reviewers with the opportunity to speak their full minds and pull no punches, and that he could work out the problem of adequate payment later. BDV to Kate Sterne, June (no day), 1936.

4. Elmer Davis to BDV, October 4, 1936. SUL.

5. Edmund Wilson, "Complaints, II. Bernard DeVoto," *New Re-public* LXXXIX (February 3, 1937), pp. 405–8.

6. Scalp hunting was, in fact, one principal temptation of the job. See BDV to Kate Sterne, February 11, 1936.

7. "Notes on the Red Parnassus," Easy Chair, *Harper's* CLXXIII (July 1936), pp. 221–24.

8. Ibid.

9. Summarized in two letters, BDV to Kate Sterne, September 8, 1936, and September (no day), 1936. Some of the difficulty was with John Farrar, who, according to BDV, "arrived in a pet." Since Farrar

did not get along with Frost—there had been a running dispute between them over domination of the Bread Loaf Conference—DeVoto's bad relations with Farrar may be put down partly to protectiveness. Any antagonist of Frost's was at that time his natural enemy.

10. "A Puritan Tercentenary," Easy Chair, *Harper's* CLXXIII (September 1936), pp. 445–48. Characteristically, DeVoto stressed the Puritan origins and survivals. He was in alliance with Frost, an "announced" Puritan, and in opposition to Brooks, Waldo Frank, and the rest of the Young Intellectuals, who found Puritanism responsible for every American ill.

11. The move, in grisly and exaggerated detail, was described to Kate Sterne on September 11, 1936. Much earlier, announcing his resignation from Harvard, he had written, "I feel pretty low, Kate. . . . I'm being kicked out of the way of life that means most to me." BDV to Kate Sterne, May 13, 1936.

12. BDV to Kate Sterne, September 21 and September 28, 1936.

13. "A Generation Beside the Limpopo," *Saturday Review of Literature* XIV (September 26, 1936), pp. 3–4.

14. BDV to Kate Sterne, September 21, 1936.

15. To Kate Sterne he confessed that, of the English Department, he had respected and been able to work with only Murdock, Miller, and Munn, but that the historians were all his pals. BDV to Kate Sterne, May 13, 1936.

Chapter 2 ·

1. "One Man's Guess," Easy Chair, *Harper's* CLXXIII (October 1936), pp. 557–60.

2. "The 42nd Parallel," *Saturday Review of Literature* XIV (October 3, 1936), p. 8.

3. "Civilization in the USA," *Saturday Review of Literature* XIV (October 3, 1936), p. 7.

4. He expected the O'Neill piece to cost the *Review* some subscribers. "But there is always the perfect retort. I can quote from some of the plays." BDV to Kate Sterne, November 17, 1936. Later he noted that the article had proved surprisingly popular. BDV to Kate Sterne, December 7, 1936.

5. As George Stevens relates the story, Doubleday, for reasons it never divulged, had issued the book on terms calculated to foreclose the possibility of reviews. But Stevens remembered that two copies of every book published in the United States had by law to be deposited in the Library of Congress, which was open to use by any citizen or any editor. He sent Canby to Washington to read and review *The Mint*. It was the only review the book got. Doubleday, Stevens said, was dismayed and annoyed to have its plan, whatever it was, blown

up, but could do nothing to block publication of the review. When it was later published in an edition meant to be read, *The Mint* fell quietly dead. Stevens to WS, June 16, 1971 (tape). DeVoto told the story in "For the Record," Easy Chair, *Harper's* CCX (June 1955), pp. 12–13 plus.

6. "Passage to India," *Saturday Review of Literature* XV (December 5, 1936), pp. 3–4.

7. Stevens remembers that essay as an editorial mistake. If it was, it was one that the editor did not acknowledge. In BDV to Kate Sterne, December 14, 1936, he remarked on the number of letters from subscribers that came in asking for "more articles by the editor."

8. BDV to Kate Sterne, January 25, 1937.

9. "Vardis Fisher in Salt Lake City," *Saturday Review of Literature* XV (December 12, 1936), p. 8.

10. Edmund Wilson, "Complaints, II. Bernard DeVoto," *New Republic* LXXXIX (February 3, 1937), pp. 405–8.

11. "My Dear Edmund Wilson," *Saturday Review of Literature* XV (February 13, 1937), p. 8. This important statement of his intellectual position DeVoto reprinted in considerably amplified form as "Autobiography: or, as Some Call It, Literary Criticism," in *Minority Report*, Little, Brown, 1940, pp. 163–89.

12. He wrote Kate that Wilson "leaned over backward" and that he could agree with more than half of what Wilson said, but that the challenge had made him think, and now he understood that his divided Mormon-Catholic youth really did explain his antipathy to dogma. BDV to Kate Sterne, February 1, 1937. He was writing, of course, before he had completed his answer, and when he had seen only a preprint of Wilson's challenge.

13. Van Wyck Brooks *On Literature Today*, New York, E. P. Dutton, 1941.

14. In *The Irresponsibles; a Declaration*, Duell, Sloan & Pearce, 1940.

15. "About Face of Mr. Stearns," *Saturday Review of Literature* XV (February 20, 1937), p. 8.

16. "Magistrate Curran's Opinion," *Saturday Review of Literature* XV (February 20, 1937), p. 8. DeVoto's favorable review of *A World I Never Made* had been quoted in defense of the book by its publishers, Vanguard Press, who had been denied advertising space for it in the New York *Times*.

Chapter 3 ·

1. "Complaints, II: Bernard DeVoto."

2. Frost referred obliquely and ambiguously to this in a letter to BDV in May 1937. Thompson, *Selected Letters of Robert Frost*, p. 444. See also *Robert Frost, the Years of Triumph*, p. 481.

3. The whole campaign is summarized by Thompson in *Robert Frost, the Years of Triumph*, in Chapter 33, "Strike That Blow for Me." Key letters from Frost are in *Selected Letters of Robert Frost*, pp. 452–53 and 455–56.

4. *Selected Letters of Robert Frost*, pp. 443–45.

5. Robert Hillyer, "A Letter to Robert Frost," *Atlantic* CLVIII (August 1936), pp. 158–63.

6. Robert Hillyer, "A Letter to the Editor," *Saturday Review of Literature* XIV (October 10, 1936), pp. 14–15.

7. For a blow-by-blow account of the squabble, see Hillyer to BDV, September 8, September 15, September 29, October 1, October 10, October 19, and November 23, 1936; and BDV to Hillyer, September 28, October 7, October 14, and November 13, 1936. SUL. Thompson discusses it in *Robert Frost, the Years of Triumph*, pp. 478–79, but he errs in saying that the Hicks parody was written in answer to "A Letter to Robert Frost," in the *Atlantic*. It was written to ridicule "A Letter to the Editor," the poem Hillyer wrote originally with DeVoto's name attached. DeVoto sent the parody on to Hillyer on November 13, indicating that he would not publish it unless it was cut, and then only on the Letters page. It did not appear in *New Republic* until almost a year later, when Hillyer's book came out.

8. Granville Hicks, "A Letter to Robert Hillyer," *New Republic* XC (October 22, 1937), p. 308.

9. Frost acknowledged the galleys on December 29. "I sat and let Elinor pour it over me," he wrote DeVoto. "I took the whole thing. I thought it couldn't do me any harm to listen unabashed to my full praise for once in a way." *Selected Letters of Robert Frost*, pp. 452–53. The essay was published as scheduled, as "The Critics and Robert Frost," *Saturday Review of Literature* XVII (January 1, 1938), pp. 3–4.

10. *Robert Frost, the Years of Triumph*, pp. 477–81.

11. F. O. Matthiessen, letter to the editor, *Saturday Review of Literature* XVII (February 5, 1938), p. 9. See also *Robert Frost, the Years of Triumph*, p. 489.

Chapter 4 ·

1. He told Kate Sterne he had (BDV to Kate Sterne, September 6, 1937). Stevens remembers no such offer.

2. See Section III, Chapter 5, note 31.

3. James Bryant Conant to BDV, June 18, 1937. SUL.

4. BDV to Kate Sterne, July 5, 1937.

5. Kate Sterne to BDV, between July 5 and July 16, 1937.

6. BDV to Kate Sterne, July 16, 1937.

7. BDV to Kate Sterne, September 6, 1937.

8. The Kate Sterne correspondence, one of the best indexes of DeVoto's state of emotional health, is fairly ebullient from September until December 5, when he reported a series of migraines. It was only later, when he was summarizing the whole *Saturday Review* experience for Kate, that he recalled the fall of 1937 as a time of failure. It is possible that he did not realize at the time how far down the morale of the staff had gone. George Stevens corroborates the decline in morale but does not precisely date it.

9. In a long letter to Kenneth Murdock, February 13, 1938, SUL, DeVoto made a statement of his side of the case.

10. George Stevens to WS, June 16, 1971 (tape).

11. Canby, *American Memoir*, p. 403.

12. BDV to Kenneth Murdock, February 13, 1938. SUL.

13. According to DeVoto (BDV to Kate Sterne, February 7, 1937), Davis actually accepted what he thought an offer to become editor, only to find that there was nothing to accept.

14. The effort was led by Kenneth Murdock. See Murdock to Thomas Lamont, February 14, 1938, and Murdock to L. J. Henderson, same date, SUL. Letters from Murdock to BDV, the last dated March 12, 1938, record the progress of the effort and its dimming hope.

15. BDV to Kate Sterne, December 15, 1937, and January 5, 1938.

16. DeVoto's version of the arrangement is expressed in BDV to Kate Sterne, January 17, January 24, and February 7, 1938. George Stevens' recollections of the same events are contained in Stevens to WS, June 16, 1971 (tape), and March 6, 1972.

Chapter 5 ·

1. BDV to Charles Townsend Copeland, January 21, 1938. SUL.

2. BDV to Crane Brinton, March 2, 1938. SUL.

3. BDV to Kenneth Murdock, February 1, 1938. SUL.

4. "Enlightened Research," *Saturday Review of Literature* XV (April 10, 1937), p. 8.

5. Murdock's letters are the principal source. See Chapter 4, note 14, above.

6. "A Puritan Tercentenary."

7. BDV to Murdock, February 26, 1938. SUL.

8. Hillyer to BDV, no date. SUL.

9. They are listed in Thompson, *Robert Frost, the Years of Triumph*, p. 699. The reunion with Wilbert Snow seems to have been purely accidental. I find no correspondence between them, and no mention of Snow in DeVoto's letters.

10. BDV to Kate Sterne, March 27, 1937, says that Charles Lark has swung the balance against Clara and the rest of the Estate and that DeVoto is finally at work on the papers.

11. A copy of the agreement is among the DeVoto Papers at SUL.

12. "On Moving from New York," Easy Chair, *Harper's* CLXXVII (August 1938), pp. 333–36.

13. May Davison Rhodes, *The Hired Man on Horseback. My Story of Eugene Manlove Rhodes*. Introduction by Bernard DeVoto. Houghton Mifflin, 1938.

Chapter 6 ·

1. See Thompson, *Robert Frost, the Years of Triumph*, pp. 682–86, where Frost's relations with Bread Loaf are recapitulated.

2. Thompson, *Selected Letters of Robert Frost*, Frost to BDV, April 12, 1938, pp. 470–71.

3. BDV to Kate Sterne, April 25, 1938.

4. I report here what I remember of the evening, or what I think I remember. Thirty-four years and much subsequent rumor and discussion have been hard on certainty. Add that at the time I was green and somewhat awe-struck, and that I understood little of what was going on.

5. My memory retrieves the discomfort and some of the aftermath of the session in Treman, but not DeVoto's rebuke. Avis DeVoto believes there was one. BDV to Kate Sterne, September 2, 1938, describes the outburst of Frost's "demon" and indicates that he himself was greatly upset by it, but does not specify what he said.

6. The aftermath of the trouble in Treman is remembered by Kay Morrison, who had to cope with it, as I have repeated it here. She is not sure about the eating of the cigarette, or about the precise time when the incident was supposed to have happened, but finds it completely in character. Kay Morrison to WS, May 13, 1972.

7. *Selected Letters of Robert Frost*, p. 481, headnote.

8. BDV to Kate Sterne, September 11, 1938.

9. Avis DeVoto to WS, March 11, 1972.

10. *Selected Letters of Robert Frost*. Frost to BDV, ca. October 20, 1938, pp. 481–82.

V "PERIODIC ASSISTANCE FROM MR. JOHN AUGUST"

Chapter 1 ·

1. BDV to Kenneth Murdock, February 13, 1938. SUL.

2. *Troubled Star, Collier's* CII (September 3 to November 5, 1938).

3. His letters to Kate Sterne during this period, especially one of October 7, 1938, express dissatisfaction with the Coolidge Hill house, but profound satisfaction with the regained Cambridge life.

4. BDV to Kate Sterne, October 25 and October 31, 1938.

5. BDV to Kate Sterne, December 23, 1938, and no date (from context January), 1939.

6. BDV to Kate Sterne, no date (January), 1939.

7. Henry Reck to WS, October 2, 1970.

8. BDV to Kate Sterne, February 20(?), 1939.

9. BDV to Kate Sterne, October 16, 1939.

10. The notion of fiction as a healing fantasy, a substitute not for reality but for other, more destructive fantasies, grew on DeVoto when he was analyzing the "Great Dark" manuscripts among the Mark Twain papers. His letters to Kate Sterne, especially that of January 20, 1939, report the excitement with which he and Dr. Barrett were unraveling the symbolism of these fragments. The articulated hypothesis was published as "The Symbols of Despair" in *Mark Twain at Work* and later in *The World of Fiction.*

11. "Freud's Influence on Literature," *Saturday Review of Literature* XX (October 7, 1939), pp. 10–11.

12. The correspondence dealing with this disagreement does not seem to have been preserved among the DeVoto Papers, but the wrangling was reported to Kate Sterne in letters of April 26, May 14, and May 23, 1939.

13. "Thou and the Camel," *Cosmopolitan* (July 1939), pp. 58–61.

14. Eugene Saxton to BDV, October 19, 1938. SUL.

15. "Aftermath of a Cocktail Party," *New Republic* LXXXXIX (June 28, 1939), p. 218. DeVoto told the story as a glum joke on himself. BDV to Kate Sterne, July 11, 1939. A letter from Samuel Eliot Morison to Avis, December 18, 1955, after DeVoto's death, reveals that he was DeVoto's source for the story.

16. "Millennial Millions," *Saturday Review of Literature* XX (August 26, 1939), pp. 3–4.

Chapter 2 ·

1. Again the most uninhibited account is in his letters to Kate Sterne. BDV to Kate Sterne, July 13 and July 30, 1939.

2. The letters of November and December 1936 are much concerned with the problem of books too ponderous for the sick or frail.

3. "The Paring Knife at the Crossroads," Easy Chair, *Harper's* CLXXVIII (April 1939), pp. 557–60. Considerably later, another article dealing in part with the same subject ("Why Professors Are Suspicious of Business," *Fortune* XLIII (April 1951) brought a fan letter

from an American woman resident in France, along with the gift of a carbon-steel chef's knife. A correspondence grew up between her and Avis and eventually led to a visit by the lady and her husband. She took charge of the kitchen with such authority that Avis suggested she write a cookbook, and arranged an option contract with Houghton Mifflin. When the first installment of the cookbook came in, a year later, it turned out to be several hundred pages on fishes and sauces. Deciding that American women did not cook that way, Houghton Mifflin let the manuscript go, whereupon Avis sold it to Alfred Knopf, a notable gourmet. It was a large result to come from one small paring knife; the lady's name was Julia Child.

4. BDV reported the uproar to Kate Sterne with delight. He loved to stir up that particular breed of lions. BDV to Kate Sterne, September 11, 1939.

5. BDV to Kate Sterne, no date, but from context end of January 1940.

6. *The Adventures of Tom Sawyer*. By Mark Twain. The text edited and with an introduction by Bernard DeVoto. Limited Editions Club, 1939.

7. Bernard DeVoto, *Minority Report*, Little, Brown, 1940.

8. *Mark Twain in Eruption. Hitherto Unpublished Pages About Men and Events*. By Mark Twain. Edited, and with an introduction, by Bernard DeVoto. Harpers, 1940.

9. It was published serially in *Collier's* CV (May 25 to July 27, 1940) and issued as a book by Little, Brown in the fall of 1940.

10. Bernard DeVoto, *Mark Twain at Work*, Cambridge, Harvard University Press, 1942.

11. "Anabasis in Buckskin," *Harper's* CLXXX (March 1940) pp. 400–10.

12. "The Engulfed Cathedral," Easy Chair, *Harper's* CLXXX (March 1940), pp. 445–48.

Chapter 3 ·

1. These were, in the order of their publication, "Letter from Santa Fe," Easy Chair, *Harper's* CLXXXI (August 1940), pp. 333–36; "Notes from a Wayside Inn," Easy Chair, *Harper's* CLXXXI (September 1940), pp. 445–48; "Road Test," Easy Chair, *Harper's* CLXXXI (October 1940), pp. 557–60; "All Quiet Along the Huron," Easy Chair, *Harper's* CLXXXI (November 1940), pp. 669–72; and "Main Street Twenty Years After," *Harper's* CLXXXI (November 1940), pp. 580–87.

2. Granville Hicks, with Richard M. Bennett, *The First to Awaken*, Modern Age Books, 1940.

Chapter 4 ·

1. BDV to William Briggs, July 11, 1940, and BDV to Eugene Saxton, same date. SUL. These were written in hot reply to Briggs (Briggs to BDV, July 11, 1940), who had forwarded Clara's objections and her derogatory comments about DeVoto.

2. Saxton to BDV, July 12, 1940. SUL.

3. Briggs to BDV, September 26, 1940, SUL, enclosed Clara's letter modifying her earlier stand, and indicated that he thought it covered all future publications from the manuscripts. Unfortunately, relations between Clara and DeVoto never became cordial, and when she removed Charles Lark as lawyer for the Estate, they deteriorated still further. See Section VII, Chapter 2.

4. BDV to Kate Sterne, July 14, 1940.

5. BDV to Kate Sterne, August 5, 1940.

6. BDV to Mattingly, June 15, 1938. SUL.

7. BDV to Kate Sterne, August 28, September 13, and September 29, 1940.

8. BDV to Kate Sterne, undated, but from context end of October 1940.

9. John August, *Advance Agent*, Little, Brown, 1942. It ran in *Collier's* CVIII (July 5 to August 30, 1941). A double-agent story, it is without much question the liveliest and best of the John August serials.

10. BDV to Kate Sterne, June 12, 1941.

11. BDV to Kate Sterne, June 30, 1941. For a discussion of the Phi Beta Kappa speech and its later repercussions, see Section VI, Chapter 2, "Fools, Liars, and Mr. DeVoto."

12. BDV to Kate Sterne, September 13, 1940. DeVoto did not at first take to the title. In his letters he continues to refer to the book as "Empire." This he appears to have thought somehow more expressive of its subject, "a cross section of western expansion at the moment of its highest potential," "the beginning of the process by which the American nation was created." BDV to Kate Sterne, September 29, 1940. Though he yielded to persuasion on this book, he returned to the "Empire" notion in his third history, *The Course of Empire*.

13. These had been discovered by one of his former students and colleagues, Mason Wade, and were edited and published by Wade with considerable advice from DeVoto. Mason Wade, ed., *The Journals of Francis Parkman*, Harper & Brothers, 1947.

14. On September 30 DeVoto sent in his pro-forma resignation from the Easy Chair to *Harper's* new editor, Frederick Lewis Allen, on the theory that a new editor should have the chance to start clean. Allen promptly rejected it.

Chapter 5 ·

1. In a letter commenting on DeVoto's rebuke to Dorothy Thompson, "a lady sort of like Boadicea," Davis, at the end of 1942, urged DeVoto to start including Washington in his social commentary. "Little they know of Washington who only Cambridge know." Davis to BDV, November 24, 1942. SUL. By March of the next year, when he had left CBS News to become a bureaucrat, the two were exchanging long letters that indicated a singular and happy agreement on matters of civil rights, politics, literature and the literary, and the (dubious) future of democracy. In discussing the suppression and distortion of war information, DeVoto either made himself available to air some of Davis' uneasinesses or supplied the public cues that Davis could then take advantage of. Crippled by political infighting, overzealous security, Congressional stinginess, and the hostility of much of the press, the OWI was a thankless job from which Davis ultimately escaped into the American Broadcasting Company. His ironic and disillusioned and yet stoutly democratic views were expressed even before the United States entered the war: ". . . Those who call on God at present seem to me to be making a big mistake; it would be just as well not to attract the divine attention to this planet." Davis to BDV, July 23, 1943. SUL. Though their personal contacts were intermittent and limited to DeVoto's trips to New York and Washington, Davis was intellectually and temperamentally closer to him than most of his friends.

2. In all these negotiations Davis was his confidential adviser and at times go-between.

3. DeVoto reported the final blowup to Kate Sterne on April 25, 1944.

4. Buck defused any possible faculty opposition by hooking the marriage of the two schools to a pay raise for all but a handful of the highest-paid professors.

5. By accident rather than design—or by reason of the uneasiness that his reported truculence aroused in bureaucrats—he ended up with the absolute independence of mind and pen that would have been impossible if he had succeeded in getting a wartime job in Washington.

6. "What to Tell the Young," Easy Chair, *Harper's* CLXXXII (May 1941), pp. 669–72.

7. "Wait a Minute, Dorothy," Easy Chair, *Harper's* CLXXXVI (December 1942), pp. 109–12.

8. "Toward Chancellorsville," Easy Chair, *Harper's* CLXXXIV (April 1942), pp. 557–60; "Lincoln to the 164th Ohio," Easy Chair, *Harper's* CLXXXIV (May 1942), pp. 669–72; "Sedition's General Staff," Easy Chair, *Harper's* CLXXXV (June 1942), pp. 109–12; and,

on the question of full and frank war information, especially "Give It to Us Straight," Easy Chair, *Harper's* CLXXXV (August 1942), pp. 333–36.

9. Willkie quoted the Easy Chair in a Concord speech in March 1944. Later he wrote requesting historical information on news policies in earlier wars. "Fear of the Coming Peace," Easy Chair, *Harper's* CLXXXVIII (March 1944), pp. 344–47, gave Willkie another campaign issue: the fear that America would fall into totalitarian methods of dealing with postwar problems.

10. Among them his friend and former pupil Arthur Schlesinger, Jr., who kept him informed about doings beyond the front office.

11. *The Easy Chair*, Houghton Mifflin, 1955.

Chapter 6 ·

1. Considerably cut and patched, these appeared in the issues of July through November 1942 and immediately involved DeVoto in a stiff exchange of letters with Oliver LaFarge, who accused him of being a Manifest Destinarian and imperialist.

2. BDV to Kate Sterne, May 9, 1943. Repeating Cambridge gossip, DeVoto told Kate that one footnote on the historical dispute between Webb and Shannon (in which DeVoto took Webb's side, Schlesinger Shannon's), had cost him Schlesinger's vote for the Pulitzer prize.

3. Paxson's review appeared in *The American Historical Review* for October 1943; Gabriel's in the New York *Times Book Review*, March 28, 1943; Hofstadter's in the *New Republic*, May 3, 1943; and Smith's in the *New England Quarterly*, Spring 1943.

4. In selecting *The Year of Decision: 1846* as a Book of the Month, Henry Seidel Canby asked that the first chapter, which he thought complex and confusing, be rewritten. DeVoto rewrote it gladly enough, but could not entirely eliminate the difficulty. Many years later, writing to his friend and physician Herbert Scheinberg, he remarked, "I wrote the book deliberately with the technique you will soon perceive. The technique forfeits nine out of ten readers. My theory is, however, that the tenth will get much more out of it than he would if I had used a different and easier technique. I was trying to suggest, as well as prose enables a writer to suggest, that all these actions were occurring at the same time." BDV to Dr. Herbert Scheinberg, April 26, 1955. HS.

5. *The Year of Decision: 1846*, p. 4.

6. Explaining himself to his Ogden librarian friend Madeline McQuown, DeVoto pointed out that his histories (he had then published only two) were literary histories, conceived and executed like novels, and that they made use of two techniques, the test boring and

simultaneousness, that other historians were going to learn and borrow. BDV to Madeline McQuown, January 3, 1947. SUL.

7. BDV to Mattingly, June 15, 1938. SUL.

8. Quoted in Lawrance Thompson, *Robert Frost, the Years of Triumph*, p. 730.

9. BDV to Mattingly, summer(?) 1933. SUL.

10. *The Year of Decision: 1846*, pp. 7–8.

11. Compare his advice to Mattingly (BDV to Mattingly, June 15, 1938. SUL) never to forget that the reader was in there working too: "In narrative fewest is best, and you don't have to tell everything, for if anyone is with you at all, he is half a yard ahead of you."

12. Dale L. Morgan to WS, May 10, 1970.

VI BLOWS GIVEN AND TAKEN

Chapter 1 ·

1. Under the will of Mr. Will Patten of Indianapolis, an endowment was provided to support an annual visiting professor who would spend several weeks on the Bloomington campus. "The purpose of this prescription is to provide an opportunity for members and friends of the University to enjoy the privilege and advantage of personal acquaintance with the Visiting Professor." In the event, not many at Indiana found DeVoto's acquaintance a privilege that they much enjoyed. Detail about DeVoto's feelings during his stay comes from his letters to Kate Sterne and from the notebook jottings he made at the time of Frost's visit. The notebook is in the Stanford Library safe, with the Sterne letters.

2. Kay Morrison, who would have been the first to know if Frost contemplated a change of biographers, never heard a hint of such an intention (Kathleen Morrison to WS, May 13, 1972). On the other hand, considering the way he encouraged DeVoto's essay "The Critics and Robert Frost," Frost may well have hoped that DeVoto would write a critical book about him.

3. BDV to Robert Frost, June 7, 1943. DCL.

4. Robert Frost to BDV, marked in Frost's hand: "To DeVoto— rough draft—date lost." DCL. A letter from BDV to Kate Sterne indicates that by June 24 DeVoto had received no answer, and so it is clear that Frost waited three weeks, perhaps longer, to reply.

Chapter 2 ·

1. The Phi Beta Kappa address, never published, exists as a typescript among the DeVoto papers at Stanford.

2. Van Wyck Brooks, *On Literature Today*.

3. Sinclair Lewis, "Fools, Liars, and Mr. DeVoto," *Saturday Review of Literature* XXVII (April 15, 1944), pp. 9–12. In reprinting the exchange as "The Great Feud" in *The Saturday Review Treasury*, Simon & Schuster, 1957, John Haverstick and the *Saturday Review* editors call the argument "a classic in the annals of the magazine." One is not quite sure what "classic" means in that context. It sounds perilously as if the editors thought the spectacle of one eminent literary man vilifying another was good for business.

4. BDV to Norman Cousins, May 8, 1944, and again May 19, 1944. SUL.

5. Malcolm Cowley to BDV, April 15, 1944. SUL.

6. BDV to Cowley, April 22, 1944. SUL. The story that DeVoto tells about his visit to Hans Zinsser he had already told to Kate Sterne on December 14, 1942, nearly a year and a half before the controversy over *The Literary Fallacy* erupted.

Chapter 3 ·

1. DeVoto's more official accounts of the progress of the *Strange Fruit* case (the Easy Chairs for May and July 1944 and February 1945, and "The Decision in the *Strange Fruit* Case; and the Obscenity Statute in Massachusetts," *New England Quarterly* XIX [June 1946], pp. 147–83) are supplemented by a saltier and less objective running account in his letters to Kate Sterne. In this last series of indignations, he is considerably more infuriated at the Booksellers Association than at the Watch and Ward and the outright censors.

2. Boston *Traveler*, April 4, 1944.

3. Malcolm Cowley, "In Defense of the 1920's," *New Republic* CX (April 24, 1944), pp. 564–65.

Chapter 4 ·

1. BDV to Kate Sterne, January 5, 1944.

2. BDV to Elmer Davis, March 28, 1944. SUL. The tone of this letter is sour and disillusioned. DeVoto indicates that Davis is to the left of where he himself is, but that the New Deal is away off to the right of both, and cynical and self-serving to boot, playing cynical games with Davis and the OWI, pretending that the OWI is responsible for war news and then not permitting it to be. He offers Davis a program: "The way to get an informed public opinion . . . is to inform the public."

3. From November 1943 onward, DeVoto's letters to Chamberlain show an increasing frustration, beginning with the letter of November 30, when he explained why Rosy Chapman's list of Mark Twain

papers could not be absolutely precise because thousands of pages were illegible scraps; proceeding through the December 17 letter in which he offered to resign if Chamberlain held him to legalistic permissions in quoting from the papers; and reaching a climax in his letter of May 27, 1944, in which he again asked to be released, but agreed to a New York meeting if everything could be settled in that one session. His letter to William Briggs of Harper's, dated May 28, repeats with brass and percussion his complaints against the administration of Chamberlain and against Henry Hoynes of Harper's, whom he blamed for some of the difficulty. One gets the impression that throughout this period, while he was impatiently waiting some definite word from the Army or Navy, and later, while he was up to his neck in the *Strange Fruit* and Lewis controversies, the Mark Twain Estate was simply a pest, a cloud of gnats that kept distracting him from his more vital concerns.

4. BDV to Commager, April 30, 1944. SUL.

Chapter 5 ·

1. My account of this episode is taken from the extensive correspondence on the subject among the DeVoto papers at Stanford, and from the recollections of Lovell Thompson and Paul Brooks, who represented Houghton Mifflin in this negotiation and who had dealings with Reves both before and after it.

2. DeVoto often adopted the pose of being an amateur, not a member of the historians' guild, untrained in the mysteries and without an official badge; and sometimes he used his amateur standing as the base for attacks on the professionals, and sometimes he seems to have felt a real inferiority in the presence of their trained competence. Actually, as he admitted in his letter to Commager, he knew as much as anybody about the areas where he admitted knowing anything; and in all the areas around these areas of expertise he had one indispensable qualification: he knew who the real experts were, and did not hesitate to ask their guidance. So here, on the spur of the moment, in the first days of his enthusiasm, he went infallibly to the people who could tell him most: Dale Morgan, Charles Camp, Robert Cleland, and the Missouri Historical Society, which held many records of the fur trade. In the course of his research he discovered another indispensable source, Professor Robert Taft of the University of Kansas, who knew more about the painters and illustrators of the early West than anybody alive. With Taft's considerable assistance, gratefully acknowledged, he turned the Appendix on "The First Illustrators of the West" into a seminal essay and emphasized what too many historians had ignored: the historical value of representational art. Professor Taft himself in

1953 made a monumental contribution to that field with his *Artists and Illustrators of the Old West.*

3. BDV to Charles Curtis, November 1, 1944. SUL.

4. If Reves had no legal agreement with Mrs. Porter, he could not make one with DeVoto to write a partial text for a book composed of Miller's paintings, Mrs. Porter's biographical essay on Miller, and her account of how she happened to acquire the Miller paintings. Charles Curtis to BDV, December 6, 1944. SUL.

5. Once the arrangements were finally made, and DeVoto settled down to writing what would become *Across the Wide Missouri*, Mrs. Porter's contribution was revealed to have been minimal, and she began to resent being, as she thought, pushed aside. When *Across the Wide Missouri* received the Pulitzer prize, in the spring of 1948, she sent DeVoto a little note—"Am I entitled to a *small* slice?"—and was distressed by the fact that he acknowledged McGill James of the Peale Museum, who had put on the first Alfred Miller show before Mrs. Porter saw the paintings, as Miller's discoverer. Still later, in lectures before women's clubs, she referred to the book as a "collaboration" between herself and DeVoto, and by implication took the small slice she thought she was entitled to. It was one such statement, in Kansas City on August 13, 1951, that Houghton Mifflin objected to. The Kansas City *Star* on October 6 printed a correction of its report of Mrs. Porter's August 13 talk.

6. *Across the Wide Missouri*, p. 384.

7. DeVoto suspected that Bonneville was probably an American agent, just as he had earlier (correctly) suspected that the British traveler Frederick Ruxton was a British agent, and just as he suspected that Sir William Drummond Stewart was in the West in the 1830s for something besides sport.

8. BDV to Edward Ely Curtis, June 10, 1944. SUL.

9. *Across the Wide Missouri*, p. 363.

10. BDV to Catherine Drinker Bowen, February 21, 1945. SUL. The letter is reprinted in Mrs. Bowen's *Biography: The Craft and the Calling*, Little, Brown, 1969, pp. 106–7.

11. *Across the Wide Missouri*, pp. xi–xii.

12. Houghton Mifflin's records indicate a sale, up to the third quarter of 1971, of just under thirty-three thousand copies.

Chapter 6 ·

1. Not counting the *Collier's* serial *Life Begins So Soon*, never published in book form.

2. BDV to Kate Sterne, March 7, 1944.

3. BDV to Mattingly, February 5, 1945. SUL.

4. BDV to Clifton Fadiman, March 8, 1945. SUL.

5. BDV to Marshall Best, December 22, 1945. At the time of this letter, DeVoto still had a week's work to do on the introduction. This was his last Mark Twain book, since he resigned from the curatorship before completing the projected volume of letters.

6. In two consecutive Easy Chairs, February and March 1946. These essays, starting as a review of J. G. Randall's *Lincoln the President*, took issue with what DeVoto called the "revisionist" position: that the Civil War was avoidable, that the radicals, reformers, and northern extremists were responsible for it, that Stephen A. Douglas was its tragic hero in that his ideas failed to persuade the hotheads, and that compromise ought to have settled the issues. At the same time, the revisionists upheld the principle of secession. The correspondence contains some acrid exchanges, after publication of these Easy Chairs, between De-Voto and (especially) Avery Craven, author of *The Coming of the Civil War*.

7. BDV to Catherine Drinker Bowen, January 13, 1947. SUL.

8. BDV to Mattingly, January 31, 1947. SUL.

9. BDV to Madeline McQuown, January 3, 1947. SUL.

10. Ibid.

11. *Mountain Time*, Little, Brown, 1947, p. 347.

12. BDV to Kate Sterne, October 16, 1939.

13. In this manuscript, given the weak title *Assorted Canapés*, the Frost figure appears as an egomaniacal Harvard professor, so self-obsessed and self-pitying that no one unaware of DeVoto's intentions would ever recognize him as drawn partly from Frost.

VII FULL CAREER

Chapter 1 ·

1. The Easy Chairs from No. 87 (January 1943) through No. 167 (September 1949) did not carry titles, though some of them may be titled from DeVoto's notes and all were given identifying titles in Robert Edson Lee's "The Easy Chair Essays of Bernard DeVoto: A Finding List," *Bulletin of Bibliography*, Vol. 23, No. 3 (September–December 1960), pp. 64–69.

2. BDV to Mattingly, June 4, 1946. SUL.

3. The itinerary was laid out in advance for Robert Coughlan of *Life*, April 29, 1946, and reviewed in retrospect for Mattingly, July 4, 1946. SUL.

4. In the issue for August 1947. "From the heart," Avis says of that article, and is a little unhappy that I use it as evidence of DeVoto's greenness about some aspects of the West. But his very excitement

about the desert crossing is the best evidence of how new it was. In fact, he had left the West before the automobile was nearly as common as it later became. His family was neither well enough off to travel for pleasure, nor inclined to be footloose. What is at least as important, DeVoto's imagination during his early years did not reach westward; it reached eastward. If any of those three conditions had been reversed, he would probably have crossed the desert, by night and by day, at least a half dozen times in his boyhood, instead of discovering it for the first time at the age of forty-nine.

5. BDV to Mattingly, August 1, 1946, SUL, recapitulates the itinerary after Portland. BDV to Robeson Bailey, August 11, 1946, from Boise, is full of the euphoria of "great experiences."

6. The Easy Chairs for August, September, October, and November 1946 and January 1947; "The Anxious West," *Harper's* CXCIII (December 1946), pp. 481–91; "The West Against Itself," *Harper's* CXCIV (January 1947), pp. 231–56; "Historian on Tour," *Woman's Day* (June 1947), pp. 38–39 plus; "Roadside Meeting," *Woman's Day* (July 1947), pp. 34–35 plus; "Night Crossing," *Woman's Day* (August 1947), pp. 28–29 plus; and "The National Parks," *Fortune* XXXV (June 1947), pp. 120–35.

7. For example, his letters are full of the excellence of the steaks at Dempsey's, in Great Falls; and he made such friends there that the proprietors airmailed him some Montana beef after his return. Nevertheless, though DeVoto always commented on the food along his routes of travel, he was no such gourmet as Alfred Knopf. His lusts stopped with steak, salad, and honest varieties of cheese.

8. Olsen continued to be a source of information on the doings of the stockmen and other enemies of the national forests. Because he feared that these enemies might retaliate politically either upon individuals or upon the service, DeVoto kept his sources completely confidential, and much of the correspondence dealing with his long effort against the stockmen was destroyed by Avis after his death.

9. See Arthur Schlesinger, Jr., "The Citizen," in *Four Portraits and One Subject: Bernard DeVoto*, Houghton Mifflin, 1963, p. 56.

Chapter 2 ·

1. *Assorted Canapés* (manuscript, in several versions). SUL.

2. Theodore Morrison to WS, October 5, 1972. After reading what was then a quite lugubrious manuscript, Mr. Morrison reminded me with complete justice, "After all, it was a *pleasure*—certainly exasperating at times and not unmixed—to spend an evening at 8 Berkeley Street."

3. "Go Ahead and Holler," *Reader's Digest* (November 1943), p. 34.

See also his rebuke to Dorothy Thompson, "Wait a Minute, Dorothy," Easy Chair, *Harper's* CLXXXVI (December 1942), pp. 109–12.

4. As he told Mina Curtiss of Smith College, who had written saying she hated to defend so bad a book as *Amber*. BDV to Mrs. A. T. Curtiss, October 14, 1946. SUL.

5. BDV to Dixon Wecter, October 12, 1946, and BDV to William Briggs, October 18, 1946. SUL.

6. A copy of the quitclaim, drawn by Curtis and dated October 25, is among the DeVoto papers. DeVoto sent it to Chamberlain on October 28. On November 8, on Curtis' advice, DeVoto refused to sign the alternative agreement that Chamberlain had sent him. It is not clear just when Chamberlain signed the quitclaim, since several DeVoto letters both to Curtis and to Dixon Wecter are undated, though clearly written during December 1946. By the paper's terms, the Estate acknowledged receipt of all papers, manuscripts, documents, etc., and did dismiss and discharge DeVoto forever from all debts, actions, causes of action, etc., and did express its complete satisfaction with the work of said DeVoto, and granted said DeVoto the right to quote from all manuscripts, papers, documents, etc., in books or lectures or writings generally.

7. DeVoto took this obligation so seriously that when the initial advertising copy was sent him, and he found it feeble, cheap, and inadequate, he made a special trip to New York and rewrote the copy from scratch. Ray C. Dovell to WS, November 2, 1962.

8. The dispersal of the judges, at first thought an advantage because of the regional differences in point of view represented, proved to be a serious handicap to prompt action, and once again DeVoto, willing to be a decision maker in times of crisis, found himself frustrated by the need to await votes from the judges or approvals from the New York office. In December 1947, in an attempt to simplify procedures and cut expenses, the History Book Club let Dobie and Holbrook go from its panel of judges. On March 30, 1948, DeVoto resigned and Arthur Schlesinger, Jr., with him. (BDV to Ray C. Dovell, March 30, 1948. SUL.) There was never any serious ill feeling, and he was never disillusioned in the possibilities of the History Book Club—only with the machinery of its formative period.

9. Mattingly to BDV, October 10, 1946, contains a four-page essay on the Mesta, with bibliography.

10. For the Roosevelt-Pinchot years, see Gifford Pinchot, *Breaking New Ground*, Harcourt, Brace, 1947. For the struggle between Major Powell and the "irrigation clique," see Wallace Stegner, *Beyond the Hundredth Meridian*, Houghton Mifflin, 1954, pp. 294ff.

11. A letter from John W. Spencer, Regional Forester of the Rocky

Mountain Region, January 22, 1947, expresses the half-incredulous joy of many Westerners at what DeVoto had managed to do.

12. For this clash between private and public interest, viewed against the background of long-range land policies, see Louise Peffer, *The Closing of the Public Domain,* Stanford University Press, 1951.

13. The proceedings, as DeVoto saw them, are summarized in the Easy Chair for January 1948. The correspondence with Arthur Carhart, Struthers Burt, Charles Moore, Olaus Murie, Kenneth Reid, and Lester Velie is full of rumor, strategy, and counterstrategy over a period of two years and more, particularly before the election of 1948.

14. The Advisory Board for National Parks, Historical Sites, Buildings, and Monuments was created by act of Congress on August 21, 1935, to advise the Secretary of the Interior on matters relating to natural and historical areas. A part of the New Deal rescue operation, it was from the beginning conservationist in membership and sympathies, and has continued to scrutinize bureau actions and departmental policies in the light of the broad public interest. Its membership has by statute contained a proportion of naturalists, historians, architects, and publicists, and some of the most effective conservationists (though less frequently the politically embattled ones) have served on it. Traditionally, the Board has met in April and October in Washington, with occasional field trips to actual or potential national-park areas. One practical result of DeVoto's membership was his access to early and confidential conservation information. Another was that, in his trips around the West, he could count on enthusiastic co-operation from the National Park Service as well as from his old friends of the Forest Service.

15. At first, because of other commitments, DeVoto felt that he could not accept the invitation from President Robert Stearns to come to Boulder to receive the degree, but he indicated that he treasured the honor as the only recognition that had come to him from his native region. BDV to Robert Stearns, May 21, 1948. SUL. To Arthur Carhart, on June 3, he wrote that the honorary degree from Colorado, which he had by then found himself able to accept, "pleases me a damned sight more than the Pulitzer Prize did." A combination of respect, liking, and gratitude led him the following October to urge Stearns as a potential Secretary of the Interior. BDV to Harold Ickes, October 12, 1948. SUL.

16. BDV to Kenneth Reid, June 3, 1948; BDV to Olaus Murie, July 27, 1948; BDV to Arthur Carhart, December 24, 1948.

17. The first of these, appearing in the *Atlantic* in July, coincided with DeVoto's double assault in the July *Harper's;* the three represented a formidable frontal attack on the stockmen's position.

18. Thus his proposal of Stearns as Secretary of the Interior and his preparation of resistance against potential Republican appointees. See BDV to a Mr. Ray, July 19, 1948; BDV to Senator Richard Neuberger, October 11, 1948; and BDV to Harold Ickes, October 12, 1948. SUL.

19. DeVoto reported the stockmen's small triumph, with rueful amusement, to Arthur Carhart. BDV to Carhart, June 3, 1948. SUL.

20. Published as "The Desert Threat," *University of Colorado Bulletin* XLVIII (July 1948), pp. 3–4, 6–10.

21. See BDV to Jonathan Forman of *The Land Letter*, July 27, 1948; BDV to *Farm Journal*, September 28 and October 12, 1948; BDV to a Mr. Ayars, October 5, 1948; and BDV to a Mr. Schwan, October 12, 1948. SUL.

22. As witness a letter to Lee Hartman, May 3, 1937, SUL: "If the history of magazines in America demonstrates anything, it demonstrates that the most valuable business asset a magazine can have is a reputation for editorial independence."

23. BDV to Frederick Lewis Allen, July 15, 1948. SUL.

Chapter 3·

1. "Restoration in the Wasatch," *The American Scholar* XVIII, No. 4 (October 1949), pp. 425–32. Reprinted in *Reader's Digest*, December 1949, as "The Lesson of Davis County."

2. BDV to Anne Ford (who wrote publicity for Houghton Mifflin), May 22, 1950. SUL.

3. "Shall We Let Them Ruin Our National Parks?" *Saturday Evening Post* CCXXIII (July 22, 1950), pp. 17–19 plus. Reprinted in *Reader's Digest* (November 1950).

4. The fight over the Dinosaur dams was the first major conservation battle in the career of David Brower, then of the Sierra Club, now of Friends of the Earth. Largely through his urging, I edited for the Sierra Club to be published by Knopf the first of the Sierra Club's "fighting books," *This Is Dinosaur*. That book, published in 1955, contained the final statements of many of the arguments that DeVoto had stated energetically in 1950.

5. BDV to Ray C. Dovell, March 30, 1948. The last straw was the club's refusal to go along (because of price) with a unanimous choice by its judges. But that was merely the last of many frustrations, brought on by many things including his own overloaded schedule. It is not unlikely that his resignation from the History Book Club was partly conditioned by his recent appointment to the National Parks Advisory Board and his increasing involvement in the conservation wars.

6. Fischer, a good friend of DeVoto's and the *Harper's* editor who

would succeed him in the Easy Chair, expressed a similar sentiment to me when I was working in the office of Secretary of the Interior Stewart Udall. Same old thing, he said of some conservation propaganda I was trying to sell him. Same thing Benny was always writing. Conservation tactics and editorial requirements are not always congruous, though DeVoto contrived to make them so very often.

7. The most uninhibited of these letters, addressed to William Sloane but meant for discreet Bread Loaf consumption, has had to be fumigated and put away with the Kate Sterne letters.

8. George Ball to WS, August 25, 1971.

9. The desire is almost wistfully present in many letters through the summer and fall. See BVD to Mattingly, July 30 and October 17, 1952, and BDV to Mahonri Young, August 21, 1952.

10. In conversation. Mr. Schlesinger kindly hunted through his campaign diary for records of DeVoto contributions, but was able to find only one: a Seattle conservation speech, drafted by DeVoto and reworked by DeVoto and David Bell.

11. BDV to Mattingly, September 30, 1952. In this same letter he corroborates Schlesinger's judgment. He has been writing speeches, he says, but not much remains in. "Stevenson's prose is his own."

12. On the testimony of Alfred Knopf, DeVoto refused to attend when Secretary Douglas McKay invited the Board to lunch in the Secretarial dining room. Knopf, Ray Hall, Ralph Chaney, and others who served with him remember DeVoto as an informed, outspoken, and effective member of the Board.

13. "Billion Dollar Jackpot," in February, "The Sturdy Corporate Homesteader," in May; "Heading for the Last Roundup," in July; and "Let's Close the National Parks," in October.

14. "Parks and Pictures," in February; "Intramural Giveaway," in March; and "And Fractions Drive Me Mad," in September. The last two deal with the proposed reclamation dams in Dinosaur National Monument.

15. "Wild West," *Holiday* XVI (July 1954), pp. 34–43 plus.

16. "Conservation—Down and on the Way Out," *Harper's* CCIX (August 1954), pp. 66–74. This had just appeared when DeVoto met Adlai Stevenson in Missoula to brief him on western problems, and formed the basis for the lesson.

17. "One-Way Partnership Derailed," in January, and "Current Comic Strips," in May.

18. "Hell's Half Acre, Mass.," in September, and "Outdoor Metropolis," in October. There was another paean to his adopted country in "New England," *Holiday* XVII (July 1955), pp. 34–47.

19. Congressional Record—Senate, July 29, 1957, p. 11,663. Neuberger proposed renaming the Clearwater National Forest for DeVoto.

Chapter 4 ·

1. BDV to Mattingly, May 2, 1949. SUL.
2. Principally "English 37," *Saturday Review of Literature* LXVI (June 26 to September 4, 1937); "From Dream to Fiction," Easy Chair, *Harper's* CLXXVIII (January 1939); and "The Threshold of Fiction," Easy Chair, *Harper's* CLXXX (January 1940). Chapter V is reprinted from *Mark Twain at Work.*
3. BDV to Mattingly, September 11, 1949. SUL.
4. *The World of Fiction,* p. xi.
5. Ibid., pp. 33–34.
6. Ibid., p. 44.
7. Ibid., p. 54.
8. Ibid., p. 131
9. Ibid., p. 298.
10. See John Sutton Tuckey, *Mark Twain's "Mysterious Stranger" and the Critics,* Wadsworth Publishing, 1968.
11. Houghton Mifflin became DeVoto's publisher after 1947. In that year Little, Brown published *Mountain Time,* and Houghton Mifflin "borrowed" DeVoto for *Across the Wide Missouri.* But DeVoto's closest friend at Little, Brown, Alfred McIntyre, had by then retired, and his friendship with Raymond Everitt had cooled. Moreover, Paul Brooks and Lovell Thompson at Houghton Mifflin had made such a magnificent book of *Across the Wide Missouri* that DeVoto felt impelled to move from 34 Beacon to 2 Park. A rumor that got blown up by the yellow press later asserted that DeVoto and Arthur Schlesinger, Jr., had left Little, Brown because of the increasing dominance there of Angus Cameron, who was too sympathetic with the far Left for their taste. Schlesinger did leave for precisely that reason (Schlesinger to Alfred McIntyre, December 21, 1947), but DeVoto just as specifically denied that he did. (BDV to Arthur Thornhill, November 2, 1951. SUL.)

Chapter 5 ·

1. John Bakeless, *Lewis and Clark, Partners in Discovery,* William Morrow, 1947. DeVoto reviewed it in the New York *Herald Tribune Books* XXIV (December 21, 1947).
2. BDV to Mattingly, November 16, 1948. SUL.
3. Mattingly to BDV, December 5, 1948. SUL.
4. BDV to Mattingly, December 2, 1948. SUL.
5. Ibid.

6. BDV to Mattingly, September 11, 1949. SUL.

7. "Due Notice to the FBI.," Easy Chair, *Harper's* CXCIX (October 1949), and "For the Wayward and Beguiled," Easy Chair, *Harper's* CXCIX (December 1949).

8. BDV to Mattingly, October 28, 1950. SUL.

9. BDV to Mattingly, December 4, 1950. SUL.

10. Mattingly to BDV, December 15, 1950. SUL.

11. Mattingly to Helen Everitt, April 10, 1951. SUL.

12. BDV to Mattingly, April 17, 1951. SUL.

13. Mattingly to BDV, March 1 or 2, 1952. SUL.

14. Commager's review appeared in the New York *Herald Tribune* Books for November 23, 1952; Webb's in the *Saturday Review of Literature* XXXV (November 22, 1952); and Smith's in the New York *Times* Book Review, November 23, 1952.

Chapter 6 ·

1. The first Cady Hewes piece appeared in *Woman's Day* in August 1949. Between then and the end of DeVoto's life, twelve more under that nom de plume were published. In 1956 Houghton Mifflin collected them into a volume, *Women and Children First*.

2. The death of Joseph Kinsey Howard, shortly after the Montana Writers' Conference, depressed him. On December 27, 1951, he did something totally uncharacteristic: he begged off writing an article he had promised Mattingly, remarking incidentally how strange it was to be without book.

3. Apart from the dating in the text, I have not bothered to locate the details of the negotiations between Brandt and certain editors. The Brandt & Brandt file is intact and chronological.

4. He did, however, try one last story, "The Link," which exploited the emotional relationship stemming from one of the Cambridge divorces with which he was familiar. He asked Brandt to try it on *Harper's* or *Atlantic* under a pseudonym, perhaps hoping to prove that he could make those pages as a total unknown. Brandt tried to make him some bigger money with it, and after several rejections sold it to *Esquire*, which published it in July 1954 under the name of Frank Gilbert. It comes closer to being an "uncommercial" story than any of his stories except perhaps the early "Search for Bergamot," and it contains not one remaining shred of the sensitive show-off named Bernard DeVoto.

Chapter 7 ·

1. BDV to Mina Curtiss, October 14, 1946. SUL.

2. "Year-End Megrims," The Easy Chair, *Harper's*, CC (February 1950), pp. 27–30.

3. Easy Chair, *Harper's*, CXCIX (September 1949), pp. 76–79.

4. There is no point in multiplying instances beyond those contained in R. H. S. Crossman, ed., *The God That Failed*, Harper & Brothers, 1950.

5. "And the D.A.R.," letter to the editor, *Harper's* CCXI (September 1955).

6. Easy Chair, *Harper's* CXCIX (July 1949), pp. 62–65.

7. In the issue of December 1949.

8. BDV to Carey McWilliams, March 27, 1950. SUL.

9. "The Ex-Communists," *Atlantic* CLXXXVII (February 1951), pp. 61–65.

10. The two attacks by McCarthy, both in October 1952, were mainly attributable to DeVoto's involvement in the Stevenson campaign. Arthur Schlesinger, Jr., and others were attacked at the same time.

11. BDV to Mattingly, February(?), 1954. SUL.

Chapter 8 ·

1. In particularly busy times, Avis might answer some of the fan mail, but even if she did, and even though he learned to utilize most of one day of the week dictating to a secretary and cleaning up the accumulation of letters, there was rarely a day without a number of letters to deal with by typewriter or by application of his favorite Estabrook ⚹313 pen nib. And he had no gift for writing brief notes. If he was involved at all, he was involved totally, and total involvement often meant a letter of four, five, or six single-spaced pages. Sometimes, in replying to an argumentative or challenging letter, he wrote what amounted to an essay—four or five thousand words. One of his secretaries, Parian Temple, saved her shorthand books, and after DeVoto's death, retyped all the letters in them for the Stanford library, so that for a period in the late 1940s we have every letter he dictated. Samplings indicate the bulk: On January 22, 1947, twenty-two letters, all a page or more in length; on March 31, sixteen, several of them long, on July 14, ten; on September 25, twenty-two. There is hardly a day without several—and these notebooks tell nothing of the letters he knocked off by himself, or the cards he scribbled on trains and airplanes, or the quick notes he wrote from the Harvard Club or the Century when he was in New York.

2. To Alfred McIntyre, before leaving on that trip, he had promised a "travel" book about the West as well as an anthology of western writings; neither ever got put together. After the completion of *The Course of Empire* and the Lewis and Clark *Journals*, DeVoto began to think seriously about a book that would tell all about the West:

geography, climate, resources, myths, enough history to make the myths intelligible, delusions, character, prognosis. Some of it was to be cannibalized from Easy Chairs and other essays, and other parts would have been used as Easy Chairs, as "Birth of an Art" was, if he had got them written. It is possible that if he had lived he might have made it into a powerful book, for the bite came into his prose and the precision into his organization on the second or third time through the typewriter. But it seems to me more likely that it would have been a kind of omnium gatherum, a collection of things already said, and better, when the heat was on him.

3. I am indebted to Dr. Scheinberg for the loan of his personal and medical files on DeVoto, as well as for a reminiscent and explanatory tape and a look at the movie footage he shot while on the western trip with DeVoto and Stevenson in 1954. All details of their association come from one or another of those sources.

4. DeVoto became increasingly convinced that the 160-acre limitation of the Reclamation Act—the clause that limits individual benefits from any reclamation dam to the water that will serve 160 acres—was obsolete and unworkable, partly because the competing bureau, the Corps of Engineers, was bound by no such limitation and partly because the 160-acre homestead was not viable under modern farming conditions. The limitation was a survival of the effort of Major Powell (and through Major Powell, of W J McGee and other early conservationists) to prevent monopoly of land through monopolization of water. In his last year, feeling that monopoly was not being prevented, DeVoto began to urge that the Democratic Party convene a meeting or series of meetings in the West to reconsider all the assumptions of reclamation and land and water use in the West, especially the Bureau of Reclamation's linking of power sales to water conservation. This was the theme of "One-Way Partnership Derailed," Easy Chair, *Harper's* CCX (January 1955).

5. DeVoto proposed some such excursion in a letter to Adlai Stevenson on May 19, 1954 (SUL)—a letter in which he enclosed a carbon of his forthcoming article "Conservation—Down and on the Way Out" and proposed conservation as a great opportunity for the Democratic Party. Stevenson tentatively accepted on June 11, and DeVoto then put his Missoula Forest Service friends to work on the preparations.

6. Dr. Herbert Scheinberg to WS, tape.

7. A carbon of these, with a note promising more later, is among the DeVoto papers.

8. After their somewhat stiff-legged co-operation on Americana Deserta from 1929 to 1931, DeVoto and Knopf saw little of one another for some years. They seem to have met personally when DeVoto was

editing the *Saturday Review*. By the early 1940s Knopf had formed the habit of calling on DeVoto for advice about western books, as well as for western travel tips. By the end of the 1940s Knopf was a confirmed western enthusiast and DeVoto his mentor. Early in 1949, by virtue of his recent appointment to the National Parks Advisory Board, DeVoto was able to give Knopf introductions to numerous informed Western-ers, and in 1950 he was instrumental in getting Knopf appointed to the Board, of which he later became chairman. Their terms overlapped by nearly four years, and they worked together effectively on conserva-tion issues.

9. When on a tour, DeVoto much preferred to travel by car. When he went lecturing, he flew if he had to, but went by train if he could. Though he frequently grumbled about deteriorating rail service, he grumbled profitably: train travel is the subject of several Easy Chairs.

10. This was the prestigious Penrose Memorial Lecture, which he delivered before the American Philosophical Society on April 21, 1954. It was published in the *Proceedings of the American Philosophi-cal Society*, Vol. 99 (August 30, 1955), pp. 185–94. Its thesis is one of the "historical ideas" of which he had written to Mattingly: that the Lewis and Clark expedition was an act of conscious imperialism on Jefferson's part—that he was "playing for the continent" from the be-ginning.

11. Some of the titles: "The Easy Chair," "The Professional Writer," "Some American Symbols," "Safeguarding Our National Wealth." Reactions, as reported to the Leigh agency, varied from enthusiasm to a sour request from Dallas to "spare us any more of these aging smarties."

12. The Easy Chairs for April 1951, December 1949, and March 1948, plus "Listen, Sister," by Fairley Blake, *Atlantic* CLXXXVIII (July 1951), pp. 90–92.

13. *The Hour*, pp. 21–22.

14. Ibid., pp. 42–43.

15. Ibid.

16. For remembrances of the Sunday Evenings I am indebted to Dr. Gregory Rochlin, Dr. Molly Brazier, Paul Buck, Kenneth and Elea-nor Murdock, Arthur Schlesinger, Jr., the late Elizabeth Kennedy, and, of course, Avis.

17. In the DeVoto papers there are a few letters on conservation is-sues to Congressman John F. Kennedy. In one bilious aside, he once called him "as handsome a baby-kisser as Nixon, but less dangerous."

18. "Freud's Influence on Literature," *Saturday Review of Litera-ture* XX (October 7, 1939), pp. 10–11.

Chapter 9·

1. The medical details are from Dr. Scheinberg's file.

2. BDV to Dr. Scheinberg, May 5, 1954. HS.

3. Kay Morrison reports him as having been extremely gloomy during his visit.

4. William Sloane to WS, December 4, 1972.

5. Theodore Morrison to WS, October 5, 1972.

6. Because of the twentieth anniversary of his occupancy of the Easy Chair, and the celebration that friends organized about it, the weeks preceding his death were the weeks when he experienced the warmest praise of his life. In the Personal and Otherwise column, *Harper's* eulogized him in "Portrait of the Artist as an Old Bear." They said his coronary melting point was considerably under that of maple sugar; they said he was less bear than armadillo or porcupine—shy, and therefore armored or prickly; they said "he collects underdogs the way a blue serge suit collects lint—all the while emitting roars of exasperation."

7. Boston *Herald*, November 16, 1955.

8. Samuel Eliot Morison to Avis DeVoto, December 18, 1955. SUL.

INDEX